A History of Modern Germany 1800–2000

For Lars, Marie-Isabel, Paula, and Philip-David

A History of Modern Germany 1800–2000

Martin Kitchen

Blackwell
Publishing

© 2006 by Martin Kitchen

BLACKWELL PUBLISHING
350 Main Street, Malden, MA 02148-5020, USA
9600 Garsington Road, Oxford OX4 2DQ, UK
550 Swanston Street, Carlton, Victoria 3053, Australia

The right of Martin Kitchen to be identified as the Author of this Work has been asserted in
accordance with the UK Copyright, Designs, and Patents Act 1988.

First published 2006 by Blackwell Publishing Ltd

4   2007

Library of Congress Cataloging-in-Publication Data

Kitchen, Martin.
   A history of modern Germany, 1800–2000 / Martin Kitchen.
      p. cm.
   Includes bibliographical references and index.
   ISBN-13: 978-1-4051-0040-3 (alk. paper)
   ISBN-10: 1-4051-0040-0 (alk. paper)
   ISBN-13: 978-1-4051-0041-0 (pbk. : alk. paper)
   ISBN-10: 1-4051-0041-9 (pbk. : alk. paper)
   1. Germany—History—1789–1900.   2. Germany—History—20th century.   I. Title.

   DD203.K58 2006
   943.08—dc22

                                                                        2005006165

A catalogue record for this title is available from the British Library.

Set in 10 on 13 pt Sabon
by SNP Best-set Typesetter Ltd, Hong Kong
Printed and bound in Singapore
by C.O.S. Printers Pte Ltd

The publisher's policy is to use permanent paper from mills that operate a sustainable forestry policy,
and which has been manufactured from pulp processed using acid-free and elementary chlorine-free
practices. Furthermore, the publisher ensures that the text paper and cover board used have met
acceptable environmental accreditation standards.

For further information on
Blackwell Publishing, visit our website:
www.blackwellpublishing.com

Contents

Plates

Acknowledgments

I am most grateful to Andrew MacLennan, with whom I have worked so profitably and enjoyably on many projects, for suggesting that I should write this book. It has proved to be a taxing but rewarding experience.

Tessa Harvey and Angela Cohen were long-suffering and confident guides through the detritus of the postmodern. My thanks are also due to Louise Spencely, whose expert editing has saved me from many an ambiguity and infelicity of style, and who set me right with Helmuth and Helmut: Schmidt and Kohl.

I would also like to thank the following for their expertise and courteous help in tracking down the illustrations: Harald Odehnal (Konrad Adenauer Stiftung); Michel Schneider, Andre Castrup, and Gabriele Lutterbeck (Friedrich Ebert Stiftung); Norbert Ludwig (Bildarchiv Preussischer Kulturbesitz); Martina Caspers and Peter Vier (Bundesarchiv); Barbara Schäche (Landesarchiv Berlin); Katrin Peters-Klaphake (Deutsches Historisches Museum); and Christian Stutterheim (Bundes Presse Agentur).

My two greatest debts are to my wife, my "*Wortschatz,*" who has taught me so much about Germany and the Germans, and to my students at Simon Fraser University, who have helped make the study of German history so infinitely rewarding.

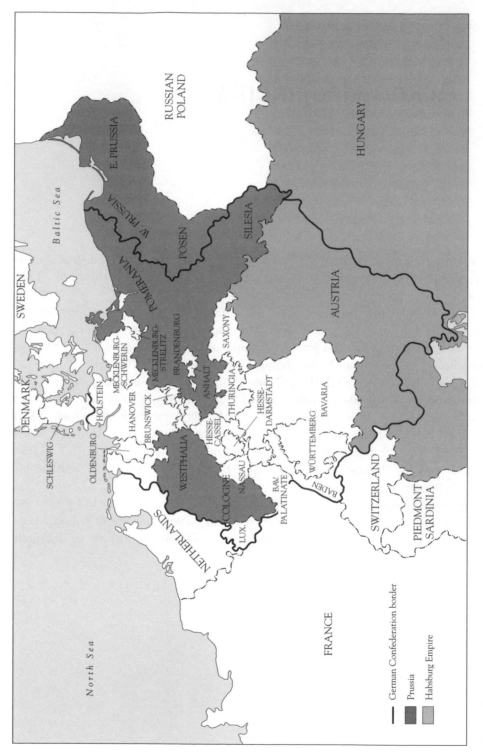

Map 1 Germany, 1815

German Confederation border
Prussia
Habsburg Empire

RUSSIAN POLAND

HUNGARY

E. PRUSSIA

Baltic Sea

W. PRUSSIA

POSEN

SILESIA

SWEDEN

POMERANIA

AUSTRIA

DENMARK

MECKLENBURG-STRELITZ

MECKLENBURG-SCHWERIN

BRANDENBURG

SCHLESWIG

HOLSTEIN

OLDENBURG

HANOVER

BRUNSWICK

ANHALT

SAXONY

THURINGIA

HESSE-CASSEL

HESSE-DARMSTADT

NETHERLANDS

WESTPHALIA

COLOGNE

NASSAU

LUX.

BAV. PALATINATE

WÜRTTEMBERG

BAVARIA

BADEN

SWITZERLAND

PIEDMONT SARDINIA

FRANCE

North Sea

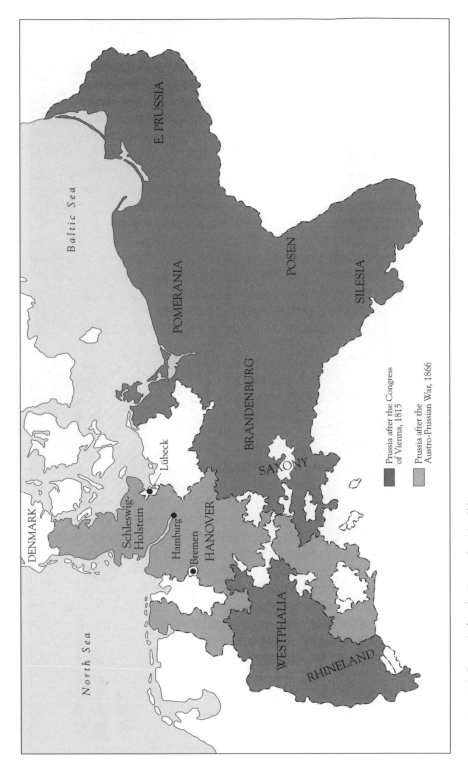

Map 2 Prussia before and after the Austro-Prussian War

E. PRUSSIA

Baltic Sea

POMERANIA

POSEN

SILESIA

BRANDENBURG

SAXONY

DENMARK

Lübeck

Schleswig-Holstein

Hamburg

Bremen

HANOVER

WESTPHALIA

RHINELAND

North Sea

Prussia after the Congress of Vienna, 1815

Prussia after the Austro-Prussian War, 1866

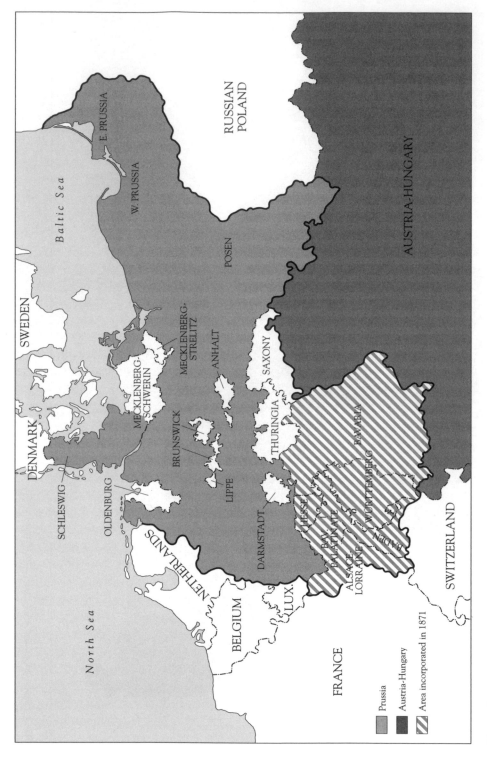

Map 3 Germany, 1871

RUSSIAN POLAND

AUSTRIA-HUNGARY

E. PRUSSIA

W. PRUSSIA

Baltic Sea

POSEN

SWEDEN

MECKLENBERG-STRELITZ

MECKLENBERG-SCHWERIN

ANHALT

SAXONY

THURINGIA

BRUNSWICK

DENMARK

LIPPE

SCHLESWIG

OLDENBURG

DARMSTADT

HESSE

BAVARIA

WÜRTTEMBERG

BADEN

BAVARIAN PALATINATE

ALSACE LORRAINE

North Sea

NETHERLANDS

BELGIUM

LUX.

FRANCE

SWITZERLAND

Prussia

Austria-Hungary

Area incorporated in 1871

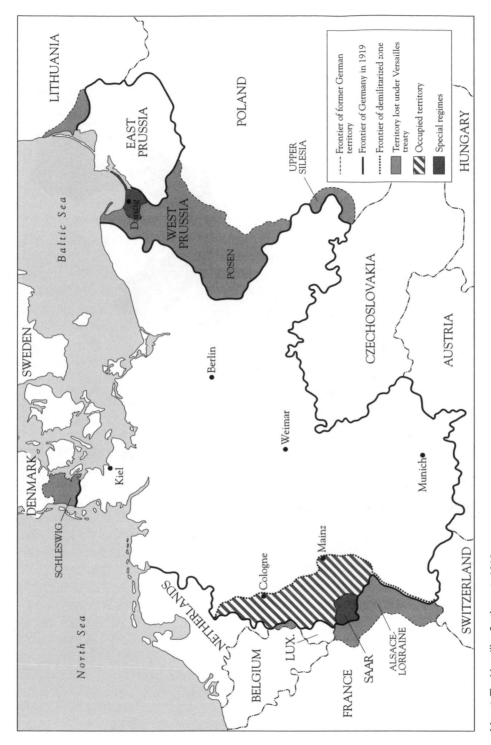

Map 4 The Versailles Settlement, 1919

Legend:

- Frontier of former German territory
- Frontier of Germany in 1919
- Frontier of demilitarized zone
- Territory lost under Versailles treaty
- Occupied territory
- Special regimes

Map 5 The division of Germany at Potsdam, 1945

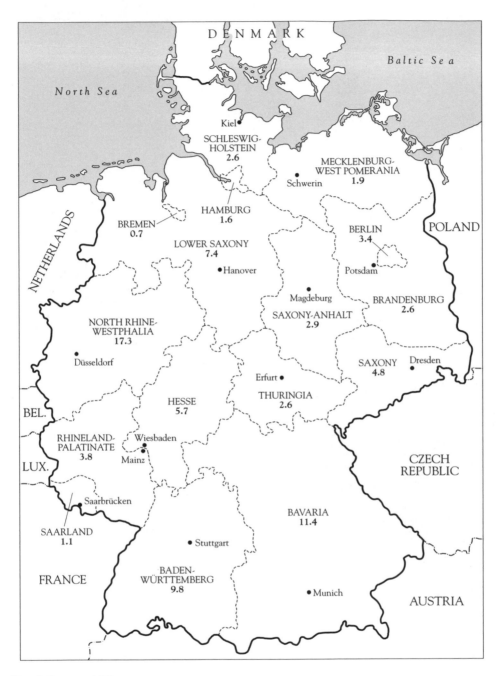

Map 6 Germany, 1993

Introduction

In 1800 Germany was a ramshackle empire, made up of hundreds of petty principalities, free cities, and ecclesiastical and aristocratic estates, which ever since 1512
had borne the impressive title of the Holy Roman Empire of the German Nation.
Voltaire caustically remarked that it was neither holy nor Roman, and certainly
not much of an empire. As for German – the word really did not mean much at
that time.

Among the German states only Austria and Brandenburg-Prussia counted for
anything, and Prussia was not even part of the empire. The empire had many virtues,
its federal constitution providing a model to the founding fathers of the United
States, but it was in a state of steady decline and was impervious to reform. It was
overrun by the armies of revolutionary France and reorganized under Napoleon.
The historian Thomas Nipperdey begins his monumental history of nineteenth-
century Germany with the catchy phrase: "In the beginning was Napoleon." Like
most such aphorisms it is a half-truth. This was no second creation, but it did mark
the end of the empire and a significant transformation of Germany's political geo-
graphy. Napoleon forced 16 of what the great reformer Baron vom Stein contemptuously called "petty sultanates" into the Confederation of the Rhine, thereby
greatly enhancing Bavaria, Württemberg, and Baden in the hope of creating a third
Germany to offset Prussia and Austria. These states were reformed on French lines,
adopting the progressive Napoleonic code of law, whereas in Prussia the reforms
were designed to strengthen the state so as eventually to free those provinces that
were under French occupation. These reforms and the struggle against France were
to lay the foundations of Prussian strength in the new century, and to lead to the
formation of the new Germany in 1871.

A somewhat vague notion of a German national identity was first articulated in
the eighteenth century and was centered on the linguistic and cultural peculiarities
of the German-speaking world. It was abstract, humanistic, cosmopolitan, philo-
sophically rarefied, and apolitical. The intense hatred of the French, caused by the
revolutionary and Napoleonic wars, along with the unacceptable behavior of the
French occupying troops, soured this early nationalism. Cosmopolitanism turned

into an arrogant feeling of cultural superiority. The apolitical became a reactionary obsession with a mythological German past. The rarefied was distilled into an impenetrable, but intoxicating obscurity. The new nationalists hoped that when the wars were over a powerful united Germany would emerge, but their hopes were dashed at the Congress of Vienna when they were overridden by the imperatives of the great European powers.

Britain and France preferred to accept the changes made by Napoleon, and completed his work by creating a German Confederation comprising the 39 remaining states. There was neither a head of state nor a government, but simply a federal assembly to which the member states sent their representatives, with Austria providing the chairman. The solution was acceptable to the Austrians, for they were the senior partners, and Metternich appeared to be firmly in charge as he imposed his reactionary and repressive policies on the Confederation.

Outward appearances were deceptive; whereas Austria failed to set its house in order by tackling the serious problems of a multinational empire at a time when national sentiments were becoming inflamed, Prussia was laying the foundations of its future economic strength. The Rhineland, which Prussia had been awarded at the Congress of Vienna much against its will, since it was a backward and Catholic area, became the center of Germany's industrial might. The Customs Union (*Zollverein*), founded in 1834 under Prussian leadership, made many of the German states economically dependent on Prussia, and created a market that was soon to challenge British supremacy. Capital moved northwards as Austria declined. All that was needed was some form of unification for Germany to be the most powerful nation on the Continent.

Metternich introduced a number of repressive measures, but he was unable to contain the various groups that clamored for constitutional reform, liberal nationalism, and radical change. Following the example of the French there was a revolutionary upheaval in Germany in 1848. A national assembly met in Frankfurt and was immediately confronted with the fundamental and perplexing questions "Who is a German?" and "Where is Germany?" There was at first general agreement that Germans were people who spoke German and, in the words of the patriotic poet and historian Ernst Moritz Arndt, who was born a serf and was thus a personification of the fundamental changes in the social fabric, Germany was "wherever German is spoken." On second thoughts this raised more problems than it solved. Were the proudly independent German-speaking Swiss really Germans? What about the Alsatians who spoke German but had French citizenship? Then there were the hundreds of thousands of Polish-speaking Prussians. Were they honorary Germans simply because there was no Polish state? A similar question was raised about the Czechs in the Austrian provinces of Bohemia and Moravia; and there was some discussion about whether Jews should be treated as equal citizens, or whether the German people needed to be protected against these threatening outsiders.

Most of the delegates to the Prussian parliament wanted a greater German solution, that is to say a Germany that included Austria. Such a Germany would, they hoped, be strong enough to protect and later absorb the German minorities on its borders in Holland, Luxemburg, Schleswig, Switzerland, and Alsace-Lorraine. Such ideas came up against the national aspirations of Poles and Czechs in the east, and were hastily dropped in the west for fear of confronting France. Whereas German liberals had traditionally championed the Polish struggle against Russian autocracy, they suddenly changed their tune, and denounced any suggestion that the German minority in Poland should be absorbed in a backward and uncultured nation. Similar accusations of treason were levied during discussions over the Czech lands, Northern Italy, and Schleswig. Healthy national egotism triumphed over any concern for other peoples' right to national self-determination. Precious few liberals realized that the denial of the rights of others to national self-determination undermined their own claims, and that victory over insurgents in Italy, Hungary, Bohemia, and Poland greatly strengthened the forces of reaction. It was a fatal flaw of this new form of nationalism that it was based on ethnicity rather than the acceptance of a shared sense of values and respect for a common legal system. One hundred and fifty years after the revolution of 1848 a Russian who could not speak a single word of German, but who was born of parents that claimed to be of German descent, had an automatic right to German citizenship, whereas a German-speaking child born of Turkish parents in Germany had no such claim. In spite of recent reforms of the immigration laws a residue of this heritage is still painfully apparent.

The men of 1848 were only free to deliberate and decide by majority vote as long as Austria and Prussia were busy dealing with their own immediate problems. Once the reaction had triumphed in both states the parliamentarians were ordered to pack their bags and returned to their respective states. In the years that followed, Austria and Prussia jockeyed for position within the German Confederation, until Bismarck was appointed Prussian chancellor and immediately set about settling the German question with blood and iron. First he defeated Denmark, and thus won over many liberal nationalists by finding a German solution to the Schleswig-Holstein question. Next he provoked a crisis with Austria, which was rapidly and soundly defeated, and then formed a federation of the German states north of the river Main under Prussian leadership. The process of German unification was completed with the defeat of France in 1871.

Very few people realized the dangers of national unification by such violent means, prominent among them Friedrich Nietzsche. After all, Greece, Serbia, and Italy were all founded by "blood and iron," and most nations were forged in civil wars. The new German empire had a parliament elected by universal manhood suffrage, which was far more than the "fig leaf of absolutism" as the socialist leader, August Bebel, claimed. Bismarck, its founding father, pronounced Germany to be "saturated;" once his great gambling streak was over he was anxious to keep the peace, and he knew that the other European powers were ever watchful of this prosperous and powerful newcomer.

The new empire, which some dubbed "The Second Reich," was a loose confederation of states, much like that which it had replaced, but it was one that was dominated to an increasing degree by Prussia. The military had always played a dominant role in Prussian society, and the Prussian army, having won three wars in quick succession virtually unaided, was admired, adulated, and emulated. Helmuth von Moltke, the greatest military genius since Napoleon, was widely regarded as a demi-god. The army was virtually free from parliamentary control since the war minister was not answerable to parliament, and the budget only came up for approval every seven years. The kaiser jealously guarded his power of command and protected the army from outside influences. Such was the social prestige of the army that Bismarck remarked that "human beings start at the rank of lieutenant."

Bismarck, often painted as a diplomatist of genius, left a fatal legacy. He permanently alienated France by agreeing to the annexation of Alsace and Lorraine, and then earned the hostility of Russia, first by his alliance with Austria-Hungary and then by triggering a trade war. His ill-considered dabbling in imperialism made the British increasingly wary of the new Germany. When his successors began to build a battle fleet, Britain, humiliated in the Boer War, sought continental partners and joined the Franco-Russian alliance, thus realizing Bismarck's "nightmare of coalitions."

Bismarck's domestic policies were as divisive as his foreign policy was hazardous. He painted a lurid picture the Reich's putative enemies, foremost among whom were the Social Democrats, but which also included Catholics along with the French, Poles, Alsatians, Danes, and whenever politically expedient, the Jews. With such a comprehensive catalog of opponents a majority of citizens were considered to be aliens, and only Protestant conservatives were deemed to be true Germans. The system began to fall apart at the seams as powerful liberal and democratic forces confronted a hidebound conservatism, backed by a racist and anti-Semitic populism. When war began in August 1914 these social and political tensions were temporarily overcome in a remarkable display of national unity, but as the war dragged on the nation fell apart. When the Western Front collapsed in the late summer and autumn of 1918, immediately following the spectacular success of the spring offensive, most people were shocked and taken by surprise. The army high command had concealed the true picture, and accused the democratic forces of stabbing the army in the back, thus causing the country's downfall.

Germany was left truculently defiant of the Treaty of Versailles and was determined to undo a peace settlement that was harsh enough for everyone to feel that it was grossly unfair, but actually so feeble that it could never be enforced. Germany's determination to undo the peace settlement was partly concealed by the Treaty of Locarno in 1925 and its subsequent admission to the League of Nations. The country was once again accepted into the community of nations as a great power, but for most Germans this was not enough. A severe economic crisis combined with a complete breakdown of the political system enabled Adolf Hitler and his National Socialists to agitate to increasing effect. Resistance to the Nazi menace was weakened by the inability of the democratic forces to settle their acute differences in order to reach a workable compromise in the face of a common danger, and by the folly of conservatives who imagined that they could use Hitler to serve their own purposes.

As soon as he was appointed chancellor, Hitler rapidly established a one-party dictatorship and his opponents were terrorized into submission. Once he was firmly in command he began systematically to tear up the Treaty of Versailles. Military service was introduced in 1935, and occupations took place of the Rhineland in 1936, Austria and the Sudetenland in 1938, and Bohemia, Moravia, and Memel in 1939.

The Nazis provided a radical and horrific answer to the perennial question "Who is a German?" Bismarck's old enemies – the Social Democrats, the politicized Christians, the left-leaning liberals – were forced into exile or locked away in concentration camps. The Polish elite was systematically murdered, millions of others enslaved. The much-vaunted "racial community" was purged of all elements which were considered to be dangerous and debilitating, such as the mentally and physically handicapped, habitual criminals, homosexuals, Gypsies and Jews, who were segregated, sterilized, or murdered.

Hitler's appalling vision could not be realized without a major war, which it at first looked as if he might win, despite the warnings of the more levelheaded of his generals. Through a deadly combination of ideological frenzy and bureaucratic efficiency, Hitler perpetrated a crime of unimaginable horror, which he believed was his greatest achievement and a legacy for which succeeding generations would be grateful, and which left behind a world in ruins, with tens of millions of dead, among them six million Jews.

In 1945 Germany was a pile of rubble with a starving population, a little Germany between the Rhine and Oder, once again a power vacuum, divided into four occupation zones. As a result of the imperatives of the cold war the country was divided into a democratic and capitalist state in the West and a Stalinist planned economy in the East. Western Germany was treated leniently – some would argue far too leniently – by the Western powers, encouraged in its determined efforts to develop a parliamentary democracy and a liberal market economy. Although a great many former Nazis had their crimes and misdemeanors overlooked, an extraordinary effort was made to confront the past, and no country has ever made such an effort to atone for its crimes.

Whereas the economy of the western Federal Republic grew at an astonishing rate thanks to the exceptional efforts of a generation determined to start anew, the eastern German Democratic Republic (GDR) was mismanaged so as to be virtually bankrupt by the early 1980s. As the Soviet empire crumbled the GDR was left isolated as a post-Stalinist dictatorship. Abandoned by the Soviet leadership, the regime collapsed and, as a result of the first free election for 57 years, the country opted to unite with the Federal Republic. On October 3 1990 Germany was thus reunited, but the gulf between the two Germanys remained alarmingly wide. Few had realized the hopeless state of the East German economy, the antiquated infrastructure, the extent of ecological devastation, the appalling state of public health and housing, to say nothing of the psychological effects of almost 60 years of dictatorship, snooping, censorship, and repression. The staggering cost of reconstruction placed a heavy burden on the West German taxpayers, who regarded the easterners as indigent, surly, and ungrateful. Easterners in turn resented this arrogance, and felt that they had been colonized by a selfish bunch of greedy materialists.

The process of unification is still far from complete. The walls that have been built in peoples' heads and hearts have to be broken down and the disparities between East and West overcome. But the prospect of a democratic and dynamic Germany, fully integrated into the European community, free from any dangerous ambitions, is a reassuring reminder that the country has learnt from its past mistakes and is determined to build on the democratic traditions that are also part of its troubled past.

German history is also the story of German historians, for they have shaped the way we see the German past. Leopold von Ranke, who established history as professional discipline, boldly asserted that a scientific and objective approach to the past could reveal, in his famous phrase, "How it actually was" (*wie es eigentlich gewesen*), was born in Thuringia in 1795, when the old empire was on its last legs. He witnessed the Napoleonic invasion and the redrawing of the map of Germany. The process of recovery was long and painful, and yet by the time that Ranke died in 1886 Germany had been united to form the most powerful and wealthiest state in Europe. Having lived through such an extraordinary series of events, it is hardly surprising that Ranke and his many disciples believed that the proper object of historical study was the state, its origins, its development, and its interactions with other states. It is wholly understandable that German historians, working at a time when the national question was foremost in peoples' mind, should thus assert the "primacy of foreign policy" (*Primat der Aussenpolitik*). The German question remained at the center of historians' attention with the country's defeat in the First World War and subsequent truncation in the Treaty of Versailles. Then came the Third Reich, total defeat, and the division into two antagonistic states. It took many decades before this approach to the past, which remained dominant at least in Germany until the 1960s, was seriously challenged. With the reunification of Germany the whole question of the German state is once again on the agenda, resulting in some remarkable neo-Rankean scholarship, notably Heinrich August Winkler's two-volume study *The Long Way to the West* (*Der lange Weg nach Westen*).

It was not until the 1960s that the younger generation of German historians began to reject the Rankean approach to the study of history. Very few were directly influenced by the works of the hugely influential "Annales" school; instead they rediscovered the works of a number of highly talented émigré historians such as Eckart Kehr, Arthur and Hans Rosenberg, Georg Hallgarten, and Alfred Vagts. They were politically engaged on the left, influenced by Weber and by Marx as reworked by the Frankfurt School into critical theory. Their self-proclaimed aim was to create a "historical science beyond historicism" (*Geschichtswissenschaft jenseits des Historismus*). Above all they saw history as a critical and emancipatory discipline. Theirs is a therapeutic model of historical discourse. They accepted that the historian has a grave moral responsibility and ostentatiously shouldered the burden of guilt for Germany's recent unfortunate past. The result was a mirror image of the old nationalist historical legacy, which saw a glorious tradition stretching from Luther to Frederick the Great to Bismarck and reaching its apotheosis in the foundation of the Reich in 1871. Now the legacy was that of the anti-Semitic and reactionary Luther, of the militaristic Great Elector, of the authoritarian Frederick the Great, and of the Bonapartist Bismarck, coupled with the disjuncture between economic modernity and political backwardness in the Kaiserreich, and the traditions of dreamy inwardness and deference to authority, all of which factors culminated in the bestiality of National Socialism.

It is hardly surprising that since 1945 the central question confronting historians was how a highly civilized country, which vaunted its moral and cultural superiority, and saw itself as the "land of writers and thinkers" (*Dichter und Denker*), could sink into the deepest depths of fanaticized barbarism. The answer to that question was quite simple. That a concentration camp commandant could love Goethe and Beethoven is proof that culture is no safeguard against barbarism. A possible answer was offered by those, like the historian A. J. P. Taylor and the journalist William Shirer, who suggested that there was a long tradition of aggressive nationalism, anti-Semitism, authoritarianism, hero-worshipping, and slavish obedience to authority that made something like National Socialism inevitable.

This enduringly popular explanation is, of course nothing of the sort. What seems in retrospect to be inevitable was the result of an almost infinite number of contingent variables. National Socialism may not have been the inevitable outcome of German history, but Hitler did not descend from the heavens as he does in Leni Riefenstahl's remarkable documentary on the Nuremberg party rally of 1934, *Triumph of the Will*. There were many factors at work that made National Socialism possible, and heavy burdens from the past resulted in an astonishing lack of resistance to a regime that trampled on all the positive traditions that Goebbels dubbed "the ideas of 1789." There is some truth in the argument that National Socialism was the fruit of certain trends that were common to all of Europe. It is also true that at least in part it was a response to Russian Communism. But none of this implies that Germany was not fully responsible for what happened between 1933 and 1945, or that National Socialism was not fully grounded on some unfortunate traditions in Germany's past. Above all, National Socialism was certainly not an "accident," as some historians have argued.

Fortunately there is much more to German history than the search for the origins of National Socialism and the analysis of the 12 years that it was in power. There is also the strong and vibrant liberal and democratic tradition to which this book pays tribute, and which makes a nonsense of the claim that National Socialism was the result of some fatal flaw in the German character. Such an idea is unable to account for the fact that these "awful" Germans, with their ghastly atavistic inheritance, now live in what is, for all its many obvious faults and shortcomings, an exemplary democracy, securely integrated within Europe, and free from any territorial ambitions.

When we talk of Germany we tend to think of it as a powerful monolith, when in fact for most of the period under discussion it was a loose federation of widely different states. Even the Wilhelmine empire comprised four separate kingdoms, with four separate armies, and a number of semi-autonomous entities, and it was only in the 12 years of National Socialism that the country was a centralized state. Regional differences were, and still are, extremely strong. Protestant Prussia was different from and antagonistic toward Catholic Bavaria. Rhinelanders had precious little in common with Pomeranians or Holsteiners. Local loyalties, summed up in the uniquely German concept of "*Heimat*," whether to proudly independent cities like Hamburg or Frankfurt, or to town, or village, remain powerful and are reinforced by local customs and practices.

The great nationalist historians concentrated on Prussia, for it was the driving force behind unification, and they glorified Bismarck's Germany, which was dominated by Prussia. Subsequent historians continued to write as if the history of Germany was the history of Prussia writ large. Some of Lamprecht's acolytes, who concentrated on cultural history, studied local history and customs as part of the National Socialist *völkisch* project, but it was not until after the Second World War that serious regional and local histories, which give us an inkling of the complexities and richness of German history, were written. Detailed studies provide a timely reminder that different Germans experienced the history of their country in widely different ways. A miner in the Ruhr, a university-educated lawyer in Berlin, a Bavarian farmer, and a Frisian fisherman lived in worlds that were poles apart. The set of relationships between men and women underwent a sea change in the period under review. It is difficult to imagine that from such widely differing circumstances something as all encompassing as a national character or the "German mind" could ever be constructed.

I make no apologies for writing a narrative history. History, as the word suggests, is essentially about telling a story. It is, with all due respects to the postmodernists, about a series of real events set into chronological order so as to show how one thing led, subject to however many eventualities, to another. For many years this approach has been dismissed by those who attempted to apply rigorously theoretical approaches derived from the social sciences to the study of history. In recent years historians have returned to a narrative approach, without which 200 years of German history would make no sense, and would dissolve into a series of unconnected events, trends, and data.

The Oxford philosopher, J. L. Austin, well known for his sardonic wit, once said that one might be tempted to call oversimplification the occupational disease of historians if it were not their occupation. I am all too aware of the many oversimplifications, omissions, and oversights in this book. Some are inevitable, others excusable, the rest entirely my fault. My one wish is that readers will find the story I have to tell of interest, and that reading it will inspire them to look elsewhere for further insights. To this end I have appended a short bibliography of works in English.

1

Germany Under Napoleon

Writing at the turn of the eighteenth to the nineteenth century, the whimsical German writer Jean Paul commented that providence had given the French the empire of the land, the English that of the sea, and to the Germans that of the air. He would have been at a loss to define what exactly he meant by the "Germans" and most likely would have found the question pointless. It could hardly have been confined to those who lived in the territory of the Holy Roman Empire of the German Nation, for that would have excluded a large number of German speakers, including the Prussians. Nor would he have included all those areas where German was spoken. The German empire indeed existed in the air. It was a threadbare patchwork of innumerable political entities from the European states of Austria and Prussia to the fiefdoms of the imperial knights, imperial monasteries, independent towns, and even villages.

All this was to change under the impact of the French revolutionary wars and above all of Napoleon. The French seized all the territory on the left bank of the Rhine, and in 1803 the map of Germany was redrawn as a result of the lengthy deliberations of an Imperial Deputation which did little more than add its seal of approval to a plan presented by the French and Russians. The deputation's Conclusions (*Reichsdeputationshauptschluss*) of February 25 1803, resulted in the secularization of the territorial possessions of the Catholic Church, including those of the Prince Bishops of Mainz, Cologne, and Trier, although the Archbishop Dalberg of Mainz, a crafty politician, retained his princely estates and his electoral title, was made Grand Duke of Frankfurt, and continued in office as chancellor of an empire that was soon to vanish. A host of smaller units were "mediatized" and absorbed by the larger states under the guise of compensation for territory lost to the west of the Rhine. The remains of once influential states such as the Electoral Palatinate vanished overnight. More than three million Germans were given new identities and most of the "petty sultanates," which had been the butt of Jean Paul's mordant wit, disappeared. The southern and southwestern states profited the most from these changes. Bavaria, Baden, and Württemberg were greatly strengthened as a counterweight to Prussia and Austria, but such power as they had resulted from their dependence on France. Clearly the empire was now doomed, and Dalberg's efforts at reform proved to no avail.

Shortly after the publication of the Conclusions France and England once again went to war. The French promptly occupied Hanover, which was in personal union with England, and thus directly threatened Prussia in spite of the provisions of the Treaty of Basel of April 1795 which guaranteed the neutrality of northern Germany. The southern German states were determined opponents of an empire that constrained their sovereignty and joined in with their French masters in an attack on Austria in 1805. On October 17 Napoleon scored a great victory over the Austrians at Ulm, but four days later Nelson destroyed the French fleet at Trafalgar in the most decisive naval victory in history. Britain now had absolute command of the seas, and Napoleon had no alternative to a land war on the Continent.

The southern German states were rewarded with spoils from the Habsburg Empire. Bavaria and Württemberg became kingdoms, Baden and Hessen-Darmstadt grand duchies. Napoleon's adopted daughter Stephanie Beauharnais was married off to the odious Karl, grand duke of Baden. The Holy Roman Empire was formally dissolved in 1806 and in July of that year the south German states where reorganized in the Confederation of the Rhine, a military alliance with the Emperor Napoleon in the self-appointed role of protector. The majority of the tiny states which had remained independent after the Conclusions were now absorbed by their larger neighbors.

Brandenburg-Prussia remained quixotically defiant in its isolation, its army a pathetic shadow of Frederick the Great's, its leadership decrepit and incompetent. The French made short shrift of them at the twin battles of Jena and Auerstedt in October. The once powerful Prussian state collapsed, Berlin's chief of police announcing that: "The king has lost a *bataille* and it is the responsibility of all citizens to remain calm." The phrase "Ruhe ist die erste Bürgerpflicht" (a citizen's prime responsibility is to remain calm), and the clear distinction made between the king and his subjects, was a classic expression of the spirit of Brandenburg-Prussia.

After an indecisive battle against the Russians at Preußisch-Eylau in early 1807, Napoleon smashed the tsar's army at Friedland in June, and peace was concluded at Tilsit. Prussia nearly vanished from the map of Europe and only survived because of the intervention of the tsar, and Napoleon's calculation that a buffer state between France and Russia might be desirable. Prussia lost all its territory west of the river Elbe, much of which went to make up the Kingdom of Westphalia for Napoleon's worthless brother Jérôme, and the smaller duchy of Berg was awarded to his brother-in-law Murat. Prussia was stripped of its recent acquisitions of Polish territory which became part of the new Grand Duchy of Warsaw. It was obliged to pay horrendous reparations and was subjected to French occupation until such time as they were paid in full.

The map of Germany had thus been radically redrawn and Prussia reduced to insignificance. In 1802 Hegel wrote:

All component parts would benefit from Germany becoming a state, but such will never come about as a result of deliberations, but only of force that is in tune with the general level of education and combined with a deeply and clearly felt desire for the need for unification. The common mass of the German people along with the estates, who only know of the separation of the various regions and who think of unification as something quite foreign to them, must be brought together by a conqueror's power. They must be coerced into regarding themselves as belonging to Germany.

Napoleon, Hegel's "world spirit on horseback," destroyed the old empire and inaugurated a new period in German history. Small wonder that Hegel stood in awe of the French emperor, as did so many of his great contemporaries, but his admiration remained on a lofty philosophical plane, and there were only a few opportunists and disgruntled ideologues who came to terms with the sordid reality of French domination.

The empire was a ramshackle affair, but it had many virtues, and most found it far more congenial than revolutionary France. Benjamin Franklin admired its federal structure and argued that it should be used as a model for the constitution of the United States. The old empire was destroyed by blood and iron, just as some 70 years later the new empire was to be created by the use of force. Germany was subjected to Napoleon's will, and his empire was now greater than that of Charlemagne. Only an uneasy Austria remained semi-independent.

The German economy was seriously disrupted by Napoleon's continental blockade that attempted to exclude British goods. German smugglers were so successful that the French felt obliged to occupy Holland and the German coast as far as Lübeck in 1810, but British goods still found their way in, and the French took draconian measures against those found in possession of such contraband. This only served to fuel resistance to the French occupiers and strengthened national self-consciousness which was further exacerbated by the "Continental System," which subordinated the German economy to French needs. The traditional export of wood, wool, grain, and linen to England was now rendered virtually impossible, but some manufacturers seized the opportunity afforded by the exclusion of British competition and thrived, only to be ruined after 1815 when British goods once again flooded the German market. All Germans were affected by sharply rising prices, by heavy taxes, and by frequent controls by the French authorities.

By 1808 the Confederation of the Rhine was forced to provide Napoleon with 119,000 soldiers, thus placing a further burden on the unfortunate Germans. French officials supervised the minutest details of each state's administration, a rigorous censorship was applied, and the nationalist opposition was hunted down. In such circumstances it is hardly surprising that attempts to give the Confederation of the Rhine a federal constitution failed. The southern German states, on whom the obligation to provide troops fell hardest, jealously guarded what remained of their sovereignty and the French did not wish to risk further alienating their German vassals for fear that they might emulate the Spanish and rise up against a despotism that proclaimed itself to be a harbinger of liberty, equality, and fraternity.

The uprising in Spain was an inspiration to many Germans, particularly in Prussia which, although it had not been forced to become a member of the Confederation of the Rhine, was suffering terribly under the burden of reparations. It had been confidently assumed that the French would not demand more than a grand total of 20 million francs. The final bill was for 154 million. The end of the occupation, the staggering cost of which the Prussians were obliged to pay, was thus postponed indefinitely. The first minister, Baron vom Stein, at first had argued in favor of trying to meet the French demands, but once he heard of events in Spain he argued in favor of a popular revolt against French rule. He was a singularly poor conspirator, the French got wind of his schemes and secured his instant dismissal. Stein's property was seized, but he managed to escape to Bohemia having been tipped off by a friendly French official. Henceforth he was a major figure in the European struggle against Napoleon. Leading military reformers, such as Scharnhorst and Gneisenau, also discussed a comprehensive reform plan to be coupled with a revolt against French rule.

Although the Prussian government would not entertain such schemes, Napoleon felt obliged to make some concessions to ease this mounting tension. In the Treaty of Paris of September 1808 reparations were somewhat reduced and the occupation was ended, but some 10,000 French troops remained to guard military roads and to man the fortresses on the Oder. The costs were borne by Prussia, and were more than the state could bear. Prussia's finances were in a parlous condition and not even Hardenberg, who was appointed chancellor in June 1810, was able to improve the situation significantly, for all his considerable administrative talents. Frederick William III, never the most decisive of monarchs, relapsed into a torpor on the death of his resourceful and immensely popular queen Luise in 1810. The queen was to become the object of a romantic cult, with poets such as Novalis as its priests. She was transformed into an idealized daughter, wife, and mother, and Gottfried Schadow's erotically charged statue of the young Luise with her sister Friederike was withheld from public view until the revolution of 1848 heralded the beginning of a less prudish age. This masterpiece of German classicism suggests that there was much more to Luise than a prototypical bourgeois *Hausfrau*.

Austria did not have to labor under such onerous conditions and played a more proactive role. Count Philip Stadion, the first minister, was a conservative southern German, but he was also a fervent patriot. He hoped to mobilize popular sentiment throughout Germany and inspire a war of liberation that would result in the rebirth of the German empire. It was a heady vision that appealed to many of the great writers and publicists of the age such as Kleist, Friedrich Schlegel, and Gentz. Metternich, another prominent conservative who was ambassador in Paris, agreed that Austria could not afford to sit and wait for France to strike once again and had to act. Even the emperor was infected with such nationalistic rhetoric, and the Archduke Karl appealed to all German patriots to join in the struggle against France and for a reborn empire.

The poetic notion that the people would arise and a storm would be unleashed was hopelessly unrealistic. The regular army was no match for Napoleon's and the new Territorial Army (*Landwehr*) was militarily worthless. This fact was somewhat obscured by Napoleon's first defeat at Aspern in May 1809 as he attempted to cross the Danube. Jubilation at this surprising victory was premature. Support from the other German states was minimal. Some adventurers, like the Prussian Major Schill, joined in the fray. Frederick William III closed his ears to entreaties from the military reformers demanding he declare war on France. There was a poorly organized peasants' revolt in Westphalia but most Germans remained passive bystanders. Napoleon crossed the Danube at night, exploited the division between the two Austrian armies and confronted the Archduke Charles' army at Wagram on June 5. Charles fought well and the first day was indecisive, but on the second Napoleon's brilliant use of artillery resulted in a crushing defeat. Shortly afterward Napoleon entered Vienna.

The only successful revolt was in the Tyrol, which had been annexed by Bavaria in 1805. Andreas Hofer, supported by the Archduke John, led a brilliant guerilla campaign in the mountains and defeated the French and Bavarian forces in a rapid series of engagements. But this was a traditional, Catholic, and regional movement at odds with the spirit of the age. Hofer was eventually captured and executed in Mantua along with Major Schill and the patriotic publisher Palm. They became the first three martyrs of the German cause, whose memory was recalled in the 22-year-old Ludwig Uhland's "*Ich hatt' einen Kamaraden*" which became an immensely popular patriotic anthem, and which was later to be appropriated by the nationalist and militaristic right.

In the Peace of Schönbrunn Austria ceded further territories and was obliged to pay crippling reparations. All of Europe was now under Napoleon's sway and only Spain offered fierce resistance to the French in a guerilla war, the ferocity and brutality of which was immortalized in Goya's shattering etchings. Austria sought to appease and accommodate Napoleon who became the emperor's son-in-law, having been rebuffed by the tsar, whose sister he had hoped to marry. Metternich, who always put security above legitimacy, encouraged Napoleon's social climbing, in the hope that the marriage would spare Austria from further depravation.

Russia was always an uneasy partner for Napoleon and there were so many points of disagreement between the two states that conflict seemed increasingly likely. Austria and Prussia now had to choose between the two sides. Metternich felt that Russia was unlikely to be able to withstand an invasion and proposed giving France limited support so as to come out on the winning side. In Prussia there was a fierce debate between the patriots, with Gneisenau as their fiery spokesman, who pleaded for an alliance with Russia and a popular uprising, and the king who dismissed such romantic notions as "mere poetry." Napoleon demanded the right to march his forces across Prussia and insisted that 20,000 men from the Prussian army, which had been reduced to a mere 42,000, should take part in the campaign. Hardenberg saw no alternative but to accept these humiliating conditions. The reaction among the patriots was instant. About one quarter of the officer corps resigned their commissions, among them Clausewitz and Boyen who went to Russia. Even the chief of police, Justus Gruner, offered his services to the tsar. Frederick William

III no longer enjoyed the loyalty of many of his most prominent officials, who now saw themselves as serving the nation and the people rather than the monarch. Such was the force of revolutionary ideas that they affected even those who were the most ardent opponents of its Bonapartist manifestation.

The Age of Reform

Although outwardly Prussia seemed weak and feeble, and its government aimless, the period from 1806 to 1811 was one of astonishing and rapid reform. Drastic changes were needed were the state ever to free itself from French domination. But it was not simply a matter of power politics. The French Revolution had swept aside the old aristocratic society based on the estates, and replaced it with the bourgeois concepts of freedom and equality. These were notions fraught with contradictions, as critics never tired of pointing out, but there was a general recognition that a state could only survive if the people identified with it to some degree, if its subjects became citizens, if the gulf between the state and society were bridged.

These were revolutionary ideas, as conservative reformers like Hardenberg knew full well. For this reason they were determined that it should be a revolution from above, controlled and channeled by the bureaucracy, so that the state could be immunized against a revolution from below. It was to be a revolution based on the rule of law, the application of logical reasoning, and concern for the good of the state. A monarchical government was to be given a degree of popular legitimacy in order to avoid the horrors of revolutionary democracy and a reign of terror.

Although there had been some efforts at reform before 1806, it was the virtual collapse of the Prussian state in that fateful year that convinced all but the most purblind of conservatives that drastic changes were needed. The Prussia of Frederick the Great had been an exemplary absolutist state, an example to the rest of Germany, a European power of consequence. But by 1806 Prussia was lagging behind the southern German states, its sclerotic social order hopelessly out of tune with the times. Reformers, who for years had been urging major changes but who had been blocked by an aristocracy determined to defend its privileges and by a reluctant monarchy, now seized their opportunity.

The reformers were inspired by Kant's lofty concept of individual rights, obligations, and reasoned self-interest that was taken up by such influential figures as Fichte and Pestalozzi. The individual citizen was to come of age, be self-actualizing, free from the restraints of a hierarchical society, free to develop his own talents and abilities, free to contribute to the common good. The enlightened absolutism of the old regime was to be replaced by the enlightened absolutism of the self, which lay at the heart of the liberal humanism of the bourgeois epoch. Obligations were doubtless emphasized at the expense of rights, but for many this vision of the new man was exciting, for others terrifying. When combined with the economic theories of Adam Smith it was to condemn the old order to extinction. Since the motive force behind the reforms was to free Prussia from the French, the reforms aimed to strengthen patriotic and nationalistic sentiments, thus further subordinating individual liberties to a common cause. It was an ambitious program that aimed at a thorough overhaul of the state. The administration was to be rationalized and careers open to the talents. The economy was to be released from the shackles of the past, and "*Manchesterismus*" was to be its guiding principle. The army was to be reformed and promotions based on talent rather than on social status. Society was to be freed from the restrictions and inequalities of the old order, and there was to be full equality before the law, thus unleashing the creative power of the people in the service of a common cause.

So much for the lofty ideals; reality was somewhat different. There was considerable resistance to reform in some quarters, particularly at court and among conservative aristocrats. There were also many differences between the reformers themselves. Baron vom Stein, who was principal minister from 1807 until his dismissal at Napoleon's command in the following year, was the initiator of the reform movement. As an imperial knight with an impeccable aristocratic lineage he detested the absolutist state and urged the devolution of power, and the strengthening of traditional rights and privileges. He was also suspicious of economic liberalism which he felt could lead to the sacrifice of individual rights to the exigencies of the market. By contrast Hardenberg, who became chancellor in 1810 and remained in office until his death in 1822, believed in the centralization of state power and a liberal economic policy. He was less troubled than Stein by moral and philosophical concerns, and argued that with the guarantee of property rights, equality before the law and fair taxation, the individual should be able to fend for himself, and would recognize the need for the firm guiding hand of an autocratic state.

The first priority was the reorganization of the administration. The late absolutist state was a shambolic affair with no identifiable areas of competence, a myriad of conflicting interests and institutions, and no clearly defined order of government. The chaotic old cabinet system was swept aside and the king could now only act through his ministers. The absolutist state gave way to bureaucratic governance. Under Stein ministers were treated as equals in a collegial system. He had hoped to create a council of state, composed of a wide range of prominent people, to act as a kind of surrogate parliament and to keep a watchful eye on overly ambitious ministers. Hardenberg had no sympathy for such ideas and created the office of chancellor which controlled the access of subordinate ministers to the king.

At the local level Prussia was divided into districts (*Regierungsbezirke*) each with an administration (*Regierung*) in which the District President (*Regierungspräsident*) was treated as a first among equals. Prussia was thus a federal state with each district enjoying a degree of autonomy, where eventually the president was responsible to the local diets (Landtage) which were introduced in 1823/4. They were based on the estates and thus dominated by the aristocracy. Only those who had owned property for many years were eligible to vote, thus many highly educated men were disenfranchised. Church affairs, education, health, and road building were among the presidents' other responsibilities. At Stein's insistence there was a strict division of powers between the judiciary and the executive. Beneath the districts were the circles (*Kreise*), which were supervised and controlled by the District President. At this level Hardenberg hoped to realize his étatist vision. A state-appointed director was to take the place of the *Landrat*, who was elected by the local aristocracy. He was to be assisted by an administration elected by the aristocracy, the towns, and the peasantry in equal parts, and by a state-appointed judge. Gendarmes were to take over the function of local policing thus putting an end to the aristocracy's right to police their own estates. Aristocratic resistance to these proposals was so strong that they were shelved, and the old order remained entrenched on the land. The *Landrat* remained as an organ of a patriarchal–feudal order, and, given that there were only 1,300 policemen in all of Prussia, the policing rights of the aristocracy further strengthened the old order. Bourgeois who purchased aristocratic estates were denied all of the special privileges that went with them, and in the Rhineland aristocratic rights that had been abolished were reestablished, causing much bitterness among the bourgeoisie. Tensions between the aspiring middle class and the aristocracy were more noticeable in Prussia than elsewhere in Germany.

Stein's notion of self-government as a counterweight to an all-powerful state was best realized in the towns. Ancient rights and outmoded privileges were abolished and the administration of justice was now in the hands of the state. The towns became self-governing. A college of electors was chosen by districts rather than by estates, this passive voting right given to all who met certain minimal requirements of property, profession, and length of residence. Active voting rights were more restrictive. The propertyless, soldiers, and Jews were not regarded as burghers and were excluded from participation at either level. Councilors who were paid a salary were elected for a term of 12 years, honorary councilors for six years. Both the mayor and the salaried councilors had to meet state approval. The reform of municipal government resulted in the creation of a highly professional class of civic administrators, and served as a model for similar reforms in other European states. But it was not an unmitigated success. Like most other reforms during this revolution from above, it was ordered from on high, it did not result from pressure from below. Its emancipatory effect was thus of little consequence. Furthermore, since it did not coincide with similar reforms in the countryside the divisions between town and country were further accentuated.

The most radical of the reforms in Prussia was the liberation of the peasantry from the remnants of the feudal order. Serfdom was repugnant to enlightened bureaucrats and its abolition was seen as striking a blow at the very foundations of the absolutist, aristocratic, social order. Stein entertained the romantic notion that the brutish and enslaved peasantry would become proud yeomen and worthy citizens who would form the backbone of a revitalized nation. Added to this mixture of Kantian morality and Rousseau's romanticism came of a large dose of Adam Smith's economic liberalism. It was argued that only if property and labor were freely brought to market could an economy flourish. Aristocratic estates henceforth could be freely bought and sold so that wealthy bourgeois could invest in the land. Serfs would become wage laborers. A traditional, aristocratic, semi-feudal society was to give way to capitalist agriculture.

Once again the impetus for reform came from above, from the liberal bureaucracy, and not from below. There were precious few instances of peasant protest
prior to the reform, indeed some peasants regretted the passing of a familiar patriarchal order. Similarly, few aristocratic landowners realized the opportunities that
a free market economy offered. Resistance to reform was so strong that it was only
after the collapse of Prussia in 1806, when the state was faced with a crippling economic burden, that Stein was able to sweep all objections aside. On October 9 1807,
only ten days after his appointment as minister, he issued the "October Edict" that
announced the abolition of serfdom in Prussia by Saint Martin's Day (November
11) 1810.

The peasants were now free subjects before the law, able to own property, marry
as they wished, free to move and to practice any trade or profession. Aristocrats
were also free to sell their estates and to enter professions that had previously been
reserved for the bourgeoisie. In theory a society based on the estates was replaced
by a class society which allowed for a high degree of social mobility. In practice
there were many remnants of the old regime and no edict could ever fundamentally
alter the habits, customs, and mentality that had been ingrained over generations.
Nevertheless, this was a radical step forward that changed Prussia in a number of
ways. Many aristocrats sold their estates to bourgeois entrepreneurs and the close
association of the aristocracy to the land was now little more than a romantic myth.
By mid-century about half of the aristocratic estates had passed into bourgeois
hands. As elsewhere in Europe wealthy entrepreneurs longed to become country
gentlemen, but although some were subsequently ennobled, unlike England where
titles did not pass on to younger sons, a strict segregation of classes was maintained
and intermarriage between aristocrats and bourgeois was extremely rare. The peasantry was no longer protected by the obligations owed by lords to their serfs, and
the pressure of population caused widespread poverty on the land. Conservative
opponents of reform argued that capitalism resulted in benevolent feudal lords being
replaced by rapacious creditors who bled their wretched victims white. They were
well organized, with their exclusive representative bodies and their own banking
system, to say nothing of their close ties to the court and to the upper echelons of
government. They prepared to fight back as soon as the state of emergency had
passed. Many concessions were made to the aristocracy. Cheap credit was made
available to landowners who were suffering the consequences of drastically falling
prices for agricultural produce. The law of 1810 governing the treatment of servants and laborers (*Gesindeordnung*) was hardly in the spirit of the reformers. Land-
lords kept their manorial courts, were permitted to mete out corporal punishment,
and could demand unquestioning obedience from their underlings. They kept their
exclusive hunting rights, were given many tax exemptions, and could appoint the
local minister and schoolmaster. The law turned a blind eye when aristocrats fought
duels, a way of settling disputes denied to lesser breeds. The entrenched powers of
the aristocracy were such that there were strict limits to reform.

A particularly intractable question was that of appropriate compensation for the
loss of feudal obligations. This could hardly be in the form of immediate money

payments since the peasantry was miserably poor and the state overburdened with debt. Compensation, in the form of land, was even harder to determine. A decision was therefore postponed, and it was not until 1821 when the reaction was winning the upper hand, that a commutation was finally put into effect. Landowners were compensated either by the transfer of land or by the payment of rents. They further profited from the conversion of common lands into private property, and by a land settlement designed to bring about a more rational allocation of acreage. Stein and Hardenberg's vision of a proud yeomanry was thus never realized, and few liberated peasants were able to survive as independent farmers. In the part of Prussia east of the Elbe the Junker estates profited considerably as a result of the liberation of the serfs, and it remained an area of large estates rather than modest farms. This was to have far-reaching social and political consequences. In the Prussian provinces west of the Rhine, where the Napoleonic code had been applied, the smaller farmers were in a far more favorable position. For all its shortcomings and injustices the reform on the land was a vital step forward in the process of modernization. Agricultural capitalism replaced a feudal cooperative mode of production. Custom, habit, and tradition gave way to scientific farming and double-entry bookkeeping. The larger estates were reorganized into effective productive units that swallowed up many a small farm that failed to compete. But the reform was incomplete. The manorial estates retained many of their ancient rights and privileges within the context of a modern economic order.

The reformers placed economic freedom above individual freedom. Land could be freely bought and sold. The power of the guilds was broken by the Trade Edict (*Gewerbeordnung*) of 1810. The legal distinctions between town and country were abolished. Church lands were secularized, and much of the royal demesne placed on the market. Hardenberg's determined efforts to reform the tax system so as to make it both equitable and evenhanded were only partially successful. A purchase tax on selected items met with fierce resistance and was later abandoned. Taxes on businesses were applied in both town and country, but the opposition of the Junkers was so strong that an attempt to make them pay equal land taxes failed. In 1811 and 1812 a one time income tax with a marginal rate of five percent was introduced, but this occasioned frantic protest by the wealthy against the violation of the private sphere by the state and the malicious assault on private property rights. In 1820 a "class tax" was introduced which combined a poll tax with a sort of income tax. This, combined with the remaining forms of indirect taxation, was a particularly heavy burden on the poor, and contributed to the growing disparities of wealth and income.

There was one issue on which the reformers and the conservatives could agree. Prussia could never be liberated without fundamental improvements in the army. The Prussian army, once the finest in Europe, had failed to keep pace with fundamental changes both in military science and in society at large. It had failed miserably in 1806. Its tactics were outmoded, commissions in its superannuated officer corps were given on the basis of birth rather than ability, and the men were subjected to brutal discipline. Foreign mercenaries made up at least one third of its personnel, and it existed as an institution separated at every level from the society around it. The reformers, with Scharnhorst at their head, were determined to bridge the gap between the army and society, and convert the downtrodden and mindless soldiers into self-actualizing patriots to whom the highest ranks and honors were open.

For this to be possible soldiers had to be respected as autonomous subjects, equal before the law, and no longer subjected to inhuman punishment. The fact that the army was drastically reduced by the French gave the reformers a golden opportunity to cut out much of the dead wood from the officer corps. Henceforth commissions were to be awarded by competitive examination, and promotions likewise were no longer to be based almost exclusively on length of service. Gneisenau waxed poetically on the power and the genius that slumbered in the lap of the nation, and which would soar on eagles' wings once the fetters of custom and class were removed. Archconservatives like Yorck, although a modernizer of the army with his mastery of light infantry tactics, was appalled. He argued that an attack on the privileges of the aristocracy would lead to an attack on the legitimacy of the monarchy and smacked of Jacobinism. His objections were swept aside and his fears soon proved to be unfounded. A conservative institution like the Prussian officer corps could never be so radically reformed. Old prejudices in favor of the traditional aristocratic families who had served the state for generations were too deeply entrenched. Many young aristocrats were men of considerable talent, and had little difficulty in passing the rigorous examinations required to gain a commission and climb the ladder of promotion. Scharnhorst and Gneisenau might have been bourgeois, but Clausewitz and Boyen came from distinguished old families.

These reforms were all based on the liberal and democratic principle of universal military service, which was designed to create a people's army, in contrast to the standing army of the autocratic state. Predictably, the idea of a nation in arms was anathema to the conservatives, but many bourgeois reformers also felt that this was going too far along the road to equality and marked a general leveling down of society to its lowest common denominator. The king had little sympathy for the romantic notion of a people's war, and feared the reaction of the French should universal military service be put into effect. It was thus not until 1813, when Prussia was again at war, that all men of age were called up to serve the nation in arms. A territorial army (*Landwehr*) was also formed with a solidly bourgeois officer corps, unlike the regular army in which the aristocracy still predominated. The ideals of the reformers were most fully realized in the *Landwehr*, which was passionately supported by the liberals and equally intensely detested by conservatives for decades to come. The proposal to arm all remaining males from the age of 15 to 60 in a *levée en masse*, without uniforms and with elected officers, appalled most respectable citizens. They denounced the guerilla bands foreseen in this *Landsturm* as Jacobins who posed a greater danger to Prussia than they did to its enemies. The suggestion was therefore dropped and the reformers concentrated on the *Landwehr* as the realization of their vision of a people's army. Under Boyen's army bill of September 1814 all those eligible for military service were to serve three years in regiments of the line and then two years in the reserve. They were then obliged to serve in the first division of the *Landwehr* until the age of 32 and the second until the age of 50. All those who did not serve in the regular army had to join the *Landwehr* at the age of 20. The educated bourgeois could serve one year in the regular army after which he became an officer in the *Landwehr*. There was thus a clear distinction between an aristocratic and conservative regular officer corps and a bourgeois and liberal *Landwehr*. Conflict between the two was thus almost inevitable.

The practical military results of the reforms did not meet the reformers' expectations. Admittedly, Prussia was able to field an army of over a quarter of a million men, it was better trained, its staff work greatly improved, and some units, particularly in the *Landwehr*, were fired by an idealistic and patriotic spirit. On the other hand such enthusiasm was by no means general; there were large numbers of desertions and there was fierce resistance by the regular officer corps to universal military service. The notion that in 1813 "a people arose, a storm burst forth" is a romantic myth. Amid widespread indifference the conservative forces braced themselves to undo the work of the reformers. They were largely successful, but the bourgeoisie had made important inroads into the old order, and the outcome of this struggle was no foregone conclusion.

The reformers insisted that a society of free citizens with careers open to the talents had to be well educated. Throughout Germany the educational system was in disarray. In the universities the professors were tedious pedants, hopelessly out of touch with the times. The student body was indolent, debauched, and given to outbursts of mindless violence against the unfortunate townsfolk. Schooling was equally abysmal, without supervision, organization, or control from central authority. Ill-qualified and miserably paid teachers used brutal discipline to drill a few vestiges of an elementary education into their hapless pupils. The great educational reformers such as Fichte, Pestalozzi, and Wilhelm von Humboldt took up Kant's ideal of the autonomous self-actualizing individual and argued that education should not be directed toward fulfilling the demands of the state, the market, or tradition, but should be an end in itself. The development of a spontaneous, critical, and imaginative subject was more important than training for a profession or trade. The practical objectives of the enlightenment were to give way to the subjective ideals of neo-humanism. Education was not to be the preserve of a small elite but was to be universal. Only thus could the many-sided talents that slumbered within the nation be awoken. Even the king, who could hardly be described as an intellectual, was captivated by such ideas and announced that: "The state must make up in the intellectual sphere for what it has lost in physical power."

The University of Berlin, founded in 1810, was based on these principles. Knowledge was to be pursued for its own sake regardless of any practical application. An interdisciplinary education in the humanities was designed to create well-rounded individuals rather than narrow specialists. In his inaugural address as rector Fichte announced: "The true life-giving breath of the university. . . . the heavenly ether is without doubt academic freedom." This was an expression of the all too often derided German notion of freedom as inward, subjective, and metapolitical. In fact the reformers who espoused these lofty ideas were eminently political. They looked in horror at the enormities committed in the name of freedom, and insisted that a people could only be genuinely free by thoroughgoing individualization. Tuition was free, there was no fixed curriculum, and no set number of years of study. Dialogue between teacher and pupil and the common pursuit of pure knowledge was the sole requirement. For all the protestations to the contrary, it was an elitist concept that aimed to replace the old aristocracy of birth with a highly educated meritocracy. It largely ignored the exigencies of the nascent industrial age and set as a new ideal the gentleman scholar.

Obviously all was dependent on state support. The reformers argued that the state had a moral obligation to educate its citizens according to their precepts. In return for this hands-off policy the state would be strengthened by the optimum development of individual capabilities. It was a lofty ideal, a dream of the higher bureaucracy and professoriate who worked closely together. It ignored the fact that changes in the structure of the state would necessarily lead to changes in its attitude to education. The age of reform was to be of limited duration and the state was soon to reassert its authority and use the educational system to strengthen its hold over the citizenry.

The Prussian school system was also reformed with two levels. The preparatory school (*Elimentarschule*) led to the grammar school (*Gymnasium*). These latter were self-consciously elite institutions which, like the universities, emphasized the humanities, particularly Greek and Latin. All teachers were required to have university degrees. A school leaving certificate, known as the *Abitur*, was introduced in 1812, and soon became the prerequisite for entry to university. By 1816 there were only 91 grammar schools in the whole of Prussia, which replaced the much more numerous but also much smaller Latin Schools. Teachers in the elementary schools (*Volksschule*) were also required to have a diploma from a teacher training college (*Normalschule*), where they absorbed a modified version of the teachings of the great Swiss educational reformer Pestalozzi. Reform of these schools, in which retired Prussian NCOs had flogged a rudimentary education into their unfortunate charges, took much longer, but at least a step had been taken in a promising direction. A separate ministry of education, which kept a close eye on the schools, was eventually established in 1817.

The aim of all these reforms was the creation of a modern bourgeois state free from the privileges of the estates and provincial particularism. This could not be done overnight, and the reforms ran far ahead of social reality. For this reason they only went half way, and only when society changed could there be any serious discussion of a modern constitution. The state was still dependent for money on the institutions of the old regime in which the privileges of the estates were anchored, and this proved an effective barrier to thoroughgoing reform. An aristocracy jealous of its privileges thus had effective means of frustrating the centralizing and modernizing intentions of the bureaucracy.

For all their limitations the reforms were the most ambitious and comprehensive in Prussia. In the Confederation of the Rhine the contradictions and frictions were even more severe. On the one hand Napoleon hoped to consolidate the moderniz-ing achievements of the revolution, but he also set out to exploit these subject states for funds and soldiers, and reward his followers with estates carved out of them. The south German states were faced with the additional problem of integrating the many disparate territories they had recently absorbed under a centralized adminis-tration, and under a common set of laws. Baden had increased four-fold and Württemberg had doubled in size as a consequence of the Napoleonic reordering of Germany. Bavaria now included 80 autonomous political entities that had to be integrated. They set about this task in the traditional manner of the absolutist state by bureaucratic and administrative control and rational planning by the centralized state. Here there was hardly a whiff of Kantian humanism, and the democratic notions of the French revolution met with little response in the upper echelons. Gov-ernments were reorganized, but rather than create collegial systems, the powers of absolutist ministers such as Montgelas in Bavaria and Reizenstein in Baden were greatly enhanced.

In the course of the territorial changes in southern Germany Catholic Bavaria absorbed large numbers of Protestants, whereas Protestant Baden now had a Catholic majority. True to enlightened absolutist traditions, the state maintained strict control over the churches and mounted a campaign against religious excesses. In both Bavaria and Württemberg pilgrimages were forbidden, miracles were not to be mentioned in homilies, and even the public display of Christmas cribs was outlawed as part of the campaign against superstition and fanaticism. In Württemberg pietism was similarly outlawed as a pernicious form of mysticism. But at least full religious equality was recognized in these states, and the often excessive struggle against religious enthusiasm was matched with an admirable degree of interdenominational tolerance.

In Bavaria, Württemberg, and Baden the first priority was the ordering and organization of the new territories, the abolition of local privileges and exemptions, and the tightening of central control. Given the heavy burden of debt that rested on all of the states in the Confederation of the Rhine a fundamental reform of the fiscal system was essential. Educational reforms lagged far behind those in Prussia and the military authorities had no truck with notions of a people in arms, prefer-ring a lengthy term of service in a conscript army. The most dramatic and far-reach-ing changes in southern Germany resulted from the secularization of church lands. In Bavaria half of the land was in the hands of monastic orders. This was taken over by the state and sold off at rock bottom prices to the peasantry, with only the forests remaining largely under state control. Unlike Prussia, where the liberation of the serfs had benefited the large estates, land reform resulted in the creation of a large number of small farms and modest peasant holdings.

There were other equally significant consequences of secularization. The seques-tration of church lands was a major step forward in the creation of a modern secular state and the impact on the church was equally dramatic. Higher ecclesiastical offices were no longer the preserve of the aristocracy. The church, which was now sup-ported financially by the state, turned away from worldly affairs and concentrated on its spiritual mission. As in Prussia the aristocracy lost some, but by no means all of their ancient privileges. With the collapse of the old empire the mediatized imperial aristocracy retained a special status within the sovereign state, and the thoroughgoing reform of property rights was blocked by the determined rearguard action of the privileged. Even in states such as Westphalia and Berg, where the *Code Napoléon* was imposed, compensation was demanded for the abolition of feudal rights. Since neither the state nor the peasantry had the money to meet such requirements these rights remained in force.

The great jurist Anselm von Feuerbach, the moving spirit behind the Bavarian penal code of 1813 which was a model of progressive legislation, argued that the logical consequence of these reforms and the establishment of bourgeois freedom was that the state should have a constitution. But Feuerbach was ahead of his time, and was soon to be pushed aside in the reaction that followed Napoleon's defeat. The Bavarian constitution of 1808 allowed for the indirect election of a National Assembly by a highly restrictive franchise, and guaranteed the independence of the judiciary, certain individual rights, and the rule of law. But the National Assembly never met. A similar institution, for which the Westphalian constitution of 1807 provided, met only twice.

Thus in the Confederation of the Rhine many ancient privileges were abolished, particularism was largely overcome, bourgeois freedoms were strengthened, and the rule of law asserted. The individual was thus partially freed within the context of a centralized bureaucratic state which was reinforced by a vigilant police force. Traces of the old oligarchy remained, but the old order of the estates was gradually being replaced by a class society, and although the principle of equality before the law was still largely theoretical, at least it was placed on the agenda. Similar reforms were carried out in Baden under Reitzenstein's forceful leadership, in Nassau and in Württemberg, where King Friedrich asserted his absolutist rights against the estates, but also against the people. Many areas, such as Saxony and the smaller north and central German states, were virtually unaffected by reform. In Westphalia and Berg the reforms remained largely on paper while the French occupiers squeezed all they could from their subjects.

The Prussian reform movement was inspired by the desire to bridge the gap between the state and society, and to involve the citizens directly or indirectly in the affairs of state. Southern German *étatisme*, although determined to overcome the outmoded rights of the estates and to modernize society, was deeply suspicious of the dangerous potential of popular sovereignty. The consequences of these differences were somewhat surprising. The tradition of the reforming state lived on in southern Germany and provided a congenial atmosphere for the liberal bourgeoisie. In Prussia the old order found it far easier to reassert itself after 1815.

Austria was virtually untouched by reform. The emperor Joseph II, the very model of the enlightened absolutist, had attempted to modernize the state in a series of fundamental reforms but every move was blocked by the determined opposition of the privileged. All his efforts to centralize the multi-ethnic empire had failed. In the Napoleonic era every proposed reform smacked of Jacobinism, and lacking any urgent need to concede either to external or internal pressures, precious little was changed. Prompted by Philipp Stadion, the principal minister from 1805 to 1809, some of the earlier reforms, such as new codes of civil and penal law, along with changes in elementary education and local government, were carried to their conclusion, but in general this was a period of stagnation in Austria which left it lagging far behind Prussia and the southern German states. Modest reforms were carried out in the army along similar lines to those in Prussia. After Austria's defeat at Wagram in 1809 and the subsequent Treaty of Schönbrunn, Austria fell into an administrative torpor while inflation ran wild and the national debt grew to the point where the state was virtually bankrupt. The resumption of war in 1813 compounded these problems, and the Austria of 1815 emerged victorious but financially crippled and in an administrative shambles.

Unlike Prussia, where the king was restrained by a council of state and by a powerful chancellor, the Austrian emperor Francis I attempted to rule as an absolute monarch. But he was permanently lost in the minutiae of administration and lacked any clear political vision. Metternich was given the title of chancellor in 1821, but his powers were largely restricted to foreign affairs. This hopeless muddle became even worse when Francis died and was succeeded by his dimwitted son Ferdinand I. The affairs of state were now conducted by a committee in which Metternich and his rival Kolowrat effectively canceled one another out. Austria was administered, but it was not ruled. The aristocracy retained its privileges, agricultural reform was stopped in its tracks, the middle class became increasingly frustrated, and Austria became a dreary police state in which intellectual life was stifled. Some of Goethe's writings were banned, Schiller's works were heavily censored, Grillparzer was constantly in trouble, and a number of Beethoven's songs were forbidden because their English words were deemed a threat to public order.

The War of Liberation

Of the 600,000 men in Napoleon's *Grande Armée* that marched against Russia in 1812 about one third were Germans. By the end of the year there were only some 100,000 demoralized remnants who staggered back to Poland. The tsar, against the advice of his generals, decided to continue the fight westwards and finally rid Europe of the Napoleonic menace. On December 30 the Prussian General Yorck signed the Convention of Tauroggen with the Russians by which the troops under his command no longer accepted orders from the French. Yorck, an ultraconservative opponent of reform, was a glowing patriot. He had acted without the knowledge of the king and with the intent of joining the Russians to drive the French out of Germany. Frederick William III was outraged at this act of mutinous insubordination and cashiered the general. Yorck took no notice and cooperated with Stein in recruiting soldiers in East Prussia to fight the French. The king continued to dither, negotiating first with the French then, urged on by the patriotic forces, with Austria and Russia. Finally at the end of February 1813 he signed an alliance with Russia whereby he agreed to cede part of Prussia's Polish provinces to Russia in return for territorial compensation elsewhere in Germany. He responded to a wave of patriotic enthusiasm by announcing a people's war in his appeal "To My People," calling for universal military service and organizing volunteer units known as the Free Corps, made up largely of the urban middle class. The poorly trained and ill-equipped Territorial Army (*Landwehr*) was an ineffective fighting force. A new medal for valor, the iron cross, was struck as a symbol of the struggle for king and fatherland. Patriotic enthusiasm was confined almost exclusively to the eastern provinces of Prussia that were not occupied by the French. Elsewhere there was a general indifference, although there were protests in Westphalia and Berg, both states being under direct French domination. Some of the northern ports, which had suffered badly under the Continental System, also witnessed some unrest. The states of the Confederation of the Rhine remained passive. In Vienna Metternich prudently arrested demonstrators calling for a popular uprising against the French.

For the Prussian patriots the war was now a struggle of the German people against a foreign tyranny. The German princes who had allied with Napoleon were regarded as traitors to the national cause. The tsar, who combined woolly-headed notions of national liberation with a careful calculation of Russia's interests, was much taken by these ideas and was encouraged by Stein, who became his unofficial advisor on German affairs. It was Stein who drafted the text of the Proclamation of Kalisch which outlined allied war aims. They included the restoration of a reformed German empire with a constitution that was to reflect the "quintessential spirit of the German people" and the freedom of the German princes and people. Russia as guarantor of the New Germany would be in a powerful position to determine its future, but with a notoriously unpredictable tsar it was unclear what lay in store.

The first engagements of the campaign did not go well for the new allies. They were defeated at the battles of Großgörschen and Bautzen, and driven out of Saxony. Napoleon failed to follow up on these successes and agreed to an armistice in order to build up his forces. Meanwhile a number of states joined Britain in the Great Coalition, but these did not yet include Russia and Prussia, and Metternich was still hesitant to commit Austria to the allied cause. Metternich, ever suspicious of the heady nationalist and popular spirit among some of the coalition partners, gradually eased away from France until in June 1813, with the Convention of Reichenbach, he joined the coalition which now included both Russia and Prussia. The war aims with respect to Germany were agreed upon at Teplitz in September. They included the restoration of the 1803 frontiers in northwestern Germany and of the Rhine frontier. Metternich's concept of a war to restore the balance of power in Europe had triumphed over notions of liberation, freedom, and nationalism.

After some initial engagements the Saxon army was left demoralized and Bavaria withdrew from the Confederation of the Rhine, its territorial integrity guaranteed by Metternich in the Treaty of Ried, a treaty that was later to be denounced by nationalist historians as blocking the way to national unification. The two armies finally clashed at Leipzig from October 16 to 19, 1813. Napoleon suffered a crushing defeat in this "Battle of the Nations," but it was something of a Pyrrhic victory with both sides losing about 60,000 men, and the coalition armies failing to follow up their success, thus allowing Napoleon to escape.

The question now was whether the war should continue. After the Treaty of Ried with Bavaria similar arrangements were made with Baden, Württemberg, and the other member states of the Confederation of the Rhine. The Confederation thus ceased to exist, but the Napoleonic territorial settlement in southern Germany remained in force. Once again Metternich had managed to ensure that the exigencies of security took precedence over legitimacy. This was enough for Metternich, who now hoped to treat with the French. However the slogan "The Rhine is a German River and not Germany's Frontier" met with fervent popular response, and the Prussian hawks demanded an all-out war to destroy the tyrant.

Napoleon rejected Metternich's peace feelers thus solving the immediate problem, but the debate as to how the war should be pursued caused severe strains within the coalition. Thanks to the energetic engagement of Castlereagh and Metternich, the Coalition was stitched together and once again agreed upon a set of war aims, which included the requirement that France should withdraw to its 1792 frontiers, and Germany should have a federal structure. Allied troops entered Paris at the end of March 1814 and Napoleon abdicated. The Treaty of Paris of May 30, 1814, was free from vindictiveness, leaving France within its 1792 borders and a major player within the European balance of power.

The future of Europe was to be decided at the Congress of Vienna, a glittering assembly of crowned heads, diplomatists, adventurers, and beauties. Their aim was above all to create a stable Europe based on a broad interpretation of the principle of legitimacy. No one thought it possible to turn the clock back to pre-revolutionary times, and there was general agreement that the Napoleonic territorial settlement in southern Germany should be accepted. Where stability seemed threatened legitimacy had to give way. Britain and Austria agreed that a strong and independent central Europe was desirable as a bulwark against both France and Russia. Prussia was clearly to play a critical role within this constellation, and would have to be compensated in the west, given Russia's claims on its Polish provinces. Prussia's main aim was to annex Saxony, a state that had remained faithful to its alliance with Napoleon. Castlereagh and Metternich were favorably disposed toward this idea since they were concerned about the tsar's ambitions in Poland. The Russians were adamantly opposed to this suggestion, and Frederick William III, anxious not to antagonize his ally, ordered Hardenberg to distance himself from Castlereagh and Metternich.

After much acrimonious debate Prussia lost most of its Polish territory to "Congress Poland" and was awarded approximately half of Saxony. Prussia's gains in the west were even more significant. In order that Prussia should protect Germany's western frontiers it was given the Rhineland as far as the Saar and the Nahe. This resulted in fundamental change in Prussia. The country was now divided between its western and eastern portions with their widely different cultures, traditions, and religions. It was imperative for the state to attempt to resolve these differences since such resolution, if successful, would necessarily lead to Prussian hegemony in northern Germany. There were further far-reaching consequences of this settlement. The Rhineland was soon to prove to be the most valuable piece of industrial real estate in Europe, and was to be the basis of Prussia's economic might. That Prussia was given the task of defending Germany's borders against any revival of French military might further underlined the importance of the army. The unequal development at every level between the Prussian homeland and its newly won western provinces was to cause many severe problems in the years ahead.

Prussia's role in Germany was thus strengthened, while Austria concentrated more on the Tyrol and Italy. Bavaria was unable to find any support for its attempt to become a third force in Germany by absorbing Frankfurt and Mainz. Prussia thus emerged as the big winner, although this was not apparent at the time, since Austria's political influence was far greater. Austria, with England's support, had limited Russia's influence in Europe and Prussia's in Germany. The Federal Act of June 8 1815, signed only ten days before the battle of Waterloo, created a loose confederation of states rather than a federal state. There was no federal army and not even a federal court. There was only one federal institution, the Federal Council (Bundestag), where delegates from the member states met to discuss matters of internal security. Austria's dominant position was emphasized in that it provided the permanent president of the Council.

Apart from repressing its critics, the Confederation was a toothless affair. It did nothing to overcome the economic divisions within Germany, failed to take the initiative in transport policy, and did not create a common currency. It was equally passive in legal matters. When the people of Hesse appealed to it against their grotesque prince, who had swept aside all the French reforms and restored the *ancien régime* to the point of insisting that wigs should once again be worn, the Confederation did nothing. The Vienna settlement asserted the rights of the states and their legitimacy against the demands of liberals and nationalists. In the short term it provided stability, but the seeds for future conflict were already sown. It brought a long period of peace, but it could not contain the democratic and nationalist forces that threatened it. Combined with the territorial changes in Prussia which resulted in further contradictions and discord, these were ultimately to severely limit the conservative restoration.

The peculiarities of the German situation were such that there was from the outset a distinction between the concepts of state and *Volk*. On the one hand the theoretically impartial, rational, and regulatory function of the state had been brought to a high level of efficiency in a number of the German states. On the other there was the confused, romantic, and antithetical notion of the *Volk* that should not be confused with the politicized British or French notion of "the people" or "the nation." The *Volk* was unique with its own ethical imperatives, its customs, and its culture. The state, by contrast, was the embodiment of the universal and rational principles of the enlightenment. The French republican notion of the state was that it expressed, however imperfectly, the will of the nation. The nation was not based on ethnicity, but was defined by the acceptance of the obligations and the rights of citizenship, and on the collective will to be a nation. That a specifically republican culture with it own myths and discursive strategies might develop was devoutly to be wished, but it was something that followed upon the creation of the nation-state. In Germany the nation, in the form of the *Volk*, preexisted the nation-state, and it was only after the Napoleonic invasion that the demand was made that nationality should take on a political form, either by identification with the existing states, or by the creation of a pan-German nation-state. In this manner the gulf between the state and the *Volk* could be bridged.

For this to be possible the concepts of both *Volk* and state had to change. The *Volk* had to be politicized and thus become truly a nation, and the state had to be infused with the notion of nationhood. The idea of the distinctiveness of the nation and its moral and cultural superiority originated with Fichte and Hegel, and was later to be expounded by the political historians Leopold von Ranke and Heinrich von Treitschke. Hegel asserted that the state was the highest form of ethical life to which humans could aspire, with each state as a self-contained ethical being, so that no law could mediate the relations between states. The Hegelian dialectic asserted that self-consciousness required the existence of the non-self, and thus for the individual to identify with the state there had to be other, antithetic states. The state, as the highest moral instance could, if necessary, demand the ultimate sacrifice of the individual. Were that not the case, it would be nothing more than a contractual arrangement which would not enable the individual the means of moral self-realization and the transcendence of the self by identification with a higher ethic. The notion of the state as the highest ethical being was thus combined with the notion of the *Volk* as a unique cultural entity and was dangerously intoxicating. When combined with later notions, such as Social Darwinism, it could become lethal.

2

German Society in Transition: 1800–70

Germany shared in the dramatic Europe-wide population expansion which began in the latter part of the eighteenth century. Many factors contributed to this demographic explosion. The removal of traditional impediments to marriage resulted not only in a marked reduction of the number of bachelors and spinsters, but also allowed couples to marry somewhat younger, thus increasing the wife's effective period of fecundity. In spite of the harsh punishments meted out on unwed mothers, bastardy rates were astonishingly high. Ten percent of births in Protestant Berlin at the beginning of our period were illegitimate. In Catholic Munich the figure was as high as 20 percent. Other factors played a role. There were no great epidemics during this period, and the outbreaks of cholera in the nineteenth century did not cause anything like the same number of deaths as in the past. It was not until mid-century that physicians like Rudolf Virchow began a serious examination of the social causes of disease. Nutrition improved, as did the weather. There were significant medical improvements, including vaccination which was made compulsory for smallpox in Bavaria in 1807 and in Prussia in 1817. There was a higher standard of personal hygiene, a drop in infant mortality, and a slight decline in the death rate. But the most important factor of all was that couples made conscious decisions to have large families. Demographers have come up with all manner of ingenious explanations for this, but none are convincing. Perhaps it is appropriate that the motives behind this most personal of decisions should remain a mystery.

It has been estimated that the population of the German Confederation in 1816 was just under 33 million. By 1865 it had risen by 60 percent. During this period about three million Germans emigrated, most of them to the United States. Although there are considerable regional differences in all these figures, the average expectation of life was terribly low in spite of many improvements. In the old Prussian provinces it hovered around 25 during the first half of the century, and in the Rhineland provinces it was about 30. Only in the latter part of the century was there an increase in life expectancy, to 35.6 for men and 38.5 for women between 1871 and 1880. It was therefore a very young society, with at least one third of the population under the age of 15.

Given the high rates of infant and adolescent mortality the average age at death is somewhat misleading and subject to wide deviations. Thus in 1800 the average marriage lasted for 20 years and ended with the death of one of the partners. Most households consisted of husband and wife and underage children. In the wealthier classes there would be a number of servants, in artisan families there would also be an apprentice or two. Extended families of three generations were exceptionally rare, even in rural areas, although peasant households were considerably larger than urban ones. Children left the home early to learn a trade or enter service and thus became part of another household.

The household performed many functions. As a farm or artisanal enterprise it was a place of work. It was obliged to perform many of the functions that are now taken over by the state. It did its best to look after the health of its members, stood by them when times were bad, and tended them in their old age. As the peasant or the artisan grew more prosperous the division between the core family and those who worked for it became more clearly defined. Servants were now summoned to their masters and mistresses by a tug on a bell-rope. But in rural areas society was still open and transparent, social control oppressive, and the private sphere severely restricted. In the towns the ideals of bourgeois privacy were more easily realized.

In such circumstances it is hardly surprising that romantic love played precious little role in the choice of a partner. One sought a spouse of appropriate social standing and of impeccable reputation, who was known to be reliable, hardworking, and honest. Mutual respect and a sense of obligation were the foundations on which the family rested. This could turn into genuine affection, but familial relations were mostly stiff, formal, and rigid. In urban areas there was a slight loosening of convention among the petite bourgeoisie. Some even went as far as to address their spouses by their first names.

The wealthier bourgeois families followed the example of their English counterparts in separating the family as far as possible from the outside world of work, society, and even the wider family. Within this secure and propertied class there was slightly more room for romantic love, affection, and personal fulfillment. This more often than not was the stuff of romantic novels, but it was an ideal which, partly because there were so many obstacles in its way, had a wide appeal. Gradually the purely pragmatic reasons for the choice of a partner were replaced by subjective and emotional considerations. The public was giving way to the private, and marriage as an institution was slowly undermined. Hegel pointed out the dual nature of the family. It is partly based on subjective and personal considerations, but it is also an institution hallowed by custom. Since both the subjective and personal are exposed to the vagaries of change, the greater the emphasis placed on these elements, the more the permanence of the institution is challenged. The highly respectable Biedermeier family thus had within it the seeds of its own destruction.

The term "Biedermeier," used to describe the artistic tastes of the period from 1815 to 1848, was first coined between 1855 and 1857 when the popular magazine *Fliegende Blätter* published the poems of a fictitious author "Gottlieb Biedermeier," written by Eichrodt and Kußmaul. The restrained simplicity of an

Plate 1 A Biedermeier interior. © BPK

Plate 2 The Biedermeier family. © BPK

essentially bourgeois style was echoed in the literature of the time in the works of Franz Grillparzer, Adalbert Stifter, Theodor Storm, Annette von Droste-Hilsdorff, Ludwig Uhland, and Eduard Mörike. The emphasis here was on detailed, objective, awe-inspiring descriptions of the otherness of nature, which was far removed from the earlier romantic view of nature as a sentimental reflection of the self. In political terms the same period is known as the "pre-March," a reference to the revolution in 1848 which began in Germany in March. Thus, whereas the Biedermeier writers were conservatives, the radical authors in the group "Young Germany" belong to the pre-March.

The privacy of the family was also emphasized in changing attitudes toward death. Formalized acceptance of a natural event sweetened by a Christian eschatology that took the sting from death and denied the grave its victory was replaced by informal and subjective expressions of grief. The deceased hardly mattered for, as Schopenhauer remarked with characteristic irony, after one's death one was what one was before one was born. The family that was left behind had a deep sense of loss, privation, and abandonment and planted in the graveyard their family totem, on which the names of succeeding generations were inscribed. Ritualistic visits to the family grave with its overtones of ancestor worship provided some solace in an age when religious convictions were waning, and strengthened a sense of family identity. Hopes for a life after death were gradually replaced by projection onto children and grandchildren, thus further emphasizing the central importance of the family.

These were also the exciting "wild years of philosophy" when Hegel, Feuerbach, and the young Marx wrestled over the rich inheritance of Kant, Fichte, and Schelling. At the heart of the matter was the emphasis on the autonomous self, on the subject, whether it was the individual, the intellect, the body, nature, or the proletariat. The absolute was in the subject. Philosophers were intoxicated by the creative possibilities of this brave new world, only to become disillusioned when fresh problems arose. It was all very well to repeat the mantra "being determines consciousness," but what exactly was meant by "being?" Were not human beings increasingly the victims of their own creations, in the form of alienation? Was not alienation an integral part of the creative process? Could one still have faith in progress, or did one have reason to fear one's self-made history? Was it still possible to believe in reason, or was it merely the obedient messenger boy of some higher power? The counterattack was led by Hegel's bitter rival, Arthur Schopenhauer, whose *The World as Will and Idea* appeared in 1844. His philosophy of the irrational, of resolute inwardness and refusal – in his own words, of "wailing and gnashing of teeth" – was largely ignored during his lifetime, but was profoundly to affect Nietzsche and Heidegger, and in the age of Auschwitz, the Gulag, and Hiroshima his influence was profound, and remains so among the postmodernists.

The new emphasis on the individual and the subjective resulted in a modest change in women's role within the family. Schiller's ideal of the conscientious "*Haus-Frau*" gave way to a grotesque idealization of an ethereal womanhood by the romantics. The Biedermeier ideal was that an educated, intelligent, and impeccably mannered wife should devote herself to the family, provide comfort and affection for its members, and avoid any conflict with her spouse. The patriarch's role was to go out into the wider world and provide for the family; his wife's duty was to ensure that the family was an island of peace and harmony amid the stressful world of the marketplace, politics, and the professions.

As more and more families began to enjoy a relatively prosperous bourgeois existence women no longer had to do onerous physical work around the house. They could devote more time to education and to cultivating their literary, musical, and artistic tastes and talents. This resulted in a revival of the romantic version of the feminized woman. She was weak, hyper-sensitive, a bundle of nerves, given to fainting fits and sudden headaches, to be revived by smelling salts and calmed by liberal doses of laudanum.

Yet for all this the very fact that husbands left the house to go to work meant that women effectively ran the household and were responsible for the upbringing of the children, thus gaining a measure of independence and scope for self-realization. Many used this position of power and influence to undermine patriarchal structures. The hen-pecked husband was as much a feature of the age as was the stern paterfamilias, and many a man of substance was driven to distraction by a wife who used her feminine weakness as a powerful weapon. The ideal of partnership and the division of labor within the harmonious family was all too often shattered by the caprices and intractability of human nature.

Some women led astonishingly independent lives in spite of all these social constraints. There were a number of remarkable women who ran brilliant salons. Prominent among them were Henriette Herz, Dorothea Mendelssohn, Sarah Levy, and Amalie Beer, all of whom came from Jewish backgrounds. This was not the result of the emancipation and integration of German Jews, quite the contrary. It was precisely because they were outsiders that they were able to provide the neutral ground on which people from different stations in life could meet as equals. The most prominent of these salons was that of Rahel Levin. Her marriage to the equally charming and intelligent Prussian diplomat Varnhagen von Ense was one in which the ideals of mutual love, openness, and understanding were fully realized. After a year of marriage she wrote to a friend: "My great joy is that I don't even notice that I am married! In everything, big and small, I am free to live and feel as I will. I can tell Varnhagen everything and be completely truthful, and that fills him with happiness and joy. I make him happy too, I alone." Unlike the luxurious salons in Paris with their lavish receptions and carefully selected guest list these were positively austere. Tea was served in very modest surroundings and the door was open to all comers. The bourgeois salon thus replaced the court as a center of intellectual discourse, the bourgeoisie thus scoring yet another success over the old order.

Actresses, singers, and female writers guarded their independence, and widows, such as Arthur Schopenhauer's extraordinary mother Joanna, enjoyed an exceptional degree of freedom. Respectable bourgeois women played an important role in education, charity organizations, and the Protestant Church, and were thus able to play fulfilling roles outside the family. It was not until the 1830s that women were permitted to work as nurses in men's wards. Here again Catholic nuns and Protestant deaconesses were at the forefront in breaking down old prejudices and conventions.

Ideas of female emancipation which originated in France did not reach Germany until the 1830s and were eagerly espoused by the writers of the "Young Germany" movement, who were enthusiastic advocates of free love. Some, like Ferdinand Lassalle's lover the Countess Sophie Hatzfeld, followed the example of George Sand and donned male attire and ostentatiously smoked cigars in public while indulging in vigorously heterosexual affairs in semi-private.

Biedermeier Germany was exceedingly prudish and viewed emotionalized sexuality with deep suspicion. The aristocratic libertines of earlier times were seen as monsters, and the sexual adventures of the likes of Goethe and the Young German writers were viewed with disgust. Karl Gutzkow's *Wally the Skeptic*, published in 1835, was a polemic in favor of sexual freedom which landed the author in jail for its "despicable representation of the faith of the Christian community." Protests at this judgment resulted in a number of writers being sent into exile, among them Heinrich Heine. Girls were kept in total sexual ignorance, and boys were simply warned of the dire consequences of masturbation. Joanna Schopenhauer was horrified at the way in which highly regarded married men in France openly flaunted their delicious mistresses. As in Victorian England, the bourgeoisie viewed extramarital sex as the distasteful habit of a degenerate aristocracy and the result of the crude animal lusts of the lower classes. Prostitution thrived, since men with an overwhelming desire to do bad things chose to do them with bad women. Wilhelm von Humboldt, who preached and practiced a marriage based on love, partnership, and mutual respect, was a regular visitor to houses of ill fame.

Childhood was a construction of the eighteenth century, and Jean-Jacques Rousseau its impassioned advocate. His appeal to women to breastfeed their infants, and his insistence that children had rights and specific needs, met with a wide response. It was generally recognized that children needed affection, consideration, and encouragement. Relations between parents and children became gradually more relaxed and informal, the familiar "Du" form was now more widely used, discipline was less rigid, and punishments were less harsh. Books were now written specifically for children, but as Heinrich Hoffmann, the brilliant psychologist and author of *Struwwelpeter* (1844), pointed out they were mostly "altogether too enlightened and rational, falsely naïve, unchildlike, untruthful and artificial." In 1816 Friedrich Froebel opened a school in Griesheim near Darmstadt which aimed at the spontaneous and natural development of a child's talents, principles which he developed in his major work *Human Education*, published in 1826. In spite of fierce opposition, particularly from the Catholic Church, in 1836 he opened the first "Kindergarten" at Blankenburg in the Harz mountains.

Critics felt that children were being pampered and smothered by motherly love, and, although they were by nature selfish, rebellious, and vicious, were absurdly idealized as little angels. The conflicts between the desire to express love, affection, and concern, and the need to educate, discipline, and where necessary punish, led to increasing tensions between parents and children which, by the end of the century provoked Sigmund Freud to make some wild speculations about the human psyche.

Bourgeois households were attended by a number of servants, as were those of the wealthier tradesmen. Servants lived in their own quarters separated from the core family, and were underpaid and overworked, without rights or legal protection. In the Biedermeier period a large percentage of the population was employed in domestic service. It has been estimated that about 45 percent of the citizens of Vienna were servants in the 1820s. Later on in the century there was a marked decline, as the number of servants employed per household dropped, and industrialization provided opportunities to earn higher wages. Many of these servants were young girls from the countryside who learnt respectable bourgeois ways during their period of service and became in turn respectable wives and mothers. In this way much of the working class was gentrified to a certain degree. Bourgeois attitudes were also strengthened in that children were used from an early age to being waited upon and to giving orders.

The vast majority of Germans lived in conditions far removed from the comforts of the bourgeois household. There was precious little room for self-fulfillment, emotional development, or even basic privacy in poverty-stricken and overworked lower class families. Children were put to work as early as possible and left home at an early age. Bourgeois reformers like William Heinrich Riehl looked at these families with horror. They wrote of drunken and heartless husbands who brutalized their wives and children, of women working long and crippling hours in addition to their household duties, and of children who received little besides abuse. By mid-century about one-quarter of German women were gainfully employed, about half as domestic servants, most of the rest as factory workers or on the land. Women's wages were roughly half those of men. Although the situation was never as appalling as it was in Britain, child labor was widespread. By 1840 some 17 percent of the factory workers in Chemnitz were children. Although no accurate figures are available, it is safe to assume that the percentage of children working on the land was still higher.

This was a period of fundamental transformation in social life. The dramatic changes in the mode of production occasioned by the industrial revolution resulted in equally remarkable changes in social life. The most obvious was the separation of domicile and place of work. With the exception of all but the most genteel of farmers and a dwindling number of handloom weavers, there was a clear distinction between the two. Life in the home was rendered more pleasant by technical advances such as the invention of the cooking stove that replaced the open fire, and of gas lighting and linoleum. "Lucifers," or safety matches, which first appeared in 1829, were a frequent cause of accidents, as Hoffmann pointed out in *Paulinchen*, which was based on a true story. Flush toilets did not appear on any great scale until the 1860s and then almost exclusively in urban areas. The greater mobility of labor meant that the vast majority of people no longer owned their own house or cottage, but rented apartments in the cities and towns.

Housing conditions for the majority of the population were appalling. Single agricultural laborers lived like animals in barns and lofts, their married workmates in filthy two-room hovels. Workers in the towns lived in dreadful conditions, packed into tiny apartments or squalid row houses, in attics and cellars. Only in the 1860s did some industrialists such as Friedrich Krupp begin to build model housing so as to ensure a steady supply of reliable workers.

The bourgeois lifestyle was comfortable but restrained. There were fewer rooms designed for lavish entertainments, and the center of the house was now the living room, which was aped by the petite bourgeoisie with their "front rooms" used only on special occasions. The elaborate Louis Seize style of furniture, as made by the Roentgens father and son and the Spindler brothers, was no longer in favor. The Biedermeier style was discrete, lacking in decoration, well proportioned, light, and practical. By the 1830s it began to give way to a more ornate style in the gothic revival or neo-renaissance manner with plenty of plush and heavy dark woods. A similar change can be seen in architecture, from the restraint of the Biedermeier to the flamboyance of the historicist style.

It was not until the 1830s that the alluring Empire fashion, with its pronounced décolleté, seductive draping, and glimpse of ankle, gave way to a more prudish style in which the body was hidden away in yards of material, and a tiny waist and wide hips were accentuated. By mid-century the crinoline swept all before it, providing rich material for caricaturists and satirists. Men's fashions went through less of a transformation. They favored a simple cut and dark colors, and elegance was expressed in the quality of the cloth and tailoring. Artists and radicals donned some-what outlandish bohemian outfits, and nationalists set about designing the folk costumes of a mythical past.

Town and Country

The combination of industrialization and rapid population growth transformed the cities and towns. The population of Berlin rose from 172,000 in 1800 to 419,000 by 1850. That of Stuttgart increased from 18,000 to 47,000 in the same period and that of Düsseldorf from 10,000 to 27,000. As the towns expanded the old city walls disappeared, thus ending the abrupt distinction between town and country. Towns were now clearly divided into districts according to social status, with the rich and powerful in the west, the poor workers in the east, and the lower middle class to the north and south. The towns were soon also to be divided by railway lines, the poor living on the wrong side of the tracks.

Towns were also transformed by the increasing number of public buildings, from ministries to museums, railway stations to schools, universities to law courts. Shopping arcades, and later department stores, revolutionized the retail trade. There was precious little planning or control. Traditional restrictions on the sale and transfer of land were removed, and now market forces were only curbed by health and safety regulations. Banks made handsome profits as the demand for mortgages grew. It was not until mid-century that the towns began to take over responsibility for public utilities, although Vienna had placed the water supply under civic control as early as 1803. The great fire in Hamburg in 1842 gave Gottfried Semper, an architect of genius, an opportunity to put aesthetic considerations above cost effectiveness in his plans for the reconstruction of the inner city. Munich was also fortunate to have monarchs who wished to beautify their capital, and ministers like Montgelas who could realize their vision. The Maximilian and Ludwig streets are their lasting monuments. In most German cities the city fathers imposed a rigorous and unimaginative geometric uniformity that saved money, but was dull and lifeless.

Germany was still an overwhelmingly agricultural land and thus vulnerable to the frightful effects of a poor harvest, which were far worse than anything experienced even in the worst crises of industrial society. The famine of 1816/17 was a major catastrophe in Germany, as it was throughout Europe, and the effects of the potato blight of 1845/7 were as horrific as they were in Ireland, awakening the conscience of the nation to the sufferings of the poor, and helping to trigger the revolutions of 1848.

There were, however, major improvements in agriculture thanks in large part to the efforts of Albrecht von Thaer, a Hanoverian doctor who studied English scientific agriculture and popularized these theories in his model farm in Mödlin in Prussia, and through the publication of his four volume study *The Principles of Rational Agriculture*, published between 1809 and 1812. In the introduction to his magnum opus he gave a lapidary definition of his intents. Agriculture was in his view "a profession the purpose of which is to make a profit or to earn money by the production, and sometimes the processing of vegetable and animal substances." This thoroughly capitalist aim was to be achieved by scientific breeding, an improved system of the rotation of crops, and double entry bookkeeping. The farmer thus became as much an entrepreneur as the industrialist, much to the horror of conservatives who felt that the farmer was part of God's order, bound by moral obligation, the backbone of society, and not a mere tradesman.

The great chemist Justus Liebig (1803–73) discovered the process whereby plants extracted nourishment from the earth and realized that this nourishment had to be replaced. Plants needed to be fed in the same way animals did, and in this sense plants were "made" just like industrial goods. Thaer's rotation of crops led inevitably to a decline in productivity if the phosphoric acid, potash, and lime absorbed by successive crops were not replaced. Liebig was blind to many factors, such as the importance of climate, crop rotation, and the need to add nitrogen to the soil, and some argued that he was merely echoing the earlier work of Karl Sprengel (1787–1859), but he was a scientist of genius who counted among his discoveries chloroform and the three basic organic compounds – fats, carbohydrates, and proteins – to say nothing of Liebig's Meat Extract. He was the founding father of the fertilizer industry, which was to begin in the 1860s and in which Germany was to be preeminent.

Rapid improvements in agricultural machinery, much of which came from England, along with further refinements in breeding stock coupled with a significant increase in the amount of land under cultivation, contributed to a steadily increasing output. Agriculture was still dependent on climatic conditions and was highly vulnerable to disease so that this favorable trend could easily be brutally reversed. Nevertheless, contrary to the teachings of the Reverend Thomas Malthus, agricultural production increased more rapidly than did the population in the first half of the century.

The state played an active role in spreading these new ideas by the foundation of a number of agricultural colleges, as well creating model farms, combating the spread of animal diseases, improving drainage, redistributing land, and encouraging agricultural associations and fairs such as Munich's "*Oktoberfest*," which was founded in 1810. Eager to keep up to date with the latest discoveries and theories, farmers joined these clubs and associations and subscribed to a host of agricultural journals. Smaller producers sought to keep pace by forming cooperatives which were given financial support by the local savings banks based on the cooperative principles of Friedrich Wilhelm Raiffeisen, whose work began in response to the appalling agricultural crisis of 1845/7. German farmers thus embraced modern capitalist methods of farming and estate management, but their mentality was rooted in an earlier age and acted as a brake on the development of fully-fledged bourgeois –capitalist agriculture that would have resulted in an even more impressive rate of growth. There was thus a curious dissonance between ideology and praxis which intrigued Max Weber but would have stumped Karl Marx.

The vast majority of the rural population was made up of poverty-stricken agricultural workers, who possessed little besides a tiny potato patch, and landless day laborers. Although for most people life on the land had always been wretched their lot had worsened since, but not necessarily because of, the reforms. Their numbers had increased disproportionately to the rest of the population, thus debasing the value of their labor, and their ranks were swollen by heavily indebted peasant farmers who were unable to survive in a more competitive and capital intensive environment. Enclosures forced them to resort to poaching and the illegal collection of firewood for which they were severely punished. In southern Germany sympathetic gamekeepers were often known to turn a blind eye to these miscreants. It was not until much later in the century that job opportunities in the industrial sector, improved transportation, and emigration offered major relief to the pressing problem of rural poverty. This was partly offset in Prussia by the law (*Gesindeordnung*) which restricted the farm workers' freedom of movement, and their right to organize, as well as permitting outrageously long working hours. Only the more prosperous small farmers could afford a scrap of meat, and even then certainly not more than once a week. Most peasants lived on potatoes without salt, bread, soup, and milk. It is small wonder that tensions mounted on the land and exploded in widespread violence in the revolutionary years of 1848/9.

Peasant demands were quite different from those of urban radicals. They protested against concrete abuses and against the remnants of feudal injustices, as well as against new injustices resulting from the reforms, and demanded the restoration of ancient rights. They had no sympathy for the liberal and democratic ideas of the townsfolk and could never make common cause with them. They in turn could readily agree with Karl Marx's comments about "the idiocy of rural life," and despised the peasantry for their reactionary conservatism, their anti-capitalism, their clericalism, and their profound distrust of the state and its bureaucracy.

In much of Germany there was thus a sharp distinction between town and country. There were deep cleavages of status, class, and wealth in rural areas but they were partly transcended by a way of life in which there were certain shared values and a feeling of community. The countryside was conservative and liberal townsfolk were never able, and were often even unwilling, to win support for their ideas in rural areas. The strength of agrarian conservatism was such that it profoundly affected the development of Germany in its development toward a modern democratic state.

The Industrial Revolution

It is hardly surprising that the industrial revolution came to Germany decades later than it did to England. Most of the states of the German Confederation protected their domestic markets with high duties and tariffs, and the larger states had a number of internal customs barriers. The transportation network was inadequate and thus further protected inefficient markets. Germany was constantly plagued by war, it lacked the stimulus of overseas colonies, and had inadequate natural resources. Conservatives looked on the English experience with horror and saw industrialization as the direct cause of poverty, urban squalor, crime, and social unrest, to say nothing of a vulgar, pushy, and enormously wealthy class of industrialists, bankers, and speculators. A new word, "*Pauperismus*," entered the German language, and years later Friedrich Engels' classic study of the condition of the working class in England was to find high praise in conservative circles. Conservatives did all they could to stave off the day when Germany would follow the English example, blaming widespread poverty on a rapacious bourgeoisie. Liberals took the view that the remnants of feudalism and aristocratic landowners were responsible and argued that the state had failed in its obligations toward the disadvantaged.

In spite of this aristocratic–conservative opposition to industrial society, some aristocrats seized the opportunities offered by new techniques and machinery. This was particularly true of Silesia, where magnates such as Count Henckel zu Donnersmarck and Prince Hohenlohe founded industrial enterprises without concern for loss of caste by soiling their hands with trade. They had access to sufficient capital to set up shop, and although technically they lagged far behind the English and were quite unable to meet the domestic demand for iron, they were decades ahead of the bourgeois entrepreneurs in the west.

The Ruhr was soon to overtake Silesia as an industrial center. With ample coal resources, a greatly improved transportation network, and a liberal economic atmosphere, it was congenial to innovative entrepreneurship, and with its solid traditions of craftsmanship was well equipped to meet the demands of the machine age. On the left bank of the Rhine where French law had been imposed, it was relatively easy to form a limited liability company. Elsewhere the authorities viewed such methods of capital accumulation with the deepest suspicion. They felt that it encouraged wild speculation, favored irresponsible management and channeled capital away from government bonds and investment in agriculture. The first joint-stock bank in Germany based on the model of the French Crédit Mobilier, the Schaffhausensche Bankverein, was founded on the initiative of the Camphausen-Hansemann ministry in 1848 to bail out the Schaffhausen Bank, which had failed due to a series of bad investments in the Rhineland. Until then entrepreneurs could only borrow modest sums from private banks or foreign investors, but most enterprises were self-financing and thus under-capitalized and highly vulnerable. Railways and inland shipping needed such large amounts of capital that they could only be financed by joint-stock companies and the success of many such ventures gradually wore down resistance to the notion of limited liability. A number of major banks were founded along the same lines. They included Gustav Mevissen's Darmstädter Bank and the Rothschilds' Österreichsiche Kreditanstalt both founded in 1855. The Discontogesellschaft opened in the following year. These new banks handled all manner of business from small individual accounts to long-term investments in industry. The ties between big banks and big industry were very close and there was soon a complex web of interlocking directorships and investments which ensured that the two sectors would work closely together for their mutual benefit.

The reforms of the Napoleonic era not only led to a revolution in agriculture but also did much to break down the social, political, and legal restraints on industrialization. The drastic reduction in the number of petty states reduced the number of internal trade barriers. The Continental System protected German industrialists against British competition and western Germany profited from its close ties to the French market. But this was outweighed by the negative effects of war, the disruption of traditional trade patterns, widespread poverty, and shortage of capital. Once the wars were over English manufactured goods again flooded the market and German firms which had mushroomed in past years went under. States pursued rigorously deflationary policies and no changes were made in a tax structure which favored the larger landowners. Precious little encouragement was given to industry apart from removing customs barriers and spending money on roads and waterways. Railways were initially private companies, but the state soon began to see the need to become involved in this revolutionary form of transportation. Liberal civil servants managed to persuade governments that Germany could only hope to catch up with Britain if technical education was made widely available in Technical Universities and Polytechnics. This initiative was only really to bear fruit much later when, in the second industrial revolution, Germany was to overtake Britain as an industrial nation. In western Germany the French started chambers of commerce, the success of which resulted in the formation of similar institutions elsewhere.

The first steam engine in Germany was used on August 23 1785. It was the result of industrial espionage by a Prussian official who had been sent to England to examine the Watt engine, and was operated by an English mechanic, Mr Richards. This soon became the pattern. Expensive English machinery was imported and was operated by highly-paid English mechanics. High costs, shortage of capital, and an ample supply of cheap labor meant that the mechanization of industry was painfully slow. By 1846 97.8 percent of looms were still operated by hand within the borders of the Germany of 1871. In such conditions the German textile industry could not possibly hope to compete with Britain.

The iron industry also limped behind Britain. As late as 1837 less than ten percent of Prussia's iron was produced in coke-fired furnaces when the process had been in widespread use in England for decades. The puddling process, which was in wide use in England from the 1780s, did not reach Silesia until 1828. It was not until the 1840s that large-scale modern ironworks, such as those of Stumm on the Saar, Hoesch at Eschweiler, and the Friedrich-Wilhelm Hütte in the Ruhr, were founded. Krupp astonished visitors to the Great Exhibition in London in 1851 with his display of a block of steel weighing two tons, a technical marvel that wounded the pride of British industrialists. The railway boom which began in the late 1830s created a tremendous demand for iron and steel which German producers were soon able to meet. Coal production also increased dramatically to meet the greatly increased demand from industry. In the first half of the century the number of workers in the iron, steel, and coal industries trebled. Demand from the railway sector in Germany played the role of the cotton industry in England in stimulating the industrial revolution.

The first railway in Germany, which ran between Nuremberg and Fürth, was opened in 1835. It was a mere six-kilometer stretch but it made a handsome profit. Four years later a line was opened from Leipzig to Dresden. A rash of similar links between major urban centers followed in a frantic and somewhat haphazard attempt to turn a quick profit. The state intervened in an effort to bring some order into this chaos and to build those linking stretches that were essential but unprofitable. Some lines were proposed in order to stimulate economic activity in remote areas, the best known of which was the Eastern Railway (*Ostbahn*), the debate over which played an important role in the political crisis of 1848 in Prussia. The transportation revolution in Germany was not confined to the railways. Enormous efforts were made to improve the navigability of the great rivers, the most remarkable of which was the widening of the Rhine at Bingen from nine meters to up to 30 meters, thus allowing ships to sail from Rotterdam to Basel. Similar improvements were made to the Danube, Isar, and Ruhr. New inland ports, such as Duisburg-Ruhrort and the Bavarian town of Ludwigshafen, built across the river from the rival port of Mannheim, became major centers. Canals were also built, the most important of which was the Ludwigskanal which linked the Main to the Danube.

The relatively modest progress of the German economy in the first half of the century provided the preconditions for the great leap forward in the third quarter. In almost every sector there were spectacular increases in output during this period. Germany led the world in the industrial application of major discoveries in organic chemistry. The 1860s saw the creation of companies that were soon to conquer world markets, such as Bayer, the Badische Anilin- und Sodafabrik (BASF), and Hoechst.

This was not merely an advance in terms of output figures and profits, the industrial revolution marked a significant advance for society as a whole. There remained areas of underdevelopment, there were still vast disparities and injustices, and many lagged behind, but the standard of living of the vast mass of the population improved significantly. The problems of pauperism, mass unemployment, chronic food shortages, and the pressure of population growth if not overcome, were at least significantly reduced. The gloomy prognostications of the Malthusians gave way to a somewhat starry-eyed faith in technical progress.

Industrialization also created new problems, injustices, and forms of domination: wild fluctuations in the business cycle, overcrowded towns, the creation of an industrial proletariat with all its problems, socialism and the class struggle, relative impoverishment, and alienation, a problem first skillfully dissected by Hegel. It also created a whole new class of white-collar workers as management became more complex and clear distinctions were made between production, research, and administration. By the 1860s ten percent of the workers at the Siemens factory were clerks. At the same time the distance between management and workers became greater, ownership remote from the workplace, and patriarchal relationships were replaced by a cold and impersonal bureaucracy. Alienation was thus the result not merely of a rapidly changing society in which old certainties were destroyed, or of the division of labor within the factory. The depersonalization of the worker due to the new concept of time dictated by the machine, the anonymity of the worker on the production line, the widespread practice of piecework, the regimentation of work, and the permanent threat of instant dismissal resulted in feelings of helplessness and anxiety.

Poverty was still a major concern and many remedies were put forward. They ranged from encouraging emigration to stringent birth control, from a suspension of the freedom to practice a trade to a belief that industrial growth would provide the wealth that could then be more evenly distributed. While some argued for wide-ranging social legislation banning child labor, shortening the working week, and guaranteeing a minimum wage, others felt that charitable organizations were sufficient to relieve most of these problems. It was not only socialists like Karl Marx who thought in terms of the class struggle. Lorenz Stein believed that only a socially conscious monarchy could mediate the conflicting interests of bourgeoisie and proletariat. Amid all the many different recipes for solving what was to become known as the "social question" there was a general agreement that the state should keep its distance and let Adam Smith's "invisible hand" work its magic. Later in the century this central tenet of liberalism became increasingly open to question as the economy manifestly failed to meet the pressing needs of the indigent.

During the pre-March the bulk of production was artisanal. Craftsmen, who were the backbone of the old middle class, became demoted by industrialization to what was to be labeled the "petite bourgeoisie" or "*Kleinbürger.*" By the 1830s there was a dramatic increase in the number of artisans who lived barely above the subsistence level and struggled on in frantic competition with mechanized industrial production. By the mid-1840s they became the tragic scavengers on the garbage

Plate 3 The suffering of the Silesian weavers. © BPK

heap of economic history. In 1844 the Silesian handloom weavers, driven to desperation by a catastrophic fall in prices that led directly to mass starvation and a
typhus epidemic, rose up in revolt only to be brutally crushed by the army. It was
a horrific series of events that awoke the conscience of the nation and inspired generations of socially critical artists. Heinrich Heine's passionate poem, "The Silesian
Weavers," Gerhardt Hautpmann's play *The Weavers*, and Käthe Kollwitz's harrowing series of prints are moving testimony to the lasting impact of this tragedy.
There were similar uprisings elsewhere in Germany in the 1840s, albeit on a smaller
scale, such as the "Potato Revolution" in Berlin in 1847.

The Emergence of a Class Society

At the beginning of the century artisans and craftsmen were organized in guilds,
but in many parts of Germany the French or the reformers ended their monopolis-
tic control and introduced complete freedom in the trades. Guilds continued to exist
in parts of northern Germany, in the south and in Austria, but they were greatly
weakened by the removal of industrial production from their control and many
craftsmen and artisans were no longer members of these guilds. In some trades,
such as building, the state demanded certificates of competence. Guilds continued
informally in states such as Prussia as voluntary associations. This confusing patchwork of the old and the new was typical of a transition period between modes of
production.

The guilds were to win back some of their privileges in the period of reaction after 1848, but given the industrial boom that followed, this policy was bound to fail. In many trades the once proud artisans were unable to compete with industrial production and were forced to join the ranks of the industrial proletariat. Those involved in specialist trades, such as jewelers, survived, others, like tailors who did not yet face the competition of mass produced clothes sold off the peg, were given temporary respite. With the triumph of industrial production there came a certain revival of craftsmanship in the luxury trades. A handful of tailors now made immaculate clothes for the rich.

Politically the artisans were archconservatives. They stood in determined opposition to capitalism, to free trade, and to the liberal reformers. They hoped to put the clock back to the golden age of the Meistersingers of Nuremberg, when the likes of Hans Sachs were proudly independent, commanded respect, and had a secure place in the social order. The artisans thus made common cause with the reactionaries in 1848.

Their apprentices had no sympathy for such ideas. They felt exploited and stifled by the formal and informal authority of their masters and saw little chance in the existing economic climate of ever becoming master craftsmen themselves. They gave vent to their protest by joining the ranks of the radicals and socialists. August Bebel, the founding father of German social democracy, came from such a background, and even as party leader was obliged to eke out a modest living by making well-crafted doorknobs which he sold door to door. In most cases their anti-capitalism was strongly flavored with the reactionary anti-capitalism of their masters, and they had little sympathy with Karl Marx's belief that industrial capitalism was a necessary and progressive stage of historical development.

This large class of petits bourgeois was thus unable to ally with the liberals in their struggle for constitutional and democratic reform. They were in certain respects progressive in their dislike of the aristocracy, the bureaucracy, the rich, and the powerful. They demanded more rights for ordinary people and the devolution of power, but in economic matters they were hopelessly reactionary and felt menaced by liberal demands for free trade and modernization, as well as by an industrial proletariat into whose ranks they felt threatened to fall.

In the first half of the century it would be inappropriate to talk of a "working class." Differences in status and in income were so vast as to make the concept meaningless. A skilled mechanic in a factory could make up to 50 times more than someone plying a rural trade. The turnover of unskilled factory workers was extremely high as rural workers would move to the towns to work for a few months in a factory and then return to their previous pursuits. Industrial workers still made up a very small fraction of manual laborers. On the whole they enjoyed a higher standard of living than a handloom weaver or agricultural laborer. Although there were wide fluctuations, as competition from industrial goods from England and the pressure from lower wages in the cottage industries began to diminish, real wages for factory workers began to rise by mid-century. Life was still extremely hard, but it was a great improvement on the wretched conditions in the earlier part of the century. Nor were the living conditions of industrial workers quite as frightful as they were in England. A strong tradition of patriarchal concern for one's workers, the result of a mixture of Christian charity and calculated concern to maintain a reliable and loyal workforce, alleviated many of the worst social consequences of industrialization. But theirs was still a precarious existence. They worked staggeringly long hours in wretched conditions and lived under the constant threat of industrial accidents, disease, death, and impoverished old age. In 1870 factory workers averaged 78 hours of work in a six-day week. It was not until the 1880s that the state intervened to offer some protection in the form of insurance benefits, and once again Germany was years ahead of Britain in this respect. Industrial workers were torn out of a network of traditional relationships which had not yet been replaced by a new set by means of political parties, trades unions, and associations. It was to be some time before a specifically working-class consciousness began to form. It played no role by mid-century, for all Karl Marx's fond hopes.

The new class of industrial magnates came from a variety of backgrounds. There were industrialists from the higher nobility in Silesia and Bohemia, but elsewhere they came from humbler stock. The iron and steel barons like Krupp, Stumm, and Hoesch had begun as artisans, as had the great engineers Borsig and Henschel. Mannesmann and Stinnes had been merchants, and so had Camphausen and Mevissen. David Hansemann, the banker, entrepreneur, and Jack of all trades, was born in the manse. Georg von Siemens' father was a civil servant who heartily disapproved of his son's banking profession, which in his view entailed a loss of caste. He referred to his son, a director of the Deutsche Bank, contemptuously as a "clerk."

As they grew in wealth and confidence the industrialists, merchants, and bankers began to see themselves as men of distinction and rank. They contrasted their bourgeois virtues, their sense of obligation, and their unflagging diligence with the aristocracy and their absurd emphasis on social status, their snobbish exclusivity, and pretentiousness. They disliked the officer corps with its aristocratic values and made sure that their sons avoided military service. They were unable to marry off their daughters to aristocrats without royal permission since, in an effort to preserve the estate, aristocrats were only permitted to marry within their own ranks. A few exceptions were made. Krupp and Stumm obtained royal consent for their daughters' marriages to a von Bohlen and a von Kühlmann, but insisted that their lowly family names be hyphenated with those of these illustrious aristocrats. In the process of what has been called "the feudalization of the bourgeoisie" men like Krupp, who had made immense fortunes, built palaces and gave magnificent receptions; but rather than aping the aristocracy they were in fierce competition with them and refused to be ennobled. Some, like Thyssen, maintained the earlier, more frugal lifestyle, but later generations could not resist the temptation to keep up with the Krupps.

In the pre-March these men were liberals, opponents of aristocratic privilege, and demanded a constitution. They resented all the bureaucratic hindrances to the freedom of the market, especially the resistance to the formation of joint-stock companies. They were also acutely aware of the social dangers posed by poverty and employed young Dr Karl Marx to address this problem in the pages of their *Rheinische Zeitung*. But precious few of them were active in politics, and left that time-consuming business to the well-educated members of the professions.

The upper echelons of the civil service formed a privileged class that was intensely conscious of its superiority over those they regarded as mere tradesmen and mechanics, however wealthy they might be. Wealth had yet to become the measure of social prestige. They were close to the sources of power, could marry into the aristocracy virtually without hindrance, enjoyed handsome tax relief, and with their own courts of honor were clearly distinguished from the ordinary bourgeois. The aristocracy, the officer corps, and the higher civil servants formed the pinnacle of society in the pre-March, and some of the residual privileges of the civil servants are still enjoyed in Germany today.

Within the bourgeoisie those who had a university education, known then and now as "*Akademiker*," also enjoyed certain privileges that came from their educational qualifications. They formed an educated middle class – the "*Bildungsbürger*" – who regarded themselves as the standard bearers of German culture and who looked down on the "*Besitzbürger*," who had little to show for themselves besides property. Lawyers, doctors, apothecaries, and evangelical ministers were ex officio members of this exclusive group. Education was the key to social advancement, and since there were precious few scholarships, it was virtually impossible for those without the means to enter the ranks of the educated middle class.

Germany was a patchwork of small states with striking regional differences and was divided along religious lines. The process of creating a unified German nation was thus complex, lengthy, and incomplete. The *Bildungsbürger* played a key role in this process in that they accepted a common culture and a common set of values, which was given political expression in liberalism. The industrial proletariat was also to have a certain sense of solidarity that transcended the regional and the religious and was the driving force behind the socialist movement.

The vast majority of the population of Germany possessed little beyond their labor power. They were agricultural laborers, servants, factory workers, and the like, living on wretched wages in squalid conditions. Having no property they had no civil rights. In Frankfurt am Main in 1811 only one-third of the population were classified as "burghers." Below them was a substantial class of beggars and vagabonds whose ranks grew alarmingly due to the pressure of population. It was only in the second half of the century that industrialization provided steady employment for much of this surplus population. Workers were strictly forbidden to form associations in an attempt to redress their grievances, but gradually many conservatives, Bismarck among them, felt that granting workers the right to form associations would win them over to the monarchy and would also help to clip the wings of an increasingly arrogant and pushy bourgeoisie. But it was not until 1869 that a limited right of association was permitted in Prussia.

The Jewish Community

One of the great achievements of the French Revolution was to grant equal civil rights to Jews. In Germany west of the Rhine, and in the states under French control, the Jews were emancipated. Archbishop Dalberg of Mainz followed suit in the Duchy of Frankfurt. Most of the German states considered that this was far too radical a step and felt that Jews should be integrated into society by a gradual process of improvement and enlightenment. The Prussian reformers had no sympathy for such reservations. They argued that all citizens should have equal rights as well as equal obligations. Hardenberg and Humboldt managed to secure full civil rights for Jews in Prussia in 1812, the only major exception being that they were still unable to obtain positions in the civil service, except as teachers. The Prussian delegation joined with Metternich at the Congress of Vienna in an attempt to emancipate all the Jews within the German Confederation, but this radical step was strongly opposed by many of the smaller states.

Prejudice and discrimination remained firmly entrenched in German society and intensified in the postwar years. Jews were widely seen as the representatives of a new and threatening age and there were a number of anti-Semitic riots in which peasants and petits bourgeois gave vent to their discontents. The emancipatory edicts of 1812 were not applied in the new Prussian provinces so that a number of crippling restrictions remained and almost 40 percent of Prussian Jews were still without civil rights. Jews were excluded from the student fraternities and from the officer corps. They were unable to teach in the universities and it became increasingly difficult for them to become schoolteachers.

Many factors stood in the way of emancipation. Governments feared the reaction of the mob to anything that seemed to favor the Jews. In Prussia the ideology of the Christian state made no provision for Jews. In southern Germany the objections were economic rather than religious. Only in Electoral Hesse did the process of emancipation continue. By the 1840s well-educated Germans felt that the continued discrimination against Jews was intolerable and most of the remaining injustices, inequalities, and restrictions were removed in 1848 virtually without debate. Peasants and petits bourgeois once again expressed their fury in isolated instances of atavistic violence, but they were hopelessly out of touch with the times, relics of an older form of anti-Semitism, and not harbingers of the new racial anti-Semitism.

In spite of many hardships and injustices, and although many chose to emigrate to the United States, the number of Jews in Germany grew in the course of the nineteenth century. In 1820 there were about 270,000 Jews in the territory that was to become the German Empire, half of whom lived in Prussia, mainly in Posen, West Prussia, and Upper Silesia. By 1850 the number had risen to 400,000 and by 1869 to 512,000. Comparable figures for Austria were 85,000, 130,000, and 200,000.

During this period there was a steady movement of Jews away from the country into towns such as Berlin, Vienna, Frankfurt, Prague, and Cologne. In Frankfurt and Prague about ten percent of the population was Jewish.

At the beginning of our period the majority of German Jews were desperately poor, eking out a wretched existence as peddlers, cattle-dealers, and moneylenders in the country, and as tailors, pawnbrokers, and shopkeepers in the towns. Very few Jews enjoyed a comfortable bourgeois life, and the Rothschilds were an extremely rare breed. By 1871 there had been a remarkable change in the fortunes of German Jewry. In spite of many restrictions and obstacles the vast majority now enjoyed a comfortable and secure living in the professions, in banking and commerce, as respected shopkeepers and craftsmen. Only a small number were still living at the margin.

This remarkable instance of upward social mobility was due solely to the industriousness, determination, inventiveness, and thrift of the Jewish community. They were determined that their children should get the best possible education so that, whereas Jews made up only about 1.3 percent of the population of Prussia in 1866, no less than 8.4 percent of grammar school pupils were Jewish. Very few chose to be baptized, even though this would have removed almost all obstacles to advancement. By 1848 only 1.5 percent of Prussian Jews had taken this route, the others continued to practice their religion while assimilating into the educated and cultured bourgeois world of liberal German nationalism. There was a dramatic change later in the century so that by 1914 one-third of the Jews in Berlin and Hamburg had either married a Gentile or had been baptized.

For many Jews the process of assimilation was a means of escape from a social and cultural ghetto, but it necessarily involved a degree of secularization, a rejection of the dead weight of tradition, and a concentration on the spiritual and philosophical nexus of religion at the cost of a ritualized way of life. Reform Judaism thus found an enthusiastic following in Germany, much to the alarm of the traditionalists who argued that their faith was becoming emaciated in the futile hope that Jews would be accepted as equals in the Gentile world.

The distance between Jews and Gentiles narrowed, but was never bridged. For many the Jews represented a threatening modernity, a world of red-in-tooth-and-claw capitalism where wealth was the sole criteria of worth, of critical thought, of rootless cosmopolitanism, and a rejection of tradition. Many drew a distinction between the abstract Jew to whom full equality of rights should be granted, and the real Jew whose otherness was disquieting and even repulsive. The novelist Gustav Freytag was a principled liberal who unequivocally championed Jewish emancipation, and yet he drew a hideous caricature of the Jews in his highly successful novel *Credit and Debit*. His characterization of Poles is equally unflattering. Somewhat later even Theodor Fontane, a quintessential liberal, described a sympathetic old Jewish moneylender in his novel *Der Stechlin* as being corrupted by the new materialist age and possessing a cloven hoof. By the 1860s there were grounds for optimism that Jews would be fully accepted as a valuable part of German culture and that the old stereotypes would be dropped. The remarkably courageous and liberal popular novelist Eugenie Marlitt, whose writing in the mass-circulation middle-class magazine *Gartenlaube* was enormously successful, drew sensitive and affectionate portraits of Jews. There were no repeat performances of the mob violence against Jews such as had occurred in 1848, and the virulent new political anti-Semitism had yet to find an echo.

The widespread feeling of insecurity which found one expression in outbursts of anti-Semitism was the result of the inevitable problems caused by a society in the process of rapid change. The old certainties of a society based on the estates, where each knew his place and where the individual was subsumed in the community, was being replaced by one in which the individual appeared disoriented, isolated, alienated, and no longer protected by a corporate society. A myriad of associations sprang up to fill the gap left by the disappearance of older forms of social cohesiveness such as the corporations and the guilds. Glee clubs and gymnastic associations, educational societies and charitable organizations, art appreciation groups and volunteer firefighters contributed to a rich associational life in Germany that was to survive until the Nazis put an end to it. These associations played a vital political role, and as national organizations contributed significantly to the creation of a national identity. They were associations of free individuals, and not part of a preordained social order. Some, like the Museum Association, excluded all but the educated, but here at least aristocrats and bourgeois could meet on common ground. Others, like the gymnasts, were outspokenly radical and opened their doors to all comers. Working-class associations began to articulate class-specific needs.

Since political associations were strictly forbidden in the German Confederation with the Carlsbad Decrees of 1819, many of these associations, especially the gymnasts and the glee clubs, played a political role and thus soon fell foul of the law. The very fact that the clubs were often national gave them a liberal hue. There was a marked increase in the political activity of the clubs in the 1840s, and after the revolution of 1848 they were the seedbeds of the political parties and associations that were henceforth to play such an important role in this new bourgeois society.

3
Restoration and Reform: 1815–40

The war years had aroused great hopes for change and equally intense fears. There were those who hoped that the reforms would continue in peacetime, and those who felt that they had already gone too far. Although the vast mass of the population of Germany was indifferent to the outcome of the struggle between these two factions of reform and restoration, the outcome was to have a profound effect on the course of German history.

At the Congress of Vienna it was agreed that each of the German states should have provincial diets. The wording of the act was extremely obscure. It spoke of "constitutions based on the estates" (*landständische Verfassungen*) but quite what that involved, and precisely what role the confederation was to play in the constitutional question, was left vague. Metternich wanted the German states to adopt the Austrian model of provincial diets, with a council of state at the center of government. The south German states saw this as a backward step, and were determined to consolidate their constitutional advances toward representative government.

Metternich's secretary, Friedrich Gentz, produced a powerful memorandum in 1819 in which he drew a clear distinction between "provincial diets" and "representative constitutions," insisting that the latter were incommensurate with the Federal Act. The Federal Council (Bundestag) in Frankfurt disagreed, and decided that it had no business interfering with the constitutional arrangements of the member states. The states wished to assert their independence from the confederation, and thus set to work drawing up constitutions before one was imposed on them from above. This proved to be only a temporary setback for Metternich. Student unrest provided an excellent excuse to call a halt to further constitutional reform.

In spite of these difficulties constitutional progress was made in southern Germany, particularly in Bavaria, Baden, and Württemberg, all of which had gained considerable amounts of new territory which needed to be integrated into the state, a process that could best be realized by means of a constitution. In these states 80 members of the old imperial nobility demanded special rights and privileges in their mediated territories. Many of these were granted under article 14 of the Federal Act. Their estates amounted almost to states within the state. They were given their places in the upper chamber, but it was thought prudent to restrain their powers by creating a largely bourgeois second chamber. In spite of these constitutional checks, the fate of these mediated territories depended on individual whim. Donaueschingen flourished under the Fürstenbergs. Some of these lofty aristocrats, like Prince Wilhelm Ludwig von Sayn-Wittgenstein, were dyed-in-the-wool reactionaries, whereas others, such as Prince Karl von Leiningen, were liberals.

Some states gave in to the mounting pressure for constitutional reform because they all faced severe financial problems in the immediate postwar years, and some form of representative body was felt to be an expedient means of collecting new taxes. Civil servants also wanted to curb the administration of the state from the capricious whims of absolutist princes, and the princes not infrequently supported the notion of constitutional reform as a means of preserving their sovereign rights against the encroachments of the confederation. The Bavarian constitution of 1818 was in part designed to reinforce claims to the Palatinate on the right bank of the Rhine. Baden, which also claimed the territory and which was about to be entangled in a difficult succession problem, proclaimed a new constitution only a few weeks later. In 1819 the lengthy struggle in Württemberg between an enlightened monarch and the estates, which jealously guarded their rights and privileges, was put on hold with the promulgation of a constitution.

The country that, more than any other, was in dire need of a constitution was Prussia, which was now a patchwork of disparate territories stretching from Memel to Aachen, and sharply divided culturally, religiously, and economically between the western and eastern provinces. Protestant Prussia was now two-fifths Catholic, of whom about half were Poles. The great reforms since 1806 were incomplete, and the restorative forces that were concentrated around the crown prince and his reversionary interests were gradually gaining the upper hand. Frederick William III was never the man to give strong leadership and he shunned a confrontation with his son and the powerful ministers who surrounded him. Administrative changes took the place of constitutional reform. The entire country was divided up into provinces, each with a president who, although he was appointed by the central government, enjoyed a high degree of independence. The regions thus each maintained their own distinct identities. Rhinelanders might now be Prussian citizens, but they did not cease to be fiercely independent, and highly critical of their fellow Prussians from Brandenburg. Liberal civil servants, who admired the legal reforms that the French had brought to the Rhineland, managed to stymie a move to introduce the far less progressive Prussian code in the region. Regionalism often went hand in hand with nationalism. A Rhinelander who did not wish to be considered a Prussian felt quite comfortable as a German.

The reformers managed to secure the creation of a council of state, an idea that had been vigorously supported by Stein, but they did not succeed in their ambition to create some form of representative body for the entire state. Some even doubted whether it would be possible in such a heterogeneous state as Prussia. The demands for constitutional reform were strongest among the liberal bourgeoisie of the Rhineland, with Joseph Görres as their outstanding spokesman, but the reform movement was seriously hampered by the inability of the various factions to settle their differences over what form the constitution should eventually take. When these differences became irreconcilable, Metternich, with the full backing of the tsar, took drastic action against the radicals with the Carlsbad Decrees of 1819. Hardenberg and Wilhelm von Humboldt, both of whom favored a constitution, became bitter rivals, Humboldt complaining that the chancellor had excessive powers. Hardenberg in return accused Humboldt and his supporters of being sympathetic to the revolutionaries and forced Görres into exile. Hermann von Boyen, the great military reformer, felt obliged to hand in his resignation when the king demanded drastic reforms of the *Landwehr*, thus threatening the principle of a citizens' army that was so dear to him. Wilhelm von Humboldt was dismissed later that year, as were a number of other prominent reformers. The hunt for "demagogues" and "Jacobins" emboldened the opponents of reform to the point that even Hardenberg was denounced as a dangerous radical. The movement for constitutional reform was buried with the chancellor in 1822 and Prussia remained a state without a constitution until 1848.

Student Radicalism

Foremost among the demagogues and radicals who supported the movement for constitutional reform were the intensely nationalist student fraternities and the equally passionate gymnastic clubs founded by Friedrich Ludwig Jahn and Friedrich Friesen. These radical nationalists affected an absurdly "Germanic" appearance, with distinctive hats and clothes, straggly beards, and a dreamy gaze toward distant horizons. Lonely figures so attired populate the paintings of the masterly romantic artist Caspar David Friedrich. They were often boorish, were unattractively contemptuous of all foreigners, and prone to a virulent anti-Semitism. The first student fraternity (*Burschenschaft*) was founded in Jena in 1815. They demanded drastic reform of the stuffy universities with their outmoded curricula, and they were inspired by a vision of a democratic and free community, but they were also fiercely nationalistic and rejected the cosmopolitanism of an earlier generation of students. Although precious few of them had actually fought in the wars of liberation, they adopted the black, red, and gold colors of the Lützow Free Corps, as well as their motto: "Honor, Freedom and Fatherland." In October 1817 the *Burschenschaften* organized a festival at the Wartburg in Eisenach to mark the third centenary of the reformation and also to celebrate the battle of Leipzig of 1813. It was attended by some 500 students from various universities and by a handful of sympathetic professors. On the first evening some of Jahn's more radical followers built a bonfire onto which were thrown various items symbolic of militarism and feudalism, such as a corporal's swagger stick, a plaited wig, and a pair of corsets, along with the works of certain writers deemed to be "un-German," among them those of the

Plate 4 Gymnasts attending the Wartburg Festival 1817. © BPK

popular dramatist August von Kotzebue, who also acted as one of the tsar's informants on German affairs. A year later the various fraternities joined together to form
a national organization with a somewhat confused program which combined the
ideals of the French Revolution, such as freedom, national unity, and representative
government, with a political gothic revival which had an intensely romantic han-
kering after an idealized vision of the medieval empire and a mythical past. At the
universities of Jena and Giessen there were small groups of German Jacobins who
were devoted followers of one Karl Follen, who taught at Giessen. They called for
a centralized republic that would be the expression of the people's general will, to
be created if need be by violence.

Metternich was horrified when he received reports of the Wartburg Festival and
was convinced that the *Burschenschaft* was a serious threat that had to be eliminated. At the European Congress of Aachen in 1818 he requested that the universities should be placed under close supervision, but he met with stiff opposition from
Wilhelm von Humboldt, who held academic freedom to be sacrosanct. For once

Plate 5 Student representatives burning reactionary books and symbols. © BPK

Hardenberg gave him full support. In March the following year one of Karl Follen's fanatical followers, the theology student Karl Sand, stabbed Kotzebue to death at his home in Mannheim. Shortly afterward a senior civil servant in Nassau was murdered by an apothecary known to be close to the radical student circle at Jena, known as "The Blacks" (*die Schwarzen*). There was much sympathy among liberals for Sand's actions. As is so often the case, the victim was blamed for the crime. Görres announced that "despotism" was the root cause. A distinguished theology professor felt that Sand had acted out of conviction and pureness of heart. Sand died as a martyr to the national cause and his wily executioner, a man of democratic convictions, built a garden shed in a vineyard outside Heidelberg out of the timber from the scaffold. It soon became a popular place of pilgrimage.

Metternich decided to take firm action against the universities and the radical press, which he held to be a serious threat to the confederation, but he came up against a certain resistance from a number of the member states to any encroachments on their sovereignty that such a step would inevitably involve. The Prussian authorities made a number of arrests, among them Jahn and Ernst Moritz Arndt. The great theologian and philosopher Friedrich Schleiermacher, who had expressed his sympathy for the radical students, was placed under close police observation. Metternich met the Prussian king at Teplitz to discuss the situation and then called a meeting of the heads of the major German states at Carlsbad in August. They agreed upon a program to crush the radical movement which was rushed through the Bundestag in an extremely dubious and hasty manner, and was promulgated on September 20 1819 as the Carlsbad Decrees. The universities were placed under close police surveillance and any professor found expounding views deemed to threaten the institutions of the state or public order was to be dismissed. The *Burschenschaft* was banned, and all its members were disbarred from the civil service. Newspapers and pamphlets were all to be censored. However, books longer than 320 pages were felt to be too expensive for general consumption, and were not subject to pre-publication censorship until 1842. A commission was established in Mainz to unearth revolutionary activities. The confederation could intervene in any state that refused to enforce these measures or which was threatened by revolution. Virtually the sole function of the German Confederation was now to crush radical dissent.

Metternich tried to go one step further and stop the movement for constitutional reform, and revoke some of the more progressive constitutions. Here he was frustrated by resistance from Württemberg, Bavaria, and Saxony-Weimar, but he was able to push through measures that made constitutional changes exceedingly difficult. The implementation of the Carlsbad Decrees varied in severity from state to state. They were rigorously enforced in Prussia and in Austria. Radical students were given lengthy prison sentences and many prominent professors were rusticated. Gymnastics were strictly forbidden. Fichte's fiercely nationalistic *Speeches to the German Nation* was not permitted to be reprinted. In 1827 the Mainz commission released a report that was greeted with hoots of derision. Schleiermacher, Arndt, and Fichte were said to have inspired the "demagogues" who had also been encouraged by Stein, Hardenberg, and the other great reformers.

Germany Under Metternich

Life in Germany in the 1820s was repressive and dreary, but Metternich's attempt to turn the confederation into a police state was only partly successful. The system was inefficient, somewhat absurd, and the loose federal structure offered areas of relative freedom. The German tendency to look inward was further enhanced in the Biedermeier period, and an atmosphere of apolitical resignation and philistine domesticity prevailed. This in turn exasperated those who could not make their peace with existing conditions, and gave rise to a fresh wave of radicalism. The most serious challenge to the Metternichian system came not from radical students and fanatical Jacobins, but from liberalism. The German version of liberalism was heavily influenced by Kant in that it stressed the rights and obligations of the autonomous individual and the need to work toward emancipation from the imperatives of the state, the bureaucracy, and one's station in society. This was seen as a duty and obligation, a lengthy process toward an unspecified future, where each would realize his own vision of reason and of freedom, and where a consensus could be reached through rational discourse. Most liberals, particularly in southern Germany, had serious reservations about a liberal capitalist economy, with its concomitant social problems, that could so clearly be observed in England. They felt that stability and social harmony were far more important than economic growth, and they hankered after a cozy pre-industrial society. Germany's foremost political economist, Friedrich List, took the opposite view, and argued that only a modern industrial society could provide the wealth that alone could provide the means to relieve the problems of poverty and want. The great entrepreneurs of the Rhineland, such as Ludolf Camphausen and David Hansemann, Gustav Mevissen and Hermann von Beckerath, were in full agreement. As Karl Marx was to comment, German liberalism, with its ambivalence about modernity, was very long on theory and very short on practice. It was a state of mind rather than a political program. As Kant had argued, freedom existed for them in the realm of ideals and obligations, rather than in the real world of politics and society.

In more practical terms this involved a demand for restricted popular sovereignty, the strict limitation of state intervention, the rule of law before which each was equal, guarantees for basic individual rights, the right of association, and the separation of powers. A system whereby that which is not expressly permitted was forbidden had to be replaced by one in which everything was permitted except that which was expressly forbidden. The franchise was to be limited to the educated and the propertied, and not frivolously wasted on those who were unable to form an intelligent opinion, and who had no material stake in society. Even then there could be no agreement on whether or not the democratic rights of a majority could be reconciled with individual rights, and from the very outset this was to be a fundamental problem at the very center of the liberal worldview. There was the uneasy feeling that liberty and equality were irreconcilable, but whereas conservatives believed that these twin ideals led inevitably to a reign of terror, liberals hoped that with reason, moderation, and compromise this horror could be avoided. They remained, however, extremely cautious, and rejected utopian blueprints in favor of modest and gradual reform.

German liberals faced another dilemma. They were in favor of a lean state that intervened as little as possible in the daily lives of its citizens, but the state was in most instances run by liberal bureaucrats bent on the destruction of the last vestiges of an autocratic and feudal system. However, the state also stifled free speech, trampled on academic freedom, and violated the fundamental rights of its opponents. The state was thus part ally, part foe, and was viewed with the utmost suspicion, since liberals were aware that they alone, and not the state, could realize their vision of a free society. Gradually the conviction grew among liberals that society should free itself, and not be liberated by civil servants, however enlightened and progressive they might be. They did not want a revolution from above, and were alarmed at the prospect of a revolution from below; they wanted gradual reform in the interests of the educated, propertied, and politically-aware middle classes. They were to be partially frustrated in this ambition as Germany found its own distinctive path toward modernization.

The creation of a bourgeois society in Prussia was in part the work of the state. The reforming civil servants of the Napoleonic era had done much to encourage modernization. When the reaction set in after 1815 the liberal bourgeoisie lost all confidence in the Prussian state. State and society were now on a collision course. As a bourgeois society was formed with its market economy, its rationalism, its pluralism, and its individualism, old social ties were sundered and social cohesion was threatened. To many, religion no longer provided helpful signposts on life's journey. The marketplace was alarmingly free and unforgiving. New social divisions became increasingly threatening. Society was no longer held together by tradition, by a clearly defined social hierarchy, or by divine sanction, but increasingly by the use of a common language and a sense of belonging to a common culture. Such a society provided fertile ground for the new religion of nationalism which offered a fresh and exhilarating sense of community. Nationalism implied a real or imaginary nation. A nation can be based on consent, on the right of citizens to choose their nationality and by implication their right to govern, or on a common ethnicity, language, or culture. Germany was not a nation in the former sense since one could not become a German by obtaining a German passport; one could only be German if one were a member of the German people (*Volk*).

Nationalism

German nationalism was fueled by the wars against France, and by the French occupation of the western states. It was also driven by the desire to create a new and freer society. It was directed against the French outside, and the despots within. The struggle against foreign domination did not of necessity go hand in hand with a liberal vision of a free people, and the contradiction between the two positions, partly obscured during the wars of liberation, was to become glaringly apparent. Although there was considerable sympathy for the French and their struggle for freedom, almost all opposed Napoleon. Goethe admired his genius, and Hegel managed to convince himself that he was the world spirit on horseback, an instrument of historical change that could no more be condemned than an earthquake or volcanic eruption. But they were isolated figures. Beethoven crossed out the dedication of his *Eroica* symphony. Görres, who had been a Jacobin, now took solace in contemplation of Germany's medieval greatness. Fichte, the erstwhile ultraradical, became a rabid nationalist and the outpourings of this great philosopher of nationalism descended to the level of crude and apocalyptic rantings that have a vile foretaste of things to come. The idea of the organic state to which the individual citizens were subservient, and in which alone they could fully realize themselves, had widespread appeal. Arndt, to whom nationalism was the "religion of our time," and the teutonomane Jahn, trumpeted this message. Even such levelheaded men as Stein and Humboldt were swept away on this wave of nationalism. Schleiermacher managed to convince himself that since the German people (*Volk*) was God's creation, to serve it was to serve its maker. Kleist, who had suffered an acute identity crisis on reading Kant, temporarily overcame his ontological anxieties by wallowing in an ecstatic nationalism and indulging in an orgy of hatred of the French in his play *Hermannschlacht*.

During the period of restoration after 1815 many wondered what they had been fighting for. Memories of the "national awakening" of 1813 began to fade, and a search began for a national identity. Architects built in the "German" style, but there was some uncertainty whether this should be gothic or Romanesque. Painters churned out canvases of Germany's heroic past and writers penned historical novels. Monuments were erected to all manner of figures from Hermann to Gutenberg and Mozart. Luther was seen as a uniquely German figure, and Protestants claimed that their religion was the only one appropriate for a true German. Ludwig I of Bavaria built Walhalla as a Germanic pantheon of the great figures of the past. In 1842 Frederick William IV ordered a magnificent celebration to mark the beginning of the final phase of the building of Cologne cathedral, one of the great monuments to Germany's former glory.

Opinions were divided as to what form the new Germany should take. Goethe, who remained true to the cosmopolitanism of the eighteenth century, thought that it should be a cultural community based on the model of ancient Greece, and thus did not require the formation of a nation-state. Local patriotism and regionalism were deeply entrenched, and had been strengthened in the southern German states that had profited from the Napoleonic reordering of Germany. But there were countervailing forces. The remarkable number of national associations and festivals, the mushrooming of the national press, lively communication between the great universities, reforms of primary and secondary education, and a much greater mobility all served to strengthen a sense of supra-regional belonging. Virtually all liberals were nationalists. They sharply criticized the smaller German states and demanded a united Germany. Freedom and unity was their rallying cry, although there was some disagreement as which of the two was the more important. They attacked the confederation for its failure to create a common currency and common weights and measures, for not removing the plethora of customs and tariff barriers, and for not developing a rational transportation policy. There was also general agreement that the new Germany would be a federal state, but there were only vague notions of how it would be organized, and what would be the relative roles of Austria and Prussia. That Austria was part of Germany was indisputable. The Austrians certainly considered themselves to be Germans, but this feeling had precious few political consequences. Austria and Bohemia formed a significant part of the German Confederation, but the Germans saw it as a right due to their cultural superiority to rule the multinational Habsburg Empire. Liberal Austrians had some sympathy for the national aspirations of Hungarians, Italians, and Poles but they were not seen as pressing concerns. They regarded any similar sentiments by the Slav peoples within the empire as patently ridiculous. None thought of abandoning the empire and merging into a united Germany.

Liberals stood for the principles of the French Revolution, at least in its earlier and moderate phase, and were sympathetic toward the Greeks in the 1820s, the

Poles in 1830/1, and the Swiss in 1847/8. Conservatives were utterly opposed and argued that the liberal call for freedom would lead inevitably to chaos and terror. Order and stability were, in their view, the essential preconditions for real freedom, and the alternative to order and stability was revolution. There could be no middle way. In place of the endless squabbles and the clash of irreconcilable points of view that liberals were pleased to call democracy, there had to be a traditional and legitimate authority that existed by the grace of God. "Authority not majority" was the rallying call of conservatives. The notion of progress was seen as a vain illusion. That one could slice off heads in the name of reason showed that society needed to be guided by a religiously-sanctioned authority that was impervious to utopian hubris. German conservatism was poles apart from the progressive conservatism of Edmund Burke and much closer to the black reactionary fulminations of de Maistre and Bonald. For conservatives the urban middle class was the greatest danger. Capitalists, intellectuals, and liberal civil servants, with their dangerous talk of the rule of reason and their calls for a constitution, were at odds with the mass of the people who simply wanted peace and quiet in an ordered, hierarchical community in which everyone knew their place, in what Karl Ludwig von Haller dubbed the "patrimonial state." This attack on the bourgeoisie won conservatives considerable support from artisans and peasants, who were losing ground as Germany rapidly became an industrial society. Conservatives denounced economic liberalism for bringing with it alienation, the separation of capital and labor, the breakdown of traditional ties, and the creation of a hydra-headed and soulless bureaucratic state. It is fascinating to observe how closely many of their attacks on bourgeois society resemble those of later socialists. For the likes of Adam Müller, Friedrich Schlegel, and Görres in his final incarnation, to call this bleak and inhuman society "free" was a cruel mockery. Conservatives were every bit as vehement in their denunciation of nationalism. For them it was a flagrant violation of legitimate, time-honored, and sovereign rights, the brainchild of a godless bourgeoisie. They were particularists, supporters of the German Confederation dominated by Metternich, and of the Europe of the Holy Alliance.

Constitutional Developments

Prussia in the pre-March had no constitution, was authoritarian, penny-pinching, and efficient, but it was not a police state, nor was it subject to the whims of its rulers. Even if its legal codes limped behind those of its more progressive neighbors, at least the rule of law prevailed. It was a state that was run by an honest, hard-working, and capable civil service, but it was no longer in tune with middle-class aspirations as it had been in the period of reform. Austria was an ossified police state in which the liberal bourgeoisie was a tiny minority. In the southern German states, where the constitutional movement had gone furthest, the pace of reform slowed down markedly. Precious little was done to modernize the economies of these states, so that the disparity between Prussia and southern Germany grew ever greater. The south had constitutions, conservative governments, and a stagnant economy. Prussia had antiquated political institutions, but a more modern social structure and a thriving economy.

The southern German states developed what came to be known as "constitutional patriotism." The states, the frontiers of which had been radically redrawn during the Napoleonic era, were defined by constitutions. These constitutions limited the power and the sovereignty of the princes, and laws could not be enacted without the consent of representative bodies. The franchise for the Landtag was indirect, limited, and unequal. A largely hereditary upper chamber ensured the predominant role of the aristocracy. The diets' powers were circumscribed and they met infrequently. Yet in spite of all these limitations, parliamentary life in southern Germany flourished to the point that the lower houses became vigorous advocates of middle-class aspirations. A peculiarity of these bodies was that about half of their members were civil servants, who became some of the most outspoken critics of the state which they continued loyally to serve. There were strict limits to the powers of the southern German parliaments. The government could dismiss them, could influence elections, and take disciplinary action against deputies, but at the same time governments did not relish confrontation and preferred stability. Parliament's control over taxation was a factor that could not be ignored and attempts to circumvent it, as happened in Baden in the 1820s, created so many difficulties that the government eventually had to give way. Once the crisis was over the Landtag in Baden made passing the budget dependent on the abolition of censorship, but the Bundestag intervened and demanded that this new censorship law be revoked. This convinced liberals that significant changes could only be made at the federal level, not in the individual states. In this manner frustration with the lack of progress toward a liberal democracy in the southern German states strengthened liberal nationalism. A series of dramatic conflicts between governments and parliaments had a profound effect on German liberalism. The relationship between government and parliament became the central constitutional question, and liberals saw themselves as a check and control over governments rather than in a governing role. They were to form a permanent opposition that kept a watchful eye on governments, and made sure that the people's rights were respected. This resulted in constant conflict between governments and parliaments, which meant that no progress could be made toward a liberal constitution, and liberals became increasingly frustrated.

The *Zollverein*

The only positive political event in Germany during the pre-March was the formation of the Customs Union (*Zollverein*) in 1834. At the Congress of Vienna the proposal that the Bundestag should be given the task of determining a common customs policy had not been accepted because of objections, principally from Bavaria, that this would be a violation of the sovereignty of the member states. The Customs Union was the work of Prussian economic reformers who enthusiastically accepted the idea put forward by, among others, Stein, the economist Friedrich List, and the sugar baron Johann Friedrich Benzenberg, that Germany could only develop economically if it formed a common market. An ugly customs war between Austria and the other German states following the catastrophic crop failure in 1816 made this argument very persuasive. The arduous process of forming a German Customs Union began in 1818 when all customs barriers between the various Prussian provinces were abolished. The Prussians were hardly innovators in this respect. The Bavarians had removed internal customs barriers as early as 1807, and the same happened in Württemberg in 1808, and Baden in 1812, but the Prussian officials were determined that their customs union should be extended to include as many of the other German states as possible. The law of 1818 created a free market for 10.5 million Germans but it also imposed crippling transit duties. The General German Association for Trade and Industry, the first all-German association of this sort, with Friedrich List as its very capable spokesman, began to agitate for a German customs union on the Prussian model. The confederation felt that such an institution was dangerously liberal and some of the German states were also opposed to the idea, so an alternative solution had to be found. Largely on the initiative of Baron Karl August von Wangenheim, the Württemberg delegate to the Bundestag, a southern German customs treaty was signed in May 1820 by Württemberg, Baden, Bavaria, Hesse-Darmstadt, and most of the Thuringian states. This did not amount to much, since the signatories were deadlocked for years because Bavaria demanded protective tariffs, while Baden wanted free trade.

Prussia, under the exceptionally able leadership of the minister of finance, Friedrich von Motz, and the economics expert in the Foreign Office, Albrecht Eichhorn, was determined to extend the Prussian customs union to northern and central Germany. Motz's vision went far beyond the purely economic. He believed that the smaller German states were doomed to backwardness and that Germany therefore had to be unified. Austria, burdened with all the problems of a multinational empire, was quite incapable of taking a leadership role in this respect; therefore Germany had to be united under Prussia by means of a customs union. Motz argued that customs dues were symbolic of political divisions, therefore if they were abolished political unity would necessarily follow. Not all Prussian officials agreed with Motz's liberal vision, but they all saw the necessity of bringing the two halves of the Prussian state together in one free-trading zone, and of abolishing all the enclaves within this patchwork of provinces. This proved to be a long and difficult task. It was not until 1828 that Anhalt finally admitted defeat in a customs war and joined the Prussian Union. Electoral Hesse and Hanover, which stood between Brandenburg-Prussia and the western provinces, fiercely resisted all attempts to win them over. The Prussians now looked south, and later in the same year managed to convince Hesse-Darmstadt to join, thus establishing a foothold south of the river Main. Austria and many of the other German states began to get exceedingly nervous and were determined to resist the Prussians. Egged on by Austria and France, a Middle German Customs Union was formed, comprising Saxony and some of the Thuringian states, Electoral Hesse, Hanover and Brunswick, Nassau, and Bremen.

In southern Germany Bavaria and Württemberg formed a customs union, also in 1828. Prussia won over two of the Thuringian states with a generous offer to improve the roads, and then in 1829 signed a trade treaty with the Southern German Union. Two years later Electoral Hesse finally gave way, so that a bridge was built between the eastern and western provinces. In 1833 negotiations between the Prussian and southern German unions were finally concluded, Prussia having made substantial concessions, and the resulting union was named the *Deutscher Zollverein*. Saxony and the Thuringian states joined the party shortly thereafter and the *Zollverein* was formally inaugurated at midnight on New Year's Eve 1834. In the following years some of the smaller states joined in, so that by 1842 28 of the 39 German states were members. Hanover, Braunschweig, and Oldenburg remained aloof. The *Zollverein* greatly strengthened Prussia's position in Germany, but it did not make a little German solution under Prussian leadership inevitable. Members had the right of veto and were free to leave at will. The *Zollverein* states could always appeal to Austria for help, and most of them were to support Austria against Prussia in the war of 1866. On the other hand Prussia's rapidly growing industrial might gave it a preponderance of power within the customs union, and eventually in Germany.

The Congress System

Germany was an important diplomatic arena in which most of the powers had a direct interest: Russia as guarantor of the Vienna settlement; Britain because of the personal union with Hanover; Holland and Denmark because of their stake in the confederation. From time to time France would cast a greedy eye on the Rhine frontier. The German Confederation itself counted for nothing on the international stage. It had no foreign ministry and no foreign policy. Of the German states only Austria really counted, so that inasmuch as Germany had a foreign policy it was that of Metternich and of Austria. Prussia's prestige paled by comparison. The principles of Metternich's foreign policy were straightforward. He wanted to maintain the conservative order, ensure stability, and preserve Austria's position as a great power. The problem was that it became increasingly difficult to pursue all three aims at once, and ultimately the enterprise was doomed to failure. Metternich was shrewd enough to know that his system's days were numbered, but he was not statesman enough to adjust to meet the challenges of a rapidly changing society. All he could hope to do was to hang on as long as possible, and put off the evil day when the system would collapse. Eighteen forty-eight came as no great surprise to him, and he congratulated himself that the revolution had come so late in the day.

He was a firm believer in summit diplomacy. After the Congress of Vienna a series of congresses were regularly held to strengthen cooperation between the European powers and to discuss common security problems. But the powers had divergent interests. Britain was less concerned with questions of legitimacy and conservative restoration, was sympathetic to the national aspirations of subject peoples, and concentrated on maintaining the balance of power in Europe. Principles were not to be allowed to get in the way of achieving this aim. Tsar Alexander I was wildly unpredictable, with his half-baked mystical views about a new order for Europe. The British were determined to keep the Russians in check, and Metternich was anxious to maintain good relations with Britain to this end. At the same time, Austria was Russia's neighbor and Metternich hoped that, by convincing the tsar to pursue more levelheaded and conservative policies, conflict could be avoided. Russia and Austria might agree on armed intervention against revolutionary movements in Italy, Spain, and Portugal, but the British government would have nothing to do with this. Britain withdrew from the Congress system and from 1822 merely sent observers. Castelreagh committed suicide that year, and the new foreign secretary Canning was strongly opposed to the Holy Alliance. He enthusiastically endorsed revolutionary national movements in South America, and in 1826 "called the New World into existence to redress the balance of the old."

Given their conflicting national interests Austria and Russia could hardly remain close allies. Nicholas I, who succeeded his elder brother in 1825, and who was married to Frederick William III of Prussia's daughter, was an appalling despot who resolutely followed what he considered to be the national interests of Russia. Along with the British he supported the struggle for Greek independence. The British wanted to stop Greece from becoming a Russian protectorate. The Russians wanted to weaken the Ottoman Empire, whereas Metternich supported the Sultan for reasons of legitimacy. With both Britain and Russia on opposite sides over the eastern question and his system in ruins, Metternich's influence over foreign affairs was minimal.

The Revolutionary Movements

In 1830 the revolution now came closer to home. The July revolution in France triggered a series of uprisings throughout Europe. Belgium broke away from the Netherlands. There were numerous revolts in Italy. In Poland there was a major uprising against Russian rule. England and France let it be known that they would not tolerate any intervention in Belgium, and in any case the Austrians had their hands full in Italy, and the Russians had theirs full in Poland. The creation of an independent Belgium was another major setback for Metternich. It had proved possible to stop the formation of a Belgian republic, and French aspirations to turn Belgium into a quasi-protectorate had been frustrated, but the principle of legitimacy had been thwarted and others could well be tempted to follow the Belgian example. The impact of the July revolution was also felt in Germany. Heine, who was spending the summer on Heligoland, spent sleepless nights, and imagined rudely awakening the "portly snoring philistines" from their torpor. In Brunswick there were protests against the heavy-handed absolutist regime of Duke Karl, who had taken away the consultative rights of the estates in 1827. When the duke refused to make any concessions, a mob of artisans, workers, and youths set the palace on fire and he fled. The Landtag declared him incapable of ruling and his brother was appointed regent. The duke attempted to return, but was stopped by army units supported by the militia. After a peasants' revolt in 1832 a constitution was promulgated which strengthened the representation of the middle classes and peasants, and lessened the influence of the aristocracy.

The Elector of Hesse, William II, was one of the worst despots in Germany. He outraged the bourgeoisie by aping the ancien régime and by flaunting his mistress. Demonstrations were held in Kassel, Hanau, and Fulda calling for a diet. A volunteer militia was formed, and there were widespread protests against all manner of abuses. As in Brunswick, artisans and workers were the most active and the bourgeoisie used this fact to argue that a constitution was essential in order avoid a civil war between haves and have-nots. The elector gave way and appointed a Landtag which promptly demanded that he abdicate. The crown prince was made co-regent, and a constitution was adopted which was by far the most progressive in all of Germany. There was a single chamber elected by a reasonably wide franchise and dominated by the bourgeoisie and peasantry. It was the only parliamentary body in Germany that had the right to initiate laws and to veto emergency decrees.

The protest movement in Saxony was multifaceted. Most agreed that the antiquated system of government needed to be drastically overhauled and society modernized, but this was mixed with confessional squabbles and artisanal protests against industrialization. After a series of protests a reform ministry was appointed, but it was soon under pressure to get on with the job. The result was a new constitution in 1831 which, although not nearly as progressive as that of Electoral Hesse, was a significant step forward.

Hanover also was the scene of violent manifestations against the reactionary regime of Count Münster. In the university town of Göttingen the tutors (*Privatdozenten*) led a rebellion that had to be suppressed by the army. The government decided to act. Münster was dismissed and discussions were begun with the diet over a constitution that came into effect in 1833. It made few concessions to the urban liberals, but they took some comfort in the fact that taxes had been reduced and the peasantry finally freed from their feudal obligations.

There were no such dramatic upheavals in southern Germany in 1830, but the liberal opposition was encouraged to take a bolder stand and there were a number of demonstrations in favor of Polish independence, the largest of which was in Munich, which was broken up by the army. Radical groups were emboldened by these events in 1830, and in 1832 a huge meeting was held at Hambach in the Palatinate organized by a recently formed "Press and Fatherland Association." Between 20,000 and 30,000 attended, making this the largest political demonstration to date in Germany. They waved the black, red, and yellow German flag, along with the white eagle of Poland. They were mostly artisans and peasants, but a number of students attended, along with some representatives from France and Poland. They listened to a series of rousing speeches calling for a democratic "legal revolution" that went far beyond liberal constitutional reform, for the emancipation of women, and for the formation of a German nation-state. The tone of these speeches was cosmopolitan and far removed from the rabid German nationalism of the Wartburg festival. A number of smaller demonstrations were held elsewhere in Germany and there were isolated instances of violence. Even moderate reformers, such as Heinrich von Gagern and Karl Rotteck, agreed with the authorities that this was all the work of misguided demagogues. At Metternich's prompting Bavaria declared a state of emergency, and an ancient field marshal was sent to the Palatinate to round up radicals and uproot the many liberty trees which had been provocatively planted throughout the region. Most of the ringleaders of the Hambach Festival managed to escape arrest. One month later the Bundestag passed the "Six Articles" which drastically limited the rights of the diets and established a Control Commission to ensure that these provisions were rigorously enforced. A federal law was proclaimed which tightened censorship and banned all political associations and meetings.

The protest movement continued in spite of these measures. In the following year there were celebrations in the Palatinate to mark the anniversary of the Hambach Festival. In Frankfurt am Main a group of students from Heidelberg led an attack on the main guardhouse. It was a dramatic gesture designed to trigger a general revolt in which the Bundestag building would be seized, the delegates arrested, and a revolutionary council formed. As is so often the case, the citizenry wrote the whole episode off as a student prank, and regarded it with amused detachment. The authorities did not share this indifference. The army was sent in and six soldiers were killed, along with one student. Metternich then pressed through further repressive legislation. A Central Office for Political Investigation was formed which began work at once tracking down radicals. Within ten years 2,000 investigations had been conducted. The Prussian authorities took drastic measures. Two hundred and four students were arrested, most of whom were given lengthy jail sentences. Thirty-nine were condemned to death. Membership of a student fraternity was now regarded as high treason.

In 1835 the police unearthed a network of radical intellectuals and artisans from Giessen, Marburg, and Frankfurt who called for a violent overthrow of the existing order and the creation of a republic based on popular sovereignty and genuine equality. The brilliant young dramatist Georg Büchner was the outstanding spokesman of this group and in his *Hessian Courier* of 1834, which he co-authored with Friedrich Ludwig Weidig, he coined a slogan that was to become an overworn cliché in left-wing circles: "Peace to the cottages! War on the palaces!" Büchner managed to escape arrest and fled to Zurich where he died of typhoid in 1837 at the age of 24. The liberal bourgeoisie who lived neither in cottages nor in palaces were horrified at these inflammatory notions and sympathized with the authorities in their determined pursuit of dangerous radicals. Had they read Büchner's masterly study of the complexities and moral ambiguities of the French Revolution in his drama *Danton's Death*, or his harrowing analysis of the structures of social control and psychological dependency in *Woyzeck*, to say nothing of his gentle mockery of the old order in his comedy *Leonce and Lena*, they would have been less indignant.

Büchner was one of a number of gifted radical writers in the 1830s which included Heine, whose political verse expressed his love–hate relationship with Germany, and who gave vent to his ironic wit in language of unparalleled brilliance and clarity. Heine and Ludwig Börne were the leading figures of a literary movement known as "Young Germany," the writings of which were banned by the Bundestag in 1835 for immorality and blasphemy. The immediate cause of this drastic action was the publication of a novel by Karl Gutzow, *Wally the Skeptic*, which attacked the hypocrisy of the churches, and preached free love and the emancipation of women.

The "Young Germans" were politically naïve, and few of their literary works are of much value. Only Heine combined literary genius with an astonishing ability to analyze the malaise of his times. History more often than not has proved him right. Heine and Börne were the most prominent of the German exiles in Paris. They were among the founding members of the "German People's Association" (*Deutsche Volksverein*) formed in Paris as a branch of the Press Association. It was disbanded by the police in 1834 and a hard core of radicals formed the "Union of Outlaws" (*Bund der Geächteten*); a few years later a splinter group called the "Union of the Just" (*Bund der Gerechten*) was formed which espoused an inchoate communism and with which the young Karl Marx was soon in contact. Its most prominent figure was William Weitling, a journeyman tailor living in exile in France and Switzerland, who, in a series of books, propounded his version of utopian socialism. It was a pre-industrial fantasy in which the industrial proletariat played no role. His messianic vision, in which property and money would be abolished and in which Jesus was seen as the original communist, was to be realized through social revolution. It is thus through the Young Germans and their naïve utopian flights of fancy that the Hambach Festival can be seen within the context of the European socialist movement.

Prussia and Austria remained remarkably quiet during these troubled years, but attempts in Electoral Hesse to turn back the clock were strongly resisted and there was permanent tension between the government and the Landtag. Popular pressure forced the regent to dismiss the fiercely reactionary first minister Ludwig Hassenpflug, the brother-in-law of the Brothers Grimm of fairytale fame, but succeeding ministries were no great improvement and Electoral Hesse remained high on the list of states deserving of liberal opprobrium.

Hanover's personal union with England ended in 1837 when Queen Victoria became Queen of England and the arch-reactionary Ernst August of Cumberland ascended the throne. He refused to take an oath to the constitution, dismissed the diet, and declared the constitution null and void. Shortly afterwards, seven prominent professors at Göttingen proclaimed their loyalty to the constitution, whereupon they were instantly dismissed. When warned of the possible consequences of removing such distinguished scholars as the Brothers Grimm and the historians Dahlmann and Gervinus, the king made the disturbingly perceptive remark that professors, like whores, can always be had for money. The "Göttingen Seven" were now the heroes of German liberalism. They were fêted as men of principle who upheld constitutional rights against princely caprice. These were no stone-throwing rowdies or fervid demagogues, but largely apolitical professors who had the courage to denounce the king's willful action. Baden and Bavaria supported the Hanoverian opposition's appeal to the Bundestag to right these wrongs, but the majority of the German states supported Metternich, who sympathized with Ernst August's coup, which was thus sanctioned by the confederation. A new constitution was introduced in 1840, but it was a far less liberal document than the earlier version, in that it greatly reduced the powers of the diet to which ministers were no longer responsible.

For all the repression, intellectual and political life in Germany was far from being stifled. The very fact that Germany was a confederation meant that the atmosphere in the various states varied widely. The Göttingen Seven might have been dismissed in Hanover, but those that so wished had no difficulty in finding a chair at another university. It was also in the period of the Carlsbad Decrees and the Six Articles that the main political movements in Germany became clearly delineated into conservatives, Catholics, liberals, democrats, and socialists. Conservatives were antinationalist, felt that the confederation should exercise its full powers against liberals and radicals, and argued that Austria and Prussia should work closely together against the forces of change. The Prussian statesman Joseph Maria von Radowitz was the first to see that conservatism could indeed be reconciled with nationalism and was to argue that Prussia should assert itself within a reformed confederation.

Catholics, unlike Protestants, also began to be seen as a distinct party. The relative roles of church and state had been redefined by the French Revolution and by secularization. The church wanted to be free from state interference, but at the same time have a decisive influence over such central issues as education and the family. Catholics thus opposed the secular and authoritarian state, but also anticlerical liberals, with their individualism and their vain belief in the unlimited power of reason. This argument was to continue throughout the century and was to be brilliantly recreated in the debates between Naphta and Settembrini in Thomas Mann's masterpiece *The Magic Mountain*.

Catholics came into direct conflict with the state in Prussia when, in 1803, the government required that east of the river Elbe children of mixed marriages should be brought up in the religion of the father. According to Tridentine practice, children of marriages between Catholics and Protestants had to be brought up as Catholics. In 1825 this requirement was extended to all of Prussia, including the predominantly Catholic Rhineland. Although the Pope urged restraint, there was widespread resistance to the law, and in 1837 the Bishop of Cologne was arrested for publicly denouncing it. He and a number of other bishops became heroes in the eyes of all their coreligionists. In 1840, at the beginning of his reign, Frederick William IV gave way to his Catholic subjects and the church won a major victory over the state, thus giving political Catholicism a major boost. A number of Catholic associations were formed, pilgrimages attracted large numbers and had distinct political overtones. Joseph Görres published another brilliant pamphlet, *Athanasius*, which provided a program for political Catholicism. He argued that since parties were an essential part of the modern constitutional state, Catholics should organize themselves to struggle for their rights. These ideas were developed in a new journal *The Historical-Political Pages for Catholic Germany* published in Munich. Görres and his friends waged war on the bureaucratic and authoritarian state, on the liberal heirs of the French Revolution out to destroy all in their wake, on Godless socialism, and above all on the Reformation, which lay at the root of all modern evil. Görres, the onetime radical, was now firmly in the camp of Catholic conservatism, dreaming of reconstituting a corporate society of a long gone age.

The majority of German Catholics were little concerned about the philosophical questions of individualism and rationalism which separated the ultraconservatives from the liberals. They sympathized with Catholics in Poland and Ireland who were struggling for national independence. They supported the liberal demands for freedom of expression, freedom of association, and a diminution of state power. Some went even further and sharply criticized industrial society as the direct cause of poverty, depravation, and alienation. They demanded state intervention to protect the working class from the grosser forms of exploitation, encouraged the working class to organize to further their interests, and played an active part in workers' education. Adolf Kolping founded the Journeymen's Association in 1845 to provide for the needs of working men on their travels. Later in the century Bishop Ketteler of Mainz was to develop social Catholicism into a major political movement.

On the national question the vast majority of Catholics were federalists, anti-Prussian, and for a greater Germany that included Catholic Austria. They all agreed that the interests of the church were their paramount concern, and refused to allow differences between conservatives and liberals to compromise their position on this cardinal issue. Political Catholicism laid the foundations for a genuine people's party in which Catholic princes and Catholic workers, Catholic conservatives and Catholic liberals, Prussians and Bavarians, could work together for common goals. Conservatives represented the interests of the old elite, the liberals those of the new, but the Catholic movement transcended this division and had no clearly defined class bias. Here were the beginnings of the Christian Democratic movement that was to play such an important role in European politics. Unfortunately this division between Catholic and Protestant liberals greatly weakened the liberal movement in Germany, and thus strengthened the conservative camp and put a brake on the development of parliamentary democracy.

The liberals distanced themselves ever more from the radicals. They were deeply suspicious of the radical call for equality. While accepting that equality was the essential precondition of freedom, they were keenly aware that equality could also destroy freedom. They had before them the example of the French Revolution which had clearly demonstrated the totalitarian aspects of egalitarianism, and de Tocqueville's study of American democracy, published in 1835, was widely read in liberal circles. Liberals had a horror of revolution and of the rabble, whom the radicals aroused with their fiery rhetoric.

As liberalism moved to the right it ceased to be a purely bourgeois movement and appealed to a number of aristocrats such as Heinrich von Gagern, Prince Karl zu Leiningen, and Anton von Schmerling, who were to play important roles in the revolution of 1848. All agreed that the existing state of affairs needed to be drastically changed and that Germany should become a nation-state with a liberal constitution, but there was considerable disagreement as to how the new Germany should look. Liberalism was also given a boost by what the great nationalist historian Heinrich von Treitschke called the "intellectual diets" – the national meetings of intellectuals and scientists, doctors and school teachers, lawyers and linguists, singers and gymnasts. These occasions were highly politicized and laden with national pathos, in particular the meetings of *"Germanisten,"* who reveled in ancient Germanic language and lore. By the 1840s there were regular meetings of a purely political nature in which liberals from all over Germany met to discuss matters of common concern, but it was not until late in the decade that a national newspaper, the *Deutsche Zeitung*, was founded in Heidelberg.

Whereas liberals argued that a natural state of inequality resulted from an unequal distribution of intelligence and talent, radicals insisted that this resulted from an unequal distribution of power. They called for popular sovereignty, a republic, and a parliament elected by direct and universal suffrage, and without the division of powers with its checks and balances. If necessary, these goals should be attained by violent revolution. The intellectual standard bearers of this radicalism were the Young Hegelians, who used the powerful tool of the Hegelian dialectic to criticize existing conditions and to demonstrate how the real diverged from the rational. David Friedrich Strauss and Ludwig Feuerbach mounted a massive attack against organized Christianity. Strauss' *Life of Jesus* (1835) presented Christ as a purely mythical figure whose existence as a human being was largely irrelevant. Feuerbach went one step further and proclaimed that God was a creation of man, rather than the other way round. This idea was taken up by two Young Hegelians, Karl Marx and Friedrich Engels, who in their *German Ideology*, which they wrote in 1845 but which remained unpublished, took Feuerbach one step further and argued that his materialism was an "ideology" in that it failed to see that the need for religious self-mystification could only be relieved by a social revolution necessitated by the contradictions within society. Moses Hess and Karl Grün presented their version of "true socialism" in direct contrast to William Weitling's mystical vision of a future society, but it also existed purely in the realm of ideas. Karl Marx savaged all these unfortunate utopians in a series of brilliant essays. Philosophy of this ilk, he proclaimed, bore the same relationship to social change as masturbation to sexual intercourse. Marx and Engels, with their catchy phrase "the history of all hitherto existing society is the history of class struggle," with which the "Communist Manifesto" begins, and with the proletariat as the universal class, were far ahead of their time. In 1848 such a class barely existed in Germany.

Radical poets were every bit as influential as the philosophers. They included Hoffmann von Fallersleben, the author of *"Deutschland über Alles,"* who published his ironically titled *Unpolitical Songs* in 1841; Ferdinand Freiligrath, who loudly proclaimed the revolution in such verses as "*Ça ira*" of 1846; the ubiquitous Georg Herwegh, who counted among his friends Turgenev and Bakunin, Herzen and Belinsky, Marx and Heine; and finally Richard Wagner, whose mother-in-law was one of Herwegh's many mistresses. Frederick William IV was so intrigued with Herwegh that he invited him to an audience in 1840, but on reflection thought it prudent to exile him. Herwegh then moved to Paris where he entranced his wide circle of brilliant friends and admirers.

4
The Revolutions of 1848

Eighteen forty was a turning point in Germany in two respects. Fredrick William IV ascended the Prussian throne, and the Orient crisis of that year marks the beginning of a new phase in German nationalism. High hopes were pinned on the new Prussian king. He was known to be a pleasant person with a lively intelligence, who was highly critical of the bureaucratic and authoritarian Prussian state of the Frederician tradition. He thought in somewhat romanticized German national rather than Prussian terms. He was a man of compromise who sought to heal the political divisions within the country, and to end the unfortunate conflict with the Catholic Church over mixed marriages. To this end he began his reign by pardoning Jahn and Arndt, the "demagogues" of 1819, and appointed three of the Göttingen seven to chairs at Berlin University. The great reforming war minister of the Napoleonic era, Hermann von Boyen, was reappointed at the ripe old age of 70. Censorship was relaxed, the policing powers of the Confederation reduced, the Germanizing policy toward the Poles in Posen was relaxed, and an accommodation was reached with the Catholic Church. In a series of amazing speeches, which were remarkably short in substance and gave rise to no end of misunderstandings, but which contained memorable rhetorical flourishes, he somehow managed to articulate many of the leading ideas of the time in a manner that was pleasing to almost all except Metternich and the tsar. Unlike his father, he enjoyed genuine and widespread popularity. In these early years of his reign it seemed to go almost unnoticed that he was profoundly conservative and had a deep distrust of the liberal bourgeoisie with their demands for a constitution.

Eighteen forty was also a critical year for the German Confederation. Cooperation between Prussia, Austria, and Russia against Polish nationalism in 1830 had resulted in the formation of an alliance of the three states aimed at crushing revolutionary movements, and also with an eye to dividing up the European spoils of the Ottoman Empire. But within a few years the situation once again changed dramatically. In 1839 Mehemet Ali, an Albanian warlord and master of Egypt and Syria, won yet another decisive victory over the Ottomans at Nezib, and it seemed that Constantinople might well fall. England, Russia, and Austria now found themselves united in support of the Ottomans against Mehemet Ali and his French allies. Acre fell to the British in 1840, Mehemet Ali lost Syria, and the French suffered a major diplomatic setback.

In an ill-considered moment of frustration, the France of Louis Adolphe Thiers, a Marseillais and historian of the French Revolution, demanded a revision of the 1815 settlement and the Rhine frontier. Germany prepared for war, France was forced to back down in a "diplomatic Waterloo," and Thiers resigned. His successor Guizot, another historian–politician, announced that he intended to seek "reconciliation with Europe" and urged his fellow-countrymen to concentrate on making money. The crisis triggered a wave of German nationalism the likes of which had never been seen before. Poets churned out reams of patriotic verse, which was rapturously received by an excited public. The most famous was Nikolaus Becker's "Song of the Rhine," which warned the French to keep their hands off this sacred German river. It was set to music by countless composers and enthusiastically sung by glee clubs throughout Germany. Hoffmann von Fallersleben's *"Deutschlandlied"* with its strident nationalism and which was to become Germany's national anthem when set to Haydn's music, was also written at this time. Equally popular was Max Schneckenberger's "Watch on the Rhine," with music by Karl Williams.

Eighteen forty thus marks a decisive point in the development of German national consciousness. Germany saw itself as the country of the future, that would defend itself against the "Romanism" of France and the "Slavism" of Russia by becoming an industrial giant with an invincible army and a superior culture. Germany was united in a wave of anti-French nationalism which momentarily covered over all major political differences, as many liberals and even radicals reconsidered their cosmopolitanism. But old divisions were bound to reappear, and many liberals and radicals remained true to their ideals of international solidarity. Eighteen forty, however, does mark a new stage in the development of the tensions between national sentiment and liberal demands. The outburst of nationalism in France in 1840 quickly disappeared, but not in Germany. The political landscape of Germany was changed forever.

Frederick William IV was also swept along by this wave of national sentiment. He enthusiastically supported the movement to complete Cologne cathedral, the building of which had ceased in 1559. Here he saw an opportunity to reconcile the Catholic Church and the Prussian state, the monarchy and the people, and Prussians and Rhinelanders, and give a dramatic demonstration of the unity of the German princes in defense of the German Rhine. He and Archduke John of Austria, whose patriotic credentials were impeccable, and who traveled to Cologne with Metternich, were the principal speakers at a massive rally in September 1842 to mark the laying of the foundation stone. Frederick William IV gave a typically rousing speech and was followed by the archduke who announced: "As long as Prussia and Austria and the rest of Germany, wherever German is spoken, are united, we shall be as strong as the rocks of our mountains." This was reported in the press as: "No longer Prussia and Austria, but one Germany, as solid as our mountains." The archduke was a remarkable man. He had led an army against Napoleon at the age of 18, when he showed both courage and skill. A life-long admirer of Rousseau, he detested Metternich and all that he stood for. He married a postman's daughter and was happiest living the simple life in the mountains. He showed wisdom and justice as a provincial governor and was loved and respected for his intelligence and evenhandedness. The faulty reporting of his speech made the already popular archduke into a national hero.

Frederick William IV saw himself as somehow mediating between God and the people, but there was no place within this mystical relationship for what he dismissed as "principles scribbled on parchment." At the beginning of his reign both the East and West Prussian diets, which were dominated by the liberal aristocracy, respectfully requested the completion of the constitutional process which had begun in 1815. The king turned this request down. Liberal demands became more strident, and soon their publications were censored, but charges of lèse majesté and high treason were dismissed by sympathetic magistrates. Frederick William was shrewd enough to realize that the constitutional question would not simply fade away, and besides he needed money in order to finance a national railway network. In 1842 the "United Committees" (*Vereinigte Ausschüsse*) were convened, attended by representatives of the provincial diets, membership of which was strictly according to the estates. The new body agreed that a comprehensive plan for the railways was necessary, but felt that it was not an appropriate body to vote on the financing of such a huge project. The provincial diets saw this as the golden opportunity to secure some sort of national parliament. After years of agitation during which demands for freedom of the press, legal reform, and budgetary control became ever louder, the king ignored Metternich and the tsar's objections and called a "United Diet" in February 1847. All the members of the provincial diets came to Berlin to discuss the budget. They were assured that they would meet on a regular basis and that a smaller body, known as the "United Committee" (*Vereinigter Ausschuss*), would be periodically consulted about future legislation. The liberals did not think that this went nearly far enough, but they accepted it as being at least a step in the right direction.

More than 600 delegates met in Berlin. All were men of substance, more than half were aristocrats, and 70 came from the very highest ranks of the nobility. Yet in spite of all this blue blood, it was a remarkably liberal body. It agreed wholeheartedly with the government's schemes to build the *Ostbahn*, a railway from Berlin to Königsberg, and to the proposal to create credit institutions to help the peasantry free themselves from their remaining debts resulting from compensatory payments at the time of the emancipation. But the delegates demanded a high price. By a two-thirds majority they demanded that the United Committee would have to be abolished and insisted on a guarantee that the United Diet should meet on a regular basis. As the liberal Rhinelander David Hansemann phrased it: "Once money is involved, good-naturedness disappears." The king promptly sent the United Diet packing, and in doing so strengthened the determination of the united front of aristocrats, bourgeois, and farmers to push for constitutional change. The constitutional question was thus a pressing issue, even in somewhat anachronistic and conservative Prussia.

An increasingly self-confident bourgeoisie was the standard bearer of the new industrial society that was developing in Germany and which set the tone in the years between 1815 and 1848. They faced the intractable forces of the old order, the harsh repression of the Metternichian system, and the irksome supervision of the bureaucratic and authoritarian state. The dynamism of the new clashed with the immobility of the old, giving rise to frustration and radicalism on both sides. There was little pragmatism on either side, there were wide divisions within the ranks, and a latent tendency toward the impractical and the doctrinaire.

These political and ideological divisions were made all the more acute by pressing social problems as Germany went through the painful and disruptive process of industrialization. The economy failed to provide for the needs of a rapidly rising population. Proud artisans had their livelihoods destroyed by power-driven machinery. Crop failures resulted in famine and disease. Millions were wrenched free of old social structures and were lost at sea in an unfamiliar and threatening world. Old certainties were shattered and new remedies had yet to be suggested for the individual lost in an increasingly pluralist society. Small wonder then that many grew impatient with the liberals' self-absorbed legalism and sought a radical and even revolutionary solution.

As in 1830 it was events in Paris that triggered a series of uprisings in Germany in 1848. Louis Philippe lost his throne on February 24 and three days later there was a mass meeting in Mannheim addressed by the radical Friedrich Hecker and the liberal Karl Mathy. They demanded freedom of the press, freedom of assembly, trial by jury, a militia, and a German national parliament. On March 1 a deputation went to Karlsruhe to present these demands, accompanied by a vast crowd, some of whom were armed. The Grand Duke of Baden at first refused to negotiate, at the same time turning down an offer of military assistance from Prussia. He then formed a new ministry, which included the liberal leaders, who began to implement most of their original demands. Similar pressure was exerted on many of the German states and in most instances with a similar outcome. Elections were held, liberal ministries appointed, constitutional changes set in train, and the remnants of the old feudal order abolished. There was precious little violence and it was only when governments resisted that force was used. The mob stormed the town halls in Frankfurt and Munich, but it was only in Prussia and Austria that there were serious confrontations between the people and the military.

There were mass demonstrations and violence in Vienna on March 13 and the situation soon got out of hand. Passions ran high, in the working-class areas there was something approaching a proletarian revolution, looting was widespread, and a considerable amount of property was destroyed. The bulk of the citizenry supported the rebels, as did the Citizens' Guard. The army's intervention was singularly half-hearted. With the government under attack in Northern Italy, Hungary, Prague, and Lower Austria, and with a frantic run on the banks, Metternich's career was clearly at an end. To general rejoicing he fled the city, and the army was withdrawn. The city was now in the hands of radical students and their working-class supporters. The Austrian government proposed a constitution on the Belgian model, but this was totally unacceptable to the radicals, who insisted that a constitution was a matter for the people to decide by means of a constituent assembly to be elected by universal suffrage. On May 15 the Academic Legion, the Workers' Association, and the National Guard forced the government to agree to their demands, and the court moved to Innsbruck. A Committee of Public Safety on the Jacobin model was formed in Vienna under Adolf Fischhof, while Innsbruck came under pressure from the ultra-radicals in the capital. The government was reformed to include a number of prominent opposition figures.

There was also Jacobin or, in the widely used phrase of the day, "communist" agitation in the Prussian Rhineland. In Cologne the prominent radical doctor Andreas Gottschalk called for the establishment of a revolutionary committee, but an enthusiastic crowd of some 5,000 was broken up by the army, much to the relief of the liberals. After a series of smaller demonstrations in Berlin and a series of clashes with the military in which a number of people were killed, and after the fall of Metternich, Frederick William IV decided to make a conciliatory gesture. He abolished censorship, promised that the United Diet would reconvene, and that Prussia would at last be given a constitution. A large crowd gathered outside the royal palace in Berlin on March 18 to greet the news joyfully and urge that these measures should be implemented as soon as possible. There was growing irritation with the presence of large numbers of armed troops, and the crowd demanded that they be withdrawn. The garrison commander, General von Prittwitz, regarded this as a menacing attack on the king's power of command and on the very foundations of the Prussian military state, and ordered his men to break up the demonstration. Only two shots were fired, it was unclear by whom, but that was enough to trigger a bloody street battle. Barricades were erected and by the next day more than 230 people lay dead.

Conventional military wisdom was that if the army was unable to storm the barricades within 24 hours it should be withdrawn and lay siege to the town. Prittwitz accordingly requested that the fighting in Berlin be stopped. Although hard-liners, led by the king's brother William, regarded this as craven submission to the mob, Frederick William was appalled at the heavy death toll and was determined to defuse this highly explosive situation. On March 19 he attended the funeral of those who had died on the barricades and took part in a ceremony in which the palace guard was handed over to units of the citizens' militia. Prince William, the leader of the military party, joined Metternich and Guizot in exile in England. On March 21 the king rode through the streets of Berlin wearing the gold, red, and black armband of the liberal nationalists, and, although he refused to be addressed as "emperor of Germany," he gave his most famous and typically gnomic speech in which he announced to an enraptured crowd that "Prussia dissolves into Germany." One week later he appointed a new ministry under two prominent liberals from the Rhineland, Ludolf Camphausen and David Hansemann. The Prussian ultraconservatives, Bismarck prominent among them, were appalled at the triumph of the

Plate 6 Street fighting in Berlin on the Night of March 18/19, 1848. © BPK

western liberals and laid plans for a counterrevolution. The revolutionaries had won the first round, but they were divided among themselves, unclear in their aims, and the king, on whose support they depended, was uncertain, hesitant, and under constant pressure from the army and the royalists.

In Prussia the revolution was largely urban, but in many parts of Germany, particularly in the southwest and in Thuringia, there were peasant uprisings. They were directed against the great landowners, the administrators of the demesne lands, and Jewish money lenders and cattle dealers. Deeds were burnt, taxes were left unpaid, poachers had a field day, committees of public safety were formed, and in Wiesbaden thousands of peasants demanded that noble estates be taken over by the state and divided up among the people. These peasant uprisings had precious little in common with the urban revolts. Their social composition, their aims, and their choice of methods were quite different. Urban liberals were appalled by this violence in the countryside and condemned the peasants' lack of respect for private property. In some instances liberal governments sent in the troops to restrain the peasantry. On the other hand they sympathized with the demand that aristocratic privileges be abolished and that the last vestiges of feudalism be removed. Once that was achieved, to varying degrees, peace and quiet was restored and the peasantry, and thus the vast majority of Germans, had no further interest in the revolution. Constitutional reform and the national question were of little consequence to them, and only in very rare cases were urban radicals able to mobilize rural discontents to win support for their cause.

The proletariat, on whose behalf Marx and Engels wrote the Communist Manifesto in 1848, failed to live up to their high and wholly unrealistic expectations. Far from forming the vanguard of a socialist revolution, workers indulged in an orgy of Luddism. In some industrial centers machines were smashed, and steamships and railways taken over by the workers. They participated in the demonstrations in the larger towns and fought on the barricades in Berlin, but in other areas the workers remained remarkably passive. The artisans and their apprentices were far more active, and shared the proletariat's passionate hatred of industrialization to such an extent that the two groups are virtually indistinguishable.

In a complex dialectic, the violent protests and political demands of the peasantry, industrial workers, and artisans lent weight to the peaceful demands of the urban notabilities. But at the same time there was a wide divergence over both aims and methods. Furthermore, there was not one revolution in Germany in 1848, but several. The revolutionary movement was decentralized, thus weakening the movement for fundamental change in the Confederation, and making its outcome even more uncertain. In each of the states liberals were sore afraid of being overtaken by radicals and socialists, and worried that the movement for constitutional reform and national reconstruction might be swept aside by a social revolution. The very fact that governments had given way so easily and quickly to their initial demands raised the question of where power resided. Was it in the studies of the urban intelligentsia or in the street? The liberal ministries were determined to halt the social revolution, but they were also keenly aware that it was popular violence that had brought them to power. The old regime having capitulated, they now had more to fear from the radicals as the revolution entered a new phase in which the national question began to be addressed.

The Frankfurt Parliament

On March 5 a diverse group of mainly southwestern politicians met in Heidelberg to discuss the next move. They included the radical republicans Hecker and Struve, and the moderate liberal monarchist Heinrich von Gagern. They were able to agree on little else than that a "Pre-Parliament" should be formed from representatives from the various diets to meet in Frankfurt and set the ground rules for an all-German election. Shortly afterwards, the Bundestag in Frankfurt appointed a 17-man committee to discuss federal reform.

The Pre-Parliament began its discussions on March 31. Five hundred and seventy-four delegates, mainly from the south and west of Germany, and with only two from Austria, were soon divided into two hostile camps. The liberals wanted to create a parliamentary monarchy in close consultation with the Bundestag; the radicals wanted a republic with executive and legislative powers invested in a revolutionary convention. There was general agreement, however, that the decision

Plate 7 A meeting of the National Assembly in the Paul's Church in Frankfurt September 16, 1848. © BPK

as to the form of the future Germany should not be decided by such an unrepresentative body as the Pre-Parliament, but by a new body elected on a broad franchise. The moderates hoped that it would be possible to create a united and free Germany in consultation with the existing governments, and shied away from outright confrontation and unilateral action. Hecker and Struve would have none of this. On April 12 they proclaimed a provisional republican government in Constance, and marched on Freiburg with some 6,000 armed supporters. Federal troops had little difficulty in crushing this ill-organized rebellion on April 20 and Hecker fled the country. Robert Blum, the leader of the moderate left, denounced the rebels for betraying the republican cause by robbing it of its democratic legitimacy. Marx and Engels were even stronger in their condemnation of this ill-considered putsch.

The elections for a national assembly were organized by the individual states, so that the number of those eligible to vote varied widely. Nevertheless, by the standards of the day a remarkably large number of men, somewhere between 75 and 90 percent depending on the state, were able to go to the polls. Since there were no political parties that could articulate sectional interests, most of those elected were prominent figures in the local community. The parliament, which met in the Paul's Church in Frankfurt, was made up largely of civil servants, lawyers, and university graduates. Among the almost 800 members there were only four artisans

and one peasant. Ten percent were aristocratic and 49 professors played a prominent role in the debates. The social composition of the parliament resulted not from
bias in the electoral system, but reflected the social esteem in which the academic
professions were held. Members of state parliaments, such as the Prussian Landtag,
tended to come from slightly lower down the social scale, largely because the more
prominent citizens preferred to go the Frankfurt Parliament. Women were not represented in either the national or state parliaments, but they played an active role
in 1848 by participating in demonstrations and by organizing a number of women's
groups. This in turn provoked a misogynistic reaction, and complaints were widespread that women were getting out of hand.

Ultraconservatives and ultra-radicals were scarcely represented, and there was a
relatively small Catholic faction relative to the strength of political Catholicism in
the March days. The various political factions were named after the inns where they
met: conservatives in the "Café Milani," moderate liberals in the "Casino," left-
liberals in the "Württemberger Hof," Robert Blum and the democrats in the
"Deutscher Hof," and Hecker's radicals in the "Donnersberg." Of these the
"Casino" faction was by far the largest with about 130 members, including most
of the distinguished professors, such as Droysen, Dahlmann, and Waitz. When
the debate centered on whether Germany should include or exclude Austria – the
großdeutsche/kleindeutsche question – the Greater German faction met in the
"Mainlust," the Little Germans in the "Weidenbusch."

The Frankfurt Parliament set about creating a new Germany with an appropriate constitution, but there was wide disagreement as to how this could or should
be done. A functioning executive was obviously essential, but it was unclear whether
the new parliament had sovereign powers and what should be its relationship with
existing federal institutions, as well as with the member states of the Confederation.
Heinrich von Gagern offered a compromise solution between the conservative call
for consultation with the states and the radical republican demand for a sovereign
parliamentary executive committee. He suggested that the widely popular Archduke
John of Austria should be appointed "Reich Administrator," thus giving the parliamentary system a monarchical coping, and hopefully reconciling the radical
demand for parliamentary sovereignty with conservative dynastic concerns.

Gagern's proposal was accepted by the overwhelming majority of the delegates
in the Paul's Church, including a number of prominent radicals. The states accepted
the decision and the Bundestag handed over its powers to the archduke, who
promptly appointed Prince Karl Leiningen, Queen Victoria's half-brother and a
prominent German Whig, as minister-president, with the like-minded Austrian
Anton von Schmerling as minister of the interior and the strong man in the new
government. This new government had widespread popular support, but it was virtually powerless. It had no money, no offices, no civil service, and no army. It was
wholly dependent on the good will of the member states of the Confederation and
this was highly questionable. When the new minister of war, the Prussian General
von Peucker, ordered that the various armies should swear an oath of allegiance to
the archduke and hoist the national flag, Austria, Prussia, Bavaria, and Hanover

promptly refused. An attempt to build a German navy was an equally embarrassing flop.

For the moment the Frankfurt Parliament filled a power vacuum in Germany. Austria was wholly absorbed in suppressing uprisings throughout its multinational empire, and Prussia was still reeling after the March days. But the worthy parliamentarians failed to realize that they had to seize the opportunity and act expeditiously before the counterrevolution recovered from the initial shock. As Bismarck was later to remark, the men of 1848 spent far too much time with resolutions and majority votes. They debated the constitutional question for six months. At the beginning of July they began discussing highly theoretical questions of fundamental rights, and it was only at the end of October that they at last addressed practical issues, such as where the frontiers of the new Germany would be, and how the state should be organized. Without a state questions of fundamental rights, however important they might be, were of little consequence.

The question "Where is Germany?" was almost impossible to answer. Linguistic, cultural, geographical, and historical boundaries did not coincide, and there were many enclaves with significant minorities. In the Habsburg Empire the Germans were a tiny minority. The problem became acute when, on March 21, the Danes annexed the Duchy of Schleswig. The Germans in the duchy resisted, claiming that by ancient law the duchies of Schleswig and Holstein could not be separated. They formed their own government which was recognized by the Frankfurt Parliament, and which invited the Prussians to send troops to protect them. The Prussians readily obliged and the Frankfurt Parliament applauded the move, announcing that Germany was now at war with Denmark and that the Prussian army was acting on its behalf. At this point the British government intervened and persuaded the Prussians to withdraw from Schleswig, whereupon the Frankfurt Parliament denounced Berlin for betraying the German people and the German national cause. Under pressure from England and Russia and with a Danish naval blockade, Prussia signed the Peace of Malmö at the end of August, which established a new government in the duchy with Danish participation. The peace was denounced by the Frankfurt Parliament, particularly by the left, as a dastardly breach of faith by Prussia, and the ratification of the treaty was rejected by a vote of 238 to 221, thus forcing the Leiningen government to resign. Some radicals, Marx among them, dreamt of a revolutionary war against Denmark, Prussia, and Russia, along the lines of the French revolutionary war of 1792. This was hopelessly unrealistic, given Germany's precarious position both internally and internationally. The Frankfurt Parliament prudently reconsidered the vote and finally ratified the treaty by a narrow majority.

Another pressing problem was that of Poland. The new Prussian government promised to reorganize the Prussian province of Posen in favor of the Poles and favored an independent Polish state. Before any changes could be put into effect the two nationalist movements were in conflict, and Polish militia units clashed with the Prussian army. Posen was now divided into Prussian and Polish regions. The Polish issue was debated in Frankfurt, where there was precious little sympathy for the Poles. The democrat William Jordan spoke for many when he talked of the "empty-headed sentimentality" of the pro-Polish faction, and argued that Germans should think in terms of "healthy national egotism" (*Volksegoismus*), since cultural superiority gave them every right over the backward Poles. Karl Marx and the radical left were in full agreement with this denunciation of a fatuously melodramatic cosmopolitanism. By a vote of 342 to 31 the parliament voted that the bulk of Posen should be considered part of the new Germany.

The Frankfurt Parliament took a similarly robust attitude toward Czech national aspirations. The Czech leader, yet another historian, Franz (Frantisek) Palacky, turned down the suggestion that Bohemia should be part of Germany and argued that Czechs were better served by remaining within the multinational Habsburg Empire. The delegates in the Paul's Church would have none of this. Bohemia had been part of the Holy Roman Empire of the German Nation and was within the Confederation; therefore it was clearly German. The same attitude was taken toward South Tyrol, when a delegate from the Trentino suggested that it too should break away from Germany.

The acerbic nationalism and arrogant feeling of cultural superiority of the Frankfurt Parliament is singularly unattractive, but is far removed from later manifestations of German national sentiment. No claim was made for Alsace or for areas in the Baltic outside the bounds of the Confederation, where there were substantial German populations. Furthermore, the Frankfurt Parliament was mindful that minority rights within the new Germany should be respected. On the other hand there was a lot of heady talk of Germany as the future European superpower that would turn its mighty army against the barbarous Slavs as the newborn nation had its baptism of fire. Much of this was little more than hot air, and overcompensation for Germany's pathetic weakness, but it betrayed a disturbing cast of mind. Monsters were slumbering in Germany that only the keenest of minds, such as the poet Heinrich Heine and the novelist Gottfried Keller, were able to detect.

The Frankfurt Parliament was plagued not only by the national question, but also by the social problems of a society in the process of fundamental change. An artisans' congress was held in Frankfurt in an attempt to put pressure on the parliament. Politically the artisans were mostly liberal democrats, but economically they were archconservatives. They were anti-capitalist and anti-industrial. They hankered after the pre-industrial society of guilds and proud master craftsmen. They called for an ordered brotherhood under a protective and interventionist state. It was the long gone world of Hans Sachs and the Meistersinger of Nuremberg.

The working classes were also active in 1848. Workers' Associations (*Arbeitervereine*) sprang up all over Germany, and at the end of August a national congress organized by Stefan Born, at that time a disciple of Karl Marx, was held in Berlin at which an umbrella organization called the "Workers' Brotherhood" was formed. It was a reformist rather than a revolutionary organization, which stood for working-class solidarity, the formation of unions and cooperatives, and above all for education. It called for "social democracy," by which was meant fair wages, justice for all, and a humane and caring society. Obviously there were widely differing views on how these ideals could be realized, but there was general agreement when Born denounced "dreamers who foam with rage" and urged a moderate and pragmatic approach. The intellectual giants of the socialist movement, Karl Marx and Friedrich Engels, ignored the Workers' Associations, and their Communist League played no role in the revolution. They had precious few followers and their articles in the *Rheinische Zeitung* did not resonate among the nascent working class.

Meanwhile the forces of the counterrevolution began to organize and prepared to strike back. In Prussia the "camarilla" around the crown prince was tirelessly active. The Gerlach brothers, Ernst and Leopold, founded an ultraconservative newspaper soon to be known as the "Iron Cross" (*Kreuzzeitung*) because of the medal printed above its title: *Neue Preußische Zeitung*. This was to become the authoritative voice of Prussian conservatism. The Junkers formed an association to further their interests, and met in what came to be known as the "Junker Parliament" to discuss matters of common concern. The army was solidly behind the counterrevolution and longed to seek revenge for the humiliation it had suffered in March. Their attitude was succinctly put in the title of an influential pamphlet: "Soldiers Are the Only Remedy for Democrats."

The radicals had been crushed in April in Baden, but they were still active in the Paul's Church, where they continued to demand the creation of a republic based on popular sovereignty. They railed against the conservatives and the liberals, and issued Jeremiads about the horrors of the counterrevolution. They were disillusioned with parliamentary procedures and hoped to push the revolution forward by extra-parliamentary activism. In short, they called for a second and more radical revolution in which the will of the people would be directly expressed by means of a Jacobin dictatorship. Some 200 delegates representing radical associations from throughout Germany, as well as some delegates to the Paul's Church, met in Frankfurt in mid-June under the chairmanship of Julius Fröbel, the nephew of the founder of the Kindergarten. They decided to form a national democratic and republican movement with a distinctly totalitarian flavor and with its headquarters in Berlin. They gained considerable support from the disaffected lower orders, who were yet to feel the effects of an economic upturn, but it was the acceptance of the Malmö armistice by the Frankfurt Parliament that brought matters to a head. On September 18 a radical mob stormed the Paul's Church, which was defended by Austrian, Prussian, and Hessian troops. Eighty people were killed on both sides, including the conservative deputies General von Auerswald and Prince Lichnowsky, whereupon the Archduke John placed the city under martial law. It was a richly significant scene: the Frankfurt Parliament could only continue to exist as long as it was still tolerated by Austria and Prussia. The violence in Frankfurt, particularly the brutal murder of two deputies, discredited the radicals in the eyes of most Germans and the subsequent uprising in Baden led once again by Hecker and Struve, who blamed the rich and the Jews for the failure of the revolution, had precious little popular support. It was quickly suppressed by the miniscule Baden army. Elsewhere in the southwest there were murmurs of discontent but little violence. Moderate liberals were terrified by the prospect of further violence and felt obliged to join forces with the conservatives to combat the radicals, thus stopping the revolution in its tracks.

The vast majority of Germans agreed with them in prioritizing law and order over freedom and due process. The radicals refused to give up the struggle and at the second Democratic Congress, which was held in Berlin at the end of October, they pronounced the Frankfurt Parliament illegitimate and demanded new elections. But by this time the counterrevolution was virtually complete in Vienna and Berlin, and the radicals were hopelessly divided among rival factions.

There had been an uprising in Prague on June 12 of unemployed workers and a poverty-stricken rabble led by a motley crew of socialists, democrats, and students, who protested against the decision of the Slav Congress to press for a federal Austria in which the Germans no longer would have a monopoly of political power. These radicals were not at all certain what they wanted, but they agreed that the Slav Congress had not dared go far enough down the path to revolution. The military commander in Prague, Prince Alfred von Windischgrätz, waited for a couple of days before striking with full force. It was all over by June 16, by which time 400 people had been killed. The Germans in Bohemia applauded Windischgrätz's savage suppression of the Czech radicals. Wealthy Czechs were relieved to see the end to a dangerous threat to their property, and heralded the victory of Austrian troops over Czech nationalists as a victory of the Habsburg Empire over German nationalism. The radicals in Vienna read the situation in much the same way. They were delighted to see the Czechs take a beating, but also knew that this was a significant victory for Vienna over Frankfurt and that their revolution was now very much on the defensive. The Austrian army was also victorious against the seriously divided Italians. The 82-year-old Count Josef von Radetszky, immortalized by Johann Strauss in the eponymous march, crushed the Italians at Custozza on July 27 and rode in triumph through the streets of Milan. German nationalists fêted Radetszky's victory and failed to realize that this was a significant victory for the counterrevolution. The revolutionaries in Vienna were professed liberals and democrats, but they were also fierce German nationalists, and this was their undoing. They applauded when the uprisings in Italy, Bohemia, and Hungary were crushed, but they seemed blind to the fact that they too would be swept away by the very same forces. Furthermore, they had precious little support in the countryside. Devout peasants were appalled at their anticlericalism, and with their conservative cast of mind had little sympathy for radical ideas.

Elections went ahead throughout the Habsburg Empire, with the exception of Hungary and Northern Italy, for a parliament (Reichstag). Of the 389 delegates, 160 were Germans and 190 Slavs. It was a moderate body made up of civil servants, lawyers, doctors, and priests, as well as a considerable number of peasants. Its first act was to abolish all remaining vestiges of feudal obligations, whereupon the peasants lost all further interest and returned home. With a largely powerless Reichstag, Jacobin radicals hunting down enemies of the people, and workers becoming increasingly restless with an economy in chaos amid so many uncertainties, the situation was more than confusing when the court returned to Vienna in the summer. There were frequent outbursts of spontaneous violence, but the government was gradually gaining the upper hand. The National Guard was brought under its control and the Committee of Public Safety disbanded. Radicals both in Vienna and in Germany began to talk of a Thermidorian reaction and were keenly aware that the fate of the German national enterprise depended on the outcome of the power struggle in Austria. Some of the leading figures of German radicalism, among them Karl Marx, Robert Blum, Friedrich Hecker, and Julius Fröbel, went to Vienna in the certain knowledge that it was here, and not in Frankfurt, that the future of Germany would be decided.

Events in Hungary precipitated a fresh crisis. The Magyars had established a fiercely nationalistic parliamentary government which claimed exclusive rule over the historic lands of Saint Stephen. The Czech, Croatian, Romanian, and Ruthenian minorities protested vigorously, and on September 12 the Croatian Ban, Baron Josip Jellacic, led an army against the Hungarians, thus precipitating a civil war that had the tacit approval of the imperial government, whose representative in Hungary had been murdered. Jellacic had the support of most factions within the empire, except for the left, who supported the national claims of Germans, Poles, Italians, and Magyars, but not of other Slavs or Romanians.

A number of radical troops from Vienna mutinied when ordered to march against the Hungarians on October 6, thus precipitating a pro-Hungarian riot in Vienna by those who felt that the Magyars had the same right to a national identity as did Germans. The war minister, Count Theodor Baillet de Latour, was strung up on a lamppost. The court once again fled the capital, as did most of the delegates to the Reichstag. Another Committee of Public Safety was formed, but it was all somewhat absurd. The "Supreme Commander" was one Wenzel Messenhauser, an obscure literary figure who was more interested in the theater than in the exercise of dictatorial powers. The Polish General Bem, an exotic adventurer from a bygone age, who was later to fight valiantly for the Hungarian national cause, was put in command of the ragtag guards. Robert Blum was made an honorary member of the Academic Legion and promptly demanded that a further 200 reactionaries should be "latoured." The radical left was in control of the capital, but still had no support in the rest of the country, and with the Hungarians under attack they could get no help from that quarter. For Windischgrätz October 6 was the signal to act. Alongside Jellacic and his Croats he marched against Vienna. Two thousand were killed in a ferocious struggle. The opportunistic and cowardly Viennese gave Windischgrätz a hero's welcome, thus foreshadowing Hitler's triumph in 1938, and the general set about ridding the city of what he was pleased to call a "hoard of snotty-nosed tykes." In fact the counterrevolution was relatively mild. Only 25 people were executed, among them Robert Blum. The flagrant violation of his immunity as a member of the Frankfurt Parliament made him the leading martyr to the German liberal and national cause, but it also was a dramatic demonstration that both causes were lost.

Windischgrätz's brother-in-law, Prince Felix zu Schwarzenberg, was appointed to head a new government. He was a politician of considerable stature, a reforming conservative who realized that times had changed, that much was wrong with the old order, and that the aristocracy was far from possessing a monopoly of wisdom.

He enlisted the help of some remarkable commoners, among them Alexander Bach, who had fought on the barricades in Vienna, and the brilliant shipping magnate Baron von Bruck, the son of a Rhenish petit-bourgeois. At the beginning of December the mentally defective emperor was persuaded to abdicate in favor of his nephew, the 18-year-old Francis Joseph, who was to reign for the next 68 years. The Reichstag was permitted to continue its constitutional deliberations in the small Moravian town of Kremsier, where it produced an admirable constitution which, although the empire was still to be dominated by the Germans, gave a considerable degree of autonomy to other nationalities. The monarchy "by the grace of God" refused to accept a constitution resulting from parliamentary debate, and unceremoniously dismissed the Reichstag. A monarchical constitution was then promulgated which borrowed some of the more progressive ideas from the parliamentary version in order to placate the liberals. It insisted on the indivisibility of the empire, thus rejecting the notion that Austria would be divided by a greater German solution, and repudiating all Hungarian national aspirations. The liberal clauses in the constitution were never put into effect, and the reaction reigned triumphant in a permanent state of emergency.

The empire was a unitary state on paper but not in reality. Piedmont once again went to war in early 1849, only to be crushed at Novara. In the spring Hungary, having beaten off Jellacic's Croats, declared its independence under the somewhat indecisive leadership of the liberal republican Lájos Kossuth. It was only when the Austrians, with great reluctance, called upon the tsar for assistance, that the Hungarians were finally defeated. One hundred ringleaders were executed, and many more given lengthy jail sentences. Kossuth lived on until 1894, having resigned in favor of the military leader General Görgei and, after the Russian victory at Temesvár, escaping to Turkey. In European liberal circles Austria now stood condemned as being both weak and brutish.

The situation in Prussia was far less complex than in the Austrian Empire, but it was not without similarities. The king hoped to reach some compromise agreement with the National Assembly over the constitutional question. The Berlin Parliament was a somewhat more radical body than the Paul's Church and insisted on its sovereign rights, and was thus in direct conflict with the king. As in Vienna there was constant pressure from the radical democratic working classes and the unemployed, who frequently clashed with the bourgeois Citizens' Militia (*Bürgerwehr*). In June Prince William, the "Grapeshot Prince," returned to Berlin as a delegate to the National Assembly and the atmosphere grew increasingly tense. On June 14 the mob stormed the Berlin arsenal, the Citizens' Militia was unable to control the situation, and the army had to be called in from Potsdam. The reactionaries called for the dismissal of the National Assembly, but the king felt this would be too drastic a move.

On July 26 parliament published a draft constitution. It was a moderate, liberal document, but one that was unacceptable to conservatives and the left alike. The National Assembly insisted that the army be bound by the constitution and in the struggle over this central issue the moderates in the assembly found themselves caught between the reactionaries and the radicals. The king took a step in the direction of the reactionaries and then a step back in the direction of compromise. The assembly's position began to harden as it called for parliamentary control over the judiciary and police, and the abolition of aristocratic titles, along with all orders and titles and the king's right to rule by the grace of God. The mob grew restless and there were sporadic outbursts of violence. The moderate reforming minister-president General Pfuel saw his hopes for compromise dashed, and resigned at the end of October. His place was taken by Count von Brandenburg, who favored a Little Germany with the Prussian king as emperor. The arch-reactionary Otto von Manteuffel was minister of the interior. The National Assembly was promptly adjourned, but refused to move. General Wrangel marched his troops into Berlin and proclaimed martial law. The National Assembly and the Citizens' Militia were disbanded. The reaction was now in full command. Not a shot was fired, not a drop of blood spilt. On December 5 the king granted a constitution which, to the extreme annoyance of the conservatives, bore a distinct resemblance to that proposed by the National Assembly. It was a shrewd move. It eased tensions and bought time. The line to Frankfurt was not broken, and the German question was left open.

The Constitutional Question

While the counterrevolution was near complete, discussions continued in Frankfurt over the constitution. It was finally voted upon on December 20, but the cardinal issues of whether Germany should include Austria and who should be the head of the new nation-state were left open. It was a moderate and liberal document that upheld principals of equality before the law, civil rights, and the abolition of all remaining vestiges of the feudal system. It was resolutely liberal on economic issues. Radicals were disappointed that it did not address the social question, that it was not more robustly democratic, that the influence of the churches was not to be curbed, and, a favorite demand, that the Jesuits were not to be turfed out of Germany. The new Germany was to be a federal state, but the framers of the constitution could find no solution to the problem of overcoming the disparities between the component states. Should the smaller entities be mediatized, or the large states like Prussia divided up into smaller federations? Although the existing situation was highly unsatisfactory it was decided to leave things as they were and hope for the best. There were to be two houses of parliament, a *Volkshaus* which would be democratically elected, and a *Staatenhaus* in which the individual states would be represented. The suffrage question was not settled until the beginning of March 1849, and many liberals voted for universal, direct, manhood suffrage in the confident hope that this would make it impossible for the Prussian king to accept the imperial crown.

There were few republicans in the Frankfurt Parliament, and even those who inclined toward a republican solution realized that it would be impossible to abolish all the existing monarchies within the Confederation. They favored what came to be called a "republican monarchy." Monarchs should exist by the grace of the people represented in parliament, not by the grace of God. Their model was the Glorious Revolution of 1688. But who was to be emperor? Should he be elected as in the old empire? Should parliament elect an emperor who would then establish a hereditary dynasty? Should Austria and Prussia take turns in appointing an emperor, or should one or the other ruling house rule in perpetuity? All this was highly theoretical, as was most of the discussion in the Paul's Church, since in the last resort the answer to the German question lay in the outcome of the struggle within and between Prussia and Austria.

The majority of delegates to the Paul's Church assumed that the Habsburg Empire was on the point of disintegration, and that therefore German Austria and Bohemia would willingly join in the new Germany and work out some form of personal union with what was left of the multinational empire. This was a hopelessly unrealistic position. Austria could not possibly be both part of a German great power and remain a great power outside the new Reich. A Greater Germany would have necessitated the dismemberment of the Habsburg Empire. With the counter-revolution in Austria nearly complete, on November 27 1848 Schwarzenberg proclaimed the indivisibility of the empire, and thus put paid to any hopes for a greater German solution. In March the following year he proposed that the entire empire should be included in the new Germany. This was totally unacceptable since Germany would then be dominated by Austria, a state in which the vast majority of the population was not even German.

The *kleindeutsche* solution was now the only possible answer to the dilemma. Its leading advocate, Heinrich von Gagern, became minister-president in mid-December, but Schmerling and his *großdeutsche* supporters were still numerous and hopeful that the Austrians might be persuaded to change their minds. German nationalists, among them many on the left, felt that Austria could not possibly be excluded and many felt it could well do without its non-German provinces. South German Catholics detested Protestant Prussia and identified with their Austrian coreligionists. Many feared that a Little Germany would provoke Russia and Austria to intervene and that the country would then be under the knout.

Prussia on the other hand might be reactionary and militaristic, but at least it was a thoroughly German state and had gone through an impressive series of reforms. It was rational state, at least in the Hegelian sense, the architect of the *Zollverein*, soberly Protestant, certainly not a threat, even prepared it seemed to "dissolve into Germany." Schwarzenberg's intransigence led to a mass desertion from the *großdeutsche* cause and even Schmerling defected in March. By now it was a case of either a Little Germany or none at all. On March 28 Frederick William IV of Prussia was elected Emperor of the Germans, with 290 votes in favor of the motion and 248 abstentions. The ruling elite in Prussia favored acceptance, provided that the franchise was changed, provision made for an absolute veto, and the election accepted by the princes, but Frederick William was adamantly opposed. He saw himself as a king by the grace of God and refused to accept a crown that was made of "muck and mire," a "dog collar with which they want to chain me to the revolution of 1848." It was an unthinking and intensely emotional response, but subsequent events make it seem unlikely that even a compromise solution would have had much of a chance of success.

Heinrich von Gagern still hoped that a compromise was possible, but it was rejected both by Frederick William and the majority in the Paul's Church. The Frankfurt Parliament now began a gradual process of dissolution. Austria and Prussia withdrew their delegations, Saxony and Hanover followed suit. A rump parliament of intransigent radicals moved to Stuttgart where they were soon chased away by a contingent of the Württemberg army. There were isolated outbursts of violence in favor of the constitution and in protest against the reactionary course. Barricades were erected in Dresden and were graced with the presence of such luminaries as the anarchist Michael Bakunin, the opera director Richard Wagner, who had just finished *Lohengrin*, the great architect Gottfried Semper, whose magnificent opera house had been opened in 1841, and the socialist Stefan Born. Prussian troops were called in to crush the uprising and fierce fighting ensued. Rebels managed to install a temporary government in the Palatinate and a colorful assortment of radicals from all over central Europe rushed to its support. Once again the disorganized and ill-disciplined radicals were no match for the Prussian army, and the uprising was soon suppressed. In the Rhineland Friedrich Engels was able to put the relationship between theory and praxis to the test in a series of riots that were soon mastered by the Citizens' Militia. Defeated barricade fighters, mercenaries, and idealists now rushed to Baden for a last ditch stand. Here the Prussian army took somewhat longer to repress the revolt, but the final outcome was never in any doubt. There followed a series of treason trials and summary executions. Every tenth man captured in the fortress town of Rastatt was shot. The brutality of the Prussians in Baden left a lasting trauma and bitter hatred, and there was a fresh wave of emigration, mainly to the United States.

Frederick William having turned down the imperial crown, the Prussian minister-president Radowitz now proposed a Little German union. Agreement was reached at the end of May with Saxony and Hanover to create a federal Little Germany, and in the following weeks most of the other German states approved this scheme. Bavaria was adamantly opposed to the idea of excluding Austria, and Württemberg did not relish the idea of a Germany dominated by Prussia. Saxony and Hanover had made their agreement contingent on the approval of all the other German states, and thus now withdrew their support. The Prussians went ahead regardless, and elections were held, on a strictly limited suffrage, in January 1850 for a parliament that met in Erfurt. The Erfurt Union had precious less support and Schwarzenberg was determined to destroy it. He put forward a proposal for a greater German union in which Prussia would have special status, but would still be subordinate to Austria. Radowitz turned this down, and Austria and Prussia were now on a collision course. The Austrians sponsored a congress to restore the German Confederation and set up a Bundestag in Frankfurt, but it was boycotted by Prussia. Electoral Hesse, which was in a state of turmoil with the Diet, the judiciary, the bulk of the civil service, and the officer corps in adamant opposition to a series of unconstitutional and reactionary measures proposed by the government, appealed to the Bundestag for help. The Danish government also asked for federal assistance against an intransigent and revolutionary local government in Holstein. Austria and Bavaria agreed to send troops to assist both governments. Prussia saw this as a direct threat to its western provinces and mobilized its army.

Frederick William was never enthusiastic about the Erfurt Union, had no desire to antagonize Austria, and was under massive pressure from the tsar to back down. He therefore dismissed Radowitz, but still insisted that Austrian troops should be withdrawn from Electoral Hesse. After several weeks of tension the Prussians suddenly capitulated and, at Olmütz on November 29 1850, signed a treaty with Austria in which they agreed to disband the Erfurt Union. But Schwarzenberg had to agree to a fresh round of negotiations for the reformation of the Confederation, and was thus unable to push through his scheme for an Austrian-dominated Germany.

For most Prussians Olmütz was an ignominious humiliation, but there was one notable exception. Otto von Bismarck poured scorn on the armchair warriors who were prepared to go to war for an absurd little state like Electoral Hesse, and for the Erfurt Union which subordinated Prussian interests to those of the member states. He argued that Prussia's national interests would be far better served in a revived Confederation. Bismarck, in this savagely witty speech, clearly articulated his belief that Prussian policy should be based on realpolitik rather than party politics. It was a belief to which he was to hold true for the rest of his remarkable career.

5

The Struggle for Mastery: 1850–66

As after 1815, the German Confederation now set about undoing most of the liberal achievements of 1848. Constitutional reforms in the individual states were revoked and in many instances new constitutions were promulgated that were far less liberal than those in effect before 1848. In some instances, such as Württemberg and Electoral Hesse, this was achieved by a coup, and the proclamation of martial law. Only in Baden was a liberal regime able to continue unchanged, but even here the heavy hand of the Confederation could still be felt. A federal law of 1854 placed severe restrictions on the freedom of the press and of assembly throughout Germany. In Catholic states, particularly in Austria, the reaction negotiated concordats with the church that strengthened the church's hand in matters such as education, marriage, and the family. Protestant states followed Prussia's example, and also strengthened the role of the church in the daily life of the citizenry.

The attempt to turn the clock back was only partially successful. The last vestiges of feudalism had been removed, and a lasting achievement of the revolution in Prussia had been the formation of the first joint-stock bank. Attempts to revive elements of the guild system by protecting artisans against the challenge of industrial capitalism were bound to fail in the long run, due to the harsh realities of the market. Constitutions were still in place, however much they might have been modified, and many influential figures were determined to win back their lost freedoms and rights. The concordats provoked a strong liberal reaction, and in Protestant states there was a wave of anticlericalism that obliged the states to give way. Liberals were most active in the smaller German states. Reactionary authoritarianism was at least partially tolerable in a strong and efficient state like Prussia with its booming economy, but was insufferable in insignificant, incompetent, and miniscule political entities such as Brunswick, Oldenburg, or Hesse-Darmstadt.

The counterrevolution went further in Austria than in any of the other German states. In 1851 the constitution of March 1849 was revoked, and the young Emperor Francis Joseph ruled as an absolute monarch after Schwarzenberg's death in the following year. The army acted as a police force under the ministry of the interior and martial law was enforced in regions deemed to be infected with liberalism. Attempts were made to centralize the state, and the special privileges accorded to the Magyars were withdrawn. But even in Austria the revolution left a lasting impact. The peasants were freed under very favorable conditions, and the selfish demands of the landowning aristocracy were largely ignored. The minister of education, Count Leo von Thun, continued the reform of schools and universities to admirable effect. The minister of trade, Baron von Bruck, an economic liberal, did much to modernize the economy, but his aims were overly ambitious. Along with Schwarzenberg, he hoped that Austria could take over the *Zollverein*, thus creating an Austrian dominated Mitteleuropa that would control the trade routes to India via Trieste and Egypt, and force the Prussians to accept high protective tariffs in an economic Olmütz when the *Zollverein* treaties were renegotiated in 1852. However much they might dislike Prussia, the smaller German states were keenly aware of the benefits of membership of the *Zollverein* and access to the North Sea ports. The Prussians skillfully headed off the Austrian bid to join the *Zollverein* on their terms, and even forced them to lower their tariffs with vague promises of a trade agreement. Austria's gross mishandling of the Crimean crisis further weakened its position, prompting hotheads like Bismarck to demand an all-out assault on Prussia's great rival, but Manteuffel's conservative government was determined to stick to strictly economic issues and not stir up a hornet's nest of liberalism and nationalism.

Austria's attempts to centralize the state, along with the concordat of 1855 which made Catholicism to all intents and purposes a state religion, were opposed by all those who still hoped for a greater Germany. The nationalities were also disaffected. Centralization meant control from Vienna by Germans. All civil servants, judges, and army officers had to speak German, and only the German texts of laws were valid. Resistance to the concordat was also widespread. But the relative weakness of the Habsburg Empire was due less to discontent among the nationalities and the German nationalists than to the parlous state of its finances. Taxes were increased, expenditure reduced, the economy boomed, but none of this was sufficient to reduce the huge deficit left over from the Metternich era, which was compounded by the military operations against the revolutionaries of 1848 and by the mobilization during the Crimean War. Austria simply could not afford to play a great power role, and the cost of the war in Italy in 1859 was the final straw.

Prussia at last had a constitution with universal suffrage, although it was singularly unequal and indirect, since voters were divided into three classes according to the amount of taxes they paid. In 1849 4.7 percent of voters chose one-third of the electors, the next third were elected by 12.6 percent of those eligible to vote, and the remaining third by 82.7 percent. Less than 22 percent of those eligible to vote actually bothered to do so in 1852. The upper house (*Herrenhaus*) was the preserve of the landowning aristocracy. The army was outside the constitution and could proclaim martial law. It was directly responsible to the king, who also had the power of veto and the right to rule by decree.

Prussia in the years of reaction was a police state, its symbolic figure the chief of Berlin's police, Carl von Hinkeldey. An army of snoopers and informers rooted out communists and democrats, the press was muzzled, and liberally-minded civil servants were dismissed. On the other hand, the reactionary government enacted a considerable amount of social legislation including the control of child labor, factory inspection, and sanitation measures. Hinkeldey was known to be on the side of the poor, and was immensely popular. He did much to stop rack-renting and to enforce health regulations. Thousands attended his funeral in 1856. Otto von Manteuffel's government, with its pliant diet of docile civil servants, an independent executive that could count on the support of the bureaucracy and the army, and his conscious efforts to win popular support, was typically Bonapartist. It was thus never a full-blown reactionary government and did not set out to undo all the achievements of 1848.

Eighteen forty-eight marked the end of the cooperation between Austria and Prussia in the German question that had characterized the Metternichian era. Otto von Bismarck, as Prussia's representative to the Bundestag, was determined to resist Schwarzenberg's attempts to bring the entire Habsburg Empire into the Confederation, for this would mean a Germany dominated by 70 million Austrians. The Prussian-controlled *Zollverein* was a powerful counterweight to Austrian pretensions, and Bismarck was able to frustrate Austria's attempts to dominate the Bundestag and to strengthen its authority over the member states.

The Crimean War

In 1853 Britain, France, and Piedmont went to war with Russia and landed a joint force in the Crimea. Both sides in the conflict were eager to recruit Austria and Prussia. Opinion was sharply divided in Austria as to which side would best serve Austria's interests. Ultraconservatives wanted an alliance with Russia and an agreement over spheres of influence in the Balkans. Some wanted Austria to remain neutral and arbitrate a settlement. Others, prominent among them the foreign minister Count Karl von Buol-Schauenstein, hoped to join the Crimean coalition and thus reduce Russia's influence in the region. In April 1854 Austria managed to persuade member states of the Confederation, Prussia among them, to sign an alliance in support of their efforts to put pressure on the Russians. In the summer Austria and Prussia delivered an ultimatum to Russia to withdraw her troops from the Danubian Principalities (present-day Romania). Russia complied and the principalities were occupied by Ottoman and Austrian troops. Austria now upped the ante, making fresh demands of the Russians. These were refused and the Austrians mobilized, thus obliging the Russians to keep a substantial force in the region. It was not until the end of the year that Austria formally allied with the coalition, promising to fight if the Russians did not give way. Buol now entertained the fantastic idea that Prussia would join Russia, and Austria could then ally with France and go to war with Prussia. France could take the Rhineland, Austria would get back Silesia – a province wrested from Maria Theresa by Frederick the Great. But Buol had powerful opponents who soon gained the upper hand. They pointed out that the treasury was empty, the Russians could very well invade, and that the allies refused to change their war aims to meet Austria's demands.

The Prussian elite was similarly divided. Archconservatives wanted an alliance with Russia. Manteuffel was for strict neutrality, since Prussia had no interest in the Eastern question. Prince Friedrich, second in line to the throne, and his supporters, usually called the "*Wochenblattpartei*" after their newspaper, wanted to join the Western powers. A member of this group, the Prussian diplomat Count Albert von Pourtalès, suggested to the British government that Prussia would join the coalition if Britain would lend its support to Prussian efforts to exclude Austria from Germany. Britain turned this proposal down, for it still hoped to get Austrian support. The Prussian ambassador, Baron von Bunsen, also hoped that by joining the coalition Russian hegemony in Eastern Europe would be ended, Poland would be restored, and Prussia's position in Germany enhanced. Once again the British government did not want to risk alienating Austria, and the "*Wochenblattpartei*" lost the king's favor, resulting in Bunsen being recalled and the war minister Eduard von Bonin, another prominent figure among the Westerners, losing his job. Prince Friedrich protested vigorously against Bonin's dismissal and the king reacted by taking away his nephew's commission, whereupon Friedrich's wife, one of Queen Victoria's daughters, fled back home to England. Clearly there could be no question now of Prussia joining the coalition, there was little enthusiasm for joining the war on Russia's side, and Prussia remained neutral. In December 1854 Austria called upon the Confederation to mobilize in accordance with the April agreement, but Bismarck had little difficulty in frustrating this move. Austria was left isolated, and Prussia scored a major victory that partly overcame the shame of Olmütz. Bismarck had argued that Austria's interests in the Balkans were not a German concern, and that Prussia's great rival was now allied with Germany's archenemy, France. Prussia, by contrast, had no interests outside Germany. Austria had succeeded in alienating both sides in the Crimean conflict, and thus played no role in the peace conference in Paris. Prussia was also ignored, but was considered weak rather than devious. The Crimean War resulted in a marked decline in Russia's power and influence in Europe. The France of Napoleon III now took center stage, but was soon to be eclipsed by a Prussian-dominated Europe. Austria had alienated Russia without earning any gratitude from France, and was left isolated. Prussia managed to preserve the conservative understanding with Russia, and had given the Confederation forceful leadership during the December crisis of 1854.

The Italian Question

Austria was soon to suffer another severe setback, this time in Italy. In 1858 Napoleon III signed a treaty with Piedmont-Sardinia with the intent of driving Austria out of northern Italy and uniting the country. The Piedmontese premier, Cavour, skillfully provoked Austria into a declaration of war in April 1859. The Austrian army was under-financed and ineptly led, and was defeated at the battles of Magenta and Solferino by a French army whose senior commanders were equally incompetent, but whose troops and subordinate officers showed considerable courage and dash. Austria's defeat in Lombardy placed Germany in a precarious position. Friedrich Engels spoke for many when he asked whether Napoleon III would make a bid for the Rhine now that France was firmly established on the Po. Austria called for support from the Confederation. Prussia was willing to go part of the way to meet Austria's request, but demanded a high price. Prussian support was made dependent on being given an equal voice to Austria in the Bundestag, command over the troops on the Rhine, and hegemony in northern Germany. Austria believed that the Confederation was obliged both constitutionally and through sheer self-interest to become involved, and was thus unwilling to make any concessions to Prussia.

Napoleon III was anxious not to become involved in a lengthy war, and quickly negotiated a preliminary peace at Villafranca in July. Prussia was thus saved from the awkward choices of whether and how to intervene. Austria handed over Lombardy to the French, but kept Venetia. Napoleon then gave Lombardy to Piedmont-Sardinia, and received Savoy and Nice in compensation. In Germany there were some who argued that Prussia should now seize the opportunity to create a Little Germany. They ranged from Bismarck, who had been sent as ambassador to Saint Petersburg to cool his heels, to the socialist leader Lassalle, and from the liberal-conservative "*Wochenblattpartei*," to radicals such as Ludwig Bamberger and Arnold Ruge. But the vast majority of Germans were anti-French, and sympathized with Austria. They argued that all Germans should stick together and resist the French. For Marx and Engels Napoleon III was the arch-villain, and so he was for ultraconservatives like Ernst Ludwig von Gerlach and Friedrich Julius Stahl.

It was thus a confusing situation, made all the more complex by Napoleon III's baffling policies. German nationalists admired Cavour and hoped to emulate the Italians, but the process of Italian unification greatly strengthened France, and thus threatened Germany. They were angered by both Prussia and Austria. Prussia, they felt, had demanded too high a price, and had left Austria in the lurch. Austria had given in to France too precipitously, and should have waited for the Prussians to come her aid. This latter charge overlooked the fact that Austria could not have afforded to be saved in Italy by Prussia, for this would have greatly enhanced Prussia's standing in Germany.

The Crimean and Italian wars gave fresh impetus to liberals and nationalists. Their hopes were also raised when Crown Prince William became regent in October 1858, his unfortunate brother, who was always somewhat unbalanced, having become completely deranged. William was a conservative, the "grapeshot prince" of 1848, but he was a fervent Little-German nationalist, opposed to the archconservatives and even prepared to swear by the constitution. His government was liberal-conservative, bent on healing the differences among the elites, and determined to preserve their status by judicious reform and a generous social policy. William had spent all his life as an army officer, and was determined to reform the army so as to lend weight to an active and independent Prussian foreign policy. Education was to be overhauled, and the churches ordered to stay out of politics. This was a program that was broadly attractive. Conservatives were delighted, and liberal hopes ran unrealistically high, since they overlooked some of William's more conservative utterances. Bismarck urged the regent to open up to the liberals so as to create a broad consensus that would greatly strengthen Prussia in the eyes of liberal Germans. The regent took note, but felt it prudent to move Bismarck from the Bundestag to Saint Petersburg, lest he cause too much trouble with Austria in the midst of the Italian crisis.

The "New Era" in Prussia

The "New Era" began cautiously. Moderate reforms were passed and pressure was placed on the appalling regime in Electoral Hesse to reinstate the constitution of 1831, but in the ranks of the liberals disappointment was growing. Reforms in Austria under Schmerling, a leading figure in 1848, greatly strengthened the role of the German and liberal urban middle class who were fervently Greater German and anti-Prussian. Liberal governments were installed in Bavaria and Baden, and elsewhere in Germany conservative regimes became more relaxed. Prussia was thus in no way unique. A new generation was coming to power which agreed with Bismarck that a conservative regime could no longer do without popular support. It was also a reflection of the social changes that had taken place in Germany, as a liberal bourgeoisie grew in strength only to find that they were soon to be faced with the threat of an organized working class. The social question was being redefined in the industrial age, and could not be answered in terms of ultraconservative nostalgia for a bygone age.

The "New Era" was a period of dramatic economic change. This was the take-off period of industrialization in Germany during which, in spite of sharp fluctuations and even crises, there was a general improvement in living standards. The truly appalling problems of poverty that marked the early part of the century had been mastered. Industrialization absorbed large-scale unemployment, the crisis of the late 1840s was overcome, and from the 1860s the situation of the industrial working class improved. Artisans and craftsmen adapted to the industrial age by forming cooperatives, by greater specialization, or by becoming highly skilled industrial workers. The peasantry also profited from this general prosperity and from improved agricultural methods. But it was the bourgeoisie that really began to thrive, with the wide range of job opportunities offered by an industrial society, and by the handsome profits to be made on the stock exchange.

It would be a serious error to imagine that this process, whereby society was being transformed from being agricultural and rural to become modern, urban, industrial, and commercial, was not fraught with problems and subject to serious disjuncture. New and sharper class distinctions were apparent as the artisan class slowly eroded. Some became entrepreneurs and entered the ranks of the bourgeoisie; others sank into the anonymity of the urban proletariat. Industry was seriously undercapitalized, bankruptcies were frequent, and the stock market collapsed in 1858. The process of modernization was fraught with difficulties, as traditional

Plate 8 German industrial might: a rolling mill in Saarbrücken c. 1870. © BPK

mentalities and structures struggled to adapt to alarmingly new conditions. Many were left by the wayside, but there was remarkable growth between 1850 and the early 1870s from which most profited. It was a society on the move, but not one in which social revolution was incubated.

As society changed so did politics. The old equation of liberal change versus conservative status quo, the people and the crown, "us" and "them," no longer held good. The complexities of a modern class society were such that alliances had now to be made that crossed traditional lines of class and ideology. Napoleon III and Bismarck gave vivid examples of how revolutionary means could be used to achieve conservative ends, much to the bewilderment of contemporaries and to the bafflement of many a historian. It took some time for the liberals to recover from their crushing defeat in 1848. It is perhaps surprising that the term "realpolitik," which is usually associated with Bismarck, its greatest practitioner, was actually coined by a liberal, August Ludwig von Rochau, in 1853. He insisted that the greatest weakness of the Liberals in 1848 was that they were out of touch with the real world: they were dreamers, idealists, and doctrinaire theoreticians. They had to abandon their idealistic and romantic notions of the German past, and to get in tune with the new philosophy of positivism, empiricism, and materialism. Politics for Rochau was all about power, for without power no ideals or political goals can be realized. Liberalism was the political expression of the aspirations of an increasingly self-confident bourgeoisie determined to become the dominant political class, and that meant a concentration on economic concerns rather than ideals and moral issues. The bourgeois world of the New Era was infused with liberalism. Professors and civil servants, school teachers and Protestant pastors, businessmen and lawyers joined the great national liberal associations, and subscribed to liberal journals such as Heinrich von Sybel's *Historischer Zeitschrift*, the *Preußischer Jahrbücher*, which was soon to be the mouthpiece of Heinrich von Treitschke, or Gustav Freitag's *Grenzboten*. Most of the disillusioned radicals who remained in Germany also joined the liberal ranks, and the liberals won wide support from ordinary people in the many national associations that still flourished in Germany: the glee singers, gymnasts, and marksmen. For all the divergences of opinion and social status the liberals formed a coherent and influential force that no politician could afford to ignore.

Wherever there were elected diets the liberals formed a majority, and Prussia, with its three-class electoral system, actually gave an advantage to the well-established bourgeois. Most liberal politicians came from the bourgeois elite, and were deeply suspicious of the masses. They needed their support and their votes, but were acutely aware of the dangers of rabble rousing and demagogy. They hoped to educate the masses to become responsible citizens and to close their ears to the siren calls of popular democracy and socialism. Some left-wing liberals put their faith in the people, but they too denounced those democrats who sought to mobilize the masses. However, for the moment such concerns were hardly pressing. There was a general political apathy, precious few bothered to make use of their franchise, and politics was the concern of a small elite. Prosperous businessmen lent their support to the movement and, as in 1848, the politicians themselves for the most part were university-educated professionals, most of them civil servants and lawyers. Liberals were traumatized by the experience of 1848, which showed how easily parliamentary democracy could descend into Jacobin terror. In the New Era they were less concerned with strengthening parliament than with ending the dominant influence of the aristocracy and the military over the government. Most liberals had abandoned their dislike and distrust of the state. A state that was free from all antiquated absolutist tendencies, and in which enlightened liberals had an ascendant influence by means of a liberal constitution, could be a force for the good, a guarantor of law, order, and individual freedom. Now it was not only the right-wing liberals who doubted that parliaments were sufficient to overcome social and political conflicts, and who feared that too much freedom could well result in anarchy. Left-wing liberals still argued in favor of universal suffrage and insisted that the masses could be trusted to vote for men of substance and culture. The right had less faith in the common man and pointed to France, where a plebiscitary democracy had resulted in a Bonapartist autocracy. Bourgeois values were seen as universal values and the vast majority of liberals distinguished themselves sharply from the lower orders, whom it was hoped would benefit from general prosperity and gradually reach a cultural level that would enable them to join the universal class. There was also disagreement over the role of the state in the economy. Most wanted to leave everything to Adam Smith's "invisible hand," but some intellectuals, such as Treitschke, felt that the state would have to intervene in order to ensure a degree of social justice. There was one thing on which both wings could agree, and that was that national unity was the absolute priority. Without unity there could be no real freedom.

As Rochau had preached, nothing could be achieved without gaining power. The liberals of the New Era mostly took the approach of the Old Liberals of 1848: power could only be won by cooperation and compromise, not by confrontation and demanding all or nothing. Left-liberals argued that they represented the people, that governments could no longer ignore the will of the people, and that therefore they could act as a power pressure group, without unleashing the unpredictable and perilous forces of radical democracy. These divisions within the liberal movement were a reflection of the heterogeneity of Germany, the transitional phase of social development, the lack of a common political culture, regional and religious differences, and the still unsolved German question. Liberals could circle their wagons when they came under attack, as in Prussia under Bismarck, or Bavaria and Baden when faced with clerical and conservative reaction. Once the pressure was off they were too divided over the questions of a Little or Greater Germany, and the awkward issue of which was to be privileged: freedom or unity. They thus found themselves obliged to ally either with Prussian or Greater German conservatives if they were not to be condemned to utter powerlessness. It was that extraordinary outsider Bismarck who was to decide the two major questions that faced the liberals, and in doing so split the movement irrevocably.

Changes in conservative attitudes were far less dramatic. There was a gradual awareness that throne, altar, and landed estate were not sufficiently strong to preserve the social order. Many conservatives argued that they should reach out to the peasantry, the craftsmen, and the artisans, and all were in opposition to the rapaciously modernizing bourgeoisie and their academic hangers-on. Lorenz Stein, with his idea of a "social monarchy," and Hermann Wagener, the proponent of an energetic social policy, were to have a profound effect on later developments: Lorenz Stein on William II and Wagener on Bismarck. Such ideas rendered the period of reaction after 1848 far less grim than it has often been painted, for conservatives began to realize that they had to have a degree of popular support. Bismarck, more than any other conservative, knew that the bourgeois-liberal modern world was a reality that could not be wished away. He took a leaf out of Napoleon III's book and with ruthless realism achieved conservative ends by means that were far from conservative.

The Origins of Social Democracy

A new factor in the social equation was the rise of an industrial working class – an army of the propertyless who possessed nothing but their labor. In 1848 the proletariat scarcely existed outside the brilliant imagination of Karl Marx. Even by the 1860s when an independent labor movement began, there was still no class-conscious proletariat as society was in the final stages of the long transitional phase from artisanal to industrial production. Communist groups and workers' associations had been ruthlessly suppressed after 1848, but in the New Era liberals began to organize workers' educational associations in an effort to win the support of craftsmen and workers to their struggle against the established powers. Liberals believed that education would provide the answer to the social question by providing workers with the skills needed to succeed, an understanding of the broad issues of the day, and an access to the riches of higher culture. Education would inoculate them against socialist ideas and help them understand the community of interests between capital and labor. Some liberals went further, and argued that workers should be taught to think critically, to challenge established authority, and to become active participants in the democratic movement for change. Socialists were to take up these ideas and workers' education was to play a central role in the labor movement. The left-liberal Hermann Schulze-Delitzsch, the leading figure behind this liberal approach to the working class, believed that bourgeoisie and proletariat had a common interest in an economy unshackled from state control, since the benefits from increased national wealth within a liberal nation-state would be shared. He believed that any friction between capital and labor could be overcome by cooperatives, both for production and retail. These ideas were imported from England where Robert Owen's ideas had been disseminated by the London Co-operative Society, and put into practice by the Rochdale Pioneers in the 1840s. These were utopian ideas but they had a powerful resonance among socialists, in spite of Karl Marx's stern disapproval. Ferdinand Lassalle, the founding father of German Social Democracy, launched a ferocious attack on Schulze-Delitzsch, but he still argued that cooperative labor was the answer to all economic and social evils. Even Bismarck, with his distaste for capitalist entrepreneurs, was favorably disposed toward cooperatives. Most of these schemes proved unworkable, but some success was achieved with cooperative savings banks that provided modest loans for working people.

Liberals took a patronizing attitude toward the working class and argued that they should be educated up to their level before being regarded as equal partners. Workers were excluded from the National Association by a hefty annual subscription. Suggestions that concessions should be made to enable workers to join were bluntly rejected. On the other hand the National Association sponsored a workers' delegation to go to London for the World Exhibition. It was decided that the delegation should report back to a workers' congress. A committee was struck in Leipzig to discuss the form this congress should take, but its conclusions were alarming to liberals. They called for an independent labor movement and appealed to Ferdinand Lassalle to write a reply to Schulze-Delitzsch's denunciations of a labor movement cut loose from the liberals. Lassalle was a radical democrat and intellectual, a flamboyant bon vivant and dandy, a captivating orator, and a charismatic and dictatorial leader. His "Open Response" of March 1 1863 is one of the key texts of social democracy. Lassalle's central contention was that his somewhat vague vision of socialism could only be achieved by universal suffrage. The ballot box, and not revolution, was the only way forward. Since 1848 liberals of all shades were no longer the driving force behind the national revolution, and furthermore he believed

Plate 9 The founders of German Social Democracy. © Friedrich Ebert Stiftung

that differences between capital and labor were irreconcilable. According to his "iron law of wages" – a notion upon which Karl Marx poured his vitriolic scorn – the working class was condemned never to rise above a minimum subsistence level. Only when society was organized into productive cooperative associations of the workers themselves, financed by the state, could this misery be overcome. Lassalle believed that the working class should take its destiny in its own hands, and argued that the nation-state had a vital role to play in the creation of a just society. Lassalle's state socialism was thus an odd mixture of radical democracy, Bonapartism,

Plate 10 August Bebel. © Friedrich Ebert Stiftung

and fervent nationalism. His important contribution to the labor movement was his insistence that the liberation of the working class should be the task of the working class itself and that all links to Schulze-Delitzsch's liberals should be severed. The Leipzig Committee accepted Lassalle's report, which became the program of the General German Workers' Association (ADAV), which had Lassalle as its president. This was not only the first independent national working-class political organization, it was also the first modern political party in Germany. Many workers' associations were not prepared to make such a radical break with the left-liberals; they were suspicious of state power, especially in its Prussian manifestation, they remained Greater Germans in the tradition of 1848, and were understandably confused by Lassalle's inchoate ideas. When he was killed in the following year following an absurd affront to a crack marksman over his fiancée, which resulted in a duel which was little more than a suicide, the party, now numbering some 3,000 members, began to fall apart. But Lassalle's influence on the labor movement in Germany was profound. A number of trades unions were formed in the 1860s, and a series of strikes marked a further radicalization of the working class. Lassalleans, with their "iron law of wages," felt that trades unions were a futile waste of time and effort. Liberals, who were anxious to lure workers away from the ADAV, were more sympathetic, but this in turn threatened the liberal alliance with business interests. The Social Democratic Workers' Party (SDAP), founded by August Bebel and Wilhelm Liebknecht at a congress in Eisenach in 1869, was formed in staunch opposition to the ADAV. The Eisenacher's largely Marxist program appealed to radical workers, trade unionists, and to Greater German radicals who could not stomach the Lassalleans' Little German and pro-Prussian policies. Even as late as 1869 the socialist movement was hardly the "specter that is haunting Europe," as Marx and Engels had claimed it to be as early as 1848. There were some 3,000 Lassalleans, and Bebel and Liebknecht had even fewer followers. During the New Era the central issues were the national question and army reform in Prussia.

The Constitutional Crisis in Prussia

On becoming regent in 1858 William had made it clear that he was determined to make some drastic changes in the Prussian army which were long overdue. Nothing had been done to improve the army since the great reforms of the Napoleonic era, and in spite of a dramatic increase in population from 11 to 18 million its size had remained the same. The army was minute when compared to those of Russia, France, and Austria. Mobilization during the Crimean War had shown up some serious deficiencies. Above all, the *Landwehr* needed a complete overhaul. It had proved thoroughly unreliable in 1848, some units having sided with the rebels. Its officers were poorly trained and over-aged, the men were ill-disciplined, and it needed to be better integrated into the regular army. William also believed that service in the army should be increased from two to three years. Three years were needed to turn citizens into soldiers, to convert disgruntled liberals into loyal subjects, to make a clear distinction between the civil and the military, and to professionalize an army that was based on the liberal principle of universal military service. The largely aristocratic officer corps saw itself as the monarchy's Praetorian Guard standing outside the constitution, ever ready to strike back against revolution, modernity, and liberalism. There was general agreement that the army needed to be reformed and its size increased, but there was considerable disagreement over the thorny issue of the role of the army, and particularly the *Landwehr*, within society. William's first minister of war, Bonin, whom the regent had instantly re-appointed, wanted to avoid confrontation with the House of Deputies (*Abgeordnetenhaus*) over the *Landwehr* and argued that a relatively independent territorial army was essential in order to reconcile the civilians with the regular army. William would have none of this, and promptly replaced Bonin with Count Albrecht von Roon, a man known not to shy away from confrontation. Roon proposed increasing army service from two to three years and the size of the army from 150,000 to 220,000. The *Landwehr* was to be reduced in size and significance, and henceforth be given regular, reserve, or retired officers. In short it should virtually cease to exist as a force independent from the regular army.

The liberals welcomed the proposed increase to the size of the army, for they were concerned about Prussia's security and also wanted a strong army to support a vigorous German policy. The cost of Roon's proposals was far from exorbitant. The great stumbling block for left-liberals was the *Landwehr*, about which they harbored fond romantic illusions. For them the *Landwehr* was a true citizens' army, the guarantee of liberal freedoms against the reactionary and aristocratic regular army. The Old Liberals were less concerned about the *Landwehr*. They were far more concerned about the three-year service, which they saw as a dangerous step toward the militarization of bourgeois society. They were determined to resist William and Roon's ambition to turn the army into the "school of the nation," intent on transforming citizens into mindless robots to be sent back to Civvy Street as loyal, pliant, and obedient subjects. Above all, the liberals were determined that the House of Deputies should have a say in military affairs and should not simply rubber-stamp the government's proposals. Step by step the army should be brought under the constitution.

The liberals were prepared to provide the money for the increases in the army, but would not agree to the proposed administrative reforms, or to the three-year service. The government counterattacked, claiming that parliament had no authority to determine the size or organization of the army. Such matters came under the king's "power of command" (*Kommandogewalt*). The question of army reform thus now became an outright power struggle between the throne and parliament. Ultras around the head of the military cabinet, Edwin von Manteuffel, hoped that this would lead to a coup d'état and the overthrow of the constitution. Most conservatives did not want to go quite so far, but they were determined to use the crisis to clip parliament's wings and to force the New Course to tack to the right. Even though liberal objections to the proposed army reforms were exceedingly modest, Roon announced that Prussia was "rotting in the sewer of doctrinaire liberalism," and he welcomed the prospect of settling accounts with the liberals once and for all. He took the money, reorganized the army, established the new units, and paraded them before a humiliated public. Left-wing liberals were outraged, both by Roon's provocative actions and by the supine attitude of the Old Liberals. A group which included Hermann Schultze-Delitzsch, the historian Theodor Mommsen, and the pathologist Rudolf Virchow formed a new party known as the Progressives (*Fortschrittspartei*), which called for major liberal constitutional reforms. In the elections in December 1861 the new party won 109 seats, the Old Liberals 91, and the conservatives were reduced to a mere 14 seats. Manteuffel called for a military dictatorship, the army rattled its swords, but William remained calm. He was determined to keep the army beyond parliamentary control, but he knew that the liberals were not a serious revolutionary danger.

Encouraged by their resounding success at the polls, the liberals now fought back by demanding to know exactly how the money they had granted for the army had been spent, whereupon the king dissolved the House of Deputies and appointed a new and conservative government. A fresh round of elections returned a comfortable liberal majority to the House. The opposition was now willing to reach a compromise, but insisted on the two-year service. William would not budge on this issue, insisting that parliament should have no say in the way that the army was organized. The conflict was now one of principal. Which side would be obliged to give way – the crown or parliament? The outcome of this struggle would be of fundamental significance to Prussia's constitutional development. Would the crown bow to parliament, or strengthen its authority in a bloodless coup? The House now refused to vote on the budget on the assumption that the government would be unable to govern without a budget, and would be forced to concede. The king and the ultras did not for a moment intend to capitulate. They came up with the ingenious idea that there was a "hole" in the constitution, since there was no provision made therein for what should happen when the House and the government were deadlocked. Most of the ministers were horrified at the proposal that they should govern without a budget, and insisted that this was blatantly unconstitutional. They knew that another election would bring no relief, and therefore begged William to give way. The king thought of abdicating in favor of his son, Friedrich. The crown prince, who was sympathetic toward the liberals, begged his father not to take this drastic step and the crisis deepened.

At this point Roon urged his friend Bismarck, who was at this time Prussian ambassador in Paris, to come to Berlin by sending a famous telegram: "Periculum in mora. Dépêchez-vous." ("There is danger in delay. Get a move on!"). Bismarck knew that his hour had come and hastened to the capital. This was one of the decisive moments in Prussian, German, and European history. It determined that Prussia would not become a parliamentary democracy on British lines, but would remain an autocratic military monarchy with a parliamentary appendage. William had serious reservations about Bismarck. He was a rogue elephant, an extremist with a brutal streak, a political gambler and adventurer, an unpredictable and highly-strung opportunist. In addition, Queen Augusta detested the man. But at the height of the crisis in 1862, William saw no alternative to the mad Junker if he wanted to govern without a budget and push through the army reforms in their original form. Bismarck pulled out all the histrionic stops, and swore that he would serve the monarch "as an Electoral-Brandenburg vassal," not as a "constitutional minister," and would preserve the full authority of the crown. At the same time he insisted that he would act as he saw fit and that he was not the creature of any man or any party. From the outset Bismarck was thus vested with virtually dictatorial powers, able at last, as he put it, to make his own music.

Bismarck appeared as minister-president before the budgetary committee on September 30, bearing an olive branch as a symbol of his willingness to reach an accommodation with the liberals to whom he had already offered three ministerial positions. But he cautioned the deputies that he intended to govern without a budget, and in the most famous of his many pithy phrases told his horrified audience that: "The great questions of the day are not settled by speeches and majority votes, that was the mistake of the men of 1848, but by blood and iron." The liberal historian Heinrich von Treitschke, who was later to become a starry-eyed admirer of Bismarck, spoke for many when he said: "it seems to me that when I hear a simple Junker like this Bismarck fellow talk of the blood and iron with which he intends to lord it over Germany, the blackguardly is only outdone by the ridiculous."

Bismarck ruled without a budget. Civil servants who raised any objections were instantly dismissed, denied a pension, and stripped of their civil rights. Prosecutors who demurred when called upon to proceed against the government's critics were given similar treatment. The press was muzzled and parliament dissolved, but the elections returned the liberals with a two-thirds majority. Bismarck continued to ignore parliament, and it was dissolved once again in May 1866, shortly before the war against Austria.

The heated rhetoric on both sides disguised the fact that liberal ambitions were exceedingly modest and far from revolutionary, and that Bismarck knew that he could not tackle the "great questions of the day" without substantial parliamentary support. He began to do so by stealing their thunder. His attitude toward the German problem was, as we shall shortly see, very close to that of the Progressives, his most outspoken critics in the House of Representatives. He was strongly opposed to Manteuffel's proposal for a coup d'état, but thought it prudent to hide his intention to win over the liberals by lashing them in public. Bismarck told Ferdinand Lassalle, with whom he got along famously, that he intended to introduce universal manhood suffrage at some future date. This was clearly no ordinary conservative, but a Bonapartist who set out to break the political deadlock by a foreign political success that would win over the liberal nationalists. This in turn was to place the liberals in an awkward predicament. They wanted both national unity and liberal freedom. Some felt that these two principals were dialectically linked, and that Prussia as part of a united Little Germany would cease to be autocratic and militaristic. Others doubted that unity under Bismarck could ever bring freedom. For the time being the German question was submersed by the constitutional crisis. In the early 1860s there had been general agreement that it could not be settled by revolution. Precious few wanted a repeat performance of 1848. Blood and iron was not yet on the agenda, with Austria humiliated after Villafranca and the tiny Prussian army in a wretched state. Reform of the Confederation seemed to be the only possible way forward.

There was no shortage of suggestions as to how the Confederation should be changed. Prussia wanted equality with Austria, with hegemony north of the river Main, plus the right to call the shots in Schleswig-Holstein and Electoral Hesse.

Given the threat to Germany posed by Napoleon III, the Prussians were prepared to cooperate with Austria. Austria was in an awkward position. It did not wish to give up its dominant position in Germany, but it also needed a strong Confederation to help strengthen its position in Venetia. It was anxious to frustrate Prussia's reform plans, but also realized that it might need Prussian support. The Austrians therefore could not decide whether to tackle the Prussians head on, or to agree to an Austro-Prussian dualism. As a result Austrian policy oscillated between these two positions. The Third Germany (Trias) was determined to resist an Austro-Prussian duumvirate, and was equally appalled by the idea of a Germany dominated by Prussia and excluding Austria. The Saxon minister-president Count Friedrich von Beust put forward a comprehensive plan in 1861 which called for a triumvirate, a strengthened federal executive, and a federal parliament. The weakness of this scheme was that the Trias was a fissiparous collection of states which Bavaria sought to dominate. Beust's ambitious scheme therefore came to nothing. Since the Austrians were unable to agree with the Prussians they now turned toward the Third Germany, but it was too late. Little German sentiment was growing. The government of Baden approached Prussia and suggested a dramatic reform of the Confederation that would include a constitution, a federal parliament, and the exclusion of Austria, which in turn would be given the assurance of military support, and would be closely associated with the new Germany. Bismarck was already thinking along much the same lines, but the Prussian government disliked the idea of a federal parliament, and still shied away from a confrontation with Austria.

Austria could mobilize considerable support against this Little German solution. Most of the Third German states now supported the idea of a common code of law and a conference of parliamentary delegates. It was even suggested that Prussia should be obliged to submit to the majority decisions of the Bundesrat, whereupon Bismarck threatened to withdraw from the Confederation, and then threatened the Austrians with war if they did not agree to parity in Germany along with Prussian hegemony in the north. Knowing that this would be totally unacceptable to Austria, he then proposed a German parliament with direct elections. The suggestion was met with a mixture of amazement, derision, and alarm. In 1863 the Austrians mounted their counterattack. They proposed a strengthening of the federal executive with a five- or six-man directory and the creation of a chamber of princes, and supported the idea of a conference of parliamentary delegates. They further suggested that if the Prussians did not agree, a new Little German Confederation could be formed without them. The Emperor Francis Joseph invited the German princes to discuss these plans in Frankfurt in August. In a stormy scene Bismarck forced William to refuse the invitation, for this was transparently a scheme to reduce Prussia to having only one voice in the directory. The Austrian plan floundered and died, due to determined Prussian opposition, but the German question still remained a burning issue. Popular opinion had been mobilized by the National Association (*Nationalverein*), founded in 1859 at the height of the Italian crisis. They were moderate liberals who supported the federal constitution of 1849 and called for the creation of a Little German nation-state, with a parliament elected by universal manhood suffrage. They saw Prussia as Germany's Piedmont that would have wide-spread popular support, but a Prussia with Bismarck as minister-president, promising "blood and iron" and trampling on Prussia's constitutional rights, was something that no liberal could stomach. From 1862 the National Association's project had to be put on hold, but this did not mean that the Greater Germans, with their German Reform Association (*Deutsche Reformverein*), won any converts. Their vision of a Germany in which Austria and Prussia could live together in harmony was hopelessly unrealistic, and liberal democrats who longed for a German parliament knew that this was impossible in a Germany that included Austria. Bismarck might have proposed a parliament out of cynical considerations of realpolitik, but Bismarck would not be there forever, and Prussia could change.

In 1860 Richard Cobden, the radical "Apostle of Free Trade" and president of the board of trade in Palmerston's cabinet, negotiated a trade treaty between Britain and France which for Prussia was both a threat and an opportunity. The "revolutionary" France of Napoleon III allied to Britain was an alarming prospect to Prussian conservatives, and almost simultaneously Prussia was approached by France for a trade treaty, and by Austria, which proposed a defensive agreement, as well as entry into the *Zollverein*. The Prussians saw a golden opportunity to exclude Austria from the customs union and face it with an economic Villafranca. A trade agreement was reached with France in 1862, opening up the French market to German industrial goods, and thus helping the economy to climb out of a severe recession. Austrian attempts to wean the southern German states away from the *Zollverein* came to naught, in spite of strong anti-Prussian sentiments in the region. Bismarck threatened to dissolve the *Zollverein* unless there was unanimous consent of all its members to the treaty. Faced with such a prospect, even the most staunchly anti-Prussian governments meekly agreed. This did not make a Little German solution under Prussian leadership inevitable, but it certainly made it more than likely. The new Germany might have been made by blood and iron, but coal and iron were its foundations.

The uprising in the Polish provinces in Russia gave Bismarck his first opportunity to strengthen Prussia's diplomatic standing. He was determined that Napoleon III should not be allowed to "form a French bridgehead on the Vistula" by helping the Poles as he had the Italians, but even more important was the opportunity to discredit the Russian foreign minister, Gorchakov, with his pro-Polish and pro-French policies. The Prussian army was mobilized and help offered to Russia in the Alvensleben Convention. There were howls of protest in Paris against Prussia. The Empress Eugenie suggested to the Austrians that they should give Venetia to Italy and in return Buol's old idea of annexing Silesia could be put into effect. France would then move up to the Rhine and Prussia would be given some modest compensation in the north. Napoleon had overplayed his hand. He had lost the understanding with Russia, which now turned toward Prussia. Bismarck was freed from pressure on two sides, and by guaranteeing Belgium was now in England's good books. Public opinion in Germany was outraged that Prussia was now on the best of terms with Asiatic despotism and had alienated France.

The Schleswig-Holstein Question

It was thus in a most uneasy situation that the Schleswig-Holstein question was once more on the agenda. In November 1863 the new Danish king, Christian IX, formally divided the duchies and incorporated Schleswig into the Danish state. German nationalists were outraged at this flagrant violation of international treaties. They demanded that both duchies should be independent from Denmark and when the son of the duke of Augustenburg, who had renounced his claim in the previous crisis, claimed the duchies he overnight became the darling of the liberal nationalists in Germany. Schleswig-Holstein Associations sprang up throughout Germany, in the first mass political movement in Germany since 1849. Bismarck had no sympathy for the baying hordes of Augustenburgers. He did not want to see a new state formed on Prussia's borders. He was fearful that the powers would intervene as they had done in 1848, and that the Russians and French would patch up their differences. He therefore insisted that the London Protocols of 1852 should be respected, and that Christian IX be recognized as the legitimate King of Denmark and Duke of Schleswig-Holstein, although the duchies should remain united. In taking this position he was denounced by the German nationalists as a vile traitor, but he could afford to ignore their emotional protests. The new Austrian foreign minister, Rechberg, was anxious to cooperate with Prussia and agreed that international treaties had to be respected. Bismarck exploited this situation to the full and dragged Austria into blindly supporting his policy in Schleswig-Holstein, even though it resulted in the loss of all support from the Trias, and forced Austria into an untenable position. This was truly a bravura piece of diplomatic wizardry. The smaller German states wanted the Confederation to go to war with Denmark, but Austria and Prussia threatened to dissolve the Confederation if their policy was not accepted. The Bundestag agreed by a majority of only one vote to an "Execution" against Christian IX's illegal annexation of Schleswig which was formally confirmed in the new Danish constitution. Federal troops now marched into Holstein, and in February 1864 Austrian and Prussian forces occupied Schleswig. They were soon in Jutland, and on April 8 Prussian troops stormed the Danish fortifications at Düppel in a dramatic and widely publicized action which won the grudging admiration of many a German nationalist.

These events were of considerable concern to the powers. Russia suspected that Napoleon III would soon become involved in the reordering of northern Europe. Palmerston was pro-Danish, but, like the Russians, was anxious to keep the French in check. Queen Victoria did not want to get involved. Napoleon III was determined to use the crisis to his advantage. A conference was held in London in April but proved fruitless. The Danes were under the illusion that they had widespread support and refused any compromise. Palmerston wanted to intervene, but since public opinion, most of the establishment, and the Queen were all deeply suspicious of Napoleon III and thus strongly opposed, he was obliged to give way. Napoleon III shied away from unleashing a European war without any allies. Russia was determined to preserve the alliance with Prussia, and Bismarck skillfully used the threat of an understanding with France to strengthen these ties. The London Conference having thus failed, the war continued, Denmark was defeated, and Schleswig-Holstein became an Austro-Prussian condominium. The Danish war was an old-fashioned, limited, cabinet war, but it caused a diplomatic revolution. Britain and Russia both now made it plain that they had no immediate interests in Germany. They stood aloof in 1866 and left France isolated in 1870. The effects within Germany were equally significant. There were complaints that Augustenburg had been betrayed, and that the rights of the people of Schleswig-Holstein to national self-determination had been ignored, but there was widespread delight at a German victory. Liberals, both right and left, began to revise their opinion of Bismarck. Treitschke no longer thought him absurd, and Sybel, Mommsen, and Droysen, his colleagues in the historians' guild, joined him in endorsing Prussian policies.

The condominium was clearly only a temporary solution, and Bismarck was determined that the duchies should be firmly under Prussian control. To this end he suggested to Rechberg that Prussia and Austria should go to war with France so that Austria could win back Lombardy and Prussia could annex the duchies as compensation. It is difficult to know how serious this proposal was, but Francis Joseph had no desire to add a large number of disgruntled Italians to his empire, and William still thought that the annexation of the duchies was altogether too risky a business. At this point Austria was finally excluded from the *Zollverein* and Rechberg, the man of compromise with Prussia, was dismissed. Austria now went over to a policy of confrontation with Prussia. It did so from a singularly weak position. It had no allies: Russia was at daggers drawn over Romania, France would demand Venetia as the price of friendship, and in Germany the Trias was alienated and Greater Germany a dead letter. In Schleswig-Holstein the Austrians now supported the claims of the duke of Augustenburg, which was a popular move in the smaller German states with their strong aversion to Prussia's hunger for power. On May 25 a Prussian crown council decided to aim for outright annexation of the duchies, even at the risk of war. Bismarck now set about preparing the diplomatic ground. Public opinion in Germany was still far too enamored with Augustenburg and an arrangement had to be made with France.

Tensions between Prussia and Austria were temporarily relieved with the Treaty of Gastein in August 1865 whereby Schleswig was to be administered by Prussia and Holstein by Austria. This left Austria in an untenable position, with Holstein sandwiched between Prussian territory, and with Prussia enjoying a number of special rights in the duchy. Austria, tottering on the verge of bankruptcy, had no alternative but to give way, but Gastein was clearly only a temporary arrangement. Austria was denounced in the Trias states for having betrayed Augustenburg at Gastein, and for apparently agreeing to divide the duchies which, according to the Treaty of Ripen of 1460, were to be joined together in perpetuity. The Prussians found every possible excuse to denounce the Austrians for violations of the terms of the treaty. By early 1866 both sides came to the conclusion that war was almost inevitable: Austria out of desperation, Bismarck for power-political reasons. He was determined to win the support of liberal nationalists for Prussia's war against

Austria, and in April 1866 put forward a proposal for federal reform. This was truly revolutionary: Bismarck the conservative was seeking an alliance with the nationalists, calling for a German parliament with universal manhood suffrage, and for the expulsion of Austria from the Confederation. It was a cunning move for it also made it unlikely that the powers would intervene. As Bismarck phrased it later, the offer of universal manhood suffrage was designed to stop other countries from "sticking their fingers into our national omelette." The problem was that the Augustenburgers and southern German liberals thought this was merely disingenuous villainy, and Greater Germans and conservatives were equally appalled. Bismarck had more success in foreign politics. On April 8, the day before he presented his reform proposals to the Confederation, he concluded an offensive alliance with Italy. It was agreed that Prussia should provoke a war with Austria within three months, and Italy would join in so as to complete the process of national unification.

Everything now depended on Napoleon III. He wanted to finish off the job in Italy, but he also wanted substantial compensation from Germany. On the other hand he did not want to see Prussia replace France as united Italy's midwife, and many of his advisors argued that France had more immediate interest in the Rhine than in the Po. For the moment Napoleon III wanted to keep his options open; then at the very last moment he reached an agreement with Austria. Austria agreed to hand over Venetia to Italy, Napoleon III agreed to remain neutral. Austria was to be compensated in southern Germany; a Rhineland state would be formed outside the Confederation and closely tied to France. Austria then brought war closer by bringing the Schleswig-Holstein question before the Bundestag, and by convening the estates in Holstein. Prussia responded by marching into Holstein on June 9 – a flagrant breach of federal law. Austria called up the Confederation to mobilize against Prussia. Bavaria, Württemberg, Saxony, Hanover, and a number of smaller states including the two Hesses voted in favor. Baden abstained; the remainder sided with Prussia. Prussia declared the Confederation dissolved and issued an ultimatum to Saxony, Hanover, and Electoral Hesse. When all three states refused to bend, Prussia attacked on June 15.

The war was immensely unpopular in Germany and it was bitterly ironic that virtually the only support for Bismarck came from the socialist ADAV, because of his promise to introduce universal manhood suffrage. Bismarck released Lassalle's successor Johann Baptist von Schweizer from jail and arranged to subsidize his newspaper *The Social Democrat*. The outcome was uncertain and most people, Napoleon III among them, imagined that it would be a long war, possibly lasting several years. Bismarck also thought this a distinct possibility, and preparations were made to stir up national revolts in the Habsburg Empire, which included a plan to bring Garibaldi first to Dalmatia and then to Hungary. Thanks to Helmuth von Moltke's operational genius the war was staggeringly short. Within three weeks the Austrian army was smashed at Königgrätz in Bohemia on July 3 when three Prussian armies, which had marched separately, came together on the battlefield – but only in the nick of time. The Austrians lost 45,000 in the battle including 20,000 prisoners, the Prussians 9,000. It was a decisive victory, but not a rout, and the bulk of the Austrian army escaped. Austria scored victories over the Italians on land at Custozza on June 24 and at sea at Lissa on July 20, but it was obvious that the Austrians were no match for the Prussians. The Prussian army was equipped with the needle gun which could release seven rounds a minute and could be fired lying down. The Austrian muzzle-loading rifle could barely fire two rounds a minute and had to be fired standing up. Austria got precious little help from its coalition partners and Benedek was no match for Moltke, the greatest military genius since Napoleon. Moltke had made full use of the railways to ensure rapid mobility and controlled his dispersed forces by telegraph.

Prussia's swift victory caught Europe by surprise. Napoleon III acted as mediator and an armistice was quickly concluded. Bismarck had no desire to humiliate Austria and the French agreed to his moderate terms: the creation of a North German Confederation under Prussia, the annexation of Schleswig-Holstein, Hanover, Electoral Hesse, and Nassau, and the creation of an independent southern German federation excluding Austria. Once Napoleon III agreed to this arrangement the Austrians were left with no alternative but to treat with Prussia. The strongest opposition to Bismarck's plan came from the king. He wanted to teach Austria a lesson, and had serious reservations about trampling on the legitimate sovereign rights of the north German states. Bismarck did not want Austria to harbor thoughts of revenge, and saw it as a potential future ally. North of the river Main he favored a revolutionary solution analogous to what had happened in Italy. William gave way eventually, after a series of heated exchanges with Bismarck.

Napoleon III tried to get some reward for his efforts, but Bismarck, who was appealing to German national sentiments, categorically refused to cede an inch of German soil. Napoleon III was without allies and had to concede, much to the disgust of his nationalist critics like Thiers. Russia was very distressed about the national-revolutionary implications of the settlement, and called for an international conference to discuss the German question. The British government was opposed to this suggestion, as was Bismarck. The French also showed little interest, and the Russians backed down. The European powers were now reconciled to the new situation in Germany and the provisions of the preliminary peace of Nikolsburg were finalized in Prague on August 23 1866. At the same time Bismarck negotiated a series of defensive alliances with the southern German states, which guaranteed their territorial integrity and stated that in the event of war their forces were to be placed under a Prussian supreme commander, thus surrendering a significant part of their sovereignty. This was a clear warning to Napoleon III to keep his hands off Germany.

Europe was thus radically changed in the summer of 1866. Austria was now excluded from the Germany of which it had been a vital part for a thousand years. The German Austrians soon shared power in the Habsburg Empire with the Magyars in the new political construction of Austria-Hungary. The Slavs were still denied an equal voice. Germany was now well on the way to becoming a nation-state, since the new order was clearly only temporary. Elections were held in Prussia on the day that the Prussian and Austrian armies clashed at Königgrätz. They were a triumph for the conservatives, who won 136 seats, having previously had only 35. Liberal mandates fell from 247 to 148. Bismarck promptly demanded an indemnity for his blatantly unconstitutional actions in the previous four years. This was granted after a heated debate, and it is a debate that still continues. For many the indemnity amounted to a capitulation by parliament to a quasi-dictator, a cowardly surrender of liberal constitutional principles. For conservatives it was a shameful kowtow to parliament. In fact it was neither. Bismarck made his peace with parliament and returned to constitutional rule, but with the army still beyond parliamentary control. For all the conservatives' complaints this was a decisive victory for the crown and for the army. On the other hand, parliament still had budgetary powers, was soon to have universal manhood suffrage, and thus had the prospect of further strengthening its position.

Political alliances were also overturned in 1866. The conservatives could not stomach Bismarck's Bonapartist tactics, his alliance with the nationalist movement, and his appeasement of the liberals, the majority of whom now supported Bismarck and formed the new party of National Liberals. They decided to abandon their utopian dreams and to work with Bismarck, to show that they were capable of governing, and to reconcile liberal ideas with a strong government in a powerful state. National unity was now given priority over liberal freedoms in the hope that liberal principles would eventually triumph in a united Germany in which Prussia would be dissolved. For the rump of the Progressive Party who remained true to their Old Liberal principles, Bismarck had debauched and corrupted the liberals into the pursuit of success, power, and a share of the spoils. They argued that a united Germany under Prussia would strengthen the old elites, block the way to further constitutional progress, and hinder the development of liberal freedoms. Tragically, the Progressives were proven right, but from the perspective of 1866 the majority of liberals were far from being unrealistic in accepting the compromise that Bismarck offered them. The alternative would have been an outright authoritarian regime that would have blocked all further development along liberal lines. Bismarck, having hijacked the liberal ideology of nationalism, left them little alternative.

6
The Unification of Germany: 1866–71

The Prussian victory at Königgrätz left many contemporaries dazed and confused. The arch-reactionary, militaristic Junker Bismarck, who had trampled on the Prussian constitution, had begun the war with a call for a national parliament based on universal suffrage and had partially realized the ambitions of the Little German bourgeoisie. Elections were held in Prussia on the same day as this decisive battle, and resulted in a crushing defeat for the liberals. There was considerable amazement when Bismarck requested from the Landtag an indemnity for the expenditure that it had refused to sanction during the constitutional crisis. It was a masterly move. Most conservatives were delighted that he had made no apology for what he had done, and implied that he would do it again if necessary. Many liberals found some comfort in that he thus acknowledged that he had ignored parliamentary rights. The indemnity made an alliance between moderate conservatives and National Liberals possible, and was designed as a conciliatory gesture toward the German states. The "Old Conservatives" were appalled that Bismarck was swimming with the tide of nationalism, constitutionalism, and parliamentarianism, and remained adamant in their opposition to his domestic realpolitik. On the other side, a number of liberals found it equally impossible to swallow Bismarck's Bonapartist strategy, and the cynicism of the indemnity. They disagreed with the National Liberals that a Germany formed under his leadership could ever become an acceptable constitutional state. Liberals in the Progressive Party voted by a fairly narrow majority against the Indemnity Bill. The Left Center voted by a two-thirds majority in favor. Only a few of those who were to join the pro-Bismarck National Liberals voted against.

Germany north of the river Main was reorganized as the North German Confederation. The princes and governments formed an upper house (Bundesrat), with a presidential committee (Praesidium), appointed by Bismarck as chancellor, forming a government. The Lower House (Reichstag) was elected by universal and secret manhood suffrage. In an attempt to exclude such dangerous elements as the "educated proletariat" and "demagogues," members were not paid. The states to the south did not form a southern German equivalent, largely due to the opposition of Baden and Württemberg. For all the economic, cultural, and confessional differences between north and south it was clear that these arrangements were temporary, and the "Main Line" along the river Main provisional. After Königgrätz the "Greater German" solution was no longer on the agenda, and the "Triad" of Austria, North and South Germany unworkable. The first major question was not whether a "Little Germany" should be created, but under what circumstances. Should unity take priority over freedom, or vice versa? Should a united Germany under Bismarck's Prussia be accepted as the unavoidable first step toward the creation of a constitutional state, or should unity only be accepted on the basis of a liberal constitution? The second major question was how the southern German states should be linked to the North German Confederation. Should this be the concern of governments or of parliaments? Should unity be achieved at one fell swoop, or piecemeal? Were an international crisis and the resort to "blood and iron" unavoidable?

Anti-Prussian sentiments resulted in strange bedfellows. Socialists and radicals were enthusiastic supporters of the idea of a nation-state, but were determined to resist its domination by a conservative and militaristic Prussia. Conservative particularists and ultramontane Catholics joined in the anti-Prussian chorus, but cocking a snook at the "Borussians" was all that united them. Archconservatives and revolutionary socialists could never agree on a solution to the national problem. Anti-Prussianism was naturally strongest in the south, but it was also prevalent elsewhere, particularly in Hamburg, Hanover, and Saxony. On the other side were the National Liberals, who argued that first Germany should be united, and only then could the constitutional question be resolved. Amid all this confusion no one had a master plan, least of all Bismarck. His main concern was the power vacuum south of the Main. He could not allow southern Germany to fall under the sway of Napoleon III, or of Austrian revisionists. At the same time he knew that the German question could only be solved by cooperation and consent, not by coercion. He had to move cautiously and was careful not to neglect public opinion. Above all, he was determined to preserve the Prussian monarchy and the authoritarian state in this radically new capitalist, bourgeois, national liberal, and constitutional world in which the relations between the European states had been drastically altered.

Military reforms in southern Germany on the Prussian model were a small step forward in the direction of a federal Germany under Prussian leadership. So too was the creation of a Customs Parliament, first with an upper house (*Zollbundesrat*) and then a Lower House (*Zollparlament*). Elections for the Customs Parliament were a disappointment for those who had hoped for a popular demonstration in favor of national unity. The particularists won a resounding and surprising victory in southern Germany. It was a vote against Prussia and a major setback for Bismarck. The National Liberals had hoped that the *Zollverein* would be the motor for national unification. They were bitterly disillusioned. Bismarck was less pessimistic. He knew that the southern German states could not afford to leave the *Zollverein*, and could write off the election results as a temporary setback. The southern German states were tied to the north economically through the *Zollverein* and militarily by a series of defensive alliances. Sharp differences between the different states, confusion, and lack of firm leadership meant that a South German Confederation, which anti-Prussian particularists along with the European states thought highly desirable, was never a serious option. The solution of 1871 was not inevitable, but for most contemporaries, whether they liked it or not, it seemed to be the most probable outcome of Prussia's victory over Austria in 1866.

Austria's exclusion from Germany, and Prussia's dominant position in central Europe was viewed by the powers with relative equanimity. The British government was far from enthusiastic about Bismarck's conservatism, but it welcomed a counterweight to the unpredictable and ambitious France of Napoleon III. Russia had tried to restrain Bismarck's territorial ambitions by calling for a European congress, but had stepped back when Bismarck threatened to play the nationalist card. It could now find comfort in the assurance that in Prussia it had a reliable conservative partner against Austria. The Austrians were absorbed with the problem of negotiating the "Compromise" with Hungary of 1867, and with dealing with the subject nationalities. These problems were so pressing that they could not possibly think of seeking revenge for Königgrätz.

For Bismarck, 1866 had only brought a temporary solution to the German problem. Having once conjured up the support of liberal nationalists, nothing short of the creation of a nation-state would suffice to integrate them in a monarchical and conservative system dominated by Prussia. Bismarck had no idea how or when this national policy could be realized, and he was secure enough to wait upon events. He was ready to seize any opportunity to secure this ultimate goal. Above all he was determined to maintain firm control and not allow liberal nationalists or public opinion undue influence. His was a revolutionary policy designed to overthrow the power-political balance of Europe, but it was to be a revolution from above that could not be allowed to slip out of his hands.

The France of Napoleon III was an unstable power that sought to overcome its chronic domestic political tensions by a dramatically adventurous foreign policy. It was thus highly unpredictable. Napoleon III was determined to assert France's hegemony over western Europe, but at the same time in line with his policy of undoing the decisions of 1815, he showed great sympathy for nationalist movements in Italy, Poland, and central Europe. Yet for all that he could hardly risk the establishment of a powerful Germany that would dominate Europe east of the Rhine. He could either try to contain Prussia north of the river Main, or support a German nation-state in return for major territorial concessions. Alternatively he could go on a confrontation course with Prussia and try to stop any further accretion of power. Napoleon lost the first round against Bismarck. He had hoped to purchase Luxembourg, which had been part of the now defunct German Confederation, from the king of Holland, who was short of cash and had no interest in the duchy. German nationalists were outraged at the proposed sale. Bismarck could not afford to alienate the nationalists, and therefore made the defensive treaties public, whereupon the Dutch king announced that he would only agree to the sale if his Prussian counterpart agreed. Bismarck wanted to avoid a direct conflict with France, and therefore put the question before the North German parliament which threw up its hands in predictable horror. Bismarck then used this reaction as an excuse to turn down the French bid but since, unlike Moltke, he did not think that the Luxembourg question was a convincing reason to go to war with France, he agreed to withdraw the Prussian garrison from the duchy and guaranteed its neutrality. Luxembourg thus ceased to be part of Germany, France was spared from total humiliation, and Europe from war. The Luxembourg crisis spelt the end of any hopes that Prussia might agree to be France's junior partner in Europe, and Napoleon III was now determined to frustrate Bismarck's territorial ambitions. Austria was the only viable partner for such a policy, but with its internal problems and its rivalry with Russia in the Balkans it was in no position to play an active anti-Prussian role. On the other hand negotiations between Paris and Vienna, coupled with England and Russia's preference for the maintenance of the status quo in Germany, obliged Bismarck to move cautiously. Thus between 1867 and 1870 there was something of a foreign political stalemate over the German question and no opportunity arose that Bismarck could exploit.

Elections for the North German Reichstag were held in February 1867. One hundred and eighty of the 297 seats were won by Bismarck's supporters – the National Liberals, Free Conservatives, and a smattering of independents and "Old Liberals." The opposition was made up of 59 Old Conservatives, 13 Poles, 19 Left Liberals, and 18 "Guelfs" – Hanoverian nationalists and champions of states' rights, confusingly known as "federalists." Once the constitution had been agreed upon fresh elections were held in August that year, resulting in little change in the relative position of the parties. Bismarck now set Rudolf Delbrück to work modernizing the economy. As a thoroughgoing economic liberal he removed all remaining trade barriers in the North German Confederation, established uniform weights and measures, abolished all restrictive practices, and, with the Trade Bill of 1869, completed the emancipation of the Jews. Finally in 1870 a common code of law was introduced. The Reichstag played a vital role in this crucial series of fundamental reforms. Prussia remained staunchly conservative and the Free Conservative and National Liberal alliance that dominated the Reichstag was seldom in the majority. The grotesquely reactionary ministers of justice and economics were replaced by men of a slightly more liberal cast of mind, but otherwise Prussia was unaffected by the liberal climate of the Confederation. The conservative, monarchical, and Borrusian tone did nothing to help the process of integrating the territories that had been absorbed by Prussia in 1866. Those who had been in opposition to the repressive regimes in Electoral Hesse and Hanover saw this as a welcome change and mostly joined the National Liberals. In Hanover the deposed king still had his supporters whose Guelph Party won the support of a number of other disaffected anti-Prussians. The proudly independent Frankfurters, whose free city had been amalgamated with Electoral Hesse and Nassau to form the new state of Hesse-Nassau, with its capital in Wiesbaden, bitterly resented their loss of independence and were fiercely anti-Prussian. Schleswig-Holstein was aloof and skeptical and remained faithful to the Augustenburgs. The Prussian administration was anxious not to offend the sensibilities of the new provinces and trod softly, allowing them a considerable degree of autonomy. The princes were given ample compensation for their losses. The major exception was Hanover, where King George V protested against the loss of his throne and formed an anti-Prussian "Guelph Legion." Bismarck made use of an emergency decree to seize the king's considerable private fortune, the interest on which was supposed to be used to combat the Guelphs. In fact Bismarck used this "Guelph Fund" as a secret slush fund for all manner of nefarious activities, including bribing the press, politicians, and princes.

Liberal reforms in the economy, education, and the law were also carried out in most of the German states south of the Main in the late 1860s. Reforms in the economy through the *Zollverein* and the Customs Parliament, along with military reforms on Prussian lines, had liberal and national implications and furthered the Little German cause. On the other side of the political divide were conservative Catholics, opponents of economic liberalism, Greater Germans, and particularists. The "patriotic" majority in Bavaria was determined to preserve the country's independence, and in Baden a vociferous minority held similar views. The Württembergers were anti-Prussian and Greater German, but, as in Bavaria, parliament was virtually deadlocked over the German question, and the government paralyzed. The situation was further complicated by fierce debates over the Vatican Council, which was to lead to a serious split within the Catholic Church in Germany. The Bavarian king refused to cave in to the anti-Prussian ultramontanes in parliament. Similarly in Württemberg the government was determined to resist the anti-Prussian democrats. Both governments thus needed an alliance with Prussia in order not to give in to parliamentary majorities. In Baden, for all the conflicts between governments and parliaments, there was a general consensus on the national question. Both agreed on the desirability of joining the North German Confederation. Bismarck viewed the southern Germans with ill-concealed contempt. He compared Bavaria, whose natives he described as a cross between human beings and Austrians, as Germany's Calabria: a primitive and backward area with which he could well do without.

The Franco-Prussian War

The gridlock over German unification was broken by events outside its borders. In 1868 the Spanish army deposed the absolutist queen and sought to establish a constitutional monarchy. The French supported a Bourbon candidate, but the military preferred the German Prince Leopold of Hohenzollern-Sigmaringen, the south German and Catholic branch of the Prussian ruling house. At first Bismarck paid little attention to the Hohenzollern candidature but by the winter of 1869, when it was clear that the Spanish were anxious to go ahead, he lent it his full support. Napoleon III used the prospect of a Hohenzollern on the throne of Spain as an opportunity to denounce Prussia's German policy as reactionary and selfish land grabbing, rather than an expression of that genuine nationalism which he wholeheartedly supported in Italy and Poland. Bismarck hoped to gain support in the south for his German policy by backing the prince and to mobilize German national sentiment by confronting France.

In April 1870 Leopold, having been cautioned by the Prussian king who wanted to avoid a showdown with the French, turned down the Spanish offer and the affair seemed to be over. Then, one month later, Napoleon III moved the ambitious and hawkish Gramont from the embassy in Vienna to the foreign ministry. Gramont hoped to strengthen Napoleon's position at home by a resounding victory over Prussia, and Bismarck welcomed the challenge. Bismarck managed to persuade the king to drop his objections to Leopold's candidature and the prince agreed to put his name forward. On July 5 Gramont denounced Prussia for attempting to revive the Empire of Charles V (an argument that Bismarck had used when trying to win William's support for the candidature) and warned that, should the Hohenzollerns persist, France would go to war. Both Britain and Russia expressed sympathy for the French point of view. Bismarck beat a hasty retreat and the candidature was once again withdrawn. The French government, emboldened by this victory, now went in for the kill. The French envoy Benedetti was sent to Bad Ems, where the Prussian king was taking the waters, to demand what amounted to an apology and a guarantee that the Hohenzollern candidature would never again be revived. William found this deeply insulting and, although he had no intention of further supporting Leopold's aspirations to the Spanish crown, flatly refused. The king sent a telegram to Bismarck reporting on this exchange with Benedetti, and Bismarck published a slightly shortened, but not significantly altered, version in the press. Contrary to Bismarck's assertion in his memoirs that he so radically altered the tone of the "Ems Telegram" that he provoked France into declaring war, the French government had already decided to go to war before the telegram was published. The "Ems Telegram" did however mobilize public opinion throughout Germany and the country was united in its determination to resist the French.

France formally declared war on July 19, and thus the defensive treaties with the south German states went into immediate effect and Napoleon III caused what he had tried at all costs to avoid – a Germany united under Prussian leadership. The Franco-Prussian War was thus in fact a Franco-German war in which the south German states, including the Bavarian patriots, gave their full and enthusiastic support to Prussia. The planned French offensive came to nothing due to poor planning and organizational chaos. After a number of bloody engagements in Lorraine part of the French army under Marshal Bazaine was trapped in the fortress town of Metz, prompting the commanding officer to remark: "We are in a chamber pot and are about to be shat upon!" The French commander Marshal MacMahon wanted to withdraw toward Paris, but he was ordered to relieve Metz. Moltke saw his chance, halted his advance toward the French capital, and encircled the bulk of the French army at Sedan. The French capitulated and Napoleon III was captured, along with 100,000 other prisoners of war. The republic was declared in Paris and on September 6 the new government announced that it would agree to a peace provided that the territorial integrity of France was respected. This the Prussians

Plate 11 The Battle of Sedan. © BPK

refused. The French republic under Gambetta created a partisan army that fought a bitter and brutal guerilla war, harrowingly described in Guy de Maupassant's stories, in a desperate attempt to stop the cessation of Alsace and Lorraine. By mid-September the Germans laid siege to Paris and by the end of January the republican government agreed to an armistice. A preliminary peace was signed on February 26 in which France was to lose Alsace and Lorraine and pay an indemnity of five thousand million francs.

Bismarck was anxious to end the war as soon as possible for fear of the reaction of the powers. This brought him into direct conflict with the military, who wanted completely to annihilate the French army and to reduce France to total subjection for at least the next hundred years. In fact the international constellation was favorable to Prussia. Britain had sympathized initially with France over the Hohenzollern candidature, but had lost patience with its increasingly bellicose policy. Austria could hardly intervene with the whole of Germany resolutely in support of Prussia. Italy resented the presence of French troops in Rome left to guard the pope. Russia harbored deep resentments about Napoleon III's support for the Poles, and this outweighed fears of the consequences of a united Germany. Although Bismarck was heartily disliked throughout most of Europe, the prospect of a French victory and consequent hegemony was far more alarming than the extension of Prussian power and influence south of the Main.

The annexation of Alsace and Lorraine was demanded by the military, applauded by the majority of Germans, and supported by Bismarck. It permanently poisoned relations between Germany and France, although Bismarck insisted they would have been every bit as strained even without these annexations. The powers saw this as an alarming sign that a defensive war had become a brutal war of conquest, and that Bismarck was aiming not only at uniting Germany, but striving for hegemony in Europe. His critics at home and abroad were loud in their condemnation of this policy, and Karl Marx shrewdly argued that he had thus sown the seeds of a European catastrophe. It obliged the European powers to regard the new German empire, which they accepted without enthusiasm, with deep suspicion. This unease at a new nation founded by blood and iron, seemingly intoxicated by victory and gorged with conquest, was shared by many intellectuals from the extremes of left and right. The massive Victory Column erected in Berlin is a dramatic representation of the spirit of the age. First designed to commemorate the victory over Denmark, it was aggrandized in 1866, and reached its final form in 1871. Surrounded by captured cannons, topped by an amply busted figure of Germania, it is decorated with a relief depicting the three wars of unification. Cretinous Danish peasants are overrun by Germanic supermen. Feeble and degenerate Austrians submit to Prussian military genius. Slovenly French soldiers, most of whom appear as colored colonial riff-raff led by a Marianne who has all the allure of a syphilitic whore, offer little resistance, while a sloppily smocked proletariat plots the Commune. The Victory Column survived the war and communism, with a Red Army soldier replacing Germania's spear with the red flag. With rich irony it served as the focal point for Berlin's Love Parade, but the bankrupt capital can alas no longer afford this extravaganza.

The Unification of Germany

It was clear to all that this Germany, swept away on a wave of national euphoria, would form a nation-state, but it was uncertain what form it would take. The south German states were anxious to retain their identity and their sovereignty. Bismarck wanted to negotiate with the princes and governments, and was determined to resist the blandishments of popular nationalism. National unity would be achieved from above, and not from below, as a federation of monarchical states, not a unitary parliamentary government. Bismarck hoped that the south German states would join the North German Confederation. In October 1870 Hesse and Baden requested membership, and Bismarck hoped that he could persuade Bavaria and Württemberg to follow suit. Faced with Bavarian resistance, Bismarck then negotiated separately in Versailles with the other states in the course of November, leaving Bavaria increasingly isolated. At the end of November the Bavarians finally gave way. Württemberg, which at the last minute had tried to win a privileged position in the new state just as Bavaria had done, capitulated two days later. The Prussian chancellor had made very few concessions. The Bundesrat was somewhat strengthened, thus giving the member states slightly more say in federal affairs. Bavaria retained an independent peacetime army, as well as a separate postal service and railway. It was also permitted to send an ambassador to the Vatican, have a separate say in the negotiation of peace treaties, and an independent right to tax beer, the national tipple.

In order to assert Prussia's supremacy over the new Germany, Bismarck was determined that the king of Prussia should be made emperor, and that the title should be offered to him by the princes, not come "from the gutter" as had been proposed by the Bundestag in 1849. King Ludwig of Bavaria was given a massive bribe from the "Guelph Fund" to persuade him to offer the imperial crown to William on behalf of the German princes. William was most unhappy about the proposed title of "German Emperor" which he felt had an empty ring about it, and wanted to be known the "Emperor of Germany," but Bismarck argued that this would cause offense among the princes, who would feel subordinated to the Prussian king. Both agreed that the other suggested title – "Emperor of the Germans" – smacked of popular nationalism and was unacceptable. The new German Empire was formally created on January 1 1871, when the various treaties were concluded. The real foundation of the Second Reich was on January 18 when William was formally proclaimed kaiser. January 18 had been the traditional coronation day of the Prussian kings since 1701, when the Elector of Brandenburg was crowned king "in" Prussia. Held in the Hall of Mirrors at Versailles, it was not quite the magnificent ceremony as represented in Anton von Werner's famous painting which was painted 14 years later, and there were many reservations and much foreboding. Most noticeable was the absence of parliamentarians and civilians. The Reich of blood and iron was proclaimed by the military, by the princes and old elite, all squeezed into military uniforms festooned with the medals of a victorious army.

The German Empire of 1871 was a curious affair destined to last a mere 47 years. It was a national constitutional state with a parliament elected by universal manhood suffrage, comprising a loose federation of quasi-independent states, the whole dominated by the Prussian military state. It was the result of a series of uneasy compromises: between the federal and the particular, monarchy and democracy, aristocracy and bourgeoisie. There was no national flag and no national anthem. It was sharply criticized by many, and won the undivided devotion of precious few. The states had wide ranging areas of competence, which included a monopoly on direct taxation and a wide range of indirect taxes, and policies on education, church affairs, and transportation. Each state had its own constitution and administration. As a federal state federal law took precedence over state law, but the states differed widely in matters of jurisprudence. The Reich was responsible for foreign policy, the military, economic and social policy, and federal law. Sovereign power was said to reside in the "allied governments" represented in the Bundesrat, with the kaiser as its hereditary president and Bismarck as chancellor serving as chairman. Prussia, which made up two-thirds of the territory of the Reich and a similar proportion of the population, only had one third of the votes in the Bundesrat, although it had a right of veto over military and constitutional matters. In practice Prussia dominated the Bundesrat, since it could easily force the smaller states to toe the line. In theory the Bundesrat had a number of significant executive powers. It had the same right to initiate legislation as the Reichstag, and no legislation could pass without its approval. The kaiser and the Bundesrat had the right to dismiss parliament and to declare war, although in practice such decisions were taken by the kaiser and the chancellor. Fundamentally it was an administrative body, made up of delegates and plenipotentiaries from the states. It did not have its own building, but was housed anonymously in the chancellery. It had virtually no staff and played no public role. Bills were prepared in the Reich ministries, or by the Prussian government, and presented to the Bundesrat at the last moment. Its inexperienced and ill-prepared members were little more than rubber stamps, since Bismarck preferred to negotiate with the states individually before launching any legislative initiative. But it was not completely powerless. It stood as a guarantee of states' rights and was determined to resist any attempts to strengthen Prussia's already excessive power within the Reich. Furthermore, it was designed to hold the Reichstag in check. The chancellor, the secretaries of state, and the Prussian ministers stood before the Reichstag as representatives of the Bundesrat, and were not answerable to parliament. No member of the Reichstag could be simultaneously a member of the Bundesrat, and thus could not be chancellor, secretary of state, or a Prussian minister. With Prussia's right of veto over any constitutional changes this was a formidable barrier to the growth of parliamentary government, as well as a means of further strengthening Prussia's domination over the empire. Federalism thus stunted parliamentary government, and those who wanted to hold the Reichstag in check were obliged to support states' rights. The states were united in their determination to resist any attempts by the Reichstag to increase its powers, since it would mean a diminution of their own rights. This determination gave a degree of coherence to this exceedingly complex and confusing constitutional structure, and also helped reconcile the states to Prussia's unique position within the Reich.

Prussian and imperial institutions were so intimately intertwined that they could hardly be distinguished. Since the king of Prussia was also president of the Bundesrat all bills put forward in that body were first discussed by the Prussian parliament. Bismarck was both Prussian minister-president and chancellor of the Reich. When these two offices were separated under his successor, Leo von Caprivi, the system proved unworkable, so that when the Bavarian Prince Hohenlohe was appointed chancellor he was simultaneously made minister-president of Prussia. Bismarck as Prussian foreign minister "instructed" the Bundesrat's plenipotentiary for foreign affairs – an office held by a Bavarian appointee – but in reality was in absolute command of imperial foreign policy. The Prussian minister of war also functioned as an imperial minister. Imperial secretaries of state worked closely with the Prussian ministries and were appointed ministers without portfolio. In these early years Prussia clearly dominated the Reich; but Prussian influence was slowly undermined by the need to make concessions to the states, by the influence of imperial secretaries of state on Prussia, by the development of a distinct federal identity and by the need for Prussia to stand together with the states to uphold the status quo, and to resist the inroads of parliamentary democracy. The dominant position of Prussia within the empire was the most important factor hindering the development of parliamentary democracy. Prussia, with its House of Peers (*Herrenhaus*) and a parliament elected by a three-class system, was dominated by the aristocracy, the military, and an ultraconservative civil service. It would be a mistake, however, to imagine that the Reich was simply Prussia writ large. A distinct national identity developed that transcended the member states. This is most clearly seen in the emergence of the kaiser as a metapolitical symbol of national unity, and in the celebration of such national triumphs as the annual "Sedan Day." At the imperial level the monarchy was constitutional, and it was often forgotten that the kaiser was also an absolutist king of Prussia, pursuing a quite different agenda. As matters of national concern became increasingly important so too did the Reichstag.

The national parliament, the Reichstag, was much more than the "fig-leaf of despotism" that the socialist leader August Bebel claimed it to be, or the powerless institution of many later historians. Although no legislation could pass without the approval of the Bundesrat – and thus in effect without that of the kaiser, the chancellor or Prussia – no bill could become law unless it passed the Reichstag. The newly founded empire needed a vast number of new laws and these laws had to be approved by the Reichstag. The government had to ensure that this approval was forthcoming. Deals had to be negotiated and concessions granted. The government also needed money, and needed it in ever increasing amounts. The approval of the Reichstag was required for the annual budget and for additional increases in revenue. Military expenditure, which accounted for the bulk of the national budget, was excepted. It was covered first by seven-year bills (Septennate), and then by five-year bills (Quinquennate), which virtually excluded parliamentary debates over the military budget. Similarly, the bulk of federal revenue came through indirect taxation and customs duties, and these were issues that seldom came up for debate. Parliament could not of its own initiative either increase or decrease taxation. Nor could the Reichstag seriously consider refusing the budget for fear of disastrous reactions from an electorate that was becoming increasingly reliant on the largesse of the state. Since the Reichstag was virtually excluded from government, its role was largely negative. Riven with party strife it could never present a determined opposition, and was further weakened by the fact that it could be dismissed at any time. Bismarck would call snap elections and turn them into Bonapartist plebiscites, thus strengthening his own position and painting the Reichstag as an unpatriotic collection of impractical prattlers, and the opposition members as enemies of the state. Yet for all this the Reichstag was still an open forum for debate in which members enjoyed parliamentary immunity. Chancellors and ministers of state could be questioned, exposed, and embarrassed, but they could not be obliged to resign. With universal and equal manhood suffrage no parliament in the world was elected on a broader franchise. Its meetings were open to the public, the debates widely reported in the press. It was thus an essential part of the public sphere, the focus of hopes for a more open society, an important counterweight to Prussian–German autocracy.

Bismarck had forged an uneasy compromise between liberal nationalism and the authoritarian state. He was determined to fashion a functioning modern state and he knew that he could not do this without the support of bourgeois society and of informed public opinion. The ultraconservative Prussian monarchy could not be strengthened without making concessions to the modern world. This he did by creating something radically new: a German nation-state. The Reichstag was an integral part of this new structure, and Bismarck imagined that it would be a grateful, pliable, and conservative institution. This proved to be a serious miscalculation. With the dramatic changes in the social structure of Germany, and the consequent rise of democratic socialism, the number of "enemies of the state" within the Reichstag grew rapidly, soon to become the largest faction. Bismarck's Bonapartist rule was doomed to be swept away because of this fundamental structural failure, but the persistent marginalization and denigration of the Reichstag was to have disastrous consequences for the development of democracy in Germany.

The Reich had no government as such. The chancellor held the only federal executive office and thus the Reich chancellery in the Wilhelmstrasse, with its ever-expanding staff, was the center of power. Until 1876 this office was run by Rudolf Delbrück, whom Bismarck made responsible for all economic and financial questions. Legislation was drafted in the chancellery, thus gradually eclipsing the Bundesrat in this regard. Federal offices were needed to deal with the increasing amount of federal legislation, and to administer such matters of federal concern as the post, railways, the treasury, and the administration of justice. A federal administration for Alsace and Lorraine was established, along with a health office, a statistical bureau, and a host of other institutions, the most important of which was the High Court (*Reichsgericht*). It took years to build up a complex federal administration with extensive executive powers which was to overshadow the states and render the Bundesrat virtually powerless. There was still no imperial government, no cabinet, and no ministries. The secretaries of state were appointed by the kaiser and were the chancellor's subordinates. Only the chancellor was "responsible" in that he was answerable to the Reichstag, although parliament could only censor him but could not secure his dismissal. Bismarck dominated the secretaries of state, and made sure that they did not confer with the kaiser without his permission. His successors were more lax, preferring a collegial system which allowed the secretaries of state a considerable degree of independence. As a result something resembling a federal government developed. This in turn created new frictions between the Reich and Prussia, and the dialectical process continued whereby the Reich became more Prussian and Prussia more federal.

The Role of the Military

The military had always played a key role in Prussia and in a Reich forged by blood and iron it was the central institution. The German Reich was a military state, and German society was permeated by the military. "Human beings," Bismarck said "begin at the rank of lieutenant." The Prussian army was by far the largest of the four armies, and although the three other "contingents" owed allegiance to the kings of Bavaria, Württemberg, and Saxony respectively, they all came under the kaiser's command in time of war; only the Bavarian army remained independent in peacetime. The three contingents followed the Prussian lead in organization, instruction, and weaponry. The military budget and questions such as those of the size of the army and length of service were settled at the federal level. The army was thus Prussian rather than German. The Prussian minister of war, as chairman of the Bundesrat's Military Commission, served as a de facto federal minister, and the military thus played an essential role in strengthening Prussia's domination over the Reich. The military was outside the constitution, beyond parliamentary control, answerable only to the Prussian king and kaiser with his absolute power of command (*Kommandogewalt*). It was every bit as concerned with the enemy within as it was with its enemies beyond the borders of the Reich. It was ready to crush a revolution, break a strike, and disperse a demonstration and even to instigate a putsch. It was not bound to consult the civil authorities before acting. All matters pertaining to personnel were dealt with by the Military Cabinet, which worked closely with the kaiser. William II was to surround himself with a number of military cronies, who formed an informal *maison militaire* of considerable power and influence, that served further to strengthen his power of command. Mere civilians, who were deemed to have no understanding of military arcana, had no place within these circles.

The Prussian minister of war had responsibility for the budget, administration, and military justice. Inevitably there was enduring friction between the ministry and the military cabinet. Since the latter was a direct expression of the kaiser's power of command, with the minister answerable to the Reichstag, a number of important responsibilities were shifted from the ministry to the military cabinet. At the same time the spiraling cost of the military, particularly after 1898 when Germany began to build a high seas fleet, meant that the Reichstag had a far greater say in military affairs. It held the purse strings, and could determine how the funds were allocated. The war minister could no longer afford to hide behind the sacrosanct power of command and had to submit to rigorous questioning by parliamentarians. This in turn alienated the war minister from the kaiser and his entourage, who were alarmed by the prospect of the army becoming subordinated to parliament, the king and kaiser thus losing his power of command. Any concession to the Reichstag was taken as a sign of weakness, so that both the war minister and the chancellor were caught between the need to appease the monarch's obsession with his power of command, and the necessity for a degree of cooperation with the Reichstag. The slightest hint of a compromise with parliament caused an immediate hardening of the military front, so that by 1914 the Reichstag was only able to make very modest gains. The army remained arrogantly aloof, intensely hostile to parliament, a state within the state.

Although the kaiser, with his power of command, had absolute control over the military, it was hopelessly divided and lacking in any sense of direction. The War Ministry, the General Staff, the Military Cabinet, and the *maison militaire* were in a state of permanent conflict one with another, with incessant wrangling over areas of competence. This was compounded by inter-service rivalry with the navy, which in turn was riven with internal strife between different offices. There was no coherent military planning, no consistency in armaments policy, no serious preparation for a war which most people in responsible positions felt was both inevitable and desirable, and virtually no effort was made to adapt to changing circumstances. Nowhere was this more blatantly obvious than in the General Staff, whose carmine-striped demigods planned and plotted in splendid isolation and consequently to disastrous effect. The war was hardly over before the General Staff began planning for a preventive war, first against France, then also against Russia. The preventive war enthusiasts in the General Staff were held in check as long as Bismarck was chancellor. He found political solutions to the crises of 1874/5 and 1886/7 when the General Staff was raring to go. Moltke's successor, Count Alfred von Waldersee, argued in favor of a war against Russia, combined with a coup d'état against the Social Democrats, during his tenure from 1887 to 1891. He too was frustrated, first by Bismarck, then by Caprivi. Bismarck fought long and hard to keep the military under political control. His successors had to deal with the saber-rattling poseur William II, and lacked the strength of character to stand up to an increasingly influential military. The kaiser bypassed the Foreign Office and relied on reports from the military and naval attachés, who painted a grim picture of the bellicose intentions of Germany's neighbors. The chancellor and the civilians were never consulted when the General Staff drew up its war plans, and were excluded from the "War Council" of 1912.

Waldersee's successor, Count Alfred von Schlieffen, turned Clausewitz on his head and argued that war was far too serious a business for politicians to have any say in its conduct. The eponymous plan, on which he worked throughout his term of office, envisaged an invasion of France through neutral Belgium and Holland. The plan was shown in its various versions to three chancellors – Hohenlohe, Bülow, and Bethmann-Hollweg – but none of these men saw fit to examine its fateful political consequences. They felt it was inappropriate for mere civilians to question the expertise of a man who was widely regarded as a strategist of genius and a worthy successor to the great Moltke. Apart from a vague plan for an offensive in the east, the "*Ostaufmarschplan*," which was never seriously considered and was dropped entirely in 1913, the German army had only one war plan: an attack on France that was almost bound to involve Britain, because of the invasion of neutral Belgium and because of Germany's naval ambitions. The proposal to invade Holland was later dropped by Schlieffen's successor, the younger Moltke.

It was not only the civilians who were excluded from discussions about the details of military planning. Germany's ally Austria-Hungary was kept completely in the dark, and it was only in 1909, during the Bosnian crisis, that hints were dropped that they were planning an offensive in the west. At the same time Moltke promised his Austrian counterpart Conrad von Hötzendorf that Germany would stand by Austria under any circumstances should it become involved in a war in the Balkans. The chief of the General Staff was here clearly exceeding his remit, and was making a political commitment of incalculable consequence. The defensive Dual Alliance of 1879 was thus converted into a blank check for Austria to attack Serbia, even at the risk of Russian intervention, at which point Germany would join in by attacking France through Belgium. Britain would then probably be involved and Europe plunged into a terrible war, the length and outcome of which many experts were hesitant to predict.

The army never consulted the navy, which in turn cooked up a series of hare-brained plans which a number of naval strategists felt were bound to fail. Neither branch of the military bothered to contemplate the consequence of failing to break the British blockade, or the failure of the Schlieffen Plan, which a number of far-sighted soldiers thought at best was a highly risky gamble, and certainly not the infallible recipe for success that Schlieffen and his epigones imagined it to be. The military Cassandras who warned that the war was likely to be very lengthy were ignored, and no preparations were made for such an eventuality. The military was determined to remain outside the constitution by insisting that the power of command was sacrosanct. It separated itself from civilians by the exclusivity of its officer corps, its code of honor, and its separate code of law. This was to lead to a series of clashes with the civilians: over the reform of military law, over the size and social composition of the army, and over its relations with the civil authorities. Every such confrontation put the role of the military in question, and whittled away at its exclusive rights. As the foundations of the military monarchy were gradually under-mined the fronts began to harden, and the temptation to risk a war in the hope of overcoming these tensions became ever harder to resist.

In the 1860s two-thirds of the Prussian officer corps was aristocratic, and in the General Staff and the more upper-class regiments the proportion was far higher. As the army expanded the percentage of aristocrats naturally declined, thus precipi-tating a lengthy debate as to whether further expansion would change the whole character of the army, water it down, and render it unreliable in the event of domes-tic unrest and revolution. Was "character" more important than "brains"? Could an army with a high percentage of liberal bourgeois officers and Social Democratic proletarians in the other ranks maintain law and order at home and pull off another Sedan? The logic of the General Staff's planners called for a mass army, and the Schlieffen Plan had no chance of success without one, but the larger the army the greater the importance of the Reichstag which held the purse strings, and the sharp division between the civil and military would become increasingly blurred. General Keim's Army League with its raucous populist clamor for substantial army increases thus was viewed with horror by the kaiser's military entourage. That the Navy League, Admiral Tirpitz's child that took on a willful life of its own, had a similar plebiscitary moment was lost on the kaiser with his obsession with battleships.

The distinction between aristocratic and bourgeois officers has often been exag-gerated, and the distinction between technically-minded modernizing bourgeois and conservative traditionalist aristocrat is inadmissible. The aristocracy, which still made up more than half the officers of the rank of colonel and above in the Prussian army in 1913, set the tone. Officers were selected not by competitive examination, but by regimental commanders. They picked men of like mind and background. Only the sons of "respectable" bourgeois with sound views were selected. Pay was so wretched that a lieutenant in the smarter regiments needed a private income. Jews were excluded. As in the British army the tradesman's entrance was tightly shut. Bourgeois officers aped the ways of their aristocratic brothers-in-arms, subscribed to a common code of honor, and resolutely refused to be outdone in overbearing arrogance and contempt of mere civilians with their vulgar materialism. The appalling young subalterns, who were so brilliantly and savagely caricatured in the satirical magazine *Simplicissimus*, were unfortunately all too common. The naval officer corps was slightly less exclusive, but here too the aristocracy was over-represented. For all the increasing importance of technical skills and training, both officer corps remained a caste rather than a profession. But it was a caste that was widely admired and emulated in a process of "double militarism," whereby civilian society panegyrized military virtues, relished the prospect of war, lent its enthusiastic support to the Army and Navy Leagues, and forced its children into miniature military uniforms. The special status of the military and its widespread acceptance was a serious impediment to a modernization of the political system and the development of civil society.

Nationalism

Bismarck continually insisted that Germany was satiated and that war had to be avoided at all costs. It was only after his fall from power in 1890 that Germany was seized by the deadly hurrah-patriotism of the imperialist age, when many influential figures put forward the preposterous argument, later to be parroted by Adolf Hitler, that the country would either become a world power or face extinction. In 1871 there was a wave of patriotic bombast, but there was no call for Germany's frontiers to coincide with linguistic borders as Hoffmann von Fallersleben's poem "Deutschlandlied" of 1841 had demanded. Greater Germany was a dead letter, with only a few isolated intellectuals like the Orientalist, cultural philosopher, and anti-Semite Paul de Lagarde worried about the fate of Germans living beyond the borders of the new Reich. Irredentist ideas first came to the fore with the formation of the Pan-German League (*Alldeutscher Verein*) in 1891, but even they did not think in terms of an *Anschluss* with Austria. German Nationalism underwent a dramatic change in 1871. Where nationalism had once been a progressive force aimed at sweeping away the old regime and furthering the cause of constitutional liberties, it was now conservative and bent on maintaining the status quo in a militarized Prussian Germany. The nation was now identified with the state, any criticism of which was denounced as unpatriotic. Political parties which demanded reform were thus condemned as enemies of the Reich. The Social Democrats were denounced as "fellows without a fatherland" and parliamentary democracy seen as un-German.

Bismarck had appealed to liberal nationalists in his bid to create a united Germany. The Reichstag was their reward, and the Reichstag was an essential part of the nation. Many conservatives, with their distrust of the new-fangled and their misgivings about Bismarck's Bonapartism, took a great deal of time to reconcile themselves with this new nationalism, in part because the heritage of the democratic nationalism of an earlier age was never completely extirpated, and the Reichstag elected by universal manhood suffrage remained its lasting monument. It stood out like a sore thumb, a provocation to the new breed of nationalists. Its supporters – Social Democrats, the Catholic Center Party and some of the Independents – were marginalized and condemned as unpatriotic. Nevertheless, for most Germans the Reichstag, and not the kaiser, was the focus of national attention, the only truly representative body of the nation with all its shortcomings, deficiencies, and divisions.

There were considerable problems involved in finding suitable occasions for national holidays. January 18, the day on which William was proclaimed Emperor, only found resonance in Prussia. The "*Sedantag*," celebrating the victory over France, soon degenerated into an unpleasant demonstration of anti-French and anti-Catholic prejudices, and was consequently boycotted by Catholics. The kaiser's birthday soon became a popular excuse for national jollification. There was no official national anthem. The "*Wacht am Rhein*" and "*Heil dir im Siegerkranz*" (sung to the same tune as "God Save the King"), both with their martial and anti-French overtones, were unofficial anthems. The "*Deutschlandlied*," set to Haydn's tune from the "Kaiser" quartet, became increasingly popular in the 1890s, by which time "*Deutschland über alles*" had taken on a singularly unpleasant imperialist and irredentist flavor. There were similar problems with a flag. The revolutionary red, gold, and black tricolor of 1848 was unacceptable. The red from this flag was added to the black and white of Prussia and used as a flag for the merchant marine. It was then adopted by Tirpitz's navy and as such became a symbol of Germany's imperial might. Germany did not have either an officially recognized national anthem or flag until the Weimar Republic, by which time neither was treated with much respect or affection.

Modern nationalism is by its very nature exclusive. Herder's admonition to rejoice in the unique features of a culture as a contribution to humanity's rich multiplicity had long since been ignored; the wishy-washy cultural relativism of the post-modern a product of the distant future. The French were now seen as the "hereditary enemy," inferior but potentially dangerous. The indolent, drunken, uncultured, and Catholic Poles could only be tolerated as helots. Their co-religionists in the Reich were condemned as ultramontane and thus un-German. Social Democrats similarly had no fatherland. Jews, as outsiders, were increasingly seen as an insidious threat to this divided, threatened, and incomplete nation. The rest of the world could only offer sordidly materialistic "civilization" and cold "intellect," whereas the Germans had the boundless riches of "culture" and the deep insights of the "soul." An open, pluralistic, civil society had little chance of emerging when raucous imperialism became a component part of a project of national integration and homogeneity in which state and society were to become one.

German nationalism was not yet directed toward Germans living outside the frontiers of the Reich, but a substantial number of non-Germans lived within these boundaries. The Poles were by far the largest of these minorities. The Prussian province of Posen had been an integral part of the old kingdom of Poland and here, as in the southern parts of West Prussia, Polish national sentiment ran high, particularly among the Polish landed nobility and an upwardly mobile Polish middle class. In Upper Silesia and the remainder of West Prussia there was a substantial Polish population, but they were in subordinate positions, exploited as miners and agricultural workers, and initially had precious little national consciousness. The same was true of the 400,000 Poles working in the Ruhr. In response to the Germanizing policies of the Prussian government these Poles developed a vigorous sub-culture, centered at first around the Catholic Church, in which national sentiment was nurtured. There was no basis for an understanding between Germans and Poles. The Poles wanted nothing short of national self-determination; the Germans were bent on creating an ethnically and linguistically homogenous nation-state. Poles, most of whom were Jews, were expelled from Metz in the middle of winter by the new prefect, Guido Henckel von Donnersmarck, who was determined to Germanize Lorraine. The poverty-stricken and ill-educated proletarian Poles could be reduced to meek submission to the Reich and reconcile themselves to becoming loyal and obedient Prussians. Much the same was true of other minority groups such as the Masurians, Kashubs, and Lithuanians. They were second-class citizens, but so were Bavarian laborers and factory hands in the Rhineland.

Bismarck insisted that language was the key to the problem. He believed that German-speaking Poles would become aware of the advantages of living in Prussia, and would become reconciled to the state and to the Reich. It was a matter of indifference to him that they should continue to speak Polish at home. Liberals, and even Karl Marx, hardly saw things differently. For them Polish aspirations were backward and reactionary. Poland was a nest of superstition, underdevelopment, and ignorance, whereas Germany for all its faults was culturally a modern, industrialized, and progressive nation. The creation of a Polish nation-state would be a disastrous step backwards. Poles should move with the times and become good Germans. Prussia was a state in which the rule of law was applied and civil rights respected. Poles were able to win some significant concessions from the Prussian authorities by legal means, and they also had the vote. But there were strict limits to their freedom to maneuver. In areas where Germans and Poles lived side by side a virtual apartheid existed. Only German was allowed to be spoken in the schools, thousands of Poles (among them a large number of Jews) were expelled from the eastern provinces, and the anti-Catholic measures of the *Kulturkampf* were rigorously enforced. In 1894 the Eastern Marches Association (*Ostmarkenverein*) was founded in opposition to Caprivi's more liberal approach to the Polish question. It succeeded in making the government take a firmer line against the Poles. The ban on Polish in schools was re-introduced. A fund was established to buy up land owned by Poles and by 1907 some 800,000 acres were settled by 14,000 German peasants. The Poles fought back by refusing to sell their land to the Commission, and by buying up German land. The end result of all this repression was that Polish national sentiment intensified and, as in Britain with the Irish question, the fronts hardened. Pleas from liberals, like the great military historian Hans Delbrück, that Polish language and culture be respected, and the futile efforts to colonize Polish areas with German peasants be stopped, fell on deaf ears.

Jews in the New Germany

The Jewish community was another significant minority group. There were just over half a million Jews living in Germany in 1871. The Jewish community was now by and large urban, bourgeois, and prosperous. By 1910 their number had grown to just over 600,000, a much slower rate of population growth than that of the community at large. Jews now formed less than one percent of the total population. This was due to two principal factors. Firstly, like other well situated and highly educated middle class people they limited their families. Secondly, marriages with non-Jews were frequent, and in about 75% of such cases the children were not brought up in the Jewish faith. Although the Kaiser William Memorial Church in Berlin was popularly known as the "*Taufhaus des Westens*" – a play on words in which the name of the magnificent department store Kaufhaus des Westens further down the Kurfürstendamm was changed to become "Baptismal House." In fact precious few Jews, other than the offspring of mixed marriages, were baptized. Those that took this step almost invariably joined the Evangelical Church. The diminution of the Jewish community by small families and mixed marriages was partially offset by the arrival of large numbers of poor orthodox Jews from Russian Poland and Galicia. These "*Ostjuden*" mostly had large families and followed the general pattern of emigration from the country to the smaller towns, thence to the cities. Thus the Jewish population of Greater Berlin grew from just under 40,000 in 1871 to over 140,000 by 1910. Other cities like Frankfurt, Cologne, Munich, and Breslau witnessed similar increases.

There were still some poverty-stricken Jewish tinkers and craftsmen, most of whom were recent immigrants from the east, but a large proportion of Jews were involved in trade and banking. About 60 percent were classified as upper-middle class, a further 25 percent middle class. Of the one hundred richest men in Prussia in 1910 29 were Jewish. In 1908 ten of the 11 greatest fortunes in Berlin were Jewish. Only a small proportion of Jews were rich, but there was a disproportionate number of Jews among the super rich. Jews were also prominent in the professions and in education. From 1886 to 1914 about eight percent of students in Prussian universities were Jewish. In Berlin they constituted up to 25 percent of the pupils in the exclusive and highly competitive grammar schools (*Gymnasien*). Jewish girls won an even higher percentage of places in such schools and made up 14 percent of female university students by 1911. In 1907 six percent of doctors, 15 percent of lawyers and eight percent of journalists were Jewish. Three years later at Berlin University Jews made up 12 percent of university instructors (*Privatdozenten*), 8.8 percent of assistant professors (*Extraordinarien*), and 2.5 percent of the professors (*Ordinarien*). About half were in the medical faculty. Clearly it was exceedingly difficult for Jews to climb the promotional ladder, but they were still "over-represented" at the top by 150 percent.

In spite of the removal of all legal discrimination against Jews many barriers to their social advancement remained. With the exception of Bavaria, they were excluded from the officer corps of the army, which was an essential precondition of social acceptance. Far fewer Jews were admitted into the civil service than had the necessary qualifications, and none reached the top positions. The same was true of the teaching profession. Precious few were admitted into the Foreign Office, but the judiciary proved to be an exception. Four percent of the judges in Prussia were Jewish, and there were two Jews on the imperial supreme court (*Reichsgericht*). Its president was a baptized Jew. Jews were excluded from most clubs and associations, including university fraternities. Even rich and influential men like Bismarck's friend and banker Gerson Bleichröder, unquestionably a member of the elite, were not universally welcome. The police chief of Lübeck argued that the nouveaux riches provoked socialism and that there was thus little to choose between Bleichröder and Bebel. Many of Fontane's characters hold similar views. Liberals waited for Jews to assimilate, to rid themselves of their minority consciousness, to shed their "otherness," but there were too many closed doors for this to be possible.

The vast majority of Jews embraced German culture wholeheartedly. They dressed like Germans, ate the same food, and embraced the ideals of the "*Bildungsbürgertum*." Reform Jews were relaxed in their Sabbath observances, broke dietary laws, brought organs into their synagogues, and gave richly bound copies of Goethe and Schiller as bar mitzvah presents. Their bible was Leo Baeck's *The Nature of Judaism*, which adumbrated the principles of a tolerant, open, and modern approach to this ancient faith. Heine remarked that "Jews are like the people among whom they live, only more so." This was certainly true of Germany, where Jews saw themselves as Germans rather than Prussians, Bavarians, or Saxons; but the fervent patriotism of German Jews was unrequited. The assimilated reform Jewish bourgeois family was far more modern in its attitudes than its gentile counterpart, and was frequently criticized on this account. There were fewer children, it was less authoritarian and patriarchal, women enjoyed far greater freedom, and it championed culture and the broadest possible definition of education (*Bildung*).

Assimilation was never complete because Jews were never fully accepted as equals. They remained outsiders and as such had a unique perspective on a society and culture that in spite of everything they loved and respected. It is thus hardly surprising that Jews played a prominent role as critics and satirists, as journalists, and in the new disciplines of sociology and psychology. The desire to assimilate and the lack of acceptance resulted in an unfortunate dichotomy between self-satisfied arrogance and self-hatred. On the one hand they were proud of their exceptional achievements and convinced of their superiority, on the other they attributed their failure to fully assimilate to their very Jewishness, and over-compensated by an exaggerated attachment to things German. The pride and touchiness of the rejected was often combined with an autogenous antipathy resulting from a feeling of frustration and inadequacy.

The vast majority of German Jews wanted to be fully accepted as Germans, while at the same time remaining true to their faith. The "Central Association of German Citizens of Jewish Belief," founded in 1893, fought against all forms of discrimination and anti-Semitism and stood, as the name of the organization made clear, for the reconciliation of German Jews and gentiles within the Reich. The result of this desire to belong while preserving a high degree of specificity was a negative symbiosis, the outcome of which depended on the attitude of the wider community. What for some Jews was assimilation, for others was acculturation. The more the Jewish community wrestled with the problem of its identity the greater became the distance from those who had no such difficulties. Very few were attracted to Zionism, which both assimilated and orthodox Jews saw as an absurd youthful revolt. By 1914 the "German Zionist Association" had only 10,000 members, most of whom were German nationalists and had no desire to emigrate. For them Zionism was a promising solution to the problem of the *Ostjuden*, whose presence in Germany they found embarrassing. Youthful Zionists, however, rejected the stuffy philistine atmosphere of imperial Germany, and dreamt of building a new and freer society in Palestine.

Throughout the first part of the nineteenth century the lot of Jews in Germany had improved greatly. Anti-Semitism was still widespread, but it was relatively muted and was far from intellectually respectable. In the 1870s a new and even more pernicious form of pseudo-scientific and racial anti-Semitism developed. Earlier anti-Semitism was rooted in the traditional animosities between Christians and Jews, in criticism of religious orthodoxy with its emphasis on living in accordance with a complex set of immutable laws and injunctions, or in the discomfort and even hatred resulting from a confrontation with otherness. Religious bigotry and fanaticism were on the wane, German Jews were emancipated and to a considerable degree assimilated, so that these older prejudices lost their potency. The new anti-Semitism was based on the belief that the Jewish people posed a biological threat to other races.

The problem lies with the anti-Semites, and not with the Jews. Anti-Semites projected their fears, anxieties, and insecurities onto the constructed figure of "The Jew." The Jewish community was highly successful and prosperous, and thus the object of envy. It was also in many respects modern, and thus representative of all the problems of the modern age. It was a distinct and remote community, and thus alien and threatening. Germany in the 1870s experienced in an acute form the crisis of the modern. Society was in a state of social and economic upheaval, values were changing rapidly, a brief period of boom was followed by a lengthy depression, and many regretted the passing of a simpler, less hectic age. In such circumstances "The Jew" was a convenient scapegoat. With a widespread disillusionment with the individualism, rationalism, and liberalism of industrial society which left so many disillusioned, frustrated, and resentful people struggling behind, anti-Semitism found widespread support. But it was not merely the illiberal, irrational, and resentful wannabes who fanned the flames of anti-Semitism. There was an intolerant and totalitarian moment within liberalism itself that allowed no space for those that did not subscribe to the liberal, Protestant, and national code. There was precious little room here for pluralism and openness. The other, whether Catholic, Socialist, Pole or Jew, was excluded.

Plate 12 The Berlin Stock Exchange. This 1889 drawing by E. Thiel was published in *Illustrierte Zeitung*, a widely circulated periodical. Many of the traders have stereotypical Semitic features

The new, virulent, and secular anti-Semitism became widespread when the speculative bubble that began in 1871 burst three years later. The *Gartenlaube* (*The Arbour*), a popular journal aimed at the petite bourgeoisie, published a series of articles blaming the stock exchange crash on Jewish speculators. Many a ribald comment was made based on the fact that the Berlin stock exchange was on the Jerusalemer Strasse. The conservative *Kreuzzeitung* ascribed the responsibility for the crash to an unsavory alliance of Jews, Bismarck, and Liberals. Such sentiments were echoed in the gutter press and in hundreds of pseudo-scientific works, the most notable of which was by Eugen Dühring, whose *The Jewish Question as a Racial, Moral and Cultural Problem* was published in 1881. The author, who was something of an academic star, is best known to posterity because of Engels' robust attack on his half-baked socialist ideas. Dühring argued that Jewish identity was racially determined and thus assimilation was impossible. No amount of baptismal water could wash away this biological stigma, and the only answer to the Jewish question was expulsion.

Anti-Semitism was also part of the new nationalist creed and was expounded in intoxicating prose by the historian Heinrich von Treitschke in the pages of the *Preußischen Jahrbücher*, a quality journal of which he was the editor. He demanded that Jews should become assimilated to the point that to all intents and purposes they ceased to be Jews. He distanced himself from the rabble-rousing popular anti-

Semitism of the day, but in doing so made his brand of anti-Semitism acceptable in "respectable" society. He admired the Jewish community for its industriousness, its culture, and its sense of tradition, but he rejected what he felt was its increasing materialism, vulgarity, and scrambling ambition. He expressed his frustration in the poisonous phrase "The Jews are our misfortune," which was to become the motto of Julius Streicher's obscene publication *Der Stürmer*. Treitschke would have been appalled to find himself in the unsavory company of the Nazis' chief Jew-baiter, but he cannot be absolved from responsibility.

The anti-modernist, anti-capitalist, chauvinistic anti-Semitism of these new "racial" anti-Semites was often combined with the older forms of religious anti-Semitism to make a particularly heady brew. Such was the case with the Christian Social (Workers') Party formed by the Protestant court preacher Adolf Stoecker in 1878. He was an electrifying demagogue who hoped to woo the working class away from the Social Democrats with a mixture of rugged Protestantism and social reform. The present malaise was blamed on Jewish speculative capitalism. Stoecker also denounced Social Democracy as a Jewish movement, and henceforth anti-Semitism became a twin-pronged attack on socialism and capitalism, both seen as part of a worldwide Jewish conspiracy. Stoecker was closely associated with William II, whose notions of becoming a "social kaiser" owed much to his ideas. But there were many misgivings at court about Stoecker, the demagogue who courted the racial anti-Semitic riff-raff. As the economy pulled out of a recession his brand of radical anti-Semitism began to lose its appeal, and rumors that he kept a Jewish mistress damaged his reputation both as a principled anti-Semite and as a man of God. Other smaller anti-Semitic parties also withered on the vine. So ended the first round of political anti-Semitism and the Jewish community breathed a sigh of relief.

Anti-Semitism was no longer a major issue in election campaigns, but it had not disappeared. It was no longer a pressing concern for the political parties, but it was deeply ingrained in a number of the associations which played such an important role in Wilhelmine Germany. The "General German Craftsmen's Association" (*Allgemeine Deutsche Handwerkerbund*), founded in 1882, represented the interests of a large group that was becoming increasingly marginalized by the victory march of industrial capitalism. This was a group that had sided with the reactionaries in 1848 for fear that the liberal market economy would result in these proud independent producers being reduced to the ranks of the proletariat. Now they seized upon the idea that industrial capitalism was "Jewish." They lent their support to Stoecker's Christian Social Party, and after its demise they trumpeted their anti-Semitism in the pages of their newspapers and at their national conventions. Similar beliefs were held by the butchers, bakers, and candlestick makers who were members of the "Imperial German Middle Class Association" (*Reichsdeutschen Mittelstandsverband*), founded in 1911, which declared all-out war on the "yellow and red internationals." White-collar employees organized in the "*Deutschnationale Handlungsgehilfenverband*" of 1893 echoed these ideas.

The "Farmers' League" (*Bund der Landwirte*) was the largest and most influential of these associations which, from its inception in 1893, adopted a harshly anti-Semitic tone. Jews were expressly excluded from membership and capitalism, liberalism, socialism, interest payments, and cattle dealing were all denounced as "Jewish." Dairy farmers coined the popular phrase "Jew tallow" for margarine. Anti-Semitism was deliberately used to whip up popular support for the league and for the Conservative Party which was its organized political wing. Relations between the league and the Conservatives were often strained. The party reluctantly realized the need to win electoral support as the Reichstag grew in importance, but it had severe reservations about the league's demagogic tactics. The league also threw its support behind anti-Semitic candidates who ran against conservatives, and the marriage of convenience between the league and party was never particularly harmonious.

Anti-Semitism was widespread in a number of other national associations and student fraternities, but it was still not considered quite respectable to be openly anti-Semitic. Fontane's Dubslav von Stechlin, the hero of his masterly novel *Der Stechlin*, felt that his honest and trustworthy Jewish moneylender has been corrupted by the vulgar materialism of the times and had grown a "cloven hoof." The sympathetic pastor Lorenzen expresses a nuanced version of Stoecker's views with which the author clearly identifies. In Fontane's *Effi Briest*, Instetten's enthusiasm for Wagner's music is said to have been due to the maestro's position on the Jewish question, coupled with his own nervous condition. Fontane as theater critic had little patience for Lessing's plea for tolerance toward Jews in *Nathan the Wise*. It would be going too far to charge Fontane, the mildest and most open-minded of men, with anti-Semitism. He deplored the vulgarity and materialism of the new Germany in such novels as *Frau Jenny Treibel*, and hankered after the good old days when life was simpler, people knew their station, and God was in his heaven. He, like his character Wüllersdorff in *Effi Briest*, resigned himself to an acceptance of the world as it was, for all the absurd conventions and customs to which society paid homage. Fontane was a liberal, certainly no reactionary, deeply suspicious of all ideologies, but the very fact that such a admirable person could even toy with the anti-Semitic camp is an indication of the insidious undertow of anti-Semitism in the Germany of his day. Not all craftsmen, shopkeepers and shop assistants, farmers, and students were anti-Semites; in fact relatively few were in any meaningful sense of the term. The Social Democratic leader August Bebel, who was himself a typical craftsman, spoke for many when he denounced anti-Semitism as the socialism of fools. France, Russia, and Austria-Hungary far outbid Germany as centers of anti-Semitism, and the sneaky underhand English brand of anti-Semitism was probably even more pernicious. But anti-Semitism was on the political agenda, was to take root and to have an unimaginably horrific outcome. For this reason it needs to be discussed in such detail.

Germany did indeed produce more than its fair share of hair-raising anti-Semitic theories. They combined the culturally pessimistic notions of the degeneration of civilization to a level of brutish mediocrity, the result of a racial struggle in which the creative Aryan Germans were undermined and enfeebled by parasitic Jews, with highly compatible social-Darwinist notions. Anti-Semites embraced race theorists and the result was a devil's brew of noxious ideas which Max Weber was to describe as "zoological nationalism." A people and the nation were formed not as the result of a historical process, as even an anti-Semite like Treitschke argued, but by blood. Hence all traces of Jewish and other non-German elements must be extirpated, Christianity rid of all traces of Judaism, the Germans should become more German, and racial purity restored. The Jew represented everything that was alien to the *Volk* and un-German. Good and creative Germans were locked in battle with evil and parasitic Jews.

Traditional anti-Semitism among Catholics was reinforced by the widespread belief that the new German Empire, with which they had yet to become reconciled, was the work of liberals and Jews. This prejudice was reinforced with Bismarck's persecution of the Catholic Church in the *Kulturkampf* in which the Jews were also felt to have had a hand. It is greatly to the credit of Ludwig Windthorst and the leadership of the Center Party that they convinced their followers that as a perse-cuted minority they should respect the rights of other minorities. As a result the Center Party earned the anathema of the anti-Semites. Whereas German Catholics thus turned their backs on political anti-Semitism, conservatives, as we have seen, instrumentalized it by means of the Farmers' League in order to win mass support. In doing so they let the genie out of the bottle. Conservative anti-Semitism, based on a snobbish attachment to rural values and Protestantism, a dislike of industrial society, socialism, modernism, and intellectuals, never sat well with rabble-rousing popular anti-Semitism. But by tolerating it and using it they nurtured a plant that was to produce poisonous fruit.

Liberals were ideologically opposed to anti-Semitism and founded the "Associa-tion for Defence Against Anti-Semitism" in 1891. On the other hand, liberals had no compunction in making electoral pacts with anti-Semites in order to block the election of Social Democrats. Of all the parties these last were the most principled opponents of anti-Semitism. Decried as the Jewish and un-German "Red Interna-tional" they had little choice in the matter; but there were elements of anti-Semitism even among socialists. As anti-capitalists they could not always desist from joining in the chorus denouncing the "Yellow International," and even Karl Marx could not overcome the temptation to make snobbish anti-Semitic jibes, remarkably similar in tone to those of Treitschke.

By the 1890s the German Jewish community had grounds for optimism. Politi-cal anti-Semitism was on the wane and there were only isolated instances of violence against Jews. Their rights were guaranteed by the law, upheld by the gov-ernment, and supported by most political parties. They had achieved positions of great distinction in all walks of life. There was still widespread discrimination and prejudice, but there was no other country where they had done so well. They looked confidently toward the future, when the last remainders of the atavistic bigotry that had plagued them for millennia would fade away, and there would be no Jewish question, no Jewish problem. German Jews were proud and even grateful to be

German. They went enthusiastically to war in August 1914 and fought valiantly for kaiser and Fatherland. Then things began to go sour. Denunciations of Jewish war profiteers and skrimshankers were combined with attacks on Jewish doves and pacifists. Jews were seen as a particularly sinister section of the "enemy within," and as bearing heavy responsibility for the "stab in the back" of 1918. The hopes of the prewar years were dashed, the future uncertain.

7
Bismarck's Germany

The construction of the German Empire was brought about by a complex series of often contradictory alliances. Liberals were wholeheartedly behind Bismarck's efforts to modernize the economy by removing all remaining barriers to the freedom of trade and commerce, to establish a uniform code of law, and to eliminate the last vestiges of feudalism from the administration. The Center Party stood for states' rights and opposed all efforts to strengthen the federal government. Liberals in turn were violently anti-Catholic and denounced the ultramontane church as hostile to the national interest, a foreign body, a nest of superstition and backwardness. Many conservatives were strongly opposed to Bismarck's enthusiasm for a capitalist market economy, particularly in the form personified by his Jewish friend and banker, Gerson Bleichröder, who became the subject of vicious attacks in the conservative *Kreuzzeitung*. They vigorously resisted his efforts to reform the administration, particularly at the local level. They had serious reservations about his attack on the Catholic Church, for in their Protestant eyes even Catholicism was preferable to Godlessness. Above all, they were appalled that a man whom they had thought was one of their own should be allied with the liberals.

Bismarck's closest associates in the early and critical years were liberals. Prominent among them were Rudolph von Delbrück, the head of his chancellery, who was known as the "chief of general staff of the free traders," the banker Otto von Camphausen as Prussian finance minister, and the fanatically anti-Catholic Adalbert Falk as Prussian minister of education. His alliance with the liberals was sealed in the common attack on the Catholic Church known as the "Battle of Cultures" (*Kulturkampf*). The Center Party, the Catholic Church's political wing, resisted all Bismarck's parliamentary initiatives, thus binding him closer to the liberals. The closer he came to the liberals, the deeper became the rift between him and the conservatives. The black reactionary Prussian of 1848, the scourge of the liberals and nationalists, now appeared as the figurehead of the National Liberals.

The *Kulturkampf*

The German Empire of 1871 was a secular state, and although the majority of the ruling elite was Protestant, it had no specific denominational affiliation. As a modern secular state it was involved in far more issues involving the individual than had been its absolutist predecessor; indeed it was legitimized by the very fact that it intervened in the personal lives of it subjects. It demanded that they sacrifice their lives in war, set the parameters within which the economy functioned, and took over responsibility for the education of the young and the welfare of the elderly and the disadvantaged. It alone had the legal right to join couples together in matrimony. Modernity involved more state and the gradual elimination of institutions that mediated between the individual and the state. This is the reverse of the situation today, when modernization implies less state, a greater degree of deregulation, and the growth of civil society. The new German Empire thus inevitably became involved in a renewed conflict between church and state, often represented as a renewal of the struggle between pope and emperor, so that "Canossa" soon became an over-worked cliché.

The Catholic Church emerged from the First Vatican Council in 1870 as anti-modern, anti-national, integralist, ultramontane, authoritarian, and fiercely opposed to liberalism and democracy in all its forms. The Franco-Prussian war broke out the day after the doctrine of Papal Infallibility was pushed through the Vatican Council, in spite of the reasoned objections of the majority of the German bishops. The French and German cardinals hurried north, cutting one another dead when they stretched their legs on the platform at Domodossola. The papacy might be infallible, but it had lost the last vestiges of its temporal power in the process of Italian unification, and one leading cleric greeted the news of Prussia's victory over France with the horrified exclamation that the world was falling apart. The enemy was no longer the emperor, but the liberals and parliamentarians, along with the secular society for which they stood. "Progress, liberalism and modern civilization" had already been roundly condemned as among the 80 iniquities listed in Pius IX's encyclical, the "Syllabus of Errors" of 1864.

The churches in Germany, then and now, were in a unique relationship with the state. Catholics and Protestants paid and pay a portion of their taxes toward the upkeep of the church. Theological faculties of universities in which priests and ministers were prepared for ordination were state funded. The state had a say in the appointment of bishops, and kept a close watch on their activities. In return the churches demanded influence over education and matrimonial law. The situation was further complicated by the divisions between Catholics and Protestants. About one third of the population was Catholic, the other two-thirds Protestant.

Liberals, whether nominally Catholic or Protestant, set out to liberate the Catholic faithful from a hidebound, reactionary, and irrational clergy. Thus they stood for secular education and for secular marriages. They were determined to reduce the influence of ultramontane priests and bishops over the church. They declared all-out war against the Jesuits, whom they saw as the storm troopers of ultramontanism. They won a number of significant victories in the 1860s in Bavaria and Baden and there were a number of anticlerical riots. The secularization trend intensified with the foundation of the German Empire, and the Vatican Council and the promulgation of the doctrine of papal infallibility were clear indications of Rome's siege mentality. In spite of this hardening of the fronts the majority of German bishops were moderate and anxious to avoid a confrontation with the new state. Their spokesman, Archbishop Ketteler of Mainz, called for cooperation between church and state, and even Pius IX, the "prisoner" in the Vatican once the French troops had left, reluctantly accepted the new Germany.

That the issue of the role of the Catholic Church became such a pressing political issue is largely due to Bismarck's reaction to the Center Party. The party was founded in 1870 to look after the interests of Catholics in northern Germany. It then joined forces with southern German particularists and anti-Prussians, along with Poles, Guelphs, and the disaffected citizenry of Alsace and Lorraine. The party thus had serious reservations about the Reich and was open to the charge of being ultramontane, and even un-German. Its great strength lay in the fact that it was the only genuine people's party in Germany. Its supporters ranged from lofty aristocrats to peasants, from industrial magnates to industrial workers, from prosperous professionals to lowly craftsmen. Furthermore it drew its support from all over the Reich, wherever there were Catholics. In the first Reichstag debate in 1871 the Center Party requested that the government should support the pope's efforts to restore his temporal power, in other words openly to confront the kingdom of Italy. Their second motion was that the fundamental rights of the church guaranteed in the Prussian constitution should be applied throughout the Reich. Bismarck, who believed that such rights should be within the jurisdiction of the states, seized the opportunity to denounce the Center Party as being solely interested in the sectional interests of the church, and not in matters of national concern. Bismarck the Protestant Junker shared many of the anti-Catholic prejudices of his estate and his coreligionists, but his antipathy toward the Center Party was based more on its opposition to the strong federal government and to the dominant role of Prussia, which were central to his vision of the new empire. It was in his very nature to seek confrontation with his political opponents, and he thus decided to launch a "preventive war" against the Catholic "enemies of the Reich." The time was propitious. The church was in turmoil after the Vatican Council. "Old Catholics" refused to accept the dogma of papal infallibility and were excommunicated, whereupon the Prussian state refused to dismiss those among them who held teaching positions in universities, seminaries, and schools, as well as chaplains in the military. This was combined with a ban on priests holding administrative positions in schools in the Polish-speaking provinces in an attempt to end their baneful influence over a basically loyal and docile population. Elsewhere in Germany the states adopted a less heavy-handed approach.

The next phase in the *Kulturkampf* came somewhat surprisingly from Catholic Bavaria, which introduced legislation at the federal level in 1871 banning priests from making subversive statements in their sermons. In addition to this "Pulpit

Paragraph," the proposal by the Reichstag majority that the Jesuit order be banned was accepted by the Bundesrat in the following year. Thenceforth the *Kulturkampf* was carried on at the state level. Adalbert Falk, the Prussian minister of education, was its most aggressive champion. He significantly reduced the influence of the Catholic Church over education, interfered in the curricula of theological faculties and seminaries, and sought greater influence over church appointments. The church fought back, whereupon the state cut off funds, closed down seminaries, and seized church property. Bishops were dismissed, imprisoned, or exiled. Catholic associations and their press were subjected to constant harassment by the police. In 1875 virtually all religious orders were banned in Prussia, with the exception of those involved in nursing and the instruction of young girls. Funds were denied to all dioceses that resisted in the "Bread Basket Law." Parishes could now elect their own priests, and the administration thereof was entrusted to lay councils. Civil marriages were made compulsory in Prussia in 1874 and in the Reich one year later. In the German states there were similar moves to secularize education, limit the activities of the religious orders, and interfere in the administration of the church. But with the possible exception of Baden these measures were nowhere enforced with the same rigor and brutality as in Prussia.

Pius IX did not hesitate to counterattack. In 1875 he threatened to excommunicate all those who obeyed these oppressive laws. Bishops and priests became popular martyrs. In Prussia almost one quarter of the parishes no longer had a priest, and eight of the 12 dioceses were without a bishop. The longer the church came under attack the more determined was the will to resist. Similarly, the Center Party, which was made up of so many conflicting interests, stood firmly united in opposition. Gradually the forces of the *Kulturkampf* began to crumble. Conservatives became increasingly concerned at the Godlessness of some of their allies and feared that the whole affair was bringing discredit upon both Prussia and the Reich. On the left the likes of Eduard Lasker were appalled at the violation of fundamental civil rights and freedom of conscience. The Center Party leader, Ludwig Windthorst, skillfully played upon misgivings in the government camp. He appealed to conservatives to uphold traditional Christian values, warned liberals of the dangers of excessive state power, and, for the benefit of the left, stressed the importance of civil liberties. Resistance was also growing at the grass-roots level. Secularization was seen as a vicious attack on a customary way of life. The almighty state tried to sweep away traditional holidays and festivities. Haughtily arrogant officials looked down upon ordinary folk as mired in a backward, superstitious, ignorant world of miracles, pilgrimages, and idolatry. They were determined to defend their little universe against the ravages of the modern. Political Catholicism thus became more radical, more populist, and paradoxically, given its constituency, more modern. With their support waning, both on the left and on the right, the liberals became even more intransigent. The *Kulturkampf* for them was a life-and-death struggle for freedom, enlightenment, modernity, the economy, the state, and the nation, against the "Black International." It was indeed for them a struggle for Culture in which no quarter could be let. They became so obsessed with this fight that they overlooked the far

Plate 13 Bismarck by Franz von Lembach, c. 1880. © BPK

more important question of changing the power structure of the Reich. They had abandoned themselves to Bismarck on whom they were now totally dependent.

Bismarck and the liberals made a curious alliance, and many differences remained between them. They could march shoulder to shoulder in the *Kulturkampf*, but the old issue of the army had not been laid to rest with the indemnity vote, and it reappeared in 1874 when Bismarck, at the urging of the military, wanted a guarantee of permanent funding for the army. This proposal for an "Eternal Law" (Aeternat) met with the adamantine resistance of the liberals who wanted to retain the system of annual budgets. The struggle was bitter but in the final resort Bismarck still needed the liberals, and they did not want to run the risk of an election. The result was a compromise whereby the army estimates were guaranteed for seven years (Septennat). The liberals lost a number of rounds with the chancellor over legal reform, but at least they were able to frustrate his attempt to broaden the concept of political offenses, punishable by law. The brilliant rhetorician and left-wing liberal, Eduard Lasker, denounced these proposals as the "rubber paragraphs," since they were open to a very wide range of interpretations. The liberals had no choice but to put up with Bismarck, stand up to his bullying tactics, try to extend the powers of the Reichstag, and wait for more propitious times. The kaiser was born in 1797, Bismarck in 1815, and their days were numbered. The crown prince, with his English wife, was known to have liberal sympathies. Liberals thus nurtured the reversionary interest, much to Bismarck's anger and disgust. Bismarck in turn detested Lasker, his outstanding opponent in the Reichstag, who opened the liberals up to the left. He therefore began to mend his bridges with the conservatives as a counterweight to the left-wing liberals. The liberals had played a significant part in molding the Reich, but now their influence was waning as Bismarck decided upon a radical change of course in economic and fiscal policy, and turned his attention to the struggle against Social Democracy.

Social Democracy and the New Germany

The socialist movement in Germany was still in its infancy, but it was growing apace. Rapid industrialization swelled the ranks of the proletariat, the movement's natural constituency. Bismarck had calculated that universal manhood suffrage would enfranchise a conservative peasantry, as had been the case in Napoleon III's France, but as Germany gradually changed from being an agricultural to an industrial society, the urban working-class vote steadily increased. In 1871 Germany had only eight towns with a population over 100,000; by 1910 there were 48. In 1871 a mere 4.9 percent of the population lived in urban areas; by 1910 this had risen to 21.3 percent. An increasing number of workers who lived in small, rural communities used the ever-expanding railway network to commute to their workplaces in industrial centers. For them the clear distinction between rural and urban was rapidly eroding. The appeal of socialism grew as boom turned to bust and the depression set in. Furthermore, the socialists, although in practice moderate and reformist, adopted a revolutionary Marxist rhetoric, which terrified the respectable bourgeoisie. Talk of the class struggle, the public ownership of the means of production and exchange, and the dictatorship of the proletariat seemed even more threatening after the experience of the Paris Commune, and with the "machines infernelles" of wild-eyed Russian, Italian, and Spanish anarchists. Such fears were deliberately fanned by Bismarck, but they were very real and understandable. The "Red Menace" was much more than an electoral ploy or a rhetorical stratagem.

There were two prescriptions for dealing with socialism. Bismarck, who always saw everything in terms of black and white, friend and foe, argued in favor of repression and had wide support in Prussian government circles. The old slogan of 1848 "only soldiers help against democrats," now read "only soldiers help against social democrats." An alternative approach was suggested by Hermann Wagener, an editor of the *Kreuzzeitung*, and a progressive conservative who wanted to open up the Conservative Party to become a genuine people's party. He argued that repression would simply strengthen the socialists and that the only solution was a comprehensive program of social reform that would do away with the grievances on which

the socialists thrived. Bismarck however wanted first to crush the socialist movement before considering social reform. The socialist leaders and Reichstag deputies
Bebel and Liebknecht were arrested in 1872, and charged with treason for remarks
they had made about the conduct of the war and the Paris Commune. They were
very well treated in a minimum-security prison; Bebel welcomed the opportunity to
at last have time to read *Das Kapital* and took great pride in the prize radishes
he grew in the prison garden. After their release the two socialist parties, the
Lassalleans and the Eisenachers, were united at the Gotha conference of 1875 to
form the German Social Democratic Party (SPD). The party's program was essentially Marxist, although Karl Marx vented his ire at the Lassallean deviations contained therein in his powerful pamphlet: *Critique of the Gotha Program*.

Liberal concerns about the violation of basic civil liberties implied in Bismarck's
proposals to combat Social Democracy further estranged the chancellor from the
party, and this at a time when the Reich was in increasing financial difficulties. The
French had paid their reparations in full and income from customs duties and indirect taxes was dwindling as the depression set in, so the federal government had to
go cap in hand to the states and ask for an increase in their supplementary payments known as "Matriculatory Contributions." The tax system was inefficient and
grossly unfair, weighed heavily on the poor, and was desperately in need of reform.
Bismarck's aim was to increase the revenues of the Reich and thus hopefully eliminate the dependence of the federal government on the states. At the same time he
hoped that the states, particularly Prussia, could alleviate the burden of local taxation and the disproportionate taxes on agriculture which were the direct cause of
so much social unrest. This implied shifting the burden of taxation from direct taxes
which went to the states, to indirect taxes which went to the Reich. He focused
exclusively on strengthening the Reich against the states and seems to have overlooked the fact that the poor would be hardest hit by increases in indirect taxation,
and that this would lead to further unrest and consequently to an increase in the
appeal of Social Democracy.

From Free Trade to Protectionism

Bismarck proposed nationalizing the railways and establishing a tobacco monopoly,
as in France and Austria-Hungary, in a further attempt to bolster federal revenue.
Such interventionist initiatives were anathema to many liberals, as were proposals
to increase customs duties, the proceeds of which would go directly to the Reich.
The depression, which began in 1873, was the first major crisis of industrial society
and had all the concomitant side effects: a stock exchange crash, rising unemployment, falling demand, bankruptcies, and widespread uncertainty, fear, and discontent. Many, both from the left and from the right, felt that the culprit was the
unbridled liberal capitalism which the Germans labeled "*Manchesterismus*." Liberalism was now discredited in the eyes of many, for them hope for the future lay
either in state intervention or in socialism.

The agrarians had long been enthusiastic free traders. They exported in large quantities, mainly to England, and in return imported British agricultural machinery. Now they faced competition from cheap grain from Russia and North America and began to clamor for protection. The same was true in the iron and steel industries where the market was swamped with imports and demand was falling drastically. Textile manufacturers were also insistent that they could not survive without a helping hand from the state. Powerful interest groups lent their enthusiastic support to Bismarck's proposals for tariff increases, chief among them the Central Association of German Industrialists (*Zentralverband Deutscher Industrieller*), founded in 1876. Economic historians have shown that the situation was far from being as grim as contemporaries imagined, and there is much talk of the "myth" of the great depression. Be that as it may, subjective factors are vital in determining behavior, particularly in the marketplace, and there can be no doubt that it was widely believed that these were the worst of times.

Tariff increases provided Bismarck with an ideal issue to help him in his change of course. They had widespread popular support, would reduce the federal government's reliance on the matriculatory contributions, strengthen the central government, and help Bismarck distance himself still further from the free-trading liberals around Lasker. The increasing importance of interest groups resulted in a corresponding diminution of the importance of the political parties. Indeed the National Liberal Party, which represented a plurality of interests, was destined to fall apart. In order to create a new political alignment Bismarck had to end the *Kulturkampf* and thus finally end his reliance on liberal support. The election of a new pope, the moderate and conciliatory Leo XIII, in 1878 provided an opportunity to end this unfortunate and profoundly damaging episode. Anti-Catholic measures were toned down, but they did not disappear. The "pulpit paragraph" remained in force, civil marriages were still compulsory, and the ban on the Jesuits was not lifted. Bismarck now drove a wedge between the pope and the Center Party. The pope, who had severe reservations about political Catholicism, at times intervened and forced the party to toe the chancellor's line. Bismarck hoped that the tensions between the pope and the party would result in Catholic voters turning their backs on the party. The party was exceedingly reluctant to take its marching orders from Rome, and the voters remained faithful. In 1886 and 1887 the Prussian government made peace with the Catholic Church in a series of measures, and the *Kulturkampf* was officially buried. The wounds took a long time to heal. Catholics saw themselves as an endangered minority, still subject to discrimination, not yet fully integrated into German society. It was not until after World War II that Catholics were fully integrated into the political process. This was another of Konrad Adenauer's great achievements.

The change of course was slow and hesitant. The first sign was the dismissal of the free-trader Delbrück in 1876. The National Liberals lost a number of seats in the elections in the following year and the Lasker wing's influence was greatly diminished. Bismarck negotiated for months on end with the National Liberal leader Bennigsen, suggesting that he become a de facto vice chancellor, but he felt that such a position would leave him seriously compromised. Bismarck's renewed attack on free trade and his proposal for a tobacco monopoly in 1878 finally convinced Bennigsen to end these interminable and fruitless discussions. A number of free-trading Prussian ministers resigned that year, among them Camphausen from finance, Aschenbach from industry, and Friedrich Eulenburg from the interior. But Bismarck was still not totally convinced of the need for and expediency of higher tariffs, or for an alliance with the Center Party. He still hoped that he could bully the National Liberals into compliance with his wishes. The political deadlock was broken when a mentally deranged journeyman plumber took a pot shot at the kaiser on May 11 1878. The would-be assassin, Max Hödel, had been briefly a member of SDAP but had been expelled for dipping his hands into the party's coffers, whereupon he had joined Stoecker's Christian Socials. Bismarck claimed that the socialists had masterminded the affair, and an anti-socialist law was placed before the Reichstag. The predictable result was another setback for Bismarck. The majority of the Reichstag refused to support this ill-considered bill which, by aiming at the curtailment of essential civil liberties, amounted in Bennigsen's words to a "war against the Reichstag." Bismarck had hoped that the liberals would abandon their few remaining principles, but he had made a serious miscalculation.

The Anti-Socialist Laws

Less than a month after the first assassination attempt, another crackpot managed to seriously wound the kaiser. The perpetrator, Dr Nobiling, an unemployed scholar and anarchist, promptly committed suicide. Bismarck seized the opportunity to deal the liberals a crushing blow. By pulling out all the stops, he bullied the Bundesrat into agreeing to dissolve the Reichstag. Bismarck fought the election campaign on a platform of anti-socialist laws and economic and financial reform, in the hope of securing a majority made up of conservatives and sympathetic National Liberals, possibly with Center Party support. With widespread discontent over the state of the economy, and with an assassination attempt on a popular kaiser lending credence to the chancellor's insistence that there was a very real revolutionary threat, and with the massive support of powerful interest groups, the campaign was successful. The National Liberals dropped from 128 to 99 seats. The Lasker liberals and the Progressives also lost seats. The two conservative parties made substantial gains, and the Center Party held its own. The result was a majority of deputies who supported the proposed tariffs, drawn from the conservatives, Center Party, and about a quarter of the National Liberals.

Using British legislation against Irish nationalists as a model, Bismarck now had little difficulty in securing a majority for his anti-socialist laws. The National Liberals, even the extreme left of the party, gritted their teeth and voted in favor, fearing that otherwise Bismarck would call another round of elections in which they would suffer further humiliation. The Anti-Socialist Laws declared Social Democracy, and any other "revolutionary" movements, to be enemies of the state, of society, and the constitution. All public activities by the party were forbidden. Its press was banned, party activists could be denied a means of earning a living, and could even be exiled. It was a draconian measure, but there were a number of loopholes. Party members could still sit in the Reichstag, they could stand for election, and could conduct electoral campaigns. Implementation of the laws was left to the individual states, and it was thus applied with widely varying degrees of severity. It was to apply for 12 years, and the debate over its renewal was to contribute to Bismarck's downfall. The laws were bound to fail, just as the *Kulturkampf* had failed. Catholics stood together against a common threat and the socialist working class showed admirable solidarity with their party. The *Kulturkampf* strengthened the Center Party, and support for the SPD increased significantly between 1878 and 1890.

Liberals in Bismarck's Germany

Bismarck had a majority in the Reichstag for tariff reform, and after lengthy debates and many unsatisfactory compromises a general agreement was reached to increase tariffs. They were very modest in the agricultural sector, and nowhere could they be called protective, but they brought in substantial additional revenue and caused a marked increase in the cost of living at a time when the depression was beginning to really hurt. Increased revenues implied a reduction in the Reichstag's budgetary control. It also meant that the Reich would no longer have to request matriculatory payments from states, so their influence over federal affairs would also diminish. The Center Party and the pro-government National Liberals, whose votes Bismarck needed to pass the legislation, were determined to frustrate his attempt to further weaken the Reichstag and the Bundesrat. The Bavarian Center Party deputy, Count Georg von und zu Frankenstein, put forward an ingenious scheme to overcome this problem. All revenues coming to the federal government in excess of 130 million marks were to be divided up among the states, and would then be returned as part of the matriculatory contributions. Thanks to the "Frankenstein Clause" budgetary rights of the Reichstag and of the state parliaments (Landtage) would thus be preserved. Bismarck thus suffered yet another defeat. He had tried to secure the financial independence of the Reich, but was unable to get increased tariffs without agreeing to the Frankenstein Clause.

The chancellor saw one positive result from the change of course. The National Liberal Party now split apart. In the final debate over tariff reform Lasker charged Bismarck with pitching the countryside against the towns, the haves against the have-nots, the producers against the consumers. He accused the chancellor of breaking the alliance of 1867 between the forces of the old and the new and of now trying to destroy the bourgeoisie and its liberal vision. The few remaining liberal ministers in Prussia now resigned. The left-liberals around Lasker, Ludwig Bamberger, and Max von Forckenbeck formed a separate party in 1880 known as the "Secession," and longed for the liberal crown prince to succeed. The Progressives, led by Eugen Richter, were also heavy losers in the election. They hoped that the "Secession" would join forces with them, but this did not happen, largely due to Richter's authoritarian style of leadership. Although most liberals were singularly pessimistic about their prospects, the chronically apprehensive Bismarck feared that his nightmare vision of a German "Gladstone government" was a step closer to becoming reality.

In the elections of 1881 there were thus three liberal parties. Although the aggregate vote for the liberals increased, the National Liberals lost a substantial number of seats. Their losses were the left-liberals' gain. In 1884 the two left-liberal parties amalgamated to form the German Independent Party (*Deutsch-Freisinnigen Partei*), under Richter's forceful leadership. It was against both "reaction" and socialism, against the increased tariffs and Bismarck's social legislation. It stood for the rights of the Reichstag, and for annual military budgets. This was hardly an inspiring program and the party was still divided over a number of issues. The new party did poorly in the 1884 election in which the call for colonies played an important role. In the run-off elections National Liberals tended to support Free Conservative candidates rather than Independents, and in the cities the Social Democrats made substantial gains at their expense.

The party lost more than half its seats in the elections of 1887 in which Bismarck pulled out all the nationalistic stops, but won almost all of them back again in 1890 in the uncertain political atmosphere after Bismarck's departure from office. Meanwhile the National Liberals leaned increasingly toward the right. They were no longer a party of the middle but were now closely allied with the Free Conservatives, united in opposition against the Center Party, the Independents, and the Social Democrats. It was a gradual process that was not completed until Bennigsen resigned the leadership in 1883. In the following year Johannes Miquel, a former Social Democrat, friend of Karl Marx, and mayor of Frankfurt, drafted the party's Heidelberg Program which placed the party solidly behind Bismarck's social policy and endorsed his anti-socialism and colonialism, as well as his position on tariffs and agricultural protection. In calling for a strong and interventionist state, it distanced the party from the Independents, and turned it into a faction of Tory democrats. It was a popular move. The party doubled its number of seats in the 1887 election as part of the "Cartel" with the two conservative parties, but German liberalism was marching resolutely down a dead-end street. Miquel could not persuade his partners in the Cartel of the need for extensive social reform, and both liberal parties were losing out to the Social Democrats as the party of change. This was not a uniquely German phenomenon. In all parliamentary democracies the fundamental choice was now between Tory Democracy and Social Democracy, in whatever guise. This shift was most pronounced in Germany because of the dramatic growth of support for the SPD. Elsewhere, as in England, liberal parties tried to revive their fortunes by an injection of social democratic ideas, but this could only postpone their final demise.

In 1879 Bismarck's hopes for a Cartel were frustrated by Bennigsen's intransigence. Memories of the *Kulturkampf* were still too vivid for it to be possible for the Center Party to ally with the two conservative parties. Bismarck therefore decided to ignore the Reichstag where possible and thus weaken the political parties. He now turned to the interest groups as a counterweight to the parties, linking them closely to various ministries and involving them in drafting legislation. The parties fought back fiercely, denounced this attempt to create a "chancellor dictatorship," and warned the interest groups of the dire consequences of their support for Bismarck's efforts to undermine the constitution. Bismarck was frustrated in his efforts to revive the old Prussian council of state and to create an imperial economic council. Only in Prussia was he able to create an economic council on which representatives from various branches of trade and industry, including workers and craftsmen, sat, and which had considerable influence over shaping legislation. His proposals for social reform were designed to make employees into state pensioners, thus turning them into docile and grateful citizens. Accident insurance, which was to be administered by a number of cooperative associations of employers (*Berufsgenossenschaften*) representing various branches of trade and industry, was also part of this attempt to bypass the Reichstag.

The unpopularity of the tariff increases and the persisting depression resulted in Bismarck suffering a severe setback at the polls in 1881, and he was left without a parliamentary majority. The Center Party, Secessionists and Independents, the Social Democrats, and a number of National Liberals were strongly opposed to Bismarck and his antiparliamentary chicanery, but they could agree on precious little else. The chancellor had no working majority, but he also did not have to face a united opposition and was able to exploit the divisions within the ranks of the disaffected. Having secured his change of course he could now afford to bide his time, continue with his plans to find ways around the Reichstag, and bully the parliamentarians with threats of dissolution and even a coup d'état. The Reichstag turned down his proposals for a tobacco monopoly in 1882 and for a spirits monopoly in 1887; both attempts were designed to make the federal government financially independent. Similarly the Center Party made its support for an increased tariff on agricultural goods dependent on increasing the revenue transferred to the states from customs duties. Other schemes for a tax on capital gains and for the nationalization of the railways met with determined resistance and had to be shelved.

Bismarck's major achievement in the 1880s was in the field of social legislation. The inspiration came from reform-minded officials, but had he not championed these ideas they would never have been put into effect. A health insurance bill passed the Reichstag in 1883, which provided benefits after the third day of a sickness up to a maximum of 13 weeks. After three years of rancorous debates this was eventually followed in 1884 with an accident insurance. Benefits amounted to two-thirds of average earnings and began on the 14th week when the sickness benefits ceased. In 1889 the Disability and Old Age Pension Act became law. The pensions were extremely modest, averaging a mere 152 marks per year in 1914, at a time when the average industrial wage was slightly more than 1,000 marks. Germany trailed far behind Britain in legislation controlling labor conditions, and France's social security system was far more advanced. We have already noted that these measures were designed to further weaken the Reichstag and strengthen the state. For this reason they were strongly opposed by liberals and the Center Party. Here was further evidence of Bismarck's Bonapartism and étatism. They fought tooth and nail against each of these bills and it is hardly surprising that it took almost a decade for them to pass. They were designed to alleviate some of the misery caused by the depression and by tariff increases, and to take the wind out the Social Democrats' sails. State socialism was proposed as an antidote to Social Democracy. The traditions of Prussian aristocratic, landowning society also played a role. The rich man should remain in his castle, but the poor man at his gate should not be too squalid a sight. Yet for all their reactionary intent, these measures were modernizing and progressive. They did nothing to halt the progress of Social Democracy, sickness benefits were ludicrously low, and as yet they did not include unemployment insurance. For all their many shortcomings they laid the foundations of the welfare state in Germany, and in the field of accident and health insurance for working men and women Germany led the way.

Class Structure

Imperial Germany was a society marked by stark differentiations of wealth, social status, and privilege. It was, in other words, a class society and as such matched the European norm. It was far removed from the relative egalitarianism of the prosperous present-day Germany, but it was also quite distinct from the earlier agrarian, pre-industrial society based on the estates. The extent to which distinctions between the haves and the have-nots increased under the impact of industrialization has been hotly debated and, although no accurate statistics are available, the evidence points to an increasing inequality of wealth, education, working conditions, housing, and health. These inequalities were gradually diminished over time, thanks to an astonishing level of economic growth, but by the 1890s this was still in the distant future. Inequalities existed not only between distinct classes, but also within them, making the very concept of class a kind of shorthand which, although generally accepted and fully comprehensible, does not do justice to the complexity of an advanced industrial society. Within the working class there were sharp distinctions between the skilled and the unskilled, as well as between urban and rural workers. The bourgeoisie included fabulously rich industrialists and the village doctor struggling to make a respectable living. How should the mason with his small construction firm be categorized, and should he be distinguished from a tailor in his tiny workshop? Where did the growing number of white-collar workers fit into this scheme? Did they form a sub-section of the bourgeoisie, known as the "petite bourgeoisie," or were they part of the "respectable" working class? Where were the dividing lines between the prosperous farmer and the small-holding peasant?

"Class" is a word loaded with ideological freight, but it is fundamentally an economic concept, applicable only in a developed, capitalist economy. It relates to wealth and to relationships to the means of production, and to the resulting way of life. This could lead to wide distinctions within a specific class. A successful farmer, although he increasingly aped the fashions of the urban bourgeois, lived in a milieu that was distinct from that of a city lawyer. A further complication was that in Germany education afforded additional status. The "educated middle class" (*Bildungsbürgertum*) comprised the very small percentage of the population with a university education, and formed a distinct caste that included senior civil servants, prosperous professionals, and impoverished grammar school teachers. There were 18,000 university students in 1869 when the population was about 45 million, rising to 79,000 by 1914 when the population was about 67 million. This is but one example of the tradition of an estate living on in a class society. The market determined the rough outlines of class, but certain groups were privileged in a manner that had precious little to do with economic status. The aristocracy was still an estate, those who played the capitalist market successfully were looked down upon as upstarts and parvenus, and professionals regarded those "in trade" as grossly inferior and unacceptable as in-laws. In a Prussian-dominated Germany the army played a unique role, prompting Bismarck's remark that a human being began at the rank of lieutenant.

The state acted as a brake on the development of a modern class society. The aristocracy enjoyed all manner of privileges, from special tax provisions and access to political power, to a monopoly on the upper echelons of the civil service and the military. Unlike the British aristocracy, which had no compunction about restoring the family fortunes by a judicious marriage with the daughter of a wealthy entrepreneur, or even an American heiress, the Germany aristocracy, with precious few exceptions – for which royal assent was required – only married their own, thus condemning many to lives of genteel and snobbish poverty. The aristocracy set the tone in certain circles, and bourgeois estate owners, army officers, senior civil servants, and students in the more exclusive fraternities often adopted their characteristic behavior, frequently to exceedingly unattractive and boorish effect. Most bourgeois viewed this behavior with disgust, and developed a distinctly middle-class culture in which a sense of social obligation, moderation, and restraint was coupled with a life of solid comfort, and which was to be the model for the future. Max Weber, who placed freedom above order, regretted that this did not go far enough, and complained that the bourgeoisie was far too much influenced by the collective values of the civil service rather than the marketplace with its individualism.

Perhaps, as in so much else, Max Weber was overly pessimistic. The aristocracy certainly set the tone in the glittering court ceremonies, in the officer corps, and in key positions in the civil service. They enjoyed many political and economic privileges, but it was the bourgeoisie that was culturally dominant. For all the talk of the "feudalization of the bourgeoisie," there was a corresponding "embourgeoisement of the aristocracy." The bourgeoisie dominated the economy, set cultural norms, determined urban life, and propagated the values of rationalism, hard work, and individualism to the point that the old concept of community was giving way to the new notion of society. In spite of all this, the bourgeoisie had no time for complacency. Its position was challenged by farmers hurt by the agrarian crisis, by artisans and craftsmen who were unable to meet the challenge of industrial capitalism, and by an organized working class with its vision of a new socialist order. The uncomfortable feeling arose that maybe it might be expedient to seek a defen sive alliance with the aristocracy in order to resist these challenges. In part this was due to the relative lack of opportunity for upward social mobility. It was possible to improve one's status within a class by learning a trade or getting a university degree, but it was exceedingly difficult to cross the class barriers. There were of course exceptions, such as the great art historian Richard Hamann, whose father was a postman and who was appointed professor at the age of 34, but such cases were exceedingly rare. Here education and training were of fundamental import- ance as the demand for skilled labor, technicians, scientists, engineers, and managers grew. A major expansion of the universities and polytechnics in the 1890s offered further opportunity for social advancement, as did the steady increase in the need for management skills. Within the bourgeoisie this resulted in a dramatic percent- age increase of entrants to the *Bildungsbürgertum* from the petite bourgeoisie in terms of percentage, but it must be remembered that this was still a small and exclu- sive group, so that the aggregate number of the upwardly mobile was still very small. There were also increasing opportunities for advancement from the ranks of the blue-collar workers into those with white collars, or for peasants to become elementary school teachers.

Class distinctions were emphasized by a conservative mentality that resisted any aspirations to better one's status or that of one's children. "What's good enough for me is good enough for you" was a widespread view, and the socially ambitious were condemned for having ideas above their station. Those who succeeded in social advancement were often snobbishly dismissive of the milieu from which they had risen, thus reinforcing class prejudice. Although the "respectable" working class began to adopt the manners, dress, eating habits, and furniture of the bourgeoisie, class distinctions remained as rigid as ever. A greater emphasis was now placed on the finer distinctions of comportment, dress, and speech between the classes and sub-classes that made up this complex, heterogeneous society that defies precise statistical analysis or sociological definition.

For all the many problems, inequalities, and setbacks, Imperial Germany wit- nessed a marked increase in the general standard of living. The first half of the nine- teenth century had been haunted by widespread under-nourishment and famine, but this was now a thing of the past. There were still individual cases of appalling dep- rivation, but the mass of the peasantry and the industrial proletariat was adequately fed, and their daily calorific intake steadily increased until the outbreak of the First World War. Bread, legumes, and potatoes remained the basic foodstuffs, but there was a marked increase in the consumption of meat. First there came a noticeable drop in the consumption of legumes, then of potatoes. Sugar was no longer a luxury, thanks to the widespread domestic cultivation of sugar beet, and consumption grew fourfold between 1870 and 1910. Meat consumption, mainly pork, rose from 22 kilos per capita per annum in 1850 to 27.6 kilos in 1879 and 44.9 kilos by 1913.

These improvements were in part due to rising real wages, since the purchase of food accounted for a sizeable part of the family budget. In 1907 it was calculated that the average working-class family spent 60 percent of the family income on food. Even more important was the revolution in the food industry and in transportation. There were significant improvements in farming techniques and livestock breeding. The provision of milk to urban areas was rationalized, condensed milk was introduced in 1884, and pasteurization began two years later. Margarine was invented in 1870 and provided a cheap source of fat for the poorer sections of society. Refrigeration revolutionized the preservation of foods so that fresh fish gradually replaced salted. The discovery of chemical preservatives greatly increased the shelf-life of many foodstuffs. Tinned vegetables first appeared in the shops in the 1870s, to be followed by meat and fish in 1880s. Knorr and Maggi introduced their powdered soups in the 1880s. In bourgeois circles food became richer and more varied, regional dietary peculiarities became less marked, and closer attention was paid to a healthy diet. By 1900 it was considered desirable to preserve a slim figure, as a new and sporting feminine image was constructed. Rural areas resisted such changing fashions, and the working class remained stolidly conservative when it came to their victuals. Diet had improved, but there was still a marked lack of vitamins and minerals, of fruit and vegetables, of milk products and fish that were later to be considered essential for health.

There were of course class-based differences in diets, but the working-class diet was gradually approximating that of the middle class. It was becoming healthier, more nutritious and more varied, and by 1900 bore a closer resemblance to today's diet than it did to that of 1850. Canteens now provided food for the destitute, and free school meals were given to the children of the poor. By contrast, factory canteens were mostly appalling, and the lukewarm swill was all too often washed down with excessive quantities of beer. A major problem in the working-class household was that the patriarchal family structure resulted in the husband getting the lion's share of the food. Wives were often ignorant of basic notions of hygiene and diet, but here too bourgeois notions seeped down, partly because many of these women had been in domestic service, and also because of the well-meaning if often intrusive efforts of various middle-class women's groups.

As the middle class prospered, the eating habits of the courts and the wealthy were imitated in luxury hotels and the finer restaurants, which provided gargantuan meals with as many as 12 courses. Such feasting was simplified and rendered more specifically bourgeois by the end of the century, by which time half the number of courses were served in "restaurants" most of which, as the name suggests, followed the French example, often with an elaborate menu in French. Those who were unable to afford such luxury went to a modest guesthouse which provided homely, bourgeois food.

Germany was a country of trenchermen, but also of tipplers. Martin Luther had said that every country has its own devil and that "our German devil lurks in a wineskin and is called drunkard." In general the bourgeoisie moderated its drinking habits as tea and coffee replaced beer, and all forms of excess were frowned upon. Alcohol consumption in the working class increased significantly with the industrial production of cheap schnapps distilled from potatoes. Considerable amounts of beer were also consumed in the workplace, and getting blind drunk on payday was a widely practiced and socially acceptable ritual. Blue-collar workers spent on average twice the amount of money on drink as white-collared clerks. In 1850 the per capita annual consumption of pure alcohol (from beer and spirits) was 6.4 liters. This increased to 10.5 liters in 1874. It then remained steady, possibly as a result of the long depression, began to drop in the new century, and fell to 7 liters by 1913. The major reason for this remarkable change was that the consumption of schnapps fell by about one-third between the 1860s and 1913, whereas that of beer rose threefold, all because of increases in the tax on spirits. Drinking habits were also regionally determined, with Rhinelanders holding the record for wine consumption, and Bavarians as the unrivalled champions in the beer stakes.

Drinking was the principal leisure-time activity for a wide section of the population, the local inn or tavern the favored site of social interaction and cultural exchange. They were also the only places available for political meetings. The various factions in the Frankfurt Parliament of 1848 were named after the bars where they met, and the Social Democrats made the tavern the locus of a specifically working-class culture. Although there was a general disapproval of excessive drunkenness, the temperance movement made little headway. Drinking was a primarily male vice that was done at the expense of women and children, and all too often led to domestic violence and unbridled sexuality. Gradually alcoholism came to be seen as a major social problem rather than as a sin, as a disease rather than as a moral transgression. By 1912 there were 48 detoxification centers and 158 centers offering help and advice. The increasing availability of cheap alcohol-free drinks helped to relieve the problem of excessive drinking, as did the gradual acceptance of coffee by the working class, even if it was of a poor quality and often made from some form of substitute. Tea was seldom drunk outside genteel circles.

Like alcohol, the consumption of tobacco increased sharply between 1870 and 1913, from 1 kilo per capita per annum to 1.6 kilos. The middle-class man smoked cigars and the working man gradually replaced his pipe with cheap cigars and cigarillos. Cigarettes first became readily available in urban areas in the late 1870s and grew in popularity, particularly among the working class. Less time-consuming than the cigar, it was an ideal accompaniment to a short break from work. The cigarette was later adopted by the fashionable youth and also, much to the horror of the traditionally-minded, by a very small number of women. Cigarettes were at first handmade, but gradually mass-production techniques were applied and cigarette-making became a major industry supported by vigorous advertising campaigns.

Diet was class specific, with a tendency toward a certain democratization of consumption, and much the same was true of clothing. People were clothed according to their social status, their occupation, their age, and marital status, as well as to their geographical location. With the invention of the sewing machine, and the subsequent mass production of readymade clothing, the movement toward the standardization of clothing was given additional impulse. This was particularly true in rural areas, where the more prosperous farmers and their wives gradually abandoned their regional dress in favor of the styles of the urban bourgeoisie. In this case the distinction between the wealthier and the poorer farmers and peasants became more clearly demarcated. The working class copied the bourgeoisie with their "Sunday best" clothes, but a clear distinction remained in quality and cut.

The bourgeoisie set the style, and here the simplification of male attire which was already apparent in the Biedermeier period continued. Color was restrained and uniform, the simple tie replaced fanciful cravats. Looser fitting jackets replaced wasp-waisted tailcoats, but collars were still starched and detachable, although the folded collar gradually replaced the high wing collar. Edward VII, as Prince of Wales, set the tone for the impeccably dressed male, a role later played by his successors Edward VIII and Prince Charles. It was he who sanctioned the replacement of tails by the dinner jacket on less formal occasions, and the top hat by the homburg. Trousers were first pressed around the turn of the century, but the Prince of Wales' curious habit of having the crease on the side found few followers. Men's hair was cut shorter and although beards were widespread an increasing number of fashionable men were clean-shaven.

Women's clothes were far more subject to the whims of fashion. The crinoline, the object of much badinage, gave way to the "cul de sac," which greatly exaggerated the buttocks, an effect enhanced by a tightly corseted waist. Skirts were long so as to cover the ankle, but the décolleté was accentuated. The dress was armless, but hands were covered, often with elbow-length gloves. By the 1870s daytime dresses were cut shorter and had sleeves, but the ankles were covered with high, laced boots. Women's dress also became increasingly informal, relaxed, and sporting. Skirt and blouse replaced the more formal dress by the 1880s, and as women took up hiking, skating, and sports such as tennis their clothing had to adapt. The emphasis was now on the new concept of "figure." That figure was the "S" form which dressmakers sought to enhance by the skillful drape of the cloth. Hair was long, but piled high. Makeup was for the exclusive use of actresses and whores.

Women's Place in the New Germany

The changes in women's fashions were a reflection of changes in women's role in society. The romantic notions of marriage as a partnership between self-actualizing equals was short-lived and the patriarchy was quick to recover the lost ground. A bourgeois woman's aim in life was to get married and have a family. This necessarily involved obligations and self-sacrifice, but it did not stifle the desire for elegance, refinement, and a lively social life. A woman's life was determined by her father, her brothers, and her husband. Men and women were unequal before the law, and were educated separately and differently. Women could not go to university and thus were unable to enter the professions; the one exception was teaching, but this only applied to unmarried women. A woman was required to relinquish her teaching post on marriage. Women were first admitted to university in Heidelberg in 1891, and by 1905 there were still only 137 women students in the universities; however, by 1914 there were 4,057. An increasing number of women from the petite bourgeoisie took clerical positions as the need for white-collar workers increased greatly due to the exigencies of advanced industrial capitalism. But the revolutionary change was the increasing number of women factory workers. Their plight awoke the sympathies of social reformers, and they were seen as an essential part of the social problem.

The women's movement was essentially a bourgeois phenomenon. It called for equality before the law, equal educational rights, access to the professions, and emancipation from patriarchal control. It accepted the notions that there were essential differences between the sexes and that a woman's principal role was to be a wife and mother. It called for equality within the context of an incontrovertible otherness, and saw men not as enemies, but as potential partners in a common cultural endeavor. To be a wife and mother, and thus fulfill the bourgeois ideal, was all very well, but what about the increasing number of unmarried women? Without access to further education or to an appropriate profession, they led an essentially parasitic and pointless life. Small wonder then that a large number of the early feminists came from their ranks, and they soon began to champion the cause of women factory workers, whose predicament was paradigmatic of the multiple problems that beset women's fate.

There were still relatively few women working in factories – just over half a million in 1882 and less than two million by 1913, the vast majority in unskilled routine jobs. Their wages averaged about 60 percent of that of male workers and they were mostly young and unmarried. Married women gradually ceased to work as their families grew, for there were precious few daycare centers where they could leave their children, and there was a stigma attached to a married woman having to work, since it was a reflection on her husband's inability to earn a living wage. Women's work was strictly regulated. They were forbidden to work at night, their working hours were limited, they were excluded from activities that demanded considerable physical strength, and were given maternal leave which by 1911 was covered by insurance payments. There has been a robust effort by feminist historians to demonstrate that all this was part of a male effort to combat the challenge presented by women in the workplace, but there is not the slightest evidence that this was indeed the case. Men feared the challenge from lower-paid female labor, but these fears were largely unfounded since industrial expansion provided a sufficiency of employment. Furthermore, these laws had nothing remotely to do with initiatives from the factory floor.

The organized women's movement began in 1865 when Luise Otto-Peters, who had first caught some public attention in 1849 when she founded Germany's first magazine specifically for women, founded the General German Women's Association (ADF). It was a middle-class organization calling for equal educational opportunities, for the right to enter the professions, and for improvements in family law. It made no political demands, such as for the right to vote. Even more conservative was the Association for the Education and Employment of German Women, popularly known as the *"Letteverein,"* which was a male society calling for the employment of women as social workers. The importance of this organization was that it thus combined the issue of the rights of women with the social question. A number of women's groups sprung up in subsequent years, the most important of which was Helene Lange's association of female teachers, founded in 1890. In 1894 many of these groups were brought under the umbrella of the League of German Women's Associations (BDF). It was still a solidly bourgeois organization, but there were some more radical elements within it, including the Association of Progressive Women's Groups, with its own newspaper, *The Women's Movement* (*Die Frauenbewegung*). This group sought contact with the Social Democratic Party, but its often strident tone did not appeal to the comrades. Radicals concentrated on three contentious issues. They demanded an end to police control over prostitution and their places of work, along with legal sanctions against their clients. They demanded votes for women, but in a moderate manner far removed from that of the British suffragettes. Lastly they called for a drastic rethinking of sexual morality. Helene Stöcker took up some of Nietzsche's notions on liberation and the freeing of the creative spirit to call for emancipation from a duplicitous morality and the emancipation of sexuality. A host of ancillary issues were addressed, including a relaxing of divorce law, improvements in the status of unwed mothers, sex education, and family planning. There were widespread differences about what forms these should take, and some tendentious issues such as eugenics were widely discussed. Although the differences between radicals and conservatives within the women's movement can all too easily be exaggerated, it was greatly weakened by the disparity of views and by frequently cantankerous debate. The radicals gradually gained the upper hand until 1908 when a fierce argument raged over the contentious issue of abortion. A special committee presented a motion calling for the abolition of paragraph 218 of the criminal code which made abortion illegal, but this was voted down by the general assembly. The arguments over a woman's right to choose versus the rights of the unborn are familiar themes, but the argument that abortion undermined the "racial health" of the nation was an distasteful novelty. The defeat of the motion was a major setback for the radicals, and the BDF now went on a conservative course.

The new leadership of Gertrud Bäumer, who had been Helene Lange's private secretary, and Marianne Weber, insisted on the difference between men and women. Whereas for them men were coldly intellectual and objective, with an abstractly mechanical view of the world that was at the root of their egotistical search for dominance, women stood for femininity and motherliness, for service, affection, and the selfless concern for others. In short they embodied the life principle. Emancipation thus would not involve equality with men, for that would involve loss of these vital feminine characteristics. Women's cultural mission was to infuse society with feminine values, which in turn implied that women should enter the teaching and healing professions on an equal basis. This triggered yet another fierce debate. Should married women continue to work? Could work outside the home be reconciled with a woman's obligations as a mother? Was there any essential difference between housework and work outside the home? How should housework be assessed, and should it be rewarded?

There was a socialist women's pressure group alongside this bourgeois women's movement. However woefully deficient he might have been in practice, Marx championed the equality of the sexes in theory, and Engels devoted part of one of his least satisfactory pamphlets to women's role in society. Socialists were in favor of the emancipation of women, but the question was for them of secondary importance, since they insisted that it could only be achieved within the context of a social revolution and the liberation of mankind. Class was of far greater importance than gender, and among women only proletarians were an object of concern. August Bebel was a champion of women's rights, and in 1879 published a hugely successful book on the subject entitled *Women and Socialism*. In this work he argued that proletarian women were doubly exploited, first as workers and secondly as women, and therefore could only be liberated when both forms of exploitation were ended. For him all those things which he saw as social evils that beset women, such as prostitution, abortion, illegitimate births, sexually transmitted diseases, and the decline in the birth rate, were all due to the capitalist system and thus could only be overcome in a socialist society. Under socialism love and sexuality would cease to be a commodity and would be free to develop. The bogus and hypocritical bourgeois family would be replaced by one based on love and free choice, and the divorce laws would be relaxed should that choice prove to have been mistaken.

Clara Zetkin was the outstanding figure in the socialist women's movement. She was a feisty character, born in a solid bourgeois family, and who had trained to be a schoolteacher. She insisted that women could only be freed by work outside the home, because only in that way could they directly experience the full horror of capitalist exploitation. For this reason, like many later feminists, she objected strongly to any special legislation that protected women in the workplace. Since she was convinced that socialism took priority over the immediate concerns of women she refused to cooperate in any way with the bourgeois women's movement, and in this she was supported by the party leader, August Bebel. As Clara Zetkin moved steadily to the left (she was to become a founder member of the German Communist Party in 1919) she became somewhat isolated within the party, but she remained editor of the Social Democratic women's magazine *Gleichheit* (*Equality*), which increased its circulation from 30,000 in 1908 to 175,000 by 1914.

The SPD's attitude toward certain important issues on the women's agenda was often problematic. The party naturally supported women's right to vote, but with little enthusiasm since they knew that they stood to lose by such a move. Socialist feminists did not call for equality within the family, but for partnership, and felt that married women should stay at home rather than go out to work. They were very dubious about birth control since they flatly rejected the neo-Malthusian argument that the social problems of the day were due to the unbridled philoprogenitive urges of the lower orders, and the eugenicists' arguments that rigorous birth control was essential to improve the race. The abolition of paragraph 218 was also not part of the party program.

There were no revolutionary changes in the status of women in the course of the nineteenth century, but there were significant improvements in their legal status, educational, and occupational opportunities, in their political influence, and in the organizational forms of their debates and demands. Attitudes toward sexuality took a somewhat different course. Here there was a gradual imposition of what came to be known as "Victorian" attitudes. Sex ceased to be seen as something natural and enjoyable and became a taboo subject, something that regrettably had to be accepted. The suppression of sexuality was an essential component of a bourgeois morality that was based on notions of obligation, duty, selflessness, altruism, and playing one's appropriate role in society. The ideal now was abstinence before marriage and then absolute fidelity toward one's partner. In an age when morality was all too often confused with sexual morality, the three cardinal sins were masturbation, pre-marital sex, and adultery. Whereas men had a bestial drive to commit all three of these sins, women were the guardians of morality who were transformed from innocent virgins into protective mothers and guarantors of respectability within the family. Women were no longer the Jezebels and temptresses who led men astray, but were seen as having a minimal sexual drive that was just sufficient for the satisfaction of their maternal instincts. Women had to be excessively feminine, men demonstrably masculine. Boyish women and effeminate men were viewed with horror and homosexuality was considered an unspeakable deviance. These ideals were also seen as specifically German. The "*Deutschlandlied*," later to become the national anthem, spoke of "German women, German fidelity." Deviations from the ideal were seen as distinctly un-German: casual attitudes toward one's marriage vows typically French, an excessive sex drive characteristically Jewish. The consequence of breaking the rules of respectability were at best a guilty conscience, at worst social ostracism, as in the case of Fontane's heroine Effi Briest, a superb study of the problems here addressed. Yet for all this oppressive prudery and woeful ignorance many people managed to enjoy sexually fulfilling partnerships. Queen Victoria thoroughly enjoyed a vigorous sex life within the context of a happy and fulfilling marriage, and only regretted that her lovemaking was frequently interrupted by the birth of yet another child. Medical men knew that the vision of frustrated men and frigid women was largely mythical, at least within the confines of marriage.

Sex and Society

Possibly the worst aspect of this unsatisfactory situation was the fact that the normative and the actual were so widely separated, resulting in a double morality. Bourgeois women were to remain pure and virginal until marriage and bourgeois men, who would never dream of marrying a woman with a past, respected this convention. Women of lesser station were fair game, were they domestic servants, peasants, factory girls, or prostitutes. There were thus two types of women: the chaste and worshipful mothers, sisters, and wives; and the hetaera: the whore and the servant girl, both of greatly inferior class, an incitement to delightful adventures, but sordid. Such women, by relieving men's sexual desires, helped preserve bourgeois women's virginity and thus played a useful role. Gladstone, a dedicated rescuer of fallen women, forcefully summed up this view when he praised the Greece of his beloved Homer on the grounds that "the society of that period did not avail itself of . . . the professional corruption of a part of womankind in order to relieve the virtue of the residue from assault." Young men from the bourgeoisie graduated from guilt-ridden adolescent onanism to spend the often lengthy years of bachelorhood in the brothel or with a mistress from the lower orders. As a result there was an appalling incidence of venereal diseases among university students, of whom Nietzsche is the best-known example, and an exceptionally high bastardy rate in university towns, with Marburg at the top of the list with 37 percent. All this served to accentuate the unhealthy separation of sex and love. Sex might be pleasurable, but it was also dangerous, dirty, and evil. It was thus something one did with bad women, even after marriage to an idealized virgin. Whereas in Paris and Vienna it was common practice to keep a mistress, married Germans favored the brothel rather than the *chambre séparé*, although by the turn of the century it became a status symbol in Berlin to subsidize the careers of successful actresses and variety artistes.

Statistics on the number of prostitutes are little more than wild guesstimates; suffice it to say that there were a large number of professionals in brothels or on the streets along with the semi-professional *belles du jour*. Although living off immoral earnings and public indecency were illegal, prostitutes were tolerated by the police, and some were regularly supervised by the medical authorities. The johns were largely, though not exclusively, middle class. A fierce debate raged over the question of prostitution which, although it was often superficial and misguided, at least raised the veil from a taboo subject. Feminists denounced the double morality of the bourgeoisie and demanded that all controls over their sisters in the sex trade be lifted. The medical profession insisted on rigorous measures to stop the spread of sexually-transmitted diseases which was then as great a problem as that of AIDs in our day. Law enforcement agencies called for a crackdown on criminality within the demi-monde. Moralists denounced prostitution as yet another glaring example of the evils of the Babylon of modernity.

The peasantry was restrained by religious sanction, by tradition, and by a concept of honor, but did not share the double morality of the bourgeoisie and was far more open and tolerant in sexual matters. Much the same was true of the urban working class, where inhibitions and sexual repression undoubtedly existed, but the consequences of the transgressions of the social norms in matters sexual were seen as misfortunes rather than as contraventions of the moral code. This in turn was all part of the secularization of society, in the course of which the rules of sexual behavior were determined not by priests and ministers, but by the medical profession.

Whereas men of the cloth had laid down what was sinful, doctors now determined what was normal. Homosexuality was clearly abnormal and a positive danger to state and society, since it was a characteristic of the effeminate, weak, and feeble. Male homosexuality was a criminal offense in Prussia and remained so under paragraph 175 of the criminal code of a united German Reich. The paragraph only covered anal intercourse, and it was not until the Third Reich that all forms of male homosexual activity, however widely interpreted, were rendered illegal. Gradually experts in the new "sexual science" began to challenge this view of homosexuality. Iwan Bloch, the author of a highly successful study *Sex Today* (*Das Sexualleben unserer Zeit*, 1907), saw homosexuality either as a byproduct of modern civilization – a view that greatly appealed to the cultural pessimists – or as an inborn trait that often affected highly intelligent and creative people, who therefore deserved sympathy. Other prominent researchers, such as Havelock Ellis and Magnus Hirschfeld, lent their support to those who demanded the decriminalization of homosexuality, and the homosexual community mounted a vigorous campaign for the recognition of their rights. The result was a slight shift toward an acceptance of homosexuality, but homosexuals were still ostracized, marginalized, regarded as perverts, and liable to prosecution. Whereas active homosexuality was unsafe in Germany, in Italy one was out of danger and there were plenty of beautiful peasant boys and fisher lads who were happy to oblige. Taormina became a gay paradise, preserved for posterity in Wilhelm von Gloeden's photographs of naked local youths, crowned with laurels and posed in a vaguely classical manner. These titillating pictures were enormously popular in certain circles and further stimulated the tourist trade. Artists also saw homosexuality as a useful weapon with which to mount an attack on hypocritical bourgeois morality. Wedekind's *Lulu* with its lesbian Countess Geschwitz, Thomas Mann's *Death in Venice*, Robert Müsil's *Young Törless*, and the poetry of Stefan George and his gay acolytes are cases in point, but it is doubtful whether they did much to change public attitudes.

An even more important factor in the gradually changing attitudes toward sexuality was what may be described as a rediscovery of the body. Throughout the nineteenth century the Greek ideal of nudity had been revered and widely consumed, whether in the form of public monuments or as soft porn for tired businessmen. The expressionlessness, the absence of soul, and the lack of individual character in Greek sculpture appealed to contemporary notions of sexuality. It was remote and depersonalized, even though a vital and alluring force. By the turn of the century there was an increased emphasis on naturalness, health, and sports. Clothes became looser and more informal, sun and water came to be regarded as health-giving, and mixed bathing in increasingly revealing costumes became commonplace. The human body was seen as something natural, vital, and even beautiful. Germans were in the vanguard of the nudist movement, which was part of a protest against modern civilization and was a Rousseauesque return to nature. The nudists were far from being sexual revolutionaries. They propagated a desexualized nudity free from false shame and lubricity. They were most upset that their magazine *Beauty* (*Die Schönheit*), with its nude photographs, had considerable appeal to Peeping Toms. The celebration of the human body further emphasized the difference between masculine and feminine. The cult of the male, often with a distinctly homoerotic flavor, particularly in the youth movement, was matched by a cult of the female as a healthy and fecund beauty. Coupled they would build a healthy, strong, and vital nation, acting as a counterforce to the destructive nervousness, concupiscence, and brutish materialism of modern civilization.

8
Germany and Europe: 1871–90

The creation of a united Germany in the course of three wars caused a revolution in the European balance of power. The new state was the dominant power in Europe, but it was surrounded by envious, resentful, and anxious neighbors who found it difficult to adjust to these new power-political realities. European states-men puzzled over the question whether Prussia-Germany would attempt further expansion or rest content within its new borders. Would the Reich threaten the peace of Europe, or would it concentrate on the pressing problems of state build-ing? Whatever the answer, Germany was no longer a patchwork of insignificant states forming a buffer between France and Russia, a deployment area for Europe's armies, but a major power likely to harbor hegemonic aspirations.

In such a situation Bismarck chose the only possible course. He had to convince the European powers that Germany was satiated, that it had no further territorial ambitions, and wanted only to live in peace with its neighbors. The German Reich had to prove that it was an acceptable newcomer among European nations, and that in finding a solution to the German problem it was not opening up any further difficulties. This was an immensely difficult problem that was made virtually insol-uble by the annexation of Alsace-Lorraine. Germany became overnight the most powerful nation in Europe and could not be fitted into the European balance of power. The annexation of Alsace-Lorraine put this delicate balance further out of kilter, and ensured the lasting enmity of France. It proved to be a disastrous legacy.

Bismarck felt that he had good reason to believe that Germany could live in freedom and peace for the foreseeable future. Republican France was crippled by reparation payments, riven with internal dissent, and was an unacceptable partner for Tsarist Russia. The Habsburg Empire harbored many resentments after its humiliation in 1866, but it badly needed support against Russia in the Balkans. Bismarck was at first determined to resist Andrássy's proposal for an anti-Russian alliance, fearing that this might drive Russia into the arms of the French. At the same time he did everything he could to hinder any attempt at reconciliation between Russia and Austria-Hungary, for that would seriously inhibit Germany's freedom of action. Russia had dynastic ties to Germany, and Bismarck was always concerned to keep the line to Saint Petersburg open. Prussia and Russia had sealed their determination to stand together against recalcitrant Poles in the Alvensleben Convention of 1863, and Russia had remained benevolently neutral over the question of German unification. On the other hand, Russia was in decline, the Pan-Slavs were gaining in influence, and the new Germany presented both a challenge and a threat.

Disraeli spoke of the "German revolution" of 1871 that was an even more significant event than the French Revolution, in that it had destroyed the European balance of power and thus threatened Britain's security. Yet by the time he was back in office in 1874 he had convinced himself that Bismarck was sincere in his desire to preserve the status quo, and that Germany was a useful counterweight to Russia and France. Britain was determined to keep out of the quarrels between Germany and France, and hoped to maintain good relations with both. There seemed to be no immediate cause for concern about Germany, and few were seriously troubled by moral qualms about the annexation of Alsace-Lorraine which, after all, had once been part of the German Empire and still had a large German-speaking community.

Germany's position was fundamentally insecure, and it is small wonder that Bismarck suffered from a "nightmare of coalitions." It was only safe provided none of the powers in the wings allied against it. It could only guarantee its security with Britain as an ally, but this would never happen because such an alliance would render Germany too powerful, and the new balance of power would be upset. Denied the possibility of such an alliance, Bismarck had no choice but to try to improve relations with both Austria-Hungary and Russia. This proved exceedingly difficult because both powers wanted Germany's exclusive support. This Bismarck could not risk for fear that the other party would turn toward France. For all its high-blown rhetoric the League of the Three Emperors of October 1873 was thus basically inconsequential. There was an affirmation of common conservative principles, and a basic agreement on the dangers posed by socialism, but differences between Russia and Austria-Hungary in the Balkans were irreconcilable, and Russia wanted to improve relations with France and offered support after its humiliating defeat. Bismarck had little to offer Russia for fear of alienating Britain, and France would clearly soon be once again a major player.

France recovered astonishingly quickly. It paid off the indemnity far quicker than anyone expected and the Germans were obliged to withdraw their troops. In 1875 the French set about reorganizing and enlarging their army. The Prussian General Staff promptly drew up plans for a preventive war and Bismarck, who rejected the idea of such a war out of hand, planned a counterattack. Constantin Rößler, a journalist known to serve as the chancellor's mouthpiece, published an article in the *Post* on April 8 1875 under the headline "Is War in Sight?" It was designed to convince the French not to go ahead with their plans for fear that it might lead to war. "The War in Sight" crisis backfired. Britain and Russia, at France's behest, denounced Bismarck's provocative behavior. There was widespread sympathy for France, and Germany's bully-boy tactics were not appreciated. France was more determined than ever to improve the army, and had won considerable sympathy.

Britain and Russia had shown that their common determination to preserve the balance of power in Europe far outweighed their many differences elsewhere. Bismarck had been taught a lesson, and he took it to heart. Any attempt by Germany to assert its hegemony was bound to meet with immediate and determined resistance.

Chastened by the experience of the War in Sight crisis Bismarck put his thoughts to paper while taking the waters at Bad Kissingen in the summer of 1877. Given the rivalries between Britain and Russia, exacerbated by Disraeli's purchase of the Suez Canal shares in 1875, between Russia and Austria-Hungary over the Balkans, and between France and Britain because of their colonial rivalry, Germany enjoyed a high degree of freedom as the "Middle Empire" in Europe. Bismarck concluded that: "All the powers with the exception of France need us and, in the foreseeable future, will be prevented from forming coalitions against us as a result of their relations one with another."

While Bismarck was drafting this Kissingen Memorandum the Balkans were once again in a state of turmoil, and his optimism over Germany's security steadily eroded, soon to turn to panic. Russia, allied with Romania, had already declared war on the Ottoman Empire in April, and eventually drove the Turks out of Europe, in spite of suffering heavy losses at Plevna in 1877. This was a battle that clearly showed the folly of attempting mass attacks against modern weaponry, a lesson which precious few officers took to heart. A greater Bulgaria stretching to the Aegean was created with the Treaty of San Stefano in March 1878. Since Bulgaria was little more than a Russian satellite, both Britain and Austria-Hungary were determined to stop this extension of Russian power and influence in a region in which they both had vital interests. The British fleet headed for the Straits to protect Constantinople, and Austria-Hungary threatened to join in an anti-Russian alliance. Europe drew back from the brink and a conference was convened to be held in Berlin. Germany had no direct interests in the Balkans and dreaded being dragged into the conflict. As early as 1876 the tsar had asked Bismarck on which side he would stand in the event of a war between Russia and Austria-Hungary over the Balkans, but he had refused to be tied down. He insisted that the preservation of the integrity of the Habsburg Empire was in Germany's vital interest, and did all he could to avoid a Balkan war. Realizing that the Treaty of San Stefano was unacceptable to Austria-Hungary, Bismarck refused to encourage them to accept its terms; at the same time he was anxious not to offend the Russians. In the long run this was an untenable position. He refused to be used either by the British against the Russians, or by the Russians against the Austrians, and strove to maintain strict neutrality. But when Russian ambitions were thwarted, and the eastern question was put before the Conference of Berlin, it seemed to the Russians that Germany was clearly biased in favor of Austria-Hungary. Bismarck as chairman of the conference announced that he intended to act as an "honest broker." This was treated by the Russians with skepticism. Gerson Bleichröder concurred, remarking that in all his years as a banker he had never come across such a creature.

From the Congress of Berlin to the Dual Alliance

The Congress of Berlin was a magnificent affair, the last old-style diplomatic meeting on the grand scale with Bismarck, Disraeli, and Gorchakov as its star performers. Bismarck's skills were widely admired, but it was inevitable that Russia would feel humiliated and frustrated. The Congress could do little more than confirm the deal that had already been struck between Britain and Russia. Anything less than San Stefano would be perceived by the Russians as a loss of face, and they were therefore bitter that the Germans had done nothing to further Russia's Balkan ambitions. The German chancellor was now a convenient scapegoat for all Russia's disappointments. Through no fault of his own Bismarck had permanently alienated Russia and the way was open for the Franco-Russian alliance which was the worst of all his nightmares. Russia continued to demand Germany's support against Austria-Hungary and against Britain. Bismarck realized that with its precarious position in the middle of Europe, Germany could not afford to take sides. That one of the powers should insist that it do just that showed up the faulty logic of the Kissingen Memorandum of the previous year.

Relations between Germany and Russia worsened in the months after the Congress of Berlin. The Pan-Slavs mounted a ferocious campaign against Germany and the ever-watchful censors allowed a number of often scurrilous attacks on the chancellor to appear in the Russian press. Tariff increases in 1879 aimed at protecting German agriculture against Russian exports were a further source of grievance. On August 15 1879, one month after the new tariffs were put into effect, the tsar sent the kaiser the "slap in the face" letter, with its harshly-worded demand that Germany come clean over its future attitude toward Russia. The tsar blamed Bismarck for the present deplorable state of relations between the two countries, ascribing it to his personal and unfounded animosity toward Prince Gorchakov. He reminded William of the singular services Russia had offered Prussia in 1870, and warned that if Germany persisted in showing such ingratitude the consequences would be "disastrous." Both the kaiser and his chancellor were deeply shocked by both the tone and content of this letter with its threats of war. William smarted under the tsar's charges and was anxious to mend fences with a conservative power for which he had much affection. Bismarck panicked, envisioning an alliance between Russia, Austria-Hungary, and France that would lead to Germany's destruction. The Kissingen Memorandum was now shown to have been mere wishful thinking. Germany needed an ally against Russia and that ally could only be Austria-Hungary. The result was the Dual Alliance of October 1879. The signatories agreed to support each other in the event of an attack by Russia and to remain benevolently neutral in any other circumstance. The treaty was to be reviewed after five years.

William was strongly opposed to Bismarck's radical break with the pro-Russian traditions of Prussian and German foreign policy, and perceptively warned that it could well lead to an alliance between Russia and France. He asked to meet the tsar in Alexandrovo at the beginning of September, in an attempt at personal diplomacy which Bismarck condemned as an "embryonic Olmütz." This initiative did nothing to improve the situation, and finally the kaiser agreed to the Dual Alliance, after yet another threat by Bismarck that he would resign, caustically remarking that the chancellor was more important than the emperor.

Bismarck presented the Dual Alliance as a revival of the German Confederation in "an appropriate contemporary form." This was putting a brave face on what he was soon to realize was a move made in haste, and with possibly fatal consequences. The master diplomat had tied his hands behind his back and spent much of his remaining time in office in Houdini-like efforts to untie them. The ink was hardly dry before he realized that a defensive treaty could be used offensively. Austria-Hungary could provoke Russia, and then appeal to Germany for help. Bismarck therefore sent numerous notes to the Vienna embassy warning that any attempts to alter the spirit of the treaty in this manner should be resisted at all costs. Bismarck's successors ignored these strictures, and the Dual Alliance was re-interpreted to mean a solemn undertaking to stand together whatever the circumstances in a poignant demonstration of "Nibelungen fealty."

The kaiser was perfectly correct in pointing out that by opting for Austria-Hungary, Germany increased the likelihood of Russia turning toward France. Bismarck knew that without Russian support, France would never attack Germany, and from 1871 the Prussian General Staff assumed that the next war would be on two fronts. His remarks to the effect that the Dual Alliance would oblige Russia to approach Germany were once again mere wishful thinking. In September 1871 he had sounded out the British government as to its attitude in the event of a war with Russia. Disraeli had been non-committal. Now the liberals were back in power, and Bismarck, with his horror of Gladstonian liberalism, did not pursue the matter. He saw no need for the moment to make a decisive choice between Russia and Britain.

The League of the Three Emperors was revived in 1881, but secretly, so as not to incense the Pan-Slavs. It still had precious little substance. Russia promised to stay neutral in the event of a war between France and Germany. Germany undertook to stay out of any conflict between Russia and Britain. For Bismarck the object was to avoid conflict between Russia and Austria-Hungary in the Balkans, and to counteract the Pan-Slav demand for closer ties between Russia and France. He imagined that he was now once again the "honest broker" between Austria-Hungary and Russia and he closed his eyes to the clouds on the horizon. While the Prussian military pondered the problems of a two-front war against Russia and France, Bismarck secured the renewal of the tripartite agreement in 1884 for another three years.

Meanwhile, in 1882 the Dual Alliance became the Triple Alliance with the inclusion of Italy. Italy had been irritated by France's annexation of Tunis in 1881, and by its exclusion from Egypt. Italy approached the Dual Alliance in an attempt to improve its position in Libya and Albania. Given the differences between Italy and Austria-Hungary in the Balkans, and the problem of South Tyrol, the treaty was of dubious value. In 1883 Romania joined the alliance hoping for protection against Russia. With the perennial problem of Transylvania, which poisoned relations between Austria-Hungary and Romania, this also hardly strengthened the alliance; nor did the tacit support of the Ottoman Empire and Spain. Germany was now at the center of two alliances with contradictory aims: an expanding system of alliances based on the Dual Alliance, and the League of the Three Emperors – the first anti-Russian and pro-British, the second pro-Russian and anti-British. Bismarck stylized this as a "game with five balls." Germany appeared to be on reasonably good terms with all the powers, with the exception of France, without making any firm commitments. It was a singularly unstable situation, and even a master diplomatist like Bismarck was unlikely to be able to keep all five balls up in the air for much longer.

Bismarck and Imperialism

In 1881 Bismarck announced: "There will be no colonial policy as long as I am chancellor." In 1871 Bismarck had treated the French suggestion that Germany take Indo-China in lieu of Alsace-Lorraine with derisory laughter. Yet in 1884–5 Germany established colonies in Southwest Africa, East Africa, Togo and Cameroon, New Guinea, the Bismarck Archipelago, the Solomons, and the Marshalls. Bismarck's motives for entering the race for colonies were many and varied. He knew that colonies were expensive, tiresome, and potential sources of conflict, but they offered certain advantages. Some of the hardship caused by the depression might be offset by providing fresh markets for German goods, assuring supplies of raw materials, and creating an autarchic trading area protected from the exigencies of world trade. The attention of disgruntled Germans could be diverted away from concerns over domestic politics by exciting them with a vision of an overseas mission. Similarly Germany's dangerously exposed position in central Europe might be overlooked by drawing attention to its overseas empire. The chancellor there-fore decided to use the colonial question as a platform in the 1884 election. He denounced his opponents for lacking both patriotism and vision, and by making colonialism the central issue he hoped to undermine the position of the pro-British crown prince, and thus lessen the likelihood of a German "Gladstone administra-tion." This too was somewhat dubious since the crown prince was an enthusiastic supporter of the Samoa project and shared much of the popular enthusiasm for colonies. Perhaps this anti-English colonial policy might open the way to improved relations with France, as seemed to be the case during the Congo Conference held in Berlin in the winter of 1884/5.

This was the heyday of European imperialism, the scramble for Africa was becoming increasingly frantic, and imperialism captured the popular imagination. Colonies were seen as an appropriate signification of great power status. The German Colonial Association (*Deutsche Kolonialverein*) was founded in 1882, with Miquel and Prince Hohenlohe-Langenburg as its most prominent members. The Society for German Colonization (*Gesellschaft für deutsche Kolonisation*) had a far less exalted membership. It was led by Dr Carl Peters, a youthful psychopath, adventurer, and rapist who set about carving out colonies in East Africa. In 1885 the two organizations were amalgamated as the German Colonial Society (*Deutsche Kolonialgesellschaft*). Colonialism was an immensely popular cause and the society soon had some 10,000 members.

Initially Bismarck hoped to involve the state as little as possible in colonial affairs. Most colonies started when the Reich guaranteed protection to merchants and adventurers who set up shop in Africa and the South Seas. Carl Peters was an extreme and unattractive example of the breed. His example was followed by Adolf Lüderitz in Southwest Africa, Adolf Woermann in Togo and Cameroon, and Adolph von Hansemann of the Diskonto-Gesellschaft in New Guinea, among a host of others. These protectorates soon ran up against the representatives of other imperialist powers, and appealed for support so that colonialists were often calling the shots in Berlin. Bismarck was content to encourage the resulting tensions with Britain, but he resented the fact that the tail was all too often tempted to wag the dog. Gradually the informal protectorates became formal colonies, and Bismarck soon lost what little enthusiasm he had for the colonial enterprise.

In 1885 the colonialist Ferry government fell in France, and the country turned its mind to revenge under the war minister Boulanger, a blustering and somewhat absurd figure known as "Général Révanche." France and Russia drew closer, and the situation between Germany and France became even more tense with the Schnaebelé espionage affair. Meanwhile an election in Britain returned the Conservatives under Lord Salisbury, who was felt to be well disposed toward Germany. Boulanger fell from office in 1887 but "the man on the white horse" still enjoyed enormous popular support and plotted a coup d'état. This turned out to be a damp squib, and he fled the country in 1889. By this time Bismarck had lost his taste for colonial exploits. Pointing at a map of Europe he told a visitor that Germany was in the center between France and Russia. "That," he said "is my map of Africa." In 1890 he laid the groundwork for the exchange with Britain of Helgoland for Zanzibar, thus indicating his desire to turn his back on the colonial empire, and concentrate once more on European affairs.

Almost all the assumptions behind Bismarck's colonial policy proved to be false. Germany's position as the "empire in the middle" was weakened by colonies, which could not be defended without building a vast fleet, which in turn inevitably led to further complications. Economically the colonies brought precious little relief. Only 0.1 percent of German exports went to the colonies, and likewise only 0.1 percent of imports came thence. By 1905 only two percent of German capital was invested in the colonies, which in turn were inhabited by a mere 6,000 Germans, most of them civil servants and soldiers. Even in the short run the returns were disappointing for the chancellor. He did not even get a majority in the 1884 elections. In the long run the colonial episode unleashed the vicious forces of nationalism, racism, and imperialism, coupled with an intensification of anti-British sentiment which was to be a major part of Bismarck's disastrous legacy. The way was opened for the hubris of "World Politics."

Bismarck's System of Alliances

Bismarck's elaborate and contradictory system of alliances began to unravel. In 1885 the German prince Alexander von Battenberg, who had been chosen as Prince of Bulgaria in 1879, was egged on by the British to annex Eastern Romelia, thus asserting his independence from Russia. Austria supported Alexander and thus acted against both the spirit and the letter of the League of the Three Emperors. Alexander was kidnapped, released, and then, under extreme pressure from Russia, abdicated in September and returned to his home in Darmstadt. In the following year another German prince, Ferdinand of Saxe-Coburg-Gotha, an officer in the Austro-Hungarian army, was elected Prince of Bulgaria. Russia refused to recognize the new prince. The League of the Three Emperors was now in ruins, the break between Austria-Hungary and Russia final.

Bismarck had tried to broker a deal between Austria-Hungary and Russia, had warned his ally that Germany had no obligations toward them under the terms of the Dual Alliance in this instance, and tended to sympathize with Russia's position in spite of massive popular support in Germany for Ferdinand. This brought him no dividends in Saint Petersburg. The Russians blamed Germany rather than Austria-Hungary for their losing control over Bulgaria, and for thus suffering a humiliating defeat in the Balkans. For the Pan-Slavs this was a repeat performance of what they had perceived to be Bismarck's anti-Russian policies at the Congress of Berlin. Once again their Balkan ambitions had been dashed, thanks to a lack of support from Berlin. Those Slavophiles and westernizers who had been arguing in favor of an alliance with France were now gaining the upper hand. Russia was still not quite ready to embrace republican France, a country that welcomed Russian revolutionaries and sympathized with Poland. The foreign minister Giers was eager to maintain friendly relations with Berlin, but the enormously influential Pan-Slav journalist Mikhail Katkov, the champion of an alliance with France, was a powerful influence. In the end it was economic forces that brought the two countries together.

Germany's protective tariffs of 1879 had adversely affected trade with Russia. Previously 34 percent of Russian exports had gone to Germany, whence came 44 percent of its imports. The situation was exacerbated by two further tariff increases by Germany, and the inevitable responses by Russia. As a result grain exports from Russia declined, and the Russians were less able to import the vital industrial goods that were essential for the modernization of the economy. Between 1879 and 1885 Germany's agricultural tariffs had trebled. This was seen in Russia as a deliberately unfriendly series of punitive measures, designed to hamstring their efforts to generate the capital needed in order to industrialize. Furthermore, up to 80 percent of Russia's source of foreign capital came from loans traded on the Berlin stock exchange, and there were powerful voices in Germany protesting against Russian countermeasures, and demanding that the export of capital to Russia should cease.

Bismarck negotiated the renewal of the Triple Alliance in February 1887, Italy having reached an agreement with Britain over the Mediterranean that was later endorsed by Austria. Bismarck now hoped to bring Britain closer to the Triple Alliance and form a front against an increasingly hostile Russia. The Mediterranean agreement formed the basis of the informal and secret Oriental Triple Alliance in December between Austria-Hungary, Italy, and Britain, which guaranteed the status quo in the Balkans and the Ottoman Empire, and as such was designed to frustrate Russian ambitions in the area. The army increases of 1886/7, ostensibly aimed at révanchist France, were also a response to closer ties between Saint Petersburg and Paris marked by discussions between the general staffs of Russia and France in 1886.

In June that year Bismarck signed the "Reinsurance Treaty" with Russia. He had always been anxious to keep the line to Saint Petersburg open, and was horrified by the widespread popular enthusiasm for a preventive strike against Russia, which was advocated by Moltke and Waldersee in the General Staff, and Holstein in the Foreign Office. He was now determined to calm things down. The initiative came from the Russians, and Bismarck jumped at the suggestion. Russia and Germany agreed that they would remain neutral in the event of an unprovoked attack by France or Austria on either signatory. Germany accepted that Bulgaria was in the Russian sphere of influence, and promised diplomatic support should Russia find it necessary to occupy the Straits. The Reinsurance Treaty was a very ambiguous affair that did not sit well with Germany's other commitments. It was against the spirit of the Triple Alliance and the letter of the Oriental agreement. It was left open to the signatories to decide whether an attack was "unprovoked." It gave Germany no protection against Russia. At best, as Herbert von Bismarck remarked, it would keep the Russians off their backs for six to eight weeks. It did nothing to solve the problem of the rivalry between Austria-Hungary and Russia in the Balkans. It was very doubtful whether it would prevent an alliance between Russia and France. At best Bismarck had achieved his aim of keeping the line open to Saint Petersburg and bought a little time, but Holstein had some justification in denouncing the treaty as "political bigamy."

Relations between Germany and Russia steadily worsened. Enthusiasts for a preventive war mounted a massive campaign in the German press. At the Foreign Office Holstein worked behind Bismarck's back and encouraged Austria-Hungary to take a firmer line against Russia. Bankers and industrialists demanded stronger retaliatory measures against Russia. Grain tariffs were raised again in 1887 so that they were now five times higher than in 1879, and further restrictions were placed on the import of meat and livestock. The Reichsbank was forbidden to make advances against Russian securities thus precipitating the panic sale of Russian bonds. Numerous Russian nationals were expelled from the Reich. The Russians responded by increasing the tariffs on industrial goods, and foreigners were forbidden to buy or transfer real estate in Russia, a measure that affected a large number of German property owners in the western provinces. Pan-Slavs lashed out against Germany and called for closer ties with France. The government, in its desperate search for capital, turned first to Amsterdam and then to Paris. The French responded by investing heavily in Russia, only to lose all in 1917.

Bismarck was clearly beginning to lose his grip. He might have imagined that he was appeasing the anti-Russian preventive war enthusiasts by increasing the pressure on Russia, but at the same time he was using these measures as a means to convince Saint Petersburg of the desirability of improving relations with Germany. He failed to realize that the time had passed when Germany could act alone. Tied to Austria he could not opt for Russia, and an alliance with France was unthinkable. An approach to Britain in 1889 failed, since Bismarck would not agree to give support to Britain against Russia in return for British support against France, and in any case Britain had no need for Germany, and Salisbury had no desire to be tied down by a formal alliance. Relations between the two countries remained good in spite of the failure of these talks.

German diplomacy under Bismarck was a one-man affair, even if at times he had to fight tooth and nail with the kaiser in order to get his way. In domestic politics he took advice, listened to suggestions, and seized upon the ideas of others. In foreign policy he acted alone according to a set of assumptions that were rapidly becoming outdated in an age of imperialism and rabid nationalism. The principles of the Kissingen Memorandum no longer applied, five balls could not be kept up in the air, and the "saturated" empire in the middle was no longer secure.

9
Wilhelmine Germany: 1890–1914

The kaiser might have been little more that the hereditary president of the Bundesrat, a monarch among many, a *primus inter pares*, but he was the lynchpin of the entire system. Bismarck had carved out a position of exceptional power to the point that there was much talk of a "chancellor dictatorship," "Caesarism," and "Bonapartism," but, as he knew full well, he was nothing without the full support of kaiser and king. For this reason he was dreading the day when William I would die, and his dangerously liberal son would succeed. The kaiser was an unimaginative and reactionary professional soldier of limited intelligence but with a strong sense for the obligations, responsibilities, and duties of his high station. This earned him the respect, but hardly the love, of his people. Over the years Bismarck bullied him into submission and he faded into the background. This earned the chancellor the undying hatred of the Empress Augusta, a princess of Weimar.

William I died in 1888, the critical "Year of Three Kaisers," aged 90. His son, Frederick III, was married to Queen Victoria's eldest daughter, who was also named Victoria. She was a strong-willed woman with liberal leanings, with which her husband was much in sympathy. But it was doubtful whether Bismarck's nightmare vision of a "German Gladstone ministry" would ever have been realized. Frederick's candidate for the role, Admiral Stosch, was hardly built of Gladstonian timber, and German liberalism had already run its course. In any case the unfortunate new kaiser was suffering from cancer of the larynx and died after a reign of 99 days. Nietzsche, certainly no liberal, proclaimed Frederick III's death to be a great and decisive misfortune for Germany. Inasmuch as his son, William II, was indisputably a great and decisive misfortune not only for Germany, but also for the rest of Europe, history was to prove this to be a sound judgment. It was a view shared by another great contemporary mind – Max Weber.

Described by his English uncle Edward VII as "the most brilliant failure in history," the 29-year-old William II was highly talented but superficial, a neurotic braggart and romantic dreamer, a militaristic poseur and passionate slaughterer of wild animals, a father of seven children and an enthusiastic womanizer, who was happiest in the exclusive circle of his homosexual and transvestite intimates.

Plate 14 William II "The Kaiser." © BPK

Bismarck said of him that he wanted every day to be his birthday. Another wit remarked that he wanted to be the bride at every wedding, the stag at every hunt, and the corpse at every funeral. His abiding hatred of England was dictated by a feeling of inferiority and his pathological hatred of his English mother, whom he placed under house arrest as soon as his father died, charging her with pilfering state papers. He attributed his withered arm, which caused him much distress, to the sinister machinations of his mother's gynecologist. This contradictory, bluster-ing, overly theatrical, arrogant yet profoundly insecure figure embodied many of the contradictions of the Germany of his day. His yearning for popularity and love of bombastic show were far from typically Prussian, but a manifestation of the new German pushiness, bluster, and aggression. The young kaiser was an exceptionally bad judge of character and ability, who surrounded himself with a deplorable bunch of advisors. The result was a standstill in domestic affairs combined with an increas-ingly ill considered, unrestrained, and aggressive foreign policy. It was a recipe for disaster.

The young emperor had long made it perfectly clear that he wished to escape from under the shadow of a chancellor who was 44 years his senior and who had long outlived his popularity. He told his cronies: "I'll let the old boy potter along for another six months, then I'll rule myself." The first bone of contention with the chancellor was over how to deal with the Social Democrats. The kaiser was temporarily much taken by the court preacher Adolf Stoecker's currently fashionable ideas. Seeing that the anti-socialist laws were a miserable failure, he announced his intention to become a "social kaiser," who would win the love of his proletarian subjects by a menu of social reforms, spiced with a healthy dose of anti-Semitism. Bismarck thought this absurd and wanted to continue with his repressive policies. In 1889 there was a massive strike of miners in the Ruhr. At its height about 140,000 miners downed tools. The army longed to have a crack at the strikers, but Bismarck held them back, hoping that the crisis would deepen and the complacent bourgeoisie would get a real shock. William II decided to demonstrate his newfound affection for the laboring masses and received a delegation of strikers. This surprising gesture worked wonders. The mine owners expressed their readiness to negotiate, and the strike was called off.

Bismarck's draft proposal for an limitless anti-socialist law was rejected by a solid majority of Reichstag deputies, including the German conservatives, whereupon the kaiser agreed to call a fresh round of elections. The result was a crushing defeat for Bismarck's Cartel. The Center Party was returned as the strongest party, and Bismarck had lost his parliamentary majority. He now proposed to reintroduce the anti-socialist measures coupled with a bill banning strikes, along with a demand for a substantial army increase. The Reichstag was to be cowed into submission by threatening to call further elections, and even the possibility of a coup d'état. In desperation he turned to his old enemy Windthorst and proposed a coalition with the Center Party, but it was too late. The kaiser refused to begin his reign on a confrontational course with the labor movement, and on March 17 1890 he requested Bismarck's resignation. This he received the following day.

Bismarck was a towering genius who left an indelible mark on Germany and on Europe, but his legacy, like that of so many truly great men, was extremely mixed. He was neither the black reactionary of left-wing myth, nor the flawless mastermind behind Germany's greatness, as his many admirers fondly imagined. He was a modernizer, a "white revolutionary," who at least partially reconciled conservatives with bourgeois liberal nationalism, who made concessions to parliamentary democracy, and supported social reforms of great consequence. But his power-hungry brutality, his lust for confrontation rather than compromise, and his inability either to delegate authority or to tolerate anyone who even approached being his equal, left a fatal legacy. He was a man of profound and even pathological contradictions, and the ambivalence and inconsistency of his own imperious personality was deeply embedded in the structure of the Reich of which he was the architect.

Bismarck once told the Reichstag that "the actual, real minister-president in Prussia is and remains His Majesty the King." This was of course only true when the minister-president and chancellor no longer enjoyed the full confidence of the

Plate 15 Bismarck Dead and Surrounded by the Ghosts of the Past. © Deutsches Historisches Museum

king and kaiser, as was the case when William II ascended the throne. The new kaiser was determined to be his own chancellor and the ministers would be his "dogsbodies." In a public address in 1891 he announced: "Only one person can be master in the Reich, I cannot tolerate anyone else!" and this claim was repeated in numerous similarly arrogant, tactless, and provocative speeches. "I shall destroy anyone who stands in my way," he announced, and somewhat later added that "a soldier must be ready to shoot his own parents." He dismissed the Reichstag as the "imperial monkey house." William II was obviously a loose cannon on deck, whom one bold historian and later Nobel Prize winner, Ludwig Quidde, compared to Caligula. He surrounded himself with a number of advisors and cronies who bolstered his neo-absolutist ambitions. Chief among them were the heads of the civil, military, and navy cabinets who were responsible for all promotions and appointments in their respective departments. Then there were the adjutants and liaison officers who acted well beyond their constitutional remit. Equally important was the circle of his intimate friends around the epicene Philipp von Eulenburg, whom his friends addressed as "she," through whom Holstein and Bülow were to gain the kaiser's ear.

The precise nature of Wilhelmine Germany has been the subject of much heated debate. Erich Eyck spoke of William II's "personal rule," but he soon came under attack by historians who argued that this was all smoke and mirrors, and that there was precious little behind the blustering rhetoric. That he had influential friends was hardly surprising or unique. After all Bismarck too had had his problems counteracting the Empress Augusta's influence on William I. Furthermore, William II was incapable of ruling. He blew hot and cold and frequently changed his mind, and this impetuosity earned him the sobriquet "William the Sudden." He was unable to work systematically, passing six months in the year traveling, rising late in the day, and spending most of his waking hours at table, taking a stroll, or enjoying the social whirl. It is small wonder that his generals were determined to do everything possible to stop this militarily incompetent "supreme warlord" leading them into battle.

Structuralist historians like Hans-Ulrich Wehler developed this theme to the point of calling William II a "shadow kaiser." In this version the political life of Wilhelmine Germany was determined by the economy, by an anonymous power structure, and by class conflicts that were played out by interest groups, the bureaucracy, and the military. The personality of the kaiser is thus irrelevant. Within the given structural determinants another figurehead would have made no difference. John Röhl has led a robust assault on this widely-held version, has withstood charges of writing "personified" history, and has done much to restore credence in "personal rule," albeit in a largely negative sense. As is so often the case in such debates the truth lies somewhere in the middle. There was indeed much tub-thumping bombast at court, and the kaiser was a loud-mouthed poseur with absolutist pretensions, but there was little of substance behind all this. On the other hand he was more than a shadow kaiser since his power and influence were considerable, but only when he chose to intervene. He had certain pet projects that he pushed through and he intervened, usually to disastrous effect, in foreign policy. Most important of all, unlike his grandfather, who left most such decisions to Bismarck, he paid considerable attention to key appointments. Bülow and Tirpitz were the kaiser's men, key players in his "personal rule." Two great crises in his reign served to clip his wings. The first was the press campaign against the court camarilla led by the mordacious journalist Maximilian Harden, who exposed the kaiser's intimate and influential friends Philipp zu Eulenburg and Kuno von Moltke as homosexuals. The second was the kaiser's humiliation over the *Daily Telegraph* affair of 1908, which led to Bülow's resignation. His successor, Bethmann Hollweg, was a bureaucrat who had worked his way up through the Prussian administration. He was neither courtier nor toady, and certainly not an instrument of the kaiser's personal rule. Nevertheless, careers depended on royal favor, and this in turn encouraged an atmosphere of lick-spitting opportunism at court, a groveling search for the favor of the All Highest. The kaiser's men, from the chancellor Bülow down, did their outmost to shield him from criticism and unpleasant reality, and were thus able to influence and even manipulate him. Temperamentally he was a modernizer and a technophile who had a horror of war, but his entourage managed to influence him to the point of making him more conservative and belligerent. Thus he was given to making grotesquely reactionary statements, and to swearing that at the next crisis he would not cave in but would lead the nation into war; all this in a pathetic attempt to show his entourage that he too was a real man.

William II's sins of commission were trivial compared to his sins of omission. Germany would almost certainly have built a high seas fleet without him, the army would have played a devastatingly reactionary role in spite of his interventions, imperialism would have been just as raucously racist were he not on the throne. He might have emphasized these trends in his outrageous speeches and public utterances, as well as in his choice of advisors and his direct interventions into the political process, but in all this he was as much a product of his times as he helped to mould them. His disastrous legacy was that he failed to provide the coordination that the system desperately needed. Nowhere was this more evident than in military affairs. The Schlieffen Plan tied the hands of the politicians. There was no proper consultation between the army and the navy, or between the Prussian army and the Bavarian, Saxon, and Württemberg armies. There was similar confusion in foreign policy. Holstein and Marschall felt that Britain would eventually realize that it needed Germany's support. Bülow favored a closer relationship with Russia. William II wavered between these two positions. His might thus have been a negative personal rule, but it set the tone of the age, as well as being the reflection of a society that was fundamentally unstable. It is not for nothing that this is called the "Wilhelmine era."

None of Bismarck's successors were men of anything like his stature and this almost inevitably resulted in a shift in power from the chancellor to the kaiser. His immediate successor, Caprivi, afforded the secretaries of state far greater freedom of action, allowing them free access to audiences with the kaiser which he did not bother to attend. This tendency became even more pronounced when he felt obliged to resign as Prussian minister-president in 1892. His successor Hohenlohe was a weak and elderly aristocrat, chosen in 1894 to bolster the kaiser's personal rule. The secretaries of state grew ever more independent from the chancellor and closer to the kaiser. Given the rivalries between the secretaries of state, both in Prussia and in the Reich, along with the simultaneous independence of the imperial and Prussian bureaucracies, and the kaiser's inability to provide decisive leadership, the system became extremely erratic and unpredictable. Bülow, who became chancellor in 1900, brought back some order and method by partially restoring the collegial structure, and this course was continued under Bethmann Hollweg.

At the root of the problem was that whereas under Bismarck Prussia dominated the Reich, the system began to fall apart under his successors. Imperial secretaries of state had been mostly Prussian ministers, and those who were not had attended meetings of the Prussian ministry of state. Now Prussia and the Reich began to part company. Prussia stuck to its conservative course, while the Reichstag pushed for

reform. Caprivi's resignation as Prussian minister-president in 1892 further exacerbated the situation, and Hohenlohe was not the man to overcome these difficulties.
The Prussian ministry of state, under the forceful leadership of the vice-president
Miquel, became increasingly independent from the Reich, where Count Arthur von
Posadowsky-Wehner at the treasury, and then at the ministry of the interior, was
the dominant figure. The imperial secretaries of state were now fully independent
from the Prussian government and their ministries, rather than their Prussian counterparts, prepared the drafts of legislation prior to presentation to the Bundesrat.
Bills were still vetted by the Prussian ministry of state, but the Reich was now
gaining the initiative. The great issues of the day – armaments and social policy –
were matters for the Reich and the Reichstag, a fact that further strengthened the
federal agencies.

Prussia still enjoyed hegemonic power in Germany. Power was centered on the
kaiser and his chancellor. The Prussian army was the most powerful institution in
the land, the Reich's bureaucracy was recruited from the Prussian administration,
and the conservative Prussian aristocracy still had immense influence, but Prussia's
influence had lessened considerably since the days of Bismarck. The importance of
the federal ministries grew to the point that one spoke of a "Reich Administration"
(*Reichsleitung*) by the end of the century, and of an "Imperial Government" (*Reichs-
regierung*) under Bethmann Hollweg. There was a corresponding decline in the influence of the Bundesrat which had been the epicenter of Bismarck's system. The
federal government frequently failed to consult the states and presented bills directly
to the Reichstag, and in some instances the support of political parties was seen as
more important than the wishes of the individual states. Once again the kaiser
echoed this trend by presenting himself not as *primus inter pares*, but as a German
emperor who regarded the other monarchs as liege lords and vassals.

The greater the importance of the federal government the greater the power of
the Reichstag. The government needed a Reichstag majority in order to push
through its legislation, and it could not get that majority without the support of the
Center Party. Above all it needed the Reichstag to agree both to how the money
was spent and how it was to be collected. The budgetary rights of the Reichstag
were strengthened as the fiscal burden increased. Nothing could be done without
making compromises and concessions with and to this Catholic party. The Center
Party thus became the most powerful party in the Reichstag, and its strength and
importance enhanced that of parliament. The Reichstag proved to be a reliable
partner for the government and an increasing number of bills were first discussed
by the parties and then introduced in the Reichstag rather than in the Bundesrat.
Even as convinced an anti-parliamentarian as Admiral Tirpitz, with his dream of
an "eternal law" for the navy, came to realize that there was no way round the
Reichstag if he wanted to build his battleships. Individual states that were unable
to get their way in the Bundesrat could always try again in the Reichstag. Relations
between Catholic Bavaria and the Center Party were particularly effective in this
respect. Similarly, when the government failed to get its way in the Bundesrat it
could always appeal to the Reichstag.

A big step forward was taken in 1906 when Reichstag deputies were paid a modest emolument. This opened the way for the creation of a professional political class, but it also furthered the process of political bureaucratization, a process brilliantly analyzed by the German sociologist Robert Michels. This had a profound effect on the SPD, the most highly organized and modern of all the political parties, which was to become the largest parliamentary party in 1912. Should it use the Reichstag merely as a propaganda forum and wait for the eagerly expected revolution as the party's chief ideologue Kautsky argued, or should it try to use the Reichstag as an instrument of social reform as the revisionist Bernstein proposed? Should it remain intransigently in opposition under the old slogan: "Not a single man, not a single Pfennig for this system;" or should it follow the example of Millerand and the French socialists and support certain proposals of the bourgeois government? The party's discourse remained resolutely revolutionary and Marxist platitudes raised the hackles of respectable bourgeois, but in practice the party was becoming increasingly reformist. In 1913 the SPD voted for the army estimates and in August 1914 the "fellows without a fatherland" supported the war effort with patriotic enthusiasm, in spite of all the antiwar resolutions of Socialist International, in which it was the largest party.

Germany was still far from having a parliamentary system whereby government was by a parliamentary majority and ministers were responsible to parliament. The Social Democrats were still regarded as pariahs. After the elections of 1912 when the Reichstag was no longer dominated by an alliance between conservatives and the Center Party, the SPD became a possible coalition partner. This was a frightful prospect for conservatives, but it was one which some members of the Center Party and the National Liberals viewed with equanimity. The time was not yet ripe for a coalition stretching from Bassermann and the National Liberals to Bebel and the SPD, and there was widespread fear among the smaller parties that a parliamentary system might be dominated by two large parties as in Britain and that they would lose their influence. But things were on the move and during the war a center–left coalition developed that was to form the basis of Germany's first parliamentary regime.

Caprivi and the "New Course"

Bismarck's successor was General Leo von Caprivi, a man who, in spite of his army rank, had for many years been secretary of state for the navy. He was an Austrian by birth, level headed, decent, conscientious, and with liberal leanings. Lacking a landed estate and many of the other trappings and characteristics of the aristocracy, he was despised by the Junkers as the "chancellor without an acre or a blade of grass." Although he was determined to uphold the authority of the monarchy and of the state, as well as being a sworn enemy of the Social Democrats, he was a man of compromise and of moderate reform. His task was not an easy one. Bismarck had far outlived his popularity, but he was a very hard act to follow. The old man in Friedrichsruh mounted a vicious campaign against the kaiser and his chancellor, and became the center of a conservative opposition. But nostalgia for the good old days of the Iron Chancellor led nowhere. Society had changed so dramatically since 1871 that the political structure he had given to the Reich was no longer either appropriate or workable. Bismarck was partially reconciled with his sovereign in 1894 and William II characteristically boasted that they could "build him triumphal arches in Vienna and Munich, but I shall always be a length ahead of him," whereupon Bismarck continued his attacks which were dismissed at court as the senile drivel of a feeble-minded old man. His memoirs, published shortly after his death in 1898, became an instant bestseller. This mendacious work was both a literary masterpiece and a massive attack on the policies of his successors. It misled generations of historians and was used as a weapon against the kaiser's personal rule, as were the numerous monuments to Bismarck that sprouted up throughout Protestant Germany, the largest and most hideous of which was built by the proudly independent burghers of Hamburg.

Caprivi was favorably disposed toward William II's momentary enthusiasm for social reform and his desire to be seen as the "social kaiser." The Prussian minister of trade, Baron Hans von Berlepsch, and the imperial secretary of state for the interior, Karl von Boetticher, worked hard to improve the lot of the working class, to give them a voice in the workplace, and to create an effective means of arbitrating disputes between management and labor. But it was all to no avail. The SPD continued to gain support and by 1893 William II lost interest in these social programs and went on a diametrically opposite course by supporting the ideas of Baron Carl von Stumm-Halberg. "King Stumm" demanded that his fellow industrialists should be masters in their own house, stern patriarchs who could demand and expect absolute obedience from the workforce, in return for which employers should ensure the wellbeing of their employees. There had been a wave of strikes since 1890, and these were to be made a thing of the past. The confrontational politics of the "Stumm era" overlooked the fact that in 1894 the Bavarian Social Democrats under Georg von Vollmar voted for the budget, thus marking the beginning of reformist politics in the party. The SPD leader August Bebel denounced this move at the party conference, but it was a clear sign that there was a possibility of integrating the industrial working class into society, and that a showdown between capital and labor as proposed by Stumm would be counter-productive.

Caprivi was open to the ideas of those who argued that Germany, as a rapidly expanding industrial nation, was hurt by high tariffs. With the clear trend toward what now would be called globalization, and which was then in certain circles described as imperialism, Germany could not afford to indulge in a neo-mercantilist policy of autarchy under the slogan of the "protection of national labor," nor could it afford to featherbed the agricultural sector. Caprivi summed up the situation with the slogan: "Either we export goods, or we export people!" The problem took on greater urgency as economic relations between Russia and France grew ever closer. The chancellor set about negotiating long-term trade agreements that would stimulate industrial exports. This in turn necessitated lowering agricultural tariffs, which was bound to upset the powerful agrarians and turn the conservatives against the government. In the winter of 1892 trade agreements were signed with Austria-Hungary, Italy, and Belgium, and ratified by the Reichstag in spite of opposition from the majority of the conservatives.

Conservatism, once a powerful political ideology, was rapidly becoming an expression of the special interests of the agrarians. German agriculture was becoming increasingly uncompetitive, prices were forced downwards by as much as 50 percent due to intense foreign competition, and many farmers were in dire straits. There were loud cries for help and a frantic search for scapegoats. The Social Democrats, with their egalitarian demands for cheaper foodstuffs, and Jewish dealers were singled out for special blame. In 1893 the Farmers' League (*Bund der Landwirte*) was formed, a populist, anti-Semitic, rabble-rousing movement that gained widespread support, particularly in the eastern provinces. A similar organization was also formed in Bavaria, known as the Bavarian Farmers' Association (*Bayerischer Bauernbund*). The Junkers had conjured up a spirit which soon got out of hand. Conservatives were dabbling with mass politics and associated with outspoken demagogues who launched a violent attack on the chancellor and his government. Many an old-style but far-sighted conservative civil servant began to worry that the sorcerer's apprentice might eventually threaten the master.

In December 1893 the trade treaty with Romania only just managed to squeak past the Reichstag and the conservatives stepped up their attacks on Caprivi. The debate on the critical treaty with Russia in March of the following year amounted to a vote of confidence in the chancellor and his policy of encouraging industry, reducing the cost of basic foods, and putting the agrarians in their place. The result was a resounding victory for Caprivi, with the parties from Bassermann to Bebel joining in support of the chancellor and his moderate policies. The conservatives fought back, promising a struggle to the death against liberal capitalism, and demanding a state trading monopoly for agricultural produce and guaranteed minimum prices. This was turned down flat by the Reichstag majority, and the fronts hardened still further. The conservatives were losing ground in the Reichstag, but they managed to hold their own in Prussia. They won major concessions in Miquel's comprehensive tax reform. The proposal to introduce death duties was rejected, and real estate was far less heavily taxed than movable capital. The three-class electoral system based on the amount of taxes paid became even more inequitable after these reforms and thus further strengthened the parties on the right.

Educational reform proved to be Caprivi's greatest headache. The conservative Prussian minister of education, Count Robert von Zedlitz-Trützschler, proposed a bill that would mark a return to confessional schools. The object behind this move was to win the support of the Center Party, which was needed in the Reichstag to ensure the passage of the trade treaties, as well as the army estimates. The proposal met with a storm of protest from the liberals and freethinking intellectuals who regretted the end of the *Kulturkampf*. The kaiser, strongly supported by Miquel, refused to accept the idea of an educational reform that was not supported by the

National Liberals, fearing the end of the cartel in Prussia. Both Caprivi and Zedlitz-Trützschler offered their resignations. Caprivi was now no longer Prussian minister-president, but remained as Prussian foreign minister so as to be able to instruct the Prussian delegation to the Bundesrat. His place in Prussia was taken by the ultra-conservative Count Botho zu Eulenburg, but Caprivi was still chancellor. Zedlitz-Trützschler's resignation was accepted.

The conservatives felt humiliated and stepped up their attacks on the government, culminating in the Tivoli Program of December 1892 with its unpleasant populist and anti-Semitic overtones. The Center Party was equally disgruntled but went on the opposite tack, attacking the government from the left. When Caprivi felt obliged to dissolve the Reichstag because of his failure to win a majority for a 72,000-man increase in the army he was left in an awkward position. The elections returned a majority of National Liberals and populists. The aristocratic conservatives suffered a severe defeat, and although the Social Democrats won the largest share of the popular vote, the Center Party had the largest number of seats.

With considerable skill Caprivi managed to push through the army estimates and won an impressive majority for the Russian trade treaty, but he had lost the confidence of the kaiser. William II disliked the chancellor's schoolmasterly tone, was irritated by the debacle over confessional schools, and was furious that Caprivi had reduced the years of compulsory service in the army from three to two years. Inspired by Stumm to take a firm stand against Social Democracy and alarmed by a wave of anarchist attacks, which culminated in the stabbing to death in Lyons of the French president Sadi Carnot by an Italian revolutionary in June 1894, the kaiser demanded immediate legislative action against the forces of revolution. Caprivi pointed out that any such legislation was the province of the individual states, but Botho Eulenburg and Miquel wanted a federal law. They knew perfectly well that the proposed "anti-revolutionary bill" (*Umsturzvorlage*) would never pass the Reichstag, and therefore plotted a coup d'état and an end to universal manhood suffrage. The kaiser's call for action was widely popular, prompting him to make yet another outrageous public address in Königsberg, calling for the forces of order to stand together against the subversives and revolutionaries. Caprivi stood firm and William II backed down, largely because of the likely reaction abroad to such an outlandish course of action, but the chancellor's days in office were now numbered.

Eulenburg went ahead with plans for anti-revolutionary legislation and a possible putsch in Prussia, but once again Caprivi won the day, this time with support from Miquel. The kaiser used an unfortunate press release that implied that the chancellor had put him in his place as an excuse to dismiss both Caprivi and Eulenburg at the end of October 1894. Thus ended Caprivi's "New Course," an imaginative and promising attempt to reform a country that was in an awkward transition period between the overbearing and ossified late Bismarckian era and the arrogant hubris of the Wilhelminian epoch. It failed because of the kaiser's fickleness, the stubbornly doctrinaire attitude of the main political parties, the excessive influence of interest groups, the alarming growth of radical populism, and the inherent structural problem of relations between Prussia and the Reich. For all his short-comings Caprivi did remarkably well, and it is exceedingly doubtful whether under such trying circumstances another chancellor would have done any better.

The first major problem confronting the "New Course" in foreign policy was the question of whether or not to renew the Reinsurance Treaty in 1890. The chancellor, along with the new head of the foreign office, Baron Adolph Marschall von Bieberstein, and the *éminence grise* of the Wilhelmstrasse, Friedrich von Holstein, agreed that this "bigamous" relationship should be ended. One objection to the treaty was that it stood in the way of an understanding with Britain. A first step in this direction was made in 1890 with the Helgoland–Zanzibar treaty for which Bismarck had already prepared the ground. Germany abandoned both the odious Carl Peters, who was widely disliked not because he had committed murder and rape but because he had an African concubine, and his co-agitator "Emin Pasha" (Eduard Schnitzer). Germany abandoned claims to Zanzibar, Uganda, and the coast of Kenya and in return received the tiny island of Helgoland, which was to provide Germany with a strategically important base for submarines in two world wars. Most Germans regarded this treaty with indifference, and only the colonial enthusiasts were outraged at what they felt was a flagrantly unequal exchange. In the following year they formed their protest group, the Pan-German League (*Alldeutsche Verband*) which was soon to become one of the most raucous and influential of Germany's many powerful interest groups.

Having abandoned the Reinsurance Treaty, Germany was perforce obliged to strengthen its ties with Austria-Hungary. The Triple Alliance was renewed ahead of time in 1891, in an effort to counter France's attempts to lure Italy away from the alliance. At the same time Germany gave an assurance of support to Austria-Hungary over the Bulgarian question, which was still a burning issue. Long-term trade agreements were made with Austria-Hungary, Italy, Belgium, and Switzerland. A somewhat half-hearted attempt to bring Britain closer to the Triple Alliance was firmly rejected. German diplomats subscribed to the "chestnut theory:" the suspicion that the British simply wanted Germany to do their dirty work for them and offer precious little in return. The Germans wanted a firm treaty with Britain, but the British had no desire to be tied to an unpredictable European partner, and did not wish to help Germany to become a hegemonic power. Relations with Britain took a turn for the worse when Gladstone returned to office in 1892. The prime minister viewed the Ottoman Empire with deep revulsion and Britain was no longer prepared to support the "sick man of Europe." Germany imagined that the British government was trying the stir up another eastern crisis, and now took over the role of protecting Turkey by supporting the Ottoman Empire's claims in Egypt, in flagrant disregard of the stipulations of the Helgoland–Zanzibar Treaty. Support for Turkey necessarily involved a further worsening of relations with Russia.

Russia viewed Caprivi's policies with the deepest suspicion. The refusal to renew the Reinsurance Treaty, the Helgoland–Zanzibar Treaty, the early renewal of the Triple alliance, closer relations with the Ottoman Empire, the army increases in 1892, and the ongoing trade war between the two countries were seen as clear evidence of a disavowal of Bismarck's more flexible attitude toward Russia. This strengthened the argument of those in Russia who argued in favor of closer relations with France. The tsar and his Danish wife were anti-German and detested William II, but they still harbored residual resentments against republican France, which was then riven by the spectacular Panama scandal. But Alexander III soon overcame his distaste for the French, the French fleet paid an official visit to Kronstadt in the summer of 1891, and the military convention of 1892 was formally ratified over the new year in 1893/4. In 1893 the Russian fleet made an official visit to Toulon in a deliberately provocative gesture against both England and Germany's ally, Italy. For Germany the threat of a two-front war had become very real.

Berlin still suffered from Bismarckian delusions that it would not be difficult to win back Russia's goodwill, since there were a number of influential figures in Russia who were appalled by the alliance with France. German diplomats were further comforted by the thought that even if England refused to draw closer, at least Germany still had a free hand. Relations with Russia were somewhat improved by the trade treaties in which the Germans made some important concessions, and also by Russia's growing preoccupation with Far Eastern affairs; but the harm had already been done, the military alliance with France was ratified, and Russo-German relations remained precariously strained.

Hohenlohe

Caprivi's successor as chancellor was the elderly Prince Chlodwig zu Hohenlohe-Schillingsfürst, a lofty Catholic magnate from Bavaria with wide administrative experience, and of liberal conservative views. He was 75, deaf, and forgetful, and certainly not the man to restrain the young kaiser, but on the other hand as a man of the old school, with the typical anti-Prussian sentiments of a southern German and with the dismissive attitude of a grand seigneur toward Prussia's "cabbage Junkers," he was not going to be content to play the role of the kaiser's man. William relied heavily on Philipp zu Eulenburg for advice as he set about appointing his own team. He was determined to get rid of Marschall and Boetticher, as well as the minister of war, Walter Bronsart von Schellendorff. The first two of these were subjected to vicious attacks from the Bismarck camp since they were held to have played a role in the great man's dismissal. Maximilian Harden sharpened his pen and supported the campaign in the pages of his magazine *Zukunft*. Boetticher was dismissed in 1897 on the grounds that he had failed adequately to protect the kaiser against a spirited attack on his "personal rule" by the left liberal Eugen Richter, leader of the Independent People's Party. The secretary of state for the navy, Admiral Hollmann, was dropped when he failed to get his way in the Reichstag over the naval estimates, when Eugen Richter and the Reichstag won yet another significant victory. The kaiser's man, Admiral Alfred von Tirpitz, took his place, with the remit to conduct a "life and death struggle" for the navy. Marschall was sent on holiday later in the year and William II's favorite, Bernhard von Bülow, became acting secretary of state. Bronsart von Schellendorff was dismissed for supporting a modest reform in the outrageously antiquated code of military law.

Hohenlohe offered his resignation over the Boetticher affair but it was refused. William II had put a number of his own candidates in key positions without even consulting the chancellor, and was determined to continue with his anti-socialist and confrontational program, in spite of the chancellor's reservations. The "anti-revolutionary bill" was reintroduced in the Reichstag at the end of 1894, having become even more repressive, so as to include the prohibition of attacks on religion, morals, tradition, and the established order. This was totally unacceptable to the Reichstag majority, and was rejected out of hand. The kaiser's intimates now talked wildly of a coup d'état to be led by the former chief of the General Staff, General Waldersee. Nothing came of this, but all social legislation was put on hold and the reform-minded Berlepsch was forced out of office. The SPD's critical attitude toward the twenty-fifth-anniversary celebrations of the foundation of the Reich provoked a storm of protest on the right and infuriated the kaiser, whereupon the Prussian minister of the interior Ernst von Köller let the police loose on the socialists; but all this only served to increase the SPD's appeal. An attempt at anti-socialist legislation in Prussia failed by a narrow margin. The fronts hardened still further over a major strike in the Hamburg docks in the winter of 1896/7. Prominent social reformers, such as the sociologist Ferdinand Tönnies and the evangelical pastor Friedrich Naumann, expressed their sympathy for the strikers. Waldersee, as corps commander in Hamburg Altona, wanted to use force to break the strike. William II sympathized, and in a public speech announced that any means, however drastic, were justified in the struggle against the forces of subversion and revolution. In further speeches he called for stern measures against picket lines. A further attempt at anti-socialist legislation was made in 1899 with the "Prison Bill" (*Zuchthausvorlage*), but it suffered an ignominious defeat, leaving the conservatives isolated in their extreme position. This was the end of the "Stumm era," and Hohenlohe's days were numbered. Bülow, whom the kaiser was grooming as his replacement, waited in the wings.

"World Politics" and Navalism

Relations with Britain had taken a turn for the worse when the kaiser sent a telegram in January 1896 congratulating President Krüger for repulsing Dr Jameson's raid on the Transvaal. This was a dramatic expression of solidarity with the Boers in their struggle against the British, and was greeted with violently anti-German tirades in the British press, but it was Tirpitz's naval building program that was really to poison relations between the two countries. The high seas fleet was the key element in the "World Politics" (*Weltpolitik*) which enjoyed widespread public support. As Max Weber said in his widely quoted inaugural lecture in Freiburg in 1895: "We must understand that the unification of Germany was a juvenile prank carried out by the nation in its old age, the expenses of which should have been saved, if it was the end and not the beginning of German power politics on a global scale" (*Welt-machtpolitik*). Germany, in short, was to join the ranks of the imperialist powers.

The newcomer had precious little room for maneuver. It could push its claims for a few marginal areas in Africa and demand equal rights in China, Morocco, or the Ottoman Empire, but at every turn it came up against the established imperialist powers of Britain, France, and Russia. When Bülow was appointed secretary of state for foreign affairs in 1897 he announced in the Reichstag, in words that echoed those of Jean Paul quoted at the beginning of this book: "The days when the Germans left the land to one of their neighbors and the sea to the other, keeping only the sky for themselves and when pure theory reigned are now over. . . . We do not wish to put anyone in the shade, but we also demand a place in the sun." Nevertheless any increase in Germany's colonial empire necessarily diminished the relative strength of other empires, and this was a particularly sensitive issue for the British, whose empire already showed marked signs of decline. German colonial ambitions, although relatively modest, were nevertheless to cast a long shadow.

Anglo-German relations were bedeviled by the contradictions between Germany's position in the center of Europe and as an aspiring imperialist power. Germany needed Britain's support in Europe against the threat from Russia and France, but its imperial aspirations were bound to place considerable strain on the relationship between the two countries. Germany wanted to ensure its security in Europe but also pursue a forceful *Weltpolitik*. Very few in positions of authority realized that these were contradictory ambitions, and most fondly imagined that the Anglo-Russian and Anglo-French antagonisms were an immutable factor in international relations, so that Britain would never join the ranks of Germany's opponents.

This contradiction was deeply embedded in the strategic thinking behind Tirpitz's battle fleet. On the one hand it was designed to protect the coastline against the Russian and French fleets and to break any close blockade. But on the other it was also intended to guard Germany's overseas empire and commercial interests, and for that to be possible naval bases were needed in remote parts of the globe. Tirpitz argued that cruisers were inadequate for either role and that a fleet of battleships was needed. The battleships were to be powerful enough not only to break a blockade and protect the colonies but also to act as a deterrent. The fleet was to be so powerful that neither Russia nor France would dare risk a confrontation and, on the principle of "if you can't beat 'em, join 'em," Germany would become an attractive potential partner.

In purely naval terms Tirpitz's plan was virtually unassailable and his views differed very little from those of sailors like Sir John Fisher, who had absorbed Alfred Thayer Mahan's teaching that great power status depended on sea power. The problem lay in the political consequences of naval building. From the outset Tirpitz saw his battle fleet as a direct challenge to Britannia's claim to rule the waves, and the "risk theory" was primarily designed to ensure British neutrality in the event of a continental war. Even before the first naval bill was debated, the admiralty envisaged Britain as a potential enemy. Anglo-German naval rivalry was soon to become the central issue, and all the other arguments in favor of a high seas fleet soon became mere propagandistic rhetoric, designed to disguise the real thrust of Tirpitz's strategy. At times Tirpitz entertained the fantastic idea that Germany could take on the Royal Navy and replace Britain as a naval power, at others he imagined that Britain would be obliged to make major concessions and accept Germany as an equal partner. At the very least the fleet would guarantee that Britain would stay out of any future European conflict. Germany did not have the financial resources or, in spite of the widespread enthusiasm among the bourgeois parties for the naval building program, the political will to build a fleet that was large enough to fulfill any of these three roles. Moreover, it never entered Tirpitz's mind that Britain might look for support elsewhere. As a result all three of Tirpitz's scenarios were to prove to be pure fantasy. Another fatal weakness was the failure to coordinate military and naval strategy with foreign policy. Whereas the diplomats thought, however ambivalently, in terms of some kind of arrangement with Britain, the army, under Schlieffen, worked on plans for a western offensive involving the violation of Belgian neutrality that was likely to involve Britain in a continental war. Tirpitz's anti-British strategy was worked out independently from the army and the chancellor was kept in virtual ignorance of strategic matters, which were never discussed with politicians.

Economic factors also played an important role in the burgeoning Anglo-German rivalry. Due in large part to Germany's spectacular achievements in the second industrial revolution, particularly in the chemical and electrical industries, the country's share of world trade was only fractionally less than Britain's on the eve of the Great War. Britain had long since ceased to be the workshop of the world, and felt humiliated by an aggressive newcomer with whom it now had a negative trade balance. Germany in return feared that the British might be tempted to put up a protective tariff wall around the empire, and the call for a place in the sun that would provide safe markets for German goods became ever more insistent. In the overly dramatic discourse of the day Germany had to become the hammer or it would be merely the anvil.

As elsewhere in the developed nations, the relationship between economic interests and foreign policy was complex and often contradictory. A consortium under the Deutsche Bank was initially enthusiastically supportive of the government's sponsorship of the Baghdad railway, a grandiose plan to link Constantinople with Basra, but it soon began to lose interest when faced with foreign competition, higher risks, and spiraling costs. Similarly, the government was unable to work up much enthusiasm for investment in the perennially dubious Chinese market. Mannesmann's mining interests in Morocco gave the tail a chance to wag the dog, while the armaments industry was given full political and diplomatic support for its efforts in the Balkans and the Ottoman Empire.

The motives behind German imperialism were many and varied and, as with other complex historical phenomena, it is impossible to establish a convincing causal hierarchy. Liberals like Gustav Stresemann, Max Weber, or Friedrich Naumann hoped that imperialism would help modernize German society, break the stranglehold of the conservative agrarian elite, provide the additional assets to enable a fairer distribution of wealth, and thus encourage the integration of the working class. Social imperialists, with Bülow at their head, saw imperialism as a glamorous project that would integrate the nation and marginalize the Social Democrats. The "Hottentot elections" of 1906, as we shall see, were to lend credence to this view, but imperialism was never such an attractive prospect for bourgeois parties and Bülow was under frequent attack from the extreme right by such mass organizations as the Pan-German League and later by the Navy League. On the other side of the equation a number of socialists, from Marx on down, saw a positive aspect in imperialism in that it brought progressive ideas to backward areas, giving the colonized the weapons for their eventual liberation and providing jobs for their working-class supporters. As the years went by there emerged a remarkably broad consensus on imperialism.

Tirpitz promptly set to work on a long-term naval building program supported by a massive propaganda effort to educate the German public. The navy's Information Office (*Nachrichtenbüro*) issued a flood of propaganda material and organized exhibitions and meetings that were addressed by patriotic "naval professors." It encouraged the formation of a Navy League (*Flottenverein*) which was soon to become one of the largest and most influential of the many powerful interest groups in Wilhelmine Germany. Tirpitz's first naval bill was debated in 1897. It was relatively modest, but it was presented as the first stage of a long-range plan to build a battle fleet. The reception in the Reichstag was mixed. Conservatives who represented agrarian interests detested this "ghastly fleet," since for them it represented nationalism, "world politics," industry, and export markets, all to the detriment of Prussia, the army, agriculture, and the old order. The bill squeaked through largely due to the support of a majority of the Center Party which was anxious to show its loyalty to the regime. In the following year Germany showed its determination to continue its naval building program by flatly refusing to agree to disarmament and international arbitration as proposed at the conference at The Hague, convened on the initiative of the tsar. The brusque and threatening attitude of the Germans caused a most unfavorable impression in the international community, as did a repeat performance at the second peace conference in 1907.

In 1897 the Germans used the murder of two missionaries in Kiautschou in order to establish a naval base in China. It was a suitable harbor with nearby coal-mines and soon boasted a fine German brewery at Tsingtao, which still produces China's best known beer. The British, who controlled 80 percent of the trade with China, resented the German presence in Shantung, but their fears were unfounded. Germany never became a major player in China and only managed to capture a fraction of the Chinese market. The former chief of the General Staff, Waldersee, was appointed to command the international force that crushed the Boxer Rebellion in 1900, but he arrived after British and Japanese troops had taken Peking. His overbearing attitude earned him the sobriquet "World Marshal," while back at home the kaiser gave another of his unfortunate speeches to German troops who were being sent to China, urging them to behave like the Huns, and adding that the Chinese should henceforth not dare to look a German in the eyes. The kaiser's discourse was now peppered with references to the "yellow peril," and the crude racism of the "Hun speech" was widely seen as further evidence of the unpredictable and pushy nature of Wilhelmine Germany.

A second naval bill was debated in 1899 that foresaw a German fleet that would be the third largest in the world, behind those of Britain and France. The proposal was sharply criticized by the agrarians on the right and by Bebel and Richter on the left. The former complained about the effects on agriculture and what they were pleased to call "the national cause;" the latter denounced the bill as a further example of the kaiser's personal rule. A number of deputies warned of a further worsening of relations with Britain, which had already been poisoned by the Boer War. In spite of such complaints the bill passed with minor revisions. It was a triumph for Tirpitz and the kaiser, and there was no further talk of the need for a coup d'état. Tirpitz had hoped that his naval building program would effectively shut out the Reichstag and, in his words, "place the social order in quarantine." He was not fully successful in this endeavor, but there was now a consensus, however hesitant in some circles, for a large navy and the strident imperialism of "World Politics."

Differences between agrarians and industrialists that were apparent in the debates over the naval bills came to a head in 1899, when a proposal to build a canal connecting the Rhine to the Elbe was debated in the Prussian House of Representatives. The kaiser wholeheartedly supported the idea, but the conservatives were in violent opposition. For them it was a floodgate through which cheap North American grain would swamp eastern agriculture. William II did not dare to dissolve the House, but he took the constitutionally highly dubious step of threatening to ask for the resignation of all representatives who were in state employ and who opposed the bill. In spite of such drastic measures the bill was rejected, and it was not until 1905 that funds were approved for the construction of part of the canal. This incident clearly showed the limits of the kaiser's personal power. As Miquel pointed out, he could not afford to break with the conservatives since he had nowhere else to turn. A break with the conservatives could not be avoided without looking after the interests of the agrarians. Their more extreme demands were clearly unacceptable, but concessions had to be made. Trading in grain futures was forbidden, strict veterinary controls were applied to imported meat and livestock, generous subsidies were provided, and tariffs increased. On the other hand there was general agreement that Germany was an industrial country and the efforts of those like Count Heinz von Kanitz, who wanted to turn the clock back with drastic measures such as a state monopoly on the sale of grain, were hopelessly unrealistic. Furthermore, the increase in the price of essential foodstuffs was causing widespread discontent and debate, all to the advantage of parties on the left. The situation was further complicated by the demands of the middle classes who felt trapped between industrialists and agrarians on one side, and by the working class on the other.

In this complex and confusing situation, where the interests of various significant groups were at odds, Miquel was inspired by Bismarck's notions of an alliance between rye and iron, and of a "cartel," to propose in 1897 a policy of "solidarity" (*Sammlung*), whereby all the "productive classes" should stand together and the differences between agriculture and industry be overcome without harming the middle classes. Conservatives would be won over to support the naval building program by tariff increases. The interests of consumers were to be respected; the Social Democrats excluded. All ideas of integrating the industrial working class by means of social reform were abandoned, the *Sammlung* being cemented by a common struggle against the Red Menace, and by collective enthusiasm for *Welt-politik*. This attractive vision of a society pulling together in pursuit of a common cause soon proved to be a fantasy, although it was to lose little of its attraction for subsequent generations, and is still peddled as a recipe for the solution of current discontents. Industrialists complained that the agrarians were being favored, the agrarians in turn grumbled that they were getting the thin end of the stick. It was a disaster in electoral terms. In 1898 the SPD increased their share of the vote from 23.3 percent to 27.2 percent. The two conservative parties lost 20 percent of their seats in the Reichstag. The National Liberals also lost seats. The Center was the largest party, and thus held the balance of power.

Bülow

In October 1900 Bernhard von Bülow was appointed chancellor. Secretary of state for foreign affairs since 1897, he had been groomed as Hohenlohe's successor. He was elegant, charming, vain, and superficial – the "minister of fine appearance" as one wit described him – but he was also a strong-willed and competent adminis-trator. He brought order to government, and ended the conflicts over competence between Prussia and the Reich by pushing aside Miquel who, as vice-president of Prussia, had carved out a personal empire. Bülow was very skillful in manipulating the kaiser, who in turn became less involved in day-to-day politics, largely due to the fact that Tirpitz, the other strong man in the government, was successful in obtaining funding for his beloved fleet. William II frequently caused havoc with his ill-considered interventions, and August Bebel claimed that each speech made by the monarch resulted in 100,000 additional votes for the Social Democrats. Bülow shielded the kaiser from mounting criticism, and sycophantically calmed the monarch's irascible and unpredictable humors. Although Bülow was at first not pre-pared to continue Miquel's appeasement of the conservatives by tariff concessions, he soon realized that there was no real alternative to *Sammlungspolitik*. At first he refused to increase the tariffs on grain, with the result that the conservatives once again defeated the Mittelland Canal project. In 1902 the government proposed tariff increases of up to 40 percent. This prompted an outburst of protest from the left, which was matched by equally inflammatory rhetoric from the Farmers' League, the Bavarian Farmers' League, and sundry other agrarian interest groups which insisted that the proposed increases were far too modest. It took a certain amount of procedural chicanery to pass the tariff bill and it did not come into effect until 1905.

The tariffs were long overdue. Years of the low Caprivi tariff and the parlous state of the world market had placed the German farmers, whether East Elbian Junkers or Bavarian peasants, in a precarious position, and they desperately needed the help afforded to the agricultural sector elsewhere. The effect of price increases on low-income groups was nowhere near as dire as had been predicted. Nevertheless, dissatisfaction with the new tariffs was expressed in the elections in 1903 in which the turnout was remarkably high. The Social Democrats made substantial gains, admittedly at the cost of the left liberals, the conservatives lost votes, and once again the Center was returned as the largest party and thus still held the balance. The Center Party used its influential position to secure modest improvements in social policy, which were enthusiastically endorsed by the energetic and progressive secretary of state for the interior, Count Posadowsky. They were also able to remove some of the remaining traces of the *Kulturkampf*. Support for the new tariffs was made conditional on the introduction of an insurance scheme for widows and orphans, and in 1904 the Bundesrat annulled the anti-Jesuit law, thus occasioning howls of protest from fervent Protestants and Godless liberals. In the following year the party managed to push through its demand that Reichstag deputies should be remunerated. None of these measures were of spectacular importance, but they all showed that the Reichstag played an increasing role within the context of Bülow's plebiscitary imperialism.

When Britain reached an agreement with France in 1904 it no longer needed to consider the possibility of winning Germany's support against Russia. Germany supported Russia in its war against Britain's ally Japan, thus prompting a violent reaction in Britain. The British press blamed the Germans for the Dogger Bank incident, when the Russian fleet fired in error upon some British fishing vessels. In February 1905 Admiral Fisher gave a provocative speech calling for a preemptive strike against the German navy. The Germans now suffered from an acute "Copenhagen complex." Hotheads in the admiralty planned to invade Denmark and Sweden and blockade the Baltic, but cooler heads prevailed, including both Tirpitz and Schlieffen.

With Russia's crushing defeat and subsequent revolution, Britain no longer had to worry about the Russian menace and the way gradually opened to an understanding between the two powers. Germany was also significantly strengthened by the Russian debacle, and the government imagined that the Entente Cordiale might now fall apart and Russia turn to Germany for support. In fact the reverse happened. The very fact that Germany was now clearly the strongest power in Europe led the British to pay closer attention to continental affairs and to seek ways to contain it. Given that France was now allied with Russia's greatest rival, Berlin imagined that there was a strong possibility of a Russo-German understanding. The kaiser visited the tsar in the summer of 1905 and signed the Treaty of Björkö, whereby the two powers agreed to cooperate in Europe for a period of one year. William II was overjoyed with the success of his personal diplomacy, but the treaty had no substance. It was in clear contradiction to the Dual Alliance, and the Russian government, which was desperately in need of French financial support, refused to renege on its commitment to its ally.

Schlieffen and Holstein now thought in terms of a preventive war against France. The situation was ideal and such a golden opportunity was unlikely to recur, but the problem remained that there was no convincing *casus belli*. The Foreign Office therefore sought to split the Entente Cordiale by provoking a crisis over Morocco. The French, with blissful disregard for international agreements, but with the blessing of the British, set about turning Morocco into a protectorate in which they would have a trade monopoly. Germany protested vigorously and called for an open-door policy in Morocco. The kaiser, much against his will, was persuaded to pay an official visit to Tangier and proclaimed his support for the sultan. Germany was unquestionably in the right, but its heavy-handed approach, far from splitting the Entente, brought the partners closer together and strengthened their determination to stand up against such browbeating. The French foreign minister Delcassé, the architect of the Entente Cordiale and advocate of France's imperialist ambitions in North Africa, was forced to resign, and an international conference was held at Algeçiras. Germany was left completely isolated and was only supported by Austria-Hungary. Some important concessions were made to internationalize Morocco, but they made no significant difference to France's dominant position. Germany had suffered a severe diplomatic defeat and Britain was now convinced that this overbearing power, with its colonial and naval ambitions, represented the major threat to European stability and to the security of the British Empire. This view was shared by the new Liberal government which took office in December 1905.

The first major clash between the Center Party and the chancellor came in 1906. The Social Democrats had long been harsh critics of German colonial policy with its severity, corruption, and brutality. The rising star in the Center Party, Matthias Erzberger, a self-appointed busy-body with a distinct demagogic streak, took up the cause somewhat to the discomfort of the party leadership, and was resolutely seconded by Hermann Roeren, an otherwise obscure deputy. The brutal suppression of the rebellions of the Hereros and the Hottentots in German Southwest Africa (Namibia) was both widely criticized and hideously expensive. A proposal for additional funding for Southwest Africa was rejected by a narrow margin after a fierce debate in the Reichstag in December 1906. Bülow promptly called for a fresh round of elections, even though both Posadowsky and Tirpitz felt that it was still possible to reach an understanding with the Center.

Relations between the kaiser and the chancellor had become increasingly strained, with William II accusing Bülow of kowtowing to the Center, a party that he detested. Bülow had been sick for six months, had only just returned to work, and was anxious to show that he was a strong man who was not dependent on the Catholics. He now set about forming the "Bülow Block" of parties that were fervently anti-socialist and anticlerical, devoutly patriotic, enthusiastically imperialist, and loyal to kaiser and fatherland. What Bebel labeled the "Hottentot election" was a disaster for the Social Democrats, who lost almost half their seats in the

Reichstag due to Block tactics in the runoff elections. The Center Party made modest gains due to the fear of many Catholics of a fresh round of the *Kulturkampf*. The conservatives and National Liberals also increased their representation, as did the Left Liberals, who were no longer in opposition after the death of the brilliantly adversarial Eugen Richter earlier in the year.

Bülow intended to convert the Block from an electoral alliance to a parliamentary coalition, thus further enhancing the importance of the Reichstag. Secretaries of state such as Posadowsky, who were sympathetic to the Center, were dismissed, to be replaced by Bethmann Hollweg, who was also appointed vice chancellor; but many conservatives preferred cooperation with the Center to an alliance with the Left Liberals. Bülow's opening to the left was distasteful to many on the right who saw the Center as the lesser evil, whereas on the left the refusal to make fundamental reforms in the Prussian electoral system meant that their allegiance was questionable. The Block was thus ever in danger of falling apart. Both left and right could abandon it at any moment, and only the National Liberals were solid in their support.

In 1907 Russia and Britain settled their differences over Tibet, Afghanistan, and Persia, and Germany could no longer imagine that it was in a position to chose between England and Russia. Germany now found itself isolated and opposed by all the great powers. Bülow's Weltpolitik was in ruins. Slavophile anti-Germans were gaining the upper hand in Russia, while at the British Foreign Office Eyre Crowe wrote his famous memorandum in which he argued that Germany was striving for hegemony in Europe and posed a threat to the vital interests of the empire. Inspired by the lessons of the Russo-Japanese naval war, Britain had begun to build the monster heavily-armed and swift Dreadnoughts in 1906. Germany immediately took up the challenge and a fresh round of naval building began which further poisoned relations between the two countries.

The Bülow Block was responsible for some minor reforms, such as the liberalizing of the right of assembly, the relaxation of the absurdly stringent laws on lèse-majesté, as well the removal of the restrictions on futures trading; but this legislative activity was wholly overshadowed by a spectacular series of scandals that rocked the monarchy. Ever since 1906 Maximilian Harden, enthusiastically abetted by Holstein, who had been dismissed from the Foreign Office and was out for revenge, began to publish a series of articles exposing a number of homosexuals in the upper echelons of the military. In 1907 he began to make similar insinuations about the kaiser's favorite Prince Philipp zu Eulenburg und Hertefeld, and the gay coterie that met regularly at his castle in Liebenberg, many of whom were close to the kaiser. Male homosexual acts were an offense under paragraph 175 of the criminal code of 1871 and there were a series of spectacular trials. Eulenburg was charged with perjury, the affair was debated in the Reichstag, and Bülow made blustering denials of the existence of a "Camarilla." The end result was that the kaiser sustained irreparable damage to his reputation.

The Eulenburg trial took place in July 1908, and in October the *Daily Telegraph* published a résumé of a number of conversations that the kaiser had had with an

English officer. The tone of these remarks was typically ill considered, blustering, and tactless. He claimed that the British had won the Boer War because they had adopted a plan which he had sent to his grandmother, Queen Victoria. He insisted that he had turned down a Franco-Russian proposal to intervene in the Boer War. He further suggested that the German navy might eventually cooperate with the Royal Navy to attack Britain's ally Japan. William had quite correctly given the text to Bülow for perusal, but it passed his desk twice unread, and it was handed to some underling in the Foreign Office who failed to see the political implications of this diatribe and gave his imprimatur. The kaiser came under a ferocious attack in the press. At the head of this attack was Maximilian Harden, who suggested that he should abdicate. Bülow offered his resignation, while at the same time washing his hands of the whole affair. He distanced himself from the views expressed in the article and placed the blame squarely on the kaiser. The leader of the conservatives begged William II to be a trifle more circumspect in future. The affair was debated in the Reichstag, with Bülow refusing either to defend the kaiser or use the crisis to strengthen the relative position of the chancellor. He managed to win the support of the Reichstag majority, the Bundesrat, and the Prussian Ministry of State, all of whom hoped that he would be able to curb the precocious monarch. Meanwhile the kaiser went off hunting with his friend Carl Fürstenberg. During one evening of jollification the worthy chief of the Civil Cabinet, Count Dietrich von Hülsen-Haeseler, died of a heart attack while dancing in front of the king-emperor in a ballerina's tutu. This terpsichorean transvestism was greeted with a mixture of ribald humor and outrage, and the kaiser's tottering reputation suffered yet another setback.

Surprisingly enough the brouhaha soon subsided. The Eulenburg and *Daily Telegraph* affairs did not cause widespread public dismay, even though they were compounded by the Bosnian crisis of 1908. It was of concern to the political and the chattering classes, not to the average voter. The kaiser's wings had been modestly clipped, but Bülow no longer enjoyed his confidence, and without this his power was strictly limited. The question as to whether it would have been possible to use the crisis to reform the system of government is open. Bülow was certainly not the man to perform such a task, and maybe it needed the profound crisis of a lost war for any fundamental changes to be possible.

Germany felt isolated and insecure and compensated for this feeling of insecurity by stepping up the naval building program, which now became a symbolic representation of its great power status rather than a carefully considered component of the country's strategic requirements. Naval planners fondly imagined that Britain would be unable to keep pace in the naval race, and Tirpitz now argued that the relative strength of the two navies should be three to two rather than two to one. This proved to be mere wishful thinking. Britain's position was greatly strengthened by the ententes with France and Russia, and the Liberal government took up the challenge. By 1908 it was clear that Tirpitz's plan could not possibly be realized.

In the wake of the Young Turk revolution and subsequent reorganization of the Ottoman Empire, Austria-Hungary decided to annex the provinces of Bosnia and

Herzegovina, which they had administered since the Congress of Berlin, even though they remained nominally under Turkish rule. Serbia, which regarded the provinces as part of a greater Serbia, saw this as a deliberate affront, and Russia, which had previously agreed to the move, now supported the Serbian position. Germany, anxious to improve relations with the Ottoman Empire, did not approve of its ally's actions and vetoed the idea of a preventive war against Serbia. Russia was in no position to give Serbia anything beyond verbal support and had to bend to German pressure to accept the Austrian move. Russia felt angry and humiliated, and anti-German feelings ran high, as they also did in France. In an exchange of telegrams between the Prussian chief of the General Staff, the younger von Moltke, and his Austrian homologue Conrad von Hötzendorf, Germany promised support should Austria-Hungary attack Serbia and thereby find itself at war with Russia. Bismarck's Dual Alliance was thus reinterpreted to be a guarantee of unconditional support for Austria-Hungary. Were Germany to go to war in support of its ally, the Schlieffen Plan would automatically go into effect and France would be attacked via Belgium. A war in the Balkans that involved Russia would thus of necessity become a European war that many prominent military minds believed would be long, inconceivably bloody, and which Germany was unlikely to be able to win.

Bethmann Hollweg

The pressing order of the day was the long overdue reform of the Reich's finances, which were strained to breaking point by the sharp increases in government expenditure, especially on armaments. Five hundred million additional marks were needed per year to balance the books and it was hoped that this could be met by an increase in taxes on such items as alcohol and tobacco, as well as death duties. It was this latter proposal that was most hotly debated. The conservatives and their allies in the Farmers' League denounced the proposed death duties as a tax on widows and orphans, and as an underhand attempt to destroy agricultural property. The Center Party, which had strong ties to agriculture, particularly in its Bavarian sister party, supported this stand. The urban middle class was determined to oppose this agrarian demagogy, and the newly-formed Hansa Association (*Hansabund*) gave its full support to Bülow's proposals; but without the support of the conservatives and the Center the chancellor was doomed. The proposed death duties were turned down by the Reichstag, in spite of the Social Democrats voting with the government on this issue. The kaiser began to prattle about a coup d'état, and Bülow once again offered his resignation. This time it was accepted. The new minister of finance, Reinhold von Sydow, then brought in a set of proposals that would cover the deficit. The death duties were dropped, to be replaced by a series of indirect taxes, and further modifications of the Frankenstein clause were approved that favored the Reich. The kaiser had no regrets in parting from a chancellor whom he no longer trusted and who relied on Social Democrats and Left Liberals for parliamentary support. Bülow's departure from office thus further strengthened the Reichstag, even though the kaiser could have kept him in office had he so wished. The crisis that led to Bülow's fall left German society deeply divided, with the middle class indignant at the selfishness of the agrarian and clerical reactionaries. The National Liberals moved to the left, but neither they nor the Social Democrats were ready to follow the recommendation of those like Friedrich Naumann who called for a firm alliance "from Bassermann to Bebel." Most National Liberals still felt that the struggle against Social Democracy was as important as the struggle against the agrarians. Some felt uncomfortably close to the red revolutionaries, and hoped that the party could restore its ties with the conservatives. The new chancellor, Bethmann Hollweg, was a conservative reformer and a man of compromise, who hoped to smooth the troubled waters. He came from a distinguished banking family from Frankfurt, his father was a professor, and the family estate at Hohenfinow was a relatively recent acquisition. A man of melancholy and pessimistic disposition which many regarded as evidence of a philosophical cast of mind, he avoided confrontation where possible and only moved into action when absolutely necessary.

In early 1911 the French responded to a revolt in Morocco by occupying Rabat and Fez. Although this was in clear violation of international agreements, the Wilhelmstrasse under Kiderlen-Wächter suggested leaving Morocco to the French in exchange for a substantial chunk of the French Congo. In order to put pressure on the French to accept this proposal he sent the gunboat *Panther* to Agadir, ostensibly to protect German interests in the region. Kiderlen turned to Heinrich Class, the leader of the Pan-German League, to provide propagandistic support for this move. Class called for the annexation of West Morocco, a suggestion which was vigorously endorsed in much of the German press, even though this was unthinkable without a war. Moltke, who felt that a war was inevitable, suggested that the moment was propitious. When France refused Germany's proposals, Germany threatened to go to war. Lloyd George, in a speech at the Mansion House, warned that Britain was ready for war and stood by France. William II and Bethmann Hollweg persuaded Kiderlen to lower the ante and the French, unwilling to risk a war without being sure of Russian support, gave way. Germany left Morocco to the French and it became a French protectorate in 1912. In return Germany was given most favored nation status in Morocco and a substantial piece of the French Congo, Germany ceding a frontier strip of Togo to the French. Germany had suffered a humiliating defeat in this ill-considered and extremely risky affair. Heinrich Class held Kiderlen-Wächter hostage, and Bethmann Hollweg came under ferocious attack in the Reichstag for having threatened war and then backed down. Bassermann accused him of engaging in the "politics of illusion," and a future chancellor, Count Georg von Hertling, argued that peace had been bought at the cost of the nation's prestige. Ernst von Heydebrand, the conservative leader and "uncrowned king of Prussia," let loose a wild tirade against Britain and France, and urged the nation to prepare for war. The Social Democratic leader, August Bebel, met with howls of derisive laughter when he suggested that the arms race would lead to a war on an unimaginable scale that would result in a catastrophic "*Götterdämmerung* of the bourgeois world." Public opinion was in an ugly and aggressive mood, and Tirpitz could count on wide support for stepping up the naval building program. Kiderlen and Bethmann Hollweg both realized that Germany had to tread softly and try to reach a détente, but they faced powerful opposition from Tirpitz, the military, the Reichstag majority, and inflamed public opinion. Support from the kaiser was barely lukewarm. Only by urging the army to press for modest increases was he able to secure a slight reduction in the navy's demands.

The British war minister, Haldane, who was educated at Göttingen and was fluent in German, visited Berlin in February 1912 and proposed a slowing down of naval building while maintaining the two to one ratio. He suggested that a three to two ratio might be discussed at some future date. He flatly rejected the preposterous German request that Britain should promise to remain neutral in the event of a continental war. Haldane's proposals were unacceptable to the kaiser and Tirpitz, and Haldane did not trust Bethmann's assurances that he was anxious to preserve the peace. The British cabinet was even more skeptical. The Haldane mission thus did nothing to improve relations between the two countries, and served further to undermine the chancellor's position.

The clamor for reform of the monstrously inequitable Prussian electoral system based on wealth could no longer be overheard. Bethmann was prepared to make some minor adjustments to the system to silence criticism without alienating the conservatives, thus making possible a renewal of the conservative–National Liberal alliance. The reform proposal was exceedingly modest. The number of voters in the first class was to be almost doubled, but was still only seven percent of the electorate. The second class was to be 17 instead of 13.8 percent, and thus 76 percent of the electorate would be represented by one third of the delegates to the House of Representatives. Even these modest changes were opposed by the conservatives and the Center, and the debate in the House of Representatives had to be called off. The National Liberals were outraged, and the conservatives were angered that Bethmann had threatened to undermine their position in Prussia. Their discontent mounted when the government introduced universal manhood suffrage in Alsace-Lorraine, a measure wholeheartedly supported by the Social Democrats. Bethmann Hollweg was now known as Bethmann Sollweg ("must go") in respectable conservative circles.

The Reichstag election campaign of 1912 was a rally against the conservative –Center alliance, although some National Liberals still felt that the struggle against Social Democracy should take precedence. A rival organization to the Hansabund, the Middle Class Association (*Mittelstandsverband*), had been formed in the previous year and supported the conservatives. The fronts hardened, and Bethmann's hopes for a liberal–conservative compromise were dashed. He held himself aloof from the election in gloomy resignation. The results were nothing short of sensational. The number of Social Democratic mandates increased from 43 to 110 and the SPD was now the largest parliamentary party, with more than a quarter of the seats. The conservative–Center block, with their allies, dropped from 211 to 158 seats and were thus the clear losers, but their opponents, with 197 seats, were divided amongst themselves. The Reichstag was deadlocked, the chancellor had no grouping with which he could work comfortably, and he had to rely on making backroom deals and compromises to which he gave the pretentious title "politics of the diagonal." Conservatives denounced him as weak-kneed and soft on socialism, he did not enjoy the confidence of the kaiser, and the left clamored for reforms which, however modest, were effectively blocked by Prussia.

The parties reacted very differently to the election. The Center sniffed the wind and edged cautiously to the left. The National Liberals, who had lost badly at the polls, moved closer to the conservatives, stepped up their attacks on the Social Democrats, and denounced the government for its lack of imperialist fervor and its failure to arm to the teeth. Young Turks in the party, prominent among them Gustav Stresemann, hoped to steer a middle course between the conservatives and the Social Democrats, a view that was shared by most of the Independents. On the left, the radicals around Karl Liebknecht and Rosa Luxemburg, as well as Karl Kautsky and the center, wanted nothing to do with the bourgeois parties. The revisionists and reformists on the right were determined to remain in opposition. Even in Baden, where Liberals and Social Democrats had worked together for a while, the two parties drifted apart. The Social Democrats were thus still pariahs, "fellows without a fatherland" in the kaiser's words, and the other parties felt that any close association with them would be the kiss of death.

It was thus virtually impossible to create a working parliamentary majority, and none of the proposed solutions were viable in the long term. The "Cartel of the Creative Estates" (*Kartell der schaffende Stände*) of 1913, made up of conservatives and the right wings of the National Liberals and the Center, was a toothless version of Sammlung. A populist appeal to the mass organizations such as the Pan-German League, the Army and Navy Leagues, and the Farmers' League to join together in an attack on the conservative reformers around the chancellor, produced little beyond a lot of hot air and unproductive sloganeering. Those in the middle of the political spectrum were too few and too weak to offer a way out of the crisis, which was virtually impossible without an opening up toward the Social Democrats. This in turn was impossible as long as the Social Democrats persisted with their blood-curdling revolutionary rhetoric that disguised their moderate, reformist stance. The conservative reformers aimed at further social legislation so as to counter the appeal of Social Democracy and reconcile the working class with the state, but the electoral success of the Social Democrats forced the reformers onto the defensive. The right demanded an all out attack on the trades unions and the SPD. The government hoped to create a reserve of social peace between the ardent class warriors on the left and on the right, but was ever sensitive to criticism that it was being too conciliatory toward the red revolutionaries, and as a result only modest efforts were made.

Armaments were still the great issue of the day and a number of pressing questions had to be addressed. What armaments strategy was best suited to Germany's needs? Which should be given priority – the army or the navy? The most difficult question was how to meet the spiraling costs of armaments. Tirpitz and the navy, smarting from Germany's humiliation having bungled the Moroccan crisis of 1911, wanted to step up the naval building program, which had been slowed down in 1908. Both Bethmann and the secretary of state for foreign affairs, Kiderlen-Wächter, hoped to improve relations with Britain, and were supported by the treasury, which was horrified by the cost of building a vast battle fleet that could take on the Royal Navy. The proposed army increases of 1911 seemed to put paid to Tirpitz's plan. Once again the role of the kaiser was critical. The Haldane mission was seen by the kaiser as an insult and affront. He ordered the German ambassador in London to wave the big stick, Tirpitz leaked his proposals to the press, and Bethmann protested that Germany was heading for war, and offered his resignation. The kaiser saw no viable alternative candidate for the post and refused to accept, but relations between the two men were further strained. The resulting naval and army bills of 1912 were relatively modest. The army was increased by a mere 29,000 men, much to the consternation of the Army League and of the proponents of a mass army such as Colonel Ludendorff. The navy was to have three new battleships by 1920. The additional cost was to be met by a prolongation of the increased tax on sugar and a tax on alcohol distilleries, the latter much to the disgust of the agrarians, many of whom produced schnapps on their estates.

By 1912 the Triple Alliance was in ruins due to fundamental differences between Italy and Austria-Hungary in the Balkans and the Middle East. The situation became extremely precarious with the Balkan War of 1912 when Serbia, Greece, Bulgaria, and Montenegro combined to drive the Ottomans out of Europe. Austria-Hungary was determined to stop Serbia from establishing a foothold on the Adriatic and therefore supported the creation of an independent Albania. Russia supported Serbia, and Europe appeared to be on the brink of war. A conference was held in London that temporarily defused the situation. Britain urged both Russia and Austria-Hungary to back down. Germany did not want to become directly involved and also urged moderation, but was determined that its ally should not be further weakened. An independent Albania was created, Serbian ambitions thus frustrated, and the crisis appeared to have been mastered. The Balkan crisis created an ugly atmosphere in Berlin. There had been a marked increase in demands for Germany to assert itself throughout the world and prepare for war. War was seen by some to be inevitable due to the fundamental differences between Teutons and Slavs, while others argued that a nation that was forged in Bismarck and Moltke's wars had become enfeebled and needed a war to restore its moral fiber. An alarming number of influential figures saw war as an inescapable component of the social-Darwinist struggle for existence between nations and races. Bestselling books such as Friedrich von Bernhardi's *Germany and the Next War*, published in 1912, both echoed and inflamed this dangerously bellicose spirit of the times.

At the height of the crisis Britain had warned Germany that it would not stand idly by should an Austrian war against Serbia lead to an attack on France. On December 8 1912 William II held a crown council attended by the military leadership. Moltke announced that Germany should go to war at the first suitable opportunity. Tirpitz wanted to wait 18 months until the fleet was ready. Moltke sourly remarked that the fleet would never be ready and that Germany should go to war "the sooner the better." The kaiser called for increased armaments and began to talk about a "racial struggle" with an "overconfident" Russia. This was a typical piece of theatrical posing and swagger, indication of a blustering lack of direction at the top rather than a clear indication of Germany's determination to go to war. There were no immediate consequences from the crown council, from which Bethmann Hollweg had been excluded, and when war broke out again in the Balkans in the following year Germany once again urged Austria-Hungary to be cautious. The victors of 1912, supported by Turkey and Romania, turned on their former ally, Bulgaria, which was promptly defeated. Germany now tried to improve relations with Serbia, and dynastic links with Romania and Greece were bolstered. A German general, Liman von Sanders, was made inspector general of the Turkish army in 1913 and given command over the troops around Constantinople. Russia protested vigorously and under intense international pressure Liman had to surrender his command. German Russophobes were incensed and Bethmann Hollweg came under further heavy attack for permitting the Reich to suffer such a humiliation.

The Balkan wars, coupled with Germany's weakened position relative to the Triple Entente, lent weight to those who argued that the Reich's armaments program was dangerously modest. In December 1912 Ludendorff presented a memorandum arguing for an army increase of 300,000 men. The War Ministry was horrified at this suggestion, fearing that it would result in an influx of dubious bourgeois into the officer corps and of Social Democratic sympathizers among the troops, making the army unreliable as a instrument of repression against revolution and domestic unrest. After much debate, from which Bethmann held himself aloof, a compromise was reached and the army increased by 136,000 officers and men. Ludendorff was posted away from the General Staff, soon to make a triumphant return to center stage. Bethmann Hollweg now had to find a way to foot the bill. He did not dare reintroduce a proposal for death duties which would have meant relying on an opening to the left. The Reichstag demanded a number of concessions in return for voting for the increased taxation to meet the enormous costs involved. These included a reform of military law, the ending of certain outmoded privileges and offices, and the refusal of funding for three proposed new cavalry regiments. The kaiser saw this as a deliberate attack on his sacred power of command and ranted and raved in a painfully familiar fashion. Bethmann threatened to dissolve the Reichstag, and much to his surprise was able to win a comfortable majority among the parties of the middle to the proposals, which were to be funded by a capital gains tax, a measure that was supported by the Social Democrats and which outraged the conservatives.

Bethmann did not enjoy his success for long. In December 1913 the Reichstag passed a vote of no confidence in the chancellor by 293 to 54. The motion had been put because of his defense of the actions of the army in Alsace-Lorraine during the Zabern affair of the previous year. A young lieutenant had insulted the Alsatians, and this had prompted civil unrest. The army proclaimed martial law and acted in a singularly brutish and insensitive manner, and a provocative speech in the

Reichstag by the war minister, Falkenhayn, had further inflamed the situation. Bethmann dismissed the vote as an empty gesture that merely showed that the liberals and the Center had made common cause with the Social Democrats. The despicable little lieutenant was tried and acquitted to general approbation, and no changes were made in the army's right to suspend civil law.

Domestic politics on the eve of the war were thus approaching stalemate. A conservative reforming chancellor could not distance himself from the court, Prussia, the military, or the conservatives. The middle parties were reluctant to seize the opportunity to strengthen their position. They could not risk refusing to pass the budget for fear of hurting their constituents, and were not yet prepared to approach the Social Democrats. The conservatives were gradually pushed aside and resorted to drumming up support from the extraparliamentary opposition, amongst whom there were calls for a counterrevolution. They were endorsed by the crown prince, who had to be called to order by his father. Others felt that a war might solve Germany's problems, however great the risks involved. Germany stood at the crossroads, and the reaction to events outside its borders was to determine the road ahead. By 1914 there were some signs of improvement in the international climate. Germany and Britain reached an agreement over the Portuguese colonies in August 1913, and in June the following year Britain agreed to German schemes for the Baghdad railway in return for an assurance that it would not go all the way to Basra. Germany also abandoned its ambitions to have shipping rights on the Euphrates and joined an Anglo-Dutch consortium as a junior partner to exploit the oil resources of the Ottoman Empire. German firms invested heavily in western Europe and there were many instances of fruitful cooperation between Germans and their future enemies. But the system was fundamentally unstable and proved incapable of mastering the crisis that lay ahead.

10

The First World War

On June 28 1914, the Serbian national day, the heir to Austrian throne, the Archduke Francis Ferdinand, and his wife, were murdered in Sarajevo. It was the work of a Serbian secret society "The Black Hand," whose head was Dragutin Dimitrievitch, a colonel in the Serbian General Staff, which stood opposed to the more moderate and flexible policies of the Serbian minister-president Pachich. It was assumed in Vienna that the government in Belgrade was at least partially responsible, and this was indeed the case. It knew of the plan, and although it did not approve, was powerless to stop it. Austria-Hungary had to act, and Germany was obliged to give its ally appropriate support.

The war party in Austria-Hungary insisted that the time had come to settle accounts with Serbia and halt the relentless decline of the country's power and influence. They were given whole-hearted support from Berlin, where the feeling was one of "now or never." Austria-Hungary was therefore given a free hand to act as it saw fit, and although it seemed highly unlikely that a war between Austria-Hungary and Serbia could be localized, even the more moderate among the leadership, headed by the chancellor, were prepared to risk a war that would involve Russia, France, and possibly Britain. The more bellicose among the military, the political elite, and the press urged unconditional support for Austria in the hope that this would indeed trigger a major European war. A number of soldiers, including Moltke, thought that a war was likely to be very long, would be unimaginably bloody, and that the outcome was uncertain. The war minister, Falkenhayn, made the grotesque remark that even if Germany perished, it would all have been great fun.

There were a number of arguments put forward in favor of going to war. Moltke and the army claimed that Germany would fall behind in the armaments race, and that they had to strike now before it was too late. Civilians argued that soon the pacifist Social Democrats would be so powerful that a war would be impossible, adding that a victorious campaign would put the socialists in their place. Bethmann Hollweg felt that a war could only be fought with the support of the Social Democrats, and not against them. Only if Russia could be construed as the aggressor would they forget the resolutions of the Socialist International against war, and support the common effort. Continued support would depend on making concessions to the party over such matters as the Prussian electoral law. The chancellor was full of foreboding, but he uncritically accepted Moltke's argument about the arms race, and managed to convince himself that this would be a preventive war.

Austria-Hungary waited until July 23 before sending Serbia a wide-ranging set of demands. The Serbian response came two days later and was so conciliatory that William II, who had previously urged Austria-Hungary to take the firmest possible line against Serbia, came to the conclusion that there was now no possible grounds for war. Vienna, however, found Belgrade's answer to the ultimatum unsatisfactory and, at 11 a.m. on July 28, declared war. On the following day Russia ordered the partial mobilization of several military districts, and egged on by his generals Nicolas II ordered a general mobilization in the night of July 30/31.

Also on July 30 Bethmann Hollweg urged Austria-Hungary to respond to the British foreign secretary Sir Edward Grey's offer of mediation. This was not part of an effort to defuse the situation, since he had repudiated the British proposal for a conference on July 27, but rather an attempt to make sure that Russia would be made to look responsible for an eventual European war. The next day Moltke, who had not yet heard that the Russians had mobilized, urged his Austrian colleague Conrad von Hötzendorf to mobilize immediately, thus prompting the famous rhetorical question by the Austro-Hungarian foreign minister Count Berchtold: "Who rules: Moltke or Bethmann?" The Austro-Hungarian army was promptly mobilized at midday on July 31. One hour later the German government announced a "state of imminent danger of war." Since Russia had not answered a German ultimatum issued on July 31, Germany mobilized on August 1, declared war on Russia, and set the Schlieffen Plan in motion. Germany officially declared war on France on August 3. On the following day, when German troops were already pouring into Belgium, Britain declared war.

Thus began what George F. Kennan so judiciously called "the great seminal catastrophe of this century." It was a catastrophe for which Germany must bear the main responsibility. The German military strengthened the war party in Austria-Hungary, and made its desperate *va banque* play for world power or annihilation. A substantial portion of the middle class lent their full support to this aggressive stance and called for a "preventive war," in spite of the fact that none of Germany's neighbors harbored aggressive intentions toward the Reich. Waverers, including the vast majority of the Social Democratic Party, were misled into believing that Russia was the aggressor and supported the government. The party had organized a number of antiwar demonstrations at the end of July, and the party press was sharply critical of the government's handling of the crisis. As the danger of war loomed larger the party leadership began to get cold feet and argued that should they adopt too critical a stance, they would face severe repression along the lines of Bismarck's antisocialist laws which still traumatized the party. That this would be a war against Imperial Russia, the despotic bastion of reaction and archenemy of all progressive forces, made it all the easier for them to cast aside considerations of proletarian solidarity and the pacifism of the Socialist International. On August 3 the SPD deputies decided by a vote of 78 to 14 to accept the government's request for war credits. Speaking for the party in the Reichstag on the following day Hugo Haase, a member of the left-wing minority, took the kaiser's words to heart when, in his throne speech, he proclaimed this to be a purely defensive war in which Germany harbored no territorial ambitions. He announced that the Social Democrats would never leave the country in the lurch in such a moment of peril, but added the warning that they would never support a war of conquest.

As Lenin, fulminating in his Zurich exile, never tired of pointing out, the SPD had abandoned class warfare and proletarian internationalism and had begun the process of reconciliation with the "ideas of 1914," the new nationalist ideology that was to form the basis of National Socialism. The brainchild of the sociologist Johann Plenge, and popularized by the Swedish constitutional lawyer Rudolf Kjellén, the "ideas of 1914" were a declaration of war on the "ideas of 1789." The rights of man, democracy, liberalism, and individualism were all rejected in favor of the truly German values of duty, discipline, law, and order. Order was to replace the anarchic libertarianism of the past century, divisions along class lines were to be overcome by a feeling of ethnic solidarity (*Volksgemeinschaft*), in which the new Social Democrats of August 1914 were welcome comrades, and socialist internationalism was to be replaced by robust national egotism. All "racial comrades" (*Volksgenossen*) were now to play a role in the building of a truly socialist society, and join in the glorious struggle of "proletarian" Germany against "capitalist" Britain.

By 1915 the war, which had ostensibly begun as a defensive campaign against Russia, had become a pseudo-socialist crusade against materialist Britain, the nation of shopkeepers and imperialists. The Tsarist Empire posed no great threat after Hindenburg, Ludendorff, and Hoffmann's great victory over the Russians at Tannenberg at the end of August 1914, and it soon became obvious that the Western Front was where the war would be decided. France was the traditional enemy and the curious love–hate relationship with Britain could easily be fanned into an intense loathing. Learned scholars became intoxicated with visions of an apocalyptic struggle between manly German militarism and sordid British capitalism. The distinguished economist Werner Sombart proclaimed the war to be a struggle between "tradesmen and soldiers," in which German militarism was inspired to fight for Beethoven's "Eroica" Symphony and "Egmont" Overture, Goethe's *Faust* and Nietzsche's *Thus Spoke Zarathustra*, against a squalid money-grubbing non-culture. He welcomed the war as an antidote to cultural pessimism and as a means to the regeneration of the race. The Catholic philosopher Max Scheler appealed to all Social Democrats to join in the struggle against the homeland of modern capitalism. He also called attention to the therapeutic effects of war on the German people. Thomas Mann was immensely relieved when the Treaty of Brest-Litovsk brought an end to Germany's war against the country that had produced Dostoevsky, and, in his *Reflections of an Unpolitical Man*, called for an all-out struggle against the "*trois pays libres*" that stood for "civilization" rather than "culture." There was an enthusiastic audience for such rubbish, and "God punish England!" replaced more conventional forms of address.

War Aims and Opposition

Since until 1916 the war was believed to be defensive, there could be no public discussion of war aims. Behind the scenes the situation was quite different. As early as September 1914 Bethmann Hollweg called for the annexation of the ore fields of Longwy-Briey, of Belfort, and Luxemburg. Belgium was to be reduced to total dependency on Germany, was to hand over Liège and Verviers to Prussia, and be given a chunk of eastern France including Calais, Dunkirk, and Boulogne as compensation. The frontiers of Russia were to be pushed eastwards and a central European economic zone was to be formed under German leadership. Bethmann's "September Program" soon became richly embroidered. The Pan-Germans called for the annexation of the Baltic States and White Russia, along with vast tracts of northwestern Russia and Russian Poland. Russian Jews were to be expelled to Palestine. The steel magnate August Thyssen and his lobbyist Matthias Erzberger called for the annexation of Belgium and the eastern departments of France, along with the Baltic States, and proposed that the Russian Empire should be split apart and the Crimea and Caucasus should be firmly under German control. A group of prominent intellectuals put forward a plan for the ethnic cleansing of Eastern Europe, and its resettlement with stalwart German peasants. Another group which included Hans Delbrück, Max Weber, Albert Einstein, and Gustav von Schmoller protested vigorously against such hair-raising fantasies, but this group, along with the Social Democrats, who opposed any annexations, formed a small minority. Bethmann Hollweg's September program was fleshed out by the liberal politician and journalist Friedrich Naumann in his book *Mitteleuropa*, which was published in 1915, and which called for a revival of the Holy Roman Empire. None of these schemes could be realized without a victory and this seemed remote after the costly failure of Falkenhayn's offensive against Verdun in 1916. The Pan-Germans and their allies mounted a massive campaign to appoint Hindenburg and Ludendorff, the heroes of Tannenberg, to the High Command (OHL). The kaiser, who saw this as a quasi-plebiscitary attack on his power of command, reluctantly gave way in August 1916. The decision to launch unrestricted submarine warfare was taken in January 1917 in spite of Bethmann's protests, and soon proved to be a serious mistake. The Allies quickly overcame the submarine menace and the United States declared war in April.

Germany now no longer had a realistic chance of winning the war, and there was widespread discontent at home. The public had been promised a resounding victory in 1914 with the Schlieffen Plan, and again two years later at Verdun. Unrestricted submarine warfare was touted as an infallible recipe for success, and the failure of the campaign was yet another bitter disappointment. The Allied blockade caused a serious food shortage, the black market thrived, and the gap between the haves and the have-nots grew ever wider. Right-wing parties blamed the Jews for all Germany's miseries. They were painted as black marketeers, war profiteers, and skrimshankers who avoided the draft. In October 1916 the Prussian War Ministry gave way to popular demand and called for a "Jewish Census." The results were disappointing for the anti-Semites and were not published. They showed that Jews served their country every bit as loyally as gentile Germans – not that this information would have changed anyone's mind – and Bethmann Hollweg continued to be seen as the "chancellor of German Jewry."

Protests against the war from the left began as early as December 1914, when Karl Liebknecht, the son of the SPD's co-founder, voted against the war credits. A number of other prominent figures, mostly from the left of the party, followed suit. This group was expelled from the Reichstag parliamentary party in 1916 and formed the "Social Democratic Working Group," a mixed bunch of opponents to the war which included Rosa Luxemburg, Klara Zetkin, and Franz Mehring on the left, and Karl Kautsky, the leading theorist of "centrism," the economist Rudolf Hilferding, and Eduard Bernstein, the founder of revisionism, on the right. The left remained loyal to the ideals of the Second International and took part in a congress in Zimmerwald in Switzerland in September 1915, at which militant socialists from the belligerent countries met to denounce their parent parties for their treacherous support of an imperialist war. Lenin excoriated the centrists and revisionists who opposed the war as weak-kneed "social pacifists," and urged that the imperialist war be turned into a civil war. Very few delegates were prepared to go quite so far and the congress ended with a unanimous called for an immediate end to the war without annexations and reparations, and a peace based on the principle of the self-determination of peoples. The group met again in Switzerland at Kienthal in the following year. The antiwar rhetoric was stepped up, but Lenin was once again left seething in vituperative isolation.

The small antiwar faction won considerable popular support in the "turnip winter" of 1916/17, when the combined effects of a poor harvest and the blockade caused widespread hunger. The situation was compounded by the "Auxiliary Labor Law" of December 1916 which forced all men from the ages of 17 to 60 who had not been drafted into the armed forces to do labor service. It was hoped that this measure would lead to the success of the "Hindenburg Program" which called for a substantial increase in armaments production. The "Auxiliary Labor Law" did not go nearly far enough for Hindenburg, Ludendorff, and Colonel Bauer, the principal architect of the bill. They wanted to militarize the economy by placing workers under military law, with strikes tantamount to desertion, and they complained bitterly that too many concessions had been made to the trades unions by creating arbitration committees with equal representation from capital and labor. Most workers felt that the unions had been co-opted and no longer represented their interests, and they resented this attempt to regiment the workforce. The February revolution in Russia and the formation of the Independent Social Democratic Party (USPD) in April 1917 marked a further stage in the radicalization of the German workers. There was a wave of strikes in which "Revolutionary Shop Stewards" first made an appearance, and in which calls for an end to the war were frequent. Two sailors were executed for mutiny, a harsh measure which only served to heighten discontent below decks.

Bethmann Hollweg, with his "politics of the diagonal," tried to defuse the situation with the kaiser's "Easter Message" in April 1917, in which a reform of the monstrously inequitable Prussian electoral law was promised once the fighting was over; but this was altogether too vague, too little, and too late. Meanwhile, Austria-Hungary, Germany's principal ally, was falling apart and desperately wanted to end the war. Negotiations were begun with France for a separate peace but these got nowhere. The new emperor Charles and his foreign minister Count Czernin now turned to the Center Party politician and perennial busybody, Matthias Erzberger, for help. Realizing that the unrestricted submarine warfare campaign had been a costly mistake, he had come to the conclusion that the war had to be ended and a large number of his party colleagues agreed. The SPD had reached a similar verdict and adopted the Petrograd Soviet's slogan calling for a peace without annexations or indemnities. In June 1917 the SPD issued an ultimatum to the chancellor to the effect that the party would vote against the war credits if he did not produce a clear catalogue of war aims. Bethmann could not afford to appear as the hostage of the socialists and refused, thus losing the support of the parliamentary majority he had enjoyed since the outset of hostilities.

On July 6 1917 Erzberger, having first consulted with members of the SPD, the Progressives, and the Center, having been briefed by Colonel Bauer on the seriousness of the military situation, and having been informed that Pope Benedict XV was about to launch a peace initiative, denounced the unconditional submarine warfare campaign and called upon the Reichstag to do everything possible to end the war. Erzberger's peace initiative marks a major turning point in German politics. The very same day the Social Democrats, National Liberals, Center, and Progressives formed a Joint Committee (*Interfraktionellen Ausschuss*) that was a significant step toward the creation of responsible parliamentary government. There were still wide differences between the parties. The National Liberals refused to accept the Petrograd Soviet's peace formula. The Center was anxious not to press the question of Prussian electoral reform too hard. The Social Democrats and Progressives wanted to push ahead with reforms and establish a thoroughgoing parliamentary regime. Meanwhile, the OHL was demanding the dismissal of Bethmann Hollweg and his replacement by a man who would do their bidding. Gustav Stresemann and the National Liberals, along with Erzberger and his supporters in the Center, agreed that the chancellor should go. The rest were largely indifferent to the chancellor's fate and his days were clearly numbered.

From Bethmann Hollweg to Michaelis

William II deeply resented the OHL's political intrigues as well as their flaunting of his prerogatives, and was furious that Bethmann's proposed successor was none other than Bülow, with whom he had become utterly disenchanted. The kaiser therefore stuck to Bethmann more out of stubbornness than conviction until July 12, when Hindenburg and Ludendorff threatened to resign unless the chancellor was dismissed. On the very same day the SPD, Center, and Progressives agreed on the text for a peace resolution. It called for a peace that would lead to reconciliation and understanding between the warring factions, in which there would be no annexations, or excessive financial or economic burdens. The resolution was not without its ambiguities but was too much for the National Liberals, who had never felt comfortable in the Joint Committee and now left in protest. Bethmann also disapproved of the resolution but was powerless to stop a debate in the Reichstag, and therefore offered his resignation that evening. Hindenburg and Ludendorff traveled to Berlin the next day in an attempt to convince the "majority parties," as they were henceforth known, to withdraw the peace resolution, but to no avail. The kaiser, who was reluctant to give way to the OHL's blackmail tactics, nevertheless agreed with the majority of his countrymen that the war could not possibly be won without the two demi-gods, and he therefore capitulated. On July 14 he appointed a relatively obscure Prussian civil servant, Georg Michaelis, as Bethmann's successor. He thus abandoned most of his few remaining sovereign powers.

The struggle was now between the OHL and majority parties of the Reichstag. It was an unequal struggle in that Michaelis was the tool of the OHL, and shared none of Bethmann's concern to achieve a broad consensus. He appointed a number of members of the majority parties to important positions in the civil administration, but the Reichstag still had no share in the responsibilities of government, and played a purely negative role. This fact was somewhat obscured by the passing of the peace resolution on July 19 by a vote of 212 to 126, and many were deceived by Michaelis' assurance that he would respect the resolution "as I interpret it." Satisfied that they had won a significant victory, the majority parties voted a few days later for the war credits.

The right was outraged by the peace resolution and in September the lawyer and banker Wolfgang Kapp, of the eponymous putsch, founded the Fatherland Party in Königsberg. The party, which saw itself as an interest group rather than a conventional political party, attracted a large number of members, particularly in the eastern Prussian provinces. A number of prominent figures lent their support, including Admiral Tirpitz, who had resigned as secretary of state for the navy in 1916 when his proposal to start unrestricted submarine warfare had been rejected. The party detested parliamentary democracy, which they saw as "hypocritical" and "English," contrasting it with something they were pleased to call "German freedom," which could only be secured by means of a "Hindenburg peace." Germany had therefore to unite in an all-out struggle for final victory in which the most exotic war aims would be achieved.

Two months later a group of moderates that included Hans Delbrück, Max Weber, and the historian Friedrich Meinecke formed the "People's Association for Freedom and Fatherland" to counter the strident propaganda of the Fatherland Party. This group called for fundamental political reform and for a peace broadly on the basis of the Reichstag resolution. It failed to attract the mass support enjoyed by the Fatherland Party, but had important contacts with the trades unions and left-wing parties, and thus did much to overcome the antagonisms between the moderate bourgeoisie and the working class. The fronts were now more clearly drawn between the proponents of a "victorious peace" and a "renunciatory peace," between a "Hindenburg peace" and a "Scheidemann peace," after its prominent Social Democratic advocate.

From Michaelis to Hertling

Meanwhile, Michaelis had gone the way of his predecessor. He had dithered on all the great issues of the day: the peace resolution, foreign policy, the Auxiliary Labor Law, franchise reform in Prussia, and how to respond to the papal peace initiative. His exceptionally inept handling of the naval mutiny lost him all the remaining sympathy of the majority parties, who now seized the initiative to secure his dismissal. Acting on behalf of the OHL, the crown prince once again suggested that he be replaced by Bülow. His candidature was vociferously seconded by Erzberger, whose party was beginning to have second thoughts about the peace resolution. The kaiser predictably would have none of this, and appointed the Bavarian minister-president Count von Hertling, a man who had more sympathy for the peace resolution than Michaelis, but who as a Bavarian patriot resisted any constitutional reforms that might strengthen the federal structure of the Reich.

Michaelis' fall was significant in that for the second time the Reichstag had played the key role in the dismissal of a chancellor. The OHL had used the Reichstag to get rid of Bethmann, but in doing so had greatly strengthened its powers. This time the OHL had played no part in the dismissal of the chancellor, and the Reichstag had done it virtually alone. Hindenburg and Ludendorff had no time for Hertling. He was a Catholic, and, even worse, he was a Bavarian. He had been appointed without them being consulted but in the end the OHL had to accept him. They treated him with unaccustomed deference, and the chancellor caused them precious few headaches. The SPD watched him closely from the other side of the fence on which the chancellor uneasily sat, making sure that he did not stray too far from the moderate course he had promised to follow.

The Impact of the Bolshevik Revolution

The Bolshevik revolution in early November 1917 caused shock waves throughout Germany. The peace resolution of the Second All-Russian Congress of Soviets was widely welcomed. However, the German working class showed no particular enthusiasm for communism in its Leninist form, and almost all socialists, even the most radical, were disturbed by the violence and brutality of its dictatorial methods; but Lenin's passionate call for an end to the imperialist war met with an eager response, not only among war-weary workers but particularly among disillusioned soldiers at the front, who were called upon to risk their lives for the absurdly unrealistic war aims of the Fatherland Party. There was virtually unanimous disillusionment with a Bolshevik regime after the violent dissolution of the constituent assembly in January. Only a handful of radicals in the extreme left-wing "Spartacus Group," which included the feisty feminist Klara Zetkin and the armchair revolutionary Franz Mehring, welcomed the move. The intellectual leader of the group, Rosa Luxemburg, was appalled, and penned the famous lines about freedom being the right to disagree, while making it plain that she too placed strict limits on the room for disagreement. She insisted that civil war was just another name for the class struggle, and that the idea that socialism could be achieved by means of parliamentary democracy was "an absurd petit-bourgeois illusion."

A wave of spontaneous strikes that began at the end of January in Berlin was inspired by widespread strikes in Austria-Hungary. In the Dual Monarchy there were clear signs of Bolshevik influence on the strikes, although the principal demands were that the peace negotiations with Russia should not become unnecessarily protracted by reason of excessive war aims, and that there should be a more equitable distribution of foodstuffs. In Berlin and elsewhere in Germany strikers were mainly concerned with these two key issues. Although the strikes were far less damaging to the war economy than were those in Britain, the Majority Socialists and the trades unions were acutely embarrassed, and did everything possible to bring them to an end for fear of being accused of undermining the war effort. The strikers denounced the military dictatorship of the OHL, and the military authorities responded by declaring a state of martial law, arresting a number of prominent figures, including a Reichstag deputy, and banning the SPD's main newspaper, *Vorwärts*. The court preacher, Bruno Doehring, denounced the strikers as "venal and cowardly creatures who have treacherously profaned the altar of the fatherland with their brothers' blood." The conservative leader Ernst von Heydebrand und der Lasa accused the strikers of treason, and held outside agitators and the complicity of the SPD to be ultimately responsible. Ludendorff preferred the use of the soldierly demotic for his public announcement: "Anyone who strikes is a cunt!" The foundations of the powerful "stab in the back" legend were thus laid in January 1918.

Lenin knew that the Bolsheviks could only remain in power if they ended the war. On March 3 1918 peace was eventually signed at Brest-Litovsk. It was a peace of unprecedented ferocity besides which the "Diktat" of Versailles pales in comparison. Russia was forced to give up the Ukraine, Finland, the Baltic States, and parts of Armenia. It lost the Trans-Caucasus and the Crimea, and was forced to pay colossal reparations. In all it lost one-third of its population and agricultural land, and an even higher percentage of many key raw materials. Even though the Treaty of Brest-Litovsk was a clear repudiation of both the letter and the spirit of the Reichstag's peace resolution, it was ratified by the overwhelming majority of deputies. The Center and Progressives voted for the treaty, the SPD, chastened by official reaction to the strikes, abstained, and only the USPD defiantly voted against.

The peace movement was temporarily silenced with the spectacular initial success of the "Michael" offensive across the old Somme battlefields, which was launched on March 21 1918. The Germans made a deep penetration on a broad front which destroyed General Sir Hubert Gough's Fifth Army, and the OHL announced that a victory was in sight that would result in a "Hindenburg peace." The more perspicacious of the German generals had serious doubts whether it would be possible to follow up these initial successes, and began to have serious reservations about Ludendorff's operational acumen and mental stability. Subsequent offensives in Flanders, on the Chemin des Dames, on the Aisne, and in the Champagne proved them to be perfectly correct. The Entente seized the initiative with the Mangin offensive in July, that was followed by a powerful blow at Amiens in the following month. By now it was plain to all that the war was lost. By September 1918 the German army's morale was broken and the number of desertions steadily mounted.

Disillusionment was also widespread on the home front. Victory had been promised in 1914, at Verdun in 1916, and again with unrestricted submarine warfare in 1917. The propaganda machine had gone into high gear in the spring of 1918, with the result that disappointment in the summer was even greater. There was a generalized disillusionment with the kaiser, the army leadership, and the government. In southern Germany, Prussia and Prussian militarism were blamed for the present wretched state of Germany, and particularist sentiments ran high. Discontent in certain sections of the working class was such that some began to fear that the Reich might go the way of Russia. Germany faced the dire prospect of defeat and red revolution.

The Revolution from Above

At this juncture the role of the SPD was crucial. The party leader, Friedrich Ebert, was determined that Germany should not emulate Bolshevik Russia, and thus suffer the chaotic disruption and horrors of a terror regime and a civil war. The clear alternative was to cooperate with the bourgeois parties and to work together for moderate reform. When faced with the alternative of revolution or reform, the SPD, for all the radical Marxist rhetoric of the party program, unhesitatingly opted for reform. Those who viewed such a choice as a betrayal of the fundamental principles of socialism and class solidarity had already left the party, and Ebert had little difficulty in persuading the parliamentary party to accept his reformist course.

It took lengthy and intense debate to get the Center to accept the idea of a constitutional monarchy, largely because they feared that the Catholic minority would suffer under a system based on majority rule. Once the National Liberals endorsed the idea of a thoroughgoing parliamentary regime and the replacement of Hertling by a more amenable chancellor, the Center dropped its objections. There was now a solid majority in the Reichstag for fundamental reform. The Joint Committee reached this agreement on September 28. On the following day Hindenburg and Ludendorff told the kaiser that the war was lost and that negotiations for an armistice based on President Wilson's peace proposals should begin at once. The OHL was now determined that the blame for a lost war should be placed squarely on the shoulders of the majority parties in the Reichstag. On October 1 Ludendorff told a group of senior officers: "We shall now see these gentlemen enter various ministries. They can make the peace that has to be made. They can now eat the soup they have served up to us!" The changeover to a parliamentary regime was part of the "revolution from above" masterminded by Admiral Paul von Hintze, a devious, blasé, and ambitious opportunist who had been appointed secretary of state for foreign affairs in July. The "stab in the back" legend that was to play such a critical role in the downfall of the Weimar Republic was thus carefully constructed in late summer of 1918.

On October 3 Prince Max of Baden, the heir to the grand duchy and a man virtually without a political profile, was appointed chancellor. Members of all the majority parties were given ministerial positions. As a result of the constitutional changes made on October 28 Germany was now a fully-fledged constitutional monarchy. The chancellor was made responsible to the Reichstag and was obliged to resign if he no longer enjoyed its confidence. War could not be declared nor peace concluded without parliamentary consent. The right was flabbergasted. Heinrich Class, the president of the Pan-German League, called for an all-out offensive on the Jews whom he held responsible for this disastrous turn of events. The League's official newspaper, the *Deutsche Zeitung*, published an article by Baron von Gelbsattel which also blamed the Jews for this "bloodless revolution," since democracy was "of Jewish origin" and was an essential ingredient of Jewry's destructive potential. At a meeting of senior officials of the League in late October Class quoted Kleist, and said of the Jews: "Kill the lot; you will not be asked the reason why at the last judgment."

The first act of Prince Max's government was to begin, at the OHL's insistence, negotiations with the United States government for an armistice. US secretary of state Lansing spelt out the conditions on October 23. They called for Germany's complete surrender and made it clear that William II would have to abdicate. The OHL, who were simply looking for a breathing space, found these terms totally unacceptable, and urged their rejection. Prince Max wrote to the kaiser saying that either Ludendorff, whom he knew to be the driving force behind the absurd idea of continuing the war, should be dismissed, or he would feel obliged to resign. Hindenburg and Ludendorff traveled to Berlin to confront the kaiser, and in a stormy scene William accepted Ludendorff's resignation. General Groener, a moderate staff officer who hailed from Württemberg, was appointed in his stead. The kaiser then left Berlin and, following Hindenburg's suggestion, traveled to headquarters at Spa.

Meanwhile, as part of the armistice negotiations the submarine campaign was stopped, whereupon the navy under Admiral Scheer, which had not ventured forth since the Battle of Jutland in 1916, decided to launch a massive attack on the Royal Navy. Scheer's motives were mixed. He wanted to save the honor of the High Seas' Fleet, which had watched idly by for two years, and above all he wanted to sabotage the armistice negotiations. It was thus an act of such gross insubordination as to amount to an attempted coup. Orders were issued, prompting mutinies first at Wilhelmshaven, and rapidly spreading to Kiel, Lübeck, Hamburg, Bremen, and

Cuxhaven, along with a number of lesser ports. The government tried to pacify the mutineers by sending Conrad Haussmann from the Progressive People's Party and the Social Democrat Gustav Noske with a promise of an amnesty. The offer was refused, and the mutiny turned into a revolution as workers joined the mutineers. On November 7 a motley crew of socialists and anarchists under Kurt Eisner seized power in Munich. The king abdicated and a republican "Free State of Bavaria" was proclaimed. On the following day, revolutionary sailors and workers took over control in Brunswick. By November 8 Düsseldorf, Stuttgart, Leipzig, Halle, Osnabrück, and Cologne were in the hands of Workers' and Soldiers' Councils. The mayor of Cologne, Konrad Adenauer, calmly announced that he fully accepted the new circumstances.

By now it was clear that the kaiser would have to go. The sailors in Kiel were the first to publicly demand his abdication. Then the prominent Social Democrat Philipp Scheidemann wrote to Prince Max at the end of October, saying that the kaiser should abdicate in order that the armistice talks should proceed smoothly. Friedrich Ebert who, unlike Scheidemann, was far from being a republican, suggested to the chancellor on November 7 that a regent should be appointed, and argued that unless William II were to go there would be a revolution. According to Prince Max he then added the famous words: "I hate revolution like the plague."

Also on November 7 the Commanding General in the Marches, General von Linsingen, decided to take decisive action against the radical left, and banned the Workers' and Soldiers' Councils which had mushroomed throughout Germany in the previous days. He also forbade any meetings sponsored by the USPD. This ran quite contrary to the more relaxed policy of the Prussian war minister General Scheüch, who had removed a number of restrictions on the right of assembly only a few days beforehand, and had released Rosa Luxemburg and Karl Liebknecht from jail. The SPD protested vigorously at von Linsingen's highhanded action and repeated its demand for the kaiser to abdicate. On the following day the Center and Progressives agreed that both the kaiser and the crown prince would have to relinquish their claims to the throne. They also agreed with the SPD's demand that the franchise, both in the states and the Reich be extended to include women. The majority of the members of the moderate parties had come to the realization that Germany was ungovernable without the SPD, and that the alternative was likely to be revolution and civil war.

The Revolution of 1918

On the morning of November 9 Otto Wels, regional secretary of the SPD in Brandenburg and a rough-hewn populist of exceptional courage and sound instincts, called for a general strike in protest against Linsingen's decree. Shortly afterwards Scheidemann resigned his post as secretary of state without portfolio in Prince Max's government. Ebert then began negotiations with the USPD, the Revolutionary Shop Stewards, and the Soldiers' and Workers' Councils, with a view to forming a government on the Bavarian model. Wels the pragmatist knew that Ebert's efforts to co-opt the extreme left were unlikely to succeed without military support. He therefore approached the Naumburg Light Infantry (*Naumburger Jäger*), a traditional regiment known for its loyalty to the kaiser. Wels appealed to the other ranks to support the Social Democrats in their endeavor to create a new republican government. He met with a warm response. The news that the Naumburger had thrown their support behind the Social Democrats was a shattering blow to Prince Max and to the OHL. At headquarters Groener had already come to the conclusion that the army would refuse to follow the kaiser in an attempt to oust the Social Democrats and that he therefore had to go. Hindenburg agreed, but refused to relay this unpleasant news to the All-Highest. In the morning of November 9 Groener told the kaiser: "The Army no longer stands behind Your Majesty!" whereupon William II expressed his intention to abdicate.

On hearing this news, Prince Max issued a press release announcing that the kaiser would abdicate, but he still hoped to save the monarchy by appointing a regent. Shortly afterwards Ebert went to the chancellery, and requested that in order to avoid unnecessary bloodshed Prince Max should hand over the office of chancellor. Prince Max insisted that the question of the regency had first to be settled, but Ebert bluntly announced that it was already far too late to save the monarchy, whereupon Prince Max formally passed on the office of chancellor to him. The war minister Scheüch agreed to stay in office, with a Social Democratic deputy secretary of state to keep a close political watch over his ministry. General von Linsingen also had to submit to the scrutiny of a Social Democratic official. Within hours the kaiser was to leave for exile in Holland, and Friedrich Ebert was now the highest authority in the land.

Born in the year of the foundation of the Reich, Ebert was a 47-year-old pragmatic moderate, an efficient administrator rather than a visionary politician. He was dull but decent, a man who realized very early on that the SPD had to reach a compromise with the moderate bourgeois parties if Germany were to be saved from chaos. He had begun life as a saddler, and had worked his way up through the trades unions to enter the Reichstag as a deputy in 1912. In the following year he succeeded August Bebel as party leader. He was not helped by an inept public relations campaign and along with his wife, who had been a cleaning lady, he was subjected to scurrilous abuse from the right, and the equally contemptible sneering of left-wing intellectuals. He was hounded to an early death in 1925. He was a convinced democrat who insisted that the future form of Germany should be decided by a constituent assembly elected by universal suffrage. Philipp Scheidemann, unlike Ebert an impressive orator and an impulsive people's tribune, did not agree. In the early afternoon of November 9 he addressed the crowds from a window in the Reichstag and announced the formation of a "German Republic." He did so largely to forestall the radical socialist Karl Liebknecht, who two hours later proclaimed a "Free Socialist German Republic." Ebert was furious with Scheidemann for thus jumping the gun, but was silenced by the Berliners' rapturous reception of his announcement.

Negotiations began that afternoon between the SPD and the USPD for the formation of a new government amid sporadic outbursts of armed violence in the capital. Ebert offered the USPD parity in an inner cabinet that would be supported by ministers drawn from the bourgeois parties who would act in a largely administrative capacity. The USPD was reluctant to join forces with the "government socialists" for fear of being tarred with the revisionist brush. Karl Liebknecht and the Spartacus Group denounced the whole concept of bourgeois democracy, and issued a Leninist call for all executive, legislative, and judicial power to be vested in the Workers' and Soldiers' Councils.

The USPD initially agreed to this plan for a Soviet Germany, but after lengthy discussions eventually agreed to a compromise solution on November 10. While still insisting that political power rested in the hands of the Workers' and Soldiers' Councils, who were holding a mass meeting at the Busch Circus in Berlin, the USPD agreed to take part in the new government, provided that it was approved by the Workers' and Soldiers' Councils. The USPD was represented on the "Council of People's Representatives" by the radical Hugo Haase, who had just been released from jail, the moderate William Dittmann, who had been sentenced to five years imprisonment for his part in the January strikes, and Emil Barth, as the representative of the Revolutionary Shop Stewards. The SPD fielded Ebert, Scheidemann, and the lawyer and Reichstag deputy Otto Landsberg. There was a fierce struggle in the Busch Circus for approval of the new government, but the radicals around Liebknecht were in a minority and grudgingly gave way. The "Council of People's Representatives" was to remain in power until a constituent assembly could be convened and was ostensibly controlled by an Executive Committee of the Workers' and Soldiers' Councils, on which the workers were represented by seven SPD and an equal number of USPD members, and the soldiers by 14 delegates without party affiliation.

For all the flaming rhetoric of the radical left this dramatic change from imperial to Social Democratic Germany happened relatively smoothly. The civil service and the judiciary were unaffected. Groener promised Ebert the army's full support in the struggle against Bolshevism and revolution. The theoretically Marxist Social Democrats provided a solid guarantee that there would be no experiments, and that they were determined to get things back to resolutely capitalist normality. The peaceful and expedite demobilization of the armed forces, the restoration of a viable peacetime economy, and the drafting of a new republican constitution were the top priorities. The old imperial order had lost its legitimacy in the course of the war and defeat sealed its fate. There were precious few royalists left, most of them to be found among the Protestant and aristocratic denizens of East Elbia, but it remained to be seen whether parliamentary democracy would take root in an environment that was far from propitious.

As yet, the Council of People's Representatives had no democratic legitimacy, and was under a permanent threat from both left and right and, as Ebert pointed out, it was in many ways the receiver of a bankrupt system. Under these circumstances it was perhaps understandable that the Council moved so cautiously as to leave themselves open to a charge of pusillanimity. They relied on an army that had no sympathy whatsoever for their ideals, and likewise on an ultraconservative civil service and on unsympathetic police forces. They made no attempt to create genuinely republican institutions such as a Republican Guard, nor did they weed out some of the more grotesquely reactionary senior members of the civil service and judiciary. With the agreement between the trade union leader Carl Legien and the industrialist Hugo Stinnes on November 15 1918, they abandoned any attempt to change property relationships. Nothing was done to tackle the problem of the excessive influence and privileges of the East Elbian landowners, and an imaginative scheme for the restructuring of the coal industry was tabled on the grounds that first the economy should be returned to normal, and only then could discussions begin as to the future.

The first All-German Congress of Workers' and Soldiers' Councils was held in Berlin between December 16 and 21, and in spite of its alarmingly revolutionary-sounding name the SPD had a comfortable majority. Karl Liebknecht and Rosa Luxemburg's hopes for a Soviet Germany were thus dashed, and a motion proposing that they be invited to attend the Congress as observers was soundly defeated. By a vote of 400 to 50 the Congress called for elections for a constituent assembly to be held on January 19. The Congress might have rejected the dictatorship of the proletariat in favor of bourgeois democracy, but in other respects it was distinctly radical. It called for the nationalization of heavy industry and a drastic reform of the army along the lines of the proposals of the Hamburg Soldiers' Council, known as the "Hamburg Points." These latter included the abolition of badges of rank, the election of officers by the men, and courts martial to be replaced by disciplinary committees appointed by the Soldiers' Councils. Groener had already made it clear to Ebert that the army's support of the new regime was dependent on the rejection of the "Hamburg Points," and there was thus no question of them being put into effect. Similarly the Stinnes-Legien agreement was an assurance that plans for a socialist economy had been abandoned.

On December 23 the "People's Marine Division," a bunch of ill-disciplined thugs who were busy plundering the palace in Berlin, took Otto Wels hostage and demanded handsome payment for their putative services to the revolution. The government called upon regular troops to settle the matter, but they failed to dislodge the marines. The troops were withdrawn and violence spread to other parts of the capital. The government was without protection, and could easily have been overthrown had not Ernst Däumig, the spokesman of the Revolutionary Shop Stewards, insisted that the German people would never forgive the radicals if they overthrew the regime on Christmas Eve. Eventually a negotiated settlement was reached, but the USPD, who were bitterly disappointed at the outcome of the Congress of Workers' and Soldiers' Councils, used the government's inept handling of the crisis as an excuse to resign from the Council of People's Representatives on December 28.

On New Year's Eve the Spartacus Group and sundry other radical socialists formed the Communist Party of Germany (KPD). In spite of Rosa Luxemburg's ardent protests, the new party resolved to boycott the forthcoming elections. A few days later the minister-president of Prussia, a Social Democrat, dismissed the police-president of Berlin, Emil Eichorn, one of the more bizarre figures in these confusing times. He was on the extreme left of the USPD, and had placed the security forces at the disposal of the People's Marine Division. The USPD and the Revolutionary Shop Stewards promptly organized a protest demonstration against what they considered to be a deliberate provocation. The KPD joined the protest, which was held on January 5. It soon got out of hand and the premises of a number of leading newspapers and publishing houses were seized by the protestors, including the offices of the SPD's party newspaper, *Vorwärts*. Carried away by totally fallacious reports that the Berlin garrison and other troops in the surrounding districts were ready to overthrow the government, Karl Liebknecht called for a general strike and the overthrow of the Ebert–Scheidemann government. The aim was to stop the elections and to create a Soviet Germany, thus making good the ground they had lost at the Congress by emulating Lenin and the Bolsheviks. The government at first tried to negotiate with the rebels, but was faced with the unacceptable demand that Eichorn be reinstated. They thus had no alternative but to crush the "Spartacus Revolt." The Social Democrat Gustav Noske, who had been appointed to the Council of People's Representatives when the USPD resigned en bloc, patched together a force of disparate elements which included volunteers from the right-wing Free Corps which successfully crushed the rebellion. Among the troops that Noske and the OHL sent to Berlin were General von Lüttwitz's Free Corps, who arrived when the fighting was over, but who acted as a police force. It was they who, under orders from Captain Waldemar Pabst, murdered Rosa Luxemburg and Karl Liebknecht. The murderers were never punished, and Pabst lived on to enjoy a comfortable pension in the Federal Republic.

The elections of January 19 1919 were a disappointment to the Social Democrats. They received 37.9 percent of the popular vote which was only three percentage points more that the united party had got in the elections of 1912. The USPD, whose radical wing had left to join the KPD, received 7.6 percent. The two social democratic parties thus failed to win the expected majority, but the bourgeois parties were divided and none of them made an impressive showing at the polls. The Center Party and the Bavarian People's Party (BVP), which had broken off from the main party in November 1918, achieved a combined vote of 19.7 percent. Erzberger's attempt to convert the party to Christian Democracy by welcoming Protestant supporters had failed, largely due to the grotesquely anticlerical antics of the Prussian minister of education, the USPD politician Adolph Hoffmann, who had raised the specter of a socialist *Kulturkampf*. The successor party to the Progressives, the German Democratic Party (DDP), got 18.5 percent of the vote. The conservatives. in their new and more populist guise as the German National People's Party (DNVP), got 10.3 percent, and Gustav Stresemann's German People's Party (DVP), the successor party to the National Liberals, received a mere 4.4 percent. Women showed little gratitude to the SPD, which had given them the vote, and gave their support overwhelmingly to the confessional parties: Catholics to the Center and BVP, and Protestants to the DNVP. The message from the electorate was clear. They wanted a resolutely democratic form of government and moderate reform. This was a clear repudiation both of the Red Revolution and of Black Reaction. They wanted parliamentary democracy based on a fruitful compromise between Social Democrats and the moderate bourgeois parties. It was a vote of confidence in the majority parties of the old Reichstag, the architects of the new republic. It was a promising beginning to a new chapter in German history.

11
The Weimar Republic: 1919–33

The new parliament met in peaceful Weimar, the town of Goethe and Schiller, far away from troubled Berlin. Ebert was elected temporary president and Scheidemann was appointed chancellor. The DDP insisted that they would only form a coalition with the SPD if the Center and BVP were included, so that the center of gravity was shifted to the right. Deliberations over a new constitution began amid mounting unrest and a wave of strikes by militant workers who made a number of radical demands, the principal being the nationalization of the coal industry. Violence was widespread. The fighting in Berlin in March left 1,000 dead. The government responded to a general strike in the Ruhr by sending in the troops. Bavaria was in a state of turmoil. Kurt Eisner was assassinated on February 21 by a young aristocrat who became an instant hero on the radical right. Munich followed the example of Béla Kun's Soviet Hungary when Ernst Niekisch proclaimed the end of the "bourgeois capitalist age" and a Soviet Bavaria. Had it not ended in a terrible blood bath, the Bavarian Soviet Republic would have been regarded as pure operetta, the object of almost universal derision. It was run by a bizarre collection of adamantine communists, dreamy pacifists, anarchic literati, and outright crackpots. Lenin took a lively interest in their activities and, with his unerring inability to understand foreign countries, imagined that Catholic, rural, reactionary Bavaria had been transformed into the standard-bearer of the German proletariat. At the Social Democratic army minister Noske's behest the White terror made quick work of the Republic, which had come under the dauntless control of the communist Eugen Leviné. Soviet Munich quickly became a hotbed of sundry right-wing extremists who blamed recent events on the machinations of world Jewry, and agitators like Adolf Hitler found a ready audience for their hateful messages. The Scheidemann government offered a few carrots to offset the sticks, but they were not enough to satisfy the radical left. A grandiose scheme for the socialization of the coal and saltpeter syndicates did nothing to alter property relationships or the powers of the owners. Works councils, however, were a significant step forward, in that they did much to overcome the crass divisions between management and labor, and they were to form the basis of Germany's exemplary industrial relations after 1945.

When the guns fell silent on November 11 most Germans confidently imagined that the peace settlement would be based on Wilson's idealistic 14 points. They had few regrets at the prospect of losing Alsace-Lorraine along with some of the Polish provinces, and even entertained the illusion that the new Austrian republic, proclaimed on November 12, would be permitted to join a greater Germany, thus completing the process of German unification. The hard-nosed realists in the OHL and their associates knew otherwise. They had negotiated the draconian peace of Brest-Litovsk on the basis of the self-determination of peoples and the rejection of indemnities and reparations, and thus were well aware that the 14 points would be interpreted in such a way as to bleed Germany white. Some argued that the harsher the peace the better. The odium of ending the war had been shifted onto the majority parties in the "Hintze Action," and they could now bear the blame for a harsh peace and thus be totally discredited. The German government was informed of the Allied peace terms on May 7, shortly after the bloodbath in Munich. They exceeded the worst fears of the direst of pessimists. That Germany should lose Upper Silesia, a large chunk of West Prussia, Danzig, and Memel, and that East Prussia should be separated from the rest of Germany, came as a devastating blow. Things were hardly better in the west. The Saar was to be placed under the League of Nations for 15 years, the left bank of the Rhine permanently demilitarized, and the entire Rhineland occupied for up to 15 years. Eupen-Malmedy was to be handed over to Belgium. An *Anschluss* with Austria was expressly forbidden. Germany's colonial empire was to be dissolved. The army was not to exceed 100,000 men. Military aircraft, submarines, and tanks were among a number of outlawed weapons. The fleet was to surrender, but it was scuttled before it reached the Scottish naval base at Scapa Flow. Ninety percent of the merchant navy had to be handed over, along with ten percent of the cattle stock and a substantial proportion of the rolling stock of the state railway. The victors were unable to agree on a final sum for reparations, but 40 million tons of coal were demanded annually. Germans were particularly incensed by article 231, which demanded that they make good the damage caused by a war which they and their allies had begun. A deliberate mistranslation of the article to read "sole guilt" (*Alleinschuld*) further inflamed a consternated public, and set off a wave of righteous indignation about the "war guilt lie."

The Scheidemann government was at first inclined to declare these terms unacceptable. Scheidemann worked himself up into a rhetorical frenzy and proclaimed: "May the hand wither that binds himself and us in such shackles!" Other leading politicians in the coalition argued that the proposed peace was merely a continuation of the war by other means, or that it would sow the seeds of further conflict. Cooler and more realistic heads soon prevailed. Groener told the government that it would be impossible to resist an Allied invasion. Scheidemann was outnumbered, and resigned the chancellorship in favor of a nondescript Social Democrat, Gustav Bauer. The Allies made minor concessions by permitting a plebiscite in Upper Silesia, and suggesting that the occupation of the Rhineland might end somewhat sooner if Germany behaved to their satisfaction. The request for a revision of article 231 met with a point-blank refusal. After a secret ballot in which the National

Plate 16 The German delegation to the Versailles Peace Conference. © BPK

Plate 17 Mass protest in Berlin against the Treaty of Versailles. © BPK

Assembly voted in favor of acceptance, the foreign minister, Hermann Müller from the SPD, and the minister of transport, Johannes Bell from the Center, signed the treaty in the Hall of Mirrors in Versailles. It was the very place where the German Empire had been proclaimed less than 50 years before.

The Treaty of Versailles was harsh and unjust, but it was neither as harsh nor as unjust as the Treaty of Brest-Litovsk. It was soon recognized as such by the Allied governments, who had been driven by their electorates which were bent on revenge, to draft a peace they knew to be fraught with problems. The process of revision, which Germany was quick to exploit, began almost immediately. Indeed Germany was in a stronger position after Versailles than it had been in 1914. With Russia in the hands of the pariah Bolsheviks it was no longer encircled. The bordering states of Poland and Czechoslovakia were hopelessly weak. The entente between Britain and France had never been particularly *cordiale*, and under the strains of a coalition war and a controversial peace it was now in tatters. Germany was still united, and the Ruhr was virtually a guarantee that it would once again be a major power. But the Treaty had a disastrous, indeed deadly, effect on domestic politics. The majority parties were blamed for accepting the "Diktat" of Versailles along with the "war guilt lie." The wooden titan Hindenburg gave his full support to the "stab in the back legend" (*Dolchstoßlegende*) which the OHL had fabricated, and announced that the army had been undefeated in the field and betrayed by the politicians. The majority parties, and with them the entire system of Weimar democracy, were henceforth denounced from the right as the "November criminals." Everyone agreed that the Treaty of Versailles had to be revised, but opinions differed on how this was to be done and how far that revision should go. On the right it was argued that revision of the treaty should also involve the overthrow of the parties most responsible for Germany's humiliation. For them the struggle to revise the Treaty of Versailles was first and foremost a fight to the death against the Weimar Republic. That was the Treaty's fatal legacy.

The new republic was a federal state, but was far more centralized than the old empire. The larger states no longer had "reserve rights" that permitted them to have their own armies, postal services, and taxes. Prussia, still by far the largest state with 60 percent of the population, was no longer a hegemonic power, and state and federal governments were now clearly separated. The fiercest debates were over the role of the president. Largely due to the advocacy of Max Weber, the architect of the new constitution, the left-liberal Hugo Preuss proposed there should be a president elected by universal suffrage whose democratic legitimation would make him a powerful counterweight to parliament. This suggestion was sharply attacked by a number of Social Democrats who saw such a strong president as a potentially Bonapartist autocrat *à la* Bismarck, or as a surrogate kaiser. Ebert might well be entrusted with such powers, but what would happen if he were succeeded by a reactionary? Most members did not share this grim view. Shaken by the recent violence they welcomed a powerful head of state who could take decisive action in difficult times. They had no objection to the president having a seven-year term of office, or to his being able to use emergency powers under paragraph 48, the latter being subject to the Reichstag's veto. The president appointed the chancellor and could dissolve the Reichstag. In a multi-party system, and with proportional representation which helped the splinter parties, this gave the president immense powers over the Reichstag.

The constitution came into effect on August 14 1919 and one week later the National Assembly left Weimar and returned to Berlin. The most pressing task of the new Reichstag was financial reform. The problems facing Matthias Erzberger, as minister of finance, were truly awesome. The war had been financed on credit, and the state was hopelessly indebted. Excessive increases in nominal wages had been granted in order to placate a dangerously discontented working class, inflation was running rife, and the Reichsbank found it difficult to resist the temptation to encourage inflation as a means of canceling part of the national debt. The situation was further complicated by the prospect of having to meet the excessive Allied demands for reparations. Erzberger set about reforming and centralizing the tax system, taxing war profiteers, increasing death duties, and introducing a one shot tax on assets and a national income tax. The net result of these reforms was to further fuel inflation. Erzberger imagined that significant increases in the tax burden would reduce the amount of money in circulation and thus cut back inflation, but the cost of higher taxes was quickly offset by higher prices. Local government authorities now depended on central government for support, and no longer relied on the sale of bonds. The result was that they were starved of funds and were soon heavily in debt.

The Kapp Putsch

Erzberger was already the bête noir of the right. He had introduced the peace resolution in 1917 and had signed the armistice. Now he was responsible for the punitive taxation of the wealthy and propertied. A scurrilous defamation campaign was mounted against him, and in January 1920 he was seriously wounded in an assassination attempt. On March 12 he felt obliged to resign. On the same day Noske informed his cabinet colleagues that a plot was afoot to overthrow the government. The coup was masterminded by Wolfgang Kapp, head of the former Fatherland Party, and by Captain Waldemar Pabst, who had ordered the murder of Rosa Luxemburg and Karl Liebknecht. Military support was provided by Baron von Lüttwitz, the commanding general of Army Group I in Berlin, and by Captain Hermann Ehrhardt, whose Free Corps Marine Brigade had fought Bolsheviks in the Baltic states with the blessing of the Allied powers. He then went on to play a leading role in the White terror in Munich. The conspiracy was coordinated by the National Association (*National Vereinigung*) under Ludendorff's patronage.

Ehrhardt's troops entered Berlin on March 13, their helmets adorned with swastikas, an ancient Indian symbol that had been adopted by a number of extreme nationalist and anti-Semitic movements. President Ebert and Gustav Bauer's cabinet prudently moved to Dresden and relied on General Georg Maercker for protection.

Kapp installed himself in the vacant chancellery, and Lüttwitz proclaimed himself commander-in-chief of the armed forces. The Kapp Putsch, which had initially been so successful, was doomed to failure because the vast majority of the ministerial bureaucracy refused to acknowledge its legitimacy. Bauer refused to negotiate with the putschists and after four frustrating days the military advised Kapp to throw in the towel. Ehrhardt's troops left Berlin on March 17. Kapp and Lüttwitz fled the country, and Ehrhardt was hidden by right-wing extremists in Munich, where he founded the terrorist group Organization Consul (OC) after his pseudonym "Consul Eichmann." After an eventful life spent largely on the run, he died in 1971 at the ripe old age of 90. Although responsible for a number of spectacular assassinations, including the deaths of Erzberger and Rathenau, he was never called to account in a court of law.

One of the persistent myths of the time is that the putsch was stopped by a general strike. A call for a general strike was issued on behalf of the SPD, although it was promptly disavowed by Ebert, who feared that it would plunge the country into a civil war. The Communists initially refused to support the strike on the grounds that the proletariat could not rush to the defense of a state that was responsible for the murders of Rosa Luxemburg and Karl Liebknecht. The party soon gave way to pressure from the rank and file and announced that it would join the struggle against military dictatorship. The strike, which was organized by the trades unions, only got going when the putsch was on its last legs. Although Kapp had fled to Sweden, the strike continued in an attempt to force the government to accept a thorough-going program of reform that would make a repeat performance of such a putsch unlikely. The government negotiated with the strikers and a compromise was reached when Noske, who had been unable to control the army, and the Prussian minister of the interior, Wolfgang Heine, resigned. The government agreed to replace unreliable police units with certified republicans, and promised to reconsider the nationalization of coal and energy. The strike was then ended.

While Kapp was in Berlin and the government paralyzed, there was unrest elsewhere in Germany. In Munich the local army commander, General von Möhl, prompted by a group a prominent figures on the extreme right, demanded of the SPD minister-president Johannes Hoffmann that he be given full emergency powers. This led to Hoffmann's resignation, and to his replacement by Gustav von Kahr at the head of a resolutely right-wing government that provided a safe haven in Bavaria for all manner of outlandish groups on the wilder shores of the radical right. In the Ruhr the KPD organized a Red Army made up of "Proletarian Centuries" that attracted men of disparate political affiliations. On March 24 the Prussian minister of the interior and Reich Commissar, Carl Severing, concluded a lengthy series of negotiations with the insurgents with the Bielefeld Agreement. The KPD would have nothing of this, and refused to end the struggle, whereupon the government sent military units to the Ruhr, which only a few days before had supported Kapp. Well over 1,000 workers lost their lives in the bloodshed that followed. The brutal suppression of the Ruhr workers had a sobering effect on the labor movement. There were no more general strikes during the whole period of the Weimar Republic, and the KPD's putsch attempt in the "March Action" in the following year was a damp squib that had no popular support.

Whereas those responsible for the uprising in the Ruhr were severely punished, those who supported the Kapp putsch were let off virtually scot-free. There was a general amnesty in August 1920 for Free Corps officers, who were then welcomed into the armed forces. Kapp returned to Germany in 1922 to face trial but died before the proceedings began. Elections were held in June that marked the end of the rule of the Weimar coalition. The SPD share of the vote fell by 43 percent. The DDP dropped by 55 percent. The Center remained relatively stable. On the left the KPD fielded candidates for the first time and only obtained 1.7 percent of the votes, but the USPD more than doubled its share so that it was only three points behind the SPD. On the right, votes for the DVP trebled, and the DNVP improved its showing by almost 50 percent.

Reparations and Inflation

Ebert found it exceedingly hard to find anyone willing to attempt to form a government, until the Center Party politician Konstantin Fehrenbach stepped into the breach and tacked together a minority government that included the Center, the DDP, and the DVP. Fehrenbach was a respected figure known for his tact and sense of humor. He had considerable political experience and had been the chairman of the Joint Committee of the Reichstag. He also had a reputation for his principled stand against the rising tide of anti-Semitism. But he was not a decisive or forceful personality and proved unequal to the weighty problems that faced his government. His task was made all the more difficult by Allied intransigence and inequity. At the beginning of May 1921 Lloyd George, on behalf of the Allies, presented the German government with an ultimatum that unless a back payment of 12 billion gold marks in reparations was made, and unless their war criminals were brought to justice, the entire Ruhr would be occupied. One billion was to be paid by the end of the month. This was no idle threat. Düsseldorf, Duisburg, and Ruhrort had already been occupied a few weeks previously when an earlier ultimatum had been disregarded. In addition the Allies finally reached an agreement that Germany should pay 132 billion gold marks in reparations, with an additional six billion for Belgium. Finding it impossible to meet these terms Fehrenbach resigned.

The crisis was rendered all the more acute by events in Upper Silesia. The Polish government refused to accept the result of the plebiscite in March 1921, in which 60 percent of the population voted for Germany, and supported Polish insurgents who laid claim to the bulk of the province. The German government responded by arming paramilitary units determined to ensure that the vote be respected and Upper Silesia be returned to Germany. The Allies managed to put an end to the fighting, and accepted a report by the League of Nations which suggested that four-fifths of Upper Silesia should be given to Poland, including certain industrial districts that had voted overwhelmingly for Germany. Also in March the KPD, supported by the

Communist International, mounted an abortive coup attempt in the Ruhr that was quickly suppressed by Severing's Prussian police.

The Weimar coalition returned to office in a minority government under Joseph Wirth. The new chancellor was something of an *enfant terrible* on the left wing of the Center Party. He was a brilliant orator, an ardent Republican, and a fervent nationalist. He was the architect of the policy, soon to be called "fulfillment," of cooperation with the Allies in the hope of being able to expose the impossibility of their demands and thus revise the treaty. The Allied demands were indeed virtually impossible to fulfill. The initial billion could only be raised by the sale of three-month treasury bonds that further fueled inflation. The problem could not be solved without a substantial tax on capital, but this was unacceptable to the Reichstag majority, even to those like Walter Rathenau who supported Wirth's fulfillment policy. If the capitalists were not going to pay then the consumers would have to foot the bill. Employees already hit by inflation would be made to suffer still further. The right mounted a massive hate campaign against the Wirth government and its policy of fulfillment. There were a number of political murders, including Erzberger's assassination in August 1921. His killers, who came from Ehrhardt's "Organization Consul," were compared to Brutus, William Tell, and Charlotte Corday in the right-wing press. Only six war criminals were brought to trial, the two most serious of whom were sprung from jail thanks to "Organization Consul." The press waxed increasingly indignant over the antics of the "Jewish swine on the Spree" and the country seemed to be heading rapidly toward civil war. At the end of August the government made use of paragraph 48 to ban a number of extreme right-wing publications that were disseminating such filth, but the Bavarian government refused to cooperate and the infant Nazi Party's *Völkischer Beobachter* continued publication.

Wirth felt obliged to resign in October when the Reichstag majority insisted that the government should step down in protest at the flagrant disregard of the right to self-determination in Upper Silesia. It was a futile gesture since no government could be formed without the Center, and Wirth was soon back in office. The outstanding figure in the second Wirth cabinet was the new foreign secretary, Walther Rathenau, who had previously served as minister for reconstruction. He was the most remarkable and most admirable personality in the Weimar Republic. As head of the family firm AEG, he was an exemplary modern manager, with a complete mastery of both the technical and the financial complexities of a vast corporation. In addition he was a sensitive and highly cultured intellectual, a perceptive essayist, philosopher, and cultural critic. He was a member of the DDP and an enthusiastic advocate of the policy of fulfillment. His first and only appearance on the international stage as foreign minister was at the Genoa Conference in April 1922. The conference was held at Lloyd George's request, ostensibly to deal with the problem of reparations and war debts, but primarily it was a desperate attempt to save his political skin. Although it was doomed to failure from the outset, largely because the United States declined to attend, it was not without significance. For the first time the Soviet Union was invited to attend an international meeting and a number of influential figures in Germany were determined to use this opportunity to strengthen ties between the two countries. As early as 1920, even before the Polish–Soviet war, General Hans von Seeckt, the de facto head of the German General Staff, an organization that had been officially outlawed by the Treaty of Versailles, and which was now known simply as the "Troops Office" (*Truppenamt*), argued that Germany could only regain the territory it had lost to Poland in close cooperation with the Soviet Union. Wirth enthusiastically agreed and both men dreamt of the destruction of Poland and a common frontier between Germany and the Soviet Union. Top secret cooperation between the German army (*Reichswehr*) and the Red Army began in 1921, soon after the Treaty of Riga obliged the Soviet Union to accept a substantial loss of territory to the victorious Poles. A few months later the head of the eastern department of the Foreign Office, Ago von Maltzan, one of Kiderlen-Wächter's protégés, began talks with Karl Radek, the German expert in the Soviet government, with a view to working out an economic agreement that would bypass the Allied syndicate to assist Soviet economic development. Rathenau was a convinced westerner and wanted nothing to do with the Soviet Union, but when the Soviet commissar for foreign affairs, Georgi Chicherin, stopped off in Berlin on his way to Genoa, substantial progress was made toward the conclusion of a treaty. At Genoa Maltzan played up the rumor that the Allies were about to do a deal with the Soviets at Germany's expense, in order to convince Rathenau to drop his objections to an alliance with the Bolsheviks. It is something of a mystery why Rathenau was so easily persuaded, against his better judgment, to take this fateful step, but, when told that Chicherin was ready to sign a treaty on German terms, he agreed to meet the Soviet delegation on Easter Sunday at the nearby resort of Rapallo. The Treaty of Rapallo was seemingly a fairly innocuous document. The signatories agreed not to make any demands on one another for war reparations or indemnities. Diplomatic relations were resumed, and most favored nation status granted.

In Berlin some conservatives objected to the acceptance of the Soviets as partners, and on the left concerns were voiced that it would ruin any chances of reaching an agreement with the Allies, but reactions to the treaty were on the whole positive, and it was ratified by a comfortable majority. The Allies, in particular the French who saw Rapallo as a repetition of crude Wilhelmine tactics and of Kiderlen's Morocco policy, were outraged and were now determined not to stand for any further nonsense from Germany. The French minister-president Poincaré publicly threatened Germany with armed intervention. Prospects for an agreement over reparations thus dissolved into the dim distant future.

Six weeks after signing the Treaty of Rapallo Rathenau was gunned down by members of Organization Consul. He was hated by the radical right as a Jew, as a man who sought a compromise with the Allies, as a political beneficiary of the revolution of 1918, and as an immensely wealthy capitalist. The republic was shattered by the death of this fascinating and complex figure. The Communists joined in the mass demonstrations organized by the unions and the two socialist parties. Wirth gave a rousing speech in the Reichstag which contained the memorable words

"The enemy is on the right" – words that were met with tumultuous applause from delegates from the left and the center. The government introduced legislation to protect the republic against right-wing terror, but it had little effect and was fiercely resisted by the Bavarian government. Offenders from the left continued to be far more harshly treated by the courts than those from the right.

Rathenau's murder was the most alarming sign of the mounting tide of anti-Semitism that was to plague the republic. "The Jew" was seen as a polyvalent evil. The fact that a number of leading figures on the left were Jewish was taken a clear evidence that the Jews were responsible for Germany's defeat. Had they not subverted loyal German workers with their Judeo-Marxist ideology, undermined the empire, over-thrown the crowned heads of Germany, and accepted a humiliating peace? Had they not avoided service at the front in order to fatten themselves with war profits? Were they not the driving force behind inflation, the black market, and fulfillment politics? In addition there were the "eastern Jews" (*Ostjuden*). Unlike the majority of German Jews they were orthodox and unassimilated. With their strange attire and alien habits, speaking Hebrew and Yiddish, they were seen as menacing foreign invaders and a sinister threat to the German race, culture, and identity. Before the war a number of *Ostjuden* lived and worked in Germany, where they were safe from the brutal pogroms of the pale. During the war many had been forced by the German army of occupation to work in munitions factories in the Reich. Others came as prisoners of war, or as refugees from Bolshevik terror and civil war. Most dreamt of emigrating to the United States and many succeeded in doing so. By 1925 there were just over 100,000 *Ostjuden* left in Germany – hardly the hordes that haunted the anti-Semites' fantasies. Anti-Semitic prejudices were widespread, but were seldom publicly voiced in respectable bourgeois circles. Student fraternities nurtured their anti-Semitic tra-ditions, and some members of the DNVP reveled in bouts of Jew-baiting, but the party had to distance itself somewhat from these creatures after Rathenau's murder, and the Prussian government banned a meeting of student fraternities in Marburg where it was intended to sing the praises of his murderers. The DNVP thus showed some restraint in Berlin, but the party's Munich branch allied itself with the German National Association (*Deutschvölkische Arbeitsgemeinschaft*), an anti-Semitic party created by dissident members of the DNVP. They were very small beer compared with Hitler's National Socialist German Workers Party (NSDAP), that was rapidly becom-ing a political force of more than local interest.

The nervousness and uncertainty caused by Rathenau's murder induced an alarm-ing hyperinflation that provided fresh ammunition for anti-Semites, political radi-cals, and assorted malcontents. Tensions between capital and labor mounted when the prominent industrialist, Hugo Stinnes, suggested to the National Economic Council (*Reichswirtschaftsrat*) that German workers should work an extra two hours per day without additional pay for at least ten years, in order to overcome the present problems. Fortunately cooler heads prevailed and the Council, which included members of a wide range of opinion from the Marxist economist Rudolf Hilferding to a number of prominent industrialists, came up with a number of pro-posals acceptable to both sides in the dispute. The eight-hour day, one of the great achievements of the revolution, remained the legal norm, and it was agreed that the government should cut back expenditure in an attempt to balance the budget. A serious attempt was also made to stabilize the mark by international loans and support from the Reichsbank. Agreement in the Council over these measures augured well for Wirth's efforts to create a coalition of parties from the DVP on the right to the SPD on the left, but all such hopes were dashed by the Social Democrats. The party had recently united with the rump of the USPD, the remainder having joined the KPD, and for fear of alienating the left by a coalition with the DVP, which they saw as the bosses' party, they decided to remain aloof. Wirth resigned as chancellor to be replaced by Wilhelm Cuno, the head of the Hamburg-America Line (Hapag). The new cabinet was largely made up of experts who, like the chancellor, had no party affiliations. Once again a government was formed without the support of the SPD, by far the most important of the parties that wholeheartedly supported the republic.

The Occupation of the Ruhr

Cuno took office in November 1922 and was soon to face a crisis that almost destroyed the republic. Ever since Rapallo the French had looked for an excuse to get back at Germany and to assert France's position as the hegemonic power in Europe. The Wirth government had been somewhat lackadaisical about reparations payments, and was seriously behindhand in deliveries of coal, wood, and telephone poles. On January 11 1923 French and Belgian troops began to occupy the Ruhr. The British government was appalled at this display of hubris and adopted an attitude which one observer described as "surly neutrality." Cuno's minority government responded to this aggressive act by calling for passive resistance. This earned him the instant and enthusiastic support of the trades unions and the SPD. Even the Communists joined in the heroic struggle against French imperialism, but were hasty to add that they were equally opposed to the gang of capitalists in Berlin. The KPD's slogan was now: "Destroy Poincaré on the Rhine and Cuno on the Spree!" Passive resistance was initially successful. Republican Germany was united as never before or subsequently, and the French were unable to extract any reparations. In March the French seized the coalmines and the railways and began the confiscation of German assets. By this time the republic was in serious financial difficulties. The Reichsbank was obliged to pay the striking workers and to grant massive credits to enterprises that had closed their doors in patriotic protest. Printing presses worked overtime as the hyperinflation got completely out of control. The exchange rate of the dollar rose from 21,000 marks in April to 110,000 by June, and the currency was soon to become utterly worthless.

As the crisis deepened there were a number of violent attacks on the invaders. Germany was soon to find a national hero in Leo Schlageter, a member of an ultraright party who was executed in May for his part in sabotaging a French train. His praises were sung by Karl Radek on behalf of the Communist International, in a dramatic speech in which he portrayed the "fascist" Schlageter as a martyr to the national cause, who lost his life in the struggle for a better future for all humanity, by taking up the cause of the working class against the coal and iron magnates. Adolf Hitler was also persuaded to join in the chorus, and Schlageter was awarded a place in the Nazi Pantheon, but his encomium paled beside Radek's. Ten years later Heidegger was to give one of his more preposterously distasteful harangues to his students at Freiburg University, where Schlageter had studied, in which he presented this unsavory figure as a model of German manhood.

It is one of the great ironies of history that whenever a communist party moved radically to the right and abandoned much of its ideological baggage it made spectacular gains in popular support. In 1923 Radek's "national Bolshevist" line met with an enthusiastic response among German workers. The KPD's membership rose by 24 percent by September and the party made significant gains in local elections. The KPD could only profit as the crisis deepened and living conditions became increasingly wretched. Was this the revolutionary situation for which Lenin and the Bolsheviks had dreamt for so long? Zinoviev, the secretary-general of the Communist International, along with Karl Radek and Trotsky, argued that it was. Stalin, as secretary-general of the Communist Party of the Soviet Union, prudently disagreed, but the triumvirate went ahead with plans for a German revolution, to take place in November, on the anniversary of the Glorious October Revolution, so as to inspire the German proletariat to greater deeds of heroism. Meanwhile the KPD was urged to join the minority government in Saxony and then ensure that the Saxon workers formed paramilitary units that would spearhead the revolution.

At long last the left wing of the SPD overcame its repugnance against supporting a government which included the DVP. Cuno's government had brought such misery to the average German that it could no longer be tolerated. Inflation had to be brought under control and the currency stabilized, national unity restored and the occupation ended. Unwilling to bear full responsibility for a policy that risked them being charged with a second "stab in the back," the majority of SPD delegates supported the national government under the DVP's strongman, Gustav Stresemann, which took office on August 13. After lengthy debate and soul searching, Stresemann's government eventually ordered an end to passive resistance on September 26. The Bavarian government immediately declared a state of emergency, whereupon Berlin invoked paragraph 48 to give the Reichswehr minister Gessler full executive powers. A struggle for power now developed between the governments in Munich and Berlin. The Nazi daily rag *Völkischer Beobachter* denounced the "Stresemann–Seeckt dictatorship" as another Jewish conspiracy, pointing out that both men were married to Jewesses and that the minister of finance Rudolf Hilferding was both a Marxist and a Jew. Otto Gessler, the DDP Reichswehr minister since the Kapp putsch, ordered the Bavarian minister-president von Kahr and the local army commander, General von Lossow, to ban the paper. In an act of defiant insubordination both men refused, leaving Berlin in an awkward quandary. Seeckt refused to take sides, just as he had done during the Kapp putsch. A military dictatorship with which some had toyed was thus out of the question. A further problem was the proposal to lengthen the working week in order to overcome the economic problems facing the republic; this was enthusiastically endorsed on the right but vetoed by the SPD. Stresemann was now under attack from the right for refusing to go ahead, and from the left for contemplating a compromise solution to the issue.

Stresemann was in an impossible situation and resigned at the beginning of October, but within four days he was back in office. Most DVP deputies were reluctant to follow the confrontational line of Stinnes and the industrialists, and the SPD showed a willingness to compromise lest worse should occur. As a result the eight-hour day was retained in principle but could be exceeded, and contract negotiations between capital and labor were subjected to compulsory arbitration. Hilferding celebrated the fact that wage contracts were no longer subject to market forces as an example of "organized capitalism" and thus a major step toward a socialist economy. With the government now in a much stronger position, Gessler demanded that General Otto von Lossow be dismissed. Kahr upped the ante by appointing him as commander-in-chief of an independent Bavarian contingent. Kahr now contemplated a national dictatorship, but was uncertain who was to be the German Mussolini. Perhaps he should aspire to this role. Seeckt was another possibility, but certainly not Adolf Hitler, who was to play a subordinate role in this drama. While he pondered this question, Kahr won considerable support throughout Bavaria by ordering the expulsion of large numbers of *Ostjuden*.

Meanwhile, Communists had been appointed to key positions in the governments of Saxony and Thuringia. The local army commander in Dresden promptly banned the Communist paramilitary wing and placed the Saxon police force under his orders. Heinrich Brandler, the leader of the KPD, acting on orders from Moscow, hoped to organize a general strike in Saxony that would trigger off the "German October," but the Reichswehr was firmly in control and the enterprise was doomed to failure. Orders were issued to cancel the uprising, but they did not reach Hamburg, where there were three days of bloody fighting before the police were able to crush the revolt. There were sporadic outbreaks of violence in Saxony which the Reichswehr had no difficulty in mastering. Paragraph 48 was now used to reconstitute the Saxon government under a commissar from the DVP. The Reichswehr marched into Thuringia shortly after the coalition collapsed, and due to considerable pressure from Berlin the local SPD broke its alliance with the Communists. That was the end of Social Democratic rule in Thuringia. The state was soon to welcome all manner of *Völkisch* movements, and as early as 1930 in Wilhelm Frick it was to have the first National Socialist minister.

The spotlight now turned once again to Munich where, on the evening of November 8, Adolf Hitler held the Bavarian triumvirate of Kahr, Lossow, and the police chief Hans von Seisser hostage by taking over a meeting in the Bürgerbräukeller, a vast and popular watering-hole. The "Beer Hall Putsch" was a badly bungled affair. The three were set free at Ludendorff's insistence, and promptly planned their revenge. On the following day Hitler's march toward the Feldherrnhalle was halted by a brief salvo from the police. Sixteen of his followers were killed and became the first martyrs of the "National Revolution," to whom homage was rendered every year on November 9, and to whose memory Adolf Hitler dedicated the first volume of *Mein Kampf*. The blood stained swastika banner became the most sacred relic of the movement. Seeckt was now formally given the full executive powers under paragraph 48 that he had enjoyed in practice since the end of September. Paradoxically, Hitler's comic opera coup helped to save the republic in that it ruined Kahr's far more threatening schemes. Kahr remained in office as Reich Commissar for Bavaria and Lossow was still in command of the local Reichswehr units. Neither was ever punished for their outrageous violations of the constitution. They quietly resigned in February 1924, having first ensured a number of additional privileges for their home state.

Stresemann and Fulfillment

Having successfully met the threats from the radical left and the radical right, Stresemann's government now set about stabilizing the mark, which was no longer worth the paper it was printed on. By November it took 4,200,000,000,000 marks to buy one dollar. In the course of an operation involving clouds of smoke and a large number of mirrors, the prominent banker Hjalmar Schacht, as special commissar for the currency, who was soon to become Reichsbank president, along with Hans Luther, the minister of finance, created a new currency known as the "*Rentenmark*." Twelve noughts were struck off the mark, so that one dollar was now equal to 4.2 Rentenmarks. Once the new currency stabilized, largely due to the government's careful housekeeping and responsible fiscal policy, international confidence was restored and the Rentenmark was converted back into marks at par in August 1924. At the initiative of the American secretary of state, Charles Hughes, a commission was struck with the banker Charles G. Dawes in the chair to reexamine the whole question of German reparations. Poincaré, whose intransigently anti-German position had brought no benefits, and had left him increasingly isolated and hoping that the United States would reward him for his cooperation by moderating their conditions for the repayment of France's war debt, readily agreed.

The SPD was outraged by the unequal treatment of Bavaria and Saxony. In Bavaria an illegal regime from the extreme right had been left untouched, whereas a constitutionally impeccable government in Saxony had been violently suppressed. Their demand that Bavaria should be given the same treatment as Saxony was rejected by the bourgeois parties, who feared that this would tear the country apart. Stresemann called for a vote of confidence, which he lost by 231 to 156, with seven abstentions. Ebert called upon the Center Party leader Wilhelm Marx to form a new government. He was a somewhat colorless Rhinelander, a dull speaker who lacked popular appeal, but he was a brilliant administrator, an open-minded pragmatist, and a man of absolute integrity. Although a devout Catholic, he was far from being a bigot. He was a man of compromise, but he always had the courage to face tough decisions. It was not for nothing that this underrated politician was the longest serving chancellor in the history of the Weimar Republic.

The Marx government was a coalition of the Center, BVP, DVP, and DDP. Stresemann served as foreign minister, and was to do so in successive governments until his premature death in 1929 at the age of 51. This was a minority government which relied on the support of the SPD and which had to take some exceedingly difficult and unpopular decisions. The new mark could not be maintained on the gold standard without considerable sacrifices being made. The middle classes had lost all their savings in the Inflation, but the government could not afford any compensation. Pay in the civil service was reduced to way below the prewar levels. The vast majority of pensioners were ruined. All those who were seriously in debt profited immensely. These included a number of large landowners, and also the state, whose war bonds were now worthless. The ranks of the unemployed swelled alarmingly and average real wages fell to a mere 70 percent of prewar levels. But although the state was relieved of this crippling burden of debt, it was totally discredited in the eyes of those millions who had patriotically bought war bonds and other government paper, and who now felt betrayed. The republicans had first stabbed the country in the back, and then robbed the little man of his savings. This was fertile soil in which radical political movements could readily take root.

Hitler and his confederates were tried in April 1924. Ludendorff was acquitted, Ernst Röhm, the head of the brown-shirted bully-boys in the SA, received three months imprisonment and a 100 mark fine. Hitler was given a five-year term, but was released by Christmas, having served his sentence in a comfortable minimum security jail at Landsberg, where he whiled away the time writing *Mein Kampf*. These absurdly light sentences were seen as virtual acquittals, thus causing jubilation on the right and consternation on the left.

The results of the Dawes commission's deliberations were published shortly after the Munich court handed down these verdicts. Germany was called upon to make annual payments of one thousand million marks in the first five years, after which time the payments were to rise to 2.5 thousand million. The creditor nations were given a degree of control over the German economy, but the pill was sweetened with a loan of 800 million marks, which was designed to help stabilize the currency. The prospect of further investments, particularly from the United States, had an immediate stimulating effect on the economy. The total sum of reparations was not mentioned, but it was understood that it would be less than the 132 thousand million marks demanded in Lloyd George's note in 1921. This looked like the dawn of a new era, in which the anti-German Poincaré was replaced by the amiable Radical Herriot, who was known to be a great admirer of German idealist philosophy, and with Ramsay MacDonald heading Britain's first Labor government.

Although Dawes was awarded the Nobel Prize for Peace in 1925, the situation in Germany was far from peaceful. The radical right and left made further significant gains in the elections of 1924. The parties in the republican center lost voters to the DNVP, whose electoral campaign was based on a repudiation of the Dawes Plan, and even the leaderless Nazis won an impressive 6.5 percent of the popular vote. Large numbers of workers turned to the KPD, which with 12.6 percent of the vote was a significant political power. Another minority government under Marx had great difficulty in gaining a majority for the ratification of the Dawes Plan, particularly the sections dealing with Allied control over the railways. Marx decided to go to the country after a series of defeats in the Reichstag, and fresh elections were held in December 1924.

The economy showed remarkable signs of recovery in 1924. Foreign investment poured into Germany, unemployment dropped dramatically, and wages rose. In such circumstances it was hardly surprising that support for the KPD dwindled and the SPD made significant gains. The Nazis and their associates, the German Nationalists, lost more than half their supporters, and were now insignificant splinter parties. The DNVP managed to improve its showing somewhat, thus making the process of cabinet building all the more difficult. After lengthy negotiations a government was formed in mid-January 1925 under Hans Luther, the energetic mayor of Essen. He was without party affiliation, and had gained a reputation as a tough and effective minister of finance. The DNVP participated in government for the first time, and soon found itself in the embarrassing situation of supporting policies it had roundly denounced during the election campaign.

A few weeks after the Luther cabinet had taken office President Ebert died. Although acute appendicitis was given as the cause of death he was the victim of character assassination. Ebert was a man who stood for compromise at a time when compromise was a dirty word. He was cruelly mocked by the KPD and the satirist Kurt Tucholsky, and on the right by everyone from Adolf Hitler to the right wing of the DNVP. He died shortly after a court in Magdeburg ruled that the charge made by a journalist, whom he had sued for libel for suggesting that he had committed high treason by supporting a strike by munitions workers in 1918, was legally admissible. Ebert won the libel case and the journalist received a three-month prison sentence, but the charge of treason broke the heart of a true patriot who had lost two sons in the war.

Among the many candidates in the ensuing presidential election were the former chancellor Marx, and the outstanding minister-president of Prussia, Otto Braun, for the SPD, who was known as the "Red tsar" and "the last king of Prussia." The KPD fielded their party chairman Ernst "Teddy" Thälmann, a bone-headed Stalinist of dubious probity, and the National Socialist candidate was General Ludendorff. In the first round of the election only Otto Braun did reasonably well with 29 percent of the vote, but he trailed behind the candidate of the DNVP and the DVP, Karl Jarres. Jarres was the former mayor of Duisburg who had been jailed for two months by the Belgians during the "struggle for the Ruhr" in 1923, and who had been minister of the interior in Stresemann's second cabinet and in both of Marx's. Although an ineffective minister, he polled 38.8 percent of the votes.

The SPD knew that they could only beat the right-wing parties in the final round if they backed a bourgeois candidate. They therefore agreed to support Marx, in return for which the Center backed Otto Braun as minister-president in Prussia. Jarres clearly had no hope of winning against such a powerful coalition and the right therefore had to find a more appealing candidate. They agreed upon Field Marshal von Hindenburg who, for the second time, was called out of retirement in spite of the opposition of the industrialists who saw him as a died-in-the-wool agrarian, and from Stresemann who feared negative reactions from abroad.

The Protestant Hindenburg's chances were greatly improved by the fact that he was supported by the Catholic BVP, who could not stomach the Center's alliance with the Social Democrats. Marx's chances were further reduced by Thälmann's refusal to step down, even though he had only obtained seven percent of the vote in the first round. Hindenburg emerged as the winner thanks to the help given him by the KPD. He received 48.3 percent of the vote, Marx 45.3 percent, and Thälmann 6.4 percent. The election of the monarchist career officer Hindenburg was a vote against the republic, just as the election of Marshal MacMahon as president of France in 1873 had been, but republicans were mostly optimistic. France had weathered the storm after all, and some argued that Hindenburg's election would oblige many on the right to come to terms with the republic. This soon proved woefully Pollyannaish. The republic shifted markedly to the right, the old Wilhelmine elites now had ready access to the president, and could easily influence events if the Reichstag once again failed to deliver the goods. Ebert had made the fatal mistake of using article 48 to pass 42 pieces of emergency legislation. It remained to be seen whether Hindenburg would do the same in similar circumstances.

Weimar Culture

Hindenburg's election was also a rejection of that exciting Weimar culture which Peter Gay reminds us was a continuation of the prewar avant-garde. Atonal music, expressionism in all the arts, the brutal realism of *"neue Sachlichkeit"* that replaced expressionism, Einstein's theory of relativity, Freudian psychoanalysis, Max Weber's sociology, Berthold Brecht and Kurt Weill's *Threepenny Opera*, Hindemith's operas *Das Nusch-Nuschi* and *Mörder, Hoffnung der Frauen*, and the Bauhaus, represented everything that was wrong with the republic. The attack on this astonishingly vital culture was not confined to primitive philistines who objected to the Bauhaus style of flat-roofed "nigger colonies," or who echoed Willibald Nagel when he wrote of *Das Nusch-Nuschi:* "Is not Pfitzner right when he says we are soiled, deceived, and trivialized by much of what calls itself recent German art? Since such thrown-together stuff like this grotesquerie can also inflict serious moral damage, it is necessary in the name of our great and pure art to protest against such bilge." Some of the greatest minds of the day also joined in the attack, among them Martin Heidegger and Carl Schmitt.

Heidegger's "fundamental ontology," his gloomy speculations over the meaning of being in a world without God in *Being and Time*, led him, in a prose which even by German standards is punishingly obscure, to an existential solipsism in which the individual was the sole site of truth in an untrue society. At last he saw reason to hope that Adolph Hitler could lead the people forward under Zarathustra's empty heavens toward a "giving of meaning amidst the meaningless." Where Heidegger saw the stifling effects of mass society that frustrated all efforts to achieve an existential "authenticity," Carl Schmitt, as the leading ideologue of the counterrevolution, protested against a destructive pluralist and democratic society that made a clear distinction between friend and foe impossible, thus resulting in sterile discourse, political horse-trading, and the impossibility of creating the "self-assertion" of the political unity of the German people. Schmitt argued that sovereignty resided in whomever had the right to declare a state of emergency. He hoped that Hindenburg, as a president elected by universal suffrage and armed with paragraph 48, would act as a powerful counterweight to a divided and cantankerous Reichstag, and become a democratically legitimized dictator. Schmitt was the outstanding spokesman for the "conservative revolution" which many hoped would follow upon the presidential election of 1925.

Schmitt's rejection of parliamentary democracy as an empty farce appealed to many on the left, and was greatly admired by the generation of 1968. Similar ideas were held in the 1920s by the "National Bolsheviks" around Ernst Niekisch. They were a bizarre collection of nationalists, anarchists, socialists, and right-wing radicals who argued in favor of close contacts with the Soviet Union and fierce resistance to the Western powers and their exorbitant demands for reparations. Comparable views were held by Oswald Spengler, the author of the bestselling *Decline of the West* and *Prussianism and Socialism*. He argued that the German people as a "master race" (*Herrenvolk*) had preserved its "predatory character" with which a small group of inspired leaders could achieve true greatness. Socialism for Spengler was identical with "good old Prussian values," in which "everyone was the servant of the state; an extremely harsh form of anti-liberal and authoritarian state." It was not enough to struggle against Marxism, equally dangerous were liberalism and parliamentarianism, which Spengler condemned as "the England within." The parallels with National Socialism are obvious, but for most of the "conservative revolutionaries" the Nazi's were too crude and low-class and their leader certainly not built of Caesarian timber. In return the Nazis ignored Spengler, who died in isolation in 1936. Niekisch was thrown into a concentration camp where he remained until liberated by the Red Army in 1945, after which he made his peace with the Communist regime in East Germany. The "conservative revolutionaries" were anti-Semites in the traditional mode, and were far removed from the obsessive, quasi-religious, and fanatical anti-Semitism of the National Socialists. Indeed in the relatively stable years after the Dawes Plan there was a distinct decline in the rabid anti-Semitism of the first years of the republic. Nevertheless Jews were widely seen as the architects of the republic, the sinister power behind a degenerate and depraved culture, and Marxism in all its forms was denounced as a Jewish ideology.

The republic had precious few defenders of note. Left-wing intellectuals treated it with a contempt equal to that of their rivals on the right. Indeed, as we have seen in the example of Ernst Niekisch, left and right could all too easily agree, and the Communists were soon to be seen arm in arm with National Socialists at demonstrations against the state they both were determined to destroy. In 1919 Max Weber had given a remarkable lecture in Munich amid the ruins of the German Empire and in the middle of a curious socialist revolution. He took up the problem posed by Tolstoy that science, for all its miracles and triumphs, for all the fundamental changes it had made to people's lives, and with its immense destructive powers, which had been so brutally shown in the war, was still unable to answer fundamental questions. How should we live? What should we do? To Weber this offered a great chance. He believed that science leaves us the freedom to make these choices independently from objective scientific laws, and he issued a timely and timeless warning against faiths masquerading as scientific truths. Ideologies such as scientific socialism and Nazi biologism were for Weber political passions dressed up as historical necessity.

Weber died in 1920 and Thomas Mann was soon to take over his role as the leading "rational republican" (*Vernunftrepublikaner*). The conservative nationalist apologist for the authoritarian Wilhelmine state in *Reflections of an Unpolitical Person* of 1918 underwent a remarkable change of heart. He made a spirited defense of the new republic in 1922, and was soon to denounce the "anti-Semitic nationalism and God-knows-what dark stupidities" of the extremist groups that mushroomed in the Munich of the 1920s where he had made his home. In his masterpiece *The Magic Mountain*, he gave a deliciously ironic analysis of the intellectual and moral malaise of the times and grim warnings of an imminent terrorism that threatened to destroy all hopes for a better future.

The historian Friedrich Meinecke shared Thomas Mann's concerns and warned that the republic, for all its obvious shortcomings, had at least managed to overcome the profound differences between the middle and working classes. He unfortunately overlooked the deep and ultimately fatal rift within the working class between communists and social democrats and concentrated on the struggle within the bourgeoisie between the right and the center. For the moment it seemed that the moderate bourgeoisie and the moderate working class, which formed the backbone of the republic, was strong enough to withstand the attacks from the right and from the left, but it was impossible to tell how long this relative stability would last, or whether it could survive another crisis like those of 1920 and 1923. Kautsky, the leading theoretician of the SPD, imagined that the parliamentary coalition of the bourgeois and proletarian parties would mark the first stage of the transition from capitalism to socialism. In fact it meant the final abandonment by the Social Democrats of socialism as an attainable goal.

Locarno

Hindenburg's election was not proof that Weimar was a "republic without republicans," but it did show that they were very thin on the ground. This gloomy fact was all too easily overlooked thanks to the striking success of Stresemann's foreign policy at Locarno in the same year. Germany, France, and Belgium guaranteed that Germany's western frontiers would not be changed by force. Britain and Italy guaranteed the agreement. The question of Germany's eastern frontiers was left open, with Germany agreeing to arbitration treaties with Poland and Czechoslovakia, with whom France signed treaties of mutual guarantee. Stresemann made it perfectly clear that he had every intention of revising the frontiers with Poland and the Soviets immediately recognized this. Moscow was convinced that Locarno was a sinister move by the western powers to turn Germany eastwards as the spearhead of an anti-Soviet crusade. Stresemann knew full well that a revision of the eastern frontiers could not even be contemplated without assuaging these fears. The Berlin Treaty of 1926 with the Soviet Union reaffirmed the Treaty of Rapallo, and guaranteed mutual neutrality in the event of an unprovoked attack on either of the contracting parties. Both parties undertook not to take part in any boycott or sanctions on the other. The treaty thus aimed to put pressure on Poland and further Germany's revisionist ambitions in the east. Germany scored a further victory over Poland in that it was not only admitted to the League of Nations but, unlike its eastern rival, was given a permanent seat on the Council. Germany's prestige was further enhanced when Stresemann, along with his French homologue Aristide Briand, was awarded the Nobel Peace Prize in 1926.

For the DNVP Locarno was a craven appeasement of the western powers, and they withdrew their support from the Luther cabinet. The treaty could only be ratified with the enthusiastic support of the SPD, but unfortunately the Social Democrats refused to join the coalition. The Luther government fell a few weeks later, over the highly emotional question of whether German embassies and consulates should be allowed to fly the black, white, and red flag of the merchant marine in place of the black, red, and gold flag symbolic of democracy and republicanism. A new minority government was formed under Marx, but the SPD stood aloof. The party had moved sharply to the left by supporting a Communist-sponsored plebiscite calling for the confiscation, without compensation, of the property of the German princes. It clung to its newly-won ideological purity and refused to compromise with its class enemies. Stresemann tried desperately to win the support of the SPD for a great coalition so as to stop an embarrassing debate over illegal armaments, but without success. On December 16 1926 Philipp Scheidemann made a sensational speech in the Reichstag in which he exposed the illegal financing of armaments and the close links between the Reichswehr and right-wing paramilitary groups which were designed to circumvent the restriction of the army to a mere 100,000 men. He also stated that the KPD was well aware that armaments forbidden by the Treaty of Versailles were being imported from the Soviet Union.

The Marx cabinet fell as a result of these revelations, but there was no alternative to yet another minority government under Marx in which the DNVP played a prominent role. The appointment of Walther von Keudell, a leading figure in the Kapp putsch who loudly professed his anti-Semitism, as minister of the interior was indication of a sharp right turn. But the fourth Marx cabinet was also responsible for the most important piece of social legislation in the history of the republic. The unemployment insurance bill of 1927 provided comprehensive coverage for all employees. It was financed by both employer and employee paying premiums equal to three percent of a worker's wages. The state was henceforth obliged to grant a bridging loan if the unemployment insurance fund fell into the red. The new system was admirably suited to deal with the problems of moderate unemployment as existed at the time, but was soon to be stretched to the limit when the depression began to be felt in following year. A substantial wage increase was given to civil servants in mid-December that was soon to prove a fiscal disaster, as some prudent deputies had warned. Among them was the future chancellor Heinrich Brüning. With an election looming their jeremiads were ignored.

Once again the government fell over a failure to reach a compromise, this time over the financing of confessional schools. The election campaign of 1928 was overshadowed by the issue of whether or not the proposed building of the pocket battleship, Battle Cruiser "A," should go ahead. The KPD demanded that the money designated for the ship should be spent on free school meals for the needy. The SPD, eager to remain in the proletarian vanguard, echoed this exhortation and was confident of a resounding success at the polls. They were not to be disappointed. The Social Democrats were the big winners in the election of May 1928, the DNVP the losers. A great coalition was clearly indicated by the results, but Stresemann had to pull out all the stops to persuade the DVP to ally with Hermann Müller and the SPD. It was not forgotten that he was the man who had put his name to the Treaty of Versailles.

The Müller government was immediately faced with a crisis in that the cabinet decided to go ahead with building Battle Cruiser "A," even though the SPD had fought the campaign in fierce opposition to the proposal. Otto Wels, who was effectively leader of the party whilst Müller was chancellor, was firmly opposed to the idea and demanded that the money be spent on school meals as the party had promised. The majority of SPD deputies were united in opposition to the plan. When the bill was debated only the chancellor and the three SPD ministers voted in favor, the parliamentary party voted against. The bill was approved, but the SPD's credibility was in ruins.

The Depression

The depression had already had a devastating effect on the economy by the spring of 1929, and it was obvious to the man responsible for supervising the collection of reparations, Parker S. Gilbert, that Germany would not be able to meet the increased payments demanded by the Dawes Plan that year. With three million unemployed by February 1929 it was unlikely that the unemployment insurance fund would be able to meet the demands made upon it. A new reparations commission was formed, chaired by another American, Owen D. Young, which met in The Hague. The resulting Young Plan, published in June 1929, reduced the annual payments and made the German government, rather than an agent, responsible for their collection, so that Germany regained its economic sovereignty. Furthermore, the plan was open for revision if Germany were to find it difficult or impossible to meet its obligations. In return for agreeing to the Young Plan the Allies consented to an early evacuation of the Rhineland. The right-wing parties mounted a massive campaign against the Young Commission, even before the final report was published. The DNVP under the press and film magnate Alfred Hugenberg, the Pan-Germans under Heinrich Class, and the veterans' organization "*Stahlhelm*" (Steel Helmet) banded together in the Reich Committee for a German National Plebiscite and called for a referendum against the "war guilt lie," and the demand that Germany be burdened with reparations until 1988. Adolf Hitler and the NSDAP joined the campaign, much to the disgust of many on the Nazi left who were horrified to see the Führer hobnobbing with a bunch of reactionaries, aristocrats, and plutocrats. Hitler's tactics paid handsome dividends. He was now in respectable company, and no longer the bohemian outsider, the failed provincial putschist. He began to focus his attention on the disaffected middle classes rather than trying to win the working class away from the "Marxist" parties. The response was immediate; money began to flow into the party's coffers and spectacular gains were made in state elections in Thuringia and Baden, and in local elections in Prussia, Berlin, and Lübeck. Wilhelm Frick was appointed minister of the interior in Thuringia, and 13 Nazis entered Berlin city council. All this seemed to have escaped the notice of politicians in Berlin.

The Plebiscite Committee managed to get just over the ten percent of eligible voters needed to support the initiative so that a referendum on "The Law Against the Enslavement of the German People" was held in December 1929. Only 5.8 million voted in favor when 21 million votes were needed for the referendum to pass, but in some districts more than 20 percent voted for the proposal.

For Communists the onset of the depression was a clear indication that the contradictions within capitalism were becoming so acute that the working masses throughout the world would soon rise up in a revolutionary war against their capitalist exploiters. The foremost task of Communist parties in this "Third Period" was the destruction of Social Democracy which they considered the "twin brother of fascism," the party of class compromise, and the capitalists' henchmen. This ultra-left course was part of Stalin's campaign against Bucharin and his associates, who had serious reservations about collectivization and the forced pace of industrialization in the Soviet Union. In the course of this campaign paranoid fears of a capitalist offensive against the homeland of the workers and peasants were whipped up to fever pitch.

Unemployment also had a shattering effect on white-collar workers such as Johannes Pinneberg, the antihero of Hans Fallada's hugely successful novel *What's Up Little Man?* (*Kleiner Mann - was nun?*), which was published in 1932. The Nazis approved of this book with its harrowing portrait of a hapless victim of plutocratic capitalism, in spite of its singularly unflattering portrait of a party activist. Communists also appreciated the fact that Pinneberg managed to survive thanks to the robust class-consciousness of his sturdily proletarian wife, whose sympathies lay with the KPD. But Pinneberg, like so many in this unfortunate situation, remained aloof from politics, refused to believe that he had suffered a shattering loss of social status, and sought solace within the closed circle of his immediate family. Such

Plate 18 Homeless men, December 1930. © Bundesarchiv

Plate 19 Homeless women, December 1930. © Bundesarchiv

people were all too susceptible to manipulation by the radical right, with their seductive promises of a better future. Siegfried Kracauer, who wrote a series of penetrating articles in the *Frankfurter Zeitung* on the problem, estimated that there were 3.5 million unemployed office workers by 1929, of whom 1.2 million were women. They were rich pickings for political swindlers and confidence tricksters.

The worldwide economic crisis, which followed four terrible years of war and the hyper-inflation of the 1920s, had a profound effect on Germany's social fabric. With the collapse of imperial Germany the last hindrances to the creation of a class society, molded by the exigencies of a market economy, were removed. It was an unfamiliar, uncertain, and pitiless world that many viewed with deep aversion. The most striking feature of this social upheaval was that it marked the end of the aristocracy's dominant role. This small group of less than one percent of the population had gradually lost ground politically, legally, and economically, as estate gave way to class in a modern industrial society. In the critical years from 1914 to 1930 it merely managed to hang on to a few favored positions in the military, the diplomatic service, and the administration, only to be reduced by the Nazi regime and Red Army to a quaint and somewhat absurd clique, providing ample fodder for the popular press.

The *Bildungsbürger*, another minute group that was scarcely larger than the aristocracy, were also profoundly affected by these changes. They lost the money they had patriotically invested in war loans, and what was left disappeared in the hyperinflation. This group was identified closely with the old regime, and found it exceedingly hard to adjust to a new political reality that was dominated by the left. In a world that was becoming increasingly specialized, there was precious little room left for the broadly educated, and mass democracy was antagonistic toward a selfconscious elite that had lost its faith in the civilizing value of a humanistic education. It withdrew into gloomy isolation, where it wallowed in cultural pessimism. Although it had been ravaged economically, this highly-educated elite still had a profound influence on public opinion due to its dominant role in the civil service and higher education, and its influence was detrimental to the creation of a healthy democratic society. The old social norms no longer applied, a familiar hierarchy had vanished, but their mental structures remained impervious to change, and the new reality appeared unstable, threatening, and based on reprehensible values. The *Bildungsbürger* longed for stability and joined the ranks of those who harbored utopian visions. Of these there were plenty, ranging from the National Socialist "racial community" to the Communists' dictatorship of the proletariat, the majority of the *Bildungsbürger* opting for various versions on the extreme right.

The five percent of the population in the economic elite survived this multiple crisis largely unscathed. In many cases they had benefited from wartime profiteering, and thanks to their material assets they had weathered the storm of inflation. They were now the objects of envy and censure, denounced on the left as capitalists and on the right as plutocrats. Yet although they had thrived under these new conditions, and nothing stood in the way of their social advancement, they felt threatened by the organized working class, and looked for an authoritarian solution to the pressing social, economic, and political problems that beset the republic. For this reason Walther Rathenau, *Bildungsbürger* and capitalist, but also a principled republican, was viewed with particular revulsion as a traitor to his class and station. The crude communist theory that Hitler was employed by this group to do their dirty work, and to destroy the republic, has absolutely no foundation in fact. Nevertheless, their search for an authoritarian solution, and their support for numerous movements on the extreme right, provided critical assistance to Hitler. Not only did they offer no resistance to Hitler, they followed him uncritically to the bitter end.

The 15 percent of the population in the petite bourgeoisie, uncomfortably trapped between big business and organized labor, its economic foundations eroded and its political convictions shattered, longed for stability, for an end to the increasingly virulent class antagonisms, and for a renewed sense of community. They found the National Socialist vision of a "racial community" irresistibly beguiling, and provided Hitler with the electoral support without which he would never have come to power.

The working class, comprising some 70 percent of the population, had suffered the worst decline in living standards since the early years of the industrial revolution during the war, but they were also the great beneficiaries of the revolution of 1918/19. They gained political power, their real wages increased considerably, they had a voice in management, and were successful in a number of rounds of collective bargaining. These remarkable gains soon began to erode. They suffered a severe setback with the defeat of the Weimar coalition. Management was determined to turn the clock back, and mounted a vigorous counterattack. The depression and subsequent mass unemployment wiped out most of their hard-won gains, and left them frustrated and prone to political radicalism. There were eight million unemployed, real wages fell by one-third, and 40 percent of the workforce was dependent on government support, all this only ten years after the deprivations of the war years. It is small wonder then that the success of Hitler's regime at putting Germany back to work won for it the loyalty of the vast majority of the working class. There were also profound changes within the working class itself. The industrial working class began to shrink, whereas the number of white-collar workers increased by one-third. Opportunities for social advancement had improved greatly, so that a number of positions in the lower ranks of the civil service, in junior management, and in the primary schools, were filled with the children of skilled workers. However, the educational system still blocked the way to further advancement in that only one percent of university students were of working-class origin.

Farmers had benefited from a doubling of prices during the war, but they had been obliged to put up with stringent government controls. From the outset they were bitterly antagonistic toward the Weimar Republic, which they saw as serving the selfish interests of the industrial proletariat and urban consumers. Hyper-inflation offered farmers temporary relief from the burden of debt, but they were soon faced with a worldwide agricultural crisis and yet another round of spiraling liability. The siren calls from the radical right were increasingly hard to resist, and farmers gave their enthusiastic support to such groups. From 1930 Protestant farmers flocked to the National Socialists, who generously promised to guarantee prices and markets for agricultural products, and whose ecstatic rodomontades about "blood and soil" and the importance of the "agricultural estate" found many a credulous ear.

In spite of these profound changes in the status of the aristocracy, the *Bildungsbürger*, and the industrial working class, the structure of social hierarchy remained remarkably resilient. What had changed was people's perception of the nature of that society. Class antagonisms existed in prewar Germany, but they were partly disguised by the trappings of monarchy, the remnants of a traditional society, regional loyalties, and ingrained deference. Much of this had now disappeared in a market economy, in which selfish social and economic interests conflicted. These struggles were compounded by socially-constructed mentalities that pitched the aristocracy against the bourgeoisie, the *Bildungsbürger* against the less educated, the traditional middle class against the proletariat. Real conflicts of interest were mixed with ritualized expressions of group identity. Such blatant antagonisms came as a great shock to all but the industrial working class, which had never doubted that this was a society riven by class. Instead of seeking for ways to overcome, or at least to ameliorate, these inevitable clashes of interest within the framework of a democratic society, all too many fell prey to Hitler's promises that National Socialism would supersede all conflicts of class and interest, and create a harmonious "racial community."

The SPD police chief of Berlin forbade all demonstrations on May 1 1929, the traditional occasion for the expression of proletarian solidarity and militancy, but the KPD ignored the ban. The police were called in and at the end of the day 32 people lay dead, 200 wounded, and some thousand arrests were made. After this "Bloody May," the KPD's paramilitary wing, the Red Front (*Roter Frontkämpferbund*) was banned nationwide. These events served as further proof to party militants that the Social Democrats were indeed "Social Fascists." This harebrained radicalism was fueled by rapidly rising unemployment, which in turn meant that a drastic reform of the unemployment insurance system was needed if the republic's finances were not to get into serious difficulties. The SPD and the unions agreed that, since the depression was causing real wages to rise, those fortunate enough to still find steady employment could be called upon to pay higher premiums. These in turn would be matched by the employers. The DVP, as the party of the employers, turned the proposal down flat and argued that benefits should be cut back. After lengthy and acrimonious debate, Stresemann managed to get his DVP to agree to abstain during the vote for a bill, to be debated in December, that called for half a point increases in both employer and employee contributions. Stresemann did not live to witness this victory, which seemed to promise the Müller government a comfortable majority.

"Black Friday" on Wall Street on October 24 1929 caused investors to withdraw funds from Germany, short-term credits were not renewed, and it was virtually impossible to borrow money abroad. Hjalmar Schacht, who had been appointed head of the Reichsbank in December 1923, used the opportunity afforded by the crisis to finally defeat his rival Rudolph Hilferding, the Marxist minister of finance, by calling for a comprehensive tax reform. In addition to the increase of unemployment insurance premiums from three to 3.5 percent, the reform included an increase in the tax on tobacco, a reduction of income tax in order to encourage savings, and massive support from the government in an attempt to rescue the country from insolvency. This was a declaration of war not only on Hilferding, who promptly resigned, but also on the entire SPD, whose gross mismanagement and largesse the power elite held responsible for the present crisis. A cabal collected around Groener as Reichswehr minister, the head of his ministerial office, General Kurt von Schleicher, and the state secretary in the chancellery, Otto Meissner. They set about planning a government that would exclude the SPD. Hindenburg was sympathetic to the idea of an antiparliamentary and anti-Marxist government, and began talks with the DNVP leaders Hugenberg and Count Kuno von Westarp to this effect. The radical Hugenberg was in favor, the more moderate Westarp against.

The Müller government survived largely because the Reichstag had to approve the Young Plan, and therefore had to reach an agreement over finance reform. A compromise solution whereby the SPD ministers agreed to increase unemployment premiums to four percent, half a point higher than previously proposed, in return for which there was to be no refund of income taxes, was rejected by the DVP, and the BVP, as good Bavarians, raised objections to an increase in the tax on beer. Hindenburg then threatened to use article 48 to secure approval of the Young Plan. The Reichstag promptly gave way and gave its approval to the Young Plan bill. The Young Plan and finance reform were thus de-coupled. Heinrich Brüning as leader of the Center's parliamentary party proposed yet another compromise to the still vexed problem of unemployment insurance premiums. He suggested postponing a decision on whether to raise premiums or lower payments until a serious reform of the entire system had been completed in the autumn. Once again the SPD ministers agreed, but the parliamentary party objected vigorously to Brüning's compromise, which they saw as a vicious attempt to destroy the welfare state, and the government was obliged to resign. Hilferding sadly remarked that the argument that the compromise had to be rejected because it implied that things would be worse in the autumn, was the equivalent of committing suicide for fear of dying. The SPD had failed to do everything possible to save parliamentary democracy in Germany at this critical juncture and must thus share a major part of the blame for its demise.

Brüning

The man chosen to convert the Weimar Republic from a parliamentary to a presidential regime was a dour 44-year-old bachelor, a devout Catholic who had served with distinction as a front-line officer, and who had a reputation for fiscal responsibility and administrative rigor. Heinrich Brüning's cabinet was well to the right of center, and within three months faced a deadlock in the Reichstag over how to deal with the budgetary deficit. This was exactly what Hindenburg and his advisors had hoped would happen, for now they were able to give the chancellor emergency powers under paragraph 48 and thus circumvent the Reichstag. The SPD objected vigorously to this misuse of a paragraph that was designed to meet genuine emergencies, not to help the government out of an awkward situation, and thus function as an ersatz constitution. They therefore introduced a motion to suspend the president's emergency powers, whereupon Hindenburg promptly dissolved the Reichstag. This meant that paragraph 48 was still in effect, and during the election campaign it was used to introduce a number of new taxes, including an increase of the unemployment insurance premiums to 4.5 percent, a poll tax, and a tax on the unmarried.

The elections resulted in a victory for the extremes. The KPD attacked the SPD as the "agents of French and Polish imperialism," and as the corrupt and treacherous "hangman's assistants of the German bourgeoisie," and increased the number of deputies from 54 to 77. The Nazi's triumph was even greater. In the last Reichstag election in 1928 they had received 800,000 votes and obtained 12 mandates. Now they got 2.6 million votes and 107 seats. Hitler's new course in 1929, combined with the political and economic crisis, thus paid handsome dividends. Some of those who voted for the NSDAP in 1930 were new voters, but most of them switched their allegiance from the bourgeois parties: the DNVP, the DVP, and the DDP. Up to ten percent of SPD voters decided the future lay with National Socialism rather than Social Democracy. Nazi voters were predominantly Protestant, from rural areas, the self-employed, civil servants, and pensioners. The unemployed looked to the Communists for help. Women tended to be more loyal to the traditional parties than men. A substantial number of workers broke ranks with the "Marxist" parties and voted for the Nazis. The brilliantly conducted propaganda campaign was careful to avoid emphasizing anti-Semitism, since this was not an issue that had much resonance among the working class. Similarly the "socialism" of National Socialism was downplayed for fear of alienating the bourgeoisie. Nationalism and the creation of a "national community" (*Volksgemeinschaft*) were the key issues. The party, unlike any of its rivals, thus managed to attract support from all walks of life and was a genuine people's party.

The elections of September 1930 mark the end of German liberalism. Stresemann's DVP made its peace with the extreme right, as did the DDP, which henceforth dropped the word "Democratic" from the party's name to become the DP. The Center Party had already moved sharply to the right under Monsignor Ludwig Kaas, who had taken over the party leadership after the poor showing in the polls in 1928. This situation left the "rational republicans" hopelessly at sea. Thomas Mann appealed to the responsible and cultured bourgeois to overlook the last remaining vestiges of Marxist rigmarole and support the SPD. Otto Braun responded positively, and called for a "coalition of the reasonable." Neither side was in the mood for compromise and appeals for reason fell on deaf ears. The bourgeois parties wanted nothing to do with the Social Democrats, who in turn detested the chancellor and his coalition supporters, many of whom saw no distinction between the "fascist" Brüning and Hitler. Most important of all, Hindenburg was determined to go ahead with his plans for a presidential regime and was not going to welcome the SPD back into the fold. The cabinet still needed a Reichstag majority and Brüning needed support from either the right or the left. Bringing the NSDAP into the coalition was still completely out of the question. They were far too "socialist" for the industrialists and bankers, the SA was seen as a challenge to the Reichswehr, and Hitler was still a wild card. There was no alternative for the SPD, which saw itself obliged to tolerate a second Brüning government. They feared another round of elections that would almost certainly make the Nazis even stronger. They could not contemplate a government that depended on Nazi support, and they were anxious to bolster Otto Braun's position as minister-president in Prussia by avoiding any hint of a conflict with the central government which might result in the Center Party withdrawing its support for Braun's SPD.

The first debate in the new session of parliament did not bode well. The Nazi deputies arrived in SA uniforms and behaved like street rowdies. The Communists ranted on about overthrowing capitalist exploitation and establishing the dictator-ship of the proletariat in a Soviet Germany. The SPD stuck to its agreement and the legislation covering the budgetary deficit passed, in return for which Brüning made certain concessions over social policy. But the SPD had to stomach an increase in the unemployment insurance premiums to 6.5 percent, along with higher duties on imports of wheat and barley. Brüning continued with his rigorous deflationary poli-cies and thereby risked losing the grudging support of the SPD. With the country on the verge of bankruptcy, in June 1931 he used presidential decrees to reduce unem-ployment benefits, along with the pensions for invalids and the war-wounded, and cut back civil servants' salaries still further. This placed the SPD in an intolerable position. The left found it impossible to continue to support a government bent on destroying all the welfare state, the right could not risk toppling Otto Braun's government in Prussia. How could the party defend democracy against the Reichstag majority, or use constitutional means when the constitution had been suspended?

Meanwhile, the economic situation worsened dramatically. The Hoover Moratorium of 1931 suspended reparations payments, but unemployment con-tinued to rise, the banking system began to fall apart, and could only be saved by using the taxpayers' money and by raising the bank rate to such an extent that it seriously impeded any chances of recovery. The International Court of Justice in The Hague ruled that the proposed customs union between Germany and Austria was a violation of the peace treaties, and thus contrary to international law. Prompted by General Schleicher, Hindenburg urged Brüning to move still further to the right in order to keep the increasingly disaffected DVP in the coalition. The chancellor obliged, but it was too late.

A mass meeting of the extreme right was held at Bad Harzburg in October 1931 and was attended by Hugenberg's DNVP, the Stahlhelm, the Pan-German League, members of a number of the former ruling houses, Hjalmar Schacht, and General von Seeckt. The former army chief was now a Reichstag deputy for the DVP and other members of party attended the meeting to show that they no longer supported

Brüning. Hitler and the NSDAP also joined the "Harzburg Front," and the SA was prominent in the march-past, but the Führer demonstrably left the platform to show that he distanced himself from the traditional reactionaries, and that he presented a genuine alternative to the tired old parties. The "Harzburg Front" reconciled the SPD to Brüning, so that a vote of no confidence from the right was narrowly defeated. The chancellor was determined to persevere with his rigorously deflationary policies, and used emergency legislation to cut back wages and prices. At the same time he rejected all proposals for priming the pump by investment in job creation, and insisted that balancing the books was his first priority. Inevitably the standard of living of the average German rapidly declined, thus fanning political radicalism.

Presidential elections were due in 1932 and the 84-year-old Hindenburg announced that he was prepared to stand for reelection. This caused the Harzburg Front to fall apart. The DNVP and the Stahlhelm put forward Theodor Duesterberg as their candidate. After agonizing for a long time Hitler decided to enter the race, but in order to do so he had at last to become a German citizen. This was done by securing an appointment as a humble civil servant in the surveyor's office in Braunschweig. The KPD put Thälmann forward on the assumption that the SPD would support Hindenburg and that the majority of their voters would be so disgusted that they would support the "red workers' candidate." The first assumption was correct, and the second totally false.

Hindenburg failed to win an absolute majority in the first round of the election in May 1932. Hitler was second with 30.1 percent. Thälmann trailed behind with 13.2 percent, and Duesterberg came last with 6.8 percent. Prompted by Moscow, Thälmann stayed in the race for the second round in order to expose the SPD as the moderate face of fascism, and as a result made a poor showing with only 10.2 percent. Hindenburg won with 53 percent, thanks to the undivided support of the SPD. The president was furious that he owed his reelection to the Social Democrats, and blamed Brüning for putting him in this embarrassing position. Hitler got an impressive 36.8 percent of the popular vote.

A few days after the presidential election, the Brüning government banned the SS and the SA. General von Schleicher had persuaded his minister, General Groener, that this step was necessary as Germany was fast slipping into anarchy. Schleicher then changed his mind and persuaded his friend Oscar von Hindenburg, who served in the same regiment, to point out to his father that the ban was most unpopular on the right. Hindenburg signed the emergency decree with considerable reluctance, and then tried to offset any possible damage by a ban on the SPD's paramilitary wing, the Black, Red, and Gold Standard (*Reichsbanner*). Groener, as minister of the interior, felt that there was no evidence to support a ban on the *Reichsbanner*, so the president's plan was stymied. As a result the president and his son, along with their *éminence grise*, were angered by both Brüning and Groener, whose days were now clearly numbered.

With spectacular gains by the Nazis in a number of provincial elections, Catholic Bavaria providing a notable exception, the KPD toned down its denunciations of the SPD and called for a "united front from below," for a common struggle against the "capitalist robbers" and "fascist hordes," but also the Social Democrats' reformist leadership. The Weimar coalition lost its majority in Prussia, but since all attempts to form a new coalition failed, largely due to the Center's refusal to work with the NSDAP, Otto Braun remained in office. Schleicher was now determined to topple the Brüning cabinet and create a new government, which would include the NSDAP. To this effect he began talks with Hitler, who demanded new elections and a lifting of the ban on the SS and SA. But it was the East Elbian Junkers who brought about Brüning's downfall. Hans Schlange-Schöningen, the man in charge of the "*Osthilfe*," a system of outdoor relief for the landed aristocracy, put forward a proposal that bankrupt estates in the east should be taken over by the state and turned into settlements that would provide work for the unemployed. The Junkers were incensed at this suggestion and the president of their organization, the "*Reichslandbund*," visited Hindenburg, who was on holiday at his estate at Neudeck in East Prussia, to voice their complaints. Hindenburg's aristocratic neighbors joined in the chorus of criticism and there was much talk of "state socialism" and "agrarian Bolshevism." The president hardly needed any persuasion to act. On his return to Berlin he immediately told Brüning that he would have to go. Brüning handed in his resignation in the course of a brief meeting with the president on May 12 1932.

Brüning was neither the villain who destroyed parliamentary democracy and paved the way for the Nazis, nor was he the conservative hero who offered a genuine alternative to both a bankrupt democratic system and a brown dictatorship. His government was little more than the moderate and parliamentary-sanctioned phase of the presidential dictatorship planned by the camarilla around the 85-year-old president. Brüning's refusal to make a deal with the Nazis, whom the right wanted to engage as junior partners in an authoritarian regime, was the real reason for his downfall. The decision to dismiss Brüning, dissolve the Reichstag, and call a fresh round of elections two years before term was a disastrous decision for which Hindenburg and the clique around him must bear full responsibility. Had they waited, the worst of the economic crisis would have passed, the radical parties would have lost much of their appeal, and the world would possibly have been spared untold misery.

Von Papen

Brüning's successor, hand picked by Schleicher, was Franz von Papen, a backbencher in the Prussian diet, who stood on the extreme right of the Center Party. He was an aristocratic ex-cavalry officer, a landowner, and accomplished horseman, well known for his impeccably tailored suits and his wide circle of influential friends. He had proved a disaster as military attaché in Washington, his career proof positive of the "Peter Principle." He was little more than Schleicher's creature, the general having secured his own appointment as Reichswehr minister in place of Groener.

The new government was soon labeled "the baron's cabinet," since it was replete with the scions of some of Germany's most illustrious families, with only three commoners in subordinate posts.

At Papen's request an election was called for July 31 and the ban on the SS and SA was lifted. The predictable result was an alarming increase in violence during the election campaign. Fights between Communists and Nazis were particularly prevalent in the industrial areas in the Rhine and Ruhr, and the government placed the blame on the Prussian minister of the interior, Carl Severing, for discriminating against the National Socialists. On July 17 a march by the SA through the communist-held district of Hamburg resulted in the deaths of 17 people, many of them killed by the police, who had been ordered to break up this illegal demonstration. Hindenburg's response to this "Bloody Sunday in Altona" was to use paragraph 48 to suspend the Prussian government, and to appoint a commissar with full executive powers. The Prussian government promptly appealed for a ruling from the High Court, but the Social Democrats were in a helpless position. With millions of unemployed, having been repudiated by the general public in the recent elections, and fearing a civil war in which they were bound to be defeated, the SPD and the unions refused to consider a general strike or massed protest against the "Prussian coup," and left it to the electorate to express their disapproval of this provocative and dubiously legal act in the forthcoming national elections. Left-wing activists were disgusted at this pusillanimous response by the leadership and the KPD, which was once again on an ultra-left tack and had abandoned the "united front from below," used the SPD's inaction as further evidence of the perfidy of the "social fascists."

On July 31 1932 the electorate once again moved to the extremes. Support for the SPD fell by a further 2.9 points and the Communists made modest gains. The National Socialists were the big winners with 37.4 percent of the vote, thus increasing their representation in the Reichstag from 107 to 230 seats. Catholic Germany and the supporters of the "Marxist" parties remained relatively immune to the siren calls from the Nazis, their increased support coming from the "bourgeois" parties and from first-time voters. Buoyed by his triumph at the polls, Hitler now demanded the chancellorship, but Hindenburg shuddered at the thought of appointing the "Bohemian corporal" and refused. Papen then proposed to Hitler that he accept the post of vice-chancellor and that after a while he would step down and make way for the Führer. Hitler was furious that he had been spurned, and swore an all-out attack on the president and the chancellor. A few days after the election, the Storm Trooper perpetrators of a particularly brutal murder of a communist in the Silesian village of Potempa were condemned to death by a special court. Hitler at once warned Papen of the dire consequences were he to soil his hands with the blood of these national heroes. Goebbels announced that the Jews were behind the sentencing of these paragons of Germanic virtue. Hindenburg decided it would be prudent to commute the death sentences to life imprisonment. He used the fact that the murder occurred immediately after the promulgation of a decree prescribing the death sentence for politically motivated murders as an excuse, and argued that the guilty men could thus not have been aware of the consequences of their actions.

The NSDAP and the KPD formed a majority in the new Reichstag, which met for the first time on August 30. Since both parties were bent on the destruction of parliamentary democracy, this meant that constitutional government was no longer possible. Klara Zetkin, an enthusiastic admirer of Joseph Stalin, was appointed president of the Reichstag for the opening session on account of her being, at 75, the oldest deputy. She announced that she hoped to live to be the president of the congress of a Soviet Germany. This pleasure was denied her. She died in exile in Moscow the following year. Hermann Göring was then elected president by a handsome majority, in accordance with the custom that the office was traditionally filled by a member of the largest party. He soon made it abundantly plain that he had no intention of making impartial rulings.

Since he had virtually no support in the Reichstag, Papen urged Hindenburg to dissolve parliament. In addition, he got the president to agree to ignore the provisions of the constitution and postpone the mandatory elections indefinitely. However, having been humiliated by the passage, by an overwhelming majority, of two resolutions proposed by the Communists, he did not dare flaunt the constitution to such an extent, and a new round of elections was called for November 6.

The Reichstag having been dissolved, Papen had to read his government's program over the radio. It called for the creation of a presidential and authoritarian "new state" based on the ideas of Edgar Jung, a prominent spokesman for a "conservative revolution." His reflections on democracy in his book *Rule by Inferiors* (*Herrschaft der Minderwertigen*) were much admired in right-wing circles, particularly in the ultraconservative "*Herrenklub*" (Gentlemen's Club). The creation of the new state involved a thoroughgoing reform of the constitution based on "national leadership irrespective of the political parties," with an upper house representative of the professions and trades, with only the president to be elected by popular suffrage, and with an end to the dualism between Prussia and the Reich. The franchise for the Reichstag elections would henceforth be decided by such factors as marital status and the number of children. Similar views were held by the group around Hans Zehrer's magazine *Der Tat* (*Action*), but here with a distinctly populist emphasis that sought an opening to the left. This group appealed greatly to Schleicher, who began to distance himself from his creature Papen, who was in thrall to Jung and the Herrenklub.

The election was held in the shadow of a strike of transport workers in Berlin in which National Socialists and Communists marched arm-in-arm, much to the alarm of middle-class electors. The result was a disappointment for Hitler's party, which lost the support of two million voters and returned 34 fewer deputies to the Reichstag. The SPD also did far worse than expected. The DNVP were the big winners, and the KPD and the DVP made significant gains. The election was thus a modest vindication of Papen's government. The conservative parties had done well, partly because of concern about the radicalism of the National Socialists, but also because certain Keynesian measures were beginning to have a positive effect on the economy. But the "baron's cabinet" was still only actively supported by about ten percent of the electorate. The Communists, who had reached the magic number of 100 seats in the Reichstag, once again entertained the illusion that this was the dawn of the Red revolution. Other more clear-sighted observers of the political scene, Josef Goebbels among them, realized that the Communists' success was a golden opportunity for the Nazis. The respectable middle class now imagined that they were faced with a simple choice between Communists and Nazis, and did not hesitate when deciding which alternative to choose.

Hindenburg wanted to continue with a presidential regime with Papen as chancellor. Papen, who had discussed the situation with a number of influential businessmen, began to toy with the idea of a Hitler chancellorship. There was mounting support for such a move among a number of industrialists, bankers, and landowners who, on November 19, sent a letter to the president suggesting that the leader of the largest single party should take over from Papen. Among those who signed this letter were Hjalmar Schacht, the banker Kurt von Schröder, and the steel baron Fritz Thyssen. Other prominent industrialists including Paul Reusch of the Gutehoffnungshütte, Fritz Springorum of Hoesch, and Albert Vögler of the Vereinigten Stahlwerke let it be known that they supported the idea, but did not want their names to appear on the letter. A large number of influential figures in the Rhine and Ruhr came to share this point of view in the course of the next few weeks, in part because they feared that the KPD would appeal to a large number of younger voters in the "national" parties, including the Nazis. The NSDAP and SPD refused to talk to the chancellor. The Center and BVP insisted that Papen should step down and that a new government should include the Nazis. The BVP suggested that Hitler should be chancellor. Realizing that he could not possibly form an effective government, Papen recommended that the president dismiss the entire cabinet. Hindenburg agreed, but still refusing to contemplate a Hitler government, hoped that Papen would somehow manage to form a new cabinet. With Papen reluctant to continue in office and Hindenburg insisting that he remain, Schleicher offered to test the political waters.

Schleicher

Schleicher first approached the Trades Union Congress (ADGB) and the SPD's parliamentary party with a promise to rescind the emergency legislation of September, which made it possible for employers to break wage contracts. The response from the union boss, Theodor Leipart, whose head was full of ideas borrowed from radical conservatives like Ernst Jünger and the "*Tat*" circle, who believed that the working class should serve the common good, was favorable. These inchoate ideas were enthusiastically endorsed by Gregor Strasser, the organizational genius of the Nazi Party and the leading figure on the movement's left wing. The SPD was not impressed and, fearing that the Communists would make political hay out of any such concessions, would not agree to postponing a fresh round of elections until the spring, on the grounds that this would be unconstitutional. Schleicher and the "*Tat*" circle now called for a front extending from Strasser's left-wing Nazis to the trades unions, but Strasser was unable to win Hitler over to the idea, and most trade unionists vehemently opposed Leipart's sharp turn to the right. Hindenburg was now ready for a showdown with the Reichstag. He wanted Papen to remain in office and promised him that he would use his presidential powers to support him, if necessary by armed force. General von Schleicher was highly alarmed at the prospect of what amounted to a military dictatorship for which the public had absolutely no sympathy, and which would undermine both the prestige and the morale of the Reichswehr. With considerable support right across the political spectrum he now prepared to oust Papen and make a bid for the chancellorship.

On December 2 1932 Schleicher ordered Lieutenant Colonel Eugen Ott to present the results of a recent war game to the cabinet. They showed that should there be a confrontation between the government and the Communists and National Socialists, the Poles would be tempted to invade. The Reichswehr and police would then be unable to master the situation. The cabinet was impressed by this hair-raising scenario and Hindenburg, horrified that the country seemed to be heading for a civil war that would result in chaos, abandoned his plans for a quasi-dictatorship and appointed Schleicher chancellor on December 3. The appointment was greeted with general relief. Plans for a hazardous constitutional experiment had been shelved, and Schleicher was known to be a man who sought compromise and who had far wider support than did his unfortunate predecessor. The major question was how he was going to deal with the National Socialists. Undaunted by their initial response, Schleicher set about trying to split the Nazi Party by offering Gregor Strasser the post of vice-chancellor; but it remained to be seen whether he would risk a direct confrontation with Hitler.

The Nazi Party now seemed on the point of collapse. Popular support was dwindling at an alarming rate, the coffers were empty, and Strasser had considerable support, particularly in northern Germany where the party was strongest. Hitler dramatically contemplated suicide were he to lose control of the party, but unfortunately this was not to be. On December 9 it was announced that Strasser had no stomach for a fight with Hitler and had resigned all his party offices. Schleicher took this as a sign that he was about to enter the government fold, but Hitler acted swiftly and decisively. That same day he called a meeting of the Gauleiter (district officials of the party), the NSDAP's Reichstag deputies, and other top officials, and won an unconditional pledge of allegiance. Schleicher's attempt to split the party had thus failed, and Strasser took off to Austria for two weeks holiday, his political career at an end. Schleicher still clung to the illusion that it would be possible to win over the NSDAP, and even imagined that Hitler and Strasser might be reconciled under his benign guidance. There were also encouraging signs that the trades unions were anxious to cooperate and to avoid a confrontation with a government that was concerned to put the country back to work with imaginative reflationary policies.

Such confidence was sadly misplaced. On January 4 1933 his two arch rivals, Papen and Hitler, met at the banker von Schröder's house in Cologne to bury the hatchet and plot their revenge. Papen agreed to try to persuade Hindenburg to dismiss Schleicher and accept a Hitler-Papen government, but it was still doubtful whether the president would agree to Hitler's appointment as chancellor. Papen then discussed the situation with some of the leading Ruhr barons. Most were satisfied with Schleicher's attempts to stimulate the economy and steer a moderate course between capital and labor. Few raised serious objections to another Papen government, but it would have to be one in which the NSDAP played a subordinate role. Most industrialists still had serious reservations about Hitler and his party. The chancellor now came under massive attack from the *Reichslandbund*, which was emboldened by its success in ousting Brüning. In all too familiar language the association accused Schleicher of pursuing a "Marxist" policy of plunder and expropriation, while kowtowing to the export industry, which had led to the ruination of German agriculture. Walter Darré, the Nazi's agricultural expert and author of *The Pig as a Criterion for Northern People and Semites, The Peasantry as the Life Source of the Nordic Race*, and *The New Aristocracy of Blood and Soil*, condemned the chancellor for "bolshevizing the German people." He also denounced Schleicher as a second Caprivi, yet another general "without an acre or a blade of grass," who vainly imagined that a solution to the economic crisis could be found by encouraging industrial exports. Hindenburg, ever mindful of agrarian interests, found his misgivings about Schleicher confirmed.

Much now depended on the attitude of the Reichstag, which was due to reconvene. Given that the government was unlikely to survive a vote of confidence, the cabinet agreed that the next round of elections should not be held within the statutory 60 days, but be postponed until the autumn, or possibly until December. An alternative was to declare a vote of no confidence invalid and to rule by presidential decree, a solution that was constitutionally acceptable under paragraph 54, and which was approved by such eminent constitutional experts as Carl Schmitt on the right, and Ernst Fraenkel on the left. The question remained open as to whether the president would agree to dissolve the Reichstag and to postpone the elections.

Schleicher's position began to erode when the DNVP parroted the *Reichslandbund* and condemned his "socialist" policies for opening the door to Bolshevism. Discussions continued in Berlin between Papen and Hitler, in the course of which Papen reconciled himself to the idea of Hitler as chancellor, and Oscar von Hindenburg dropped many of his objections to Hitler and his party. Hindenburg was warned by the Center Party and the SPD that postponing the elections would be a gross violation of the constitution, and became deeply concerned that a presidential emergency regime pending the elections would plunge Germany into civil war. He was ever mindful of Colonel Ott's dire warnings of the consequences, and it soon became clear that Schleicher, by using this underhand weapon against Papen, had dug his own political grave. The Social Democrats and the Center, the twin pillars of Weimar democracy, now set about bringing down the Schleicher government on the grounds that he threatened to violate one paragraph of the constitution. Since by now there was no viable alternative to a Hitler government, they thus paved the way for a regime that was determined to tear up the entire constitution, and to destroy parliamentary democracy once and for all. For them a Hitler government appointed according to the constitution was preferable to a temporary dictatorship under Schleicher, to say nothing of a presidential government under Papen, or even Hugenberg. Schleicher was left virtually without support and on January 28 1933 drew the necessary consequences and the cabinet resigned.

Faced with the imminent prospect of a Hitler cabinet the SPD suddenly saw the light, and the party called for a mass demonstration in Berlin against a government that was denounced as "the springboard for a fascist dictatorship." Papen busied himself persuading prominent conservatives to consider posts in a Hitler cabinet. The two outstanding problems were to get Hugenberg to serve, and to settle the question of who should be commissar for Prussia. Hugenberg's objections were largely overcome when he was offered the post of minister of finance and agriculture. Papen insisted on becoming commissar for Prussia, but accepted Hermann Göring as his deputy, with responsibility for the police force. Göring was also to be a minister without portfolio and commissar responsible for aviation. Wilhelm Frick, another member of the old guard of the Munich putsch, who as minister of the interior in Thuringia had earned a reputation as a ferocious reactionary with a blissful disregard for legality, was to continue the good work as minister of the interior. Hindenburg chose one minister himself. He swore in General Werner von Blomberg, one of the very few senior officers who supported Hitler, as Reichswehr minister even before Hitler became chancellor. Since it was the chancellor who appointed ministers this was a serious breach of the constitution.

The only remaining obstacle was to get Hindenburg to agree to Hitler's demand that there should be new elections immediately. Since neither the Center nor the BVP would agree to support a Hitler government, and since a two-thirds Reichstag majority was needed for an enabling act which Hitler insisted was essential if the government were to be effective, Hindenburg gave way. Thus in the late afternoon of January 30 1933 chancellor Hitler swore allegiance to a constitution he was determined to destroy. On the following day he asked Hindenburg to dissolve the Reichstag. On February 1 elections were called for March 5, and in the meantime Hitler could make full use of the emergency powers permitted under article 48. The conservative elite was delighted. There were only two National Socialists in Hitler's first cabinet: Wilhelm Frick, who was appointed minister of the interior, and Hermann Göring, who was as yet without a ministerial portfolio. The conservative elite still controlled the civil service, the army, and the judiciary, and enjoyed the support of the agrarians and the industrialists. Hitler the drummer boy provided the mass support that they had hitherto lacked. Papen spoke on their behalf when he announced: "He is now in our employ!" and added: "In two months' time we will have pushed Hitler so tightly into the corner that he will squeak!" The Stahlhelm leader Theodor Duesterberg, who refused a position in Hitler's cabinet, claimed that Hitler would soon be seen running in his underpants through the chancellery garden to avoid arrest. It seemed to be a perfect solution: Hitler's popularity, drive, and dynamism were harnessed by experienced and responsible conservatives.

On the left, the SPD were hamstrung by their fetishistic loyalty to a constitution which they were determined to uphold, whatever the cost. They argued that since Hitler had been legally appointed they should not be tempted away from the narrow path of legality. The KPD had no such scruples and called for a general strike against Hitler, Papen, Hugenberg, and their fascist dictatorship. With six million unemployed this call fell on deaf ears. For most contemporaries Hitler's appointment as chancellor marked an end to unseemly and unproductive party strife, and opened up the prospect of a united, powerful, and prosperous Germany. Only a few lonely visionaries realized the disastrous consequences of an appointment which was neither inevitable nor necessary, and for which Hindenburg, his intimate advisors, and the old elites must bear the major share of the blame.

12
The Nazi Dictatorship

The DNVP leader and minister of economics, Hugenberg, was soon to admit that he and his associates had completely misread the situation. The conservative elite failed to realize that behind a threadbare façade, the Weimar Republic was falling apart. Society was in the midst of a profound crisis, and for all his moderate assurances in the last few days, Hitler was a man with a fanatical determination to destroy the existing state, and establish an iron dictatorship. His clearly stated intention to call elections as soon as possible should have been indication enough to his conservative allies that he was out to destroy them, and that his assurances to the DNVP had to be taken with a truckload of salt. The Nazis had mass support, a superb propaganda machine, and the SA was more than happy to resort to violence whenever necessary. Precious little stood in their way.

At the time of the Nazi "Seizure of Power" there were some 850,000 party members. They mounted a series of torchlight processions and heralded the "National Revolution." Skeptical intellectuals like the charming Count Harry Kessler dismissed such demonstrations as a mere carnival. Others waited anxiously upon events. Most Germans were indifferent, and there was no rush to join the party. Only after the March elections was there a scramble to jump on the bandwagon. These opportunists, contemptuously known as the "March Fallen" (*Märzgefallenen*) by the old guard, were so numerous that by January 1934 the membership had almost trebled.

Hitler's first announcement of his long-term goals was made behind closed doors to a group of leading generals on February 3. He certainly did not mince his words. He promised strict authoritarian rule that would rid Germany of the "cancer" of democracy, "exterminate" Marxism and pacifism, and make Germany once again ready for war (*Wiederwehrhaftmachung*) by rearmament and the introduction of universal military service. In an ominous footnote, which most of his audience seems to have overheard, he spoke of "radically Germanizing" the east in order to carve out "living space" (*Lebensraum*). The generals, with their traditional anti-Semitism, their loathing of "Jewish Bolshevism," and their determination to rearm and to revise the Versailles settlement, were encouraged by these remarks. For all their snobbish disdain toward some of the more vulgar aspects of National Socialism, they were in broad agreement with Hitler's program, and most of them remained so until the bitter end.

On February 1 Hindenburg agreed to dissolve the Reichstag and elections were called for March 5. In the meantime Hitler could make use of the emergency presidential powers as provided in article 48 of the Weimar constitution. He could count on wide support, and he complacently remarked at the cabinet meeting on February 1 that this was to be the last Reichstag election, and there would be no return to the parliamentary system. On February 4 Hitler used the Communist appeal for a general strike as an excuse to push through an emergency decree, "For the Protection of the German People." It permitted severe restrictions on the freedom of the press and of assembly should there be "an immediate danger to public safety," or in instances where "the organs, organizations, and offices of the state and its employees were insulted or mocked." This gave Hitler and his minions discretion to silence the opposition parties during the election campaign. Appeals against the flagrant misuse of this decree could be made to the High Court (*Reichsgericht*), but by the time they could be lodged the election was long since over. Hermann Göring used the decree to the utmost in Prussia, where he had been appointed minister of the interior in the commissarial government. Otto Braun's government had been reinstated when the State Court (*Staatsgerichtshof*) ruled that Papen's coup in July 1932 was unconstitutional, so that there were now two governments in Prussia. Hitler then issued another presidential decree, "For the Restoration of Orderly Government in Prussia," and on February 6 the Prussian parliament (Landtag) was once again dissolved.

Although Göring was formally subordinate to Papen, as Reich Commissar for Prussia he promptly weeded out the few remaining democrats in the upper echelons of the Prussian civil service, police force, and judiciary. The Prussian secret police was reorganized into a separate Secret Police Office (*Geheimen Staatspolizeiamt – Gestapa*). The police were ordered to cooperate fully with the SA, the SS, and the Stahlhelm in an all-out campaign against the Communists. The SA was given carte blanche to threaten officials and make arbitrary arrests, and their hapless victims were flung into hastily improvised concentration camps. Meetings of all the democratic parties were systematically broken up, politicians were brutally beaten within an inch of their lives, and the opposition press silenced. On February 17 Göring published a decree in which he ordered the police to shoot to kill if necessary, and guaranteed that he would protect any officer who found it necessary to use his gun. Thus a former minister, Adam Stegerwald of the Center Party, was brutally assaulted during a rally in Krefeld. The Social Democratic police-president of Berlin, Albert Grzesinski, was made to fear for his life and was obliged to resign. The offices of a number of republican newspapers were torched. In all there were 69 deaths and hundreds were seriously wounded during the five weeks of the election campaign. The SA arrested some 100,000 people in the early months of 1933, and murdered about 600. There was widespread revulsion against such barbarity. Ludendorff, Hitler's brother-in-arms in 1923, wrote to his old superior Hindenburg complaining bitterly about such "unbelievable events" and claiming that this was "the blackest time in German history."

Hitler traveled tirelessly the length and breadth of Germany preaching his simple message of national redemption to vast and enthusiastic crowds. He denounced the "November criminals" who were responsible for the last 14 years of economic misery, political bickering, and national humiliation. He promised to unite the nation into a strong-willed "racial community" (*Volksgemeinschaft*) that would transcend all divisions of class and station. The economy would be revitalized in two successive four-year plans. "National rebirth" would result from reasserting family values and Christian morality. He made no concrete proposals, but he spoke with such utter conviction and passion that the crowds believed that he could be trusted. In this highly-charged emotional atmosphere what mattered was not a carefully crafted program but a spontaneous and passionate reaction. The opposition forces were so hopelessly divided, demoralized, and cowed that they could offer precious little resistance. On February 20 Hitler addressed a group of leading industrialists and told them that this would be positively the last election, and that he intended to create a strong and independent state, regardless of the outcome of the election. First he had to gain absolute power, and then he would destroy his opponents. The industrialists were delighted, and promptly got out their checkbooks, thus relieving the party of all financial worries.

At nine o'clock in the evening of February 27 smoke was seen billowing through the roof of the Reichstag. Shortly afterward a dim-witted Dutch anarchist, Marinus van der Lubbe, was arrested in the Bismarck room and promptly admitted that he had set the building on fire. The National Socialists convinced themselves that this was part of a Communist plot. Their opponents claimed that the Nazis had organized the fire in order to find an excuse to bring in further emergency legislation. The Communists soon published a "Brown Book" which purported to show Nazi complicity in the fire and which proved to be a highly effective piece of antifascist propaganda. The Nazi claim that van der Lubbe was under orders from the Communists was soon shown to be utterly false. The Communists later admitted that their "Brown Book" was a fabrication. In 1962 Fritz Tobias published a detailed study of the Reichstag fire and came to the conclusion that van der Lubbe acted alone. Most historians now accept this version, although some respected scholars still believe that the Nazis were implicated.

Regardless of whoever was ultimately responsible for the fire, the Nazis acted promptly. When Hitler was told of the fire he wound himself up into a passion and said that all Communist functionaries should be shot, and Reichstag deputies hanged. The Prussian ministry of the interior promptly set about drafting an emergency decree. On the following day the "Decree for the Protection of the People and the State" was promulgated. All the fundamental rights guaranteed in the constitution were suspended. The death penalty was extended to include a number of crimes including treason and arson. Summary arrests could be made, and the Nazis' opponents placed in "protective custody" in concentration camps. In an important step toward dismantling the republic's federal structure, Wilhelm Frick, as minister of the interior, could disregard the sovereignty of the states if he deemed that law and order were in jeopardy. This decree, which claimed to be solely directed against the Communists, was the fundamental law on which the Nazi dictatorship was based. It remained in force even though van der Lubbe's trial in September clearly showed that there was no evidence that the Communists were involved. The accused was executed in spite of the fact that arson was not a capital offense at the time he committed the crime. There was a wave of arrests throughout Germany. One hundred thousand people, mostly Communists, were arrested in Prussia, among them the prominent left-wing writers Egon Erwin Kisch, Erich Mühsam, Carl von Ossietsky, and Ludwig Renn.

In spite of all the intimidation, mass arrests, and harassment of the opposition parties, the results of the elections were most disappointing for the National Socialists. They only managed to obtain 43.9 percent of the popular vote, 6.5 points more than their best showing in the July elections of 1932. Their largest gains were in Bavaria and Württemberg, where they had previously had little support. Since the conservatives got a meager eight percent, the coalition parties had a very narrow majority in the Reichstag. Voters remained faithful to the Social Democrats and the Center Party, and the Communists did surprisingly well under the circumstances with 12.3 percent. The parties in the middle of the political spectrum were virtually eliminated. The astonishingly high voter participation of 88.8 percent showed how important these elections were to the average German.

The ballots were hardly counted when the National Socialists set about the demolition of the republic's federal structure. A two-pronged attack on local government was launched. SA thugs and party activists stormed town halls and local government offices, hoisted the swastika flag, and chased terrified officials away. The authorities in Berlin used such lawlessness as an excuse to overthrow provincial governments by using the powers vested in them by article 2 of the Reichstag Fire Decree. Commissars, often the local Gauleiter, were appointed in each of the states, and prominent Nazis replaced the police chiefs. In some areas the Nazis met with considerable resistance. The Bavarian minister-president Heinrich Held adamantly refused to give way to threats from the SA, but the local army units gave him no support when ordered from Berlin to stay out of domestic politics. Hitler's wooing of the Reichswehr on February 3 thus paid a handsome dividend. Held was now without any support, and Frick appointed the stalwart Nazi Lieutenant-General Franz Ritter von Epp as commissar for Bavaria. The commissar's protégé, Heinrich Himmler, head of the still minute SS, was made chief of police in Munich, and then took over the Bavarian secret police. Ably assisted by his ruthless and brilliant underling Reinhard Heydrich, this was the beginning of a remarkable career in law enforcement.

On March 21, the first day of spring, the regime held an impressive ceremony in Potsdam organized by Joseph Goebbels, who had recently been appointed minister of propaganda. The occasion was designed not only to mark the opening of the new parliament, but also as a symbolic gesture of reconciliation between the old and the new Germany. Representatives of all walks of life were present. Only the

Communists and the Social Democrats were not invited because, as Frick remarked with obvious relish, they had a lot of important work to do in the concentration camps. The "Potsdam Day" began with a service in the garrison church, after which Hitler was presented to Hindenburg. The humble other-ranker bowed before the field marshal. Hindenburg then saluted the empty chair where the kaiser used to sit and behind which stood the crown prince. Hitler gave an anodyne speech in which he spoke of the union of past greatness with youthful vigor. National Socialism was thus presented as the apotheosis of German history in the long and glorious tradition of Luther, Frederick the Great, Bismarck, and Hindenburg. Goebbels was well satisfied with the day's work, which he cynically described in his diary as a "jolly farce."

The atmosphere was menacing when the Reichstag met three days later in the Kroll Opera House in Berlin. The SA surrounded it, Hitler appeared in party uniform, all of the 81 Communist deputies were forbidden to attend, and 26 Social Democrats had been arrested. There was only one item of business on the agenda: a constitutional amendment that would put an end to the last vestiges of parliamentary rule, known as the "Enabling Act." Since the bill needed a two-thirds majority, all depended on the attitude of the Center Party. The leadership under Monsignor Ludwig Kaas favored an authoritarian solution to the present crisis, and feared that opposition would result in further restrictions of the freedom of the Catholic Church. Others managed to convince themselves that the bill was aimed solely against the Communists and comforted themselves with the thought that it was only to last for four years. The former chancellor Heinrich Brüning had serious reservations. After lengthy discussions, the party agreed to vote for the proposal. Otto Wels from the Social Democratic party was the only member who had the courage to speak out against the bill. His measured but passionate plea for democracy, the rule of law, and the fundamental principals of his party incited Hitler's fury, but had no influence on the outcome. There were 444 votes in favor and only 94 against. Even though the bill had been pushed through in a blatantly unconstitutional manner it was formally renewed twice, and thus provided the pseudo-legal basis for 12 years of dictatorship.

On March 31 the government used its new powers to promulgate the Provisional Law for the Coordination (*Gleichschaltung*) of the States (*Länder*) with the Reich. This gave state governments the right to pass legislation without consulting regional parliaments. State governors (*Reichsstatthälter*), who acted on instructions from Berlin, were appointed under the terms of a second bill of April 7. Hitler appointed himself Reichsstatthälter of Prussia, but delegated his authority to Göring. Thus ended the long tradition of German federalism. The new system was greatly confused by the fact that many of the Reichsstatthälter were also Gauleiter, but the state and party district boundaries did not correspond. It was typical of the Third Reich that this resulted in a confusion of state and party functions, as well as power struggles where state and district boundaries overlapped. The situation was further muddled when armaments commissars were appointed in areas which corresponded to neither the states nor the party districts. Furthermore, the Gauleiter and state governors established themselves as little Hitlers in their satrapies, paying scant attention to instructions passed down from Berlin, and considering themselves beholden to the Führer alone.

For all the talk of the unity of the National Socialist state, there was thus from the very beginning a hopeless confusion over the areas of competence of state and party, federal and state governments, and special plenipotentiaries. Hitler was in many ways a "hands off" tyrant. He preferred to let his myrmidons fight among themselves and let the strongest and fittest emerge triumphant. This corresponded to his view of life as an endless struggle, and it ensured that the Nazi movement never lost its activist dynamic by becoming bureaucratized. The end result was that the leading figures in the Third Reich were, almost without exception, a repulsive collection of brutish gangsters, corrupt place-seekers, and ruthless careerists. The advantage of this administrative Blitzkrieg was that it was possible to cut through red tape and avoid futile paper shuffling, but far too much time and energy was lost on interdepartmental rivalries and the struggle for power. In June 1934 a senior civil servant wrote to Frick: "Legally the state governors are subordinate to you as minister of the interior. Adolf Hitler is the state governor of Prussia. He has delegated his authority to Göring. You are also Prussian minister of the interior. As Reich minister of the interior, Adolf Hitler and the Prussian minister president are legally subordinate to you. Since you are the same person as the Prussian minister-president you are subordinate to yourself as Prussian minister president and as Reich minister of the interior. I am not a legal scholar, but I am sure that such a situation has never happened before."

The regime now set about the systematic destruction of the political parties that no longer had any role to play after the passing of the Enabling Act. On May 1 Goebbels staged a "Day of National Labor." On the following day the trades unions were banned. Units of the SA and SS stormed union offices and union leaders were arrested. Although most leading Communists had been imprisoned or had fled the country after the Reichstag fire, the party had not been forbidden so as to ensure that the working class vote would be split in the March election. The party was not formally banned until the end of March. Moscow appeared curiously indifferent to the destruction of the party and the martyrdom of its members.

The Social Democratic paramilitary organization "Reichsbanner," which had been involved in a series of street battles with the SA, was banned state by state. The party had been harassed since the Reichstag fire decree, its party offices raided, and its newspapers banned. The membership was demoralized and rapidly dwindled. Many of the leadership moved to Prague whence they called for an all-out struggle against Hitler's regime. The Nazis used this as an excuse to ban the party on June 22 and ordered the arrest of all those party leaders who were still in Germany.

The smaller democratic parties self-destructed, so that now only the Center Party, its Bavarian branch party (BVP), and the conservatives (DNVP) remained. Members were leaving these parties in droves, many of them joining the National Socialists. On March 28 the Catholic bishops, fearing that the state might interfere with the church, made a solemn pledge of allegiance to the Nazi state. Monsignor Kaas was in Rome discussing the details of a concordat with Papen and Vatican officials, so the party was left leaderless. Brüning took over command on May 6, but the party had no fight left in it. Under the terms of the concordat priests were forbidden to take part in politics and the Vatican thus clearly distanced itself from political Catholicism. A number of leading figures in the BVP were arrested, and on July 4 the party dissolved itself. The Center Party followed suit the next day.

The regime made quick work of the DNVP. The party leader Hugenberg caused a scandal during the London economic conference in June by demanding the return of Germany's colonies and expansion in the east, thus providing Hitler with an excellent excuse to dismiss him from the cabinet. The Stahlhelm leader Franz Seldte demonstrably joined the National Socialists on April 26 and on June 21 the Stahlhelm was amalgamated with the SA. On June 27 a "Friendly Agreement" was reached between the NSDAP and the DNVP. All conservative members of the Reichstag became Nazi party members, and all party members who had been arrested were released. The demise of the DNVP passed almost unnoticed. The Nazi daily newspaper *Völkischer Beobachter* had already announced on June 10 that the "party state" was dead. On July 14, a day of particular significance to democrats, a law was promulgated which declared the NSDAP to be the only legal party in Germany. Goebbels announced that this was the final victory over the ideals of the enlightenment and the French Revolution. But the regime made provision for plebiscites, thus showing that even dictatorships have to make, however fraudulent the means, some claim to legitimacy by securing popular consent. The spirit of 1789 was thus not quite extinguished.

Gleichschaltung

All professional associations, societies, and clubs were brought under party control as part of the comprehensive programme of "Coordination" (*Gleichschaltung*). Walter Darré, the party's agricultural expert and a long-time friend of Himmler, took control over all Germany's farmers' associations and was given the title of "Reich Farmers' Leader." He was appointed minister of agriculture at the end of June, and thus had complete control over all aspects of agriculture. On April 1 the offices of the Reich Association of German Industry (RDI) were raided by the SA, and a number of officials were dismissed, among them the vice-president Paul Silverberg who, although he was a Nazi sympathizer, was Jewish. In the following month the RDI was completely reorganized. The name was slightly changed, but the initials remained the same to give the appearance of continuity. Gustav Krupp von Bohlen und Halbach was appointed president and he, along with Hjalmar Schacht, who was reinstated as president of the Reichsbank, organized the "Adolf Hitler Fund" which collected money from industrialists for the NSDAP.

"*Gleichschaltung*" affected every walk of life. The professional organizations of doctors, lawyers, and engineers were brought under party control and henceforth there were only National Socialist beekeepers' associations and National Socialist cycle clubs. Even the village skittles teams were closely watched by the party. As a result, Germany's vigorous and varied club life withered, and people stayed at home or visited the local inn where they learnt to keep an eye out for police informants. The SA combed local government offices, the banks, and department stores in the search for democrats and Jews. A campaign began to drive women out of the professions, the civil service, and business, so that they could become the ideal wives and mothers that National Socialism demanded.

In May hundreds of university professors made an open declaration of their devotion to the new regime hoping thereby to further their miserable careers. But it was not only the second-rate who supported Hitler's dictatorship. Martin Heidegger, Germany's greatest philosopher, lauded the regime in a speech given in his capacity as rector of the University of Freiburg. It was a speech that he never retracted, although he was later to find kind words for Hitler's nemesis, Josef Stalin. His pupil, Hans Jonas, spoke of Heidegger's Nazism as a "world historical shame," and indeed the philosopher who saw man as the "shepherd of being," woefully failed to be his brother's keeper. Carl Schmitt, a renowned expert on constitutional law, provided ingenious justification for Nazi lawlessness. But he soon fell from grace because, unlike the sage of Todtnauberg, he had a wide circle of Jewish friends. This however did not stop him from addressing a meeting of German jurists with the words: "We need to free the German spirit from all Jewish falsifications, falsifications of the concept of spirit which have made it possible for Jewish emigrants to label the great struggle of Gauleiter Julius Streicher as something unspiritual." The "Law for the Restoration of a Professional Civil Service" of April 7 1933 was designed to purge the civil service of Jews and others whom the regime found undesirable. Since university professors were civil servants, it was used to rid the universities of a number of prominent intellectuals, many of whom made an incalculable contribution to the countries in which they found asylum. The systematic purge of the universities was carried out by Alfred Rosenberg's "Battle Group for German Culture," enthusiastically assisted by students in the National Socialist German Students' Association. Having one Jewish grandparent was sufficient to be considered a Jew under the terms of this law, which was soon extended to include the legal profession, doctors, dentists, and dental technicians, as well as accountants. At Hindenburg's insistence "Jewish" civil servants who had been in office before August 1 1914, who had served in the war, or who had either fathers or sons killed in the war were exempted.

Germany's rich and exciting cultural life was also brought under strict party control. In mid-February the socialist novelist Heinrich Mann was forced to resign as president of the Prussian Academy of the Arts. When the Academy was required to make a declaration of loyalty to the regime in March, Heinrich Mann's brother Thomas, along with Ricarda Huch and Alfred Döblin, resigned in protest. Other distinguished writers such as Franz Werfel and Jakob Wassermann were also forced to leave. In April a long list was published of authors whose works were banned, among whom were Karl Marx, Alfred Einstein, Sigmund Freud, and Eduard

Bernstein. Heinrich Heine was also banned, but some of his poetry, such as "The Lorelei," was so popular that it was still published. The author was said to be anonymous. In May the National Socialist German Students Association organized an "Action Against the Un-German Spirit." Bonfires were lit throughout the country into which books and newspapers were thrown. Goebbels addressed the crowds assembled around a huge bonfire in Berlin, proclaiming that the intellectual foundations of the November republic had now been destroyed. Heinrich Heine, who had witnessed similar book burnings almost a century before, uttered the prophetic words: "In the end one burns people where books are burnt."

The persecution of the Jews, which began in the first weeks of the regime, was carried out in a manner typical of the Nazis. It was a combination of uncoordinated violence from below and control from above. Bully-boys from the SA went on the rampage, vandalizing Jewish property and beating and murdering their hapless victims. Jews from all walks of life fell prey to this ever-increasing wave of violence. The reaction from abroad was immediate and robust, but this merely provoked the regime to step up its anti-Semitic campaign. Goebbels promised that he would "teach foreign Jews a lesson" for interfering in German affairs on behalf of their "racial comrades." A "Central Defense Committee Against Jewish Atrocity and Boycott Besetment" was formed under Julius Streicher, the Gauleiter of Franconia, an utterly repulsive creature even by the exceptional standards set by the National Socialists, who rejoiced in the reputation of being the movement's most brutal, scatological, and vicious anti-Semite. He was rewarded by being given the task of organizing a boycott of Jewish businesses to take place on April 1. It was not a success. The SA prevented people from shopping at their favorite stores, and there were widespread complaints about the crude excesses of the brown-shirts. Goebbels was disappointed at the lack of popular enthusiasm for his operation, and promptly called it off. Party activists continued the boycott in some areas, even though both Hitler and Frick had ordered them to stop for fear of foreign reaction.

Within a year 2,000 civil servants had been dismissed and about the same number of artists were forbidden to work. Four thousand lawyers were no longer able to practice their profession, and hundreds of doctors and university professors lost their livelihoods. For the moment Jewish businessmen were needed to help the process of economic recovery, but their days were numbered. In the first year of the regime some 37,000 German Jews emigrated, even though Jewish agencies only recommended leaving the country if an individual was in extreme personal danger. They hoped that things would calm down, and that it would be possible for the Jewish community to enjoy a degree of autonomy within the new state. It was almost impossible for the Jewish community to believe that worse would befall them. Had not Rabbi Leo Baeck described Germany as witnessing the third golden age of Judaism, following that of Hellenic Judaism in the period before the destruction of the second temple, and the second that of Sephardic Judaism before the expulsion from Spain? Did the fact that 13 of the 33 German Nobel Prize winners were Jewish count for nothing? Could the extraordinary contribution of Jews to Germany's cultural heritage simply be ignored? Others were less confident. In 1934 a further

23,000 Jews left the country. There was some reason for such optimism. Things began to settle down in the summer of 1933, by which time Hitler had destroyed the republic and had virtually absolute power. But the military, industry, and the bureaucracy still enjoyed a degree of autonomy, and Hitler was still partially dependent on them and thus could not afford to go on too radical a course. Hitler was also concerned not to alienate foreign opinion, presenting himself as a man of moderation and peace. The Nazi radicals around Ernst Röhm and the SA were deeply frustrated at such pusillanimous behavior and complained bitterly that there had been no revolutionary changes in German society.

Ernst Röhm and the SA

Thus while the SA, with about three million members, was chomping at the bit and eager to begin what they called the "Second Revolution," Hitler was trying to dampen down this radicalism, which threatened his fruitful alliance with the old elites. In an attempt to bring the anarchic violence of the SA under control greater powers were given to Himmler's SS, specialists in orderly, bureaucratic violence infused with ideological passion. The SS established their first concentration camp in a former munitions factory at Dachau near Munich. Here the regime's victims were systematically bullied, tortured, and murdered in a secluded camp, without offending the sensitive German public who found the open violence of the SA, to which they had been eyewitnesses, somewhat disturbing. At the end of June Himmler appointed SS-Oberführer (Brigadier) Theodor Eicke commandant. He was a sadistic brute who had recently been released from a psychiatric hospital for the criminally insane. He immediately began to organize the SS Death's Head units which guarded the camps, and was soon to be promoted inspector general of the concentration camps and set up his Berlin office in the Gestapo headquarters at Prinz-Albrecht-Strasse 7. The SA lost control over their concentration camps, which were henceforth administered by the SS, even though the SS was still formally subordinate to the SA.

By the spring of 1934 the conflict between the SA and the army had become so acute as to be worrisome to Hitler. Ernst Röhm had accused the regime of "falling asleep," and announced that "It is high time that the national revolution should become the National Socialist revolution." At a series of mass meetings he demanded that "reactionaries" should be weeded out from the bureaucracy, industry, and the military. He was outraged that the military had been largely spared from the process of *Gleichschaltung*, but said that its time would come. "The grey rock of the Reichswehr," he proclaimed, "will disappear beneath the brown wave of the SA." Hitler could not tolerate such a suggestion. He needed the professionals in the Reichswehr and knew full well that he could never fulfill his territorial ambitions with gangs of street-fighting men, whatever their ideological fervor and activist élan. The Reichswehr saw Röhm and his *ouvrieriste* ideas as a serious danger, and suggested that the SA should form a sort of territorial army under its close control.

Hitler felt that this solution would probably be unacceptable to Röhm, but decided to test his reactions.

The Reichswehr was more than happy to make some concessions to the new regime. The traditionally anti-Semitic officer corps was happy to purge its ranks of Jews. Admittedly this purge was far from complete, largely due to the difficulty in determining who was Jewish. Two to three thousand "pure Jews" (*Volljuden*) served in the Wehrmacht during the war, along with 150–200,000 "half-Jews," and "quarter-Jews." Most served in the ranks, but there were many officers and some 20 generals among them. In February 1934 the swastika was incorporated into military emblems. In the same month Hitler called a meeting between the Reichswehr minister, General Werner von Blomberg, and Röhm. He ordered that since the revolution was over and the Reichswehr should remain above politics, the SA should restrict its activities to political indoctrination and pre-military training. Hitler told them that a war would have to be fought to secure *Lebensraum* and that war should be left to the professionals. Röhm left the meeting in a towering rage, calling Hitler "an ignorant corporal," and vowing to keep up the struggle against "reactionaries." In a speech on April 18 he denounced "the incredible tolerance" of the regime toward "the supporters and associates of former and ancient regimes," and demanded that they should be "ruthlessly removed."

Although Hitler was still reluctant to act against his old companion-in-arms, Röhm had powerful enemies, and it was not simply the Reichswehr that was determined to frustrate his ambitions. Göring, Goebbels, and Hess were envious of his position, and Himmler and his associate Heydrich resented the fact that the SS played second fiddle to the SA. The fact that he was a notorious homosexual in a country where homosexuality was an offense under article 175 of the criminal code left him wide open to attack. Göring put together a weighty dossier on Röhm and his numerous homosexual accomplices and catamites. Reichswehr intelligence cooperated closely with the National Socialist Security Service (SD) in the search for further material to use against Röhm. It was at this time that Himmler took over control of the Prussian Gestapo and he promptly set them to work on the case.

On June 4, in an attempt to calm things down, Hitler ordered the entire SA to go on leave for the month of July. Röhm's "reactionaries" were emboldened by this obvious split among the National Socialists, and went on the offensive. Once again Papen was to play a key and characteristically disastrous role. It was obvious that Hindenburg did not have much longer to live and the question of a successor now became of pressing concern. The president had fallen seriously ill in April and had not made a complete recovery. Papen tried to convince Hindenburg to call for the restoration of the monarchy in his will. His aim was to establish a military dictatorship in which the conservative elites would keep the Nazi activists in check. On June 17 1934 Papen gave a speech at Marburg University, which had been written for him by Edgar Jung, an ultraconservative Calvinist lawyer whose hazy notions of "revolutionary conservatism" were strongly influenced by the muddle-headed corporatist speculations of Othmar Spann. The speech was a forceful expression of the conservative opposition to Hitler. Men who had colluded with the Nazis in the vain belief that they could be tamed, now realized that they had made a serious error of judgment and that Hitler had to be removed. It is doubtful whether Papen grasped the full implications of the speech that Jung had prepared for him, for it came as a bombshell. It was an outspoken attack on the regime's radicalism, violence, and lawlessness. A sharp distinction was made between conservative authoritarianism and the "unnatural totalitarian aspirations of National Socialism." The speech stated that dynamism and movement could achieve nothing but chaos, and the "permanent revolution from below" had to be brought to an end. A firm structure was needed in which the rule of law was respected and state authority unchallenged. Goebbels promptly banned the publication of this speech, and no mention was made of it on state radio. Jung was arrested and shortly after murdered, along with a number of leading figures in this early conservative resistance to Hitler's dictatorship. Jung's *spiritus rector*, Othmar Spann, as an Austrian, was temporarily spared. After the *Anschluss* he was brutally mishandled and left virtually blind.

Hitler hastened to visit Hindenburg on his estate at Neudeck in an effort at damage control, but realized that the time had come to take more drastic action. Göring, Himmler, and Blomberg decided that the SS should be set loose on the SA leadership, with the weapons and logistical support to be supplied by the Reichswehr. Hitler then called a meeting of senior SA commanders at Bad Wiessee where Röhm was taking the waters. In the early morning of June 30 Hitler arrived at Röhm's hotel in a state of great agitation, riding crop in hand, accompanied by Goebbels and SA-Obergruppenführer (General) Viktor Lutze, the police chief of Hanover, whom Goebbels described as being of "unlimited stupidity," and who was to take over command of the SA, along with an SS detachment. Röhm and his associates were arrested, taken first to the prison at Stadelheim, and then transferred to Dachau where Röhm's associates were executed that evening by the SS. Röhm was killed on the following day, once Hitler had been finally persuaded to agree to his execution.

This "Röhm Putsch," or "Night of the Long Knives," was not confined to the SA. A number of old scores were settled. Schleicher, his wife, and his adjutant were gunned down in Schleicher's own home. The former Bavarian minister-president, von Kahr, was assassinated, as was the leader of a prominent Catholic layman's group. Gregor Strasser was dragged off to the cellars of the Gestapo headquarters in Berlin where he was shot. A music critic by the name of Dr Wilhelm Schmidt was also murdered, having had the misfortune to be confused with the SA leader Ludwig Schmitt. There were a total of 85 known victims on June 30, but the real figure is almost certainly considerably higher.

The regime had taken a critical step toward a state of total lawlessness that was characteristic of the fully-fledged Nazi tyranny. Although the state had now degenerated to the level of a criminal organization, there was widespread popular support for this bloodbath. The cabinet was called together on July 3 and hastily cobbled together a law that justified these "emergency measures" that were needed to combat "treasonable attacks." These criminal acts were thus legalized after the event, and no legal action could be taken against the perpetrators. Carl Schmitt opined that "The Führer protects the law from the worst forms of abuse when he uses his position as leader to create the law in his capacity as supreme judge." He was later to extend this dubious definition of the law in the lapidary injunction that "The will of the Führer is the highest law." Most Germans were relieved that the SA, with their brutal activism, had now been brought under control by Hitler's decisive action. They forgot that law and order could not be restored by murderous disregard for the law. Even though two prominent generals had been slaughtered in cold blood, the Reichswehr was delighted that the SA had been silenced, and the generals cravenly congratulated Hitler for saving Germany from the horrors of civil war. Hitler had thus overcome all serious opposition within the Nazi movement, and his dazzling position as the omniscient and omnipotent Führer in the eyes of his countless devotees was further enhanced.

Hitler in Full Command

The cabinet met as President Hindenburg lay dying, and it was agreed that on his demise Hitler should combine the offices of chancellor and president. None of those present were troubled that this was blatantly unconstitutional, and flouted the Enabling Act. Blomberg toadishly announced that on the Field Marshal's death he would order the Reichswehr to make a personal oath of allegiance to the Führer, rather than to the constitution as had previously been the case. A number of soldiers were thus to suffer severe and genuine pangs of conscience when they contemplated resistance to the man to whom before Almighty God they had sworn total allegiance. Blomberg vainly imagined that the oath of allegiance would guarantee their independence. The generals were soon to find out that the absolute reverse was true.

Hindenburg died on August 2 1934, and Hitler was promptly appointed "Führer and Reich Chancellor." The dictatorship was now complete. On August 19 a plebiscite was held asking the German people to approve the appointment of Hitler as head of state, chancellor, supreme commander of the armed forces, and head of the judiciary, thus giving pseudo-democratic sanction to a blatantly unconstitutional move. Eighty-nine-point-nine percent voted in favor. On the following day Hitler announced that the "fifteen-year struggle for power" was completed, and that the National Socialists now controlled everything from the highest offices in the Reich to the smallest village council. This was no idle boast. All aspects of German life were now firmly under party control. At the beginning of September the sixth party rally was held in Nuremberg to celebrate this astonishing victory. Its pomp, ceremony, and menace was captured on celluloid in Leni Riefenstahl's brilliant piece of propaganda *Triumph of the Will*.

The film's title, whether deliberately or not, is misleading. Hitler did not owe his success to his iron willpower, but to a set of fortunate circumstances that offered him opportunities that he exploited adroitly. He gambled for very high stakes and lady luck smiled upon him. The social, economic, and political crises created a

Plate 20 Nazi Party rally 1934. © Bundesarchiv

situation in which a firm hand was needed. Men of power and influence imagined that they could use the little drummer boy for their own purposes, whilst the National Socialist movement developed an anarchic activist dynamic that swept all before it. Hitler the master tactician managed to stop the situation from getting out of hand, and thereby won the allegiance of the conservative elites who felt most threatened by party radicals. This was no carefully considered plan carried out with ruthless determination, but 18 months of breathless improvisation and nerve-wracking gambling for the highest stakes. The rule of law no longer applied. Parliamentary democracy had been destroyed, the separation of powers ended, the constitution was defunct, the federal system dismantled, and a number of new bodies created that were answerable neither to the state nor to the party, but to Hitler alone. Conservatives believed that with the destruction of the radicals in the SA the regime would now settle down to be firmly repressive yet predictably authoritarian, and that the road ahead would be smooth.

Once again the conservative elites had seriously misread the situation. They failed to see that behind the façade of unity there were ferocious struggles for power, conflicts over areas of competence, and bitter rivalries. The system was in a constant state of flux, and possessed an inner dynamic without which it would atrophy. It was unpredictable, anarchic, and individualistic in that the little Führers called the shots and were not bound by rules, regulations, or the law. Officials tried to interpret Hitler's will, for that was the highest law and the secret of success. The resulting situation was so chaotic that during the war Hitler's closest associate, Martin Bormann, complained that whereas the republic had been far too tightly bound with red tape, the present situation was so disorderly as to be dysfunctional. A highly complex modern state could not possibly operate effectively by attempts to interpret the wishes of an individual, particularly when the leader became progressively unhinged as the war dragged on, and his will amounted to little more than wishful thinking. Furthermore, many of the leading figures in the Third Reich were exceedingly idle and absurdly vain. In the latter stages of the war, Göring spent most of the year hunting and playing with his electric trains in his vast palace, Karinhall. Wilhelm Frick relaxed in his lakeside home on the Chiemsee. Philip Bouhler, who ran Hitler's personal chancellery, idled away for months on end at his country estate in Nußdorf. Hitler was indubitably the fount of all authority and the final arbiter, but his unbridled power did not rest solely on his willpower, and certainly not on his careful planning, but rather on the inner workings of the system, and the willingness of so many Germans to lend him their full support and absolute devotion.

The years from 1934 to 1938 appeared to be a time of tranquility and peace in Germany. The regime was authoritarian, but it seemed to have distanced itself from the radical activism of the "Years of Struggle." It had a number of striking successes to its credit, both at home and abroad. A comprehensive welfare state was created and the feeling of "Racial Community" (*Volksgemeinschaft*) was more than an empty slogan. It was widely believed in Germany and abroad that Hitler was a man of peace who had restored Germany to its rightful place in the world. However, behind the scenes the situation was very different. Hitler was systematically laying the groundwork for the realization of his schemes for conquest, expansion, and racial purification. Many in the military, civil service, and industrial elites, to say nothing of the people at large, agreed in principal with these aims, but they feared the risks involved. Hitler needed first to bring them totally under his control and bend them to his will, before he put all his chips on the table in one desperate *va banque* gamble. It was to be total victory or total destruction – Hitler would brook no alternative.

By August 1934 Hitler had absolute power. In the state there was no body or person who could check or control him. With the removal of Ernst Röhm he had unbridled authority over the party, which followed him blindly. Hitler as Führer was the awesome figure that bound this confusing and fissiparous movement together, and Goebbels' brilliant propaganda helped make him into a figure of messianic proportions, the superbly choreographed rallies becoming quasi-religious ceremonies. This could not have been done purely with smoke and mirrors, nor could the German people's longing for a savior in their hour of need be stilled without results. The regime overcame the unemployment problem, stimulated the economy, and had a series of foreign political successes that silenced most of Hitler's critics and reconciled the masses to the countless irritations of daily life. Hitler was credited with all the many successes; the failures were ascribed to his wretched underlings.

Initially the elites believed that they could tame Hitler, or, where they were unable to do so, could profit from him. They were reassured by the fact that for the first little while he played by the book as written by Brüning and Papen. But he quickly dropped established governmental routine. The cabinet met 72 times in 1933, 12 times in 1935 and never again after 1938, so that the vast cabinet room in Hitler's magnificent new Reich chancellery was never used. At none of these cabinet meetings was a vote taken. Members of the cabinet met Hitler individually, access to the Presence controlled by his assiduous head of chancellery, Hans Heinrich Lammers. Once the Enabling Act was passed Hitler's working methods became even more haphazard. When he was not rushing around the country addressing rallies, laying foundation stones, and calling impromptu meetings with sundry officials, he paid increasingly long visits to the Berghof, his mountain fastness in Berchtesgaden. Officials scurried around after him begging for his approval. The result was inevitably chaotic. One minister would secure his endorsement of legislation that contradicted that which had already been passed via another ministry. All this further strengthened Hitler's position as Führer, for he alone could reconcile such differences and order the implementation of laws so as to create the impression of order and consistency.

Hitler resisted all attempts to bring some order into this confusion, which exasperated the orderly minds of experienced bureaucrats. His instructions were often deliberately vague, so that many different interpretations were possible as to how they should be executed. Or he hesitated until one of his powerful subordinates took it upon himself to act. Amid this tangled situation there was plenty of room for ambitious Gauleiter and Reichsstaathälter to carve out empires where they reigned supreme, virtually unhampered by considerations of the law or of established practice, and with a direct line of communication to Hitler. Since Hitler took little interest in domestic politics in these early years there was ample scope for power-hungry and resourceful men to establish themselves in positions of authority and influence, and they could be almost certain of the Führer's blessing. In National Socialist Germany nothing succeeded like success. Hitler seldom intervened and he ruled at a distance. The shortcomings and failures of the regime could thus be blamed on local party functionaries, and this did nothing to undermine his status as the nation's redeemer. On the contrary: "If only the Führer knew" was a frequent response to the widespread irritations, injustices, and deficiencies.

The longing for a leader who would deliver Germany from all evil was deeply rooted both ideologically and psychologically. There was Emperor Frederick I of Hohenstaufen who, as "Barbarossa," lay buried in the Kyffhaüser mountain and who would rise again to save Germany in its hour of need. There were the Parsifals and Siegfrieds in Wagner's operas that Hitler loved so dearly. There was the deeply ingrained military spirit of Brandenburg-Prussia, the leadership ideology of the youth movement, and the widespread desire to find a substitute for the monarchy as a symbolic representation of the nation. But it was Goebbels and his propaganda machine which transformed admiration of the regime's achievements into a quasi-religious cult of the Führer. "The whole *Volk*," he proclaimed, "is devoted to him not merely through respect, but with deep and heartfelt love, because it has the feeling that it belongs to Him. It is flesh of his flesh, blood of his blood." Perhaps only someone who had been educated by Jesuits could be capable of such blasphemy. Few were able to resist enchantment by this superhuman figure. Erstwhile opponents became his devotees, and even those who remained critically distanced from him found it hard to withstand his attraction. Hitler himself succumbed totally to the myth so that this mean-spirited, cruel, and bigoted creature became convinced that he was an infallible and indispensable instrument of providence, with a world-historical mission to fulfil. Those who even today speak of the "fascination" of the Hitler phenomenon are still under the spell of this despicable megalomaniac.

The Dual State

As early as 1940 the émigré social scientist Ernst Fraenkel described this confusion of rival power centers in the state and the party as the "Dual State," and another brilliant colleague, Franz Neumann, analyzed how the normative state apparatus gradually dissolved into an "organized anarchy," with its characteristically amorphous dynamic. The dualism was not a clear cut distinction between party and state, but a highly complex intertwining of areas of competence, which led to ever-increasing radicalization both of goals and methods.

There were substantial changes within the power structure of this polycratic state. The SS triumphed over the SA in 1934, and began its rapid growth to become a state within the state, submitting the judiciary and the police to its whims. Walter Darré, although grossly inefficient, was made food tsar and minister of agriculture with extensive powers. The German Work Front (DAF), built on the ruins of the democratic unions under Robert Ley, a chronic alcoholic, had 25.3 million members by 1939. This gave Ley immense power, which he used to tackle questions of professional training, social problems, housing, and leisure-time activities. His empire thus infringed at many points on the competence of other ministries. Similarly, Fritz Todt was made responsible for building the highways and given special plenipotentiary powers that enabled him to tread on the toes of a number of ministers, principal among them the minister of transport. One of these ministers was the founder of the Stahlhelm, Franz Seldte, a bone-idle creature who had been appointed minister of labor in 1933. When Goebbels suggested to Hitler that Ley should replace Seldte, on the grounds that although he was an appalling drunk he tended to get things done, Hitler refused point blank. He argued that Seldte could always be removed, whereas Ley was in a position of such power and influence that it would be extremely difficult to dislodge him. The situation was made even more absurd in that, as Ernst Jünger pointed out, under normal circumstances none of these magnates would have even been made a junior partner in a halfway decent firm.

No one accumulated so many offices as the intelligent, jovial, sadistic, morphine-addicted, and progressively deranged Göring. He was president of the Reichstag, Prussian minister of the interior, and Prussian minister-president. He was a Reich minister without portfolio, air minister, minister responsible for hunting and the forests, commander-in-chief of the Luftwaffe, and commissar for raw materials and foreign exchange. When Hitler decided to push ahead with his autarchy plans in spite of the resistance of the central bank, the ministry of economics, and powerful voices in the private sector, he appointed Göring as head of the Four Year Plan, and as such made him a virtual dictator over all aspects of the economy.

Goebbels combined the office of minister of propaganda with that of Gauleiter of Berlin. Bernard Rust, the Gauleiter of Hanover and Braunschweig, was also minister of technology and education, even though he had lost his job as a schoolteacher because he sexually abused one his charges. He also suffered from a severe mental handicap as a result of a head wound received while serving as an infantry lieutenant during the war. Rust and Goebbels were the only Gauleiter who were also ministers. Heinrich Himmler was both head of the SS and police chief for all of Germany. In October 1939 he was made "Reich Commissar for the Strengthening of the German Race" (*Volkstums*). As such he was responsible for the brutal deportation of Jews and Poles, and the resettlement by pure-blooded Germans of the areas they had been forced to leave. This new office as a "Higher Instance of the Reich" was placed outside the law, and kept secret from the regular civil service. Himmler also became minister of the interior in 1943, and was given command over the reserve army in the following year. Some were in positions of great power without holding state office. Julius Streicher, the grisly Gauleiter of Franconia, enjoyed Hitler's absolute and unconditional support for his rabidly pornographic and sadistic anti-Semitism. Baldo von Shirach, as head of the Hitler Youth (HJ) and later Reich Youth Leader, was another powerful figure, in spite of his widely rumored homosexuality and his endless struggles with Bernhard Rust.

Hitler was obsessed with architecture and had gigantomanic plans for rebuilding Berlin. When he felt that this project was not going ahead fast enough he appointed an ambitious young architect, Albert Speer, as "General Building Inspector for the Reich Capital," vested with plenipotentiary powers over building and traffic. Speer was appointed minister of munitions on Todt's death in an airplane crash in February 1942. Meanwhile, the traditional ministries continued to work as before so that an impression of normalcy was created amid all this chaos. By 1937 the party had become a gigantic bureaucratized apparatus, with 700,000 well paid employees. It nearly trebled in size during the war as the "golden pheasants," as these gold braided officials were caustically called, found ingenious ways to avoid dying a hero's death for Führer and *Vaterland*. Party officials down to the very lowest level had the means to make the lives of ordinary people miserable, and many took great delight in doing so. The party wards (*Ortsgruppen*) were obliged to provide certificates of good conduct for civil servants, for those who requested social assistance, and for students and apprentices. No business could be started without the sanction of the party, and during the war it was the party that decided which workers were essential (UK), and therefore exempted from military service. The Block Leader (*Blockleiter*) kept a close watch on the citizenry and extracted contributions from them for party membership, the National Socialist People's Welfare (NSV), as well as for the "Winter Help" (*Winterhilfswerk*). These Nazi charitable organizations amounted to little more than state-sponsored mugging, and a large chunk of the proceeds went to build Goebbels' magnificent villa in Berlin. Money was also collected through "Casserole Sundays," whereby the proceeds of a modest one-course meal went to assist needy "racial comrades." During the war the Block-leiter issued ration cards. The opportunities for harassment were unlimited, and complaints about these vile mini-Hitlers at the bottom of Nazi midden were legion.

The SS

The most spectacular change since 1934 was the rise of the SS to become the purest expression of National Socialism. It had begun as a minute subordinate section of the SA, but by 1933 it had 56,000 members. Himmler began to build up his police empire in Bavaria, but the way ahead was blocked by Göring who controlled the police in Prussia. There began a bitter personal rivalry, with strong ideological overtones, between the two men. Göring saw the police as an organ of the state, Himmler wanted a political police force that was completely free from any form of outside control and was utterly devoted to the Führer. Heinrich Himmler was an improbable leader of this new order of ideologically-charged Aryan supermen. He was a weedy and shy little man, born in 1900, who, in spite of the permissive atmosphere of the Weimar Republic, did not lose his virginity until 1928. In gratitude for this act of mercy he promptly married his dreary Jezebel, temporarily retired from political life, and took up chicken farming. Although unsuccessful with the poultry, he channeled his agricultural expertise into an obsession with breeding and with race. His devotion to Hitler was unconditional.

The SS (*Schutzstaffel* or Guard Squad) was founded in 1923 under a slightly different name, and was reorganized in 1925. Himmler took over command of its 289 members in 1929 and set to work turning it into an elite formation. In 1931 he established the Security Service (SD) under the unrelentingly malevolent 25-year-old Reinhard Heydrich, a racial fanatic who had recently been dismissed from the navy for dishonorable conduct. Shortly after the March elections the first military formation, known as the "SS Personal Standard Adolf Hitler" (*Leibstandarte-SS* Adolf Hitler), was created under the command of Sepp Dietrich, a former butcher and bouncer whose coarseness was only partially concealed behind a heavy layer of beer-swilling Bavarian joviality. After the SS victory over the SA, the first units of the *SS-Verfügungstruppe* (Emergency Troops) were formed, which were later to be reorganized into the Waffen-SS, the military wing. On June 20 1934 the SS was made solely responsible for the concentration camps, which were guarded by the SS Death's Head Units (*SS-Totenkopfverbände*).

By the spring of 1934 Himmler had taken over the political police forces in all the German states with the exception of Prussia. Göring, who was looking for an ally in the interminable power-struggles that beset the Third Reich, decided to make his peace with Himmler and gave him control over the Prussian secret police, the Gestapo, in April 1934. Himmler was now in control of the secret police

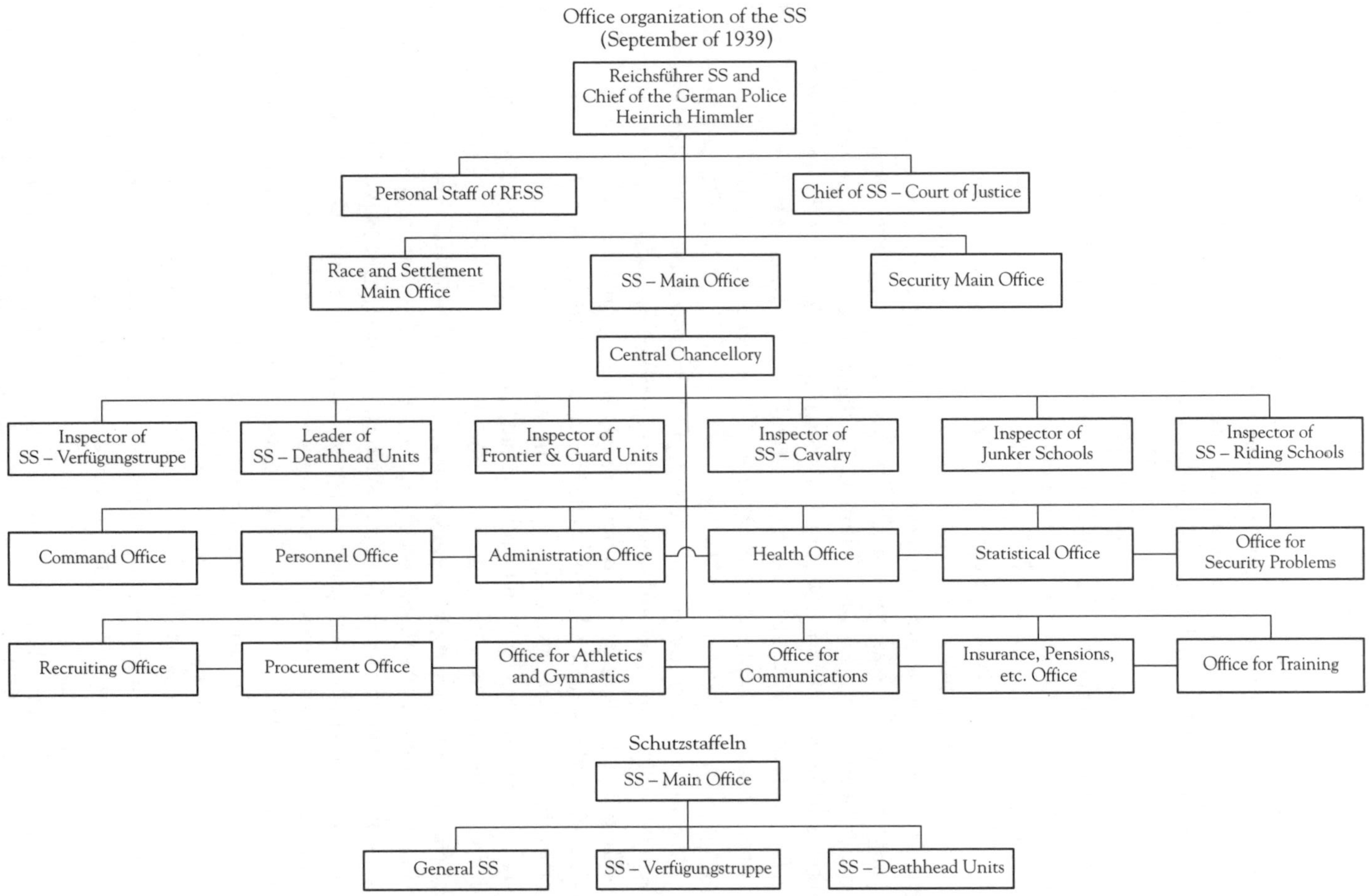

Office organization of the SS
(September of 1939)

Reichsführer SS and
Chief of the German Police
Heinrich Himmler

Personal Staff of RFSS

Race and Settlement
Main Office

Chief of SS – Court of Justice

SS – Main Office

Security Main Office

Central Chancellory

Inspector of
SS – Verfügungstruppe

Leader of
SS – Deathhead Units

Inspector of
Frontier & Guard Units

Inspector of
SS – Cavalry

Inspector of
Junker Schools

Inspector of
SS – Riding Schools

Command Office

Personnel Office

Administration Office

Health Office

Statistical Office

Office for
Security Problems

Recruiting Office

Procurement Office

Office for Athletics
and Gymnastics

Office for
Communications

Insurance, Pensions,
etc. Office

Office for Training

Schutzstaffeln

SS – Main Office

General SS

SS – Verfügungstruppe

SS – Deathhead Units

Figure 1

throughout the Reich and placed Heydrich in command. Heydrich was now head of the SD and the Gestapo, and thus of both the party and the state secret police forces. In 1936 the Gestapo was made independent from judicial and administrative control. Himmler was now given command over all the regular police forces in Germany and sported the pompous title of "Reichsführer-SS and Chief of the German Police in the Reich Ministry of the Interior." In a situation typical of the Third Reich, Himmler was thus subordinate to the minister of the interior in his capacity as state secretary in charge of the police, but as head of the SS he reported directly to Hitler. With immediate access to the Führer he could afford to ignore the minister of the interior, and the entire police force was thus beyond state control. Himmler did not see fit to even have an office in the ministry of the interior.

Himmler immediately began the reorganization of his all-encompassing empire. The police force was divided into two sections. The Order Police (*Ordnungspolizei*), which dealt with minor offenses, comprised the Safety Police (*Schutzpolizei*) and the Gendarmerie and was commanded by Kurt Daluege, a Freikorps veteran and early party member, a man of such limited intelligence that he was popularly known as Dummi-Dummi. Heydrich was put in charge of the Security Police (*Sicherheitspolizei*), which was made up of the Political Police, the Criminal Police (*Kripo*), and the Border Police. In September 1939 the party's secret police force, SD, was added to the *Sicherheitspolizei* to form the Reich Security Main Office (RSHA). Heydrich was determined to turn the SS into "ideological storm-troopers and bodyguards of the Führer's ideas." Its mission was to "keep a close eye on the political health of the body politic [*Volkskörpers*], quickly diagnose any symptoms of sickness and to immediately destroy all malignant cells." Himmler told his men that they had to steel themselves to face "the campaign to annihilate Germany's subhuman enemies throughout the entire world" which he would soon unleash. Heydrich's RSHA was divided up into numerous divisions to combat the regime's enemies and ill-wishers. There were sections dealing with such issues as communism, Marxism and its allies, reactionary movements, opposition groups, legitimists, liberalism, political Catholicism and Protestantism, sects and Free Masons, abortion, homosexuality, and racial research. Section IV B 4 was given responsibility for questions concerning "Political Churches, Sects and Jews." Its head was SS-Obersturmbannführer (Lieutenant-Colonel) Adolf Eichmann. Section IV C dealt with those unfortunates in "protective custody," Section IV D with foreign workers and hostile foreigners, and Section VII with "ideological research and evaluation." As early as 1934 Heydrich made his intentions perfectly clear. He announced that "The aim of our Jewish policy [*Judenpolitik*] must be the emigration of all Jews." He then added an even more sinister note: "Rowdy anti-Semitism must be rejected. One does not fight rats with revolvers, but with poison and gas."

The SS was thus a totalitarian organization designed to protect the German *Volk*, rid it of all undesirable elements, whether biological or ideological, and thus render it pure, strong, and healthy. Heinrich Himmler, the prim little bureaucrat known as the "Reich's Heini," was a mass of contradictions. He was a merciless mass murderer who found a visit to Auschwitz disturbing, and tried to ban hunting on the grounds that it was cruel to animals. He used every modern technique in order to extirpate the evil works of Jewish–Bolshevik sub-humans and create his atavistic dystopia, but he was full of anxieties and fears about the modern world. He wanted to turn the SS into a mystical order, living in remote castles, worshipping the ancient Germanic Gods, abjuring alcohol and tobacco, and adhering to a strictly vegetarian diet.

In order to hunt down and destroy the enemies of the Volk the regime undermined and eventually destroyed the rule of law. The law could not remain independent in a totalitarian regime, but was instrumentalized to serve its needs. Special courts were opened in each state against the decisions of which there could be no appeal. There were a number of new criminal offenses, such as "Acts Contrary to the Healthy Feelings of the *Volk*," which were open to a wide range of interpretations. The concept of the rule of law was denounced as "liberal," and was replaced by such notions as "the will of the Führer is the highest law," or "law is that which is good for the *Volk*." Whereas civil law was administered in much the same way as before, the courts outbid one another in the ferocity of their judgments in criminal cases. Members of the Communist and Social Democratic Parties were ruthlessly pursued and charged with treason. Merely listening to Radio Moscow or the BBC during the war was considered to be "preparation for treason." Sixteen thousand death sentences had been handed down for such offenses by the end of 1944. The courts also interpreted questions of "racial law" with exceptional ideological fervor.

With the Gestapo Law of February 1936 the individual citizen was left without any legal protection whatsoever. The Gestapo could define what constituted a political crime, and the courts had no jurisdiction over its activities. If the Gestapo did not approve of the judgment of a court they would simply arrest the accused and fling the hapless individual into a concentration camp. Roland Freisler, state secretary in the ministry of justice and later president of the People's Court, a sadistic former Communist commissar, threatened to deliver any judges who handed down light sentences to this "police justice." The law became even more draconian during the war, with a host of new capital crimes such as "taking advantage of the state of war."

Anti-Semitism, Racism, and Euthanasia

The persecution of the Jews provides the paradigmatic example of the lawlessness, ideological fervor, and ruthless brutality of the Nazi tyranny. It was also characteristic of the regime that it should be part of a process of gradual radicalization, and that it should be carried out in a somewhat haphazard way, as various power-centers within this polycratic system vied with one another. The very notion of the "racial community" is by definition exclusive, and from the beginning the Nazis spoke of their determination to destroy everything that was deemed to be "alien to the community" (*Gemeinschaftsfremd*), in order to hasten the creation of a pure, healthy, and superior race. The National Socialist concept of law was based on the will of the Führer and on the "healthy instincts of the *Volk*," thus all who were outside the *Volk* were also outside the law. Although Jews were seen as the greatest danger to the *Volk*, other groups were also singled out for exclusion. These included the mentally and physically handicapped, psychiatric patients, male homosexuals, Gypsies, habitual criminals, alcoholics, drug addicts, and other "asocials." This in spite of the fact that most of the leading figures in Nazi Germany fell under one or more of these categories, with the possible exception of the Gypsies. These latter were damned on three counts. They were deemed to be "asocial," "inferior," and "racially unacceptable" (*Fremdrassig*). In Berlin Goebbels declared Jews also to be "asocial," but it was difficult to charge this sinisterly powerful and deeply threatening people with "inferiority." Lesbians were only persecuted in Austria where, under paragraphs 129 and 130 of the criminal code, their proclivity was condemned as an "unnatural sexual offense." Unlike the Jews, homosexuals were not systematically hunted down and murdered, and there was an extensive homosexual subculture in the Third Reich. In the early years many homosexuals were attracted by the markedly homoerotic aesthetic of the "Movement," and a number of leading Nazis would have been in serious trouble had paragraph 175 of the criminal code been rigorously enforced. In 1935 the law, which had only outlawed anal intercourse, was extended to cover all forms of sexual activity between males, and was thus open to wide interpretation.

Compulsory sterilization of the "hereditarily sick" began in July 1933. A total of about 360,000 such operations were performed. Initially those suffering from such disorders as schizophrenia, epilepsy, manic-depression, and "idiocy" were singled out, but soon social rather than medical criteria were more often used. Habitual criminals, alcoholics, prostitutes, and tramps were also sterilized in this extensive program of "racial hygiene." The Nazis first decided what was "normal" and then set about destroying everything that did not match these criteria, in a desperate attempt to build a new society.

The regime moved a little more cautiously in 1934 since it was preoccupied with the Röhm crisis and was concerned to improve its image abroad. Julius Streicher stepped up his personal anti-Semitic campaign in his obscene publication *Der Stürmer*, which was put on public display in showcases throughout Germany from the summer of 1934. He demanded that Jews should be denied all civil rights and that marriages between Jews and Gentiles should be forbidden. In a number of instances registrars refused to allow such marriages, and appeals to the courts against such illegal actions were often in vain.

In 1935 Jews were forbidden to serve in the armed forces. Attempts to create a special nationality law for Jews failed because there was no agreement on how to define who was Jewish. Should "half-Jews," those with only one Jewish parent, be treated the same as "full-Jews," both of whose parents were Jewish? Hitler demanded clarification so that further discrimination against Jews could be put in train, and "mixed marriages" outlawed. There had been a revival of "rowdy anti-Semitism" in 1935, as a result of dissatisfaction among the ranks of the SA at the regime's refusal to carry out a National Socialist revolution. This had hurt Germany's reputation abroad, and was bad for business. Consequently there was widespread disapproval of such lawlessness. Most important of all, Hitler could not tolerate such insubordination from this dissident rabble. Anti-Semitism had to become a government monopoly, and to this end officials from Frick's ministry of the interior worked feverishly during the Nuremberg party rally drafting the "Law for the Protection of German Blood and German Honor," otherwise known as the "Nuremberg laws."

The laws made marriages and sexual intercourse between Jews and non-Jews criminal offenses. Jews were forbidden to employ female non-Jews as domestic servants. Only those German citizens who had "German or similar blood" could enjoy full civil rights. The thorny question of the definition of who was a Jew was still left open. After lengthy debates it was decided that a Jew was someone who had "three grandparents who were racially full-Jews," a practicing Jew with only two Jewish grandparents, or someone with two Jewish grandparents who was married to a Jew. Those who only had two Jewish grandparents were dubbed "Jewish half-breeds," but for the time being still retained their civil rights. Marriages with Gypsies and colored people were also forbidden. Also in 1935 the "Law for the Protection of the Hereditary Health of the German People" made it impossible for people with hereditary diseases to marry.

Although the Nazis insisted that the Jews were a race, they were thus obliged to use religious criteria for deciding who was Jewish. A grotesque and tragic exception was in the Crimea where Otto Ohlendorf, a brilliant academic economist turned mass-murderer, ordered his "Einsatzgruppe D" to kill 6,000 Tartar Krimshaks whom racial experts certified as Jewish. The Turkic Karaimen, who practiced a heterodox form of Judaism were spared. But other factors played an important role in this bizarre episode. The Karaimen had fought with the Whites in the Civil War, whereas the Krimshaks supported the Bolsheviks. For some equally unfathomable reason Portuguese Jews were also deemed to be Aryans.

The Nuremberg laws were something of a compromise and did not satisfy the more radical anti-Semites in the party. Although the Nazis continued to insist that Jews were a race, with the two exceptions above, the definition of who was Jewish was based solely on religious affiliation. It did not occur to the hordes of crackpot racial researchers and skull-measurers that there could be no other definition. Jews had already been excluded from the civil service and the professions, and by 1938 60 percent of Jewish businesses had been confiscated. The once prosperous Jewish community was now poverty-stricken and subjected to never-ending humiliation and chicanery. In April 1938 they were forced to make a full disclosure of their assets. In July they were given special identity cards. In August they were obliged to add the first names Sarah or Israel to their existing names, and their passports were stamped with a "J." German Jews thus lost their individual identity, a fact that was further underlined by the Nazi habit of referring to the Jews as "the Jew" (*der Jude*). In November Jewish children were forbidden to attend state schools.

The fresh wave of radical anti-Semitism in 1938 was particularly strong in Berlin, where Goebbels announced that the capital would soon be "uncontaminated by Jews" (*Judenrein*). He told a meeting of 300 policemen that: "Law is not the order of the day, but harassment." In the summer synagogues and Jewish shops were ransacked and the appallingly corrupt police chief, Count Helldorf, proved most cooperative with the Nazi thugs. In addition to ordering his men to make life as unpleasant as possible for Berlin's Jews, he amassed a vast fortune by confiscating the passports of rich Jews and selling them back for up to 250,000 marks apiece. Later he was to see the writing on the wall, joined the conspirators of July 20 1944, was tortured, and hanged.

The SD now decided upon a policy of "ordered harassment" (*geordneter Schikanieren*). This involved local bans on Jews from visiting public parks, theaters, cinemas, and the like. With very few exceptions Jews were banned from practicing medicine, the law, and similar professions. This placed the Nazis in a bind: on the one hand they wanted the Jews to leave Germany, on the other they had reduced them to such a state of poverty that they were unable to bear the cost of emigration. Violence, as in Austria, now seemed an attractive alternative.

On November 7 1938 Ernst von Rath, a diplomat serving in the German embassy in Paris, was assassinated by a young Polish-German Jew by the name of Herschel Grynszpan. It was an act of revenge for the gross mistreatment of his parents by the Gestapo. They were among the 75,000 Polish Jews expelled from Germany, whom the Poles promptly refused citizenship. A few obtained passages to America, the majority were interned. Rath died on November 9, the anniversary of Hitler's putsch in Munich, where the party leadership was assembled for the yearly celebrations. A "spontaneous expression of popular outrage" was carefully organized by Goebbels on Hitler's orders, and the Gauleiter let loose the SA in a nationwide pogrom euphemistically known as "The Night of Broken Glass" (*Reichskristallnacht*). It was a night of shattered lives and broken hopes, in which some 100 Jews were brutally murdered, several hundred synagogues burnt to the ground, and countless Jewish stores, apartments, and houses ransacked. Thirty thousand Jewish men were arrested and shipped off to concentration camps. That same night Himmler spoke in apocalyptic terms of a war to the death between Germans and Jews.

The majority of Germans averted their gaze while disapproving of the SA rowdies, who reminded them of the bad old days of Nazi violence, and somewhat sanctimoniously expressed their horror at the material damage that had been done. Some were concerned about the reaction from abroad. Precious few helped the unfortunate victims of this outrage. The 250,000 Jews who still remained in Germany were fined 1,000 million marks for the damage done by the SA, who were said to have been provoked. Göring seized the proceeds of all the insurance claims. Finally, all remaining Jewish stores and businesses were "Aryanized." They were confiscated by the state and sold off to non-Jews at well below their market value. Throughout the Reich all Jews were now forbidden to go to the theater, the cinema, or to public swimming pools. They were thus excluded from German society and barely able to exist.

There were clear indications that even worse was to come. The official SS magazine, the *Schwarze Korps*, called for the "extinction" and the "total annihilation" of this "parasitic race." On November 12 Göring told a meeting of senior officials that in the event of a war Germany would "first of all settle accounts with the Jews." November 9 1938 thus marked the end of the phase of pogrom anti-Semitism and the beginning of a bureaucratized and systematic approach to a "final solution." The Nazis had by now decided that "harassment" was not enough, more drastic measures were needed.

13
Nazi Germany: 1933–45

Hitler had promised to put Germany back to work, and he was true to his word. Within four years unemployment had been virtually overcome, and in some sectors there was even a shortage of skilled labor. He benefited from programs that had already been put in train by the Papen and Schleicher administrations, but the National Socialists set about them with exceptional energy and determination. Plans for a network of highways (*Autobahnen*) had already been laid, but Hitler gave this program top priority. An initial 1.7 thousand million marks were invested in road building, thus providing employment for thousands and scoring a major propaganda victory. A further 1.3 thousand million was invested in housing, and one thousand million in government buildings. From 1936 armaments were given top priority, so that expenditure on weapons increased from 720 million marks in 1933 to 10.8 thousand million in 1937. In the six peacetime years, the government spent the staggering sum of 90 thousand million marks on armaments.

Expenditure on this scale could not be covered by revenue, or offset by the six-month compulsory labor service, which was introduced in 1935. At first the regime used the same methods as Papen and Schleicher, who had financed their Keynesian schemes by bills of exchange. In May 1933 four large companies, Krupp, Siemens, the Gutehoffnungshütte, and Rheinmetall, pooled their resources and formed the Metallurgical Research Association (Mefo), with capital of 1,000 million marks. The government paid for armaments orders given to these four companies with five-year promissory notes, guaranteed by the government, and known as Mefo Bills. The government then discounted them, so that the Mefo Bills acted as a form of currency. Mefo Bills worth thousands of millions of marks thus fell due in 1938 and the government took recourse to highly dubious methods in order to pay the bill. Tax relief was offered in lieu of payment, banks were forced to buy government bonds, and the government took money from savings accounts and insurance companies. In 1937 the central bank was no longer able to control the volume of money in circulation, so that the government used the printing press to meet the cash shortage.

Concentration on rearmament meant that the government soon faced an acute shortage of foreign exchange, and consequently a severe shortage of raw materials.

Plate 21 Göring and Hitler. © Bundesarchiv

Schacht's "New Plan" of 1934 introduced strict currency controls, but they did little to stem the persistent drain on reserves. The Four Year Plan of 1936, which was designed to overcome these problems, placed the economy under strict government control and aimed at autarchy. Synthetic rubber and substitute fuel was produced on a vast scale and domestic ores exploited in an attempt to lessen dependence on foreign suppliers. Once again the party took the helm, with Göring as a virtual economic dictator setting the course. Two Gauleiter, Walter Köhler and Adolf Wagner, were made responsible respectively for the allocation of raw materials and for setting prices. Senior officers in Göring's Luftwaffe were put in charge of oil and energy. Carl Krauch from IG Farben was given plenipotentiary powers over the chemical industry, but he succeeded in keeping it firmly in private hands. Hjalmar Schacht felt that this approach to Germany's pressing economic problems was disastrous and ceased to be minister of economics in 1937. He left the Reichsbank two years later. Just as Schacht had predicted, the autarchy programme was an expensive failure. Vast amounts of capital were invested in the Buna and Leuna works near Halle, but Germany was still dependent on foreign supplies of rubber and oil. Domestic iron ore was of very inferior quality and was extremely expensive to mine and smelt, so that half of the iron ore still had to be imported. Germany was also dependent on imports of manganese, chrome, and wolfram, and was still far from self-sufficient in foodstuffs.

The regime tried to produce both guns and butter, but armaments took precedence over consumer goods. By the summer of 1935 industrial production and employment was back at the 1928 level, and there was no longer any need to prime the pump. The problems that beset the economy were now almost solely due to excessive government expenditure on armaments, and thus in spite of the remarkable economic recovery between 1933 and 1939, life remained very austere. The Nazis put Germany back to work, but the condition of the working class was still wretched, and there was an increasing number of complaints about food shortages and the paucity of the better things in life. A report in September 1935 showed that almost half of German workers earned less than 18 marks per week, which was below the poverty level. Nationwide the standard of living was still below that of 1928. Food prices were rising rapidly, placing further strain on low-income families. In 1938 meat consumption was still below the 1929 level and there was a shortage of quality consumer goods. Industrial wages did not reach 1928 levels until 1941, and then largely because of long hours of overtime rather than increases in basic wages.

Early experiments with National Socialist unions were hastily dropped. Known as "National Socialist Works Cell Organizations" (NSBO) they attracted disaffected left-wing elements who had the temerity to try to further the interests of the membership. In the summer of 1933 "Trustees of Labor" were appointed by the ministry of labor to determine wages, contracts, and working conditions. Since these officials were mostly recruited from management they looked after the interests of the employers rather than those of the employees. Robert Ley was obliged to purge the German Labor Front (DAF) of all those who hoped to create National Socialist unions, and now concentrated on the educational programs and leisure time activities run by "Strength Through Joy" (KdF). This vast organization, founded in November 1933, offered further education courses, theatrical performances, concerts, sports, holidays at home and abroad, and even cruises. The DAF was thus rendered totally docile and workers no longer had any voice in management. In November 1933 Gustav Krupp von Bohlen und Halbach agreed that businessmen should be included in the DAF. In the following year the DAF was reorganized with four "pillars:" blue-collar workers, white-collar workers, industrialists, and small businessmen. It had 40,000 fulltime staff and 1.3 million volunteers. One-point-five percent of workers' wages was deducted to cover costs.

The concessions that had been made to labor during the Weimar Republic were all revoked and a businessman was now master in his own house. The "leadership principle" (*Führerprinzip*) now applied in the business world. The "Works Führer" ruled supreme over the "Works Community." When members of various factory councils complained about this denial of all workers' rights in 1935 the system was changed so that council members were no longer elected but were appointed by the trustees. Workers were now issued with "Labor Books," which drastically curtailed their freedom of movement from one place of employment to another.

The peasantry was the darling of the Nazi propagandists, the "biological kernel" of Germany's future greatness, where "blood and soil" were one. They were susceptible to such flattery and flocked to the Nazi cause, but once the Nazis were in power they were treated in much the same way as industrial workers. Walter Darré's "Reich Food Department" (*Reichsnährstand*) exercised dominion over its 17 million members. It was a mammoth bureaucratic organization that, hydra-like, touched all aspects of rural life. It controlled production, prices, and marketing of all agricultural products. It made desperate but vain attempts to bind the peasantry to the land and stop the flight to the urban areas in pursuit of higher wages. One such attempt was the creation of "Hereditary Farms" (*Erbhöfe*), whereby peasants of "German or racially similar blood" were given entailed farms of up to 125 hectares (312 acres). This amounted to a new form of serfdom in that elder sons were tied to the soil, and the farm could not be sold. It did nothing to stop the movement away from the land and the number of those employed in agriculture dropped by 440,000 between 1933 and 1939. The result was a chronic shortage of farm laborers that could only be made good after 1939 by the use of foreign labor and prisoners of war. In spite of all these efforts, the results were somewhat disappointing. Germany managed to reduce its dependence on imported foodstuffs, and there were substantial increases in the production of certain goods. Prices rose sharply and caused widespread discontent. For all the talk of "blood and soil" it was Slav blood that worked German soil in the war years.

Extravagant promises had also been made to the middle class and they too quickly saw their hopes dashed. The National Socialists had pledged to break the stranglehold of the big department stores and help the struggling butchers, bakers, and candlestick makers. In fact the number of small businesses declined sharply. Many were simply closed down as the economy came under ever closer state control, a process that was stepped up markedly in the latter stages of the war. Others were starved of labor. The department stores were obliged to pay higher taxes but their share of the market increased. Competition from Jewish businesses was savagely ended, and many small businessmen joined the unseemly scramble to snap up Jewish property for bargain basement prices. But even this windfall did not offset the overall losses.

Women in Nazi Germany

For many years historians largely ignored the female half of the population of Nazi Germany, until feminists sharpened their pens and set to work restoring the balance. The picture that emerged was of a society run by misogynist monsters, brutal machos, and mad scientists bent on mass sterilization, in which women were cast into the depths of a gynaecophobic hell, where their only function was to bear a series of warrior children sired by callous patriarchs. Subsequent research by more level-headed social historians reveals a more nuanced picture.

For many women life in the Third Reich was indeed hellish. Jewish women suffered unimaginable horrors, as did the hapless victims of the eugenicists; and the wives, daughters, and sisters of political prisoners who were punished for crimes committed by male members of the family – a system known as "*Sippenhaft*" (clan arrest) – should not be forgotten. Nevertheless, the lot of the vast majority of women in the Third Reich improved greatly. Their husbands had a steady job, real wages were rising, admittedly from a very low level, and the future looked promising. Married couples were given a loan of 1,000 Reichmarks, provided that the woman stayed at home. One quarter of the loan was written off with each child born. Generous tax relief was given for children, and family allowances were paid with the third child, payments coming from the brimming unemployment insurance fund. Medical services for women were also greatly improved. Five million women had visited the new "Maternity Schools" by 1944, and ten million women availed themselves of the services of special advice centers. Pregnant working women were given six weeks of leave with full pay before and after a birth, a policy that was unrivaled anywhere else in the world. Free holidays were also provided for mothers and children. A large number of daycare centers were established. Generous provision was made for unwed mothers, provided of course that the offspring were of suitable racial stock. Women were appreciative of these measures, and gave the state their grateful loyalty.

If this was no hell for women, it was also no paradise, and there were many negative aspects of Nazi policy toward women. Under ideal circumstances they were to be confined to the home as mothers of racially sound children, all in the interests of eugenics, racial politics, and preparation for war. The Führer needed children, and to this end "Mother's Day," which had been instigated during the Weimar Republic, was made into the central event of the Nazi fertility cult, celebrated with great pomp, ceremony, and pathos. The "Mother's Service Medal" was awarded to those with four children and more, graded according to number of children. Motherhood ceased to be a private affair, and was seen as a public service that helped improve the racial stock and create a genuine "racial community." To this end abortions, which prior to 1933 were estimated to average 600,000 annually, were made illegal. Birth control devices were virtually unobtainable, except for Jews and other undesirables. Compulsory abortions were performed on the racially unwanted and the eugenically suspect. A new law on marriage and divorce in 1938 further reduced women's legal rights.

The birth rate increased from 14.7 per thousand in 1932 to 18.6 per thousand in 1936, but this was the result of improvements in the economy rather than ideological pressure. The number of women workers increased sharply, particularly in low-paid and unskilled positions, and this in spite of the generous loans offered to married women who left the workforce. At the other end of the scale many women with university degrees were forced to quit their jobs, and only a very limited number of women were admitted to institutions of higher learning. Women were weeded out of the civil service and were no longer permitted to practice law, or to hold senior positions in education.

National Socialist policies toward women were thus profoundly contradictory. Women were to serve the Führer and *Volk* by raising large numbers of children and tending the family home, rather than going out to work. On the other hand, with the increasing shortage of labor, women were desperately needed in the workforce. By 1937 women no longer had to give up their jobs in order to qualify for the 1,000 RM marriage loan. Large numbers of women were also employed in the various women's organizations, social services, and medical facilities, as well as being needed to staff the National Socialists' mushrooming bureaucracy. Paradoxically, this had a liberating effect. Women felt that new opportunities had opened up for them, that they were making a vital contribution to society, and that their work was appreciated.

The persistent myth that German women were chained to *Kinder* (children) and *Küche* (kitchen) can be quickly dismissed. Fifty-two percent of German women between the ages of 15 and 60 were in regular employment by 1939. In Britain, by contrast the figure was 45 percent, and in the United States a mere 36 percent. Thirty-six percent of married women and 88 percent of unmarried women were wage earners. Women comprised 41 percent of the German workforce by 1940, whereas in Britain they made up only 29 percent. Hitler persistently resisted attempts to force women to work during the war for fear that it would have an adverse effect on morale, and lead to a repeat performance of the widespread discontent in 1918, which he believed was the major reason for Germany's defeat. He refused to allow women's wages to rise so as to equal men's, and soldiers' wives were given generous allowances in order to encourage them to stay at home. Nevertheless, women took on a number of jobs that previously had been exclusively reserved for men. Female bus conductors and readers of gas and electric meters were paid the same wages as men. Women doing piecework in the armaments industry were paid on the same scale as men. The chronic shortage of doctors meant that restrictions on the admission of women to medical schools had to be lifted. In 1933 only 6.5 percent of doctors were women, by 1944 the figure had risen to 17 percent. Nine hundred thousand women were eventually forced to work in 1943, but they came from the ranks of the underprivileged. For all the talk of community, women from higher up the social scale were exempt from labor service, and Nazi Germany thus clearly remained a two-class society. With the men at the front, women had to take on a whole host of new responsibilities and with them an increased autonomy, whether it was by running the family firm, looking after a farm, standing behind the counter, or providing services for the mounting number of refugees and those left homeless due to the bombing raids.

There were 3.3 million members of the National Socialist Women's Association (*Nationalsozialistischen Frauenschaft* – NSF), led by the formidable Gertrud Scholtz-Klink, a slender, blonde, blue-eyed mother of six. She was also the head of the German Women's League (*Deutsches Frauenwerk* – DFW), which had some 4.7 million members. In addition she was head of the women's section of the DAF. She was thus the most powerful woman in the Third Reich, but she was caught in the glaring contradiction between her vision of German women as submissive wives, mothers, and housewives, and as party activists in the NSF and DFW. Scholtz-Klink was unable to find a solution to this fundamental discrepancy, and her remark that the wooden spoon was as powerful a weapon as the machine-gun was somewhat unconvincing. She was further troubled by the contradiction between her own prudish sexual morality, and the racial theories of the party which made no distinction between legitimate and illegitimate motherhood.

Women were subjected to a great deal of ideological harassment and discrimination in a male-dominated society, but they also made great gains thanks to generous social policies, and an appreciation of their contributions to society both at work and in everyday life. Gertrud Scholtz-Klink might denounce the women's movement as a "symbol of decay," Hitler write of it as a product of the Jewish intellect, bent on the systematic destruction of the Aryan race, and Goebbels announce that women were being removed from public life in order to restore their essential dignity, but they were powerless against the pressures of a society stretched to the limit. In spite of fierce political resistance, the exigencies of a terrible war were such that women gained a degree of independence that was to fuel the demand for further emancipation in the postwar years.

First Steps in Foreign Policy

At first the regime moved very cautiously in the field of foreign affairs, and with its demands for a revision of the Treaty of Versailles it hardly distinguished itself from the other parties in Weimar Germany. Calls for the restoration of Germany's status as a great power and the return of the colonies were also commonplace in conservative and nationalist circles. But from the outset Hitler was determined to create a vast empire in Eastern Europe to secure "living space" (*Lebensraum*), and he was prepared to go to any lengths to achieve this goal. His single-minded determination, his gambler's instincts, and his ruthless pursuit of long-term goals alarmed his generals, and even the most robust among his myrmidons began to waver. As Hitler played for ever higher stakes and won every time, his prestige grew, his critics were silenced, and his charismatic status as a Führer of genius was further embellished. He was thus able to manipulate the conservative nationalists and use them to help realize his vision of *Lebensraum* and the extermination of the "racial enemies" who threatened the "racial community."

The international situation was very favorable for a forceful revisionist policy. The powers were seriously weakened by the depression. Collective security was in ruins with the Japanese invasion of Manchuria and the subsequent feeble response of the League of Nations. Reparations had effectively been ended in 1932, and Brüning had got within an inch of removing the military restrictions placed on Germany by the Versailles treaty. Hitler was anxious to allay the fears of Germany's neighbors while he established his dictatorship at home. To this end he retained the aristocratic career diplomat of the old school, Konstantin von Neurath, as foreign minister, along with his secretary of state, Wilhelm von Bülow. Diplomats in the Wilhelmstrasse seemed to have ignored Hitler's alarming message to his generals on February 3 1933 and did not think that the new government meant a radical change in course. They imagined that it would be possible to pursue a somewhat more aggressive policy than that of Stresemann whereby Germany's position would be strengthened by rearmament, unification (*Anschluss*) with Austria, and the restoration of the lost colonies.

Hitler's first major public address on foreign policy was made in the Reichstag on May 17 1933, and in it he promised to respect all international treaties and obligations, and called for a peaceful revision of the Versailles settlement. For all his anti-Marxist rhetoric, and whilst he was busy murdering communists at home, he signed a credit agreement with the Soviet Union on February 25 1933, and a friendship and non-aggression treaty on April 4. On October 14 the German government took the British and French proposal at Geneva that Germany should be given a four-year trial period before reaching a general agreement on disarmament as an excuse to leave the League of Nations. This was an enormously popular move in Germany, where the League was seen as little more than an instrument whereby the victorious powers upheld the "Diktat" of Versailles. This was followed by a surprising non-aggression pact with Poland on January 16 1934 which marked a radical departure from the pro-Soviet and anti-Polish policy of the Weimar Republic since Rapallo. The Poles had every reason to be suspicious, particularly as Hitler pointed out that the treaty did not mean that there would be no frontier changes between the two countries, but they felt abandoned by their French sponsors and believed they had no other choice.

Relations between Germany and Austria were extremely tense. Most Austrians had welcomed the idea of an *Anschluss*, but they had grave reservations now that Germany was in the hands of the National Socialists. The Austrian government complained bitterly about the massive financial help given to Austrian Nazis. The Germans replied by imposing a 1,000 mark tax on any German citizen traveling to Austria. This effectively closed the border and destroyed Austria's tourist trade. The Austrians then required visas, thus making it difficult for German Nazis to cross the border. The Austrian Nazis promptly stepped up their terror campaign that culminated in the assassination of the Chancellor Englebert Dollfuss on July 25 1934. Mussolini, anxious to maintain Austria as a buffer state between Italy and Germany, moved troops to the frontier, and Hitler thought it prudent to disavow any connection with his unruly followers in Austria.

Ninety-one percent of the electorate in the Saar voted in a plebiscite to return to Germany on January 13 1935, in spite of massive antifascist propaganda in this largely working class mining area. In February Hitler invited the British foreign secretary, Sir John Simon, and the Lord Privy Seal, Anthony Eden, to visit Berlin on March 7 to discuss an Anglo-French communiqué which proposed certain measures to avoid a renewed arms race. Then only three days before the British delegation was due to arrive, the British government published a White Paper on defense that called for substantial increases in spending on the armed forces, said to be in direct response to Hitler's overbearingly belligerent tone. Hitler, buoyed up by his remarkable victory in the Saar, promptly postponed the visit, feigning an indisposition, and took great delight in thus snubbing the British government. Six days later, on March 10, Göring announced the formation of the Luftwaffe, the German air force that was expressly forbidden under the terms of the Treaty of Versailles. On March 15 the French National Assembly approved an increase in the term for military service from one to two years. Then on March 16 Hitler announced the introduction of universal military service in order to create an army of 550,000 men. Simon and Eden eventually came to Berlin on March 25. They were treated to a series of monologues, most of them on Hitler's favorite topic of the menace of Bolshevism, and were scarcely able to get a word in edgeways. When they did manage to register a complaint, they were shot down in flames. When Sir John Simon complained of Germany's breach of the disarmament clauses of the Treaty of Versailles, Hitler archly inquired whether Wellington had raised similar objections when Blücher arrived on the field at Waterloo.

The French were particularly concerned with recent developments in Germany. In reaction to the Röhm putsch in June and the Austrian crisis in the following month, they began fence-building with the countries in central and eastern Europe and made approaches to Moscow. The result was the Franco-Soviet mutual assistance pact of May 2 1935, whereupon the Soviet Union joined the League of Nations. For the Soviets this was a mighty antifascist coalition, but it was a fissiparous alliance fraught with all manner of ideological differences and conflicts of interest. Meanwhile, France's efforts to persuade Britain and Italy to stand together against German violations of the Treaty of Versailles resulted in the Stresa front of April 14 1935, which upheld the Locarno treaty of 1925, and guaranteed the international status quo.

Hitler was not in the least bit concerned. Having clearly dominated the talks with Simon and Eden, he was convinced that if he kept up a bold front the British would be accommodating. Accordingly he sent his special representative, Joachim von Ribbentrop, to London to follow up on the British delegation's visit to Berlin. He reminded Paul Schmidt, Hitler's interpreter and a keen observer of human frailty, of the dog on HMV records. He was an insufferably ill-mannered former sparkling wine salesman, whose boorish behavior soon earned him the sobriquet "von Brickendrop." He immediately demanded that Germany should be given a free hand in Europe to destroy the Soviet Union. In return Britannia could continue to rule the waves and concentrate on the empire. The British government did not take kindly to this proposal to divide the world, and threatened to cancel the talks, but eventually agreed to a naval agreement on June 18 1935, whereby the ratio of British to German surface fleets was fixed at 100 to 35. Submarines, Hitler's favored weapon, were not included. Hitler had every reason to consider this as his "happiest day." The British had single-handedly torn up the disarmament clauses of the Versailles treaty, without even consulting their French allies. The British, whose eyes were on the very real threat posed by Japan, were relieved that an understanding had been reached, and were determined to avoid any confrontation with Germany.

Encouraged by the feeble response of the British and French to Italy's aggression in Ethiopia, and taking the ratification of the Franco-Soviet treaty as a excuse, Hitler ordered the remilitarization of the Rhineland on March 2 1936, having first received assurances from Mussolini that he had no serious objections to such a move. France was in the middle of an election campaign and the government was paralyzed. The British did not feel that their vital interests were affected. On March 7 Hitler announced in the Reichstag that he had no further territorial demands. Eden told the House of Commons that there was no cause for alarm. Churchill's jeremiads were dismissed as the fulminations of an elderly politician totally out of touch with the times.

Hitler's triumph in the Rhineland helped silence those who complained about the hardships caused by the concentration on rearmament and the harassment of the churches. In the elections held on March 29, 98.8 percent voted for the "Führer's list." Hitler's descent into outright megalomania was greatly accelerated by these giddy successes. His speeches were now full of references to providential guidance, his sacred mission, and his visionary prescience, while Goebbels' propaganda machine pumped out clouds of adulatory incense in honor of this preternatural being.

After some initial hesitation Hitler, prompted by ideological and economic considerations, decided to intervene in the Spanish Civil War. He now found himself fighting alongside Mussolini for General Franco's nationalists, against the republicans in the "Marxist" popular front. Mussolini had already expressed his gratitude for German neutrality over Ethiopia by ceasing to support the Austrian Heimwehr against the National Socialists and making it plain that he now had no objections to an *Anschluss*. The Italian foreign minister, Ciano, went to Berlin in October 1936 and signed a pact of mutual cooperation. He then visited Hitler in his Bavarian mountaintop retreat, where his host proposed an offensive treaty designed to crush Marxism and to bring Britain to heel. Hitler said that the German army would be ready to go to war within three to five years. On November 1 Mussolini first spoke openly of an "axis" from Rome to Berlin, and invited other European states to cooperate.

Meanwhile Ribbentrop, frustrated that he had been unable to win over the British government, worked feverishly to secure an agreement with Japan, so as to form a triple alliance that would leave Britain isolated. Both the German Foreign Office and the Wehrmacht leadership were opposed to this idea, and there was considerable resistance on the Japanese side as well. Major-General Hiroshi Oshima, the

military attaché who was to become ambassador later in 1936, was an enthusiastic admirer of National Socialism, and fought long and hard for an agreement with
Germany. The result was the Anti-Comintern Pact of November 1936, a vague
understanding that Hitler felt might help put pressure on Britain to reach an understanding with Germany.

Rearmament was now putting an intolerable strain on the economy. There was
a chronic shortage of foreign exchange and import prices had risen an average of
nine percent since 1933. There was a shortage of foodstuffs resulting from a series
of poor harvests, so that the regime was faced with the choice of guns or butter.
Hitler was determined to keep up the pace of rearmament, and therefore supported
those who argued that domestic sources of raw materials should be exploited and
synthetic rubber and petroleum produced so as to reduce the reliance on imports.
He brusquely dismissed all concerns about the horrendous cost of autarchy, imag-
ining that it would be offset by the rich booty acquired from a war of conquest. In
a secret memorandum in August 1936 Hitler said that the country had to be ready
for war within four years, and that a series of short campaigns would then result
in an "increase in *Lebensraum* and thus of raw materials and foodstuffs."

Hitler gave vent to increasingly frequent outbursts about the necessity of finding
a solution to "Germany's space question," and of the need to settle matters by force
as early as 1938. On November 5 1937 he called a top-level meeting in the chancellery attended by von Neurath, the war minister von Blomberg, as well as the
commanders-in-chief of the army, the navy, and the air force, von Fritsch, Raeder,
and Göring. They were treated to a four-hour monologue which Hitler announced
should be taken as his testament in the event of his death. It began with a rambling
discourse on familiar topics such as social Darwinism, race and geopolitics, and the
need to strengthen the "racial mass" (*Volksmasse*) and to secure *Lebensraum*. None
of these outstanding problems could be solved without recourse to force. He then
announced that in the first stage Austria would have to be annexed, and then
Czechoslovakia would be attacked. Germany would have to be prepared to fight
both England and France should they decide to intervene. Hitler brushed aside all
objections, but realized that he would have to replace traditionally-minded men like
Neurath and Fritsch to secure the cooperation of the Foreign Office and the army
for his hazardous policy.

The *Anschluss*

In January 1938 Austrian police unearthed evidence that the National Socialists
were planning to cause so much disorder that the Germans would have an excuse
to intervene in order to restore law and order. The Austrian chancellor Schuschnigg
decided to visit Hitler in an attempt to ease the tension between the two countries.
He arrived in Berchtesgaden on February 12 1938 and was immediately subjected
to a vituperative tirade from Hitler, who accused Austria of all manner of misdemeanors including "racial treason." He warned the Austrian chancellor that he only

had to give the order and the country would be destroyed. Ribbentrop then demanded that the National Socialist Arthur Seyß-Inquart should be put in charge of home security, that there should be a general amnesty for all Nazis, and that Austria's foreign and economic policies should be coordinated with the Reich. Talks between the two general staffs should also be scheduled.

Schuschnigg felt that he had no alternative but to accept, but on his return home he called for a referendum for a "free, German, independent, social, Christian and united Austria" to be held on March 13. The Nazis saw this as a provocation, the more so since younger voters, who were highly susceptible to the movement, were excluded, and Austria descended into violent anarchy. The Austrian president Wilhelm Miklas courageously refused Hitler's demand that Seyß-Inquart be appointed chancellor, whereupon the Austrian Nazis seized government buildings in Vienna. Hitler then gave orders to his troops to cross the frontier. The German army met with a rapturously enthusiastic welcome on March 12, and Hitler made a triumphant return to his birthplace at Braunau before moving on to Linz where, impressed by the vast and enthusiastic crowds, he announced that Austria would be incorporated into the German Reich. From Linz he traveled to Vienna where he addressed an even larger crowd of ecstatic devotees. On April 10 a referendum was held in which 99 percent of those eligible, including the Austrian Socialist leader Karl Renner, voted in favor of the *Anschluss*. Austria promptly ceased to exist and became a German province known as the Ostmark. The German mark replaced the Austrian schilling, and overnight Austrians had to learn to drive on the right-hand side of the road like the Germans.

For the Austrian Jewish community these were days of horror. Austrian Nazis were even more vicious and brutal in their anti-Semitism than their German comrades, and this in turn helped to radicalize the Germans immediately after the *Anschluss*. Units of the SS and police followed behind the army, and with their Austrian supporters carried out a bestial pogrom in which thousands of innocent victims were murdered, brutally beaten, imprisoned, and their property seized. Their humiliation and savage mistreatment was savored by jeering crowds. It was a gruesome foretaste of what was to happen in Germany on November 9.

Czechoslovakia and Appeasement

Boosted by his triumph in Austria, encouraged by the supine attitude of Britain and France and by Mussolini's support, Hitler now turned his attention to Czechoslovakia. On April 21 he told the military that he would either go to war after a few preliminary diplomatic moves, or would use some incident to strike a lightning blow. He had already decided on the latter alternative and had instructed the Sudeten German leader Konrad Henlein to make demands of the Czechoslovakian government that could not possibly be fulfilled. On May 30 Hitler announced that he intended "to destroy Czechoslovakia by military means in the foreseeable future." Throughout the summer of 1938 there was widespread violence in the Sudetenland as the crisis deepened. On September 15 the British prime minister Neville Chamberlain flew to Munich to meet Hitler at Berchtesgaden, and told him that neither Britain nor France would object to parts of the Sudetenland being handed over to Germany. Hitler was caught by surprise by Chamberlain's readiness to give way and decided to take a tougher line when they met again at Bad Godesberg on September 22. He had already told the Polish and Hungarian governments that he would support their claims against Czechoslovakia, and he now told Chamberlain that he was prepared to use force if his wishes were not immediately granted.

War now seemed inevitable. Both Czechoslovakia and France mobilized. Britain prepared for war, and the Soviet Union promised support. Hitler moved seven divisions up to the Czech border. Opposition forces in Germany went into action. General Ludwig Beck had already resigned as chief of staff in August in protest against Hitler's risky policy. Now Colonel Hans Oster from military counterintelligence, and the mayor of Leipzig, Carl Goerdeler, contacted British politicians and begged that a firm stand be taken against Hitler. Much to Hitler's disgust the majority of Germans viewed the prospect of war with sullen apprehension. Prompted by Mussolini and by a further offer from Chamberlain, Hitler agreed to meet with the British and French prime ministers in Munich on September 29. Without consulting either Czechoslovakia or the Soviet Union, Chamberlain and Daladier agreed that those areas in the Sudetenland where the Germans had a majority should be handed over to Germany between October 1 and 10 1938.

In one sense Munich was a triumph for Hitler. He had gained an important industrial area, rich in natural resources, and with a highly skilled labor force. Czechoslovakia was now virtually defenseless and its economy was in ruins. But Hitler had been denied the crisis that he needed were he to destroy the country and make a triumphal entry into Prague. He was furious that Chamberlain and Daladier were seen as heroes by the majority of Germans and asked: "How can I go to war with a people like this?!" On November 10, the day after the pogrom, Hitler gave a lengthy speech to representatives of the press, ordering them to desist from all talk of peace and to steel the people for war. On October 21 1938 he issued instructions for the destruction of Czechoslovakia and the occupation of the Memel. To this end the Slovak president Monsignor Jozef Tiso was ordered to declare Slovak independence.

Nazi Germany was now on a headlong course toward war. It was driven forward by its inner dynamics and was virtually out of control. Hitler was now an absolute dictator who paid no attention to the mounting crisis in the economy, and was impervious to all notes of caution. He rambled on incessantly about a "battle of world views" and a "racial war." On January 30 1939, the sixth anniversary of the "seizure of power," he told the Reichstag: "If international Jewry in Europe and elsewhere plunge the peoples once again into a world war, the result will not be the Bolshevization of the world, and thus a Jewish victory, but the destruction of the Jewish race in Europe." Hitler now promised to create a vast German empire, one that was purified of all alien racial elements. There could now be no turning back.

Tiso slavishly obeyed his orders from Berlin and declared Slovak independence on March 14. That day the Czech president Emil Hacha traveled to Berlin in a desperate attempt to preserve the independence of his rump state. Hitler ranted and raved, and the unfortunate Hacha suffered a heart attack. Having been revived by Hitler's personal physician, Dr Theodor Morell, he was told that if he did not hand over the state to Nazi Germany it would be invaded. A shattered president then signed a document placing his unhappy and betrayed people "confidently into the hands of the Führer of the German Reich." German troops crossed the frontier that night. Hitler traveled to Prague the following day, to be met by a silent, crushed, and tearful crowd. The Czech Republic was transformed into the "Protectorate of Bohemia and Moravia," and was thus submitted to a pitiless occupation regime.

The Polish Crisis

On March 21 German troops occupied Memel (Klaipéda), German territory that had been awarded to Lithuania under the terms of the Memel Statute of 1923. This strengthened Poland's resolve to resist further German demands over the Danzig question. On March 31 the British government gave a guarantee to both Poland and Romania. Hitler was furious. On April 3 he ordered plans to be drawn up for the invasion of Poland. His 50th birthday was celebrated on April 20 with a massive military march-past in Berlin, and one week later he rescinded the Non-Aggression Pact with Poland of 1934 and the Anglo-German Naval Agreement of 1935. The next day he rejected President Roosevelt's appeal for world peace in an unrelentingly derisive speech.

Britain and France now made a somewhat half-hearted attempt to bring the Soviet Union into a European security pact, but Stalin was deeply distrustful of these two imperialist powers. Neither Poland nor Romania were at all keen to entrust their security to a power that harbored substantial claims on their territory. In May the Soviet commissar for foreign affairs, Maxim Litvinov, who was both pro-Western and Jewish, was replaced by the boot-faced Stalinist Molotov. This move was seen as a clear signal to Berlin, and was underlined by frequent mentions of Rapallo. Hitler decided to test the water. The "Pact of Steel" between Berlin and Rome did not amount to much, since Mussolini had made it plain that Italy would not be ready for war until 1943. Talks with Japan over a similar military alliance had come to nothing. He had set August 26 as the date for an invasion of Poland and he was virtually without an ally in this hazardous undertaking. Joachim von Ribbentrop, who had replaced von Neurath as foreign minister in 1938, made the first move toward Molotov, who reacted positively. Ribbentrop flew to Moscow on August 23 and was immediately taken to see Stalin. He thus became the first minister of a foreign government to meet the Soviet dictator. Agreement was reached within a few hours, once Hitler agreed that the Soviets should be given all of Latvia. The Ribbentrop–Molotov Pact, which was in fact negotiated personally by Stalin, was a non-aggression pact to last for ten years and to go into effect immediately.

In a secret protocol the Soviet Union was given a free hand in eastern Poland up to the line of the Narev, Vistula, and San rivers, along with Estonia, Latvia, Finland, and Bessarabia. The future of Poland was to be settled at a later date. After the signing ceremony numerous toasts were drunk in vodka, and the gangsters swapped what passed for jokes in such circles. These sordid jollifications lasted until 2 a.m.

On August 25, the eve of the planned invasion of Poland, Hitler suffered two setbacks. The British government finally sealed the pact with Poland, and Mussolini let it be known that he would not join in the war. Hitler nervously inquired whether the attack could be postponed. He was assured that it could be. September 1 was set as the new date. Göring warned Hitler that he should not play *va banque*. Hitler replied: "I have played *va banque* my entire life!" This time there was to be no further delay. At 4.45 on the morning of September 1 the battleship *Schleswig-Holstein* opened fire on the Polish garrison on the Westerplatte near Danzig, while Stuka dive-bombers swooped down on the city. Europe was once again at war.

War

Britain and France declared war on September 3, and the dominions followed suit a few days later, but they did nothing to help Poland. The "phoney war" in the west enabled the Germans to concentrate on a swift campaign in the east. Within a week they had reached the outskirts of Warsaw. One week later the city was encircled. On September 17 the Polish government left the country, and the Soviets invaded that very day. Warsaw capitulated ten days later, having been flattened by aerial and artillery bombardment. The next day Germany and the Soviet Union divided up the spoils of war. Lithuania was given to the Soviets; the Germans got Warsaw and Lublin. The fighting ended on October 6.

SS "*Einsatzgruppen*," made up of men chosen from the SD and from the Security Police (Sipo), followed behind the victorious Wehrmacht. They were ordered to "fight all elements behind the fighting troops who are enemies of the Reich and the German people." They immediately set to work arresting 30,000 representatives of the Polish elites who were thrown into concentration camps where they were, in Heydrich's words, "rendered harmless." On September 21 Heydrich ordered all Jews to be herded into the larger cities. Meanwhile Himmler's order to summarily execute any "*franc-tireurs*" was given a generous interpretation, and the Einsatz-gruppen indulged in an orgy of slaughter. They were given the enthusiastic support of those Germans living in Poland who were organized in "Self-Protection" (*Selbst-schutz*) units, and by detachments of the Wehrmacht. To his lasting credit the commanding general in Poland, Blaskowitz, remonstrated vigorously at this bar-barism. Hitler dismissed his protest as "childish" and the result of a "Salvation Army attitude."

In October about half of German-occupied Poland was incorporated into the Reich; the remainder was called the General Government, which was to become a reservoir of helots to serve the master race. Hitler appointed Himmler "Reich Commissar for the Strengthening of the German Race," and he immediately set about expelling all Poles and Jews from areas recently annexed by Germany. By the end of 1940, 325,000 Polish citizens had been deported, their property stolen, their place taken by Germans from the Baltic states and Wolhynia. The population was divided into four categories according to National Socialist racial criteria. At the top of the ladder came the "Citizens of the Reich" (*Reichsbürger*), made up of ethnic Germans and Poles who were deemed to be capable of being turned into Germans (*eindeutschungsfähig*). Next came two classes of "Citizens" (*Staatsangehöriger*), who were regarded as being on trial to see if they could be made into true Germans. Lastly came the six million Poles labeled "Protected" (*Schutzangehörigen*), who were to serve their racial superiors. Of these "Protected" Poles, 311,000 were shipped off to work in the armaments industry in Germany, some voluntarily, others forcibly. A further 400,000 workers were sent by 1942. Meanwhile in early 1940 the newly annexed territories were proclaimed "free of Jews" (*Judenfrei*), and the Jews were forced into ghettos in Warsaw, Kraców, Lvov, Lublin, and Radom. Large numbers of Jews were denied this temporary respite, and were murdered by the Einsatzgruppen. The Germans were determined to exterminate the Polish intelligentsia, and 17 percent of those listed as "intellectuals" were murdered. Also in early 1940 the SS built a vast concentration camp at Auschwitz, where Polish prisoners were treated as slave labor and executed at will. The first victims of systematic industrialized murder at Auschwitz were Soviet prisoners of war, Poles, and sick inmates.

On the day that fighting stopped in Poland, Hitler made a peace offer to Britain and France. It was an entirely fraudulent move, for at the same time he issued orders for an invasion of Holland, Belgium, and France to take place as soon as possible, insisting that he had first to have his "hands free" in the west before taking on the Soviet Union. The military leadership felt that this was an extremely risky undertaking, and the commander-in-chief, Walther von Brauchitsch, tried to convince Hitler to change his mind, but to no avail. Bad weather finally obliged Hitler to agree to postpone the attack on the west until May 10 1940.

Some officers close to General Ludwig Beck plotted to overthrow Hitler. Göring again made a half-hearted attempt to stop the war, because he felt that the German armed forces were not sufficiently prepared to fight what he felt was likely to be a lengthy war. A few menacing remarks by Hitler about "defeatists" among his generals were enough to silence the opposition. Then on November 9 a cabinetmaker named Georg Elser planted a bomb under the podium in the Bürgerbräukeller in Munich where Hitler was due to address a meeting of "old fighters" on the occasion of the anniversary of the 1923 coup. The bomb went off, but it missed Hitler by a few minutes.

In April 1940 the Germans invaded Norway to forestall an Anglo-French expeditionary force, and to protect the Swedish ore fields which were vital to the war economy. Operation "Weser Exercise" (*Weserübung*) was swift, economical, and met with very little resistance; but the Royal Navy managed to sink a number of German ships. An attack on Denmark, "Weser Exercise South" was an even greater success, and the whole operation was over within 24 hours.

Despite Hitler's insistence to the contrary, the delay of the western offensive worked to Germany's advantage. Thanks to the Herculean efforts of Fritz Todt, armaments production had increased by 50 percent, and the army now had an excellent plan based on the ideas of General Erich von Manstein. Army Group A was to drive its armor and motorized infantry through the Ardennes and then head for the Channel coast at Dunkirk in a "sweep of the sickle." Army Group B was to occupy Belgium and Holland and thus trap the bulk of the enemy's forces between the two army groups. Army Group C was to tie down the French forces in the Maginot Line, without actually attacking these heavily fortified defensive positions.

The War in the West

The attack was launched on May 10 and went like clockwork. The French were caught off balance by the speed of the advance, and the British forced to abandon the Continent in "Operation Dynamo," a brilliantly organized evacuation. The "Spirit of Dunkirk" became part of popular mythology, and a humiliating defeat was transformed into a resounding triumph of the British spirit. The Third republic was riven with political dissent and began to fall apart. Armistice negotiations began on June 21, pointedly in the same railway carriage in which the Germans had been forced to capitulate in 1918.

Characteristically the conquered territories were treated differently, thus creating a hastily improvised confusion of military, state, and party administrative bodies. France was divided into the occupied northern zone and a rump state in the south, with an authoritarian government in the spa town of Vichy under Marshal Pétain, the octogenarian hero of Verdun. Alsace, Lorraine, and Luxembourg were annexed and ruled by Gauleiter. Belgium was placed under military occupation. Holland was governed by a Reich commissar. Denmark was left as a theoretically sovereign state; its government remained in office, the Germans transmitting their requests through traditional diplomatic channels. Even though it was under military occupation it retained its own armed forces. Josef Terboven was appointed Reich commissar for Norway who, ordered by Hitler, tried unsuccessfully to form a credible government under Vidkun Quisling, a contemptible stooge whom, like the vast majority of Norwegians, he heartily detested.

Hitler now turned his attention to Britain. It was a frustrating problem for him. He could not understand why the British refused to make peace at a time when they appeared to be helpless. Even if Germany defeated Britain, the problem of the empire would remain. Would it fall into the hands of the Japanese or the Americans, and thus immeasurably strengthen one or even both of Germany's future rivals? He agreed with his generals that an invasion was far too risky without first gaining absolute control over the air. To this end the Luftwaffe began massive attacks on August 5. By switching the attacks on August 24 from airstrips and radar installations to civilian targets, the "Few" in RAF fighter command were given a respite, and were able to win the "Battle of Britain." The air offensive was called off on

September 17, and Hitler thus suffered his first serious defeat, as he himself was grudgingly forced to admit. Admiral Raeder now suggested concentrating on attacking British forces in the Mediterranean and the Middle East.

Barbarossa

On July 31 Hitler ordered his generals to prepare an attack on the Soviet Union, arguing that it was "England's last hope." Given that all experts agreed that the Red Army was in a state of disarray, victory was assured. Hitler said: "We only have to kick in the front door and the whole rotten structure will collapse." Goebbels was of the same mind: "Bolshevism will collapse like a house of cards." With virtually all of continental Europe under German control, the United States would not dare to intervene. Germany would then have all the Lebensraum it could possibly want at its disposal. The theory that this was a preventive war fought because the Germans believed that the Soviets were about to attack is pure fantasy, behind which lurks a sinister political agenda.

Molotov visited Berlin on November 12 and 13, and Hitler made the preposterous suggestion that their two countries should divide up the spoils of the British Empire. Molotov replied that if Germany wished to maintain good relations with the Soviet Union it would have to agree to Soviet control over Finland, Romania, Bulgaria, and the Straits, all of which were vital to the defense of the Soviet Union. Later he added Hungary, Yugoslavia, and Eastern Poland to this impressive list. Hitler was relieved that Molotov had provided him with further reasons for pushing ahead with plans for an attack on the Soviet Union, and announced that his pact with Stalin "would not even remain a marriage of convenience." On December 18 he issued "Direction Number 21 for Case Barbarossa," which stated that "The German army must be ready to crush the Soviet Union in a swift campaign once the war against England is ended."

This was to be no ordinary war. Hitler announced that it would be "a battle between world views" in which the Einsatzgruppen would destroy the "Jewish-Bolshevik intelligentsia." No mercy was to be shown to the civilian population, Himmler and the SS were given "special tasks" within the Wehrmacht's operational area involving the "final battle between two opposing political systems." In January 1941 Himmler announced that 30 million people in the east would have to be removed in order to ensure an adequate supply of food for Germany. This figure was increased to 31 million in the "General Plan for the East," which Himmler published two days after the launching of "Barbarossa." Hitler gave repeated instruction to the military not to treat the Red Army as normal soldiers, to ignore the rules of war, and give no quarter. From the very beginning of the planning stage the Wehrmacht was deeply implicated in the criminal conduct of this unspeakably frightful campaign. Most of his generals enthusiastically endorsed Hitler's demented vision of a crusade against these Asiatic-Jewish-Bolshevik sub-humans. A few remained silent. None raised any serious objections.

Plate 22 Hitler and Goebbels. This image could not be published at the time because it showed Goebbels' club foot. © DIZ Munich

A decree was published on May 13 to the effect that "crimes committed by enemy civilians" did not have to go to trial and any "suspicious elements" should be shot on the spot on an officer's orders. No German soldier was to be punished for crimes committed against enemy civilians. This was an invitation to every perverted brute and sadist to have a field day. The infamous "Commissar Order" was issued on June 6, whereby any commissar captured in battle should be instantly shot. Commissars discovered behind the German lines were to be handed over to the

Einsatzgruppen for immediate dispatch. The army objected to both these orders on practical rather than moral grounds. It was frequently argued that the Commissar Order simply strengthened Soviet determination to resist, and military discipline was severely threatened by the limitation of the army's jurisdiction in the earlier decree.

General Georg Thomas, head of the Military Economic and Armaments Office, consulted with a number of prominent civilian officials from various ministries in the spring of 1941, and came to the conclusion that the Wehrmacht would have to live off the land in the Soviet Union. It was agreed that "several million" Soviet citizens would starve to death as a result, but these worthy civil servants viewed such a prospect with equanimity. The Wehrmacht and the SS were thus substantially in agreement that mass murder on a staggering scale was a desirable necessity. In May the Einsatzgruppen were ordered to kill all Jews in the occupied territories, since they were the "biological root" of Bolshevism. Since the Wehrmacht was responsible for the logistical support of the Einsatzgruppen, once again it was deeply implicated in this indescribable crime. The much-vaunted honor of the German army was lost forever.

In mid-December 1940 Hitler ordered preparations to be made for a campaign in the Balkans in order to secure the flank of "Barbarossa" and to protect the Romanian oil fields from attack by the RAF. A pro-Western coup in Belgrade at the end of March 1941 enraged Hitler, who ordered an immediate attack on Yugoslavia and Greece. Yugoslavia capitulated on April 17, Greece four days later. Large numbers of German troops were now tied down in the Balkans in a brutish and bloody campaign against highly motivated and skillful partisans.

The Germans attacked the Soviet Union on June 22 1941, with 153 divisions totaling about three million men. Anticipating a swift campaign lasting three months, there were precious few reserves at the ready, and no preparations were made for a winter campaign. The early stages of "Barbarossa" seemed to indicate that such confidence was justified. Within a few months Army Group North was approaching Leningrad, Army Group South had reached Kharkov, and Army Group Center began its final assault on Moscow. By mid-November the Wehrmacht was within 30 kilometers of the Soviet capital. On December 5 Zhukov launched a massive counteroffensive, striking north and south of Moscow. The Germans were forced back some 100 to 250 kilometers and all hopes for a swift campaign were dashed. Having been locked in seemingly endless arguments with Hitler throughout the summer as to where the main thrust (*Schwerpunkt*) of the attack should be, Brauchitsch handed in his resignation and Hitler appointed himself commander-in-chief.

Between June 22 1941 and March 1942 the Germans lost more than one million men. Only 450,000 replacements could be found. They had also lost enormous amounts of material, and were running short of food. As early as November General Friedrich Fromm, commander of the reserve army, felt that the situation was hopeless and urged Hitler to negotiate a peace. At the same time Fritz Todt also urged Hitler to end the war because of the parlous state of Germany's armaments industry. Hitler would not hear of this, and entertained dark apocalyptic thoughts of a

Götterdämmerung. "If the German Volk is not strong enough and is not sufficiently prepared to offer its own blood for its existence," he announced portentously, "it should cease to exist and be destroyed by a stronger power."

On December 11 Hitler declared war on the United States, four days after the attack on Pearl Harbor. It was another characteristic *va banque* play and a gesture of defiance, based on the gamble that he could win a victory in the Soviet Union before the Americans could engage in the European theater. Referring to a speech made by Hitler on December 12 Goebbels commented in his diary: "This is now a world war, and the annihilation of the Jews must be the necessary consequence." It was an extraordinarily risky and totally unnecessary move, in which the gambler made his first really serious miscalculation. Or did he already realize that all was lost and was preparing for the final Götterdämmerung?

By the time the spring offensive began only ten percent of the wheeled vehicles lost could be made good. A mere five percent of the Wehrmacht's divisions were fully operational. They pushed on regardless of the fact that there was a shortage of 650,000 men, profiting from the Soviets' poor intelligence and serious operational blunders. In the summer of 1942 Army Group A of Army Group South under Hitler's direct command was ordered to head for the Black Sea and the Caucasus. The bulk of Army Group B stationed around Kursk was to push on to the Don at Voronezh and then head southeast toward Stalingrad. Paulus' Sixth Army was to break out west of Kharkov and meet up with the rest of the Army Group.

The Battle of El Alamein beginning on October 23 1942, and the subsequent American "Torch" landings on November 8, spelt an end to the North African campaign. On November 19 1942 the Soviets launched a massive counteroffensive at Stalingrad that left Paulus' Sixth Army in a hopeless situation. Now nothing short of a miracle could bring victory. Hitler was so far removed from reality that his blind faith in destiny and his own unique genius was undiminished, and such was the nimbus that surrounded the "Greatest Commander of All Time" (sometimes disrespectfully shortened to "*Gröfaz*") that precious few grasped the true gravity of the situation.

The Beginnings of the Shoah

With the invasion of the Soviet Union the Nazi persecution of the Jews entered its final and most terrible stage. When the General Government was created out of the remains of Poland, Heydrich hoped to create a "Jewish Reservation" in the Lublin area as a temporary measure, prior to a "territorial solution" of the "Jewish problem" somewhere in the east. This proved impractical as the area was simply not large enough, and the Jews were herded into ghettos in the larger cities. Hans Frank, the governor of the Protectorate, also vigorously objected to the proposal, as he wanted to make his satrapy uncontaminated by Jews (*Judenrein*).

After the fall of France, Franz Rademacher, head of section III (Jewish Questions) in the Foreign Office, suggested that the western European Jews could be shipped off to Madagascar. Eastern Jews were considered "more fertile, and would produce future generations versed in the Talmud and forming a Jewish intelligentsia." They should be used as hostages so as to silence American Jews. Adolf Eichmann enthusiastically endorsed the Madagascar plan, which had long been popular in anti-Semitic circles. It was assumed that climatic conditions on the island were such that the death rate would be exceedingly high, but with Britain still determined to fight on, and with the consequent shipping problem, this scheme had to be dropped.

Meanwhile, conditions in the overcrowded Polish ghettos grew steadily worse, and the authorities were faced with serious problems guarding and feeding their victims. Suggestions were now made by some lower-ranking SS officers that the only solution was to kill all those who were unable to work. The situation worsened still further with the invasion of the Soviet Union with its large Jewish population. There was a conflation in the Nazi mind of Jews and partisans, as well as Jews and Bolsheviks, and the Germans set about their destruction with murderous intensity. Göring, who announced that "This is not the Second World War. This is the Great Racial War," gave Heydrich plenipotentiary powers on July 31 1941 to find a "general solution [*Gesamtlösung*] to the Jewish problem in German-occupied Europe."

In September Hitler decided that all German Jews should be expelled to the General Government. They were now forced to wear a yellow Star of David, their few remaining civil rights were taken away from them, and their property was seized. Preparations were now made for the mass murder of Jews and psychiatric patients in the east so as to make beds available for those wounded on the eastern front. Among the first victims were Jews in the ghettos of Riga and Minsk, as well as the psychiatric patients in the Warthegau. The Einsatzkommandos murdered them using carbon monoxide in mobile gas chambers, or shot them in mass executions. Extermination camps were built in Belzec, Chelmno, Sobibor, and Treblinka, where gas chambers were constructed along the lines of those used to murder the handicapped in Germany in Action T4, which had begun in April 1940. The gas chambers at Chelmno were first used in December 1941.

Heydrich set December 9 1941 as the date for a major conference on "the final solution of the Jewish question," to be held in a villa Am Großen Wannsee 56–8 in Berlin, but it had to be postponed because of the Japanese attack on Pearl Harbor. The Wannsee Conference, attended by 15 party functionaries and senior civil servants from most of the major ministries, was eventually held at noon on January 20 1942. Heydrich chaired the meeting and Eichmann kept the minutes. Heydrich announced his intention to render all of Europe, including Britain and Sweden, as well as North Africa, "uncontaminated by Jews" (*Judenrein*). He estimated that a total of 11 million Jews would be deported to the east. Those who were able to work would be subject to "natural reduction." Those that survived would be given "appropriate treatment," since they would otherwise represent an exceptionally tough "germ-cell" of a Jewish revival. An exception was made for those over the age of 65 in the "old people's ghetto" in the concentration camp in Theresienstadt. This was to serve as a model institution to counter any Allied charges of the mistreatment of Jews. Joseph Bühler, Hans Frank's deputy in the General Government, requested that the "final solution" should begin there as soon as possible, since most of the Jews were unable to work, and posed a serious economic and health problem. According to Eichmann's testimony at his trial, there was a frank and open discussion of the relative merits of different methods of mass killing. The question of whether Jewish partners of "mixed marriages" or Jewish "half-breeds" should be deported was tabled. The meeting was brief and no objections were raised to this horrendous undertaking.

In one sense the Wannsee Conference was a confirmation of what had already been done. The decision to murder large numbers of Jews had already been taken and many of the death camps built. Hundreds of thousands had already been slaughtered in an orgy of the basest savagery, but now for the first time the intention to murder every single Jew in Europe was clearly expressed. There had been a number of previous "final solutions to the Jewish question," but this was the definitive "Final Solution" by means of a cold-blooded, carefully planned, industrialized, and centralized genocide, a horror unparalleled in human history.

Rudolf Höss's concentration camp at Auschwitz was now greatly expanded so as to accommodate victims from western Europe, the Balkans, and the Czech Protectorate. The original camp (*Stammlager*) was now called Auschwitz I, the extermination camp at Birkenau was Auschwitz II, and IG Farben's factory in the work camp at Monowitz was Auschwitz III. Forty thousand workers slaved away for four years in the Buna works under the most appalling conditions and all to no avail. No synthetic rubber was ever produced. Zyklon B, a gas based on prussic acid, was first used to kill Russian prisoners of war in Auschwitz I in September 1941. The first Jews were murdered by such means in February 1942. Himmler visited Auschwitz in July 1942, witnessed the entire process from selection on the ramp to gas chamber and crematorium, and expressed his complete satisfaction with the arrangements. He ordered a major expansion of Birkenau as a result of which up to 10,000 victims could be killed per day. Those who were not killed in the gas chambers were beaten to death or shot, or were victims of grisly medical experiments, rampant disease, or malnutrition. Only the very strongest and most resourceful survived.

Six million Jews were murdered in the Shoah, but they were not the only victims of the Nazi's dystopian mania. Up to three million Polish gentiles were slaughtered and at least as many Soviet civilians, in addition to the 2.1 million Soviet Jews. Also killed were 3.3 million Soviet prisoners of war, most of them by starvation. In addition about half a million Gypsies were murdered. The precise number of those who died in this horrific massacre will probably never be known. Precision hardly matters with figures such as these, except to counter wicked people who deny that it ever happened, or that the number of victims was insignificant. For those who demand an accurate count, Peter Witte has shown that exactly 1,274,166 Polish Jews were murdered in the gas chambers in the General Government by December 31 1942, in the first stage of "Aktion Reinhardt." Up to 15 million died as a result of the National Socialists' "Racial New Order," and had they won the war the number would have been infinitely higher. In the "General Plan for the East" prepared by the SS and published on June 24 1941, a "solution to the Polish question" was to follow upon the "solution to the Jewish problem." Thirty-one million people were to be "resettled," a euphemism for killed, and their places taken by ethnic Germans and racially suitable candidates for "Germanization."

The path to Auschwitz was twisted. There is no single document, verbal order, or single cause that can explain these terrible events. Every attempt to explain hardly brings us closer to an understanding and we are mindful of Primo Levi's fellow Auschwitz inmate Iss Clausner, who scratched the following words on the bottom of his soup bowl: "Ne chercher pas à comprendre." It needed a highly complex multiplicity of causes and actors for virulent, repulsive but still conventional anti-Semitism and racialism to result in mass murder on such an unthinkable scale. Food shortages were such that it was possible for deskbound experts to contemplate the removal of 30 million "useless eaters" and "ballast material." Housing shortages as a result of Allied bombing led to demands that Jews should be expelled from the Reich. Financial experts cast greedy eyes on Jewish property. Exotic plans were drawn up for the resettlement of eastern Europe. Half-crazed racial fanatics were free to indulge in their wildest fantasies, while grim specialists on economic ration-alization played with statistics and cooked up equally inhuman schemes. The ini-tiative did not always come from the SS. The Foreign Office objected to the Madagascar Plan because it was "too slow" and would "only" apply to Jews in occupied Europe. Thousands of anonymous accomplices were involved in a highly developed modern society in which the rule of law had broken down. Partial know-ledge hardly troubled the consciences of these desktop murders as they drew up their railway timetables, wrote their memoranda, gave their lectures on racial theory, made their films, studied the accounts, and interpreted the Führer's will. As the regime grew progressively more radical all restraint was cast aside. As Goebbels said: "Whoever says A must also say B. . . . After a certain moment Jewish politics [*Judenpolitik*] takes on a momentum of its own."

The Turn of the Tide

The Red Army seized the initiative in the summer of 1943 with their victory at Kursk, and kept it for the rest of the war. Meanwhile the Allied landing in Sicily meant that Italy was lost. Hitler was obliged to pull troops out of the eastern front to defend Italy, this at a time when the Wehrmacht was reeling after its defeat at Kursk. It was all in vain. Mussolini was deposed on July 25 1943 and the Italians switched sides. By the summer of the following year the Germans had been pushed back to their starting positions on the eastern front in June 1941. Vichy France had been occupied as early as November 1942, three days after the Americans landed in North Africa. The successful Allied landing in Normandy on June 6 1944 meant that Hitler's days were numbered.

The nimbus around the Führer began to fade as disaster followed disaster. The great gambler found himself holding a series of losing hands and nothing but a miracle could save him from ruin. For an increasing number of Germans an end to the horror now seemed preferable to what was becoming a horror without end. A small group of mostly aristocratic soldiers and civil servants now decided that the time had come to act to save Germany from total destruction and from sinking further into total moral turpitude. They were brave men who had virtually no support from the population at large, even though the regime had become savagely repressive at home and the tentacles of Himmler's SS reached every corner. Hitler became increasingly remote and isolated. Entry to the Presence was jealously guarded by his brutish secretary, Martin Bormann, and he was surrounded by syco-phants, court jesters, and mindless agitators. The failed assassination attempt on July 20 1944 gave this medieval despot with his warring barony a renewed popu-larity, and expressions of sympathy came from throughout the Reich. How could these wicked men attempt to kill the Führer at this moment of national peril? There was widespread approval of the bestial treatment of the conspirators, their asso-ciates, and their families, who were denounced as "reactionaries," "toffs," and "plutocrats" and subjected to a reign of terror. Many renewed their faith in their chiliastic savior.

In spite of a series of setbacks and the devastating effects of the Allied strategic bombing campaign, armaments production peaked in the summer of 1944. This was largely the result of the exceptional efforts of Albert Speer, Hitler's young archi-tect friend, who took over responsibility for this vital sector on the death of Fritz Todt in February 1942. Speer struggled against Bormann, the Gauleiters, and Reichsleiters, to create a rationalized and centralized Ministry for Armaments and War Production that favored large-scale production over the smaller enterprises much loved by the Nazis. Speer was only able to win the struggle because he enjoyed Hitler's full confidence.

The absurd proposition that Germany was a "people without space," the premise on which a war to achieve *Lebensraum* had been unleashed, was soon shown to be utter nonsense. Germany was in fact a space without people, totally dependent on foreign workers. This in turn was most disturbing to strict upholders of National Socialist racial policy, who had serious racial–political objections to such a policy, but who also had ideological objections to the employment of women. Walter Darré and his "blood and soil" disciples were deeply disturbed that, by as early as 1938, a shortage of a quarter of a million agricultural workers meant that German soil was increasingly tilled by workers from the lesser breeds. By the autumn of 1944 there were about 8.5 million foreign workers in Germany, amounting to more than a quarter of the workforce. The armaments industry was now dependent on foreign workers and prisoners of war. Of these about two million were prisoners of war, 2.8 million workers came from the Soviet Union, 1.7 million from Poland, 1.3 million from France, and 600,000 from Italy. In addition there were 650,000 con-centration camp inmates engaged in some form of labor, most of whom were Jews.

It was easy enough to put prisoners of war to work, but few of them had the skills required in the armaments industry. The recruitment of foreigners proved exceptionally difficult, and party functionaries feared that workers from the east would weaken the "racial basis of the biological strength of Germany," especially as there was an alarming number of instances of sexual relations between Aryan Germans and Slav sub-humans. This problem was partly overcome by moving a number of factories from Germany to the General Government. Workers from western Europe posed less of a biological threat, but it was feared that they might be prone to indulge in acts of sabotage.

In March 1942 Fritz Sauckel, the Gauleiter of Thuringia, was appointed General Plenipotentiary for Labor. His remit was "to ensure the ordered employment of labor in the German war economy, by taking all the measures he deems necessary in the Greater German Reich, the Protectorate, the General Government and the occupied territories." As a good National Socialist Sauckel refused to be bound by any legal norms. He adopted the Pauline principal of "he who does not work shall not eat" by taking away ration books and clothing coupons from anyone who refused to work. He called this total disregard for the law "active legitimization." His attempts to find volunteers by offering pay equal to that of German workers was not a success. Of five million foreign workers, only 200,000 came of their own accord. Primitive living conditions, malnutrition, and long working hours resulted in a noticeable decrease in productivity. Sauckel tried to overcome this by increasing wages through the introduction of piecework and by giving foreign workers a great deal more freedom. The result was a significant increase in productivity. Prisoners of war were not so easily bribed and proved exceedingly reluctant to work for the benefit of the Greater German Reich.

All foreign workers, apart from those from Poland and the Soviet Union, were given the same wages and working conditions as Germans. They thus had paid holidays, child allowances, pension contributions, and special bonuses for birthdays, marriages, and deaths. Polish and Soviet workers were given the same gross wages as the others, but they were subject to special taxes which left them between ten and 17 marks per week. Since they had to pay 1.50 marks per day for board and lodging, this left precious little over at the end of the week. Progressive taxation was so steep that no amount of overtime made any substantial difference to net wages. Sauckel significantly reduced the burden of taxation on Soviet and Polish workers. He also allowed Polish workers to travel home until a shortage of transportation made this impossible. Soviet workers were not permitted to travel, but were given a few days rest provided they could be spared from work. Sauckel soon found himself in direct conflict with the SS. He was anxious to find as many able-bodied workers as possible, and therefore insisted that they should be properly fed, housed, and clothed, and given adequate incentives to work. The aim of the SS was to kill all the millions of Soviet prisoners of war, along with the hundreds of thousands of Jews who were working for the Germans. The SS won the struggle, and millions of Soviet prisoners of war were worked until they dropped, or starved to death.

In the final stages of the war the situation of foreign workers and prisoners of war became desperate. They wandered among the rubble of the ruined cities in search of food and shelter. Many organized themselves into armed bands and had pitched battles with the security forces. Those caught plundering, in other words those who actually found something to eat, were shot on the spot. Two hundred Soviet citizens were shot in Dortmund, and in Suttrop in the Sauerland 129 men, 77 women, and two small children were murdered on the order of SS General Kammler. At Arnsburg in Hesse the SS men who refused to execute a group of Soviet women lie buried beside them amid the ruins of a beautiful Cistercian monastery. Their sacrifice is a reminder that amid these unimaginable horrors, human decency and extraordinary moral courage was never wholly absent, often occurring in the most surprising places. The tragedy is that there were so few such cases, a fact that is disguised by the comforting myth that there was a clear distinction between criminal Germans and ordinary Germans. As Carlyle wrote: "Of such stuff are we made, in such powder-mines of bottomless guilt and criminality – 'if God restrained not' as is well said – does the purest of us walk."

On December 16 1944 the last German offensive was launched in the Ardennes, against the American forces in Luxembourg and Belgium. It was a pale imitation of "Plan Yellow" of 1940 and further weakened the hard-pressed eastern front. The Americans were at first caught completely by surprise, but reserves were rushed in to halt the German advance. Brigadier General McAuliffe stopped von Manteuffel's Fifth Panzer Army at Bastogne, and to the south Patton's Third Army made a brilliant 90-degree shift north to hit the southern flank of the "Bulge." The ill-equipped and exhausted Germans fought tenaciously with inadequate air cover, relying solely on Allied fuel depots for replenishments. The odds against them were overwhelming. The Allies launched their counteroffensive on January 3 and within a few days it was clear that Hitler's final *va banque* had failed. He had expended his slender reserves that were badly needed to meet the Soviet winter offensive, which began on January 12, and the Luftwaffe had virtually ceased to exist.

Hitler returned to Berlin on January 16, spending the rest of his days huddled with his cronies in the bunker under the chancellery, where the atmosphere was claustrophobic, divorced from reality, and nightmarishly apocalyptic. Meanwhile, millions of half-starved refugees trudged westwards to escape the Red Army, which indulged in a disgusting orgy of murder, rape, plunder, and mass deportations to the gulag. Poles and Czechs joined in this appalling debauch, taking terrible revenge on their oppressors. Hundreds of thousands of Germans who suffered from this barbaric treatment must also be counted among the millions of Hitler's victims.

Hitler took to the airwaves for the last time on January 30 to give his traditional address on the anniversary of the "seizure of power." It was a poor performance, full of talk of fighting to the death against "Asiatic Bolshevism," but it was clear to all around him that the war was lost. On March 15 1945 Speer pointed out that the war economy had collapsed, not because of Allied bombing, but because of the loss of essential sources of raw materials, particularly Romanian oil, and because of the destruction of the transportation network. The Allies would soon be in the Ruhr and it was thus pointless to prolong the war. In fact it was Allied bombers that had effectively disrupted transport, and they now concentrated on the destruction of oil refineries, bridges, canals, and chemical plants.

Plate 23 Dresden after the raid. © Bundesarchiv

Allied bombing resulted in about 600,000 deaths and destroyed 3.37 million homes. It obliged the Germans to employ 800,000 people in air defense; other fronts were thus denuded of artillery, aircraft, and manpower. There was a desperate shortage of aluminium resulting from its use in fuses for antiaircraft shells. It clearly had a devastating effect on civilian morale, and there was widespread disillusionment with a leadership that failed so spectacularly to defend the fatherland. The morality of strategic bombing is questionable, but attempts by some to make men like "Bomber" Harris the moral equivalents of Heinrich Himmler are clearly grotesque.

Hitler ignored Speer's plea that the German people had to be left with some means of subsistence in the postwar world, and argued that a people who had shown themselves so weak and feeble deserved to be destroyed. To his dismay Germany's performance in this titanic clash between the races had demonstrated that his lunatic vision of the biological–racial superiority of the German *Volk* was woefully deficient. On March 19 he issued his "Nero Order," calling for the total destruction of Germany's economic infrastructure. Mercifully this insane command was seldom obeyed. The Führer's wish was no longer law.

Hitler's fifty-sixth birthday, on April 20, was a gloomy affair during which he decided he would stay in Berlin to the last. On April 29 he married his long-term and long-suffering mistress, Eva Braun. He then dictated his political testament. Even his devoted secretary, Traudl Junge, was appalled by this mean-spirited and

Plate 24 Red Army troops hoisting the Soviet flag on the Reichstag May 5, 1945. © BBK

repulsive document. Hitler and his young bride committed suicide the following day at 3.30 p.m. Meanwhile on April 23 Göring, who had removed himself to Berchtesgaden, had asked whether he could take over command, as Hitler no longer had any freedom of action. Hitler's reply was to dismiss him from the party. Himmler sent out some peace feelers, whereupon Hitler ordered his arrest. The Reichsführer-SS ended his wretched life with a cyanide pill on May 23. Goebbels failed in an attempt to sign a separate peace with the Soviets and committed suicide along with his wife on May 1, having first murdered their six children.

On May 7 Jodl signed an act of surrender at Reims. The laconic General Eisenhower reported to the Combined Chiefs that the Allied mission was over. On May 8 Keitel signed a second act of surrender along with Marshal Zhukov and Air Marshal Tedder in Berlin, and Hitler's war was thus formally ended at midnight.

It was also the end of National Socialism. The Third Reich left nothing behind it but horror: The horror of tens of millions of dead, of a continent laid waste, the horror of a great nation reduced to barbarism, moral squalor, and mass murder, soon to be crippled by guilt. It is a horror that will not go away, that refuses to distance itself by becoming history, it is the horror of the unfathomable.

The Third Reich and Modernization

The Third Reich was so irredeemably stygian that it took many years before the question could be asked whether there was anything positive that could be said about it. In 1965 the sociologist Ralf Dahrendorf presented the startling thesis that the 12 years of Nazi dictatorship had provided the impetus for a surprising degree of modernization. In 1967 the historian David Schoenbaum developed this theme and made the extravagant claim that there had been a "brown revolution," resulting in a fundamental change in mental and social structures. These ideas were either rejected or ignored by historians for a good 20 years, and were then revisited in a debate over modernization. This too got bogged down in a theoretical morass, due to methodological shortcomings, and the sheer impossibility of examining a mere 12 years using a theory that is designed to reveal long-term trends.

The question remains whether the Third Reich helped further the process of modernization, or whether it halted or even reversed it. How much of this was by accident, how much by design? Such questions can only be answered if the 12 years of the "Thousand Year Reich" are examined within their historical context between the Weimar and Federal republics, and not taken as an isolated event, a hideous historical accident, or an abrupt caesura. The problem is further compounded by the Janus face of modernization. The horrors of total war, industrialized mass murder, the misuse of science, hypertrophic bureaucracy, and propagandistic indoctrination, are all the products of modernization.

As we have already seen, a key component of modernization is the change from an agrarian to an industrial society. The Third Reich did not stand in the way of this process, in spite of the initial effects of Walter Darré's half-baked "blood and soil" ideology. As elsewhere in the industrial world, agriculture declined, there was a continued movement from the land to urban areas, and agriculture depended increasingly on government protection by means of tariffs and subsidies. Industry continued to expand, largely due to rearmament and war. Government interfered with the economy, but left the basic structures of a capitalist economy unaffected.

An increasing degree of equality of opportunity is another vital component of the modernization process. Nazi racial policy allowed no room for this democratic notion. The challenges of the modern were to be met by racial selection, not by an open meritocracy. Upward mobility for the "Aryan racial comrade" was possible through political selection into the upper ranks of the party, by the opportunities that opened up in a rapidly expanding military, and a swollen state bureaucracy. The party elite was recruited almost exclusively from the lower orders. They worked alongside the old elites, and in many instances either co-opted them or pushed them aside. The social policies of the DAF did much to improve the lot of the working class, and lessened, but did not overcome, the distinctions between blue- and white-collar workers.

Hitler, a rudimentarily-educated autodidact, had an intense loathing of intellectuals, and it is thus hardly surprising that there was a dramatic reverse to the process of modernization in the area of education. The number of university students sank from 121,00 in 1933 to 56,000 in 1939. In the technical colleges the numbers shrank from 20,400 to 9,500. The percentage of women university students fell from 15.4 to 11.6 percent, and in the technical colleges the drop was even more dramatic: from 4.6 to 1.9 percent. The result was a chronic shortage of specialists in all fields. One typical example: Germany took over the oil fields of eastern Europe, but had no engineers to operate them.

All this resulted from a profound loathing of intellectuals, a constant theme in *Mein Kampf*, and an essential ingredient in the National Socialist worldview. The expulsion of Jewish, and politically suspect, scholars from the universities caused irreparable damage to German universities, and was of incalculable value to Germany's opponents. Vital areas of research were neglected, and effort frittered away in such absurd pursuits as "race research," the hunt for the holy grail, or for Atlantis. Doctors, badly needed for public health, set about the forcible sterilization of 360,000 people, mostly women, but many of them men. They measured skulls, pickled brains, and conducted sadistic research on live subjects, thus perverting medical science in the pursuit of irrational ends.

The development of democratic processes is also a vital component of the process of modernization, and here Hitler's charismatic dictatorship marked the most dramatic break with the modern. The democratic constitution of the Weimar Republic was torn up, the rule of law cast aside, and Germany became a corrupt neo-feudal free-for-all, in which Hitler's myrmidons skirmished for status, and dispensed patronage to their slavish underlings. The "racial community," which was said to overcome the latent tensions within society, was a derisory sham. On the other hand, the traditional social hierarchy was delegitimized by this ideology, and many people felt that their longing for a social consensus, which had become acute in the latter stages of the Weimar Republic, had been largely realized in the "racial community." Subjective perception, if widely shared, takes on the form of objective fact. Class, in the form of self-perception, could vanish with effective integration into a National Socialist society. It was, after all, a dynamic society which had brought full employment, and with its spectacular successes in foreign policy had restored Germany's prestige in the world. A series of stunning victories up until Stalingrad were further evidence that the National Socialist theory of the master race was based on objective fact. The social state and consumer society, which the Nazis promised would follow upon a final victory, seemed close to realization.

Hitler himself embodied the crisis of the modern. On the one hand he loved airplanes and fast cars, shared none of his cranky followers' dislike of industry, and mastered the modern means of mass communication; but he also imagined the deadly threat posed by the modern in the form of Jewry, which embodied for him all the negative aspects of modernity. Modern technology was placed in the service of essentially atavistic ideological aims, and it was precisely the crushing defeat of those aims that removed so many of the barriers that stood in the way of modernity. The military was destroyed, the officer corps discredited, the East Elbian aristocracy robbed of any influence, all pretensions to the superiority of the German race reduced to an absurdity, and the notion that a charismatic dictator can reach the promised land, by means of a war of conquest and genocide, was finally revealed as a satanic illusion.

14
The Adenauer Era: 1945–63

Hitler's war left Germany bankrupt and starving amidst a pile of rubble. Millions of refugees, the homeless, and "displaced persons" wandered in search of their loved ones and a safe place to stay, bartering their few remaining belongings for a scrap of food. Defeat was palpable and surrender unconditional. There could be no renewed talk of a "stab in the back." There was not much doubt as to who was responsible for the war and there was little possibility of another "war guilt lie." Germany's second bid for hegemony in Europe had failed utterly and the country was now under four-power control. The Polish frontier was moved westwards to the Oder and the western Neisse, while the Soviet Union laid claim to a large part of East Prussia and to Königsberg, the town of Immanuel Kant. These arrangements were subject to revision in a peace treaty that was not to be signed for decades, by which time there could be no serious consideration of a revision.

A terrible revenge was reaped on the Germans in the east, even though it was agreed at the Potsdam Conference that they should be permitted to return to the rump Germany in a proper and humane manner. Particularly harsh treatment was meted out to the Sudeten Germans who were not covered by this agreement. Appalling acts of willful brutality were committed by people who had suffered under the Nazis' bestial occupation regime. Many got their just desserts, the vast majority were further innocent victims of Hitler's war.

Germany was now divided into four occupation zones, as agreed during the war. The Soviet zone (SBZ) extended as far west as the rivers Elbe, Werra, and Fulda. In the west, the British occupied the northern half, the Americans the south, and the French the areas contiguous to their frontier with Germany: Rheinland-Palatinate, southern Baden, and southern Württemberg. All political power was now in the hands of the Allied Control Council, and the leaders of the Third Reich who were still alive were called upon to answer for their crimes in front of the International Military Tribunal in Nuremberg. Some were concerned that these people were being tried for crimes that did not exist at the time they were committed, such as "crimes against humanity," "crimes against peace," or the crime of belonging to a criminal organization. Others felt that the Allies, particularly the Soviet Union, should also be tried for similar crimes of which they were clearly guilty, but the enormity of the crimes committed in the name of the German people and their Führer was so great that such cavils were soon forgotten. Only 12 of the main criminals were condemned to death, including Göring, Ribbentrop, Rosenberg, Keitel, and Jodl. Albert Speer was lucky to be spared, and this was done largely because of his frank admission of guilt. He and Rudolf Hess were given lengthy prison sentences. Schacht and Papen were set free.

The process of "de-Nazification" was applied with different degrees of rigor in each of the four occupation zones. The Soviets used this program to get rid of all manner of opposition elements, including dissidents within the Communist Party (KPD), "bourgeois" democrats, and "capitalists" whose property they coveted. Some 120,000 people were thrown into former Nazi concentration camps, such as Buchenwald and Sachsenhausen, and of these some 40,000 died of ill treatment. After Stalin's death in 1953 the camp at Buchenwald was cynically recycled as an "antifascist monument."

All four occupation powers made use of Nazis with desirable skills, whether as scientists, administrators, or publicists. Many opportunistic Nazis in the Soviet zone found the transition from one dictatorial form to another easy to make, whereas in the Western zones the difficulty of finding competent antifascists was such that a blind eye was all too often turned. This was particularly true of the legal profession where a large number of singularly unsavory characters remained in office. Some of the more egregious of the Nazi university professors, including Martin Heidegger and Carl Schmitt, lost their chairs, but many who were equally guilty but less prominent were soon reinstalled. The French were the most lenient in dealing with their Nazis, the Americans the most stringent, although they quickly lowered their standards as tensions with the Soviet Union began to worsen. All in all the de-Nazification program was an expensive and time-consuming failure. There were precious few devout Nazis left by 1945, degrees of complicity were hard to establish, and the need to rebuild the country was such that even those with a heavy burden of guilt were forgiven after a few years. Many serious criminals managed to avoid prosecution for many years, and some still live in increasingly secure anonymity.

The Soviets, true to their Marxist–Leninist precepts, saw the fundamental problem in class, rather than individual, terms. The Prussian Junkers were conveniently deemed to be one of the main pillars of National Socialism, and thus in 1945 the land of all who owned more than 100 hectares (247 acres) of land was handed over, without compensation, to 500,000 peasants. Principled antifascists were not excluded from this decree. A referendum was then held in which a large percentage of the electorate voted in favor of seizing the property of "Nazi activists and war criminals." Officials in the Soviet Military Administration in Germany (SMAD) were thereby given full discretion to take whatever they wanted. By early 1948 some 40 percent of industry in the Soviet zone was controlled by the occupation authorities. De-Nazification for the Soviets meant the extirpation of all remaining vestiges of capitalism, and the creation of a socialist society.

The British Labour Party, which won the general election in 1945, wanted to nationalize the larger concerns in the British zone, but this was vehemently opposed by Lucius D. Clay, the American military governor. He argued that such a far-reaching measure could not be applied simply in one occupation zone and should be left to a future German government to decide. Some large firms such as IG Farben, the Dresdner and Kommerz banks, and a number iron and steel works that had had particularly dubious dealings with the Nazi regime, were placed under trusteeship.

Whereas in 1919 Germany had been left with greatly reduced armed forces and certain types of weaponry had been forbidden, in 1945 the country was completely demilitarized. The baronial estates of the Junkers, a class that had played such a key role in German history, were parceled out. Heavy industry in the Soviet zone was nationalized, and in the west it was placed under strict control. Thus the military, the Junkers, and the industrialists lost most of their power and influence in this fundamental change in the social structure of the country which was brought about by total defeat, rather than by the 12 years of the National Socialist "revolution."

In spite of these radical changes 1945 was hardly "zero hour." Germany did not start from scratch and there were inevitably strong elements of continuity. Nevertheless for contemporaries this was a period of profound anxiety about a future that was largely beyond their control. They had hit rock bottom and longed for a normal life with a steady job, food on the table, and a roof over their heads. Most had, through bitter experience, learnt to mistrust the ideologues and pied pipers who had reduced them to this pitiful state, and wanted little more than pragmatic answers to practical questions.

The Hitler regime never managed totally to destroy the democratic spirit in Germany, which Goebbels called the "ideas of 1789," and in 1945 the democratic forces were determined not to repeat the mistakes of the Weimar Republic. There could be no place for the multiplicity of small parties that had bedeviled the republic and certainly no room for confessional politics. The Christian Democratic Union (CDU), with the former mayor of Cologne, Konrad Adenauer, as its dominant figure, was founded shortly after the war's end. Based on the former Catholic Center Party it was a non-denominational people's party of moderate conservatives. A Bavarian wing of the party, the Christian Social Union (CSU), as a follow-on of the BVP, had to play the particularist card in order to wean voters away from the conservative Bavarian Party.

Much of the leadership of the Social Democratic Party (SPD), the great historic party of the left, had been martyred during the Third Reich, but it was revived two days before Germany's capitulation at a meeting in Hanover called by Kurt Schumacher. He was a truly remarkable figure who had been severely wounded in the First World War, and had spent ten years as a prisoner in Dachau. His health was broken, he had lost an arm, and was soon to lose a leg, but his spirit was indomitable and he was an almost frighteningly charismatic figure. He was a fervent nationalist and virulent anticommunist who was determined that the SPD should also become a people's party by appealing to the middle-class voter.

Between the still distinctly clerical CDU and the still theoretically Marxist SPD were a number a local liberal parties which united in December 1948 to form the Free Democratic Party (FDP) under the leadership of Theodor Heuss, a genial Württemberger and former associate of Friedrich Naumann. He was an archetypical grand bourgeois: an honest, open, highly intelligent *homme de lettres*, but also a man who had made some serious errors of judgment in the turmoil of 1933. The split between left and right liberals that characterized German politics from Bismarck to Hitler was largely overcome, although as in any large party there were differences of emphasis and disagreements over the details of policy, none of which in these early years were of fundamental significance. The liberals were opposed to the clericalism of the CDU and the socialism of the SPD, but as the CDU became less clerical and the SPD less socialist, the FDP found it increasingly difficult to offer a serious alternative to the two main parties. Its importance resided largely in its ability to tip the scales and decide which way to turn to form a coalition government.

The first party to be formally reconstituted was the Communist Party (KPD). Its leading cadre, the "Ulbricht Group," had been carefully selected and trained in Moscow and was flown to Germany as early as April. On June 11 1945 the party published a moderate "reformist" program which proclaimed its determination to uphold the rights of private property, private enterprise, and free trade. It solemnly declared that it would be a serious mistake to force a Soviet system of government upon the German people, and called for an antifascist, democratic, and parliamentary regime that would guarantee freedom for all. This was nothing more than a cynical attempt to win over Social Democrats in support of a united front, and thus create the impression that the Potsdam formula for a democratic Germany was being respected, after which Walter Ulbricht and his minions would take over control and establish a Communist dictatorship. Many Social Democrats in the Soviet zone were understandably suspicious of the Communists, but massive pressure by the Soviet authorities resulted in a shotgun wedding between the KPD and SPD in April 1946, leading to the formation of the Socialist Unity Party (SED). Henceforth it became a criminal offense in the Soviet zone to proclaim one's allegiance to the principles of Social Democracy. Social Democrats were once again "social fascists." Two other parties, the Liberal Democratic Party of Germany (LDPD) and the CDU, were permitted, but the leadership was purged and bullied by the SMAD to the point that they obediently followed the directions of the SED.

That the KPD failed to persuade the SPD in the Western zones to work toward the "unity of the working class" was due in no small part to Kurt Schumacher's adamantine opposition. A free vote among SPD members in the Western sectors of Berlin resulted in 82 percent opposed to union, but 62 percent were in favor of cooperation with the KPD. Schumacher had always been a bitter enemy of the KPD, and could never forgive them the role they had played in bringing Hitler to power, but his attacks on the CDU were equally virulent. He denounced it as a party of clerical obscurantists and rapacious capitalists. He condemned Adenauer as a Rhineland separatist who did not care a fig for the unity of the nation. As a

Prussian Protestant he was committed to the Germany of Bismarck, whereas Adenauer as a devoutly Catholic Rhinelander harbored deep suspicions of Prussia, and is said to have asked for divine protection when crossing the Elbe since he felt himself now to be in Asia. Adenauer, the realist, knew from the very beginning that the Soviet zone was lost to the German nation for the foreseeable future. Schumacher, the romantic nationalist, refused to accept this unpleasant fact, and stepped up his attacks on his rival for his betrayal of the national cause.

The center of gravity in German politics in the years immediately after the war was well to the left. The Social Democrats called for widespread nationalization and a planned economy. The CDU in the British zone endorsed these ideas, and when Josef Kaiser, a union leader and prominent member of the resistance, called for "Christian Socialism" that would enable Germany to bridge the gap between Soviet communism and American capitalism he met with a widely positive response among party members. The CDU moved steadily to the right partly because of the mounting tensions between East and West, and also because of the influence of another of the dominant figures in these postwar years. Ludwig Erhard was an economist who had kept a clean vest during the Nazi years, had valuable connections with leading figures in industry and banking, and who was a convincing advocate of what his associate Alfred Müller-Armack called a "social market economy." He was fully committed to freedom of the market and the free play of supply and demand, but he also insisted that the state had to intervene to make sure that free competition was not unduly hindered by monopolies and cartels, and that an extensive welfare state should provide assistance to the less fortunate, overcome crass social differences, and ease the resulting tensions.

For the time being Erhard had to wait on the sidelines. Amid the ruins of 1945 there could be no question of a social market economy. With a flourishing black market with cigarettes as a basic currency, and a starving population, this was purely visionary talk. The Soviet insistence on milking Germany dry obliged the British and Americans to heavily subsidize their occupation zones. Bread was rationed in Britain for the first time so that yesterday's enemies could be fed. Millions of Americans sent CARE parcels to save Germans from starvation. Such measures could only bring temporary relief, and the refusal of both the Soviets and the French to implement the Potsdam agreement that Germany be treated as an economic whole obliged the British and Americans to rethink the situation.

The Big Four foreign ministers met in Paris in early 1946 for a lengthy series of frustrating meetings. Ernest Bevin, Britain's foreign secretary, used his remarkable persuasive skills to convince James F. Byrnes, the American secretary of state, that the two Anglo-Saxon powers should stand up to the Soviet Union and not allow French objections to German unity to stop them from going ahead to save what could be saved. On September 6 1946 Byrnes gave an epoch-making speech in Stuttgart in which he announced that American troops would remain in Germany as long as other countries left theirs. He also made it clear that the United States would no longer respect the Soviet Union's demand that industrial production in Germany for domestic use should be drastically limited. He further called for the

Plate 25 Ludwig Ehrhard. © Konrad Adenauer Stiftung

unification of all the occupation zones. Knowing full well that the Soviets would not accept, he was thus proposing the division of Germany.

In January 1947 the British and American zones were joined economically to form "Bizonia," the French still objecting to the idea of a West German state. On June 12 of that year the US president proclaimed the "Truman Doctrine," whereby the United States promised economic and military assistance to all peoples in their struggle against communism. On June 5 the new American secretary of state, General George C. Marshall, gave a speech at Harvard University in which he promised massive economic aid to Europe. The resulting Marshall Plan was accepted by Congress in April 1948. The resulting $17 billion dollars of aid to Western Europe was a dramatic demonstration of the United States' leadership of the "Free World," as well as establishing American domination of European markets. The Soviets responded by forming the Kominform, in which the states in the "anti-imperialist and democratic" camp banded together to combat the United States and its "imperialist and antidemocratic" allies. In March 1948 Britain, France, and the Benelux countries formed the Western European Union (WEU), a military alliance clearly aimed against the Soviets, who responded by promptly withdrawing from the Allied Control Council, which effectively ended four-power control over Germany. The French now dropped most of their objections to the Anglo-American plan for the unification of the Western zones, and in April "Bizonia" became "Trizonia."

The currency reform in Trizonia on June 20 introduced the German mark, ended price controls and food rationing, as well as putting the black market out of business. These measures were in large part the work of Ludwig Erhard, who had been appointed director of the economic council in the unified zones. Since prices rose far more rapidly than wages, the SPD had a field-day attacking this unpopular measure, but the economy stabilized within a relatively short space of time and the critics were soon silenced.

The Soviets responded to currency reform in the Western zones by introducing a new currency in the Soviet zone and in Berlin two days later. The feisty Social Democratic mayor of Berlin, Ernst Reuter, protested vigorously and insisted that the German mark should be circulated in the three Western sectors of the city. The three Western commandants agreed, whereupon the SMAD made it a criminal offense for East Berliners to possess German marks. Then on August 4 the Soviets blocked all road, water, and rail routes to the Western sectors of Berlin. In November the transport of goods from the Eastern to the Western sectors of Berlin was stopped. Two million Germans were now threatened with starvation. It would seem that Stalin hoped that the Western Allies would abandon Berlin, get rid of the German mark, and drop their plans for a West German state. The Western powers took up the challenge, and in a remarkable display of solidarity and American efficiency, the Berlin Airlift supplied the Western sectors for 11 tense months. A plane landed at Tempelhof airfield almost every minute, bringing more than 6,000 tons of supplies every day. The Berlin blockade strengthened America's commitment to Europe and the West's resolve to resist Communism.

The Berlin Blockade was a propagandistic disaster for the Soviets and also severely hurt the economy in their occupation zone. It was ended on May 12 1949, a month after the United States, Canada, the five states of the Western European Union, along with Iceland, Norway, Denmark, Italy, and Portugal had joined together to form the North Atlantic Treaty Organization (NATO). The United States, the sole possessor of atomic weapons, was now firmly committed to the defense of Western Europe. The victory of Communist forces in China did little to console the Soviets when their bluff was called.

Plate 26 The Berlin Airlift. © BBK

Germany Divided

There were tense discussions about the form which a West German state would take during the anxious months of the Berlin blockade. A "Parliamentary Council" was elected by the provincial governments and was entrusted with the task of working out the details of a "Basic Law" (*Grundgesetz*). This was designed to underline the provisional nature of the future state. The details of the Basic Law were hammered out by a group of experts who met in a convent in the idyllic setting of Herrenchiemsee in August 1948. Their conclusions were presented to the Parliamentary Council in September for further discussion, with Konrad Adenauer in the chair. Carlo Schmid, a genial and brilliant constitutional lawyer, social democrat, and bon vivant, who was born in France of a French mother, dominated the proceedings, and constantly insisted that a democracy should always have the courage to be intolerant toward those who set out to destroy it. In other words, the new republic should not repeat the fatal mistakes of Weimar, which had such a democratic constitution that its enemies had at least as many, if not more, rights than its supporters.

The first 20 paragraphs of the Basic Law, which guaranteed essential freedoms, were made unalterable under article 79, clause 3, so that there could be no more Enabling Acts or similar constitutional changes that would undermine democratic rule and civil rights. Similarly, a constitutional court was empowered to ban parties that were deemed to be undemocratic. A government could only be toppled by means of a "Constructive Vote of No Confidence" whereby the removal of one chancellor depended on the election of a successor. Backroom intrigues and the decisions of a president elected by popular vote, that had helped bring Hitler to power, were thus no longer possible. Henceforth parliament alone bore the responsibility for appointing a chancellor.

The issue that was most fiercely debated was over the relative powers of the states (*Länder*) and the federal government (*Bund*), and how the finances should be apportioned between the two levels of government. The Allies, the CSU, and the CDU were in favor of states' rights; the SPD and FDP wanted a strong central government. Kurt Schumacher openly defied the Allies over the issue of the financial sovereignty of the federal government, and won major concessions on this issue, much to the surprise and amazement of his supporters, and to Adenauer's disgust.

The Parliamentary Council concluded its deliberations on May 8 1949, four years to the day after Germany's unconditional surrender, and the Basic Law was accepted by an overwhelming majority, with only a handful of disgruntled Bavarians and Communists voting against. All the provincial governments, with the exception of Bavaria, voted in favor of the new law. A face-saving formula was found, special arrangements were made for West Berlin, the military governors gave their seal of approval, and the Basic Law was formally proclaimed on May 23. Bonn was chosen as a suitable capital for a provisional state with a provisional constitution. According to the final paragraph (146), the Basic Law would cease to be in effect once the German people freely decided upon a constitution.

The election campaign for the first parliament (Bundestag) was fought over the issue of the Social Democrats' version of a planned economy versus Erhard's "social market economy." The election was held on August 14 1949 and resulted in the CDU/CSU winning 31 percent of the vote, the SPD 29.2 percent, and the FDP 11.9 percent. The remaining 27.9 percent was divided up among five smaller parties, the Communist Party winning 5.7 percent and thus meeting the requirement of getting at least five percent of the popular vote in order to get a seat in the Bundestag. On September 12 Theodor Heuss, the leader of the FDP, was elected President of the Federal Republic of Germany by the members of the Bundestag and an equal number of representatives of the state governments. Three days later Adenauer was elected chancellor by a majority of one (his own) vote in the Bundestag. His government, made up of the CDU/CSU, the FDP, and the German Party (DP), had 208 of the 402 seats. In a final act on September 20 1949 the Allies formally recognized the new state, but required that all laws be countersigned by the three high commissioners. The Federal Republic was thus far from being a sovereign state.

Whereas the Western Allies saw no viable alternative to the division of Germany, Stalin still hoped to split the imperialist camp and add a united Germany to the

Soviet sphere of influence. To this end he warned the two leaders of the SED, Wilhelm Pieck from the former KPD and Otto Grotewohl from the former SPD, to move cautiously and disguise their real intentions with "opportunistic" tactics. In this cynical spirit he called for the creation of a new party in the Soviet zone which he personally named the National Democratic Party of Germany (NDPD), in which former Nazis would be welcomed and which would be encouraged to open an anti-Marxist discourse. In much the same spirit, the Democratic Peasants' Party of Germany (DBD) was formed to win voters away from the CDU and the LPDP. Both of these new parties were placed under the leadership of died-in-the-wool Stalinists.

Sergei Tulpanow, the Soviet military governor, realized by early 1948 that there was virtually no chance of uniting Germany under Soviet leadership and therefore wanted to establish a Communist regime in the SBZ as soon as possible. Walter Ulbricht, the deputy chairman of the SED and the most ruthless of the KPD's leadership, enthusiastically supported Tulpanow. They were ignored for the time being and a People's Council of Germany was convened in June 1948 to work out the details of a constitution for all of Germany. One quarter of the 400 members of the Council were Communists from the Western zones. The first draft, based on the old Weimar constitution, was presented in October and, after further revisions, was adopted on May 30 1949, shortly after the promulgation of the Basic Law and the ending of the Berlin blockade. By this time it was clear that the constitution would only apply to the SBZ. On September 27, a week after the Allies recognized the Federal Republic of Germany as a semi-sovereign state, Stalin gave the go-ahead for the formation of a state to be known as the German Democratic Republic (DDR). A constitution was passed on October 11 1949 and Wilhelm Pieck elected president. Shortly afterward Otto Grotewohl was elected minister-president with Walter Ulbricht (SED), Hermann Kastner (LDPD), and Otto Nuschke (CDU) as his deputies.

This constitution, like the Soviet constitution of 1936, was on the surface a very liberal document that guaranteed traditional civil rights, including property rights, as well as the right to strike, but a clause outlawing "rabble-rousing," "antidemo-cratic propaganda," "war mongering," and the like made all such guarantees worthless. Similarly, the marginal preponderance of the "bourgeois" parties was a charade which did not disguise the fact that the DDR was a one-party dictatorship based on the Leninist principle of "democratic centralism" in which Ulbricht was the key figure, and behind which stood the Soviet Union. The new regime marched under the banner of "antifascism," the most powerful weapon in the Communists' propaganda arsenal. The establishment of a Stalinist dictatorship was thus presented as "antifascist social transformation," and a continuation of the glorious struggle of the Soviet peoples against Nazi tyranny. The DDR, like the Federal Republic (FRG), was seen as a provisional state pending the unification of Germany when it would become an "indivisible democratic republic."

It was a striking characteristic of the new Germany that nationalism was now a left-wing cause. It is hardly surprising that the SED should call for a united Germany that was "democratic" and "antifascist," in other words Communist, but it was

Plate 27 East German Communist poster. Photo: Landesarchiv Berlin/N. N.

truly remarkable that the SPD, which had once been the leading light in the Socialist International should now, under Kurt Schumacher and Erich Ollenhauer, be fervently nationalist. By contrast, the moderate conservatives under Konrad Adenauer
were committed to a policy of integration with the Western powers, and refused to
pay the high price in the loss of freedom and security that a policy of national integration was bound to involve. Schumacher was unable to untangle the problem of
reconciling his desire for national unification with his robust democratic principles
and his passionate anti-communism, and gave vent to his frustration by denouncing Adenauer as "the chancellor of the Allies," but such outbursts brought him little
credit.

Adenauer's concern to remain on good terms with the Western Allies and the
concessions he was obliged to make over such issues as reparations, the allocation
of coal and steel in Rhineland-Westphalia, and the status of the Saar, met with opposition even within the ranks of the coalition. After a long struggle he was able to
overcome all obstacles, and remained deaf to protests that he was throwing away

what little remained of the country's sovereignty. The Federal Republic took part in the Council of Europe, the Schuman Plan and, in January 1952, the European Coal and Steel Community.

At the time all these issues seemed to be highly technical and secondary. Although they laid the foundations of the European Union, the pressing issue of the day was that of rearmament. Adenauer knew right from the outset that were the Federal Republic to play an equal role in the Western Alliance it would have to make a major contribution to its defense. Both the Americans and the British agreed, but the French were still deeply suspicious. The invasion of South Korea by the Communist North in 1950, and Ulbricht's pointed comparison of the Federal Republic to South Korea, prompted the chancellor to propose the formation of a 150,000-man West German army. The debate over rearmament was to dominate German politics for years to come. The SPD was predictably opposed and was supported by a number of influential figures in the Evangelical Church whose fervent nationalism led them to adopt a pacifist stance. The most outspoken of these was Martin Niemöller, a former U-boat commander and Free Corps mercenary who, as a Protestant minister, had fallen foul of the Nazis and had been imprisoned. A rigid and humorless authoritarian, he denounced the Bonn republic as being begotten in Rome and born in the United States.

With the Korean War in the headlines and memories of the horrors of the last war all too painfully vivid, pacifist sentiments ran high. "Leave me out" (*ohne mich*) was the prevailing sentiment among those likely to be called upon to serve. There was also the problem of how a future German army was to be integrated into a European defense structure. The French minister-president, René Plevin, proposed a European Defense Community (EDC) in which national contingents would be integrated at the battalion level and later, due to German protests and American support, at the corps level. Plans for a new German army went ahead with a de facto ministry of defense under Theodor Blank.

The Soviets were highly alarmed by these developments and decided to intervene. In November 1950 Otto Grotewohl wrote to Adenauer proposing the formation of an All-German Council to work out the details for elections in both Germanys. After lengthy debate the Federal Republic responded by calling for free elections in East and West to be supervised by the United Nations. On March 10 1952 the Soviets released a bombshell by proposing to the Western Allies that a peace treaty with Germany should be concluded that would result in a free, democratic, united, and neutral Germany. There was no mention of free elections in this note. Adenauer saw this proposal as an artful attempt to torpedo his policy of western integration and to ruin the plans for a Western European defense community, leaving Germany hopelessly weak and ending his political career. It is highly doubtful whether Stalin ever imagined that the proposal would be acceptable in Washington, London, or Paris, and it might have placed him in a somewhat awkward position were it adopted, but it was a major propaganda victory.

The Nationalists, both Social Democrat and Protestant, called for a careful examination of the Soviet proposal, but the Western Allies had already decided that it was unacceptable. The Americans and the British considered that a neutral Germany would mean Soviet hegemony over Europe. For the French the mere thought of a united Germany, in whatever form, was a horror that did not bear contemplation. For years to come the opposition continued to accuse Adenauer of having missed a golden opportunity for national unification in 1952, but history was to prove them wrong. The eventual unification of Germany met Adenauer's requirement for freedom to be combined with security. Equally importantly, the formal loss of Silesia, East Prussia, and Pomerania, which was required under the Soviet conditions, was by 1989 no longer a burning issue. The majority of West German electors would have found such terms unacceptable in 1952.

If anything the Soviet note hastened the process of western integration. Under the terms of a treaty signed on May 26 the occupation was formally ended, and a few days later the treaty creating the European Defense Community was also signed. The Federal Republic was still not fully sovereign, but Adenauer was comforted by the undertaking of the Western powers to work toward the creation of a united Germany that was integrated into the European community. All this was anathema to the opposition and Kurt Schumacher proclaimed that "whoever signs this treaty ceases to be a German." He was to die shortly afterward at the age of 57, but his spirit lived on in the lively debates over the treaty, which was not formally ratified until May 1953, by which time Stalin had died, the Soviet threat seemed to have diminished, and opposition to German involvement in a European defense community was growing apace in France.

The German Democratic Republic

Meanwhile in the German Democratic Republic "People's Democracy" was quickly transformed into one-party dictatorship. In February 1950 a Ministry of State Security (MfS – "Stasi") was created under a veteran Communist Wilhelm Zaisser, a former NKVD operative who had served as chief of staff to the International Brigade in the Spanish Civil War under the pseudonym "General Gomez." Show trials of 3,300 Nazis, war criminals, and political prisoners, including 55 members of the KPD, began in April. The SED was purged of some 150,000 unreliable elements which, in accordance with Stalin's anti-Semitic obsessions, included a number of "Zionists" and "Cosmopolitans." A hunt began for "imperialist" and "American" agents which culminated in the show trials of a number of prominent figures in the SED in 1953, which were soon to become entwined with the struggle for power after Stalin's death.

Walter Ulbricht, who was elected secretary-general of the party, announced the details of a five-year plan at the third congress of the SED in 1950. Since Stalin wanted to keep the option of a united Germany open, the DDR was deemed to still be in the midst of an "antifascist and democratic transformation," and the five-year plan was concerned with doubling industrial production, not with the creation of a socialist society. With the rejection of the Soviet initiatives in 1952 the SED set about planning the creation of a socialist society.

In fact by 1952 almost 80 percent of industry had been nationalized as "People's Own Enterprises" (VEBs). "Socialism" now meant a concentration on heavy industry, regardless of the cost, the lack of raw materials, and economic feasibility. East German planners blindly followed the outmoded and inefficient Stalinist model of industrialization, and as a result the DDR's economy was hamstrung from the start. Consumer goods were scarce, prohibitively expensive, and of extremely poor quality.

"Smashing the bourgeois educational monopoly" was considered a prerequisite to building socialism. "Bourgeois" children were barred from all forms of higher education, the universities, and new faculties for Marxism–Leninism and "Scientific Atheism" were founded. In spite of compulsory courses in historical and dialectical materialism ("*Histomat*" and "*Diamat*") 80 percent of the citizenry remained at least nominally members of the Evangelical Church, on which the Stasi kept an ever watchful eye. A number of prominent churchmen were arrested in 1953 and hundreds of young people who were active in the church were forbidden to continue their studies. Within the Communist state the churches were centers of relative freedom, in which dissent and resistance steadily grew.

The citizenry voted with their feet against these measures. One hundred and eighty-one thousand left the DDR in 1952, and contributed to and benefited from the rapid economic growth in the Federal Republic. A further 180,000 followed in the first five months of 1953. Stalin's successors – Malenkov, Molotov, and Beria – were highly alarmed at this declaration of bankruptcy, and came to the conclusion that the effort to build socialism in the DDR had been bungled and would have to stop. Their bone-headed henchmen in the central committee of the SED imagined that the economic misery could be relieved by a ten percent increase in industrial norms – in other words by making people work harder for the same pay. This resulted in widespread protests and an alarming increase in the number of refugees. The party leadership was then called to Moscow, given a severe dressing-down, and ordered to take a more lenient approach.

The Politburo of the SED now proclaimed a "New Course." Somewhat lame apologies were offered for past mistakes, promises were made to improve the consumer industries and to lessen restrictions on travel to the West. Recent price increases were rescinded, but the ten percent norm increase remained in place. For the working class this was an intolerable slap in the face. Protests and strikes began on June 11 1953, and on June 16 construction workers on East Berlin's showpiece, the Stalinallee, downed tools and marched in protest, demanding not only reduction of industrial norms but also the resignation of the entire government and free elections. The Politburo promptly rescinded the increased norms, but it was too late. On June 17 hundreds of thousands demonstrated in the major cities throughout the DDR, demanding free elections and reunification. This was the first mass protest against a communist regime, and it left the Politburo helpless and with no alternative but to appeal to the Soviets for help. Tanks rolled into Berlin, at least 50 demonstrators were killed, and thousands were arrested. The Stasi then made 13,000 arrests, but smaller strikes and protests by workers continued for months to come, in a remarkably courageous protest against an inhuman regime that cynically claimed to be a government of and for the workers and peasants. At first it seemed that Ulbricht, the main proponent of a tough line, was bound to topple, but at the end of July Beria, Stalin's bloodstained executioner-turned-reformer, was executed and the moderates in the SED lost their patron. Ulbricht promptly purged the SED and the trades unions (FDGB) of his opponents, who were branded "opposition elements," and Stasi informers worked overtime hunting down dissidents. In the end the "New Course" did lead to modest improvements in the consumer sector, but the DDR was more than ever a police state, and refugees continued to pour west.

The German Question

Given that the new American president, Dwight D. Eisenhower, and his secretary of state John Foster Dulles, did nothing to help the protesters in the DDR, there was precious little that the Federal Republic could do beyond expressing solidarity and making June 17 into a national holiday as "The Day of German Unity." Since there was general agreement among the political parties, with the exception of the KPD, which denounced the uprising as a putsch organized by the imperialist powers, a Committee for an Indivisible Germany was formed to orchestrate the ceremonies on June 17. Much to Adenauer's horror and disgust this fiercely nationalist body called for the restitution of the frontiers of 1937, a demand which threatened to undermine his policy of western integration. He distanced himself from the committee, whose "révanchist" policies provided rich material for the DDR's propagandists, but for years to come the maps of Germany that were prominently displayed in the corridors of West German trains clearly showed the German frontiers as those of 1937. The powerful lobby of expellees could not be ignored.

The Expellees Party (BHE) won considerable support by clamoring for the release of those who had been given prison sentences by the Allies as a result of the crimes they had committed during the Nazi era. They were supported by the nationalist German Party (DP) and by the Liberals (FDP). The FDP had a number of prominent Nazis in their ranks including Werner Naumann, Goebbels' secretary of state in the propaganda ministry; the Gauleiter of Hamburg, Karl Kaufmann; Ernst Achenbach, who had played a key role in the deportation of Jews from France; and SS Obergruppenführer Werner Best, plenipotentiary in occupied Denmark. There was general agreement that those who had been sentenced at Nuremberg had got their just desserts, but others were deemed simply to have done their duty as soldiers or civil servants. They now called for a general amnesty that would include such noisome characters as SS General Kurt Meyer. The SPD jumped on the bandwagon and subscribed to the myth that the army and the Waffen-SS had fought a clean war, and should not be confused with the other SS departments, who alone were responsible for all the crimes of the Nazi era. The Jewish Bund protested against this preposterous assertion, but Kurt Schumacher replied that it was inhuman to treat the 900,000 former members of the Waffen-SS as pariahs. According to a public opinion poll in 1952 an amazing 24 percent of the population still thought highly of Adolf Hitler, and 30 percent condemned the July 20 resistance movement.

Nineteen-fifty-three was an election year in West Germany and Adenauer was in a particularly strong position, which he bolstered by holding a well-publicized interview with the recently released war criminal General von Manstein, and by visiting in prison "Panzer" Meyer and General Nikolaus von Falkenhorst, both of whom had been given prison sentences for murdering Canadian and British prisoners of war. The brutal suppression of the June uprising confirmed to many voters that his firm anticommunist stand was fully justified. The economic boom caused by the Korean War, which ended in July that year, triggered West Germany's "economic miracle" (*Wirtschaftswunder*), which helped to integrate the expellees and to silence radical critics from the extremes of left and right. The dramatic expansion of the economy caused a profound change in the social structure. The flight from the land continued apace and blue collars were exchanged for white. Western Germany became a society of office workers and government employees, of unpretentiously comfortable petits bourgeois with a Volkswagen and a television set, a modest home and a secure pension. A class-conscious proletariat ceased to exist, the all-powerful captains of industry had mostly disappeared, and divisions along confessional and regional lines became blurred. Gross inequalities still existed, and were to become more pronounced, but the Adenauer era was one in which the somewhat philistine and narrow values of the modestly situated middle classes set the tone.

Adenauer's CDU/CSU won a convincing victory in the elections of September 6 1953 gaining 45.2 percent of the popular vote, 14.2 points more than in 1949. The SPD's share of the vote under the rather uninspiring leadership of Erich Ollenhauer remained virtually unchanged at 28.8 percent. The FDP, with 9.5 percent, gave Adenauer a majority, even though they had lost 20 percent of their supporters since 1949, many of whom were disgusted with a party that harbored so many Nazis. A number of smaller parties, including the Communists, failed to reach the five percent minimum, although the Expellees' Party, with its unsavory leadership of old Nazis, SA, and SS men, just squeaked in.

An abortive meeting of the Big Four foreign ministers in Berlin, beginning in January 1954, made it clear that neither side was prepared to make any concessions over the German question. Shortly after this meeting the Bundestag voted in favor of rearmament, but this was of little consequence owing to the attitude of the French. In May French forces in Indo-China met with a crushing defeat at Dien-Bien-Phu, the Laniel government fell, and his successor Pierre Mendès-France negotiated an armistice with Ho Chi Minh's Vietnamese Communists. After such a humiliation the French were in no mood to accept any diminution of their sovereignty, and the National Assembly rejected the European Defense Community by an overwhelming majority. This was a shattering blow to Adenauer who had set great store by the EDC, but France's NATO partners were determined to get the West Germans on board and had little patience with France's residual suspicions of their eastern neighbor. Italy and the Federal Republic were invited to join the Western European Union and discussions began as to the nature of Bonn's future contribution to NATO. Adenauer readily agreed that Germany would not produce ABC weapons, battleships, or strategic bombers. Much to the fury of his nationalist critics, he also agreed to an autonomous Saar, which would be economically linked to France pending a final peace conference, and subject to the Saarlanders' approval in a referendum to be held the following year. The Western Allies in return ceded a number of their rights over the Federal Republic, whose sovereignty nevertheless still remained restricted.

The Soviet Union responded to these negotiations in Paris by making a half-hearted offer of free elections in all of Germany, but when the treaties were signed Molotov, who was still foreign minister, announced that there could now be no question of reunification. A number of leading Protestants, including Niemöller and Gustav Heinemann, who had resigned as minister of the interior over Adenauer's policy of western integration, and who was to later become president of the republic, mounted a massive campaign against the Paris Treaties and rearmament. They were supported by the SPD and the trades unions. The public response was muted, and the treaties were ratified with a convincing majority. French objections to German rearmament were overcome, thanks to some skillful diplomacy by the British foreign secretary Anthony Eden, and the Federal Republic joined the WEU on June 7 1955. Two days later it became a member of NATO.

The Soviet Union responded to German membership of NATO by forming the Warsaw Pact five days later, thus placing the armed forces of all the satellite states, including the DDR, under direct Soviet command. At the same time Molotov and the three Western allies signed a treaty which ended the occupation of Austria. The new state was neutral and an *Anschluss* was forbidden, but it was in all other respects fully sovereign. At Molotov's suggestion, a summit meeting of the Big Four was held in Geneva in the summer of 1955, at which the German question was discussed at length. Much to Adenauer's alarm the Western powers proposed disarmament talks as a means of lessening tension in Europe. This implied an acceptance of the division of Germany and Adenauer's belief that western integration was the most effective way of achieving reunification on acceptable terms began to fade. His fears were largely confirmed when the first secretary of the Communist Party, and the coming man in the Soviet Union, Nikita Khrushchev, gave an inflammatory speech in East Berlin in which he said that the DDR should never give up its "socialist achievements" and made no mention of German unity. It was clear from the tame assurances of the Western powers to the contrary that the division of Germany was now accepted by both sides in the cold war. Adenauer traveled to Moscow in September in order to establish diplomatic relations with the Soviet Union. He had to accept that there would henceforth be two German ambassadors in Moscow, which was a bitter pill to swallow, but he did succeed in securing the release of thousands of wartime prisoners, which greatly enhanced his popularity at home.

On his return to Bonn, Adenauer adumbrated what came to be known as the "Hallstein Doctrine," named after the permanent secretary in the Foreign Office, Walter Hallstein. The Federal Republic henceforth considered itself to be the sole representative body of the German people, and were any third state to establish diplomatic relations with the DDR it would be considered in Bonn as an "unfriendly act." For this reason Bonn refused to establish diplomatic relations with any of the Soviet satellite states, but relations with the Soviet Union were not affected. The Hallstein Doctrine was first put into effect in 1957 when diplomatic relations with Yugoslavia were severed upon Belgrade opening an embassy in East Berlin.

Somewhat to Adenauer's surprise the people of the Saar rejected the "Europeanization" of the region in the referendum, thus opening the way for the return of the Saar to Germany, a process that was finally concluded in 1959. None of this undermined the Federal Republic's relations with Western Europe as the chancellor had feared. In 1957 the Treaty of Rome created the European Economic Community (EEC) in which the Federal Republic was to play a key role, and which was a milestone along the road to European integration.

Nineteen fifty-seven saw the beginnings of a campaign against nuclear weapons along the lines of the Campaign for Nuclear Disarmament (CND) in Britain, with the dramatic title "Struggle Against Atomic Death." Franz Josef Strauss, the dynamic young minister of defense from the CSU who was soon to become one of the dominant figures in West German politics, proposed that the German army (*Bundeswehr*) should be equipped with missiles capable of delivering nuclear warheads. The warheads themselves were to remain under American control. Many saw this as the first step toward Germany becoming a nuclear power and a number of prominent scientists, among them Otto Hahn and Werner Heisenberg, issued a stern warning of the dangers of nuclear war. For the time being the movement had precious little popular support, but thanks in no little part to substantial support from the DDR it was soon to become an important factor in the formation of a powerful Extra-Parliamentary Opposition (APO), which was to cause the major upheavals of 1968.

Nineteen fifty-seven was election year, and Adenauer was once again in an almost invincible position. The brutal suppression of the Hungarian uprising in November of the previous year lent credence to his anticommunist stand. The indexed pensions that were introduced early in the year were enormously beneficial to millions of pensioners and were extremely popular. The SPD had been obliged to vote for the measure but the credit went to the CDU/CSU. The Christian Democrats found a powerful election slogan that was pasted all over the country: "NO EXPERIMENTS!" The SPD's call for more housing was very small beer by comparison. Adenauer won in a landslide, his CDU/CSU winning 50.2 percent of the popular vote. The SPD also had a better showing with 31.8 percent. The FDP dropped to 7.7 percent. None of the other parties obtained the obligatory five percent and the insignificant Communist Party had been banned as a result of a ruling by the Constitutional Court in the previous year. The FDP managed to get 15 additional seats through the direct vote, thanks to a deal made with the CDU. Half the seats in the

Plate 28 No experiments! © Konrad Adenauer Stiftung

Bundestag were elected by proportional representation according to party lists, for which a minimum of five percent of the popular vote was mandatory, and the other half were elected by a direct vote in constituencies. Each elector thus had two votes: one for a party, the other for an individual.

Whereas Adenauer put western integration before national unification and most conservatives, particularly Catholics, turned their back on the Bismarckian Reich and spoke in high-minded tones of the values of the Occident and a united Europe from the Atlantic to the Urals, the national tradition was vigorously upheld in the DDR. Historians set to work to reveal a progressive tradition running from the peasants' war and the Anabaptists in the sixteenth century, to the brief Jacobin regime in Mainz and the glorious struggle for national liberation against Napoleon, in which progressive Germans fought alongside their Russian liberators. Later on Frederick the Great and even Bismarck were added to the list of the enlightened and the progressive. The Federal Republic was painted as the illegitimate offspring of a contrary tradition that culminated in the Third Reich, whereas the DDR held high the banner of Marx, Engels, and the working class and continued the glorious antifascist struggle.

East Germany in the Khrushchev Era

The Soviet Union graciously granted the DDR "full sovereign rights" and in January 1956 the National People's Army (NVA) was formed and integrated into the Warsaw Pact, but the country was soon rocked by the crisis triggered by Khrushchev's speech to the twentieth Congress of the CPSU in which he denounced Stalin's crimes. Ulbricht and his fellow Stalinists were at something of a loss what to do, and for a while it seemed that he might be toppled. A number of prominent dissidents were pardoned and some 21,000 political prisoners were released from jail. Widespread protests in Poland led to the release of Wladyslav Gomulka, who had been jailed as a "Titoite" in 1951, and his appointment as first secretary of the party. The Hungarian uprising in October led to the formation of a new government under the reforming Communist Imre Nagy, which called for withdrawal from the Warsaw Pact, whereupon the Soviet tanks rolled in, 2,000 death sentences were handed down, and some quarter of a million Hungarians fled to the West. With Britain and France engaged in the invasion of Egypt, the Western powers were in no position to give the Hungarians any effective support. Khrushchev could pose as the Egyptian's champion against Western imperialism, and celebrated his victory over the counterrevolutionaries in Hungary. Many Communists in the West found the revelations of Stalin's crimes and the brutality of the Soviets in Hungary hard to stomach and tore up their party cards. Those that remained in the party began the gradual process of loosening ties with Moscow, and laid the foundations of a distinctive form of Euro-Communism.

In the DDR the suppression of Imre Nagy's regime was used as an excuse for an abrupt change of course and a number of prominent "revisionists" were arrested, including Ernst Wollweber, the minister of state security. He was replaced by Erich Mielke, a particularly odious creature whose principal claim to the office was that he had murdered two policemen in 1931 on orders from the party. He was to remain in charge until the state's inglorious demise. The philosopher Wolfgang Harich, who had called for a "third way" and "humane socialism" that would avoid the injustices of capitalism and the rigidity of communist economic planning, and who had the ear of a number of key figures in the SED, was given a ten-year prison sentence.

His ideas lived on in the Prague Spring of 1968, and in the heady last days of the DDR.

Ulbricht had weathered the de-Stalinization storm and was now in full command. The economy was steadily improving and the majority of people had come to terms with a regime which, although grim, did not quite match the stereotype of a communist hell that prevailed in the West. The stream of refugees was still immense but it was diminishing, from 260,000 in 1957 to 144,000 in 1959. Encouraged by these developments, Ulbricht announced at the Fifth Party Congress in 1958 that a socialist society was in the making, in which the quantity of consumer goods per capita would overtake that of West Germany. The process of "catch-up and overtake" was to be completed by 1961. This was to be made possible in part by heavy investment in "socialist education" in which science, mathematics, and economics would be privileged. Within a year it was plain that this was all pie in the sky, and the five-year plan became a seven-year plan. At the same time it was decided to complete the process of collectivization. Forty percent of farmland had been collectivized by 1959 and by 1961 almost 90 percent was in the hands of the Agricultural Production Cooperatives (LPGs). The result was a severe food shortage and the mass exodus of peasantry to the West. The nationalization of a large number of small enterprises had a similar result. Output sank and artisans left the country. Two hundred thousand people left in 1960, most of them via West Berlin.

Meanwhile various schemes were put forward in an attempt to solve the German question. In 1956 Ulbricht presented a plan for a neutral German confederation, a proposal that was soon seconded by the Soviet Union. Adenauer responded to this dangerous suggestion by proposing that an arrangement be made with the DDR along the lines of the Austrian State Treaty. Also in 1957, the Polish foreign minister Adam Rapacki proposed a central Europe free of atomic weapons, and with minimal armed forces that would include Poland and both German states. Hugh Gaitskill, the leader of the British Labor Party, supported Rapacki's plan by proposing disengagement from central Europe and a unified and neutral Germany. The doyen of American diplomats, George F. Kennan, echoed Gaitskill's suggestion in the BBC's Reith Lectures in 1957. Much to Adenauer's alarm these proposals found wide public acceptance, but he was saved by Khrushchev's impulsive intervention. In October 1958 Ulbricht demanded an end to four-power control in Berlin so that the entire city would become integrated into the DDR. In the following month Khrushchev issued his "Berlin Ultimatum," in which he threatened that the Soviet Union and the DDR would act unilaterally if the three Western powers did not withdraw and thus end their "occupation regime" in Berlin.

This was the most serious crisis in Berlin since the blockade, and the Western Alliance began to waver. In January 1959 Khrushchev proposed a peace conference that would result in a neutral Germany consisting of two states, with a demilitarized Berlin as a free city, and with a solemn renunciation of any claim to territory east of the Oder-Neisse line. The Conservative British prime minister Harold Macmillan, who was soon to face an election and was mindful of the popularity of Gaitskill's proposals for the future of Germany, made conciliatory remarks

during a visit to Moscow. He hinted that he might go along with Moscow's proposals, and would consider opening diplomatic relations with the DDR. Even John
Foster Dulles, a close ally of Adenauer and an adamantine anticommunist, showed
signs of willingness to concede at least a fraction. But he was mortally ill with cancer
and resigned in April. Only Charles de Gaulle, who became president of the Republic on December 21 1958, was inalterably opposed to Khrushchev's proposals.

The Big Four foreign ministers met in Geneva in May and again in July, but the
only positive result of these discussions was an agreement that Khrushchev should
meet Eisenhower in Camp David in September. The communiqué issued after these
meetings spoke of the two sides' determination to preserve the peace and to continue discussions of the Berlin problem. Khrushchev no longer stood by his ultimatum, but he now knew that the West wanted to avoid a confrontation over Berlin,
and that the American president considered the present status of Berlin to be highly
unsatisfactory. The 83-year-old Adenauer could take little comfort from these
developments.

Willy Brandt

Elections were held in West Berlin in December 1958 which resulted in a victory
for Willy Brandt's SPD. He and Adenauer were the two towering figures in the
history of the Federal Republic. Born in Lübeck as Herbert Frahm in 1913 to a
single mother, he emigrated to Norway in 1933 and joined the Norwegian army in
order to escape from the clutches of the Gestapo. Later he worked as a journalist
in Sweden. He regained his German citizenship in 1948 when he adopted his nom
de plume as his official name. He endorsed the Federal Republic's membership of
NATO, and rejected his own party's plans for the future of Germany. They had been
drawn up by Herbert Wehner, a brilliant and sourly ironic former communist, and
bore a certain resemblance to Ulbricht's proposals. Shortly after his election, Brandt
addressed the NATO council in Paris in his inimitable English, and impressed his
audience with his absolute determination to stand up to Soviet pressure and ensure
that West Berlin remain an island of freedom in the heart of the DDR.

Brandt was the outstanding example of the new type of Social Democrat. He was
pro-Western, flexible, ready to compromise while remaining true to his principles,
a brilliant speaker, and a thoroughgoing democrat. Although born in the humblest
of circumstances, he enjoyed a solidly bourgeois lifestyle while never losing the
common touch. No politician was less corrupted by power, none more widely loved
and respected. His modernizing ideas were reflected in the SPD's new party program
adopted at Godesberg in 1959. The last vestiges of the Marxism that remained in
the Heidelberg program of 1925 and the Dortmund program of 1952 were cast
aside. The party endorsed the free market economy and announced that it was no
longer a party of the working class, but an open-ended people's party.

In 1960 Herbert Wehner gave a brilliant speech in the Bundestag in which he
said that the SPD fully endorsed NATO and the Western Alliance as the basis of

the Federal Republic's foreign policy. Furthermore he insisted that "a divided Germany cannot tolerate a situation in which Christian Democrats and Social Democrats are in a permanent state of mutual enmity." Wehner thus turned his back on his Plan for Germany (*Deutschlandplan*) of March 1959, and showed that the Godesberg Program, which he had played a key role in writing, marked a genuine new beginning for the SPD. Wehner was every inch a power politician who realized that the SPD would remain without influence as long as it stood in principled opposition to the CDU/CSU. The party would have to become an acceptable coalition partner for it to have any share of political power. In such circumstances there was no serious alternative for the SPD but to make Willy Brandt their candidate for chancellor in 1960. As mayor of Berlin he was a popular national figure, a youthful and even glamorous alternative to the octogenarian chancellor, a man much respected in the West, and who could appeal to all sectors of German society, except those who could not stomach the fact that he was both illegitimate and an émigré.

The next round of Big Four talks was held in Paris in May 1960, but when Gary Powers was shot down over the Soviet Union in his U2 reconnaissance plane Khrushchev walked out and announced that he would not attend another such meeting for several months to come. He promised that in the meantime he would not raise the issue of Berlin. He clearly intended to await the outcome of the US presidential elections, in which John F. Kennedy faced Richard Nixon. Adenauer breathed a sigh of relief when the Paris talks were thus abruptly ended, but he was soon to be alarmed by the diplomatic ineptitude of the young and inexperienced American president. After the abortive invasion of the Bay of Pigs in April 1961 there followed a disastrous meeting between Kennedy and Khrushchev in Vienna in June. Kennedy was sent reeling by Khrushchev's renewed threat to sign a peace treaty with the GDR and to seal off all routes to West Berlin. He returned to Washington in a highly agitated state and in the following month gave a radio address announcing a substantial increase in America's conventional forces and his absolute resolve to stand by West Berlin.

Tension over Berlin was such that refugees flooded to the West to the point that the East German economy was on the verge of collapse. At a meeting of the Warsaw Pact in March 1961 Ulbricht requested permission to cut off all routes to West Berlin, but this was denied. He renewed his plea at the August meeting of the Warsaw Pact and on August 5 he was given the go-ahead. In the early morning of August 13 1961 work was begun to seal off West Berlin with an "antifascist defensive wall," which made it virtually impossible for anyone to leave the DDR. The Berlin Wall was a declaration of the bankruptcy of the Communist system, but it led to a certain degree of stability in that the nagging question of whether to leave or not was finally settled. Planners no longer had to face the disastrous economic effects of the mass flight of what was often the best and the brightest. Snow White, as one cabaret artist in East Berlin remarked, now only had three dwarves since the other four were in the West. But at least she was not totally bereft of help.

The West contented itself with verbal protests and was relieved that West Berlin had been left untouched. August 13 was a shattering blow for Germans in both East

Plate 29 Adenauer and De Gaulle. © DPA

and West and they felt abandoned by their allies and well-wishers. Reunification now seemed nothing but a pipe dream. The two societies grew steadily apart, each taking on a distinctive identity. On the personal level families and loved ones were separated by barbed wire, minefields, and machine-gun posts. The idea of a united Germany that was free, peaceful, and secure seemed little more than an empty formula. The way ahead seemed more uncertain than ever.

The Berlin Wall was built in the middle of an election campaign in the Federal Republic in which Adenauer showed signs of losing his grip. He did not allow for a pause in the campaign when the wall was built and concentrated on scurrilous attacks on the opposition, at one point referring to his rival Willy Brandt as "Herr Brandt alias Frahm." Brandt, as mayor of West Berlin, used his position in these crisis days to the utmost and overnight became a figure of international stature. When the votes were counted on September 17 the CDU/CSU had lost almost five points compared with 1957, the SPD gained 4.4 points, and the FDP with 12.8 percent had increased their share of the popular vote by a remarkable 66.2 percent. Coalition discussions were protracted and acrimonious. The FDP wanted to maintain the alliance with the CDU/CSU but insisted on getting rid of Adenauer, who was now 85 years old and who stubbornly refused to resign. Eventually a compromise solution was found when Adenauer agreed to step down in the middle of the new parliament, and the coalition between the CDU/CSU and the FDP was renewed. The SPD, which had hoped for a national government to deal with the Berlin crisis, remained in opposition.

In April 1962 the French president, de Gaulle, successfully brought the Algerian war to an end and thus avoided what could have become a civil war in France. He then turned to Adenauer and proposed close cooperation between the two countries, particularly with respect to European defense. Adenauer made an official visit to France in July that culminated in a Franco-German military parade, and the two old men celebrated mass in Reims cathedral. De Gaulle then paid a return visit to the Federal Republic in September in which he was given a heartfelt welcome. Relations with France became a major debating point in Germany, particularly within the ranks of the CDU/CSU. The division was between "Atlanticists," like the foreign minister Gerhard Schroeder, who wanted the closest possible ties with the United States, and the "Gaullists," such as Franz-Josef Strauss, who wanted Europe to be less dependent on America. The debate between the two factions intensified when de Gaulle proposed an alliance between the two countries shortly after his visit to Germany.

Meanwhile, the crisis continued over Berlin as the Soviets harassed the air corridors, and when an 18-year-old construction worker was left by American soldiers to bleed to death on the frontier strip, having been shot trying to cross the border into West Berlin the public outrage was such that a serious incident was only narrowly avoided thanks to Willy Brandt's skillful handling of the situation. Adenauer got no support from Kennedy, and Khrushchev exploited the president's weakness to step up the pressure by stationing middle-range missiles in Cuba. Kennedy forced Khrushchev to back down in an extremely hazardous poker game that brought the world perilously close to nuclear war. The building of the Berlin Wall and the Cuban missile crisis forced both sides to rethink their positions. The Americans and the Soviets realized that it would clearly be madness to push the envelope any further, and the way was open for a gradual détente.

The *Spiegel* Affair

At the height of the Cuban missile crisis Germany was rocked by the most serious domestic political crisis in the history of the Bonn republic. The popular news magazine *Spiegel* published an article on the recent NATO exercise "Fallex 62," which had shown up some disastrous deficiencies in West Germany's defenses and a number of serious differences between the US and the Federal Republic over atomic weapons. All of this was in the public domain, but the impetuous minister of defense and chairman of the CDU, Franz-Josef Strauss, a man of dubious political morality and one of the magazine's favorite targets, was convinced that top secret documents had been leaked which endangered the republic's security. The magazine's offices were searched and sealed. A number of journalists were arrested, with total disregard for due legal procedure, in a scandalous attempt to muzzle the free press. Strauss blatantly lied to the Bundestag about his role in the affair, and, when caught out, refused to resign. Adenauer made a fool of himself by accusing the *Spiegel* of committing high treason simply to make money. The minister of the interior admitted that he had "acted somewhat outside the law," and the minister of justice confessed that he had not been informed that the arrests were to be made, as was required by the law. The five FDP ministers resigned in protest, and the party leader, Erich Mende, made it clear that the coalition could not continue if Strauss were to remain in office. A number of CDU ministers followed suit. Massive protests were held throughout the country in expressions of solidarity with the *Spiegel* journalists and in support of the freedom of the press. In the end the journalists were acquitted by the High Court of all charges, and the Constitutional Court had a tied vote on whether or not the action against the *Spiegel* was unconstitutional. Rudolf Augstein, the paper's editor, emerged from 103 days in jail to be fêted as a national hero. Strauss eventually bowed to the inevitable and resigned, his parting marked by a ceremonial parade and an effusive panegyric from Adenauer. The *Spiegel* affair marked a turning point in the history of the Bonn republic. The old authoritarian tradition of the "*Obrigkeitsstaat*," with obedient citizens meekly following orders from above, was totally discredited, and a younger generation called for a more open, liberal, and free society of autonomous subjects. The westernizer Adenauer had been overtaken by the Coca-Cola generation.

The End of the Adenauer Era

In December 1962 Macmillan met Kennedy in the Bahamas and agreed to arm British submarines with American nuclear warheads. This was designed as the first stage of the creation of a multinational atomic force (MLF), under American command, within the framework of NATO. De Gaulle took this as a personal affront and announced that France would now join the nuclear club, and would veto Britain's entry to the EEC. Shortly afterwards, on January 22 1963, the Franco-German Agreement was signed in Paris, which called for regular meetings between the two heads of government and consultation over all key issues of foreign policy and cultural and educational exchanges.

At first it appeared that the Federal Republic was now on an anti-American course, but Adenauer made it plain that the Federal Republic would live up to its NATO obligations and was interested in joining the proposed MLF. The Bonn government also supported British entry to the EEC – an empty gesture since the French veto was already in effect. The Elysée Treaty, as ratified by the Bundestag, removed all traces of anti-Americanism, and thus frustrated de Gaulle's intentions. The general suffered a further setback when the CDU/CSU decided upon Ludwig Erhard, a prominent "Atlanticist" who thought Washington and London far more important than Paris, as Adenauer's successor.

The "Atlanticists" were given a further boost when Kennedy paid a state visit to the Federal Republic in June 1963. The American president was given a rapturous welcome as he underlined the United States' commitment to the Federal Republic and when, in Berlin, he announced: "ich bin ein Berliner!" At the same time, in accordance with his recently expressed determination to "make the world safe for diversity," he urged the Germans to be patient, warning that national unification would be an extremely long process. Willy Brandt was in total accord with Kennedy. He had told his audience in Harvard in October 1962 that coexistence, détente, and communication were the keys to any progress. In July the following year he told a German audience that "a solution to the German problem can only be found with the Soviet Union, not against it." Here were the clear outlines of his future *Ostpolitik*. His close associate, Egon Bahr, had already spoken of "change through convergence" (*Wandel durch Annäherung*), which was soon to become a popular slogan. Brandt and Bahr agreed with Kennedy that the Soviet regime could not be overthrown, but it could be subject to change. As a consequence the Hallstein Doctrine, the claim that the Federal Republic was the sole representative of the German people, and the still persisting claim on land to the east of the Oder and Neisse, had both to be called into serious question.

Adenauer was not prepared to accept these arguments and thus became increasingly out of step with the times. A new crisis erupted when all nations were invited to sign a treaty banning the testing of atomic weapons, which had been concluded between the Soviet Union, the United States, and Britain in Moscow in August 1963. Since the DDR was invited to append its signature the chancellor considered this to be a form of recognition of the East German regime. His foreign minister, Gerhard Schröder, strongly disagreed, and with the support of the FDP and the opposition SPD he won the day. The Federal Republic signed the treaty in August, while formally declaring that this should not be seen as granting recognition to any regime with which it did not already have diplomatic relations. This was also the position of the US government.

Finally, after 14 years in office, Adenauer ceded his place with singular ill grace to Ludwig Erhard on October 15 1963. The 87-year-old remained as party chairman and set out to make life as difficult as possible for his successor, whom he considered to be a political lightweight. Adenauer regarded the corpulent, cigar-smoking, and incurably optimistic Erhard with deep suspicion. Erhard was a died-in-the-wool liberal, who did not share the old man's profound mistrust of his countrymen, did not seem to be concerned about the decline of Christian values that in Adenauer's view threatened to undermine European civilization, and worst of all he was a Protestant.

For all Adenauer's authoritarian style, which led many to draw a parallel with Bismarck, he left behind him a well-functioning democracy. His other great achievement was that he had integrated the Federal Republic into the Western Alliance against fierce opposition, and this was integration no longer challenged except by a handful on the lunatic fringes of left and right. At the same time he forged a close alliance with Germany's "hereditary enemy" France, which was to become the cornerstone of a new European order. He always feared that were Germany not fully committed to the Atlantic alliance and to Europe, it would once again be a loose cannon on deck, and a threat to peace and stability in Europe.

Culture in the Federal Republic

Intellectuals in the Adenauer era, most of whom were on the left, were sharply critical of a man they compared to Franco with his unbendingly authoritarian personality, his clericalism, and his narrow-minded regional patriotism. To them the Federal Republic was insufferably petit bourgeois, philistine, intolerant, and unenlightened. Adenauer had no time for art and artists, and spent his leisure hours playing boccie at his holiday home in Italy or tending his roses at his villa on the Rhine. He summarily dismissed his high-minded and finger-wagging critics as fellow travelers and stooges in the pay of the East German regime. Intellectuals and artists were excluded from politics, but they enjoyed a comfortable martyrdom while denouncing the crass materialism of the "economic miracle." In their eyes Adenauer's greatest sin was that instead of creating a new Germany, he had simply carried on where the Weimar Republic had left off. "Restoration" was the fashionable word, first coined by the left-wing Catholic journalist Walter Dirks in an enormously influential article published in 1950 in the *Frankfurter Hefte*, of which he was coeditor with Eugen Kogon, a survivor of Buchenwald concentration camp and author of powerful study of the SS state.

In fact it was the intellectuals rather than the politicians who were committed to restoration. They were pale echoes of the carping, mocking left-wingers of the Weimar Republic, whose vicious attacks had done much to destroy the democratic process. They signed countless denunciations of nuclear armaments, the censorship of pornography, and Franz-Josef Strauss, but they were uninvolved in the political process. They remained aloof and disapproving.

In striking contrast to the Weimar Republic there were no outstanding intellectuals on the right. The catastrophic consequences of National Socialism were so obvious that only a few cranks and outsiders could find anything positive in its achievements. Those who had been close to the movement, such as Ernst Junger, had long since distanced themselves from the brown rabble, and were now independent thinkers on the right who accepted the parliamentary system, although often grudgingly. It was not until the 1970s that the right was to begin to seize the intellectual high ground, although some quixotic attempts were already being made to discover the positive aspects of National Socialism.

The key literary works of this period, such as Günther Grass's bestselling *Tin Drum* (1959), the novels of Heinrich Böll, Wolfgang Koeppen, and Martin Walser, and the poetry of Hans Magnus Enzensberger, were massive attacks on the stuffiness, the complacency, and the collective amnesia of Adenauer's Germany, in which all too often righteous indignation was a poor substitute for literary merit. As time goes by much of this highly acclaimed writing seems intolerably schoolmasterly, tendentious and, in the final resort, tiresome. Very few writers dared tackle the problems of the immediate past. Hans Erich Nossak's shattering account of the bombing of Hamburg in July 1943 in *Downfall (Der Untergang)* was largely ignored, whereas Gert Ledig's superb novel on the bombing campaign, *Revenge (Vergeltung)*, was largely dismissed in 1956 as a grotesque distortion of the reality of war and was condemned as politically inopportune. He was so depressed by this reaction that he ceased to write. Along with his novel *The Rocket Launcher (Der Stalinorgel)*, published in 1955, these are two of the finest literary works to have emerged from World War II. It is only in recent years that German writers have been able successfully to tackle the German past. In *Crab Walk (Krebsgang)*, Gunther Grass uses his exceptional narrative skills to reconstruct the sinking of the *Wilhelm Gütloff* by a Soviet submarine in 1945, in which thousands of German refugees lost their lives. Uwe Timm's *My Brother as an Example (Am Beispiel meines Bruders*, 2003) is a subtle, penetrating, and poetic analysis of the heavy weight of the past on the postwar generation.

The theater, which had managed to preserve a degree of autonomy during the Nazi period, had some remarkable achievements to its credit, thanks to the efforts of such outstanding talents as Gustav Gründgens, Heinrich George, and Heinz Hilpert, all of whom had impeccable left-wing credentials. Gründgens was vilified in Klaus Mann's novel *Mephisto*, later to be made into a successful movie, but in fact it was George who made a pact with the devil, though many attributed his grotesquely Nazified outbursts to his chronic alcoholism. This fine theatrical tradition lived on in the Federal Republic, while in East Berlin Berthold Brecht was given his own theater on the Schiffbauerdamm which soon won world renown. His relations with his Communist paymasters were somewhat tense and it was often hinted that he was guilty of the terrible heresy of "formalism." When he received the Stalin prize in 1955 he prudently deposited the money in a Swiss bank, but he died in the following year, ever true to the East German regime.

The Wagner festival in Bayreuth, Hitler's favorite theatrical occasion, reopened in 1951, with some misgivings but to great acclaim. The master's works were freed of their National Socialist trappings and, under his grandsons Wieland and Wolfgang's direction, were presented in a rarified Jungian world of myth and symbolic archetypes, which even sensitive left-wingers allowed themselves to enjoy. During the Weimar Republic works by Schönberg, Webern, Hindemith, and Weill had been premiered at the Donaueschingen music festival, sponsored by Prince Max Egon zu Furstenberg. The festival was ended due first to the depression and then to the hostility of the Nazis to such "degenerate" music. It opened again in 1946 in collaboration with the Südwestfunk Baden-Baden (SWF), and was sponsored by the French occupation authorities. It soon became a forum for brilliant young composers such as Karlheinz Stockhausen and Hans Werner Henze, who began their careers in the Adenauer years. Stockhausen joined Pierre Boulez and Luigi Nono to form a trio of leading lights who inspired a whole generation of young composers. The Electronic Studio in Cologne became a major center of experiment in the new medium of electronic music. Pierre Schaefer and Pierre Henry introduced their "*musique con-*

crète" at Donaueschingen in 1953, and John Cage and David Tudor made their sensational first appearance in Europe in the following year. Masterpieces of modern music such as Messiaen's *Chronochromie* (1960), Ligeti's *Atmosphères* (1961), and Stockhausen's *Mantra* (1970) were given their first performances at the festival. Although such music never found wide acceptance, and John Cage's experiments with a prepared piano met with cat calls and hoots of derisive laughter, the Federal Republic became a major center of experimental music and encouraged a younger generation of musicians, from Helmut Lachenmann and Wolfgang Rihm on one side of an increasingly narrowing divide, to Kraftwerk and the contemporary techno scene on the other.

American pop and jazz music were enormously popular, and radio stations such as the American Forces Network and Voice of America were greatly appreciated. Elvis Presley's German fans were sent into ecstasy when he was posted to Wiesbaden as a GI. A number of up-and-coming jazz musicians also served in the US forces in Germany, and could be heard jamming in smoky cellars in Berlin and Frankfurt. Popular culture, with its freshness and individuality, was a healthy influence on the young democracy, not least because it brought forth blustering reactions from the Babbitts and cultural pessimists, and it also served to underscore Adenauer's Western orientation.

The Federal Republic had come a long way, but there was still a great deal to be done. A serious debate over the Nazi past was still confined to a handful of historians and journalists. Perhaps this dreadful time was too close and too traumatic for this to have happened so soon, and it was to be many years before Germany really came to grips with these intractable problems. Although the Basic Law accorded equal rights to men and women in article 3, this bore no resemblance to reality and German women were expected to be content with being dutiful wives, hard-working homemakers, and diligent mothers. The educational system had still not recovered from the damage done by the Nazis, and the law was in need of fundamental reform. Most serious of all, Adenauer's rhetoric about reunification in peace and in freedom rang hollow, since in the midst of the cold war this was clearly an impossibility. The time had come for a completely new approach to the German question.

15
Two Germanys: 1963–82

There was a certain relaxation of tension in the DDR after the building of the Berlin Wall. Taking his cue from Khrushchev's speech at the twenty-second Congress of the CPSU in October 1961 that revealed further horrors committed during the Stalin era, Ulbricht at last began to speak of "crimes" committed in the name of Communism. The town of Stalinstadt on the Oder was given the robustly socialist name of Eisenhüttenstadt (Iron Works Town), and was to become a showpiece of socialist architecture. Berlin's Stalinallee was renamed Marx-Engels Allee. Statues of the Soviet dictator were hastily removed. Artists and writers were allowed a small degree of freedom, so that Christa Wolf in her novel *Der Geteilte Himmel* (1963) was permitted to touch on the taboo subject of "flight from the Republic," and although it was drearily orthodox, in that socialist political correctness triumphed over love, it enjoyed a certain success in the West.

In 1963 a "New Economic System for Planning and Direction" (NÖPL) was proclaimed, which permitted the use of "economic levers" such as prices, wages, and even profit to bring a degree of flexibility into the fossilized planned economy. In the same spirit a degree of decentralization was permitted. It was hoped that a homeopathic dose of capitalism would revive a moribund economy. The results were encouraging. Productivity and gross national product rose substantially, and it seemed that a totalitarian society was gradually becoming what the West German political scientist, Peter Christian Ludz, was soon to call a system of "consultative authoritarianism." As Western scholars moved steadily to the left there was much talk of the "convergence" of the two systems. According to this theory communism and capitalism were gradually being transformed into technocracies that recognized the importance of input from society at large, and which had to take individual needs and aspirations into account. This was altogether too rosy a view of developments in the DDR, and the people were still left without a voice, but at least it was no longer a totalitarian Stalinist police state. Khrushchev fell from power in 1964 and was replaced by a "collective leadership" under the dreary Leonid Brezhnev, who presided over the inexorable economic decline of the Soviet system, hastened by excessive expenditure on the military, and by neo-Stalinist ideological sclerosis.

The new Soviet leadership ordered Ulbricht to distance himself from the New Economic System, which had failed to meet its targets and had put the economy above politics. Ulbricht promptly made the chief planner, Erich Appel, responsible for all deficiencies in the plan, which were in large part due to the failure of the Soviet Union to supply the raw materials they had promised. Appel was found shot dead in his office in December 1965. It remains uncertain whether this was murder or suicide. The Central Committee of the SED drew up a long list of past mistakes and returned to a system of rigidly centralized planning. At the same time Erich Honecker, as secretary for security, clamped down on the arts, which had become infected by the "lack of moral inhibitions and brutality of capitalist West Germany." The highly talented folk singer Wolf Biermann was forbidden to perform in public, and his friend the physicist Robert Havemann, also a prominent critic of a pro-crustean Marxism, was expelled from the SED and lost his professorship at the Humboldt University in Berlin. A reform of education added a heavier dose of Marxism–Leninism to the curriculum, and emphasized mathematics and science in the vain hope that East German youth would overtake their Western counterparts in both ideological fervor and scientific attainments.

A series of agreements over permitting West Berliners to visit East Berlin, the first of which was signed shortly before Christmas in 1963, was very much in the spirit of Willy Brandt's "step by step" approach, but there was great concern in the CDU/CSU that this would eventually lead to recognition of the East German regime. By 1966 the DDR announced it would make no further concessions on this issue unless Bonn formally recognized the East German regime. The Brezhnev administration showed no interest in improving relations with the Federal Republic, and in 1965 the majority of Arab states broke off diplomatic relations with Bonn when West Germany exchanged ambassadors with Israel. The struggle between "Atlanticists" and "Gaullists" in Germany grew all the more intense when President Johnson finally dropped the idea of an MLF, thus further weakening West Germany's diplomatic effectiveness. Then de Gaulle withdrew France's delegation from the ministerial council of the EEC, in protest against a German-sponsored plan for a thoroughgoing reform of the community's agricultural policy that featherbedded the French peasantry. The way for further European integration, which the German government supported, was thus blocked. But for all these diplomatic setbacks the economy continued to flourish, and although there had been serious deficiencies in the labor market since the Wall was built, they were largely made good by over a million "guest workers," mostly from Italy, Spain, Yugoslavia, and Turkey.

The Federal Republic after Adenauer

Willy Brandt entered the election campaign of 1965 with an outstanding team, but they were no match for Ludwig Erhard, the man so closely associated with the "economic miracle" from which almost all were profiting. The CDU/CSU were the clear winners, with 47.6 percent of the popular vote. The SPD improved their standing, but still trailed behind with 39.3 percent. The FDP suffered a major reverse with a mere 9.5 percent, but the coalition was back in government with a comfortable majority of 92 seats. Willy Brandt, the object of a scandalous press campaign that was even more vicious than in 1961, announced that he would stay on as mayor of Berlin and as party chairman, but would not stand again as candidate for chancellor.

Many thorny issues had to be resolved before a coalition could be formed, principal among them relations with the DDR and whether Franz-Josef Strauss should be allowed back into the cabinet after the *Spiegel* debacle. The new government did not get off to a good start. A proposed exchange of top-level speakers with the DDR did not come to fruition, thanks to the intervention of the USSR. De Gaulle continued to refuse to accept changes in the common European agricultural policy, and in February 1966 he announced that France would withdraw its forces from NATO. De Gaulle went on a dramatically staged state visit to the Soviet Union in June, and the debates between "Atlanticists" and "Gaullists" flared up once again. Erhard felt it prudent to go to Washington in order to reassure the Americans that Bonn was still a faithful ally, and in the hope of winning some concessions over such issues as access to atomic weapons, the offset payments for US troops stationed in Germany, and currency exchange. President Johnson refused to give way on any of these points, and Erhard returned home empty handed.

Bonn's finances were now in dire straits. Taxes had been reduced, expenditure increased, and inflation was rapidly rising. The FDP refused to accept tax increases to cover the substantial deficit, and all four FDP ministers resigned in protest. Erhard, who had never had close ties with his party, was now clearly a man of the past. The extreme right-wing National Democratic Party of Germany (NDP) won 7.9 percent of the vote in local elections in Hesse, and with Erhard as a seriously weakened chancellor in a minority government, there was much wild talk of a resurgence of the radical right and of Bonn going the way of Weimar. Erhard refused to step down until he was forced out by a "constructive" vote of no confidence that appointed the minister-president of Baden-Württemberg, Kurt George Kiesinger, as his successor. He was a smoothly charming man, an experienced politician who was always well briefed, and who had an excellent record as an effective administrator. There was however a major blot on his escutcheon. He was one of the "March fallen" who had joined the Nazi Party after the March elections of 1933, and there was much talk on the left of his appointment being further evidence of an alarming swing to the extreme right. All suspicions to this effect were lifted when the *Spiegel* published Gestapo documents which charged Kiesinger of "hindering anti-Jewish actions" and supporting "political tendencies" which "ran counter to the Führer's foreign policy."

After lengthy negotiations a new coalition was formed between the CDU/CSU and the SPD. There had been considerable resistance to the idea of a coalition with the CDU/CSU among the Social Democrats' rank and file, by the Young Socialists (*Jusos*) in the party, and by left-wing intellectuals, but Herbert Wehner and the rising star of the party, Helmuth Schmidt, were determined that the party should at last take an active part in government. In many ways it was an unsatisfactory solution and was at best a temporary measure to deal with the immediate budgetary crisis. With only the tiny FDP in opposition the extreme right and left were both greatly strengthened. The new coalition marked a major turning point in the history of the Bonn republic, but it raised more questions than it answered. A serious debate took place about the nature of the state. Was it merely a provisional structure as the Basic Law asserted? Should it be regarded as permanent, with all talk of reunification struck from the agenda? What were the obligations, if any, of West Germans to their fellow Germans in the East? Where were the boundaries of "Germany?" How was the distinction to be drawn between "state" and "nation?"

These questions were intertwined with the fierce debates triggered by discussions of Germany's past. Fritz Fischer's *Germany's Aims in the First World War* (1961) challenged the conservative historical establishment's comfortable belief that Germany bore no particular share in the blame for the outbreak of war in 1914. After a lengthy and ferocious debate Fischer and his young assistants emerged victorious. Ralf Dahrendorf's *Society and Democracy in Germany* (1965) suggested that the failed coup attempt on July 20 1944, and the subsequent terror, resulted in the destruction of the old German elite, thus opening up the "brutal path to modernity." Alexander and Margarete Mitcherlich's *The Inability to Mourn* (1967) used a Freudian approach to argue that the "brutal path to modernity" had in fact been blocked by Germany's inability to go through the painful process of dealing with collective responsibility for the crimes of the Nazi era, and thus overcome the country's ambivalence toward its past and face reality.

The "culprit generation" suffered from a collective amnesia, and remained, in the Mitcherlichs' terms, "infantile." The younger generation who had played no active role in events between 1933 and 1945, or who had been born after the collapse of the Third Reich, was to a large extent plagued by a feeling of guilt for crimes that had been committed in the name of a people with whom they had an uncomfortable relationship. They felt bitter toward their smug, self-satisfied, and morally dubious elders. The trial of Adolf Eichmann in Jerusalem in 1960/1 was an uncomfortable reminder of a past that many hoped would go away. Thanks to Fritz Bauer, the courageous and steadfast chief prosecutor of the state of Hesse, a trial began of those accused of crimes committed at Auschwitz. After four years of preparation, during which statements from 1,300 witnesses were taken, the "Auschwitz Trial" began in Frankfurt in December 1963 and lasted for 20 months. Six of the accused were imprisoned for life, 11 were given prison sentences of between three and 14 years, and three were acquitted. Many felt that these sentences were too lenient, and there was a stormy debate over quite what the trial was supposed to achieve, but it served as a shocking reminder of the appalling crimes of the Nazi era, memories of which had been suppressed. It was also an uncomfortable reminder of the active complicity of ordinary Germans in Hitler's crimes. The Auschwitz trial opened up old wounds, and fueled a fierce intergenerational clash.

Students were at the vanguard of the left-wing opposition. They were organized in the Socialist German Students' Association (SDS), which had been strongly opposed to the right turn the party had made in the Godesberg Program. It had not been sponsored by the SPD since 1961. Their theoretical journal *Das Argument* took up some of the basic notions of the "critical theory" of Theodor W. Adorno and Max Horkheimer, who had returned from exile in America and now held court at the Institute for Social Research in Frankfurt. Their rarified re-workings of Marx and Hegel provided them with an opaque language with which they imagined they could influence the structure of society from comfortable positions within the infrastructure.

The protest culture of the 1960s was the product of a saturated society. The material rubble had been cleared, and although much of the moral rubble remained, the economic miracle had brought a degree of prosperity to almost all. Jean-Luc Godard's "children of Marx and Coca-Cola" escaped this bloated and philistine world by going "underground." In a world of sex, drugs, and rock and roll, of Eastern meditation and Western Marxism, young people imagined that they were living the revolution. In fact the underground was very much above ground and, as the outstanding Marxist philosopher Ernst Bloch was shrewd enough to fear, was soon packaged and sold to the general public, as wily capitalists made huge profits from "alternative" culture.

Solidarity with Ho Chi Minh's anti-imperialist struggle for national liberation against the United States, and identification with the glamorous figure of Che Guevara, soon to become the most prominent of martyrs in the anti-colonialist cause, gave the movement an international dimension and a revolutionary flavor. Radical students in Berlin were one with their colleagues in Berkeley, Paris, and Rome. In June 1967 a mass demonstration was held in Berlin to protest against the visit of the Shah of Iran, during which a student, Bruno Ohnesorg, was shot in the head by a policeman.

The student movement accused the older generation of refusing to face the Nazi past, and retreating into what the philosopher Hermann Lübbe called a "communicative silence." They denounced the government for supporting the United States in their brutal war against the Vietcong, in which chemical weapons such as napalm and Agent Orange were used on a vast scale, and for allying with such tyrants as the Shah of Iran. When the "Great Coalition" government proposed legislation which would remove judicial and parliamentary control over the government in a state of emergency, rights which the Allies had reserved in the German Treaty of 1955, they denounced the measure as a "Nazi law" comparable to Hitler's Enabling Act. Their protest was joined by a number of prominent artists, churchmen, and intellectuals who in turn were denounced in inflammatory tones by the gutter press, in particular by Axel Springer's mass circulation *Bild-Zeitung*. In April 1968 the principal spokesman of this "Extra-Parliamentary Opposition" (APO), Rudi Dutschke, was gunned down on the Kurfürstendamm in Berlin by a house painter with a criminal record, who was an assiduous reader of the *Bild-Zeitung*. Rudi Dutschke suffered severe brain injuries from which he died in 1979.

The widespread protests at the attempt on Rudi Dutschke's life gave renewed momentum to the struggle against the emergency laws, but this was all to no avail.

The alliance with the proletariat for which they yearned came to nothing, with the stolid trades unions refusing to be associated with a bunch of rowdies. The law was passed in the Bundestag by an overwhelming majority in May 1968, in part as a response to the unruliness of the student protestors, and the SDS began to fall apart. The protest movement became even more strident. Sit-ins, teach-ins, strikes, and riots were now the order of the day. Dress and behavior became increasingly provocative. A new vocabulary made up of concepts taken from psychoanalysis, Marxism, and existentialist philosophy, with a large admixture of the scatological, was used to attack what Adorno was pleased to call the "jargon of the literal" (*Jargon der Eigentlichkeit*) used by those in power. A new violent phase began shortly after the shots were fired at Rudi Dutschke, when Andreas Baader and Gudrun Ensslin set two Frankfurt department stores on fire in protest against the "tyranny of consumption."

Before long the philosophers of the Frankfurt School realized that the protest movement was getting out of hand, as raucous demands were made that "critical theory" be put into practice. A younger sorcerer, Jürgen Habermas, issued a frenzied warning about the "left-wing fascism" of his unruly apprentices. Almost none of their mentors accepted any responsibility for having produced the intellectual justification for much of the nonsense that took place in these years. Only Herbert Marcuse continued to lend his support to the struggle against one-dimensionality from the agreeable distance of Orange County, California. Not that it really mattered. The students' "long march through the institutions" achieved very little beyond giving them more say in the running of universities by sitting on a number of immensely tedious and time-consuming committees. Those whose hearts were on the left were soon reminded that their wallets were on the right, and pursued careers in the professions, the media, and business, and were quickly absorbed into the establishment. With comfortable bank balances, they preached the virtues of their simple lives in Tuscan villas and Spanish fincas, and expressed their deep concerns about an ecosystem which, in their working lives, they did so much to endanger. Those who failed to jump on the capitalist bandwagon opted out. Protest ceased to be political and became a mere matter of what was to become known as "lifestyle." They had to wait a while until the postmodernists comforted them with the preposterous notion that their very passivity was a form of political activism.

Meanwhile the new government had to deal with the major problem of a deep recession. The key post was now that of the minister of trade and commerce, Karl Schiller. A professor of economics, a member of the SPD, and like the chancellor a former member of the NSDAP, he was a convinced Keynesian. He called for economic expansion, globalization (which had not yet become a dirty word), and the reduction of unemployment, which was fast becoming a major problem. Franz-Josef Strauss, as minister of finance, was fully in accord with Schiller, and the result was a reduction in the prime rate from five to three percent, and the release of vast sums of money for investment. Management, labor, and the state were brought together in a "Concentrated Action" to achieve "measured growth" while maintaining "social symmetry." To the radical left "Concentrated Action" smacked of Mussolini's corporatism and was denounced as a fascistoid form of bourgeois domination in the era of late capitalism. The remarkable growth of the economy in 1968 served to disguise the fact that Schiller's much-vaunted plan was actually little more than a rhetorical device. The new boom triggered a round of inflation and the prime rate was back at five percent by June 1969, rising to six percent in September. The Great Coalition passed a considerable amount of important legislation. A finance reform was followed by a major overhaul of criminal law along more liberal lines, and adultery, homosexuality among adults, and blasphemy ceased to be criminal offenses. The statute of limitations on major Nazi crimes and on murder was lifted, and in the case of lesser crimes it was extended from 20 to 30 years.

Although de Gaulle was an outspoken critic of American policy in Vietnam, and continued to make all manner of difficulties in Europe, both Washington and Paris made it clear that they would not do anything that would run counter to Bonn's policies toward the DDR and the Soviet bloc. There was considerable resistance in the ranks of the CDU/CSU to the SPD's call for a more flexible approach to the DDR, but Kiesinger kept an open mind on the issue, and when he became party chairman on Adenauer's death at the age of 91 in April 1967, he gradually convinced the party to drop its hard-line approach. In his view East and West Germany could only come closer together within the context of a lessening of the tensions between East and West in Europe. Although he refused to refer to the East German state as the German Democratic Republic, he ceased to call it the "Soviet Zone." His avowed aim was to find areas in which progress could be made in an effort to reduce tensions; these included economic cooperation, easing of movement between the two states, and cultural exchanges.

The new approach to policy toward the Soviet Bloc got off to an uneasy start when diplomatic recognition was afforded to Romania, thus for the first time breaching the Halstein Doctrine. With the megalomaniac Romanian dictator Nicolae Ceausescu pursuing a nationalist foreign policy independent from Moscow, which ensured him a warm welcome in the West in spite of his ferociously Stalinist policies at home, the Soviet Union was far from pleased with Bonn's initiative. At a meeting of the Warsaw Pact all member states were warned not to open diplomatic relations with the Federal Republic. The Great Coalition was not deterred, and later in 1967 it established diplomatic relations with Yugoslavia, even though Belgrade recognized the DDR. Cambodia, Iraq, and the Sudan recognized the DDR in 1969, soon to be followed by Syria and South Yemen. Bonn responded by declaring that any recognition of the DDR would be regarded as an unfriendly act. The DDR replied by promulgating the "Ulbricht Doctrine," whereby no member state of the Warsaw Pact could recognize the Federal Republic until it accepted existing frontiers, and the existence of two German states.

The Nuclear Non-Proliferation Treaty proposed by the USA and the USSR presented another major difficulty. Adenauer had denounced the treaty, which forbade non-nuclear countries from building their own nuclear weapons, and banned countries possessing nuclear weapons from transferring the capability to produce them, as "the Morgenthau Plan squared" – reference to the US secretary of the treasury's plan in 1944 to convert Germany into an agrarian country. Franz-Josef Strauss, in equally dramatic tones, claimed that it was a "Versailles of cosmic dimensions." Kiesinger complained bitterly that the US government failed to consult the Federal Republic over the treaty and accused Washington and Moscow of conniving at Western Europe's expense. This hard nosed approach, which left some observers amazed at Bonn's audacity, paid handsome dividends. The US became much more mindful of Bonn's legitimate concerns, particularly over the peaceful use of atomic energy, and relations between the two countries were greatly improved. At the same time, Willy Brandt as foreign minister played a key role in convincing NATO to adopt a more flexible policy toward the Warsaw Pact and to work toward a gradual reduction of armed forces on both sides of the Berlin Wall. This did nothing to ease tensions with Moscow, which continued to lambaste the Federal Republic as "révanchist" and claimed the right under the United Nations' charter to intervene in its affairs as an "enemy state." With the Soviet intervention in Czechoslovakia in 1968, in which East German troops played a supporting role without actually crossing the borders of the CSSR, East–West relations were once again put into deep freeze, and Bonn's "Ostpolitik" ground to a halt. There were widespread protests in the DDR against the country's complicity in crushing the "Prague Spring," and the parallel was drawn with 1938. The precise number of those arrested, reprimanded, or excluded from the SED is still unknown but it was certainly in the thousands. The Stasi reported some 2,000 examples of "hostile actions." All hopes for a "socialism with a human face" were dashed by Ulbricht's concept of a "socialist human community" (*sozialistische Menschengemeinschaft*), with its overtones of the Nazi "racial community" (*Volksgemeinschaft*), and which also offered a degree of social security in return for a loss of freedom. None of this deterred the champions of Ostpolitik. Willy Brandt and the SPD continued to insist that this was merely a temporary setback, and they were soon to be proven correct.

As early as January 1969 the Soviet ambassador told Brandt that his government was anxious to improve relations with Bonn. This initiative came to nothing when the Federal Republic insisted that the election of a new president should take place in Berlin. At a meeting of the Warsaw Pact in March the demand was no longer that the Federal Republic should grant formal recognition to the DDR, but merely that it should recognize its existence. The Warsaw Pact also proposed a joint conference with NATO on European security, a proposal that was strongly endorsed by Willy Brandt. A series of events in 1969 opened the way for a fresh round of détente. Richard Nixon, a master of realpolitik, was elected president. The Soviet Union was engaged in armed conflict with China and was thus anxious to improve relations with the West. Lastly de Gaulle staged his own fall from power in April, much to the relief of most in Bonn. The Federal Republic refused to give way to pressure from the US, Britain, and France to revalue the mark to offset the weakness of their own currencies. Although undiplomatic, perhaps *Bild-Zeitung* had some justification for printing a banner headline in November which read: "Now The Germans Are Number One In Europe!"

The Great Coalition had a host of critics, in spite of its many achievements. Many agreed with the philosopher Karl Jaspers that it was symptomatic of a drastic decline in democracy. With virtually no opposition there was an alarming lack of transparency, and precious little control of the executive by the legislature. The proposal to abolish proportional representation was seen by some as an indication that the coalition was out to annihilate the opposition. But at the same time there were signs that the Great Coalition was only a temporary expedient. The SPD wanted to push ahead with its Ostpolitik; the CDU/CSU had serious reservations. The opposition FDP sympathized with the SPD, and formed an alliance in March 1969 which secured the election of the Social Democrat Gustav Heinemann as president by a margin of only six votes in the third round. With a general election soon to be held it seemed that the Great Coalition's days were numbered. In the September elections the CDU/CSU dropped 1.5 points, but still won the largest share of the vote with 46.1 percent. The SPD had their best ever showing with 42.7 percent. The FDP did very poorly, and, with 5.8 percent, only just squeaked back into the Bundestag. No other party managed to clear the five percent hurdle.

Willy Brandt as Chancellor

Thanks to the energetic intervention of Willy Brandt, who was tired of the CDU/CSU's obstruction of his Ostpolitik, and of Karl Schiller, who found it impossible to work with the minister of finance, Franz-Josef Strauss, the SPD formed a new coalition with Walter Scheel's FDP. Scheel, who was on the left wing of the party, had as much difficulty in convincing his right-wing colleagues to ally with the SPD as Brandt and Schiller had in persuading Herbert Wehner and Helmuth Schmidt to end the Great Coalition. Willy Brandt presented his government's program to the Bundestag in October 1969. It called for major reforms in education which, very much in the spirit of the times, included the "removal of outmoded hierarchical structures" in the universities. The goal of Schiller's economic policy was "stabilization without stagnation." An overhaul of criminal law and the penal system was promised. In foreign policy Brandt expressed his determination to continue trying to improve relations with the East, and to reach an accommodation with the DDR.

The coalition's schemes for economic reform were soon shelved when faced with an alarming increase in the rate of inflation. The mark was allowed to float, and all levels of government were obliged to reduce expenditure. This led to a fierce struggle between the Keynesian Schiller and the deflationist minister of finance, Alex Möller, the former head of a major life insurance company. Möller resigned when ministers objected vigorously to his cutting back the budgets of their departments, and Karl Schiller, who was popular with the voters, was given a new "super ministry," which combined those of trade and industry, and finance. Never a man to hide his talents under a bushel, Professor Schiller's penchant for self-promotion now knew no bounds, as he obstinately clung to an economic theory that no longer commanded the undivided respect either of his academic colleagues or the business world.

Schiller's arrogant stewardship of his super ministry left him without allies in the cabinet. Helmuth Schmidt, the aggressive minister of defense, was constantly locked in battle with him. So too was the minister of development aid, Erhard Eppler, who called for increased taxation to finance a more generous aid program. Brandt's powerful head of chancellery, Horst Empke, urged his boss to get rid of this by now widely unpopular figure. The crunch came in 1971, when the USA unilaterally tore up the Bretton Woods Agreement, and took the dollar off the gold standard. At a conference of the ten richest countries held in December it was agreed that the dollar exchange rate of the German mark should be revalued by 13.7 percent, a measure that was supported by the Bundesbank president Karl Klasen. In March the following year, in an attempt to give a degree of stability to the money market, and to discourage the flood of speculative capital into Europe, the EEC member states agreed to the "snake," whereby the exchange rates of members' currencies could only change by a maximum of 2.5 percent. Schiller opposed these measures vehemently and handed in his resignation, which was accepted with a sigh of relief. Helmuth Schmidt, his bitterest critic, succeeded him in the super ministry, a major step forward in his impressive career.

Willy Brandt had neither interest nor expertise in economics, and had an exaggerated faith in his super minister, but he showed true mastery in foreign affairs. First he managed to persuade de Gaulle's successor, Georges Pompidou, to accept British membership of the EEC, along with that of Ireland, Denmark, and Norway. In January 1970 he proposed opening discussions on a joint declaration renouncing violence to Willy Stoph, the chairman of the DDR's Council of State (*Staatsrat*). Stoph took three weeks to consider his reply, but eventually agreed and invited Brandt to meet him in Erfurt. The talks came to nothing, but much to the fury of the East German leadership Brandt was welcomed by an enthusiastic crowd. They resolved that this should never be allowed to happen again and the next meeting between the two heads of government took place in Kassel in May. Once again nothing concrete was achieved. Brandt offered the normalization of relations between the "two German states," but Stoph insisted on full diplomatic recognition of the DDR. The significance of these meetings can hardly be overestimated. No formal agreement was reached, but at the same time each state accepted the existence of the other. The remaining problem was to agree on the precise terms of that acceptance. It was a major achievement, made possible by the full support given to Willy Brandt by President Nixon and his national security advisor, Henry Kissinger.

Meanwhile, Brandt's close associate Egon Bahr, whom he had brought with him from Berlin in 1966 and had appointed as a chief of planning in the Foreign Office and who now served as secretary of state in the chancellery, began talks with the Soviet foreign minister Andrei Gromyko. The two sides could not agree on a common formula for Germany, but the Soviets took notice of the Federal Republic's position and left the door open for further discussion. Bahr, a past master

Plate 30 Willy Brandt in Warsaw. © BPK

of secret diplomacy, pursued every opening, and in May 1970 got Gromyko to accept a letter laying out the Federal Republic's position on the German people's right to self-determination. The details of this confidential meeting were leaked to the popular weekly *Quick* by a Foreign Office official set on torpedoing Brandt's *Ostpolitik*, but this scandalous act of treachery did nothing to damage relations between Bonn and Moscow. The treaty outlawing the use of force in a revision of the Federal Republic's frontier with the DDR was signed in Moscow in August 1970, when Walter Scheel managed to get the Soviets to agree that this frontier was not absolutely immutable.

The next major step in Brandt's *Ostpolitik* was to reach an agreement with Poland. Acceptance of the Oder-Neisse frontier in perpetuity was extremely unpopular in the Federal Republic because the refugee organizations still had a powerful voice, and about one quarter of the population was opposed to the idea. Brandt and his foreign minister, Walter Scheel, ignored these objections, and a treaty was signed in Warsaw in December 1970. For Willy Brandt the renunciation of any claims to German territory lost to Poland in 1945 was the price that had to be paid for the monstrous crimes of the Nazi regime. In a remarkable and spontaneous gesture during a wreath-laying ceremony in the Warsaw ghetto he knelt in silence, his hands crossed, his head bowed as he later wrote, "before the abyss of German history and under the burden of the murdered millions." This deeply moving act of contrition was a milestone along the difficult path of Germany's confrontation with its criminal past. Willy Brandt was awarded the Nobel Prize for Peace in 1971. No one has ever been more worthy of this high honor.

In September 1971 a four-power agreement on Berlin was signed which guaranteed unhindered passage between the Federal Republic and West Berlin, but the three Western powers repeated that West Berlin was not to be considered as an integral part of the Federal Republic. The three Eastern treaties brought Moscow and Bonn much closer together, but the Soviets were concerned that this might lead to a blurring of distinctions between East and West Germany, which would eventually lead to the collapse of the DDR. Ulbricht however made some remarkably flattering remarks about the SPD in the hope of persuading Bonn to help finance his plan, labeled the "Socialist Economic System," concentrating on high technology industries in a renewed bid to overtake the West. It was both politically and economically a disaster. The DDR lacked the infrastructure and the expertise to make such a leap into the future, and capital was urgently needed for investment in less utopian schemes. A lowering of living standards was a necessary corollary, for all the high-flown rhetoric about the "socialist human community." Ulbricht was also locked in a very arcane ideological struggle with the Soviets over the precise nature of "socialism," and had the impertinence to remind them that the DDR was an independent state, and not a Soviet state like Belarus. The Soviets were also alarmed at the spectacle of Ulbricht hobnobbing with the SPD, and decided it was time to replace him with Erich Honecker, a man who was utterly loyal to Moscow and wanted no truck with the infidels in the West.

Crown prince Honecker had to wait for some time until the green light came from Moscow. In the meantime he continually intrigued against the 77-year-old first secretary, and since it was clear that he was the coming man he gained increasing support in the upper echelons of the SED. Finally, in April 1971, Brezhnev ordered Ulbricht, whose health was rapidly deteriorating, to resign as first secretary, but graciously permitted him to stay on as chairman of the council of state.

Erich Honecker was born in the Saar, was a roofer by trade, and a lifelong Communist. He had been arrested by the Nazis in 1937 and sentenced to ten years imprisonment for conspiracy to commit treason. He had escaped in 1945 and was made head of the Free German Youth (FDJ) in 1946. He was a dreary, unimaginative paper-pusher whose speeches were even duller than the ineffably boring tirades from Ulbricht. His tastes were impeccably petit bourgeois, and he was unquestioningly loyal to Moscow. He immediately dropped Ulbricht's madcap "socialist economic system," and in a new five-year plan concentrated on consumer goods and on improving the living standard of the population at large. Ulbricht's heterodox notions of a "socialist human community," and of socialism as being something other than a mere phase in the development of a Communist society, were also denounced.

Honecker now proclaimed the Federal Republic to be an "imperialist foreign country," and Johannes R. Becker's words to Hans Eisler's national anthem, which spoke of a united German nation, were no longer allowed to be sung. True to the Soviet's "two nation theory," Honecker countered the SPD's assertion that Germany was one nation consisting of two states, by proclaiming the DDR to be a "socialist state of the German nation." A fresh round in the class struggle was begun by an all-out attack on the remaining vestiges of private enterprise. Small independent businesses were converted into "People's Own Enterprises" (VEBs) resulting in a disastrous drop in productivity. While Brezhnev was urging Honecker to distance himself from the Federal Republic, he was growing ever closer to Brandt, with whom he developed a close personal relationship. Brandt used his influence on the Soviet leader to further détente and played an important role in the negotiation of the Mutual Balanced Force Reduction (MBFR) treaty. Indeed relations between Brezhnev and Brandt became so cordial that there was much concerned talk in the West of another Rapallo. Nixon harbored deep suspicions of Brandt, and Henry Kissinger, while admiring Egon Bahr's diplomatic skills, saw him as a dangerous nationalist and even as a neutralist.

Debates over the ratification of the Eastern Treaties began in April 1972, and it looked as if Brandt would not find the necessary majority. A number of members of the Bundestag from the FDP and SPD had jumped ship, and the CDU, under its chairman Rainer Barzel, who was also the chancellor candidate of the CDU/CSU, mounted a vigorous campaign against the treaties. On April 27 Barzel proposed a motion of constructive no confidence in a bid to unseat Brandt and to become chancellor. At first it looked as if he would succeed, but when the votes were counted Barzel was two votes short of victory. It would seem that the Stasi had bribed a senior member of the CSU to vote against the motion, and thus saved Brandt. The SPD in turn bribed a CDU deputy who was also a double agent, almost certainly using funds provided for this purpose by the DDR. In both cases the 30 pieces of silver were worth 50,000 marks. Brandt and his Ostpolitik were saved, but the democratic system was severely damaged.

The treaties were eventually ratified after certain revisions were made, with the CDU/CSU abstaining from a key vote. At the same time the USA, the Soviet Union, Britain, and France signed the final version of the four-power agreements which facilitated inter-German travel. But while East–West relations were thus greatly improved, the Federal Republic moved in the opposite direction in domestic politics. A law was passed in January 1972 that banned members and sympathizers with radical groups from becoming civil servants. The state had every right to make sure that people who did not accept its "fundamental free and democratic system" did not become teachers or senior administrators, but the heavy-handed approach taken to the implementation of the law caused widespread and justified criticism of what was dubbed a "ban on the professions" (*Berufsverbot*). In part this was an excessive response to the growth of radical Marxism, particularly in the universities. The Young Socialists (*Jusos*) in the SPD were trying to move the party sharply to the left, thus scaring off middle-of-the-road voters. On the wilder shores of the left Andreas Baader and Gudrun Ensslin, having served time in jail for arson, set about organizing the Red Army Faction (RAF) in 1969. Baader was once again arrested, and then sprung from jail by the left-wing journalist-turned-terrorist, Ulrike Meinhof. The group fled to Syria in the summer of 1970, where they were given expert training in terrorist methods by the PLO.

A number of people were killed in a series of terrorist attacks in 1972 on the American Army Headquarters in Germany, and the Springer building in Hamburg was set on fire. Andreas Baader was once again arrested in June, along with two other ringleaders of the RAF, Holger Meins and Jan-Carl Raspe. Shortly afterwards, Ulrike Meinhof and Gudrun Ensslin were also placed in custody. Another group with direct links to the PLO attacked the quarters of the Israeli team at the Munich Olympic Games in September, killing two athletes and taking nine hostages. The Bavarian police badly bungled an attempt to free the hostages, all of whom were killed, along with five terrorists. When a Lufthansa plane was hijacked and the passengers held to ransom, the three surviving terrorists were freed and flown to Syria. There is no evidence that any Germans were involved in this terrorist attack, but in an atmosphere of horror, fear, and uncertainty it was easy to imagine that such links existed.

Meanwhile Brandt had lost his majority in the Bundestag, due to defections from the FDP and the disappearance of Karl Schiller. In September Brandt proposed a motion of no confidence and made sure that members of the government did not vote so that the motion passed. Barzel agreed that the Bundestag should be dissolved, and elections were called for November. During the election campaign Walter Scheel traveled to China, and Egon Bahr visited Brezhnev before negotiating the "Treaty on the General Principles of Relations Between the Federal Republic of Germany and the German Democratic Republic" with his East German homologue Michael Kohl in November. This amounted to a de facto recognition of the DDR, and instead of an exchange of ambassadors "permanent representations" were established in Bonn and East Berlin. Thorny issues, such as that of reunification, were left open with a reference to differences of opinion. Both states agreed that they should be represented in the United Nations. The DDR was now free to establish diplomatic relations with any country without fear of reprisals from the Federal Republic.

The election campaign soon turned into a plebiscite over the treaty. Rainer Barzel, as the CDU/CSU chancellor candidate, said that he would not support ratification of the treaty as long as the National People's Army (NVA) continued to kill refugees attempting to cross the border, but this met with little response from the electorate. A group of prominent historians, including Karl Dietrich Bracher, Fritz Fischer, and Thomas Nipperdy signed a declaration of support for Brandt's Ostpolitik. Support also came from artists and intellectuals, and the novelist Gunther Grass campaigned tirelessly for the SPD. Young Socialists forgot their ideological differences with the party leadership for the moment, and lent their wholehearted support. Amid general prosperity Karl Schiller's spiteful attacks on the coalition's economic policy fell on deaf ears. The election was held on November 19 and resulted in a triumph for the coalition. The SPD increased its share of the vote by 3.1 points, the FDP by 2.6, and the CDU/CSU dropped 1.2 points. Willy Brandt was sadly unable to exploit his triumph. His vocal chords had been seriously damaged by his heavy smoking. He had to undergo surgery and was forbidden to speak during the critical negotiations for the new coalition. The treaty was the coping-stone of his Ostpolitik, so that there was nothing exciting left to do in foreign policy and he was loath to devote all his attention to the drudgery of daily politics. His rival, Rainer Barzel, resigned as chairman of the CDU and the CDU/CSU when the caucus voted in favor of membership of the United Nations, even though it meant that the DDR would also be admitted. His place as head of the CDU was taken by the minister-president of Rhineland-Palatinate, Helmut Kohl, while Karl Carstens became the leader of the opposition in the Bundestag. In spite of sabotage efforts by the Bavarian government, the Treaty on General Principles was ratified and went into effect in June 1973.

Brandt was under constant attack from the president of the SPD caucus, Herbert Wehner, who felt, as he said in Moscow, that "number one" was "worn out" and no longer capable of effective leadership. He also told Erich Honecker that he disagreed with the chancellor's approach to the German question. The ex-Communist Wehner told the East German leader, whom he knew as a former party comrade, that he fully understood the DDR's need to suppress dissidents and sympathized with the Soviet Union's intervention in Czechoslovakia in 1968. He felt that Brandt's vision of a united Germany was merely wishful thinking, and worked for an alliance between the working classes of both German states and a consequent "Social Democratization" of the DDR. His nationalism was thus based on class, rather than the notion of a single German nation.

Brandt was in America when he heard of Wehner's imprudent remarks, made during a reception at the German ambassador's residence in Moscow, and flew back to Bonn determined to remove him from office. This was easier said than done. Wehner was moderately apologetic and had considerable support in the party. Brandt shied away from an open confrontation and his authority was thus further undermined. The chancellor's star was now beginning to wane. He failed to persuade Brezhnev to use his influence to get the DDR to make further concessions, including agreeing to accept a ministry of the environment having its offices in West Berlin. His prestige suffered a serious blow when a parliamentary investigation committee took a close look at the bribing of opposition members in 1972, which had enabled him to remain in office. The economy was in serious trouble following the Egyptian attack on Israel in the 1973 Yom Kippur War and the subsequent decision of the Arab states drastically to cut back oil supplies. Relations with the United States became very tense when Bonn and the rest of the European Community called upon Israel to end the fighting, and to respect the United Nations resolution on the occupied territories. A wave of strikes was taken as further evidence of the government's lack of authority. The Young Socialists were once again becoming restless. Then in April 1974 a bombshell exploded when it was revealed that Gunther Guillaume, a close advisor of Brandt's in the chancellery, was a Stasi agent.

Guillaume, an officer in the East German army, had come to the Federal Republic in 1956 disguised as a refugee. He had joined the SPD in Frankfurt and had worked his way up the party hierarchy to join the chancellery staff in 1970. In 1973 he had accompanied Brandt on his annual holiday to Norway, during which time he had access to top secret NATO documents. He was so close to Brandt that he was also privy to this notorious ladies' man's amorous escapades. Suspicions were first aroused in May 1973 that Guillaume was a Stasi plant, but the authorities were singularly lax, and did not trouble to keep a close watch on him. Brandt at first wanted to resign, but he was persuaded that he should fight back. Then Herbert Wehner, who had been informed of his numerous affairs, suggested that resignation was the most prudent way out of the crisis. Brandt tendered his resignation on May 6, and appointed Helmuth Schmidt as his successor. It was a typically courageous and honorable move, and he took full blame for the fiasco. He refused to name any of those who bore a far greater share of the blame, principal among them the FDP minister of the interior, Hans Dieter Genscher.

In his five years as chancellor Brandt had brought about a revolution in the Federal Republic's foreign policy. He had normalized relations with the Soviet Union and the DDR, while remaining firmly committed to Europe and the Atlantic alliance. The Federal Republic had been in serious danger of isolation, but was now a respected ally and a daunting opponent led by a statesman of international stature. In domestic affairs he had been less successful, and the coalition's ambitious policies for reform mostly remained on the drawing board; but the balance of his chancellorship was positive, and he stands with Adenauer as a founding father of a vibrant democracy.

East Germany Under Honecker

With the signing of the Treaty on General Principles, the DDR was more determined than ever to draw a sharp ideological line between East and West Germany. Kurt Hager, the SED's chief ideologue, preached the somewhat perplexing doctrine of "socialism as it really exists" (*realexistiernenden Sozialismus*), whereby the unbridgeable differences between the "socialist state of workers and peasants" and the "continuously existing capitalist nation" in the West were emphasized. The "socialist brotherhood" between the DDR and the Soviet Union, and with the other states in the "socialist community," was another Leitmotif of Hager's propaganda offensive. The DDR also provided a safe haven and technical advice to West German terrorists. Yet in spite of this rigidity toward the West, the regime became marginally more tolerant at home. There had been a youth revolt in the DDR that paralleled similar events in the West, although the stakes were obviously much higher, culminating in the "Beat Demonstration" in Leipzig in 1965. Henceforth smuggled albums of the Rolling Stones and the Beatles were no longer considered as contraband, long hair and blue jeans were reluctantly tolerated, and an underground rock scene flourished. In 1973 Ulrich Plensdorf was permitted to publish his remarkable novel *The New Sufferings of the Young W.*, a portrait of a disillusioned, pro-Western youth with a love for "real music," as opposed to that of "Händelsohn-Bacholdy," and who wanted nothing whatever to do with the state or the party. Although very closely modeled on J. D. Salinger's *Catcher in the Rye*, it is both a forceful portrait of teenage anomie and evidence that Honecker's DDR, for all its dreary conformity and paranoid insecurity, had moved on a long way from its Stalinist beginnings.

The oil crisis also had a shattering effect on the DDR, and meant that Honecker's dogma of the "unity of economic and social policy" could only be partially realized, and that at the expense of massive deficit financing. The Soviet Union, with its grossly mismanaged economy and shortage of capital, was unable to help out the socialist countries by exploiting its huge reserves of natural resources. Mounting economic problems led to increasing criticism of the regime's ossified ideology, and resulted in an attempt to stifle all critical voices. Robert Havemann was placed under house arrest. Rudolf Bahro, a leading dissident who had compared the Politburo to the Inquisition and denounced the SED as a political police force, and whose vision of a reformed Communism earned widespread assent, was given an eight-year prison sentence in 1978 and was deported to West Germany in the following year.

Helmuth Schmidt

The Federal Republic's new chancellor, Helmuth Schmidt, was the leading light on the right wing of the party. His often overbearingly arrogant style earned him the title "Big-Mouth Schmidt" (*Schmidt-Schnauze*) and he was the bête noir of the party left, of the Young Socialists, and of the extra-parliamentary opposition. He did not suffer fools gladly, and never let an opportunity pass to demonstrate his intellectual superiority over lesser mortals. There was little that was inspiring in his resolutely pragmatic approach to politics, but none could deny that he was a man of quite exceptional intelligence, a devastatingly effective debater who, unlike Brandt, never flinched from taking on his adversaries both inside and outside the party. He was a thoroughgoing professional who had a complete mastery of all aspects of both foreign and domestic policy, and who stands head and shoulders above all other proponents of a non-dogmatic approach to Social Democracy that was later to be dubbed the "New Middle." On the debit side he was the first of a line of chancellors from Kohl to Schroeder to avoid tackling serious social issues and structural deficiencies, and who failed to address the overriding problem of a general disillusionment and dissatisfaction with politicians, the political process, and with it democracy itself. Willy Brandt had dared the people to "risk more democracy," but they had failed to take up the challenge. His successors did nothing to encourage them to have another go.

Schmidt was fully committed to the Atlantic alliance, and knew that West Germany's security depended on the United States, but at the same time he sent a clear message to the DDR that he was determined to improve relations between the two countries, provided both respected the spirit and the letter of all existing treaties. This was a difficult hand to play. The United States suffered a devastating loss of prestige in the Vietnam War, which was rapidly drawing to a humiliating close. The Federal Republic was going through a severe economic crisis owing to the oil embargo. The Soviet Union was bent on exploiting America's weakness to improve its strategic position in Europe by building up its arsenal of intermediate range missiles, having failed to reach an agreement with the USA on their limitation.

The MBFR talks in Vienna between NATO and the Warsaw Pact had got bogged down and intermediate range missiles were not subject to discussion. Nixon and Brezhnev signed the Strategic Arms Limitation Treaty (SALT) in May 1972, but it only covered long-range missiles. Schmidt did everything possible to ensure that intermediate range missiles were included in the SALT-II discussions between the US and the USSR, which began soon after SALT-I was signed. Nixon's successor, Gerald Ford, gave Schmidt a verbal assurance that he would do so, but gave no formal written confirmation of this intention. In the summer of 1975 Schmidt attended the concluding Conference on Security and Cooperation in Europe in Helsinki, and laid the groundwork for a treaty with Poland whereby 125,000 Poles of German origin were permitted to settle in the Federal Republic, in return for which Poland received substantial financial assistance. An agreement was also reached with Honecker not to rock the boat in Berlin. In a wider perspective the Soviets were pleased with the Helsinki accords in that they guaranteed the inviolability (but not the permanence) of existing frontiers in Europe; but the West had secured guarantees for human rights and fundamental freedoms which gave great encouragement to activists within the Soviet bloc.

The DDR found a lucrative way to avoid some of the more embarrassing consequences of the Helsinki accords. Tiresome dissidents like Rudolf Bahro could be shipped out to the West, others were allowed to go to West Germany on receipt of handsome payment from the Federal Republic. Between 1964 and 1989 Bonn paid 3.4 thousand million marks and secured the release of 33,755 political prisoners, an average of about 100,000 marks per head. The DDR had access to huge interest-free loans from West Germany, based on aggregate inner-German trade. Bonn helped finance major projects including an autobahn from Hamburg to Berlin and, much to the alarm of hardliners in the SED, the DDR was thus becoming increasingly dependent on the Federal Republic.

Schmidt was a close ally of Valéry Giscard d'Estaing who had been elected president of France in 1974, and he gave his wholehearted support to the French initiative calling for an economic summit of six leading industrial nations, which was held in Rambouillet in November 1975. The G-6 was to become G-7 when Canada was included at the London summit in 1976. With the US smarting after its humiliation in Vietnam and under the lackluster leadership of Gerald Ford, the Schmidt–Giscard tandem played a leading role in international politics and the Federal Republic's prestige was greatly enhanced. The coalition was much less successful in domestic politics. A comprehensive reform of the universities made little progress. The Constitutional Court blocked a reform of the law on abortion. A new law on co-determination in the workplace satisfied neither management nor labor, and both sides appealed to the Constitutional Court, only to be rejected. The labor force had a greater say in management than in any other country, but they did not have the parity on boards of directors they demanded.

A fresh wave of terrorist attacks began in November 1974 when a court official in Berlin was assassinated. In February 1975 the chairman of the CDU in Berlin was kidnapped, only to be released when the government agreed to set five convicted terrorists free and fly them to Yemen. Two months later the "June 2 Movement" seized 12 hostages in the German Embassy in Stockholm in the course of which two West German diplomats were killed. They demanded the release of 26 terrorists, including Andreas Baader and Ulrike Meinhof. This time the government refused to back down, the embassy was stormed, and two of the terrorists were killed. German terrorists were involved in an attack on the OPEC ministers in Vienna in December 1975, which was masterminded by "Carlos." They were also complicit in the hijacking of an Air France plane en route from Athens to Entebbe in Uganda in June 1976. A special Israeli antiterrorist unit freed the hostages at Entebbe, a brilliant action in which two German terrorists were killed. The terrorists labored under the curious delusion that their efforts to undermine the state would meet with considerable sympathy, particularly among the working class. In spite of the fulminations of some deluded intellectuals about the even worse threat to civil rights posed by the Schmidt government, quite the reverse was true. A general disillusionment set in, and Ulrike Meinhof committed suicide in her cell at Stammheim prison in Stuttgart in May 1976.

The Candidature of Helmut Kohl

Nineteen seventy-six was an election year and the issue of terrorism played an important role in the campaign. The CDU/CSU chose Helmut Kohl as their chancellor candidate, largely because he was not the temperamental and unpredictable Franz-Josef Strauss, who had let loose a tirade against the SPD, painting them as closet communists bent on establishing the dictatorship of the proletariat. The suggestion that the resolutely anti-communist, fervently pro-Western, and thoroughly centrist Helmuth Schmidt, was Moscow's marionette might have been accepted by the more delusional of the lederhosened denizens of Strauss' Bavarian fastness, but it was altogether too absurd for the average Ottos who made up the bulk of the electorate. Kohl was a right-winger who had opposed signing the Helsinki accords, but on the other hand he had excellent personal contacts with key figures in the SED. His supporters saw him as a pragmatist, his opponents as an opportunist. He fought the campaign under the slogan "Freedom instead of Socialism," whereas Strauss's CSU preferred the more aggressive form of "Freedom or Socialism." Although some CDU politicians felt that the attempt to paint Schmidt as a socialist would misfire, the CDU/CSU made substantial gains at the polls, but it was not quite enough to defeat the coalition. The SPD dropped to 42.6 percent and the FDP to 7.9 percent, and the CDU/CSU obtained only 48.6 percent of the vote. Strauss blamed Kohl and the CDU for failing to win an absolute majority, and announced that his CSU would henceforth fight a separate election campaign. Shortly afterward he publicly denounced Kohl as an incompetent and stupid politician who would never become chancellor. The CDU responded to this extraordinarily crass attack by threatening to found a Bavarian branch of the party, whereupon the CSU got cold feet, and reluctantly returned to the fold. The animosity between the stolid Kohl and the mercurial Strauss was to continue until Strauss's sudden death in 1988.

For all Kohl's reservations about the Helsinki accords, the SED regime was seriously worried about the consequences of what they were pleased to call the "heightened form of imperialist class war." The East German regime decided to get rid of some of their more troublesome critics, for whom they reserved a word of particular opprobrium: "individual." Prominent among these was the folk singer Wolf Biermann, who had his citizenship taken away from him while on a tour of West Germany, prompting a courageous protest from a number of the DDR's most prominent artists and intellectuals. This marked an end to Honecker's relatively relaxed attitude toward the arts, and the theory that the socialism of the DDR was a unique and self-contained form of social organization had to be dropped in favor of the Soviet assertion that it was merely a step on the way to communism. Like Ulbricht before him, Honecker tried to offset this ideological rigidity with an ambitious housing program, and a concentration on the production of much sought-after consumer goods such as cars, television sets, and washing machines. With productivity one-third of that of the Federal Republic, this was mere wishful thinking, and simply raised hopes that were bound to be dashed.

The Extra-Parliamentary Opposition

Civil liberties were also under attack in the Federal Republic, where a fresh wave of terror was unleashed. In April 1977 a senior state prosecutor, his driver, and a court guard were murdered by the Ulrike Meinhof Commando of the RAF. In July of that year the chairman of the board of directors of the Dresdner Bank, Erich Ponto, was killed in a kidnapping attempt. In September the head of the Employers' Association and the Association of Germany Industry, Hanns Martin Schleyer, was kidnapped, his driver and three policemen shot. The RAF demanded the release of 11 prisoners and a large ransom. The government played for time and took the highly questionable step of banning all contact between the terrorists in prison and the outside world, including their lawyers, as well as banning any news reports on the kidnapping. In October four Arab terrorists hijacked a Lufthansa plane flying from Mallorca to Frankfurt, and also demanded the release of the 11 prisoners. The plane flew to Rome, Cyprus, Dubai, and then Athens before eventually landing in Mogadishu where the hijackers murdered the pilot. After agonizing debates the government decided to send a special unit of the Border Guards (GSG9) to Mogadishu. The mission was brilliantly accomplished. Three kidnappers were killed, one seriously wounded, and all the hostages were released unharmed. The good news from Mogadishu was closely followed by the announcement that Andreas Baader, Gudrun Ensslin, and Jan-Carl Raspe had committed suicide in their cells at Starnheim. Many on the left were convinced that the prison authorities had murdered them, and there were demonstrations in a number of European capitals. After 43 days in the hands of his kidnappers, Hanns Martin Schleyer was murdered, his body discovered in the trunk of a car parked in Mulhouse in Alsace.

Many in the extra-parliamentary opposition had a certain sympathy with the terrorists. They could point to the fact that Schleyer had been a senior official in the SS, responsible for the exploitation of Czechoslovakia during the war, they were convinced that the Stammheim trio had been murdered, and some believed that the terrorists were part of a continuing antifascist struggle. Many West Germans were concerned at the growing intolerance of a society that lumped terrorists together with such SPD sympathizers as Günther Grass and Heinrich Böll, and there was widespread concern that the antiterrorist laws undermined the rule of law. There was some justified fear that the terrorists' attempts to reveal the Federal Republic as fundamentally "fascist" would, by such extreme measures, prove successful.

The extra-parliamentary opposition was in the process of transformation. The apolitical and selfish hedonism of late-sixties youth led to the casting off of restraints, first on sex and then on greed, as flower children became yuppies. Openly communicative and social forces became reduced to a restrictive and oppressive intimacy that put an intolerable pressure on couples that was reflected in a rapidly escalating divorce rate. On the left highly theoretical neo-Marxism was giving way to a fundamentally reactionary, naively romantic anti-modernism. Nature was seen as the ultimate good, history gruesome and unpredictable, and progress an all-consuming Moloch, a cruel delusion. The fruits of nature were pure, generous, and immediate, those of history the dubious, closefisted promises of a distant future. Trees were there for hugging, not logging. Some thoroughgoing reactionaries argued that industrial society was one huge mistake and dreamt of a return to an Arcadian paradise of cavorting nymphs and sturdy shepherds. The mother earth was to be protected from rapine and plunder. The prime evil was now no longer "fascism" or "imperialism," although these terms were still used as generic terms of abuse, but atomic energy, which became symbolic of all that was evil in a technological, profit oriented, ecologically irresponsible society.

The Brandt government had decided to build 100 atomic energy plants in 1973, and with the oil crisis that began in that year it seemed to many to be the most promising way out of an emergency situation. What seemed to the government an admirable technical solution to a weighty predicament was to others bound to end in an apocalyptic disaster. Violent demonstrations were held in 1975, and in the following year armed and masked demonstrators joined in a riot at the site of a reactor at Brokdorf in Schleswig-Holstein. A campaign was then mounted against a proposed dump for atomic waste at Gorleben. The question of atomic energy split the SPD. Schmidt was solidly in favor. Willy Brandt as party chairman was anxious not to lose the youth vote and hoped to integrate the fundamentalist ecologists into the party. Just as Brandt feared, in January 1980 a Green party was formed on the federal level which threatened to take voters away from the SPD. The Greens were from the outset an odd bunch. Some were former communists or linked to various heretical Trotskyite, Marxist, or Communist Groups (*K-Gruppen*). Others, like Joschka Fischer who was later to become foreign minister and, for a time, the most respected politician in a united Germany, were "spontaneous" (*Spontis*) stone-hurling crypto-anarchists. They were joined by sundry peaceniks, eco-friendly farmers, conservationists, and apostles of alternative lifestyles. There were Greens on the left and Greens on the right, but in the early years the weight was on the left. They insisted on "basis democracy," by which party offices rotated, no member of any legislative assembly could hold party office, and party members were to have a real and effective control over the leadership and the elected delegates. There was general agreement that ecology mattered, that peace should be given a chance, and that women should be given full and equal opportunities. The emancipation of women, the one important and lasting consequence of the upheavals in the 1960s, was already on the political agenda, but it had been largely ignored by the main parties and had become somewhat sidetracked into the thorny issue of abortion, to the detriment of other important issues.

In 1977 the delightfully brash, exuberant, and quick-witted Alice Schwarzer founded *Emma*, a feminist magazine that provided an intelligent and accessible forum for women's issues. The more strident forms of feminism led by an inevitable dialectic from liberation to a new form of dependence and sour intolerance. A form of sexual apartheid was propagated, with women's rock groups, women's theater, women's bars and cafés, and women's centers, and the dubious new discipline of women's studies provided a congenial male-free environment within the universities where, sheltered by guarantees of academic freedom, ideology could masquerade as scholarship. Lesbians took advantage of the women's movement to live openly in ways of their choice and the Federal Republic, particularly in West Berlin, soon had a rich and vibrant gay culture. Indeed to some it seemed that "the love that dare not speak its name" now found it difficult to know when to shut up. But when the first shock waves were over, gays and lesbians were readily accepted in public life and bone-headed homophobes were far too busy setting immigrant homes on fire, beating up Turks, desecrating Jewish cemeteries, and marching in celebration of Rudolph Hess's birthday to turn their undivided attention to the challenge of homosexuality.

Helmuth Schmidt's Chancellorship: The Final Phase

Helmuth Schmidt's relationship with President Carter, who took office in 1977, was far from harmonious. It would be hard to imagine two more different temperaments than the tough-minded pragmatist Schmidt and the dreamy idealist Carter. The German chancellor had ill-concealed contempt for the new president's woeful ignorance of foreign affairs, and was increasingly exacerbated by the naïve campaign of

Carter's national security advisor, Zbigniew Brzezinski, for civil rights in the Soviet Union, and for his imprudent belief that the Soviets' enemies were necessarily the West's friends. The Carter administration blew hot and cold on the neutron bomb, a grotesque weapon designed to kill people by radioactivity but leave buildings intact. Schmidt hoped that this could be used as a bargaining counter to persuade the Soviets to remove their intermediate range SS-20 missiles from Europe, but Carter eventually decided not to deploy the weapon, thus leaving Western Europe seriously disadvantaged strategically. In January 1979 Carter, Giscard d'Estaing, the British prime minister James Callaghan, and Helmuth Schmidt met in Guadeloupe to discuss a wide range of foreign political and security issues. Schmidt, who was accepted as an equal partner of the three atomic powers, played a significant role in reaching an agreement whereby the US would threaten to station intermediate-range missiles in Europe if the Soviets did not agree to withdraw their SS-20s.

Back in Germany Schmidt found, as he had predicted, considerable resistance to the proposal. Within the government the opposition was led by Egon Bahr, who argued that it would put an end to Ostpolitik, to say nothing of his plans for a European security system that would replace both NATO and the Warsaw Pact. Brandt and Wehner were in broad sympathy with Bahr's position, and the division between the two sides could only be temporarily bridged by the hope for a "double zero solution" whereby the Soviets would withdraw their SS-20s, whereupon the Americans would not deploy their Cruise and Pershing II intermediate-range missiles. The Young Socialists, under the future chancellor Gerhard Schröder, put forward a motion at the SPD party conference in 1979 that no intermediate range missiles should be stationed in Germany which, had it been accepted, would have spelt the end of Schmidt's chances in the forthcoming general election. In December 1979 NATO agreed to the US proposal to replace their Pershing Ia missiles in Europe with 108 Pershing IIs, and to station 464 ground-based Cruise missiles by 1983. One thousand obsolete atomic warheads were to be withdrawn. As part of a twin-track program negotiations with the USSR over nuclear arms reduction in Europe were to be put in train as soon as possible.

The Soviet Union invaded Afghanistan only a few days after this NATO meeting in Brussels, thus causing a serious crisis not only in East–West relations, but also between the US and its European allies. Carter and Brzezinski set out to punish the Soviets, much to the alarm of Schmidt and his close ally Giscard d'Estaing. As Schmidt pointed out to secretary of state Cyrus Vance, punishment of the Soviet Union would also involve punishing 16 million Germans in the DDR and two million in West Berlin. The German chancellor launched an unprecedented attack on the Carter administration's policy toward the Soviet Union, and called on both sides to halt the deployment of intermediate-range missiles. This triggered a bitter exchange of notes in which Schmidt got the better of Carter, and forced the president to accept his views on the missile question.

Schmidt flew to Moscow in June 1980 with US blessing, and managed finally to persuade Brezhnev to agree to bilateral talks with the United States over intermediate-range missiles. It was a diplomatic triumph which Carter generously acknowledged and which greatly strengthened the chancellor's position in the 1980 elections. Helmuth Schmidt was now unquestionably a statesman of world stature who showed a complete mastery of foreign policy, and also played the leading role in the G7 summits; but this was only a short-term victory. As predicted Carter lost to Ronald Reagan in the November presidential elections, and the new hard-line administration put the talks on hold for one year.

A wave of strikes in Poland in 1980, coordinated by Lech Walesa's "*Solidarnosc*" (Solidarity), and supported by the former bishop of Krakow, Karol Wojtyla, who had become pope as John Paul II in the previous year, raised the specter of Soviet intervention, which would have spelt an end to Schmidt and Giscard's policy of détente. Franz-Josef Strauss, as the chancellor candidate of the CDU/CSU, had little success in once again trying to paint Schmidt as a dangerous socialist, and even stooped as low as to suggest that there were certain similarities between the SPD and the National Socialists. Voters who were not particularly sympathetic to the SPD often admired Schmidt for his tough stand on nuclear parity in Europe, whereas the volatile and capricious Strauss inspired little confidence other than as an energetic demagogue. Although the CDU/CSU emerged once again as the largest party in the October elections, they lost 4.1 points and the SPD made marginal gains. The FDP won an impressive 10.6 percent. The Greens, in their first ever Bundestag election, received a mere 1.5 percent and therefore did not qualify for representation. The SPD/FDP coalition now had a clear majority in the new Bundestag of 271 as against 226 seats.

The crisis in Poland placed Honecker in an awkward situation. Outwardly he was intractable and intransigent. He doubled the amount of hard currency that visitors from "capitalist foreign countries" were obliged to exchange into the DDR's "aluminum chips," and in the "Gera Demands" of October 1980 he called upon the Federal Republic to afford full diplomatic recognition to the DDR. Privately he reassured Bonn that he was anxious not to beak off the dialogue. There were many murmurs of complaint among the SED leadership about their leader's zigzag policy, but they were all too scared of him to do anything about it. Although the Soviet leadership were not entirely happy with their myrmidon in Berlin, they knew him to be essentially a loyal vassal, and saw no pressing need to remove him.

Helmuth Schmidt's new government in Bonn faced a serious economic crisis and concomitant social problems. Unemployment rose within one year from 400,000 to 1,370,000, with inflation running at seven percent, and output falling. The Right found an easy scapegoat in the 4.6 million foreigners living in Germany and in the 100,000 asylum seekers. Politicians fulminated against "phoney asylum seekers," and the less sophisticated gave vent to their frustrations by beating up Turks. The extra-parliamentary opposition and their fellow travelers also took to violence in protest against atomic reactors, the visits of prominent American politicians, extensions to Frankfurt airport, and in support of squatters' rights. The election of Ronald Reagan triggered a fresh round of anti-Americanism in Germany, even though the president invited the Soviets to Strategic Arms Limitation Talks (START) in Geneva, and said that the US would not station Pershing Ias and Cruise missiles in Europe if the Soviets withdrew their SS-20s and other intermediate-range missiles. Reagan's rhetoric about the "evil empire," and his enthusiastic support of the Strategic Defense Initiative (SDI), further convinced the German pacifists that Reagan had no interest whatsoever in disarmament. The peace movement was skilfully manipulated by Markus Wolf, head of the Stasi's propaganda bureau, who financed the German Peace Union (DFU), a barely disguised Communist organization which included two prominent Greens, the German/American Petra Kelly and her lover, Gerd Bastian, a retired general. Markus Wolf's DFU collected some 4.7 million signatures to the "Krefeld Appeal" against nuclear weapons, among them a number of mainly Protestant churchmen who were unable to reconcile NATO's policies with the sermon on the mount.

This was a matter of great concern to the Protestant Schmidt, who was also facing increasing criticism for his wholehearted support for the twin-track policy. Like Brandt before him he was in danger of losing the support of his parliamentary caucus. He was opposed within his own ranks not only by Young Turks like the mayor of Saarbrücken, Oskar Lafontaine, but also by Willy Brandt as party chairman, who remained convinced that the Soviets posed no real threat, and that his friend Brezhnev was seriously interested in disarmament talks. Schmidt's problems were compounded by fundamental differences with the FDP over how to deal with the budgetary crisis. He wanted increases in income tax, the FDP wanted drastic cuts in expenditure on social services. At the same time Bonn was hit by a major scandal over illegal contributions to political parties in which all parties in the Bundestag were involved. The proposal for a general amnesty for those implicated in a complex series of dubious financial transactions, which involved vast sums of money, was rejected by the SPD caucus and by the SPD minister of justice. The FDP, which had the most to gain by such an amnesty, was incensed. The coalition was beginning to crumble.

Schmidt began to show signs that he was losing touch when, in spite of the mounting crisis in Poland, he agreed to talks with Honecker at the SED chief's hunting lodge. The talks got nowhere and martial law was declared in Poland while the chancellor was still in the DDR. Schmidt and Honecker went to Güstrow to admire Ernst Barlach's sculptures and to visit the cathedral. To the outside world it seemed that both men were indifferent to events in Poland, and Franz-Josef Strauss took great relish in denouncing his rival for having been so easily led by the nose. There was precious little sympathy for "*Solidarnosc*" in government circles in Bonn. It was a fiercely nationalist and Catholic movement rather than a left wing one, and Walesa was known to be something of a lightweight. Far more important, however, was the fact that events in Poland threatened the peace and stability of the Communist Bloc, and thus that of Western Europe. The Federal Republic was in the front line, and therefore was more concerned about the preservation of peace than the self-determination of peoples. Herbert Wehner even went as far as to let the DDR know that he favored a tough line in Poland and believed that violent measures were inevitable. Some of the more perspicacious observers argued that events in Poland showed that hopes for a peaceful and gradual reform of the Communist system were illusory, and that more such violent upheavals could be expected. Things had not turned out as expected, and the future had become unpredictable and alarming. In such a situation the vituperative denunciation of events in Poland coming from Ronald Reagan's America made Bonn's position even more precarious. All Schmidt could do was to try and persuade Honecker of the need for General Jaruzelski to be as forbearing as possible in the exercise of martial law.

Schmidt's visit to the United States in January 1982 was not a success. He refused to go along with the US demand for a trade embargo on Poland and was subject to such scurrilous attacks in the *New York Times* and the *Washington Post* that the president felt obliged to offer an apology. In spite of these differences Helmuth Schmidt by now had lost the confidence of those members of the SPD caucus who were sharply critical of his endorsement of American policy on intermediate-range missiles. Relations with the FDP had also been badly damaged over the issue of amnesty for those involved in violations of the law on party finance, and by differences over how to deal with the budgetary crisis. In February 1982 he called for a vote of confidence in order to clear the air. He won by a comfortable margin, and at the party conference in April two-thirds of the delegates supported his position on nuclear weapons, and his commitment to NATO and the Western alliance.

At first it seemed that the conference on Intermediate-Range Nuclear Forces (INF) in Geneva might reach a workable compromise when the US and Soviet chief negotiators took their famous "walk in the woods," and agreed to reciprocal reductions of these weapons in Europe. Then both Washington and Moscow promptly rejected this promising formula. A new and dangerous phase in the arms race began, and Schmidt's calculations that an American threat would lead to a compromise along the lines proposed by Paul Nitze and Julii A. Kvizinski in Geneva proved illusory. With his policy on nuclear deployment in ruins, Schmidt now faced a serious revolt in his own ranks led by Oskar Lafontaine, who called for the SPD to abandon the coalition, go into opposition, and begin a drastic rethinking of basic Social Democratic principles. The chancellor was outraged when there was precious little protest within the party over an inflammatory interview given by Lafontaine to the weekly magazine *Stern* in July 1983. The attack was a direct response to Schmidt's plans for a budget in which he had made a number of significant concessions to the economic liberals in the FDP, and did precious little to tackle the pressing problem of unemployment. The trades unions supported Lafontaine's position, and threatened to take action against the budgetary compromise. Noises were also coming from the FDP that they were considering abandoning the coalition, and following the example of the party in Hesse that was seeking an alliance with the CDU.

Schmidt brought matters to a head in September 1982 when he challenged Helmut Kohl to introduce a motion of constructive no confidence to be followed by a fresh round of elections. Kohl hesitated while the FDP minister of trade and commerce, Count Otto Lambsdorff, presented a position paper with which Margaret Thatcher would have been in broad agreement. It was clearly irreconcilable with even Schmidt's Laodician Social Democratic views, and was diametrically opposed to the radical program passed at the SPD's recent party conference. The chancellor was growing increasingly impatient and eager for a fight. Having got word that they were soon to be fired, the four FDP ministers resigned from the cabinet.

The vote was held on October 1 leaving Helmuth Schmidt head of a minority government, his popularity scarcely diminished, and the FDP widely regarded as traitors who had stabbed him in the back. The FDP paid the price in the elections in Hesse in September where they received a miserable 3.1 percent of the popular vote, and were therefore not represented in the provincial parliament (Landtag). Two days after the Hesse elections Helmut Kohl proposed a motion of constructive no confidence. After a lengthy and lively debate in which the CDU pitched the outspoken Rainer Barzel against the eloquent Helmuth Schmidt, the motion was carried by 256 to 235 votes with four abstentions. Helmut Kohl thus became the first chancellor to be appointed as a result of such a motion.

There was a great deal of unfinished business for the new coalition between the CDU/CSU and FDP to tackle. Scandals of party financing had to be investigated, the welfare system was in desperate need of overhaul, and fundamental changes in tax law were long overdue. It remained to be seen whether the new chancellor, who was so obviously the intellectual inferior to his glittering predecessor, who was scarcely able to formulate a coherent idea in spite of a doctorate in history, who was the butt of the intelligentsia's derision, and who was not yet in full control of his own party, would be equal to the job.

16
The Reunification of Germany

The 52-year-old Helmut Kohl was the first chancellor from the postwar generation who enjoyed, as he later put it in a characteristic phrase, "the favor of a later birth." He saw himself as the heir to Konrad Adenauer in that he was a whole-hearted supporter of European integration and the Western Alliance, as well as sharing his precursor's awareness of the implicit dangers were Germany to harbor any great power pretensions. Like Adenauer he was a provincial, in his case from the Palatinate, for whose wines and stuffed pig's bellies he had a great affection that was reflected in his gigantic frame. Unlike Adenauer he had no particular resentments against Prussia or Berlin. He focused all his attention on power at the expense of any ethical concerns, to the point of violating the constitution, his oath of office, sworn before Almighty God, and laws to which he had appended his signature. This was to lead to the disgraceful end to a distinguished and remarkable career.

After a constitutionally somewhat dubious procedure, elections were called for March 6 1983. Schmidt was no longer the SPD's front runner. He had lost the confidence of the party caucus and his health was seriously impaired, in large part because of very heavy smoking, and he had had to rely on a pacemaker since 1981. The SPD's chancellor candidate was Hans-Jochen Vogel, the highly respected, moderate, and somewhat uninspiring former mayor of Berlin. The Kohl/Genscher coalition was denounced by the left as an American stooge, but Kohl somewhat surprisingly won the backing of the French president, the socialist François Mitterand, who gave a rousing speech in the Bundestag in support of the twin-track solution. The result was a resounding victory for the CDU/CSU who received 4.3 points more than in 1980, with the SPD dropping by 4.7 points and the FDP by 3.6 points. The Greens just managed to clear the five percent hurdle by 0.6 points, and thus were represented in the Bundestag for the first time.

The new parliament was at first exclusively absorbed with a major scandal involving the largesse of the Flick industrial empire, which made use of a money-laundering outfit conveniently situated near Bonn to channel 26 million marks into the pockets of the political parties between 1960 and 1980. The state prosecutor's office had begun trying to unravel this highly complicated affair throughout 1983, but the task was made even more difficult when one of the main suspects, the treasurer of the FDP, Heinz Herbert Karry, was murdered by terrorists, and another, the SPD's treasurer Alfred Nau, died.

Although both men took a number of secrets to the grave, survivors' heads began to roll. Count Otto Lambsdorff from the FDP felt obliged to resign as minister of trade and commerce. Rainer Barzel, president of the Bundestag, also resigned when it transpired that he had received a substantial sum from the Flick empire in 1973 disguised as a fee for services rendered in his capacity as a partner in a prominent Frankfurt law firm. Helmut Kohl also came under attack for receiving 55,000 marks in cash from Flick. His skin was only saved when three leading witnesses committed perjury, as was revealed when Kohl was disgraced in a subsequent financial scandal.

Long debates were held over proposals to change the law on financing political parties, challenges were made to the Constitutional Court, and eventually a new set of rules was passed. None of this made much difference. The parties found new ways to circumvent the law and, as was later to be revealed, Helmut Kohl continued to receive illegal payments, even though he had come dangerously close to ending his political career due to such dubious activities. But the higher he climbed, the further he had to fall, and climb he did, the arrogance of power rendering him impervious to the law, as illegal millions were stashed away in secret accounts in Switzerland and Liechtenstein.

The issue of intermediate-range missiles did not disappear from the agenda while the parties argued about money. It was the central issue at the SPD's party congress held in November 1983, at which the opponents of US policy, led by Willy Brandt, engaged in spirited debate with the proponents of a tough line toward the Soviet Union led by Helmuth Schmidt. Anti-Communism *à l'américaine* had no attraction for the majority of Social Democrats, and was dismissed by Egon Bahr as mere ideology. The SPD's official statement of 1970, which had been written by extreme right-winger Richard Löwenthal, insisted that the fundamental distinctions between liberal democracy and communist dictatorship should never be overlooked in the pursuit of peace. This position was now reversed in practice, although only a small minority within the party agreed with Oskar Lafontaine that the Federal Republic should withdraw from NATO.

Now in opposition, the SPD negotiated directly with the SED and drew up a series of plans for disarmament in central Europe that were enthusiastically supported by the Social Democratic minister-president of Sweden, Olaf Palme. Such efforts were in marked contrast to the renewed arms race between the two superpowers, prompting some overly-optimistic observers to suggest that this was the beginning of a new European self-consciousness that could eventually even lead to the reunification of Germany. In fact Europe was helpless as the two giants challenged one another in what turned out to be the final round in the struggle for hegemony. The most the European states could do was to engage in damage control and hope for the best.

The Winds of Change

Kohl and his foreign minister Genscher made profuse assurances of their loyalty to the Atlantic alliance, while at the same time continuing the previous government's policy toward the DDR. The government had only been in office for a few weeks when the Bavarian anti-Communist firebrand, Franz-Josef Strauss, made a spectacular appearance in East Berlin and negotiated a credit of one thousand million marks with the extremely dubious East German entrepreneur and secretary of state for "Commercial Coordination," Alexander Schalck-Golodowski. The DDR was on the verge of financial collapse, which some feared would lead to chaos and Soviet intervention. Nothing was offered in return for the loan, although it was remarked that border guards were not quite as insufferable toward visitors as was their singularly unattractive wont. Strauss, one of the arch-ideologues of the cold war, amazed his host Honecker when he blandly stated that the age of ideology was over, and pragmatic and practical issues were now paramount. Wicked tongues suggested that financial gain was also a consideration in this extraordinary about-turn.

Massive credits from the Federal Republic enabled the SED regime to borrow from other capitalist states, thus enabling Honecker to continue in the illusion that the "unity of economics and social policy" was an attainable goal; but the DDR was now in hock to the capitalists, and was in no position to take a principled stand against the Reagan administration's nuclear strategy. The Communist Honecker trusted the conservatives Kohl and Strauss more than he did the Social Democrats, against whom he harbored bitter resentments from the good old Stalinist days of "Social Fascism," but his masters in the Kremlin kept him on a short leash. Constantin Chernenko, who took over the Soviet leadership in 1984, was suspicious of Honecker's independence and vetoed his proposed visit to the Federal Republic. But Chernenko was not long in office. He died in early 1985, aged 79. The last of the gerontocrats was succeeded by the 54-year-old Mikhail Gorbachev, who at once made it known that he was keen to reopen the disarmament talks in Geneva and reach an agreement on intermediate-range missiles. He was an apparatchik, bent on reforming rather than changing the Soviet system, and Kohl got cold comfort from the interview he was granted during Chernenko's funeral. Talks with Honecker on this occasion went far smoother, and resulted in the joint Moscow Declaration which stated that: "The inviolability of the frontiers and respect for the territorial integrity and sovereignty of all European states is the fundamental precondition for peace."

In the DDR there was a growing feeling of pride in the state's achievements, particularly in the remarkable performance of their skillfully doped athletes, resulting in a distinct national identity. In the Federal Republic the left accepted that the German nation-state was a thing of the past, whereas on the right there was constant criticism of the Eastern treaties as a betrayal of the national ideal. In a sense things were back to normal after the aberration of the Adenauer years. The right was nationalistic once again, the left antinational; but both left and right had serious problems with the question of German national identity. Most were inoculated against the more virulent forms of nationalism after the ghastly experience of National Socialism, and the concept of "constitutional patriotism," made popular by the journalist Dolf Sternberger, found wide acceptance. This tended to overlook the problem that the founding fathers of the Federal Republic defined nationality in terms of blood (*jus sanguinis*) rather than place of birth (*jus soli*). A German was someone born of German parents, not someone born in Germany. A person born in Alma Ata who could claim to be of German descent had an automatic right to German citizenship. A person born of Turkish parents in the Federal Republic did not. The fierce debates over a change in the citizenship laws in 1999 showed that this issue still remained extremely sensitive, even after reunification. Meanwhile, much ink was spilt on the difference between nations and nation-states, on whether Germany was "bi-national" or "post-national," and whether or not a "cultural nation" could encompass two German states.

These rarified and abstract debates inevitably brought up the question of the Nazi era, and it was not until the 1980s that a serious debate began as the Federal Republic at last confronted Germany's sordid past. It was then that the word "holocaust" entered everyday speech as a result of the eponymous American television serial that attracted huge audiences when it was shown in 1979. In 1985 Kohl showed a typical lack of sensitivity when he invited Ronald Reagan to visit a World War II military cemetery at Bitburg where 2,000 German soldiers lay buried. What was designed as an act of reconciliation misfired when it was revealed that 40 of the dead had been members of the Waffen-SS. Some of the damage was undone by a remarkable speech given on May 8 by Richard von Weizsäcker, who had been elected president the previous year, only three days after the Bitburg incident. He stressed that May 8 1945 should be regarded as a day of liberation and "the end of a wrong track in German history," and that the horrors suffered by Germans in the final days of the war were the direct result of January 30 1933. The president further stressed that the mass murder of the European Jews was a unique historical event and insisted that every single German "could witness what their Jewish fellow-citizens had to suffer."

Weizsäcker's speech was on the whole very favorably received, although there were a number of protests from those who insisted that ordinary Germans were wholly ignorant of what had happened to the Jews, or who suggested that the past was being dug up simply in order to further the national interests of the state of Israel. It was an article by Ernst Nolte, written in the convoluted language of a Heidegger pupil and devotee, published in the *Frankfurter Allgemeine Zeitung* in June 1986, that finally triggered a fierce debate among historians over the Nazi past. Nolte suggested that there was a causal link between the Gulag and Auschwitz and that the Nazis were Stalin's epigones, and complained that Stalinist murders were consistently ignored while Nazi crimes were discussed ad nauseam. In this version of recent history Hitler merely reacted to communist crimes and was acting, or believed that he was acting, in self-defense against an "Asiatic" threat, and therefore the burden of guilt should be lifted from Germany's collective shoulders.

Jürgen Habermas, Germany's most influential philosopher, spearheaded the counterattack on Nolte and his neoconservative admirers in the historical profession in a spirited article in the liberal weekly *Die Zeit*. He accused Nolte of removing all moral issues from Germany's historical past, of reducing Auschwitz to "a mere technical innovation," and of undermining the opening to the West based on "universal constitutional principles" of which postwar Germany could be justly proud. No new insights resulted from the subsequent *"Historikerstreit,"* in which the majority of the historical guild lined up against Nolte and his nationalist followers, but at least the attempt to rewrite German history had been stopped in its tracks. However, the problem remained that insistence on the unique nature of Nazi crimes left the Habermas camp open to the charge that they overlooked the crimes committed in the name of Communism, and the threadbare theory of totalitarianism was taken out of the mothballs in which it had been packed since the heyday of the cold war. Recognition of the responsibility for the terrible crimes of the Nazi era could also lead to a perverse form of nationalism. German crimes were unparalleled, and German atonement equally unique.

While the *Historikerstreit* raged, fundamental changes were taking place in the relationship between the United States and the Soviet Union. Mikhail Gorbachev knew that something had to be done to stop the Soviet Union's rapid decline. Talk of "Glasnost" (openness) and "Perestroika" (restructuring), coupled with insistence on the need for democracy, was singularly vague, but was at least indication of a certain loosening of the stranglehold of dictatorship. Ronald Reagan, who had been reelected in 1984, was also in difficulties arising from the Iran-Contra affair, and was under attack from the Democratic majority in the House of Representatives. Gorbachev and Reagan almost reached an agreement to withdraw all nuclear weapons from Europe during their meeting in Reykjavik in October 1986, but this came to nothing when Reagan refused to abandon his beloved "Star Wars" project. Four months later, the Soviet Union announced that it no longer linked the removal of intermediate-range missiles to SDI, and the INF Treaty was signed in Washington in December 1987.

The course of relations between the Soviet Union and the Federal Republic was far bumpier. Gorbachev did not react kindly when Kohl compared him to Goebbels in an interview given to *Newsweek*, and Genscher had to use all his redoubtable diplomatic skills to smooth the severely troubled waters. Indeed he went so far in his efforts to appease the Soviet Union that he was severely criticized in Washington and London for harboring dangerous illusions about the new Russia.

The Bundestag elections, which were held in January 1987, were a disappointment for the CDU/CSU. Kohl remained in office, but the two parties dropped 4.7 points and booked their worst result since 1949. The SPD under the leadership of the estimable but lack-luster Johannes Rau also lost votes. The FDP and Greens both made substantial gains. In his address to the new Bundestag Kohl expressed his determination to further the dialogue with the DDR, but added that he could never reconcile himself to "the Wall, the shoot-to-kill order, and barbed wire" on the inner-German border. He called for the drastic reduction of intermediate-range nuclear missiles in Europe and for parity in defensive weapons between East and West.

The strained relations between Moscow and Bonn were greatly improved thanks to the sterling efforts of Weizsäcker and Genscher during a state visit to the Soviet Union in July 1987. Shortly afterward, the SPD and SED produced a joint paper on "Arguments over Ideology and Mutual Security," in which the parties agreed to disagree within a framework of open discussion and by avoiding reciprocal recriminations. The SED thus opened the door to discussion, admittedly within strict limits, of the "failures and disadvantages" of "socialism as it really exists." On the other side, the SPD allowed that the dictatorial regime in the DDR was a legitimate form of government, but it was one that was very definitely open to criticism.

In September 1987 Honecker made a historic visit to the Federal Republic, during which he was accorded full honors. Nothing concrete came from the visit, other than an agreement on environmental control that had been negotiated before Honecker arrived. Kohl's masterly speech at a banquet in Bad Godesberg offered encouragement to those who hoped that closer relations with the DDR would bring concessions, without alienating those who felt that he had already gone too far in appeasing the Evil Empire's satrapy. As for Honecker, even Oskar Lafontaine, a fellow Saarlander and his most influential supporter in the SPD, could only find "respect" for this prissy little man. Given that the DDR had recently abolished the death penalty, and had become much more generous in allowing its citizens to visit the West for compassionate reasons, there was a general feeling that, although Honecker was not even remotely likeable, the devil was perhaps not quite a black as he had often been painted. On the other side of the Wall the Stasi reported that Kohl's speech and remarks by other politicians in the host country had raised unrealistic hopes, and the restrictions on travel to capitalist countries were causing mounting discontent.

Willy Brandt and a number of leading figures in the SPD, among them Oskar Lafontaine and the mayor of Hamburg, Klaus von Dohnanyi, hoped that the historic division of the labor movement between Communists and Social Democrats would gradually be overcome. The Italian and Spanish Communist parties had jettisoned their Leninist baggage and, as "Eurocommunists," were virtually indistinguishable from Social Democrats. Gorbachev, with his "Glasnost" and "Perestroika," seemed to be moving in the same direction. But the belief that the SED would metamorphose to this extent was an illusion. Gorbachev was intent on reforming rather than transforming the CPSU, and Honecker was convinced that even this was going too far. The DDR was to remain a bastion of orthodoxy as the Communist world gradually became more receptive to new ideas.

The CDU/CSU was far more concerned with nuclear weapons than with the finer shades of Marxist dogma. Franz Josef Strauss, and Manfred Wörner who served as minister of defense between 1982 and 1988 before becoming secretary-general of NATO, agreed with Ronald Reagan and Margaret Thatcher, prime minister since 1979, that the obsolete US "Lance" missiles needed to be replaced immediately. Hans-Dietrich Genscher, on the contrary, argued that disarmament talks should begin before the new missiles were deployed. Kohl remained undecided for a long time, but even though the hawkish George Bush was inaugurated in January 1989 and fielded a team that included the hardliner James Baker as secretary of state and the uncompromisingly combative Dick Cheney in charge of defense, he felt it prudent to support his foreign minister so as not to endanger the coalition.

Genscher, who instantly became one of the leading bêtes noirs of the Bush administration, had a number of allies. Although the French were not involved in the military side of NATO, they were always ready to cock a snook at the Americans and therefore gladly lent their support. A number of NATO allies were also mindful that détente was as much their concern as defense, and backed the West German foreign minister's stand. These included Italy, Spain, Greece, Belgium, Luxembourg, and Denmark. The leading proponent of "Genscherism," as the dove-like position was contemptuously dubbed on the other side of the Atlantic, was the Norwegian foreign minister Thorvald Stoltenberg. He played an important role in helping Genscher negotiate an uneasy compromise at the NATO meeting in May 1989, when it was agreed to postpone deployment of the new missiles until 1992.

The doves in Bonn had forced the hawks in Washington to back down, and NATO announced its determination to work toward the creation of a new peaceful environment in Europe. Although Gorbachev was still justifiably suspicious of the US administration, and appeared unwilling to take up the challenge, dramatic changes were taking place in Eastern Europe. In 1986 Gorbachev disowned the "Brezhnev Doctrine" which severely limited the sovereignty of the socialist states, and replaced it with what was to be called the "Sinatra Doctrine," whereby members of the Warsaw Pact were given a degree of freedom to do it their way. The socialist states tested the waters with due caution. In Hungary János Kádár fell from power in May 1988, and was replaced by a reformer. In April the following year the entire Politburo was replaced. A number of prominent reformers were among the new members. Discussions began in Poland in early 1989 about recognizing "*Solidarnosc*" and thus beginning the process of genuine democratic reform. Czechoslovakia was once bitten in 1968, and was thus twice shy. The DDR remained resilient to the winds of change. Any signs of opposition were promptly suppressed. At the annual Liebknecht–Luxemburg Demonstration in East Berlin in 1988 a few intrepid souls carried signs with Rosa Luxemburg's famous words: "Freedom is always freedom for those who think otherwise." The offenders were arrested, even though Luxemburg's notion of freedom of expression was confined to party members and was hardly a liberal manifesto. In November 1988 the Soviet publication *Sputnik* was removed from the newsstands. It had published the text of the secret protocol to the Molotov–Ribbentrop Pact of August 1939, whereby the two gangsters had divided up the spoils. The SED could not tolerate such an insult to the memory of the Soviet Union's glorious antifascist struggle.

The SED's intransigent attitude to these changes prompted a fresh round of discussions of the German problem. A group of moderates in the CDU under the chairmanship of the secretary-general of the party, Heiner Geissler, produced a document for the 1988 party congress which spoke of one German nation that was divided into two states, and which insisted that freedom was the precondition for unity and not the price that had to be paid. For the right-wing and its mouthpiece the *Frankfurter Allgemeine Zeitung* this was an outrageous watering-down of the concept of "nation," which overlooked the absolute priority of reunification. For Willy Brandt and most of the SPD, renewed talk of reunification was little more than the revival of the dangerous illusions harbored at the height of the cold war. He warned that behind the idea of "reunification" was the pernicious belief that it would be possible to restore the German frontiers of 1937, and felt that the most that could be hoped for was that the Federal Republic and the DDR would gradually develop closer relations. Egon Bahr was somewhat more optimistic, and envisioned the two superpowers withdrawing from central Europe, thus creating the preconditions for the unification of the two German states.

When the issue was debated in the Bundestag in December 1988, the SPD's party chairman Hans-Jochen Vogel praised Geissler's paper and denounced the Bismarckian delusions of the CDU/CSU's caucus chairman, Alfred Dregger, the spokesman for the right wing. Vogel's notion of "unity" was based on shared historical, cultural, linguistic, and emotional experiences, and had little to do with the state as such. This point was seconded by another SPD speaker, Gerhard Heimann, who pointed out past German efforts to combine freedom and unity, as in 1848 and 1871, gave little cause for optimism, and that it was time to learn to live with a Germany that consisted of more than one state. Helmut Lippelt for the Greens argued that the whole notion of reunification should be abandoned since it restricted Bonn's freedom of action, and by posing a threat to the DDR strengthened Honecker's hand in resisting Soviet calls for reform. This antinationalist view was strongly supported by Oskar Lafontaine in his book *The Society of the Future*, published in 1988, in which he argued that German nationalism was "perverted," and that therefore the country could play a unique role in helping to build a supranational Europe. A united Germany for Lafontaine would be a step backwards to the grim era of the nation-state and away from Europe. Europe would save Germany from its appalling past, and Germany, by searching for atonement for the worst of crimes could, by a redemptive dialectic, play a leading role in the new Europe. In its guilt lay its strength, and the division of Germany was a blessing in that it marked the end of the German nation-state, which had caused so much misery and devastation. These views were shared by many in Lafontaine's postwar generation who felt that the DDR was not a part of Germany.

At a time when talk of reunification was the preserve of a mere handful of neo-conservatives, a series of dramatic events in Eastern Europe placed the issue high on the agenda. In February 1989 discussions began in Hungary on the introduction of a multiparty system, and in June the frontier with Austria was opened. There was now a gaping hole in the iron curtain. The reforms in Poland were hardly less surprising. Solidarnosc was officially recognized, the market replaced a state-planned economy, and an element of democracy was introduced into the political system, which resulted in a triumph for the opposition. Solidarnosc won 99 of the 100 seats in the senate, and all of the 35 percent of the seats in parliament that were open to free election. The new minister-president Kiszczak Mazowiecki was one of Walesa's closest advisors. The DDR was unaffected by these reforms. In February 1989 a man was shot while try to cross the Berlin Wall. Protests against the rigged local elections were brutally suppressed by the Stasi and the police. In June deputies in the People's Chamber (*Volkskammer*) denounced the "violent and bloody actions of the enemies of the constitution" committed by the victims of the Tiananmen Square massacre. This was clear warning that any similar demonstrations in the DDR would be treated in like manner.

A few days after the people's representatives issued this drastic message, Mikhail Gorbachev made an official visit to the Federal Republic. He was given an even warmer welcome than that afforded to George Bush a mere fortnight previously. The joint communiqué at the end of the visit referred to the right of all peoples freely to determine the social and political system in which they wished to live. At a press conference Gorbachev made the gnomic remark that the Wall could disappear once "the preconditions were removed that caused it to be built," and went on to say that the division of Germany was a "reality," but that the future would decide what would happen.

Shortly after his return to Moscow from his triumphant visit to the Federal Republic, Gorbachev played host to Honecker, whom he warned that the major problems that faced the socialist countries could only be solved by democratic means. Honecker took no notice of this admonition, and blandly replied that the SED always discussed matters with the people, and that the DDR's admirable social services guaranteed that the people were content. Faced with this flat refusal to make any concessions, the Soviets became increasingly concerned that the situation in the DDR would become explosive. But the SED was also faced with an intractable dilemma. The DDR was clearly defined as an antifascist and socialist alternative to the Federal Republic. What possible legitimacy could there be for the continued existence of a separate capitalist German state?

Unification

The disenfranchised citizens of the German Democratic Republic began to vote with their feet. They poured into the offices of the Federal Republic's permanent representative in East Berlin in the hope that they would be able to travel to the Federal Republic. They did the same in the West German embassies in Budapest, Warsaw, and Prague. In the course of a secret meeting near Bonn on August 31, the Hungarian minister president Miklós Németh and foreign minister Gula Horn assured Kohl and Genscher that citizens of the DDR would be permitted to cross the border to Austria within a couple of weeks. By the end of the month 25,000 had taken advantage of this opportunity to move to the Federal Republic. At the end of September Genscher managed to get the SED regime to agree that the 6,000 DDR refugees in the Prague embassy could travel freely to the West. The 700 refugees in Warsaw were also permitted to leave.

The DDR now began preparations for the celebration the fortieth anniversary of the foundation of the state. The frontier with Czechoslovakia was closed on October 3 in order that the jollifications should not be marred by the unsightly spectacle of a mass exodus of the disaffected. The news was met with outrage and dismay, and on the following day the railway station in Dresden was occupied by people hoping to leave what to many now seemed like a prison. The police met with a hail of stones, a squad car was set on fire, and there were a number of injuries on both sides.

The majority of the opposition groups did not want to leave the DDR, but called for far-reaching reforms. The most important of these groups was the New Forum (*Neues Forum*), an open discussion group rather than a political party, which owed its popularity to the fact that it was free from ideological preconceptions, and left all the major issues of the day open to discussion. An application for official recognition was made to the ministry of the interior but it was promptly refused. Another group, Democracy Now (*Demokratie Jetzt*) called for democratic socialism in the DDR, and invited the citizens of the Federal Republic to follow suit and create a socialist alternative to a consumer society. The Democratic Beginning (*Demokratische Aufbruch*) was closely associated with the Evangelical Church, and was ecological and pacifist rather than socialist. The opposition was infused with an essentially Protestant ethic, even though many of the leading dissidents were not members of the church. They insisted on the primacy of individual conscience, regarded the division of Germany as just punishment for Nazi crimes, and disapproved strongly of the materialism of the West.

Opposition to "socialism as it really exists" was so widespread that the Stasi was unable to stop the increasing number of demonstrations in favor of democratic reform, even though the opposition groups and the Evangelical Church were riddled with their agents and informants known as "unofficial colleagues" (IMs). Among these were Ibrahim Böhme, who was to become party chairman of the newly constituted East German Social Democratic Party (SDP), and Manfred Stolpe, who was to become minister-president of Brandenburg in a united Germany and later federal minister of transport. Leipzig, a city of 500,000 inhabitants, became the center of opposition when the first of the Monday demonstrations was held on September 25, in which about 10,000 people took part. The police were very restrained, and used only the very minimum of coercion in dispelling the tail end of the demonstration. The authorities could not risk a bloodbath on the eve of the national celebrations. On the following Monday a crowd of 20,000 sang the "*Internationale,*" with particular emphasis on its call for human rights, and demanded democracy. The Stasi reported that it had had to use force in order to disperse the hard core of this "concentration of people," who were still taunting the police with "slanderous insults" after nine o'clock in the evening. Twenty arrests were made.

Gorbachev arrived in East Berlin on October 5 for the national celebrations. In his formal address he attacked those in Bonn who wanted to restore the frontiers of 1937, lavishly praised the achievement of the Workers' and Peasants' State, and expressed his confidence that the SED leadership would find appropriate solutions to the problems of the day. Behind closed doors he urged Honecker and the SED to move with the times but met with a stony response. Wherever he appeared in public intrepid souls shouted "Help us Gorbi!" A demonstration of some 1,000 persons in East Berlin on October 7 was broken up with extreme violence and 547 people were placed in custody. There was some concern that the Monday demonstration scheduled in Leipzig for October 9 would end in bloodshed. Undeterred by these fears, Kurt Masur, principal conductor of the Gewandhaus Orchestra, read a declaration to a crowd estimated at 70,000 which called for peaceful dialogue. It was signed by six prominent local figures, including three district secretaries of the SED. The crowd chanted slogans such as "We are the people!" "Gorbi, Gorbi, Gorbi!" "We're staying here!" and "Stasi go home!" but the police and paramilitary forces did not intervene. East Berlin had left it to the local authorities to take whatever action they deemed appropriate, and that evening Egon Krenz, deputy chairman of the council of state, said that the "Declaration of the Six" was acceptable. Krenz had the backing of the Soviet Ambassador in East Berlin, and instructions were sent to Soviet forces in the DDR that they were not to intervene. The SED had thus finally given way to popular pressure and a critical turning point had been reached. Honecker and his henchmen, Erich Mielke and Günter Mittag, had wanted a "Chinese" solution to the Leipzig demonstrations, but they were blocked at every turn by a group of moderates around Krenz who were determined to open up the way to fundamental reforms. Honecker was obdurate in his refusal to make any concessions. The Krenz faction won a major victory over the old guard at meetings of the Politburo on October 10 and 11. Honecker came under direct attack at a meeting of local party secretaries on October 12, where there were even calls for his resignation. The Monday demonstration in Leipzig on October 16 was the largest ever, with a crowd of 120,000, and there were smaller demonstrations in Dresden, Halle, Magdeburg, and East Berlin.

By now a number of prominent rats, Erich Mielke and Günter Mittag chief among them, began to leave the sinking ship, and Honecker's days were clearly numbered. No one supported him at the Politburo meeting on October 17 and on the following day he was stripped of his offices as secretary-general, member of the Politburo, and secretary of the Central Committee, "for reasons of health." Egon Krenz was appointed secretary-general, and in his first public address he announced that the SED would find a political solution to all outstanding problems, that socialism would not be put in question, and that he fully supported Gorbachev's policy of perestroika. Restrictions on travel to "socialist brother-states" would be either lifted or "modified." Ten thousand people took advantage of this between November 1 and 3 and traveled to West Germany via Czechoslovakia. From November 3 anyone who had an identity card and enough petrol could drive from anywhere in the DDR to Munich. The Wall had, to all intents and purposes, fallen.

Krenz, for all his toothy grin and professions of reforming zeal, was far too closely associated with the system to win the confidence of the civil rights activists, who well remembered his praise of the Chinese authorities for their robust treatment of dissidents, his active role in rigging local elections, and his encouragement of the police to take firm action against the demonstrators. Protest demonstrations spread throughout the country and 300,000 took part in the Monday rally in Leipzig on October 30. In the following days the mighty began to fall one by one, but this did nothing to appease the reformers. On November 4 a massive demonstration was held in East Berlin and carried live on TV. Among the speakers were the novelist Christa Wolf, the playwright Heiner Müller, a lawyer and rising political star Gregor Gysi, and, somewhat surprisingly, the spymaster Markus Wolf. The latter met with catcalls and whistles. The SED regime was now on the brink of collapse.

On November 7 Willy Stoph's government resigned. The next day all the members of the Politburo followed suit, and their replacements included a number of reformers, including Hans Modrow, the party boss of Dresden, who was appointed chairman of the council of ministers. The Central Committee of the SED met on November 8 and listened in horror to a series of reports to the effect that the state was virtually bankrupt. Some party stalwarts suddenly realized that they had been persistently lied to over the years, and their blind faith in the SED was shattered. In large part this was the unforeseen result of Bonn's Ostpolitik. Massive credits had allowed Honecker to continue fostering the illusion that "social and economic policy" could go hand in hand. Outwardly the DDR was by far the most prosperous of the socialist states, the envy of others in the socialist brotherhood, but from the early 1970s it was obvious to all those who had access to the true figures that the economy could only be set to rights if there was a drastic and politically unacceptable drop in living standards. Outward prosperity had enabled Honecker to resist calls for reform, with the result that pressure built up within society that could eventually no longer be contained.

The most pressing and immediate problem was that of refugees. The Czechoslovakian government had complained that its resources were seriously strained by the flood of people in transit to the Federal Republic. On November 9, the Central Committee agreed that the press secretary of the Council of Ministers should announce the opening of the border to the Federal Republic with effect from November 10. Krenz gave a copy of this order to the press secretary of the Central Committee, Günter Schabowski, who was on his way to a press conference to be held at 6 p.m. At this meeting the foreign press was informed that all border crossings would be opened with immediate effect. He prevaricated when asked what would happen to the Wall.

Associated Press announced shortly after 7 p.m. that the border was open. This was repeated on West German television shortly afterwards, and Tom Brockaw relayed this historic news to the viewers of NBC. The Bundestag interrupted its session, and after a series of emotional speeches the members joined together to sing the national anthem. Kohl, who was in Warsaw on November 9, hurried home, anxious not to miss the boat as Adenauer had done when the Wall was built. East Berliners poured across the border to the West and the border guards were at a loss to know what to do. Berlin was once again one city and Berliners celebrated this happy occasion throughout the night. November 9 1989 was the happiest day in German history but it could not be celebrated as a national holiday. The Weimar

Plate 31 The Berlin Wall November 10, 1989. © BPK

Republic had been proclaimed on November 9 1919, but the Hitler putsch in Munich took place on November 9 1923, and the horrific pogrom that goes under the unfortunate name of "The Night of Broken Glass" also happened on November 9 1938.

A mass rally was held in the John F. Kennedy-Platz in front of the Schöneberg city hall in West Berlin on November 10, at which Kohl urged patience, caution, and careful consideration of the import of these recent dramatic events. The crowd did not receive the speech well and the chancellor was frequently interrupted by whistles and hoots of derision. Hans-Dietrich Genscher, Willy Brandt, and the mayor of Berlin Walter Momper, were more favorably received. None of these speakers made any reference to national unity; although Willy Brandt repeated the famous remark "that which belongs together is now coming together" in a number of interviews that day, the phrase was not included in his speech. The opposition groups in the DDR were still strongly opposed to the idea of reunification, as were

Plate 32 Helmut Kohl

the SPD and the Greens in the West. For many, particularly in the Evangelical Church, the division of Germany was the mete and proper punishment for the sins of the past. The prominent Green politician Joschka Fischer, who was to become foreign minister of a united Germany, argued that a German nation-state had caused two world wars, had built the gas chambers and crematoria at Auschwitz-Birkenau, and should never be revived. Hans Modrow, who was appointed chairman of the council of ministers in the DDR in mid-November, argued that speculation about unification was "unrealistic and dangerous," although he did call for close cooperation between the two German states. The majority of artists and intellectuals in the DDR imagined that it would be possible to create a model socialist state that would avoid all the disadvantages of naked capitalism and of communist rigidity, thus realizing the dreams of a "third way" dear to socialist critics of the Soviet system. Ordinary citizens were not impressed by this utopian vision and, to the horror and dismay of the critical left, wanted to wallow in Western materialism. A public opinion poll taken toward the end of November showed that 70 percent of the population of the DDR favored unification, although the majority felt that the new Germany would have to be neutral.

In a move that caught everyone by surprise the Soviet Union let Bonn know that it favored some form of federation of the two German states. Kohl promptly unveiled his "Ten Point Program" in a speech to the Bundestag on November 28, in which he proposed a German confederation, adding that Germany would be unified if that was the people's wish. The SPD supported Kohl's initiative. The

Greens remained opposed. Neither François Mitterand nor Margaret Thatcher had been given prior knowledge of Kohl's speech, and both were outraged. The Israeli prime minister, Yitzak Shamir, had already warned that a united Germany would be so strong that it might be tempted to kill a few million more Jews. Moscow was also outspoken in its criticism of Kohl's speech, which went far further than the loose confederation it had proposed. Gorbachev denounced it as "dyed-in-the-wool révanchism," and the foreign minister Eduard Shevardnadze even went as far as to suggest that not even Adolf Hitler would have made such a proposal. George Bush was the only major statesman who wholeheartedly supported Kohl's initiative, and set only one condition for his continued endorsement: a united Germany would have to remain a member of NATO.

Bush met Gorbachev in Malta and reaffirmed his support for German unification, adding that he regarded the Oder-Neisse frontier as inviolable: a point that Kohl had pointedly failed to mention in his speech, and which had been picked up by the SPD. The president then traveled to Brussels for a NATO summit to discuss the German question on December 4. Margaret Thatcher and the Italian minister president, Giulio Andreotti, were alone in their opposition to Bush's proposal for a united Germany that would be a member of NATO and the European Community, and which would remain within the borders of the two existing German states. Kohl continued to refuse to make a commitment to the Oder-Neisse line on the grounds that it was an issue to be settled at a peace conference, and it took the combined skills of German and French diplomats to produce an ingenious communiqué that skirted the issue. Mitterand's reservations about German unification were partially overcome by major concessions to France's position on economic and monetary policy within the European Community. Kohl agreed to sacrifice the German mark to the euro before the political unification of Europe as the French demanded. Both NATO and the European Community now supported the idea of a united Germany, although Paris and London still harbored serious reservations. Moscow was implacably opposed. Helmut Kohl had risen magnificently to the occasion, and this often maladroit power-brokering politician had become a leading statesman. Even though Paris, London, and Rome were less than enthusiastic about the idea of German unification, Kohl could count on Washington's wholehearted support. Opposition to his policies from the Greens and the post-nationalists in the SPD around Oskar Lafontaine did not cause him a serious headache. The Soviet Union remained the major obstacle to the realization of his audacious project.

Meanwhile in the DDR the SED imploded, the old guard charged with corruption and abuse of their official positions. All but Honecker and the foreign policy expert Hermann Axen were imprisoned. Honecker had been diagnosed with cancer and Axen was in Moscow undergoing an operation. The implausible Krenz lost his job, having floundered around helplessly for seven weeks. On December 7 the "Round Table" had its first meeting in Berlin, when representatives of seven civil rights groups and the Evangelical and Catholic churches began discussions with the SED and the allied "Bloc Parties." The opposition groups hoped that the Round Table would serve as an interim parliament and a constituent assembly, the SED that it would give a degree of democratic legitimacy to the Modrow government, and act as a safety valve for the malcontents. Both sides rejected the notion of unification with the Federal Republic. If the SED were to survive it would have to be drastically reformed. A first step in this direction was taken at an extraordinary party congress held in December at which the party adopted a new acronym – SED/PDS – the addition standing for "Party of Democratic Socialism." Gregor Gysi, the brilliantly eloquent advocate of reform, hoped thus to steer the DDR through the Scylla of Stalinist, centralized Communism and the Charybdis of monopoly capitalism.

The East German CDU, under the new leadership of Lothar de Maizière, regarded itself as a socialist party, but when it left the "Democratic Bloc" at the beginning of December all mention of socialism was dropped, and the party expressed its faith in a socially conscious market economy with a strong ecological commitment. Unlike the SED/PDS, the CDU supported the notion of a confederation of the two German states while avoiding use of the term "reunification." The Liberal Democratic Party of Germany (LDPD) traveled along the same route. At first it professed its faith in "socialism with a human face" but soon embraced an "ecological market economy." It followed the lead of Democratic Beginning (DA) in accepting the idea of a united Germany within the existing frontiers. DA's commitment to a united Germany, admittedly as a bloc-free and neutral state, was strongly opposed by some of its most prominent members, who resigned in protest. Another small party, Democracy Now, proposed a three-stage plan for German unification. The Federal Republic was first called upon to achieve a higher degree of social justice and ecological responsibility. Then the two states would join together in a confederation with dual German citizenship. Finally, a plebiscite would be held to determine the final form of a unified, federal, and demilitarized Germany.

All the parties were completely out of touch with the mood of the vast majority of the people. They wanted nothing to do with utopian visions of a "third way," and demanded a united Germany. They waved the black, red, and gold flag of German liberal nationalism and of the Federal Republic. They sang the long forbidden words of the DDR's national anthem which spoke of Germany as a "united fatherland." Helmut Kohl went to Dresden to meet Hans Modrow. His masterly public address was given an ecstatic reception, the crowds chanting "Helmut, Helmut, Helmut!" "Deutschland, Deutschland!" and "unity, unity!" The political parties gradually realized which way the wind was blowing, and trimmed their sails accordingly. Kohl returned home convinced that the DDR was on the verge of total collapse.

The Stasi had already changed its name but not its spots. The Office for National Security (AfNS), immediately dubbed "Nasi," began to destroy particularly sensitive documents dealing with such issues as the use of chemical and biological weapons, and the construction of concentration camps for dissidents, and began looking for secure jobs for those colleagues who were likely to be called to account when the state collapsed. Hans Modrow dragged his feet when the Round Table called for an immediate halt to such activities, and there was widespread fear that the SED was trying to get back in the saddle. A massive demonstration against the Nasi in mid-January 1990 got out of control, the crowd stormed the Ministry of State Security in the Normannenstrasse, and a considerable amount of damage was done. There was convincing evidence that the riot had been provoked by the Nasi in order to give them an excuse to crack down. It now looked as if the revolution was getting out of control and both the Modrow government and the Round Table did all they could to calm the situation down by joining together in a coalition "Government of National Responsibility." The Round Table took this step with a heavy heart, but there seemed to be no alternative. The country was in a state of near anarchy, the economy was in ruins, the people were leaving in droves, and social tensions were growing ever more intense. It was agreed that elections for a national assembly should take place on March 18, some three weeks earlier than had been originally planned.

Modrow, who insisted that the DDR should remain an independent state, was now told by Gorbachev that the Four Powers agreed that the unification of Germany was not in question. This was made public when he went to Moscow on January 30 and the press release left Germans in East and West stunned, but when they recovered from the shock they realized that they had been tricked by Gorbachev and Modrow. Moscow, knowing full well that the US, the French, and the British would find this unacceptable, insisted that a united Germany would have to be neutral. Modrow announced the plan for unification on February 1. Bonn's reply was cautious. Kohl proposed fundamental structural reform of the DDR's economy and the introduction of the German mark at the earliest possible date. There was no mention of an interim confederation of the two states as Modrow had proposed. The all-powerful Bundesbank and hosts of experts were horrified at Kohl's suggestion. Given the appalling state of the East German economy the expense would be prohibitive, but Kohl insisted that political considerations were paramount, not the least of which was that it would give an enormous boost to the chances of the East German CDU in the forthcoming elections. Thanks to an initiative from the US State Department, a formula was now generally accepted that the question of German reunification should be the subject of "Two-plus-Four" discussions. Genscher insisted on strict adherence to that order: first the two Germanys, then the four powers. The outstanding issue was that of neutrality, but Gorbachev hinted to James Baker that he was somewhat more flexible on this issue than had previously been the case. Kohl returned greatly encouraged from his visit to Moscow in early February, and decided to push ahead.

Modrow went to Bonn cap in hand on February 13, but Kohl refused to grant him the massive credits he needed to keep the DDR afloat. At a meeting with Bush and Baker at Camp David ten days later, he reluctantly accepted the American view that a united Germany should be part of NATO and thus abandoned Genscher's earlier idea that only the former DDR should remain neutral, with the Federal Republic staying within the alliance. The Bush administration knew that they had Gorbachev on the run, and were determined to up the ante. For 40 years the stability of Europe had rested on the division of Germany, and now the stability of Europe was seriously endangered by that very division. Time was of the essence in this dramatically new situation. Would Gorbachev and Shevardnadze be able to hang on to power? Would the DDR dissolve into political and economic chaos? Would everything be slowed down by interminable discussions about whether unification should take place under article 23 or article 146 of the Fundamental Law? Would the growing frustration over the protracted process lead to violence? How would the SPD react now that Oskar Lafontaine, the strongest opponent to a swift process of unification under article 23, had won a resounding victory in the Saarland elections and was thus virtually certain to be the SPD's chancellor candidate in the forthcoming elections? Willy Brandt enjoyed enormous popularity in the East, but his position was undermined by the constant jeremiads from Lafontaine, who prudently only made rare visits to the DDR. Would the Round Table stick by its refusal to accept the *Anschluss* of the DDR under article 23? Would Modrow be able to continue his campaign to protect "socialist achievements" from the rapacious hands of West German capitalists?

Much depended on the outcome of the election to the new People's Chamber (*Volkskammer*), the first free election in the Eastern provinces for almost 60 years. In the course of the campaign Modrow pleaded for a slow process of unification so that the great achievements of the Workers' and Peasants' State could be preserved. These turned out to be the "right to work," which amounted to little more than the right to hang around the workplace with nothing to do. The "right to free education and further education" already virtually existed in West Germany. The other great achievement was the right to a free abortion. The election results surprised all the experts. With a turnout of 93.4 percent, 48 percent voted for the CDU and allied parties. The SDP (the East German SPD), in spite of rosy prognostications, only managed to get 21.9 percent of the vote and did best in Berlin. The PDS followed behind with 16.4 percent, the Free Democrats got 5.3 percent, and the dissident group Association 90 (*Bündnis* 90) achieved a mere 2.9 percent. The workers and peasants had voted for the CDU. Party functionaries, civil servants, dutiful intellectuals, and other privileged groups had voted for the PDS, in the hope of keeping their snouts in the trough. The result was an overwhelming popular endorsement for unification with the Federal Republic at the earliest possible opportunity. The Round Table's vision of a "third way" was shown to be a pipe dream for which there was virtually no popular support. The people turned their backs on the theoretical achievements of socialism and looked forward to enjoying the material achievements of capitalism. That many, if not most, found it difficult to adjust and were often bitterly disappointed is no vindication of the well-intentioned utopians of the "peaceful revolution," who attributed the peoples' refusal to heed their call to the machinations of US imperialism, West German capitalists and their lackeys, and the consequent "false consciousness" of the proletariat.

Concern in the West over the results of these elections was largely confined to the left. They had long hoped that the Federal Republic would become more like the DDR, now they feared that the DDR would be simply swallowed by the materialist Moloch. Peoples' minds would turn away from building a new socialist state and focus on acquiring Golf GTi's and video recorders. Jürgen Habermas sounded the alarm that the Federal Republic's antinationalist identity would become prey to an arrogant "DM nationalism" that would thwart the creation of a genuine multicultural society. Habermas agreed with Lafontaine that the reunification of Germany should be postponed until there were no more nation-states left in Europe. For this lofty idealist Auschwitz meant that a future Germany could only be based on universal civic principles. Germany's "post-traditional identity" should consist of the way in which the public discursive argument over the interpretation of "constitutional patriotism" was put into practice. Now Germany threatened to turn away from this supranational project and from the ideal of discourse without domination.

The CDU was the clear winner in the elections, but Lothar de Mazière felt that under the circumstances only a national government was appropriate. This placed the SDP in an awkward situation. The party chairman, Ibrahim Böhme, was an opponent of unification, and therefore of a grand coalition, and had the powerful support of the SPD's chancellor candidate, Oskar Lafontaine. Böhme was disgraced when the West German magazine *Spiegel* revealed that he had been in the regular employ of the Stasi. His place was taken by Markus Merkel, who was in favor of joining the coalition, and by this time even Lafontaine agreed that the SDP should take part in government. Lothar de Mazière had no difficulty in accepting the SDP's conditions for participation in his government: recognition of the Oder-Neisse frontier, a neutral Germany, and the inviolability of the post-1945 land reform. This latter point was driven home by the Soviets in a communiqué that stated that all the economic measures taken by the Soviet Military Administration (SMAD) between 1945 and 1949 were legal and under no circumstances could be reversed. No agreement could be reached on whether the DDR should simply join the Federal Republic, or whether there should be a new constitution sanctioned by a plebiscite.

The first major problem to be addressed by the new government was the negotiation of a treaty on monetary and economic union. The Federal Republic paid an enormously high price. Wages and pensions were henceforth to be paid in German marks at par with the worthless East German currency. People between the ages of 15 and 59 could exchange 4,000 East German marks at par, those aged 60 and above 6,000, and children 2,000. Massive loans were given to cover pensions and unemployment benefits. The Kohl government pretended that this could be financed by a balanced growth in the economy, but they were deliberately deceiving the electorate in the West by having them believe that unification could be had on the cheap. The entire infrastructure of the country was in a disastrous state of decay. Experts estimated that only one-third of East German enterprises was capable of making a modest profit. Forty years of neglect had resulted in ecological depravation on a staggering scale. Kohl's finance minister, Theodor Waigel, refused to consider increased taxation to meet what he knew would be the horrendous cost, on the grounds that this would hinder the growth that he vainly hoped would cover the costs. The Federal Republic took on the DDR's burden of debt that was estimated to be in excess of 600 thousand million marks. In addition it was prepared to under-write the risks of the newly created Public Trust (*Treuhandanstalt*) which had responsibility for the privatization of state holdings and the return of private prop-erty to its lawful owners. This also proved to be a costly business. The trust was landed with a pile of largely worthless property that was sold off at often derisory prices, and when it finally wound up its affairs it was 256 billion marks in the red. Three-quarters of the workforce lost their jobs as a result of these transfers. Such industrial concerns as showed a chance of turning a profit were often bought up by foreign companies, whereas West German industry was largely concerned to avoid any competition from the East and therefore showed a certain lack of enthusiasm for hunting for interesting investment opportunities. Many enterprises, such as the Wartburg motor works in Eisenach, were beyond redemption and were simply closed down. Smaller firms were often sold to local management. East Germany was thus effectively de-industrialized, a process quite unique in the history of an industrial nation. Today 15 percent of workers in the East are employed in indus-try, in the West 30 percent. Since Kohl and his finance minister Waigel had already managed to tot up a budget deficit of 490 thousand million marks in 1989, the Federal Republic was now in hock to the tune of over one million, million marks. As Lothar Späth, a shrewd Swabian conservative who managed to turn East Germany's optical company Jenaoptik into a going concern, remarked: "Helmut Kohl did everything right politically, and everything wrong economically." But Kohl was now at sea, courting popularity in East and West, refusing to admit that serious mistakes had been made, turning down every imaginative suggestion for a way forward, and reduced to repeating worn-out appeals for solidarity and patient endurance. At every attempt to save a few pfennigs the SPD accused the chancellor of "social clear cutting." In 1993 his minister of labor rose to his defense in the Bundestag, indignantly announcing that: "Per capita welfare payments have increased by 12 percent since 1989. The gross domestic product has dropped by 15 percent during the same period. . . . We are second to none as a welfare state." Never was a truer word spoken.

The high rate of potential unemployment in the East had been disguised by the state policy of keeping workers on the payroll, even though they often had nothing to do. With the introduction of a capitalist market economy, up to 20 percent of the workforce found themselves without a job. This situation was exacerbated with the introduction of the German mark in the East. Since export production was almost exclusively for markets in the East this resulted in an inflation of prices that were unsustainable, and a number of firms were consequently put out of business. Nine hundred thousand workplaces, amounting to ten percent of the total work-force, depended solely on trade with the Soviet Union. The unproductive and anti-quated industries of the East were totally unable to compete with Western firms on the domestic market. The government tried to relieve the situation with make-work programmes, by encouraging early retirement, and by providing funds to save firms from bankruptcy. By 1994 50 percent of East German workers had participated in a make-work programme, and 60 billion marks had been spent on such measures by 1997. But it was all to no avail. Unemployment continued to rise and remains today one of the greatest social problems.

This gross mismanagement was a godsend to the SPD's electoral campaign. They won victories in state elections in North Rhine-Westphalia and Lower Saxony, and thus had a majority in the Bundesrat and could veto the State Treaty designed to coordinate the two economies. Lafontaine, who had been seriously wounded in an assassination attempt by a deranged woman, wanted to stop the treaty, but the majority of the SPD was in favor, provided that a number of amendments were made. Lafontaine threatened to step down as chancellor candidate but was eventually persuaded to change his mind. In June 1990 the State Treaty was passed in the Bundestag and the People's Chamber by overwhelming majorities. In the Bundestag 35 Greens and 25 Social Democrats voted against. In the Bundesrat only the Saarland and Gerhard Schroeder's Lower Saxony voted against the treaty. For all the problems involved in the treaty, had Lafontaine and Schroeder prevailed, Germany would have been plunged into a state of political and economic chaos. Neither was able to provide a viable alternative to the Kohl government's costly and fiscally irresponsible policies, and politically there was none available.

Economic and monetary unity was now complete, but a political solution had still to be found. In early March, the Soviets insisted that a unified Germany as a member of NATO was totally unacceptable, as was the idea of unification under article 23. Mitterand insisted that the Oder-Neisse frontier had to be formally accepted as a precondition for unification. Margaret Thatcher's Britain harbored grim visions of a "Fourth Reich," that were only partially assuaged when a report on a meeting at Chequers between the prime minister and a group of experts, which included such distinguished scholars as Gordon Craig and Fritz Stern, was leaked to the press. Discussions centered on whether the Germans were congenitally aggressive, arrogant, egotistical, overly sentimental, and suffered from a massive inferiority complex. The experts concurred that the Germans had learnt their lesson and had created a stable and lively democracy, but there was some concern that a united Germany might be tempted to throw its weight about and suffer twitches of a *"Drang nach Osten."* The news of this meeting met with a storm of protest in the German press, and ruffled feathers were only partially smoothed when some of the wise men averred that the negative comments were only with reference to Bismarck's Germany. Repeated instances of crude Hun-bashing in the British press and an astonishing outburst by Nicholas Ridley, the minister of trade and industry, comparing Kohl to Hitler, did nothing to improve matters. The Iron Lady was disappointed that she did not get the support at the Chequers meeting for which she had hoped, and now began to rethink her position. Her opposition to unification was no longer quite so adamantine. Mitterand feared that a united Germany would be an economic colossus that would overshadow France, and managed to force Kohl to make a number of concessions on Europe along the lines suggested by Jacques Delors, the ambitious and assertive French head of the European Commission. Kohl thus had to abandon his hopes of strengthening European institutions in return for French support.

The Soviet Union was now beginning to fall apart at the seams. The economy was on its last legs and Lithuania proclaimed its independence in March 1990. KGB troops were promptly dispatched to the republic and fuel supplies were cut off. The Warsaw Pact had virtually ceased to exist. The Soviets could not tolerate another blow to their prestige, and Shevardnadze dug in his heels, refusing to even contemplate a united Germany as a member of NATO. But Moscow was also in desperate need of immediate financial assistance and, given that the United States refused to help as long as the blockade against Lithuania continued, turned to Bonn for help. Kohl immediately agreed, and a loan of five thousand million marks was granted in May under the clear understanding that concessions were expected on the outstanding issues with respect to German unification. In fact Gorbachev's political survival depended to a large extent on economic support from Bonn. Of this he was well aware, and he was prepared to pay the price. Much to the alarm and amazement of many of his closest associates, Gorbachev decided that he would have to accept German membership of NATO as the price for continued financial support from the West. He traveled to Washington at the end of May, where Bush told him that under the Commission on Cooperation and Security in Europe (CSCE) agreements all countries were free to choose the alliances to which they wished to belong, and that this should also apply to a united Germany. To general astonishment and delight, Gorbachev agreed. Kohl could hardly believe his ears when Bush relayed the good news via telephone.

Everything now depended on the future relations between the Warsaw Pact and NATO, and on the extent to which the CSCE could be strengthened. It soon became clear that the Soviets had no fundamental objections to German membership of NATO, provided that it changed with the times. NATO met in London in July and announced that it planned drastic reductions of both nuclear and conventional weapons in Europe, and thus watered down the doctrines of "Forward Defense" and "Flexible Response" on which its strategy had previously been based. This concession, coupled with the success of Mitterand and Kohl's appeal to Lithuania to withdraw its declaration of independence, greatly strengthened Gorbachev's hand against his critics at the twenty-eighth Congress of the CPSU, which was in session at the same time as the NATO meeting in London.

There were still a number of obstacles in the way of unification. Gorbachev was acting with arrogant disregard for all the institutions of the Soviet Union and, although he still had the power to do so, his resentful critics were looking for an opportunity to fight back. The issue of how long Soviet troops were to remain stationed in the DDR had to be settled, as had the question of the upper limit to be set for the Bundeswehr. How much Danegeld would the Federal Republic be called upon to pay for its independence? How long would France, Britain, and the DDR be prepared to stand on the sidelines while Kohl, Gorbachev, and Bush decided the fate of Europe? Were not the fears of those who saw a united Germany as a potential menace justified?

Negotiations between Bonn and East Berlin for a unification treaty had begun even before the State Treaty had been signed. There was general agreement that unification should go into effect on December 2 1990, the day set for elections in the

Federal Republic, so that all Germans could vote for a new Bundestag. Here again there were a number of thorny issues to resolve. Should the capital of the new state be in Berlin as the East Germans insisted, remain in Bonn as the Western states hoped, or move to Frankfurt as some historians suggested? How would the financial arrangements between the federal government and the states be structured? To what extent should the Fundamental Law be modified to include such issues as ecology, public health, and culture, or even an obligation to help the poorest countries? How could two very different laws on abortion be reconciled? Should the five percent clause for elections apply nationwide, or should the DDR be regarded as separate?

Given the rapid collapse of the DDR's economy, de Mazière saw no alternative to unification at the earliest possible moment. He visited Kohl, who was on holiday at the idyllic Wolfgangsee in Bavaria, and suggested that all-German elections should be held on October 14, the date on which local elections were to be held in East Germany. Kohl agreed, but the problem now was how to hold elections in the Federal Republic before the designated date of December 2 1990. Kohl was prepared to have a vote of constructive no-confidence, thus repeating the constitutionally dubious move of 1982, but the president, Richard von Weizsäcker, insisted that a constitutional amendment was required. Since Oskar Lafontaine felt that the SPD's electoral chances would be much better the later the election, it would not be possible to get the two-thirds majority needed for a constitutional amendment. The elections were therefore to be held on December 2.

The next decisive step was taken in the early morning hours of August 23, when the People's Chamber voted overwhelmingly for unification with the Federal Republic under article 23 of the Fundamental Law with effect from October 3 1990. The PDS voted against the motion, its leader Gregor Gysi expressing his anger that the German Democratic Republic thereby ceased to exist. The unification treaty was formally signed in Berlin on August 31 by the ministers of the interior of the DDR and the Federal Republic, Günther Krause and Wolfgang Schäuble. Both men had tried to keep the Stasi archives under lock and key on the grounds that they contained an enormous amount of sensitive material. Civil rights activists in the DDR fought vigorously against this suggestion, and resolutely argued that the regime's shabby past should be put on public display. The result was the creation of a special Stasi archive in East Berlin under the direction of a highly respected pastor from Rostock, Joachim Gauck. The "Gauck Office" was the last great triumph of this dedicated group of courageous men and women who had done so much to topple a discredited political system. Since the unification treaty left a number of constitutional questions open, the SPD had no problems voting for ratification in the Bundestag. The opposition of the PDS to the treaty did not hinder its ratification in the People's Chamber.

Germany Unified

The question of German unification was now settled, and October 3, the "Day of German Unity," was henceforth a national holiday. But the Two-plus-Four talks had still not been concluded. The Soviet Union demanded 36 thousand million marks to cover the cost of withdrawing their troops from Germany. Kohl managed to beat Gorbachev down to the point of accepting 12 thousand million marks, plus three thousand million in interest-free credit. The final round of talks in Moscow almost came unstuck when the British and Americans insisted that NATO should have the right to station troops in the former DDR. At the last moment Genscher managed to come up with a compromise formula that was satisfactory to the Soviets. The foreign ministers then signed the treaty on September 12. On October 1 the four powers formally renounced their occupation rights and Germany became a fully sovereign state. Four days later a united Bundestag ratified the Two-plus-Four treaty and one after another the signatories then also ratified the treaty. Last in line was the Soviet Union on March 4 1991. The treaty went into effect nine days later. Elections were held on October 14 for the parliaments (Landtage) in the five new provinces in the former DDR. They were a triumph for the CDU. Brandenburg was the only state that was won by the SPD, with Manfred Stolpe as the new minister-president. Kohl and the CDU/CSU could now look forward confidently to the elections on December 2.

There followed a series of treaties between the new Germany and the Soviet Union, Czechoslovakia, and Poland. At a CSCE summit in Paris on November 19 NATO and Warsaw Pact leaders signed a treaty on Conventional Forces in Europe (CFE), in which both sides agreed to a substantial reduction of their non-nuclear weaponry. A covenant was also signed by all concerned outlawing the use of force except in self-defense or when otherwise sanctioned by the United Nations charter. Gorbachev, who was under fierce attack from Boris Yeltsin for accumulating too much power, and who was soon to abandoned by Shevardnadze who also accused him of establishing a dictatorship, wooed Bush in Paris by assuring him of his support in the Gulf, Iraq having invaded Kuwait on August 2.

As expected the election results on December 2 were a triumph for the Bonn coalition. The CDU/CSU obtained 43.8 percent of the popular vote. Buoyed by Genscher's enormous popularity, the FDP secured 11 percent. Oskar Lafontaine had totally misread the mood of the country and his SPD got only 33.5 percent. This came as a shattering disappointment after the party's wins in North Rhine Westphalia, Lower Saxony, and the Saar. The electorate was deaf to his warnings of the severe economic problems that would face a united Germany which, compared with Kohl's Panglossian vision of a "blooming landscape" in the East, which he had promised on May 18 1990, when he signed the treaty on the monetary, economic, and social union with the citizens of the DDR, appeared to be little more than sour grapes. The Greens also suffered as a result of their critical attitude toward the reunification process. The party received less than the mandatory five percent in the West, but in the East their alliance with the dissidents in Association 90 (*Bündnis* 90) put them just over the five percent hurdle. Nationwide the PDS received only 2.4 percent of the popular vote, but in the East with 11.1 percent they obtained 17 seats as a special concession in this first all-German election.

There were bitter recriminations in the SPD over the party's disastrous showing at the polls. The party split along broadly generational lines, with the nationalist older age group led by Willy Brandt pitched against Lafontaine and the post-nationalists. Lafontaine charged his critics with having a racial (*völkisch*) vision of nationhood, which he contrasted with Ernst Renan's French republican definition of the nation as a "daily plebiscite." He still believed that a German confederation could have been the first step toward the creation of a European confederation. This mixture of wishful thinking and muddled logic met with precious little resonance in the party at large, and the brilliant maverick Lafontaine was left increasingly isolated, wounded, and resentful.

A decision still had to be reached about the capital of the new Germany. Many argued that it should remain in Bonn, a town which looked to the West and which had been the capital of the first successful democracy in Germany. Supporters of Bonn regarded Berlin as symbolic of Prussian militarism, and of great power illusions. They could also point to the enormous expense of moving. Those who argued for Berlin remembered the Blockade, the Wall, and November 9 1989, and insisted that it was here that the two German states should come together. Bonn was far too remote from the five new provinces. Germany's wealth was in the West, so that at least the East should enjoy the political and economic benefits of a capital city.

The majority of leading politicians in Germany were in enthusiastic support of Berlin. Lafontaine and his post-national supporters were firmly against. Politicians whose power base was in the West, such as Johannes Rau for the SPD, Norbert Blüm for the CDU, and Count Otto Lambsdorff for the FDP, argued for Bonn. A free vote was held in the Bundestag on June 20 1991, and was a narrow victory for Berlin, with Berlin getting 338 votes to Bonn's 320. Deputies from the former Federal Republic voted in favor of Bonn by 291 to 214, those from the former DDR voted 124 to 29 in favor of Berlin. The move from Bonn to Berlin was subject to numerous delays, and was not made until 1999. The idea that some of the ministries could remain in Bonn soon proved unworkable. Fears that with Berlin as its capital, the new Germany would turn its back on the European Community proved unfounded. The ghosts of the old Berlin had long since been exorcized.

The new Germany was no loose cannon on deck as some had feared. It was an integral part of the European Community and with the Treaty of Maastricht, which was negotiated in December 1991 and signed in the following February, Germany's sovereign powers were further reduced. Monetary union meant that the mighty Deutschmark would be replaced by the euro, and the all-powerful Bundesbank by a European central bank. Europe was to have a common foreign and defense policy. Henceforth the frontiers between the member states of the European Union were open. Some concerns had been expressed that the choice of Berlin as a capital would lead to a centralization of power and that provincial rights would be weakened. In fact the provinces were given increased powers under the Maastricht Treaty, and Bavaria, North-Rhine Westphalia, and Baden-Württemberg were now able to make direct representation to Brussels.

Some modification of the Basic Law was necessitated by unification, and the opportunity was taken to make some long overdue changes. Provision was made for the Federal government to hand over certain sovereign rights to the European

Union, the provinces were given further powers, the Bundesrat was strengthened, and the role of the Bundesbank had to be amended. At the same time the rights of the handicapped were added to article 3, and the state was constitutionally bound to protect the environment.

These reforms were very modest and did not go far enough for the left, who had hoped that a raft of questions such full employment, minority and animal rights, and the nature of civil society would be addressed. Fortunately the argument prevailed that a constitution should not be stuffed full of rights and aims, for that would lead to an interpretative nightmare, and place an intolerable burden on the Constitutional Court. One long-overdue piece of reform failed because of resistance from the CDU/CSU. It was still not possible for the Bundestag to dissolve itself by a vote of simple no-confidence and the jiggery-pokery of a manipulated vote of "constructive" no-confidence remained the only way for a government to call new elections.

One of the most hotly disputed provisions of the Fundamental Law was article 16, section 2, which stated that "right of asylum is to be given to the politically persecuted." This admirable clause was written when memories of the horrors of Nazi oppression were all too vivid, but now times had changed. With the collapse of Communism and the removal of Western European frontier posts, Germany became a haven for refugees. In 1985 there had been just over 70,000 asylum seekers in the Federal Republic, but by 1992 there were 438,191, along with tens of thousands of illegal immigrants. According to very generous criteria only 4.5 percent qualified as "politically persecuted." This situation was exploited by extremist right-wing groups, and there were a number of ugly attacks on foreign workers and asylum seekers resulting in several deaths. The CDU, CSU, FDP, and SPD agreed that the process of examining claims for asylum should be speeded up, and that those who did not meet the criteria should be promptly deported. This did nothing to stem the stream of applicants. Clearly something had to be done, but it proved impossible to uphold article 16.2 in a pristine form, while trying to relieve the intolerable strain occasioned by the fact that 78 percent of asylum seekers in the European Community landed up in Germany. Everything depended on the attitude of the Social Democrats. The party program denounced any attempt to change the constitutional guaranteed right of asylum, but the rank and file demanded drastic action against those with bogus claims. It was with a heavy heart and severe pangs of conscience that the party decided to vote in favor of a constitutional amendment. The FDP was in a similar dilemma, and, when the vote was taken on June 26 1992, more than 100 delegates from the SPD and FDP broke ranks and voted against the proposal. Emotions ran very high that day and opponents to the amendment cordoned off the area around the parliament building in Bonn, so that many delegates had to be ferried across the Rhine in order to be able to vote. The whole incident was most unfortunate in that principal appeared to have bowed to expedience, and it looked as if the government had given way to pressure from the extreme right.

A singularly uneasy answer was found by designating all Germany's neighboring countries as "safe," from which refugees could therefore not claim asylum. This meant that only those who arrived by air had any right to claim asylum. The right of asylum thus remained, but any claims for the revision of unfavorable decisions had henceforth to be made from outside the country. The result was that there was a dramatic and immediate drop in the number of asylum seekers.

Another emotionally charged issue was that of abortion. Article 31 of the unification treaty called for a common law on this tendentious issue. It took five years to reach another uneasy compromise, between the rights of the unborn and the freedoms of individual women. The issue was resolved by the Constitutional Court, which ruled the draft law to be unconstitutional. In the court's view the termination of a pregnancy in the first 12 weeks remained illegal, but should not be subject to prosecution. Medical insurance schemes should not be required to pay for abortions, except in cases of rape, or when either mother or child were liable to suffer undue harm. Before an abortion could be performed the woman had to undergo a medical consultation, at least three days before the operation, the aim of which should be to preserve life. An attempt by the Catholic Church, under the energetic and inspired leadership of Archbishop Lehmann of Mainz, to take part in this consultative process, was frustrated by orders from the Vatican, and the good bishop was pointedly kept waiting before his long overdue elevation to the college of cardinals.

With the collapse of the iron curtain there was a dramatic increase in crime that provided the popular press with ample sensational and lubricious copy on prostitution rings, drug dealers, and gangs of car thieves. The government was under considerable pressure to act and was determined to show that it meant business. In October 1994 the Secret Service (BND) was given the right to pass on information gleaned from telephone tapping to the prosecuting authority. Accused were henceforth permitted to turn state's evidence in the fight against organized crime. Four years later, shortly before a general election, the SPD supported a bill which permitted the police to use electronic devices to pry into private houses, for fear that otherwise the party would be seen as being soft on crime. The FDP similarly abandoned its liberal principles for fear of severe electoral repercussions. The objections of a number of prominent figures in the party were overruled by a vote by the membership.

Rancorous debates over such emotional issues only served to make the severe hangover after the first euphoric rapture over unification infinitely worse. The economic desolation in the East was far grimmer than even the most pessimistic of experts had imagined. There was virtually nothing that could be saved from a hopelessly backward industry, decrepit infrastructure, and a ravaged environment. A completely fresh start had to be made, and the expense was astronomical. The situation was made worse by the unions demanding huge wage increases that the Eastern economy could not possibly sustain, and by greedy speculators who invested billions in what soon turned out to be worthless projects.

Unification was politically, culturally, historically, and from the point of view of national and international security, a resounding success. Economically it was an unmitigated disaster. The Federal Republic now took over a piece of virtually worthless real estate in which 70 percent of the housing stock was in a state of advanced decrepitude, where industrial productivity was one-third of the Western norm and industrial assets were so run down as to have negative value of hundreds of billions of marks, and which was contaminated to an unimaginable degree, with air pollution levels seven times that of the Federal Republic and 50 percent worse than Hungary's. The 27.5 million fully employed workers and two million self-employed in West Germany now had to support their unproductive compatriots in the East and provide the wherewithal for the 47 percent of the adult population dependent on the social services. Since only 18 billion of the 113 billion marks transferred annually from West to East were invested, the drain on the West German economy was horrific. The West undoubtedly dominated the East politically, but economically the East bled the West white to the point that the economic power center in the former Federal Republic witnessed a steady decline in capital stock and services. It was a situation which one witty journalist described as "kohlonialism."

Initially the cost of unification was met by accruing a massive burden of debt. Politically this was the easy way out, since the Federal Republic's finances were in excellent shape, and it seemed only fair that the cost should be spread over several generations. There was however a major problem in that the government had insisted on very strict "convergency criteria" as a prerequisite for the introduction of a common European currency. These required that the total national debt should not exceed 60 percent of gross national product, and that new debts should not surpass three percent of GDP. A decision had therefore to be made about whether to take on the immediate burden of meeting the cost of reunification, or to place the creation of the euro in jeopardy.

A further difficulty was that with massive unemployment in the East the unemployment insurance fund was rapidly depleting, and an aging population resulted in a sharp rise in the cost of providing pensions. Neither was offset by an increase in income tax or capital gains. The government was also faced with the enormous additional expense of financing its contribution to the Gulf War, which amounted to 18 thousand million marks. Since the vision of a dramatic upswing in the economy in the East proved to be an illusion there was no alternative to an increase in taxation. Purchase tax was increased, as were taxes on oil and tobacco. Most controversial of all was the new "solidarity tax" of an additional 7.5 percent on incomes in the former Federal Republic.

The cost of unification was borne unevenly and was the cause of considerable resentment. The average wage earner in the West was by far the hardest hit, whereas civil servants, the self-employed, and the wealthy got off relatively lightly. The gap between rich and poor, which was increasing as a result of the structural changes in a highly developed economy, was thus further widened. Corporate taxes were reduced in order to encourage investment in the East, and West German industry profited immensely from the dramatically increased demand for consumer goods in the East. Bitterness over what appeared to be a deliberate government policy of featherbedding the rich was compounded by resentment at having to pay for ungrateful easterners. This was matched by bitterness in the East over what seemed to be the arrogance and condescension of westerners.

One thousand and thirty-one billion marks were transferred from West to East between 1991 and 1998, in order to replace an infrastructure that was in a far worse state of decrepitude than had ever been imagined, and to provide a welfare system that was comparable to that of the former Federal Republic. Since much of this vast sum was spent in consumption rather than investment the economic consequences were dire. Even though wages were far lower in the East, the total cost of labor was higher relative to productivity. In 2002 wages were 77.5 percent of the Western level, but productivity was only 71.1 percent. Eastern Germany is now the least attractive area for investment in the European Union.

The Kohl government pursued a far-reaching policy of deregulation and dena-tionalization. The German Federal Railway was privatized in 1994, and in the following year the postal service was divided up into three private companies: Telekom for the telephone system, Postbank for banking, and the Deutsche Post. The government still held a majority of shares in all these new companies, but a process of privatization was set in motion which was to be continued by Gerhard Schröder's SPD and Green coalition, which came to power in 1998. The ending of the monopolies for the post and telephone service, and on gas and electricity, has resulted in a dramatic fall in prices in some sectors, most noticeably the cost of telephone calls.

A further strain on the economy was caused by the fact that since both the birth and death rates were dropping, German society was rapidly becoming one domi-nated by pensioners, resulting in the increased need for care of the aged. The FDP felt that the cost of such care should be carried by private insurance, but the pas-sionate minister of labor, Norbert Blüm, the staunchest advocate of the CDU's com-mitment to the welfare state, insisted that it should be handled by the state. The premiums for the old age care insurance act of 1994 are paid in part by employees, and partly by employers. In spite of vigorous protests from the unions and churches, the cost to employers was partly borne by the abolition of one national holiday. Helmut Kohl knew perfectly well that the full cost of the scheme would only begin to hurt after the election in 1998, possibly after the end of his term in office.

The social structure and mentalities of the two Germanys were so very different that misunderstanding between "*Ossis*" and "*Wessis*" was inevitable. A few enterprising souls seized the opportunities offered by a free market economy and prospered, but most found it extremely difficult to adjust to the dramatically changed circumstances. Many gave vent to their frustration by beating up foreigners and joining right-wing extremist groups. Members of the old *nomen-klatura* who had enjoyed many privileges, and who owed their position more to political reliability than to their skills and abilities, had no place in the new Germany, and were deeply resentful at their loss of status. The gap between East and West became ever wider and it soon became a journalistic cliché to remark that the Berlin Wall had been replaced by a wall in people's minds. In April 1993 a survey showed that 85 percent of the inhabitants of the former DDR and

71 percent of those in the West felt that the two Germanys still had conflicting interests. Only 11 percent of easterners and 22 percent of westerners thought of themselves as being part of one Germany.

Most of the East German leadership escaped punishment for the crimes committed by the regime. Honecker was arrested and charged with authorizing the shoot to kill order on the frontier, but he was suffering from cancer of the liver and was deemed unfit to stand trial. He left for Chile, where he enjoyed a certain popularity for having offered asylum to victims of Pinochet's unmerciful dictatorship. He died there in 1994, at the age of 81. Willi Stoph's state of health was also such that proceedings against him were halted. Erich Mielke was charged with murdering two policemen in 1931 and was given a six-year prison sentence. He served less than two years and died in 2000. Three members of the Politburo, including Egon Krenz, were given prison sentences of up to six and a half years for their part in passing the shoot to kill order. Two border guards were given suspended sentences for killing people trying to escape. Hardest hit were people who lost their jobs in the civil service, the judiciary, and the universities. They were mostly replaced by "*Wessis*," thus providing further grist to the PDS's propaganda mill according to which unification was an *Anschluss*, the East a mere colony of the West. The PDS's campaign against the "westernization" of the five new provinces found considerable resonance among these embittered and disillusioned losers. Since there was no dramatic improvement in living standards in the East after unification, in spite of the extravagant and irresponsible promises of some Western politicians, many began to look back on the good old days of the DDR and there was a wave of "Ostalgia." "*Ossis*" relapsed into familiar mental structures, "*Wessis*" indulged in what Jürgen Habermas dubbed "the chauvinism of prosperity."

The DDR was a secular society in which less than 30 percent of the population belonged to the two major Christian denominations. In the West more than three-quarters were at least nominally either Protestant or Catholic. This difference was reflected in widely different moral standards and cultural practices in the two Germanys. There were also profound differences in an understanding of the German past. The Federal Republic looked back to the liberal democracy of the Frankfurt Parliament and to the conspiracy to assassinate Hitler on July 20 1944. The DDR's ideological premise was antifascism, and the SED claimed to be in the direct line of descent from Marx's Communist League and Lenin's Bolsheviks. In the West there was an intensive debate over the Nazi past, and the burden of guilt for Auschwitz was terribly heavy. For the East the only victims of Nazism that counted were members of the Communist Party, Nazism was considered a problem for the West, and not for the sturdy antifascist workers and peasants in the DDR. Whereas historians in the West examined the roots of National Socialism and asked where Germany had gone wrong, their colleagues in the DDR painted a positive picture of the German past whose heroes were Luther, Frederick the Great, and even Bismarck. The principal villains were the SPD, who had betrayed the revolution in 1918, misled the working class, and left the way open for monopoly capitalists to put Hitler in command.

In 1992 the Bundestag established a commission to examine the history and nature of the SED regime. The report was published two years later on July 17, the anniversary of the uprising in East Germany in 1953. The conclusions from this lengthy document were mostly unexceptional. The DDR was described as a dictatorship which had changed considerably over the years, but which remained a totalitarian regime under the firm control of the SED. Strong objections were raised on the left to the use of the term "totalitarian," which had so often been used in the past to lump Communism and National Socialism together, and thus overlook the profound differences between the two dictatorial systems. The charge that a triumphant liberalism was reverting to the crude rhetoric of the worst phases of the cold war was somewhat lamely countered by the assertion that "totalitarianism" only referred to both regimes' claim on the whole individual. On the other hand, however absurd the suggestion that the DDR was similar to the Third Reich, there was still the awesome problem of undoing the harmful results of more than 40 years of Communist dictatorship following upon 12 years of National Socialism.

The new and fully sovereign Germany was soon faced with some exceedingly difficult decisions that made many hanker after a return to the time when the Federal Republic was subject to a degree of four-power control and restraint. The Kohl government's first priority was to further the process of European integration. Germany and France provided the driving force behind the decisions taken at Maastricht in December 1991 which brought the European states closer together, and which established a European citizenship which gave all holders of a European passport the right to vote and eligibility for office at the local and European level in any of the member states of the European Union. The Treaty of Maastricht, signed in February of the following year, created a common market which was to begin on January 1 1993, and it was agreed that a common European currency should be introduced in three stages, the euro to replace national currencies on January 1 2002. The majority of Germans were opposed to abandoning the German mark, which was Europe's strongest currency and a symbol of the country's astonishing postwar prosperity. Germany's thriving export industries welcomed the change to the euro, and most Germans accepted the new currency as the price that had to be paid for German reunification. Monetary union was one pillar on which the new Europe was to rest; the other two were a common defense and security policy, and co-operation in domestic and legal policies, which included the formation of a European police force (Europol). The Maastricht Treaty upheld the principle of subsidiarity, a concept associated with the French president of the European Commission, Jacques Delors, but which came directly from Catholic social teaching, especially the encyclical "Quadragesimo Anno" of 1931, whereby the European Union had only a subsidiary function in that it could only perform functions that could not be resolved satisfactorily at the local level. It was hoped that an inflated bureaucracy in Brussels could thus be avoided, and that citizens would have an effective voice all the way down to the local level. Accordingly the European Parliament was given additional fields of competence, but not enough to satisfy the German government, which wanted to strengthen the democratic element within the European Union. A further step toward European integration was taken with the Schengen agreement, which removed passport controls on the frontiers between those countries which signed on, and which increased the degree of political cooperation between them.

There was widespread concern that the more Europe became integrated, the less authority remained with national parliaments. In spite of the principle of subsidiarity there was a severe democratic deficit. The European Parliament was virtually powerless, so that people hardly bothered to turn out to vote in European elections, and far too many decisions were made behind closed doors by national governments. Since unanimity was required for the Council of Europe to make any binding decision, resort was taken to arcane language and scholastic argument that left the normal citizen utterly bemused. Clearly something had to be done to ameliorate the situation and the word "transparency" became the new euro-mantra. The requirement for unanimity might have made some sense when the European Union consisted of only six members, but now there were 15 and with the proposed opening up to the East there would soon be 27. For all the talk about transparency, precious little improvement resulted from the Amsterdam conference held in June 1997. The only concrete decision was to create, at German insistence, a European bank independent from political control and modeled on Germany's Bundesbank. The solidarity pact, agreed upon at this conference, set rigorous criteria for stringent fiscal policies for member states in order to ensure that the euro would be as stable a currency as the mark. The pact was more honored in the breach than in the observance, particularly by its strongest advocates, Germany and France. A certain degree of flexibility was introduced in that states were now freer to integrate at varying degrees, whereas earlier they were required to keep in step.

One of the Kohl government's greatest achievements was to reassure the world community that the new Germany had no intention of asserting itself as a great power, and that it was firmly committed to the European project and to close cooperation with the United States. A major test was soon to come. Germany's allies expected that a significant contribution would be made to the Iraq war, fought under the auspices of the United Nations as a response to Iraq's invasion of Kuwait. According to the constitution the Bundeswehr could only be used to counter a direct attack on the Federal Republic, or in certain instances of internal emergency. What part, if any, therefore should or could Germany play in Operation Desert Storm? There was widespread opposition to the war in Germany, especially from the younger generation, and there was a dramatic increase in the number of those who refused to do the obligatory military service. Genscher decided that material help should be offered to the United States, Britain, and Israel, but that German troops should not be involved, thus leaving the Federal Republic open to the charge that it was trying to buy its way out of its military obligations by indulging in check book diplomacy, with a handsome contribution of 18 billion marks. German fighter planes were deployed in southern Turkey, because should Iraq attack a NATO member the *Bundeswehr* was bound to respond. Resentment, particularly in the United States and Israel, at Germany's reluctance to become involved was heightened by massive demonstrations against a war that was denounced as further proof of American imperialism. A number of prominent voices on the left denounced the facile comparison of Saddam Hussein to Hitler as a glib excuse to go to war on behalf of the major oil companies. Oskar Lafontaine claimed that Germany bore the mark of Cain after the crimes of the Nazi era and should never be the cause of further bloodshed. Others argued that with the end of the cold war Europe should sever its ties with the United States and that NATO, which in their view was rapidly becoming little more than America's unpaid foreign legion, should be dissolved.

The debate over Germany's participation in the Gulf War was still raging when Yugoslavia began to fall apart and NATO became actively involved in the area. The people of Sarajevo were submitted to a siege lasting years, and the massacre at Srebrenica horrified the civilized world and forced many a pacifist who had opposed intervention in Iraq to rethink. Nowhere was this more strongly felt than in Germany, where hundreds of thousands of refugees arrived, each with a horrific tale to tell. Since the Russians supported their Slav brothers in these criminal undertakings, there was no hope of the Security Council approving any action, as had been the case in the Gulf War, and President Bush's vision of a "new world order" proved to be nothing more than wishful thinking. This forced the government to make a radical change in foreign policy which some described as "normalization," others as "militarization." In 1993 German AWACs patrolled the airspace over Bosnia-Herzegovina and naval vessels took part in the blockade of the former Yugoslavia. For the first time the Federal Republic's armed forces were on active duty. The SPD and the FDP argued that this was unconstitutional, and appealed to the Constitutional Court. The court rejected this argument, and in 1994 ruled that the *Bundeswehr* could take part in humanitarian or military missions out of area, provided that a simple majority in the Bundestag supported such action. German military medics also took part in the UN intervention in Cambodia in 1992/3 and the *Bundeswehr* provided logistical support in Somalia. In 1995 the Bundestag debated whether German troops should participate in a special NATO force that was to be on the alert for rapid deployment in Bosnia-Herzegovina. The CDU/CSU and FDP were in favor, the majority of the SPD, most of the Greens, and all the PDS were opposed. Once again the familiar argument was trundled out that, after Auschwitz, Germany was obliged to eschew the use of force. Four years later the SPD stood this argument on its head when Auschwitz was used to justify participation in the badly bungled intervention in Kosovo in an attempt to stop the genocide. The autonomy of Kosovo, a province that had an Albanian majority, had been rescinded, and Serbia began the gruesome process of ethnic cleansing. European public opinion was outraged at the grisly reports of mass murder in Kosovo and demanded that something should be done. Only a small minority clung to the argument in favor of a German foreign political *Sonderweg*, and denounced the intervention as an aggressive war in defiance of international law. SPD and Green whips made sure that the opponents of intervention did not get the chance to speak in the Bundestag, and the number of negative votes and abstentions was far from representative of the full extent of opposition to the intervention. Gregor Gysi, on behalf of the

PDS, challenged the constitutionality of the intervention in Kosovo, but the Constitutional Court ruled in favor of the government, and upheld the right to send troops out of area, provided that it was within a system of collective security such as NATO. The constitutional question was now settled, but the issue of sending troops into active service abroad was still highly contentious. When the question of sending *Bundeswehr* troops to Afghanistan was debated in 2001, Chancellor Schröder had to resort to the ultimate measure of a vote of confidence in order to get the narrowest of majorities.

The Federal Republic was at last in tune with its allies, but there were signs that the country was no longer prepared to play quite such a modest role in foreign affairs and wished to assert its independence. Germany, as the third largest contributor to the United Nations, felt that it was entitled to a seat on the Security Council. Prompted by a similar request from Japan, Genscher's successor Klaus Kinkel made a formal request to this effect at a meeting of the General Assembly in 1992. It was turned down, and repeated efforts have been made subsequently, all of them to no avail. Of far greater concern to Germany's allies was the precipitous and unilateral diplomatic recognition accorded to the former Yugoslavian provinces of Croatia and Slovenia. The British press, always eager to have a go at the Hun, denounced this as a sinister revival of Germany's desire to dominate Europe. In fact the Kohl government made this ill-considered move for short-term domestic political reasons, rather than to deal a blow to Serbia as in 1914, as some irresponsible commentators suggested. Germany was to fall seriously out of line with the United States over the invasion of Iraq in 2003, but this time the majority of Europeans supported Germany's position as a wave of anti-American sentiment swept the continent.

One particularly thorny problem remained after reunification – Germany's future relations with Russia. One year after the fall of the Berlin Wall the two countries signed a mutual non-aggression treaty and an agreement was reached on the return of art treasures which had been stolen in World War II. In the winter of 1990/1, Gorbachev's experiment in reform communism was in ruins and the Soviet Union began to fall apart at the seams. Food shortages became chronic and Germany lent massive support to help a starving country. The state, churches, charitable organizations, and private donors mounted the largest aid campaign in the history of the republic. It was a munificent vote of thanks for Soviet support for German reunification. Relations between Germany and Russia remained cordial even after the fall of the Soviet Union in December 1991, in large part due to the friendship between Kohl and Gorbachev's rival and successor, Boris Yeltsin. Indeed relations were so close that there were some horrified murmurings in European chancelleries about a revival of Rapallo.

By contrast, relations between Germany and its immediate neighbors, Poland and the Czech Republic, were far from cordial. At issue was the brutal expulsion of Germans from both countries at the end of the war, and the refusal of these governments to make any sign of regret for some such injustices. In spite of the efforts of various refugee organizations the German government strongly supported Polish and Czech applications for membership in the European Union, and both countries received substantial sums in government aid. Most Germans were either indifferent to the issue, or felt that, given Germany's murderous occupation policy in World War II, the country was hardly in a position to demand apologies.

By 1998, when the country once again went to the polls, the electorate no longer had any confidence in Helmut Kohl, whose promises had all been broken and who no longer provided a convincing vision of the future. The national debt had increased by 65 percent during his chancellorship, unemployment had risen by 60 percent and economic growth had ground to a halt. He was no longer the states-man who had achieved national unity, he was the politician responsible for Germany's decline. National unity had been achieved, and the country thereby weakened. The SPD had a convincing chancellor candidate in Gerhard Schröder, who had won a resounding victory in the state elections in Lower Saxony, and who, like US President Bill Clinton and Britain's Tony Blair, fought the campaign on behalf of what he chose to call the "new middle." This was where the swing votes lay, and there were more such votes than at any time since the 1950s. Pollsters predicted a victory for the Social Democrats, but were surprised that it was so decisive. With 35.1 percent of the vote, Kohl's CDU/CSU had its worst showing since 1949. Since the CDU's sister party, the CSU, received over 40 percent of the vote in its home state, this was clear indication that Kohl's unpopularity was the key factor in the Union's defeat. Nationally the CDU got 28.4 percent of the vote, the CSU 6.7. Their coalition partner, the FDP, also lost votes, whereas the Greens, with 6.7 percent, advanced to become the third largest party.

These elections were a turning point in the history of the republic. This was the first time that a chancellor had been turned out of office as the result of a general election. The Greens entered government for the first time. The SPD was, for only the second time, the strongest party, and therefore selected the president of the Bundestag. Since the successor party to the SED, the Party of Democratic Socialism (PDS), just managed to secure enough votes to return delegates to the Bundestag, for the first time for many, many years there were five parties in parliament. With the election of a social democratic government Germany fell in line with most of the other major European countries.

Schröder, whom his supporters see as a pragmatist and his detractors as an opportunist, was the chancellor candidate. The party secretary was Oscar Lafontaine, a maverick on the left of the party. The SPD thus chose as its election motto "Innovation and Social Justice;" this won the party the active support of the trades unions, and the tacit support of the Catholic and Evangelical churches, which issued a joint statement decrying the widening gap between rich and poor and calling for a more just society. With a comfortable majority in the Bundestag as well as in the Bundesrat, and with the president, Johannes Rau, a party comrade, the new chancellor was in an unassailable position to implement the changes he promised. However things soon began to unravel. Lafontaine was both minister of finance and party secretary. In his former capacity he was subordinate to the chancellor, in the latter his superior. Ideologically and temperamentally far apart, they were bound to clash, and they were soon at daggers drawn. The SPD was sadly lacking in experience after 16 years in opposition to Kohl's chancellorship and made a series of crass initial blunders. The parliamentary party was riven with dissent, as deputies took sides in the battle between the party secretary and the chancellor. There were a series of disastrous local elections in which the party lost heavily. Then in March 1999 Lafontaine made a characteristically spectacular gesture, resigning his positions as minister and as party secretary. Schröder promptly assumed the office of party secretary, and thus was in a strong position. This was the normal state of affairs in German politics, for Helmuth Schmidt was the only chancellor who had previously not held the two offices.

Schröder's position was further strengthened when it was revealed that the former chancellor was involved in a spectacular scandal involving millions of marks in illegal party funds. He was succeeded as party leader by Angela Merkel, an East German, and the first woman to head a political party. Kohl's designated successor, Wolfgang Schäuble, was too heavily involved in the scandal to be a serious candidate, and was shunted off to the sidelines. Many of the old guard resented the new leader and she became the butt of numerous tasteless jokes, leaving her isolated in her inexperience. At first she showed little interest in, or understanding of, economic affairs, and was soon to make a colossal blunder in supporting George W. Bush's invasion of Iraq, and it is unlikely that she will gain much gratitude from that quarter for this ill-considered step. But she is quick to learn and adapt. Honest and trustworthy, she is woman of exceptional intelligence, with an admirable strength of character and an uncluttered mind. She has grown remarkably in stature and enjoys the support of a number of bright young politicians. This bodes well for the future. The FDP also went through a leadership crisis in which Wolfgang Gerhardt, who wished to continue the alliance with the CDU, was replaced by Guido Westerwelle, who saw the party as a potential partner for the SPD in the elections in 2002. A salesman rather than a leader, a polemicist rather than a thinker, inexperienced and uncertain which way to turn, his appointment was also a first, for the new party leader was openly homosexual.

With the opposition in disarray the new government decided to win the support of the trades unions by increasing the length of time that sick workers remained on the payroll, and greatly strengthened the protection given to workers from dismissal, even in small firms. This won Schröder the support of the SPD's traditional voters in the working class, but it increased the cost of labor, and unemployment continued to rise. This was an alarming statistic for a chancellor who promised that he would halve the unemployment rate. Similarly, he saved the giant construction company Holzmann from bankruptcy in 1999 with a huge guaranteed loan. This saved a number of jobs in the short run, but did nothing to slow down the overall increase in the unemployment rate. These moves may have done nothing whatsoever to help the economy, but they ensured that the chancellor was given a warm reception at the party congress in December.

Schröder and his team realized that a change of course was necessary if the problem of unemployment was to be seriously addressed, and that without a major overhaul of an appallingly wasteful and prohibitively expensive welfare state nothing could be done to ameliorate the system. He had lost his faith in the unions and fired his minister of labor, a former functionary in Germany's largest union. He was not replaced, and the ministry of labor was combined with that of economics. Schröder appointed his friend Peter Hartz, head of personnel at Volkswagen, as his special advisor with a remit to reduce the rate of unemployment to two million. There was much highly technical talk and a CD-ROM was produced suggesting a number of exciting remedies, but unemployment continued to rise. The government remained complacent behind this smokescreen, for it was people with a job who decided elections, not the unemployed. The unemployed have no lobby and were kept quiet by generous unemployment benefits. The employed remained blissfully unaware of the fact that by increasing the cost of labor and making it more diffi-cult for employers to dismiss them, the government was in fact making it more likely that they would lose their jobs. In spite of a rapid increase in unemployment and an alarming series of bankruptcies, the SPD/Green coalition won the election in 2002. Now there was no alternative but to take strong measures and drastically reform unemployment benefits and welfare support in the Hartz IV program. It remains to be seen whether these measures have the desired effect. As I write these lines effective unemployment in Germany has reached a record 6.5 million, and shows no immediate signs of dropping. Critics maintain that Hartz IV does not go to the root of the problem. The labor market is shackled by a multitude of hide-bound restrictions and an excessively intrusive anti-discrimination law. Protection against wrongful dismissal has reached the point of absurdity. Labor costs have not been reduced, so that companies move their enterprises to cheaper markets.

Germany was governed by a conservative government for 36 years and by a social democratic government for 19 years, and it made precious little difference who was at the helm. Since the mid-1970s the country has been in steady decline, a process that was greatly accelerated by the process of unification. At times the rate of decline has been slowed down, but no government has been able to stop it. What are the factors standing in the way of reversing the process?

A major part of the problem lies in the relationship between the federal and state governments. No chancellor, whatever his majority at the polls, has full control over the budget. Control over the budget lies somewhere between the two houses of par-liament, the Bundestag and the Bundesrat, and some taxes, such as income tax and value added tax, are shared between the federal and state governments. Neither the Western occupying powers nor the German states wanted to have a strong central government. This was no doubt understandable in a country which had too much power at the top and suffered 12 years of National Socialist dictatorship, but it has proved to be a disaster at a time when political leadership is badly needed, and it has contributed significantly to a widespread disillusionment with the political process. The situation is rendered even worse by the fact that decisions made by the government can be referred to the Constitutional Court in Karlsruhe, a process that can hold up legislation for months or even years. In short, the powers of the Bundesrat should be drastically reduced. It should no longer be a sort of adjunct government and should become, as Adenauer suggested, part of a system of checks and balances, analogous to the British House of Lords. A recent attempt to strengthen central government failed owing to the states' refusal to relinquish their control over education.

Part of the problem undoubtedly lies in the fact that half the seats in the Bundestag are elected by proportional representation, so that leading political figures simply slide up the party list and never have to face the electorate directly. Politicians all to easily become party functionaries, out of contact with the people. Election by majority vote in constituencies brings politics far closer to the ordinary voter. In the German system only the second-rate stand for election by majority vote, and they show no concern for the well-being of their constituents. Numerous suggestions for a majority voting system were made by politicians as various as Helmuth Schmidt, Herbert Wehner, and Hans-Georg Kiesinger, but they were always blocked by the FDP, which knew perfectly well that this would spell the end of the party. Were such a measure taken today the FDP would disappear, and this would be no great loss. The party of Theodor Heuss, Thomas Dehler, Hans-Dietrich Genscher, Walter Scheel, and Lord Dahrendorf no longer has such prominent figures, and is little more than a political lobby whose excessive power resides solely in its ability to tip the scales in an election. The Greens would also vanish, and they too would hardly be missed, their concerns over the environment and minority rights having already been taken over by the major parties, their pacifism an infantile reflex. Once the founding fathers have vanished the party will soon reveal that it has nothing much to offer.

The first priority for any government of Germany, however elected, is drastically to reduce the rate of unemployment. This simply cannot be achieved without major changes in the labor market. Successive governments, of whatever hue, have systematically increased unemployment and welfare payments, and have financed these by increased contributions by management and labor, thus making labor costs ludicrously high and seriously endangering the competitiveness of the German economy. The labor market should be there to create value, not feed an obese welfare state. Similarly, access to welfare payments must be limited to those in real need. A welfare mix of state and private schemes needs to replace a sclerotic nationalized system that functioned well in the days of full employment and a burgeoning economy. In days when the national economy has virtually ceased to exist, where labor is highly mobile, when an increasing number of people work part-time, when a service economy has replaced an industrial economy, and with a dramatic increase in the proportion of the population which is past the age of retirement, such a system cannot possibly work. The labor market can no longer sustain the welfare state and the burden must be more equitably distributed. In 2000 Germany spent the equivalent of 18 percent of gross domestic product on welfare, and took the equivalent of 0.8 percent of GDP from tax on wealth such as death duties or real estate taxes. By contrast Britain paid out the equivalent of 7.5 percent of GDP on welfare and took 4.3 percent of GDP out of taxes on wealth. Britain's remarkably healthy labor market is testament to the inefficiency of the German system. If the labor market only had to bear the cost of accident and unemployment insurance, the cost of labor would be reduced by hundreds of billions of euros. Supplementary payments on wages in Germany are the highest in the world. They have to be drastically reduced. The Red/Green coalition has tinkered with the system, all to no avail. The time has come for radical, some would say revolutionary, reform.

Some steps in this direction have already been taken. With an increasingly aged population, the labor market is unable to pay the full cost of pensions and the pension fund has to be topped up from other sources. The Red/Green coalition has increased these subsidies from 51.4 to 77.2 billion euros. With mounting unemployment, the unemployment benefit fund has to be similarly subsidized. It was been calculated that if subsidies continued to rise at this rate, by 2050 the state will have to allocate 80 percent of the budget to the pension fund. The result would be a state without schools, police, garbage removal, or social services. Clearly this is an absurdity; the alternative would be for employees to finance their own pensions from the money saved from erstwhile contributions, and they would still obtain the guaranteed state pension that is financed out of general taxes. Red/Green have made a small step in this direction with the introduction of the "*Riester*" pension: a low-risk, and therefore modest, investment designed to top-up the guaranteed state pension. A similar system could also be applied to medical insurance: on the one hand a state-sponsored scheme, guaranteeing basic medical care, on the other a private scheme for additional coverage.

There is also room for major changes in Germany's complex tax system, which favors the rich and further hurts the poor. Taxes on real estate and death duties are one-quarter of those in the USA and one-fifth of those in Britain. If such taxes were introduced in Germany at the US level, they would be sufficient to pay all unemployment benefits. The burden of taxes on labor is so high because when the state was young there was virtually nothing else to tax. Income taxes and corporate taxes, by contrast, do not act as a brake on the economy. When times are good the minister of finance rakes it in, when they are tough he too has to tighten his belt. Germany's income tax laws are of a mind-boggling complexity and need to be radically simplified. They contain far too many loopholes for the wealthy, for which there is no possible justification. Much has to be done, but the leadership is sadly lacking. Germany desperately needs the "pragmatism with vision" which Schröder promised when he first took office.

Much to the sorrow of those who dreamt of a post-national Europe, Germany has become a nation-state, but one integrated into the European Community, and an increasingly uneasy partner in the American hegemonic project. It is a worthy heir to the admirable liberal, constitutional, democratic, social, and federal traditions of German history. In spite of appalling scandals involving party financing which, among other things, resulted in Helmut Kohl's career ending in disgrace, and the gross featherbedding of self-serving and unprincipled politicians, the old Federal Republic was a decent and functioning democracy that was viewed by its citizens not with overwhelming pride, but by a healthy skepticism. It was a state that scrupulously guarded the fundamental rights of its citizens, and with a new law on citizenship that went into effect on January 1 2000, an element of the democratic *lex soli* was introduced that watered down the exclusive and highly dubious *lex sanguinis*, Germany thus moving closer to the Western democracies. Thanks to Adenauer's insistence on firm ties with the West, and Willy Brandt's pragmatic approach to an opening to the East in his Ostpolitik, Germany was able to combine national unity with democratic freedoms, unlike Bismarck's Germany of 1871. The old Federal Republic, which the historian Karl Dietrich Bracher had justifiably called a "post-national democracy among nation-states" became, to the alarm of many on the left, a nation-state among nation-states with the absorption of the "international" DDR. It remains to be seen how the new Germany will wrestle with the myths, heroes, and villains of its past, and whether it will be able to find a positive sense of national identity. Much is still to be done, for the nation-state will long remain with us, in however changed and weaker a form. The force of circumstances was such that Germany was unable to undertake the mission, for which many hoped in 1990, to lead Europe forward to a post-national utopia. This version of a German *Sonderweg* was not to be, and the country was left with the daunting task of facing up to similar responsibilities and obligations as its allies. None of the old excuses will wash, and the self-satisfied comforts offered by a bad conscience over a criminal past no longer offer protection against the need to face up to the burdens and vexations of normalcy.

Bibliography

GENERAL WORKS

Berghahn, V. R. *Imperial Germany 1871–1914* (Oxford, 1994).
——*Modern Germany: Society, Economy, and Politics in the Twentieth Century* (Cambridge, 1987).
Blackbourn, D. *History of Germany 1780–1918: The Long Nineteenth Century* (Oxford, 2003).
Carr, W. A. *History of Germany 1815–1945* (London, 1987).
Craig, G. A. *The Germans* (Harmondsworth, 1978).
——*Germany 1866–1945* (Oxford, 1981).
Fulbrook, M. *German History Since 1800* (London, 1997).
——*History of Germany 1918–1990: The Divided Nation* (Oxford, 2002).
Macartney, C. A. *The Habsburg Empire 1790–1918* (London, 1968).
Mann, G. *A History of Germany since 1789* (London, 1968).
Nipperdey, T. *German History from Napoleon to Bismarck, 1800–1866* (Dublin, 1996).
Orlow, D. A. *History of Modern Germany 1871 to the Present* (Englewood Cliffs NJ, 1987).
Ramm, A. *Germany 1789–1919* (London, 1968).
Sheehan, J. J. *German History, 1770–1866* (Oxford, 1989).
Sked, A. *The Decline and Fall of the Habsburg Empire 1815–1918* (London, 1989).
Wehler, H.-U. *The German Empire 1871–1918* (Leamington Spa, 1985).

NINETEENTH CENTURY: SPECIFIC WORKS

Albisetti, J. C. *Secondary School Reform in Wilhelmine Germany* (Princeton, 1983).
Allen, A. T. *Feminism and Motherhood in Germany 1800–1914* (New Brunswick NJ, 1991).
——*Satire and Society in Wilhelmine Germany* (Louisville, 1985).
Angress, W. T. *Stillborn Revolution* (Princeton, 1963).
Applegate, C. *A Nation of Provincials. The German Idea of Heimat* (Berkeley, 1990).
Augustine, D. L. *Patricians and Parvenus: Wealth and High Society in Wilhelmine Germany* (Oxford, 1984).
Bade, K. J. (ed.) *Population, Labour and Migration in 19th and 20th Century Germany* (Oxford, 1987).

Barclay, D. *Frederick William IV and the Prussian Monarchy 1840–1861* (Oxford, 1995).

Barkin, K. D. *The Controversy over German Industrialization 1890–1902* (Chicago, 1970).

Berghahn, V. R. *Germany and the Approach of War in 1914* (London, 1973).

Best, G. *War and Society in Revolutionary Europe 1770–1870* (London, 1982).

Billinger, R. D. *Metternich and the German Question. State Rights and Federal Duties, 1820–1834* (Newark, 1992).

Birnbaum, K. *Peace Moves and U-Boat Warfare* (Hampden CT, 1970).

Blackbourn, D. *Class, Religion and Politics in Wilhelmine Germany. The Centre Party in Württemberg before 1914* (London, 1984).

——*Populists and Patricians* (London, 1987).

Blackbourn, D., and G. Eley *The Peculiarities of German History* (Oxford, 1984).

Blackbourn, D., and R. Evans (eds.) *The German Bourgeoisie* (London, 1991).

Blanning, T. C. W. *The French Revolution in Germany* (Cambridge, 1983).

Breuer, M. *Modernity within Tradition: The Social History of Orthodox Jewry in Imperial Germany* (New York, 1992).

Brose, E. D. *The Kaiser's Army: The Politics of Military Technology in Germany During the Machine Age, 1870–1918* (Oxford, 2001).

Bry, G. *Wages in Germany, 1871–1914* (Princeton, 1960).

Bucholz, A. *Moltke, Schlieffen and Prussian War Planning* (Oxford, 1991).

Campbell, J. *The German Werkbund. The Politics of Reform in the Applied Arts* (Princeton, 1978).

Carsten, F. L. *Revolution in Central Europe, 1918–1919* (London, 1972).

——*War against War: British and German Radical Movements in the First World War* (Berkeley, 1982).

Cecil, L. *The German Diplomatic Service, 1871–1914* (Princeton, 1979).

Chapple, G., and H. Schulte (eds.) *The Turn of the Century: German Literature and Art, 1890–1915* (Bonn, 1981).

Chickering, R. *Imperial Germany and the Great War* (Cambridge, 1998).

——*"We Men Who Feel Most German." A Cultural Study of the Pan-German League* (London, 1984).

Coetzee, M. S. *The German Army League* (Oxford, 1990).

Comfort, R. A. *Revolutionary Hamburg* (Stanford CA, 1966).

Craig, G. A. *The Politics of the Prussian Army 1640–1945* (Oxford, 1955).

——*The Politics of the Unpolitical. German Writers and the Problem of Power, 1770–1871* (Oxford, 1995).

Crampton, R. J. *The Hollow Détente. Anglo-German Relations in the Balkans* (London, 1979).

Desai, A. V. *Real Wages in Germany, 1871–1914* (Oxford, 1968).

Dube, W.-D. *The Expressionists* (London, 1972).

Eley, G. *Reshaping the German Right* (London, 1980).

Epstein, K. *The Genesis of German Conservatism* (Princeton, 1966).

——*Matthias Erzberger and the Dilemma of German Democracy* (Princeton, 1959).

Evans, R. J. *Death in Hamburg: Society and Politics in the Cholera Years, 1830–1910* (Oxford, 1987).

——*The Feminist Movement in Germany, 1894–1933* (London, 1976).

——*Rethinking German History* (London, 1987).

——(ed.) *The German Underworld* (London, 1988).

——(ed.) *The German Working Class* (London, 1968).

—— (ed.) *Society and Politics in Wilhelmine Germany* (London, 1978).

Evans, R. J., and W.R. Lee (eds.) *The German Family* (London, 1980).

——(eds.) *The German Peasantry* (London, 1986).

Eyck, F. *The Frankfurt Parliament 1848–1849* (London, 1968).

Feldman, G. D. *Army, Industry, and Labor in Germany, 1914–1918* (Princeton, 1966).

——*The Great Disorder. Politics, Economics and Society in the German Inflation, 1914–1924* (New York, 1993).

Ferro, M. *The Great War 1914–1918* (London, 1973).

Fischer, F. *Germany's War Aims in the First World War* (London, 1967).

——*War of Illusions: German Policies from 1911 to 1914* (London, 1975).

Franzoi, B. *At the Very Least She Pays the Rent. Women and German Industrialization* (Westport CN, 1985).

Frevert, U. *Women in German History* (Oxford, 1990).

Gatzke, H. *Germany's Drive to the West* (Baltimore, 1950).

Gay, P. *Freud, Jews, and Other Germans* (Oxford, 1978).

Gay, R. *The Jews of Germany* (New Haven, 1992).

Geiss, I. *German Foreign Policy, 1871–1914* (London, 1976).

——*July 1914. The Outbreak of the First World War: Selected Documents* (New York, 1967).

Gellately, R. *The Politics of Economic Despair. Shopkeepers and German Politics 1890–1914* (London, 1974).

Gerschenkron, A. *Bread and Democracy in Germany* (Ithaca, 1989).

Gerth, H. H., and C. W. Mills *From Max Weber* (London, 1974).

Gray, M. *Prussia in Transition: Society and Politics under the Stein Reform Ministry of 1808* (Philadelphia, 1986).

Grebing, H. *The History of the German Labour Movement* (Leamington Spa, 1985).

Guttsmans, W. *The German Social Democratic Party 1875–1933* (London, 1981).

Hackett, A. *The Politics of Feminism in Wilhelmine Germany, 1890–1918* (New York, 1979).

Hamerow, T. S. *Restoration, Revolution, Reaction: Economics and Politics in Central Europe 1815–1871* (Princeton, 1958).

Hamilton, N. *The Brothers Mann* (London, 1978).

Hardach, K. W. *The First World War* (Berkeley, 1977).

Heckart, B. *From Bassermann to Bebel* (New Haven, 1974).

Henderson, W. O. *The Rise of German Industrial Power, 1834–1914* (Berkeley, 1975).

——*The State and the Industrial Revolution in Prussia 1740–1870* (Liverpool, 1958).

——*The Zollverein* (London, 1939).

Herwig, H. H. *The First World War. Germany and Austria-Hungary, 1914–1918* (London, 1997).

——*The German Naval Officer Corps* (Oxford, 1973).

——*"Luxury Fleet": The Imperial German Navy, 1888–1918* (London, 1980).

Hickey, S. *Workers in Imperial Germany: Miners in the Ruhr* (Oxford, 1985).

Horn, D. *The German Naval Mutinies of World War I* (New Brunswick NJ, 1969).

Hull, I. *The Entourage of Kaiser Wilhelm II* (Cambridge, 1982).

Jarausch, K. H. *The Enigmatic Chancellor. Bethmann Hollweg and the Hubris of Imperial Germany* (New Haven, 1973).

Jevalich, P. *Munich and Theatrical Modernism* (Cambridge MA, 1985).

Joll, J. *The Origins of the First World War* (London, 1984).

Jones, L. E., and J. Retallack (eds.) *Elections, Mass Politics, and Social Change in Modern Germany* (Cambridge, 1992).

Kaplan, M. A. *The Making of the Jewish Middle Class. Women, Family, and Identity in Imperial Germany* (New York, 1991).

Kehr, E. *Battleship Building and Party Politics in Germany, 1894–1901* (Chicago, 1973).

——*Economic Interest, Militarism, and Foreign Policy* (Berkeley, 1977).

Kennedy, P. M. *The Rise of Anglo-German Antagonism, 1860–1914* (London, 1980).

——(ed.) *The War Plans of the Great Powers, 1880–1914* (London, 1979).

Kitchen, M. *The German Offensives of 1918* (Stroud, 2001).

——*The German Officer Corps, 1890–1914* (Oxford, 1968).

——*The Political Economy of Germany 1815–1914* (London, 1978).

——*The Silent Dictatorship. The Politics of the German High Command under Hindenburg and Ludendorff, 1916–1918* (London, 1976).

Knodel, J. *The Decline of Fertility in Germany, 1871–1939* (Princeton, 1974).

Kocka, J. *Facing Total War. German Society 1914–1918* (Leamington Spa, 1984).

Kraehe, E. E. *Metternich's German Policy.* 2 vols. (Princeton, 1963–84).

Krieger, L. *The German Idea of Freedom* (Boston, 1957).

Lambi, I. N. *The Navy and German Power Politics* (London, 1984).

Laqueur, W. *Young Germany* (London, 1962).

LaVopa, A. *Prussian Schoolteachers: Profession and Office, 1763–1848* (Chapel Hill, 1980).

Lerman, K. A. *The Chancellor as Courtier. Bernhard von Bülow and the Governance of Germany, 1900–1909* (Cambridge, 1990).

Levy, R. S. *The Downfall of the Anti-Semitic Political Parties in Imperial Germany* (New Haven, 1975).

Lidtke, V. L. *The Alternative Culture* (Oxford, 1985).

——*The Outlawed Party* (Princeton, 1966).

Makela, M. *The Munich Succession. Art and Artists in Turn-of-the-Century Munich* (Princeton, 1990).

Mann, T. *Reflections of a Nonpolitical Man* (New York, 1983).

Masur, G. *Imperial Berlin* (London, 1971).

Mayer, A. J. *The Politics and Diplomacy of Peacemaking* (London, 1968).

McClelland, C. *State, Society, and University in Germany, 1700–1914* (Cambridge, 1980).

McLellan, D. *Karl Marx* (New York, 1973).

Meyer, H. C. *Mitteleuropa in German Thought and Action* (The Hague, 1955).

Mitchell, A. *Revolution in Bavaria* (Princeton, 1965).

Mombauer, A. *Helmuth von Moltke and the Origins of the First World War* (Cambridge, 2001).

——*The Origins of the First World War. Controversies and Consensus* (London, 2002).

Mommsen, W. J. *Imperial Germany 1867–1918. Politics, Culture and Society in an Authoritarian State* (London, 1995).

——*Max Weber and German Politics* (Chicago, 1984).

Moses, J. A. *The Fischer Controversy in German Historiography* (New York, 1975).

——*The Politics of Illusion* (London, 1975).

——*Trade Unionism in Germany from Bismarck to Hitler.* 2 vols. (Totowa NJ, 1982).

Mosse, G. *The Crisis of German Ideology* (London, 1966).
—— *The Nationalization of the Masses* (New York, 1975).
Mosse, W. *Jews in the German Economy* (Oxford, 1987).
Nettl, J. P. *Rosa Luxemburg.* 2 vols. (Oxford, 1966).
Neuberger, H. *German Banks and German Economic Growth, 1871–1914* (New York, 1977).
Nichols, J. A. *Germany After Bismarck: The Caprivi Era, 1890–1894* (Cambridge MA, 1958).
Nipperdey, T. *The Rise of the Arts in Modern Society* (London, 1990).
Noyes, P. H. *Organization and Revolution: Working-Class Associations in the German Revolutions of 1848–49* (Princeton, 1966).
Paret, P. *The Berlin Secession* (Cambridge MA, 1980).
—— *Yorck and the Era of Prussian Reform, 1807–1815* (Princeton, 1966).
Pascal, R. *From Naturalism to Expressionism. German Literature and Society 1880–1918* (London, 1973).
Pinkard, T. *Hegel: A Biography* (Cambridge, 2000).
Pulzer, P. G. J. *The Rise of Political Anti-Semitism in Germany and Austria* (New York, 1964).
Retallack, J. N. *Notables of the Right* (London, 1988).
Ringer, A. (ed.) *The Early Romantic Era. Between Revolutions: 1789 and 1848* (London, 1990).
Ringer, F. *The Decline of the German Mandarins* (Cambridge MA, 1969).
Ritter, G. *The Schlieffen Plan* (London, 1958).
Ritter, G. A. *Social Welfare in Germany and Britain* (Leamington Spa, 1983).
Rogoff, I. (ed.) *The Divided Heritage. Themes and Problems in German Modernism* (Cambridge, 1991).
Röhl, J. C. G. *1914: Delusion or Design? The Testimony of Two German Diplomats* (New York, 1973).
—— *From Bismarck to Hitler. The Problem of Continuity in German History* (London, 1970).
—— *Germany Without Bismarck: The Crisis of Government in the Second Reich, 1890–1900* (Berkeley, 1967).
—— *The Kaiser and His Court: William II and the Government of Germany* (Cambridge, 1994).
—— *Kaiser William II, New Interpretations: The Corfu Papers* (Cambridge, 1982).
—— *Wilhelm II: The Kaiser's Early Life, 1859–1888* (Cambridge, 1998).
—— *Wilhelm II: The Kaiser's Personal Monarchy, 1888–1900* (New York, 2004).
Röhl, J. C. G., and N. Sombart (eds.) *Kaiser Wilhelm II: New Interpretations* (Cambridge, 1982).
Rosenberg, H. *Imperial Germany* (Boston, 1964).
Roth, G. *The Social Democrats in Imperial Germany* (Totowa, 1963).
Ryder, A. J. *The German Revolution of 1918* (Cambridge, 1967).
Sackett, R. E. *Popular Entertainment, Class, and Politics in Imperial Germany* (London, 1982).
Sagarra, E. A. *Social History of Germany 1648–1914* (London, 1977).
—— *Tradition and Revolution: German Literature and Society, 1830–1890* (London, 1971).
Schoenbaum, D. *Zabern* (Garden City, 1982).
Schorske, C. E. *German Social Democracy, 1905–1917* (Cambridge MA, 1955).

Schulze, H. *The Course of German Nationalism: From Frederick the Great to Bismarck, 1763–1867* (Cambridge, 1991).

Sheehan, J. J. *The Career of Lujo Brentano* (Chicago, 1966).

——*German Liberalism in the Nineteenth Century* (Chicago, 1978).

Smith, W. D. *The German Colonial Empire* (Chapel Hill, 1978).

——*The Ideological Origins of Nazi Imperialism* (New York, 1986).

——*Politics and the Sciences of Culture in Germany, 1840–1920* (New York, 1991).

Sperber, J. *The European Revolutions, 1848–1851* (Cambridge, 1994).

——*Popular Catholicism in Nineteenth-Century Germany* (Princeton, 1984).

——*Rhineland Radicals. The Democratic Movement and the Revolution of 1848* (Princeton, 1991).

Spree, R. *Health and Social Class in Imperial Germany: A Social History of Mortality, Morbidity, and Inequality* (Oxford, 1987).

Stachura, P. D. *The German Youth Movement, 1900–1945* (London, 1981).

Steinmetz, G. *Regulating the Social: The Welfare State and Local Politics in Imperial Germany* (Princeton, 1973).

Stern, F. *The Politics of Cultural Despair* (Berkeley, 1961).

Stevenson, D. *French War Aims Against Germany, 1914–1919* (Oxford, 1982).

Strachan, H. *The First World War*. Vol. 1 (Oxford, 2001).

Struve, W. *Elites against Democracy* (Princeton, 1973).

Tal, U. *Christians and Jews in Germany, 1870–1915* (Ithaca, 1974).

Tampke, J. *The Ruhr and Revolution* (London, 1979).

Teich, M., and R. Porter, *Fin-de-Siècle and its Legacy* (Cambridge, 1990).

Veblen, T. *Imperial Germany and the Industrial Revolution* (London, 1915).

Vincent, C. P. *The Politics of Hunger: The Allied Blockade of Germany, 1915–1919* (Athens OH, 1985).

Voegelin, E. *Science, Politics and Gnosticism* (Chicago, 1968).

Volkov, S. *The Rise of Popular Antimodernism in Germany: The Urban Master Artisans, 1873–1896* (Princeton, 1978).

Watt, R. M. *The Kings Depart* (London, 1969).

Weiss, P. J. *Race, Hygiene, and National Efficiency* (Berkeley, 1987).

Whalen, R. W. *Bitter Wounds. German Victims of the Great War, 1914–1939* (Ithaca, 1984).

Williamson, J. G. *Karl Helferrich, 1872–1924: Economist, Financier, Politician* (Princeton, 1971).

Winter, J. M. *The Experience of World War I* (London, 1988).

Wohl, R. *The Generation of 1914* (Cambridge MA, 1979).

Woycke, J. *Birth Control in Germany, 1871–1933* (London, 1988).

1919–33

Abrams, D. *The Collapse of the Weimar Republic. Political Economy and Crisis* (Princeton, 1981).

Balderston, T. *Economics and Politics in the Weimar Republic* (Cambridge, 2002).

——*The Origins and Course of the German Economic Crisis, November 1923–May 1932* (Berlin, 1993).

Bessel, R. *Germany After the First World War* (Oxford, 1993).

Carsten, F. L. *The Reichswehr and Politics 1918–1933* (Oxford, 1966).

Childers, T. (ed.) *The Formation of the Nazi Constituency, 1918–1933* (Totowa NJ, 1986).

Eichengreen, B. *Golden Fetters. The Gold Standard and the Great Depression, 1919–1939* (New York, 1992).

Evans, R. J., and D. Geary (eds.) *The German Unemployed. Experiences and Consequences of Mass Unemployment from the Weimar Republic to the Third Reich* (New York, 1987).

Feldman, G. D. *The Great Disorder. Economics, Politics, and Society in the German Inflation, 1914–1924* (Oxford, 1983).

Fergusson, N. *Paper and Iron. Hamburg Business and German Politics in the Era of Inflation, 1897–1927* (Cambridge, 1995).

Feuchtwanger, E. J. *From Weimar to Hitler: Germany 1918–1933* (Basingstoke, 1993).

Fritzsche, P. *Rehearsals for Fascism. Populism and Political Mobilization in Weimar Germany* (New York, 1990).

Gay, P. *Weimar Culture: The Outsider as Insider* (London, 1974).

Harsch, D. *German Social Democracy and the Rise of Nazism* (Chapel Hill, 1993).

Haxthausen, C. W., and G. Suhr (eds.) *Berlin: Culture and Metropolis* (Minneapolis, 1990).

Heiber, H. *The Weimar Republic* (Oxford, 1993).

Herf, J. *Reactionary Modernism: Technology, Culture and Politics in Weimar and the Third Reich* (Cambridge, 1984).

Holtfrerich, C.-L. *The German Inflation, 1914–1923. Causes and Effects in International Perspective* (New York, 1986).

James, H. *The German Slump. Politics and Economics 1924–1936* (Oxford, 1986).

Jones, L. E. *German Liberalism and the Dissolution of the Weimar Party System, 1918–1933* (Chapel Hill, 1988).

Kershaw, I. *Weimar: Why Did German Democracy Fail?* (London, 1990).

Keynes, J. M. *The Economic Consequences of the Peace* (London, 1919).

Kneische, T. W., and S. Brockmann *Dancing on the Volcano: Essays on the Culture of the Weimar Republic* (Columbia SC, 1994).

Kolb, E. *The Weimar Republic* (London, 1988).

Kunz, A. *Civil Servants and the Politics of Inflation in Germany, 1914–1924* (Berlin, 1986).

Lane, B. M. *Architecture and Politics in Germany 1918–1945* (Boston, 1985).

Laqueur, W. *Weimar: A Cultural History 1918–1933* (London, 1974).

Lee, M., and W. Michalka *German Foreign Policy 1917–1933: Continuity or Break?* (New York, 1987).

Lee, S. J. *The Weimar Republic* (London, 1998).

Michalski, S. *New Objectivity: Painting, Graphic Art and Photography in Weimar Germany, 1919–1933* (Cologne, 1994).

Mommsen, H. *The Rise and Fall of Weimar Democracy* (Chapel Hill, 1996).

Nichols, A. J. *Weimar and the Rise of Hitler* (Basingstoke, 1991).

Nolan, M. *Visions of Modernity: American Business and the Modernization of Germany* (New York, 1994).

Plummer, T. G. *Film and Politics in the Weimar Republic* (New York, 1982).

Schuker, S. A. *American "Reparations" to Germany, 1919–33: Implications for the Third World Debt Crisis* (Princeton, 1988).

Stachura, P. D. *Unemployment and the Great Depression in Weimar Germany* (Basingstoke, 1986).

Stark, G. *Entrepreneurs of Ideology: Neoconservative Publishers in Weimar Germany* (Chapel Hill, 1981).

Webb, S. B. *Hyperinflation and Stabilisation in Weimar Germany* (New York, 1989).

Whalen, R. W. *Bitter Wounds. German Victims of the Great War, 1914–1939* (Ithaca, 1984).

1933–45

Arad, Y., Y. Gutman, and A. Margaliot (eds.) *Documents of the Holocaust* (Jerusalem, 1981).

Arad, Y., S. Krakowski, and S. Spector (eds.) *The Einsatzgruppen Reports* (New York, 1989).

Balfour, M. *Withstanding Hitler in Germany 1933–1945* (London, 1988).

Barkai, A. *From Boycott to Annihilation. The Economic Struggle of German Jews 1933–1945* (Brandeis, 1989).

——*Nazi Economics. Ideology, Theory and Policy* (Oxford, 1990).

Bauer, Y. *The Holocaust in Historical Perspective* (London, 1978).

Benz, W. *The Holocaust* (New York, 1999).

Bergen, D. L. *Twisted Cross. The German Christian Movement in the Third Reich* (Chapel Hill, 1996).

Bracher, K.-D. *The German Dictatorship* (London, 1970).

Breitmann, R. *The Architect of Genocide. Heinrich Himmler and the Final Solution* (London, 1991).

Browning, C. *Ordinary Men. Reserve Battalion 101 and the Final Solution in Poland* (New York, 1993).

——*Paths to Genocide* (Cambridge, 1994).

Bullock, A. *Hitler. A Study in Tyranny* (London, 1964).

Burleigh, M. *Death and Deliverance. Euthanasia in Germany c. 1900–1945* (Cambridge, 1994).

——*The Third Reich* (New York, 2000).

Burleigh M., and W. Wippermann *The Racial State. Germany 1933–1945* (Cambridge, 1991).

Conway, J. S. *The Nazi Persecution of the Churches 1933–1945* (London, 1968).

Deist, W. *The Wehrmacht and German Rearmament* (London, 1981).

Farquharson, J. E. *The Plough and the Swastika. The NSDAP and Agriculture in Germany 1928–1945* (London, 1976).

Fest, J. *Hitler* (London, 1974).

Friedländer, S. *Nazi Germany and the Jews. The Years of Persecution 1933–1939* (London, 1998).

Gellately, R. *The Gestapo and German Society* (Oxford, 1988).

Glantz, D. M. *Barbarossa. Hitler's Invasion of Russia 1941* (Stroud, 2001).

Gorodetsky, G. *Grand Delusion. Stalin and the German Invasion of Russia* (New Haven and London, 1999).

Graml, H. *Anti-Semitism in the Third Reich* (Oxford, 1992).

Grossmann, V. *Life and Fate* (London, 1985).

Herbert, U. *Hitler's Foreign Workers. Enforced Foreign Labour in Germany under the Third Reich* (Cambridge, 1997).

Hiden, J., and J. Farquharson *Explaining Hitler's Germany* (London, 1989).

Hilberg, R. *The Destruction of the European Jews* (New York, 1983).

Hildebrand, K. *The Third Reich* (London, 1984).

Hoffmann, P. *The History of German Resistance to Hitler 1933–1945* (Montreal, 1996).

Kershaw, I. *Hitler 1889–1936. Hubris* (London, 1998).

——*Hitler 1936–1945. Nemesis* (London, 2000).

——*The "Hitler Myth". Image and Reality in the Third Reich* (Oxford, 1987).

——*The Nazi Dictatorship* (London, 1995).

Kitchen, M. *Nazi Germany at War* (New York, 1995).

Klemperer, V. *I Shall Bear Witness. The Diaries of Viktor Klemperer* (London, 1998–9).

Koonz, C. *Mothers in the Fatherland – Women, the Family, and Nazi Politics* (New York, 1987).

Longerich, P. *The Unwritten Order: Hitler's Role in the Final Solution* (Stroud, 2001).

Marrus, M. *The Holocaust in History* (Jerusalem, 1981).

Marrus, M., and R. Paxton *Vichy France and the Jews* (New York, 1983).

Müller, K.-J. *The Army, Politics and Society in Germany 1933–1939* (Manchester, 1987).

Mulligan, T. *The Politics of Illusion and Empire. German Occupation Policy in the Soviet Union 1942–43* (New York, 1988).

Nekrich, A. M. *Pariahs, Partners, Predators. German-Soviet Relations 1922–1941* (New York, 1997).

Noakes, J., and G. Pridham (eds.) *Nazism, 1919–1945. A Documentary Reader* (Exeter, 1983/98).

Overy, R. J. *The Air War, 1939–1945* (London, 1980).

——*Göring. The Iron Man* (London, 1983).

——*The Nazi Economic Recovery, 1932–1938* (Cambridge, 1996).

——*Russia's War* (London, 1997).

——*Why the Allies Won* (London, 1995).

Paucker, A. *Jewish Resistance in Germany. The Facts and the Problems* (Berlin, 1991).

Trunk, I. *Judenrat. The Jewish Councils in Eastern Europe under Nazi Occupation* (New York, 1972).

1945–2000

Balfour, M. *Germany, The Tides of Power* (London, 1992).

Baring, A. *Uprising in East Germany* (New York, 1972).

Berghahn, V. R. *The Americanisation of West German Industry, 1945–1973* (Leamington Spa, 1986).

Burns, R. *German Cultural Studies: An Introduction* (Oxford, 1995).

Carter, E. *How German is She? Postwar West German Reconstruction and the Consuming Woman* (Ann Arbor, 1997).

Childs, D. *The GDR. Moscow's German Ally* (London, 1988).

——(ed.) *Honecker's Germany* (London, 1985).

Dahrendorf, R. *Society and Democracy in Germany* (London, 1968).

Dennis, M. *German Democratic Republic. Politics, Economics and Society* (London, 1988).

——*Social and Economic Modernization in Eastern Germany from Honecker to Kohl* (London, 1993).

Elsaesser, T. *New German Cinema: A History* (London, 1989).

Fulbrook, M. *Anatomy of a Dictatorship. Inside the GDR 1949–1989* (Oxford, 1995).

——*The Two Germanies 1945–1990. Problems of Interpretation* (London, 1992).

Glaessner, G.-J. *The Unification Process in Germany: From Dictatorship to Democracy* (London, 1992).

Glaessner, G.-J., and I. Wallace (eds.) *The German Revolution of 1989: Causes and Consequences* (Oxford, 1992).

Goodbody, A., and D. Tate (eds.) *Geist und Macht. Writers and the State in the GDR* (Amsterdam, 1992).

Humphreys, P. J. *Media and Media Policy in Germany: The Press and Broadcasting since 1945* (Oxford, 1989).

James, H., and M. Stone (eds.) *When the Wall Came Down: Reaction to German Unification* (New York, 1992).

Jarausch, K. H. *The Rush to German Unity* (Oxford, 1994).

Jarausch, K. H., and V. Gransow (eds.) *Uniting Germany. Documents and Debates, 1944–1993* (Providence, 1994).

Kaes, A. *From Hitler to Heimat. The Return of History as Film* (Cambridge, 1989).

Kolinsky, E. *Women in West Germany: Life, Work and Politics* (Oxford, 1989).

——(ed.) *Between Hope and Fear: Everyday Life in Post-Unification East Germany: A Case Study of Leipzig* (Keele, 1995).

Kramer, A. *The West German Economy* (Oxford, 1991).

Larres, K., and P. Panayi (eds.) *The Federal Republic of Germany since 1949: Politics, Society and Economy Before and After Unification* (Longman, 1996).

Lewis, D., and J. R. P. McKenzie (eds.) *The New Germany: Social, Political and Cultural Challenges of Unification* (Exeter, 1995).

Maaz, H.-J. *Behind the Wall: The Inner Life of Communist Germany* (New York, 1995).

McAdams, A. J. *Germany Divided: From the Wall to Unification* (Princeton, 1993).

McCauley, M. *The GDR since 1945* (London, 1983).

Merkl, P. H. (ed.) *The Federal Republic of Germany at Forty-Five: Union Without Unity* (London, 1995).

Nicholls, A. J. *Freedom With Responsibility* (Oxford, 1995).

Osmond, J. (ed.) *German Reunification: A Reference Guide and Commentary* (Harlow, 1992).

Philipson, D. *We Were the People: Voices from East Germany's Revolutionary Autumn of 1989* (Durham NC, 1993).

Pommerin, R. (ed.) *The American Impact on Post-War Germany* (Providence, 1995).

Pond, E. *Beyond the Wall: Germany's Road to Unification* (Washington, 1993).

Pulzer, P. *German Politics. 1945–1995* (Oxford, 1995).

Rogers, D. *Politics After Hitler. The Western Allies and the German Party System* (London, 1995).

Scharf, C. B. *Politics and Change in East Germany* (Boulder, 1984).

Schwarz, H. P. *Adenauer. From the German Empire to the Federal Republic* (Oxford, 1995).

Sinn, G., and H.-W. *Jumpstart: The Economic Unification of Germany* (Cambridge MA, 1992).

Smith, E. O. *The German Economy* (London, 1994).

Smith, G. *Democracy in Western Germany: Parties and Politics in the Federal Republic* (Aldershot, 1986).

Sontheimer, K., and W. Bleek *The Government and Politics of East Germany* (London, 1975).

Thomanek, J. K. A., and J. Mellis (eds.) *Politics, Society and Government in the German Democratic Republic: Basis Documents* (Oxford, 1988).

Turner, H. O. *The Two Germanies* (New Haven, 1987).

Turner, I. *Reconstruction in Post-War Germany: British Occupation Policy and the Western Zones, 1945–1955* (Oxford, 1989).

Von Hallberg, R. *Literary Intellectuals and the Dissolution of the State: Professionalism and Conformity in the GDR* (Chicago, 1996).

Woods, R. *Opposition in the GDR under Honecker, 1971–85* (London, 1986).

Zelikow, P., and C. Rice *Germany Unified and Europe Transformed: A Study in Statecraft* (Cambridge, 1995).

Index

Note: page numbers in italics refer to illustrations

Also of Interest

History of Germany, 1780-1918
The Long Nineteenth Century

SECOND EDITION

DAVID BLACKBOURN
Harvard University

"David Blackbourn … has transformed the historiography of modern Germany."

Times Higher Education Supplement

Series: Blackwell Classic Histories of Europe
2002 / 480 pages / illustrations
0-631-23196-X PB £17.99 / 0-631-23195-1 HB £65.00

History of Germany 1918-2000
The Divided Nation

SECOND EDITION

MARY FULBROOK
University College London

This accessible study traces the dramatic social, cultural and political tensions in Germany since 1918. The second edition incorporates the results of recent research, an epilogue covering the years 1990-2000, and updated bibliography.

Series: Blackwell Classic Histories of Europe
2002 / 352 pages / illustrations
0-631-23208-7 PB £16.99 / 0-631-23207-9 HB £65.00

Blackwell
Publishing